# #1

# TRIGUN YASUHIRO NIGHTOW

## DEEP SPACE PLANET FUTURE GUN ACTION!!

内藤泰弘
**YASUHIRO NIGHTOW**

TRANSLATION
**JUSTIN BURNS**

LETTERING
**STUDIO CUTIE**

DARK HORSE MANGA

DMP
Digital Manga Publishing

PUBLISHERS

## MIKE RICHARDSON
## AND HIKARU SASAHARA

EDITORS

## TIM ERVIN
## AND FRED LUI

COLLECTION DESIGNER

## DAVID NESTELLE

English-language version produced
by DARK HORSE COMICS and
DIGITAL MANGA PUBLISHING.

# TRIGUN vol. 1

Published by
Dark Horse Manga
A division of Dark Horse Comics, Inc.
10956 S.E. Main Street
Milwaukie, OR 97222

www.DarkHorse.com

Digital Manga Publishing
1487 West 178th Street, Suite 300
Gardena, CA 90248

www.DMPBooks.com

To find a comics shop in your area, call the Comic
Shop Locator Service toll-free at 1-888-266-4226

First edition: October 2003
ISBN: 978-1-59307-052-6

10 9

Printed at Transcontinental Gagné, Louiseville, QC, Canada

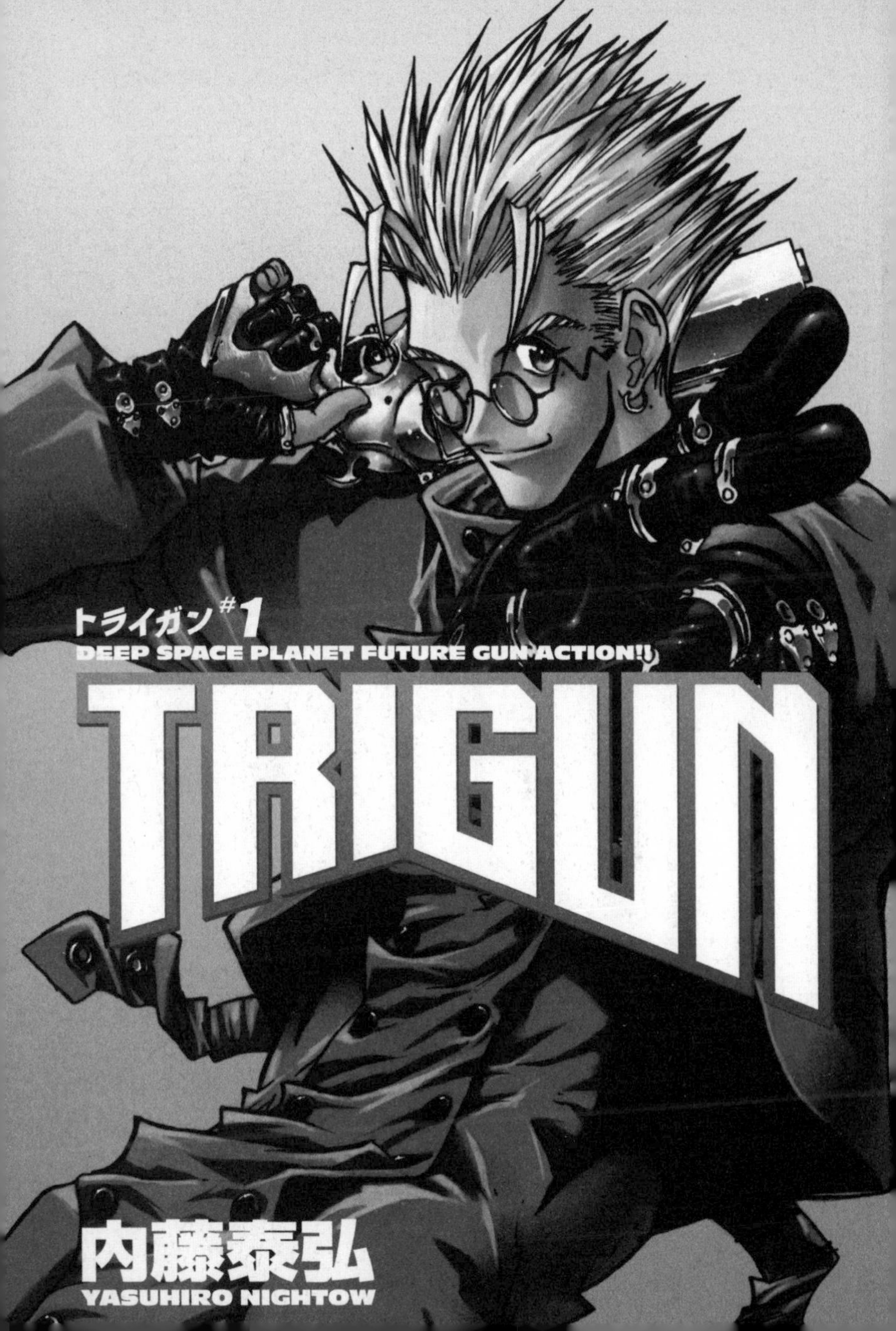

トライガン #1

DEEP SPACE PLANET FUTURE GUN ACTION!!

# TRIGUN

内藤泰弘

YASUHIRO NIGHTOW

# #1 TRIGUN YASUHIRO NIGHTOW
## DEEP SPACE PLANET FUTURE GUN ACTION!!
# CONTENTS

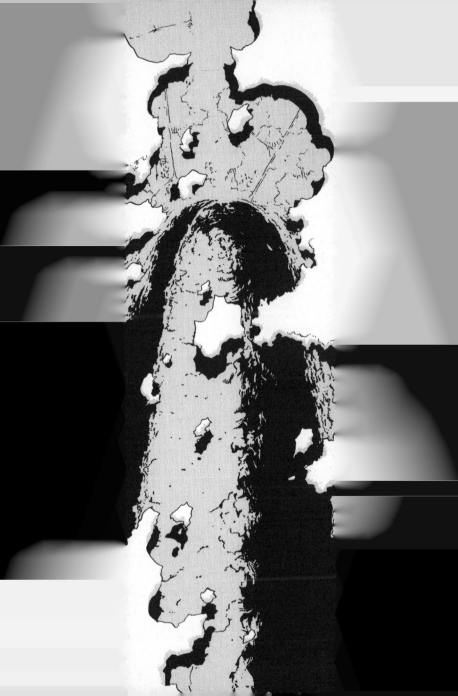

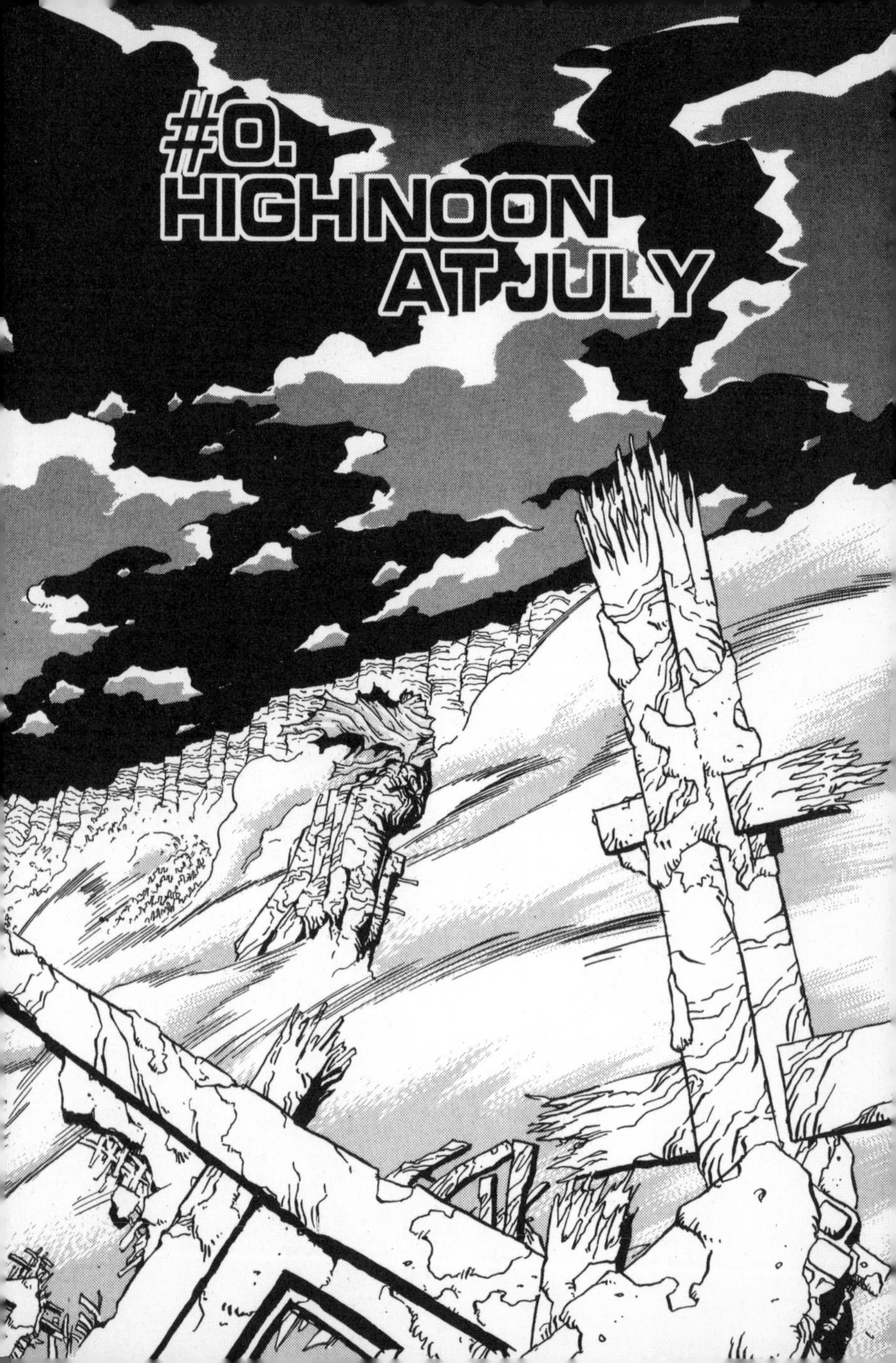
#0.
HIGH NOON
AT JULY

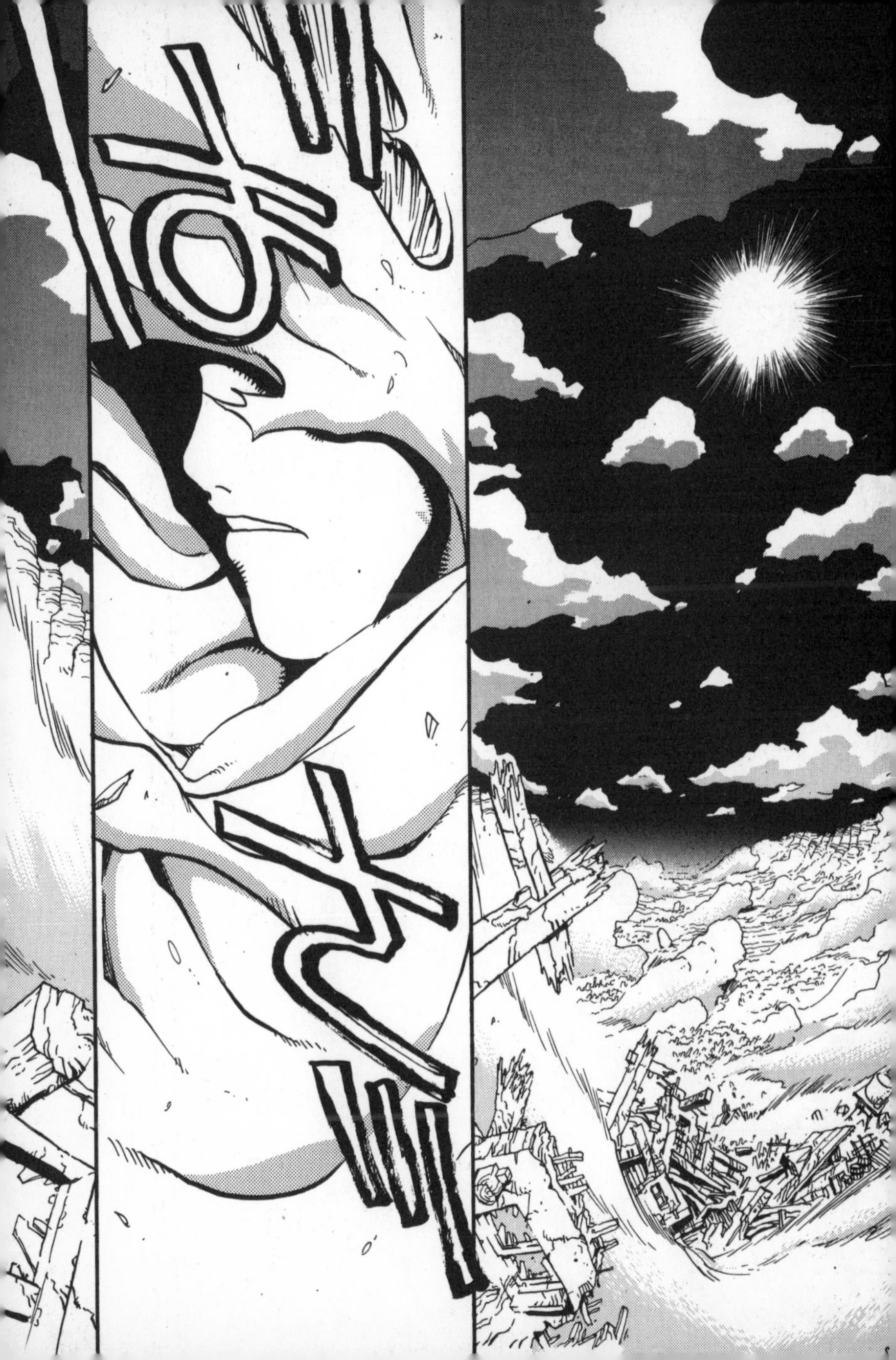

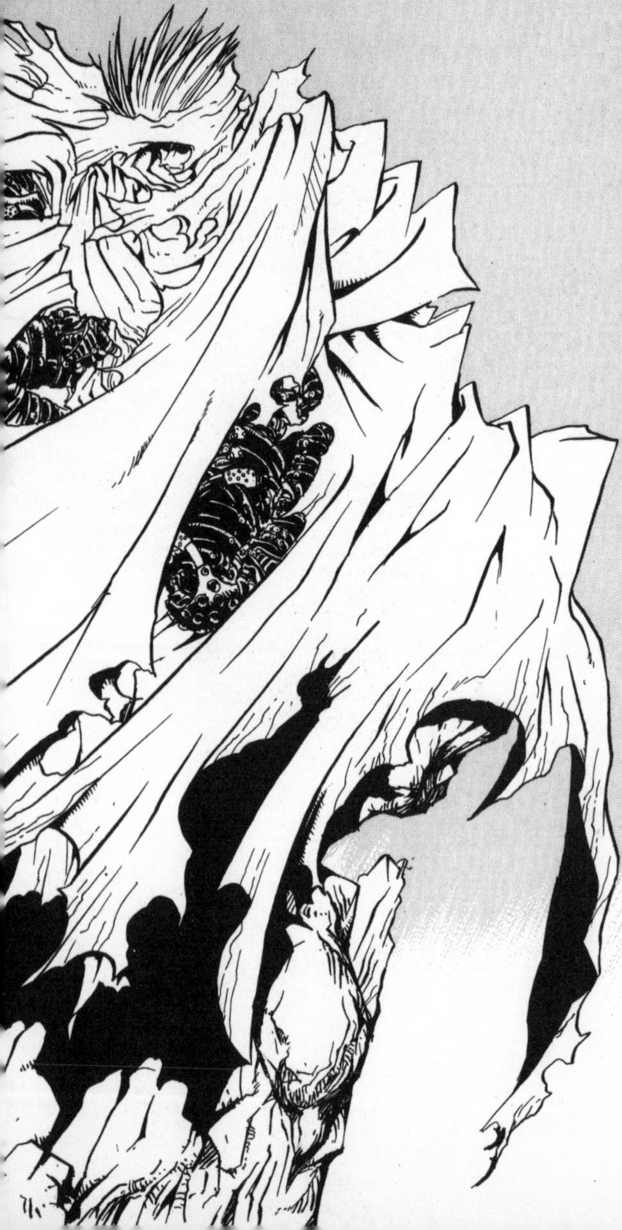

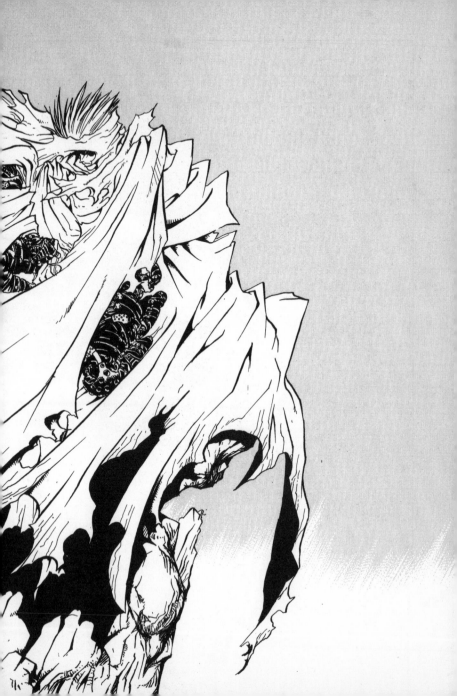

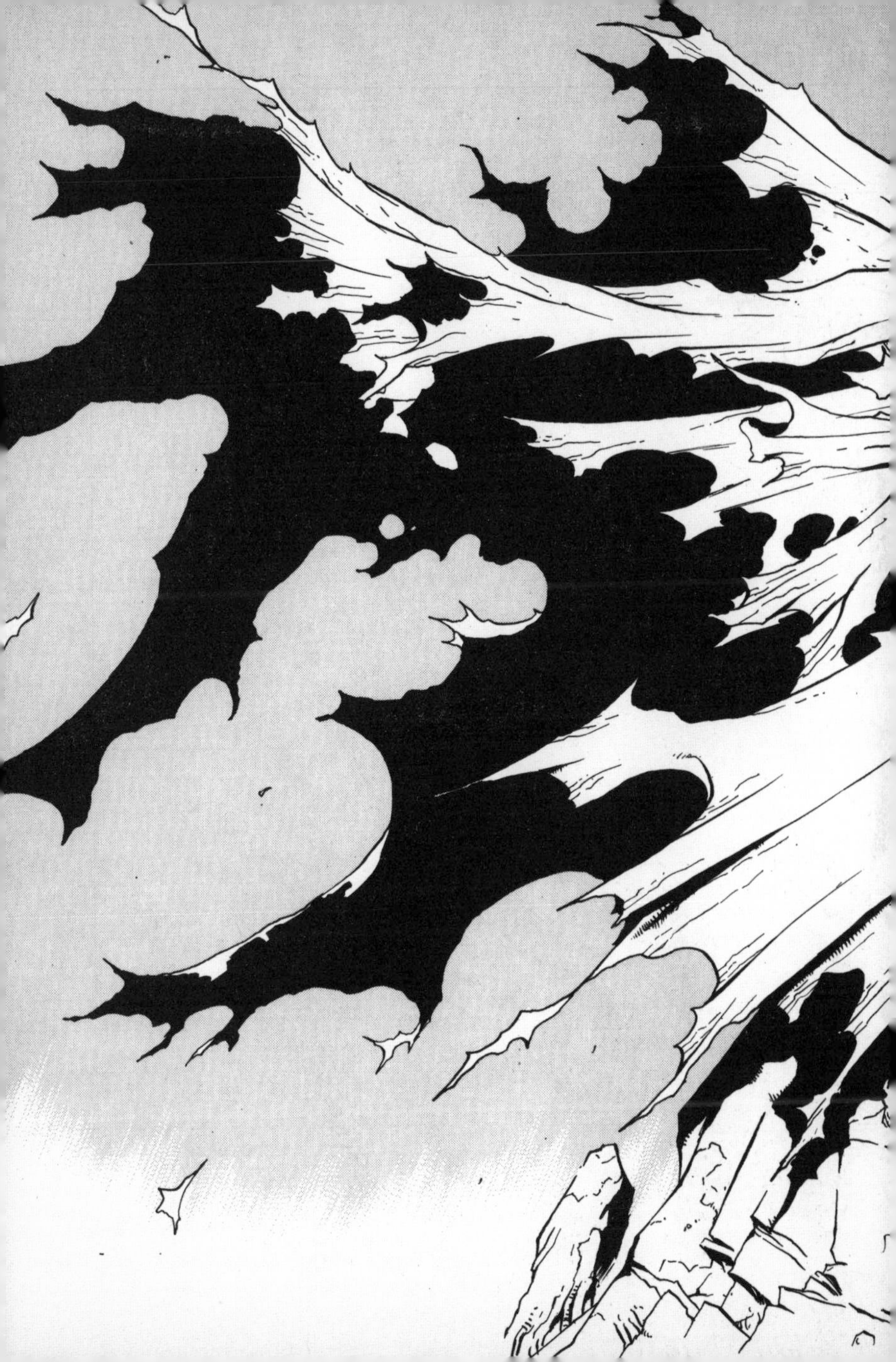

LONG AGO, IN A YET UNSEEN TIME, IN A FARAWAY PLACE...
THE SAME SONG OF HUMANITY STILL SANG.

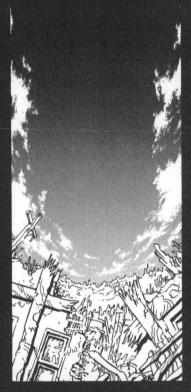

## #0. HIGH NOON AT JULY/END

# 1

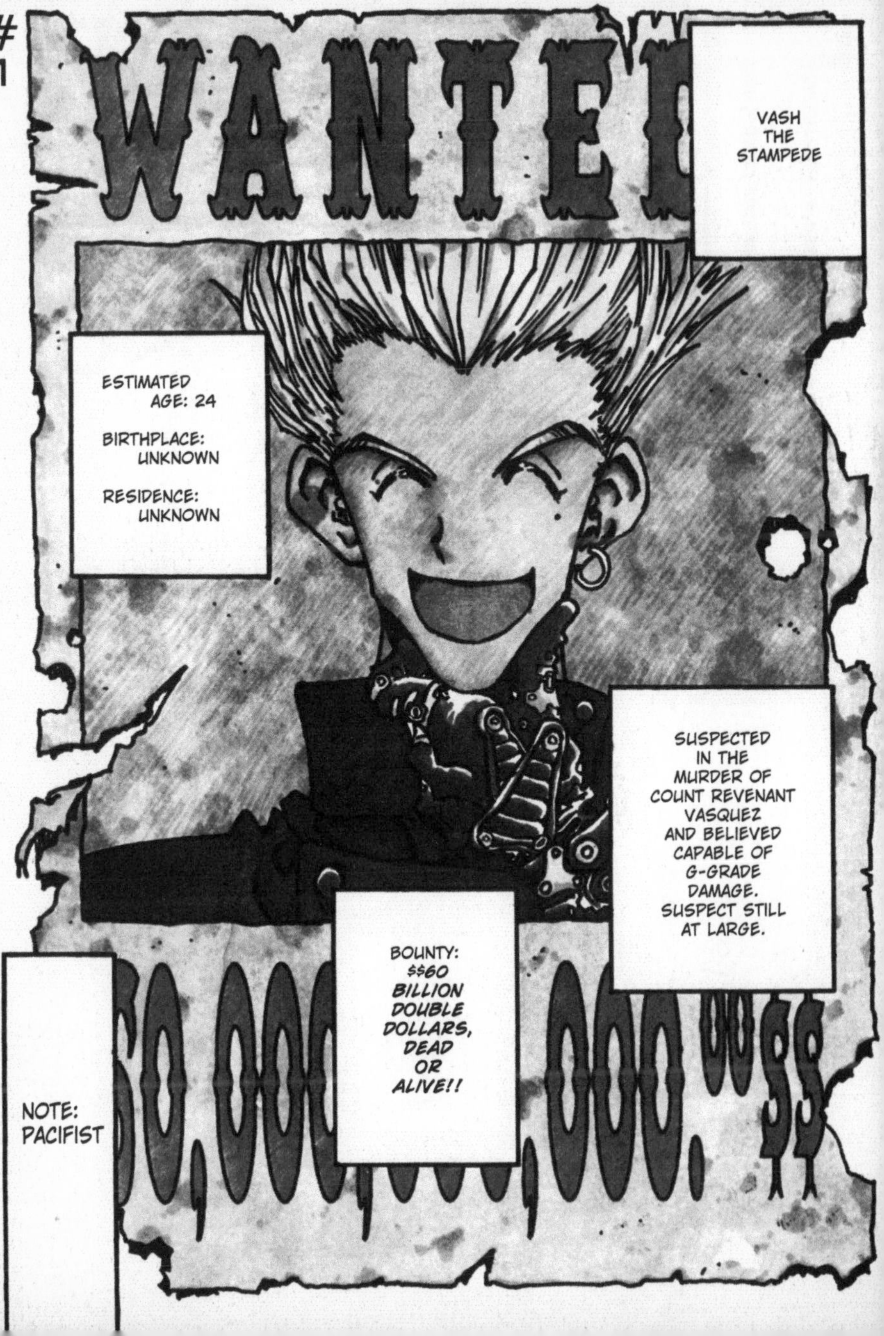

VASH THE STAMPEDE
ESTIMATED AGE: 24
BIRTHPLACE: UNKNOWN
RESIDENCE: UNKNOWN
SUSPECTED IN THE MURDER OF COUNT REVENANT VASQUEZ AND BELIEVED CAPABLE OF G-GRADE DAMAGE. SUSPECT STILL AT LARGE.
BOUNTY: $$60 BILLION DOUBLE DOLLARS, DEAD OR ALIVE!!
NOTE: PACIFIST

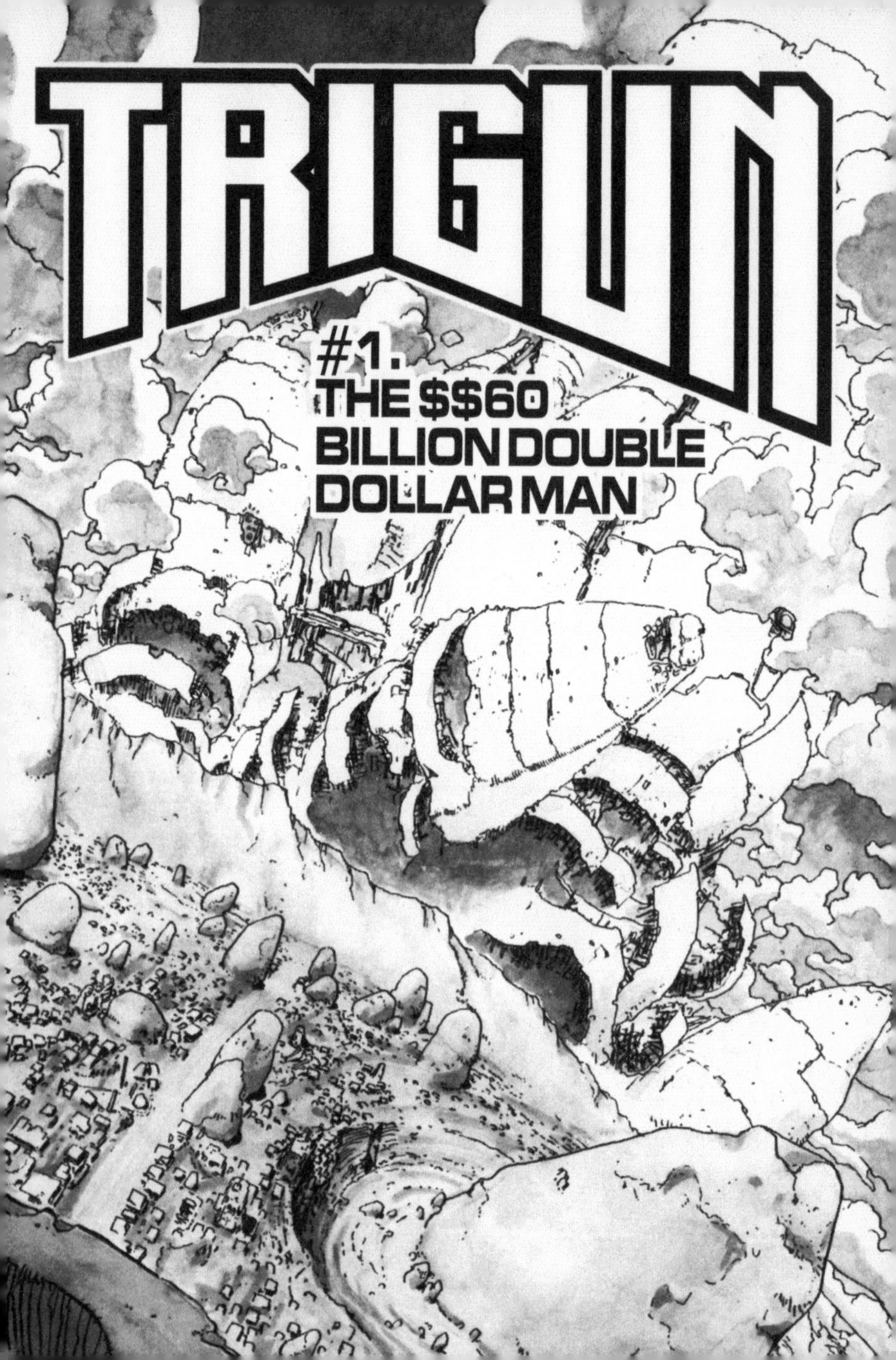
TRIGUN
#1.
THE $$60
BILLION DOUBLE
DOLLAR MAN

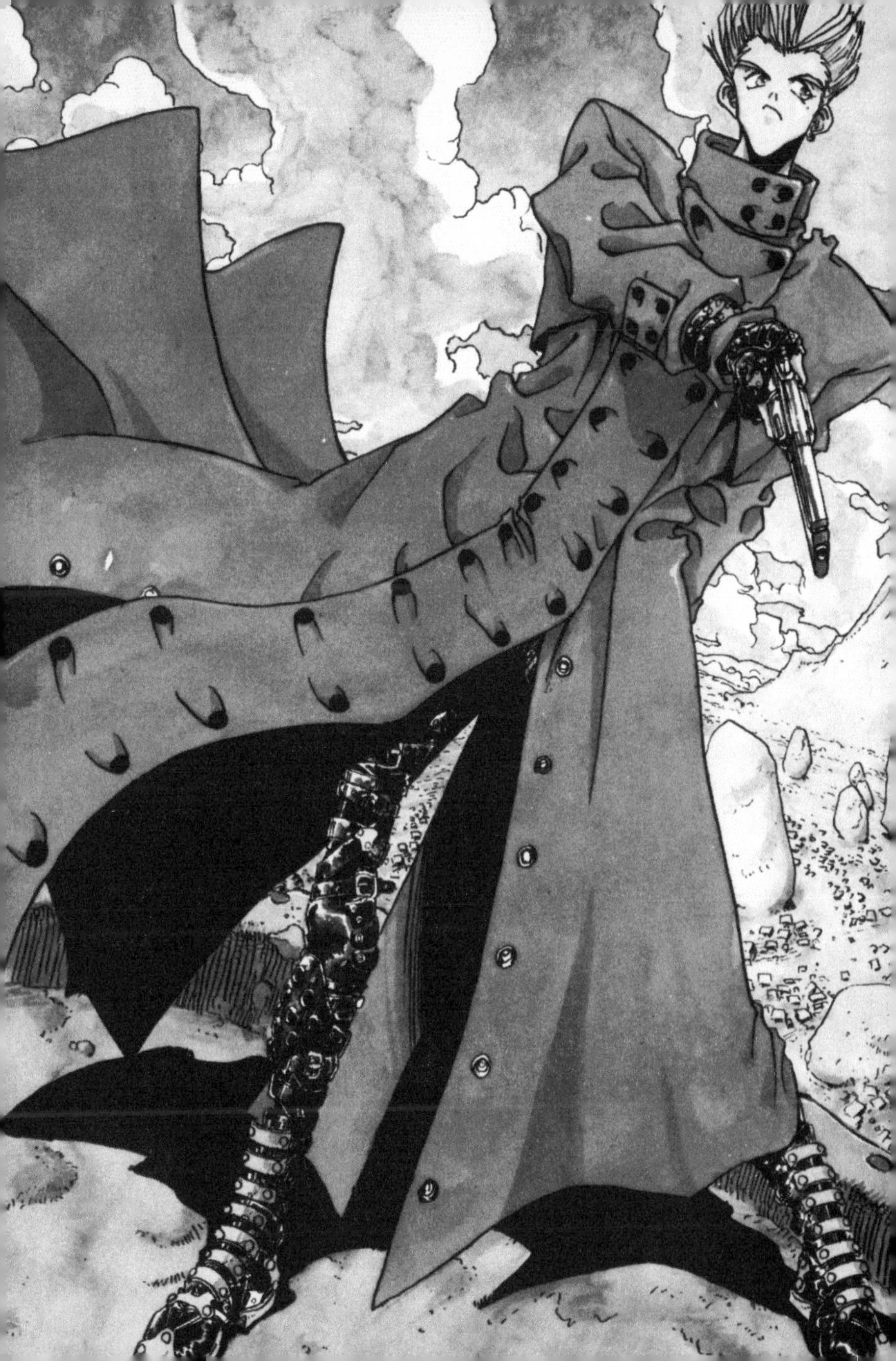

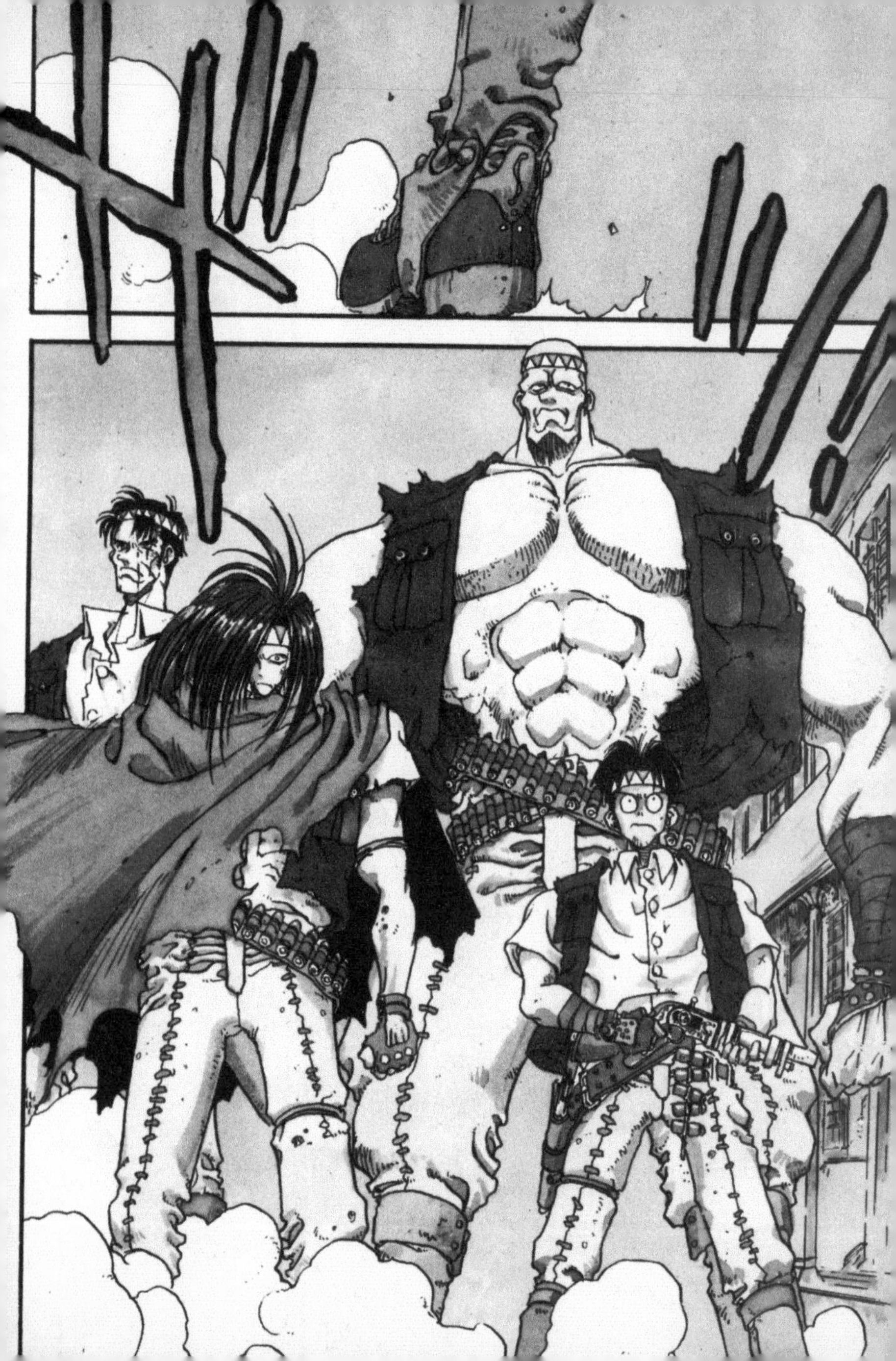

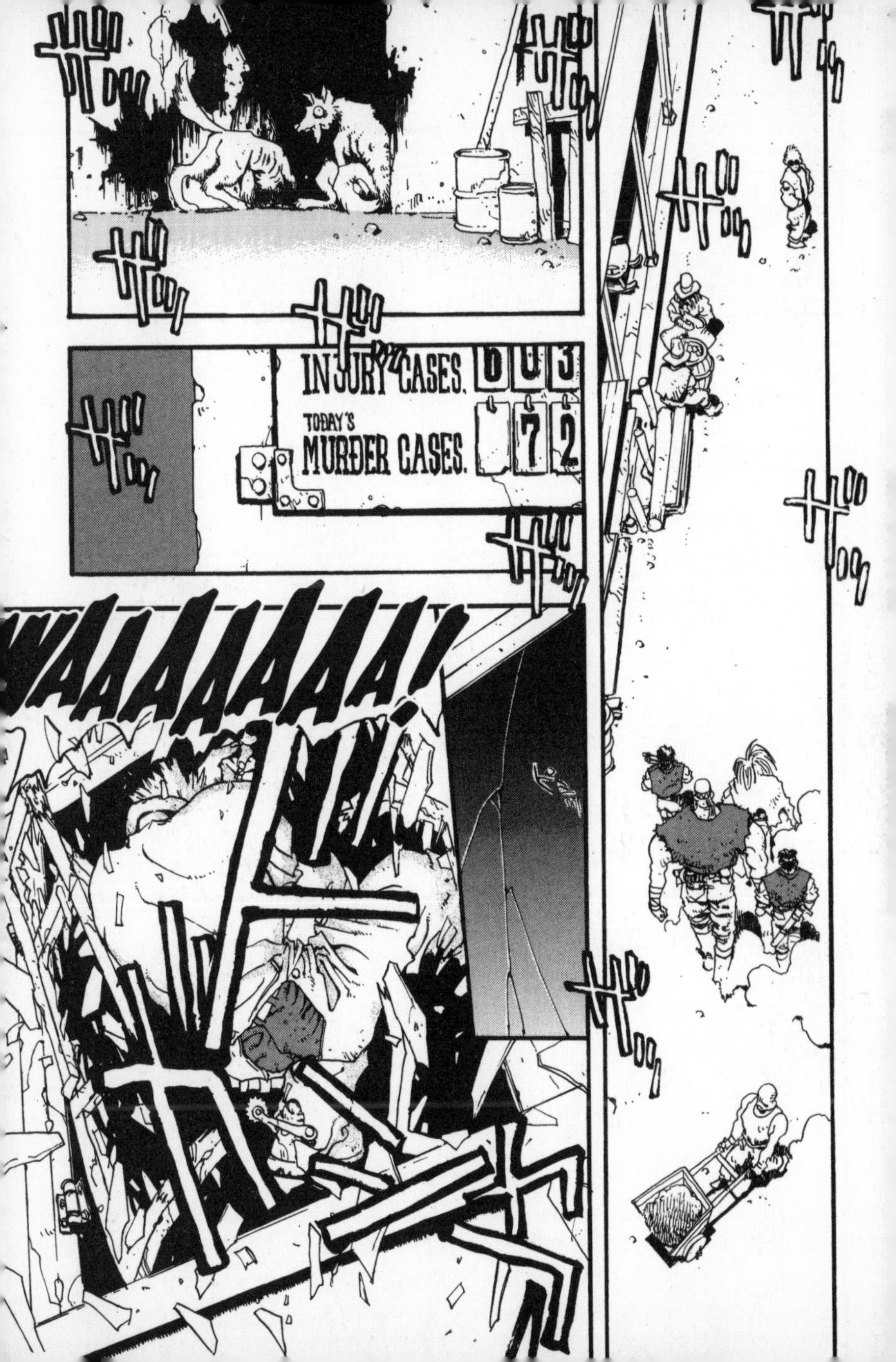
INJURY CASES. 003
TODAY'S MURDER CASES. 72
WAAAAAAAA!

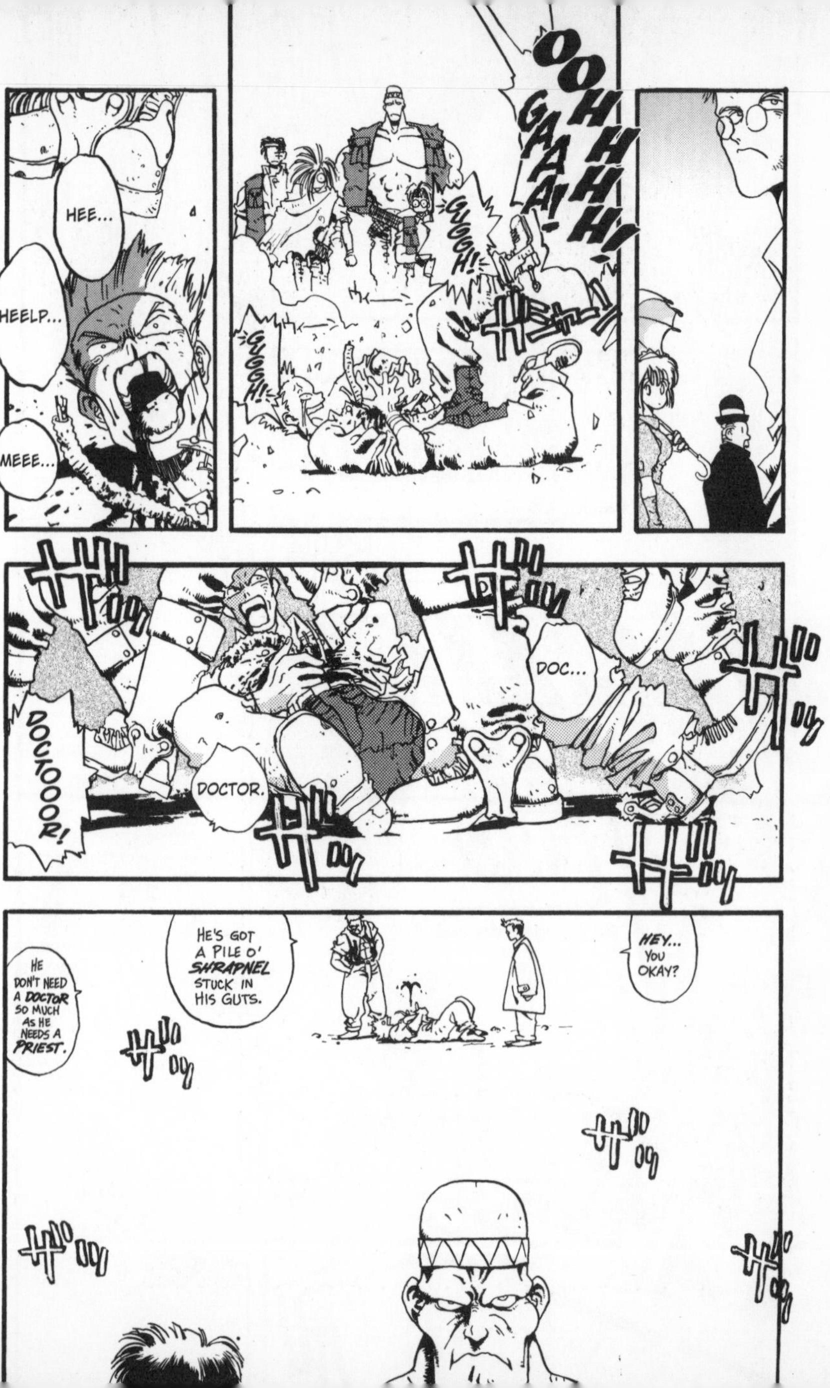
OOHHHHH!
GAAAA!
GUGGH!!
GUGGH!!
HEE...
HEELP...
MEEE...
DOC...
DOCTOR.
DOCTOOOOR!
HEY... YOU OKAY?
HE'S GOT A PILE O' SHRAPNEL STUCK IN HIS GUTS.
HE DON'T NEED A DOCTOR SO MUCH AS HE NEEDS A PRIEST.

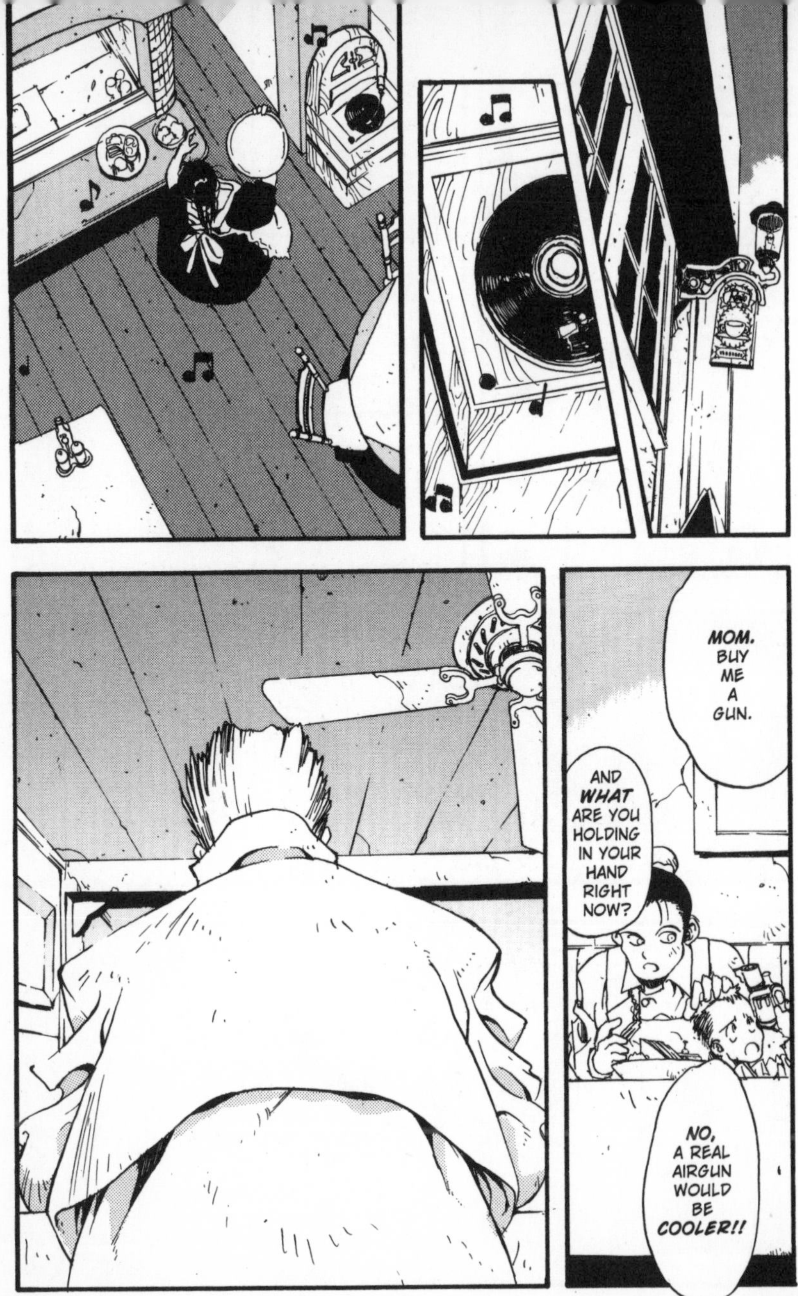
MOM. BUY ME A GUN.
AND WHAT ARE YOU HOLDING IN YOUR HAND RIGHT NOW?
NO, A REAL AIRGUN WOULD BE COOLER!!

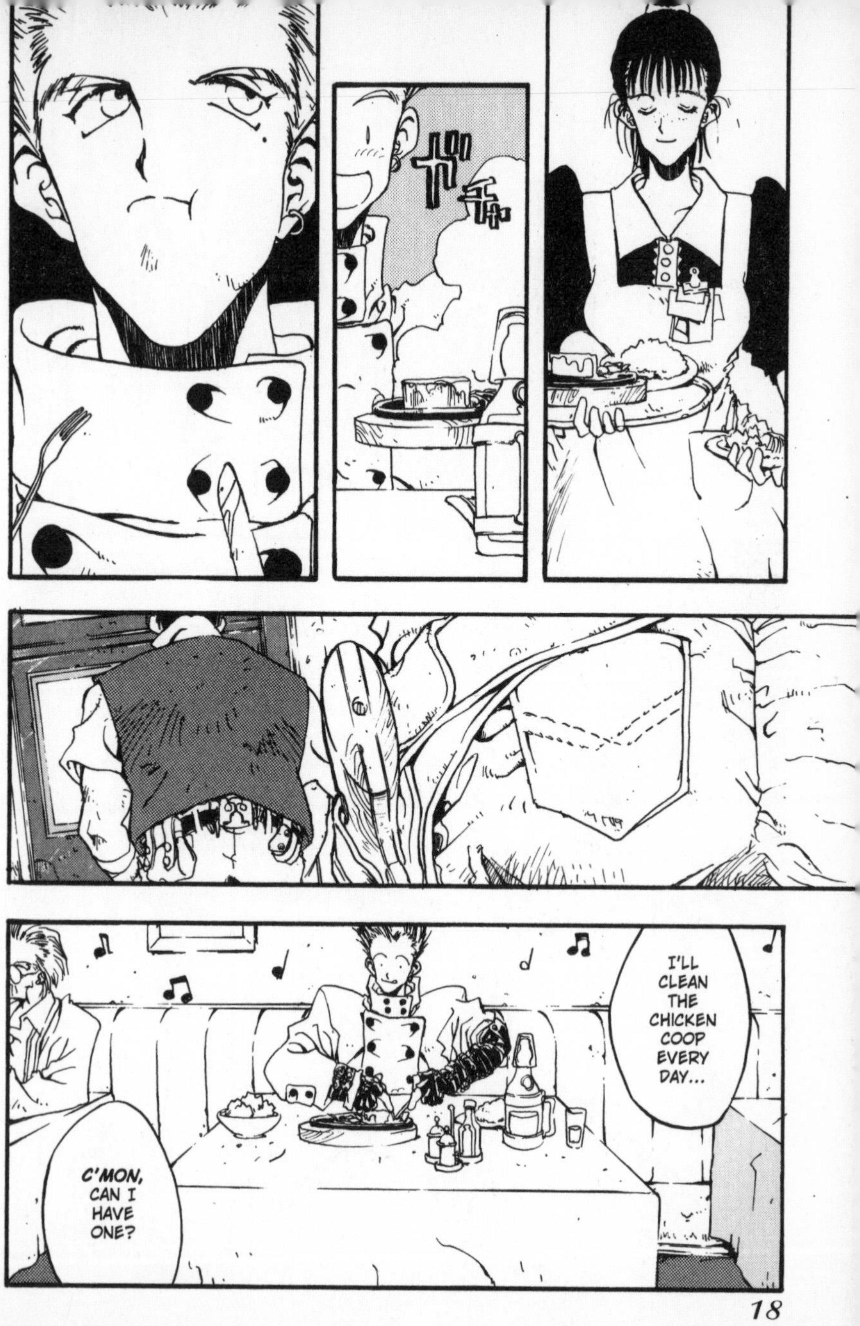
ガチャ
I'LL CLEAN THE CHICKEN COOP EVERY DAY...
C'MON, CAN I HAVE ONE?

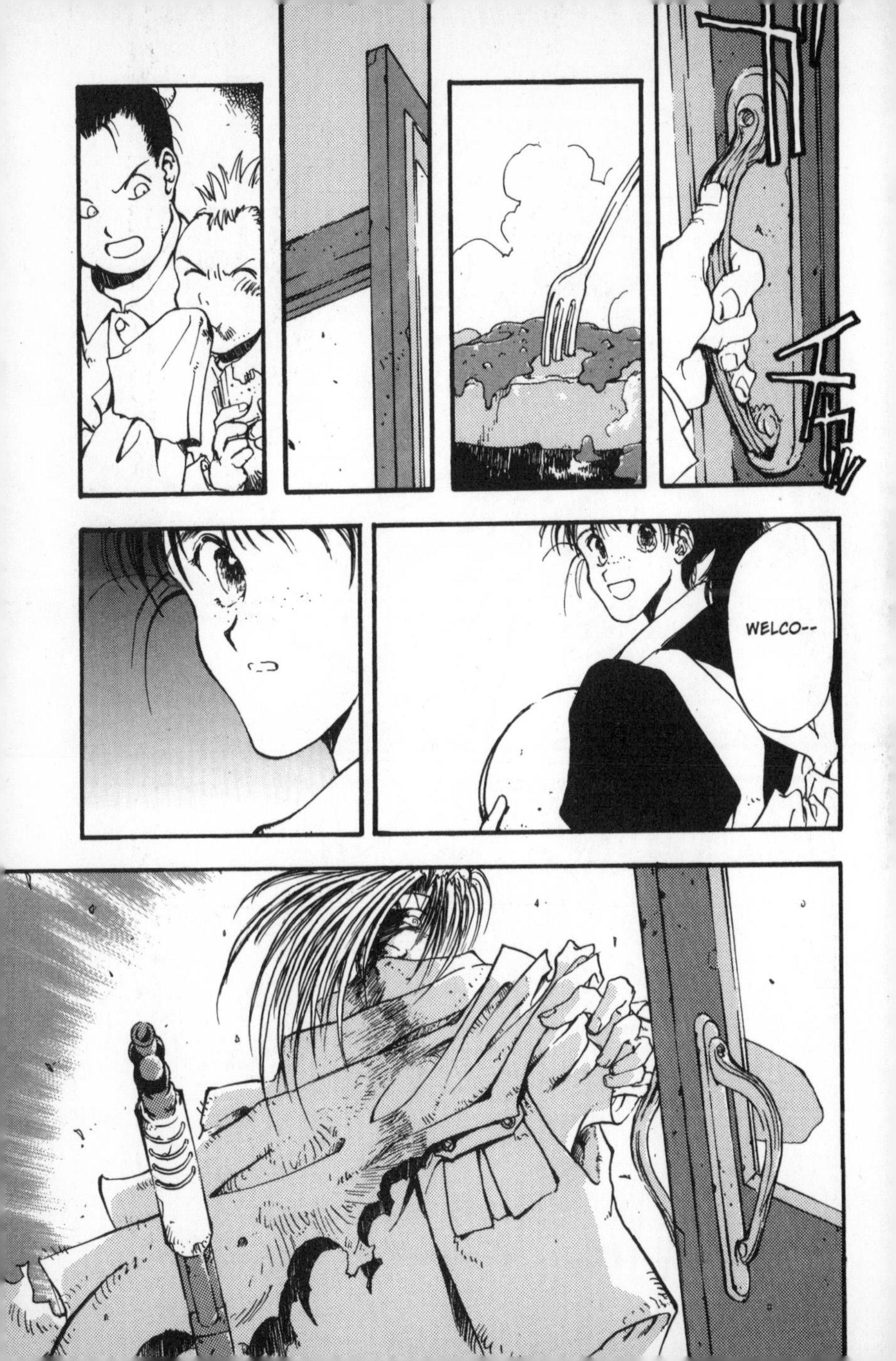
WELCO--

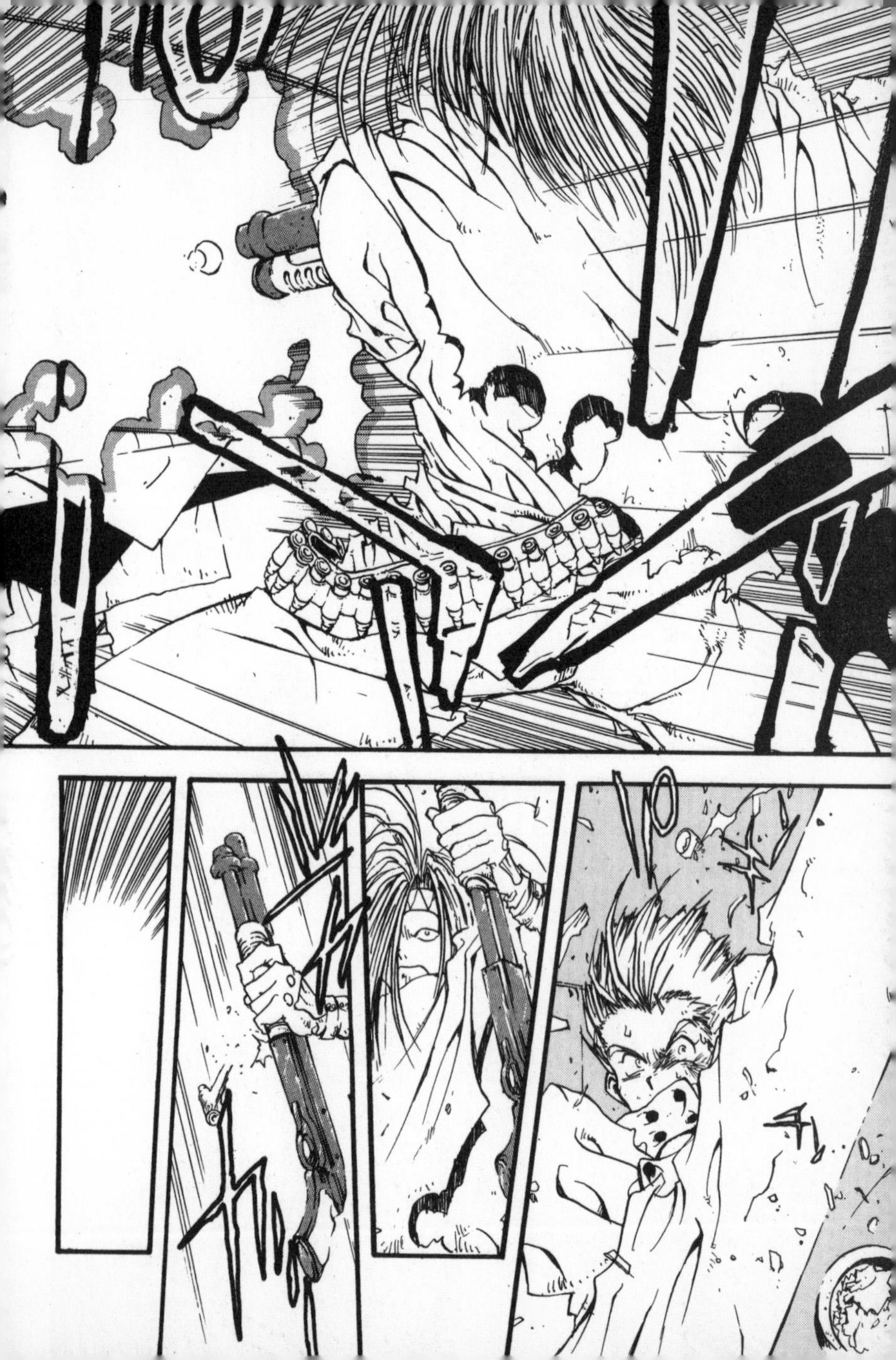

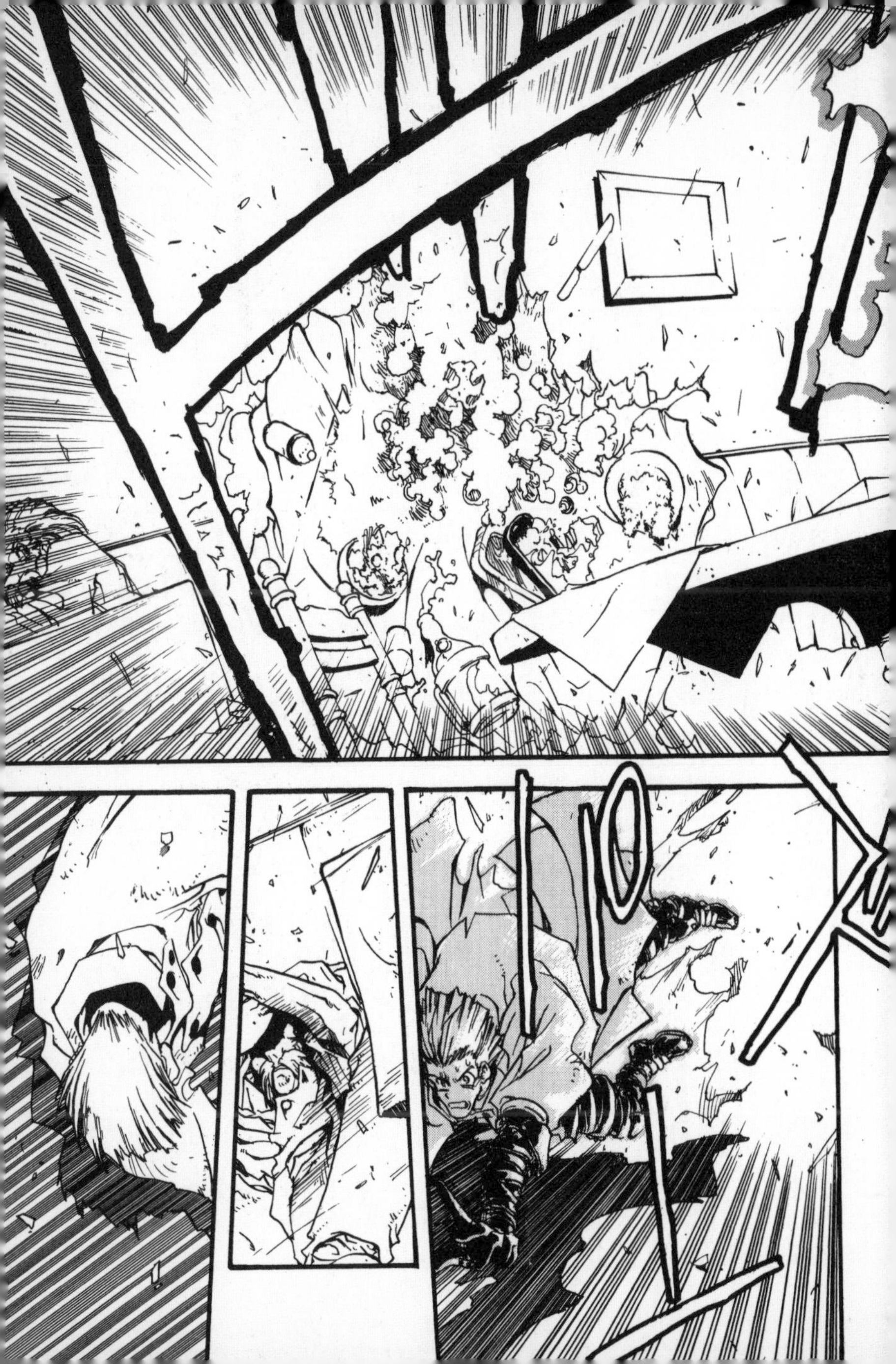

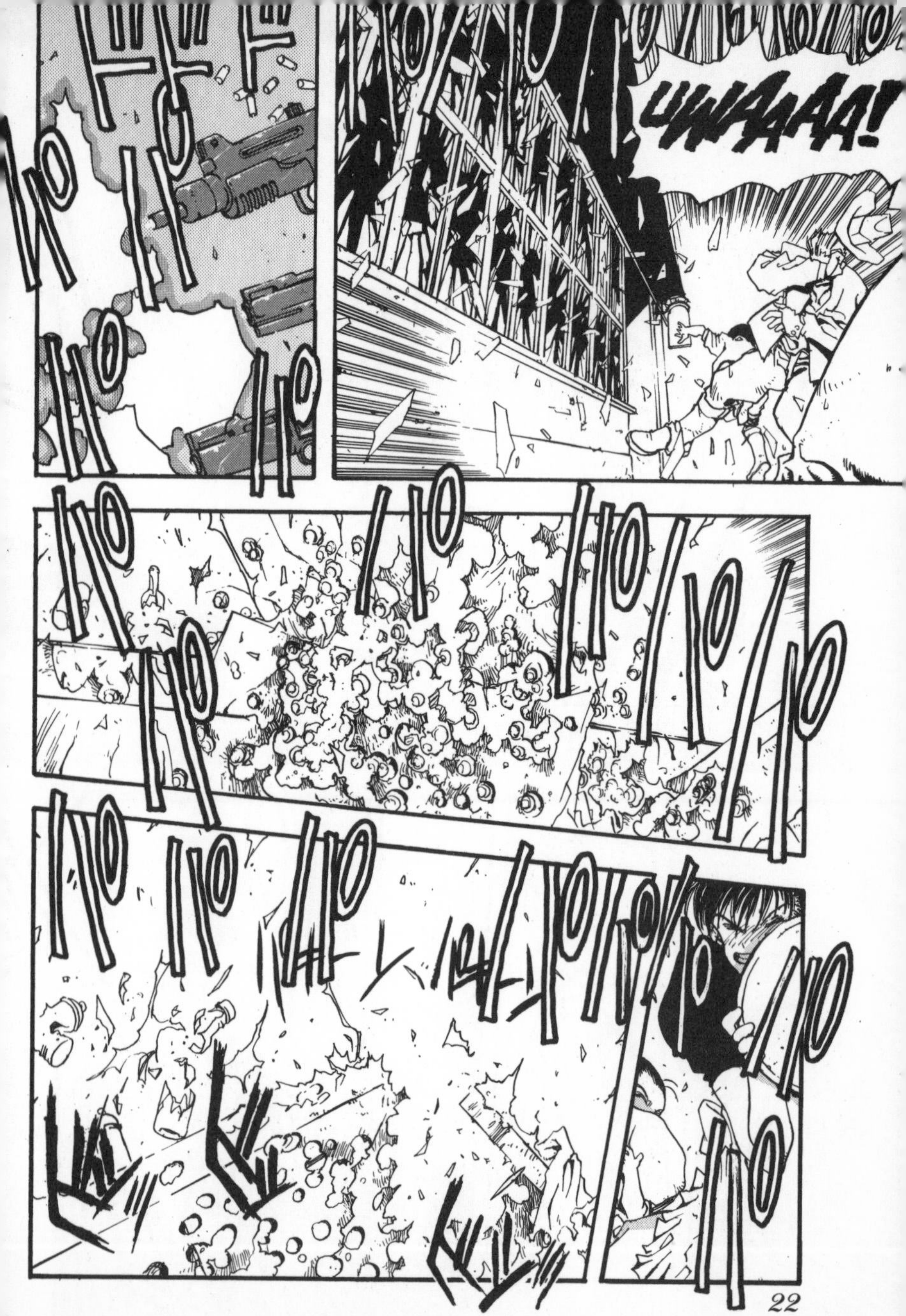
UWAAAA!

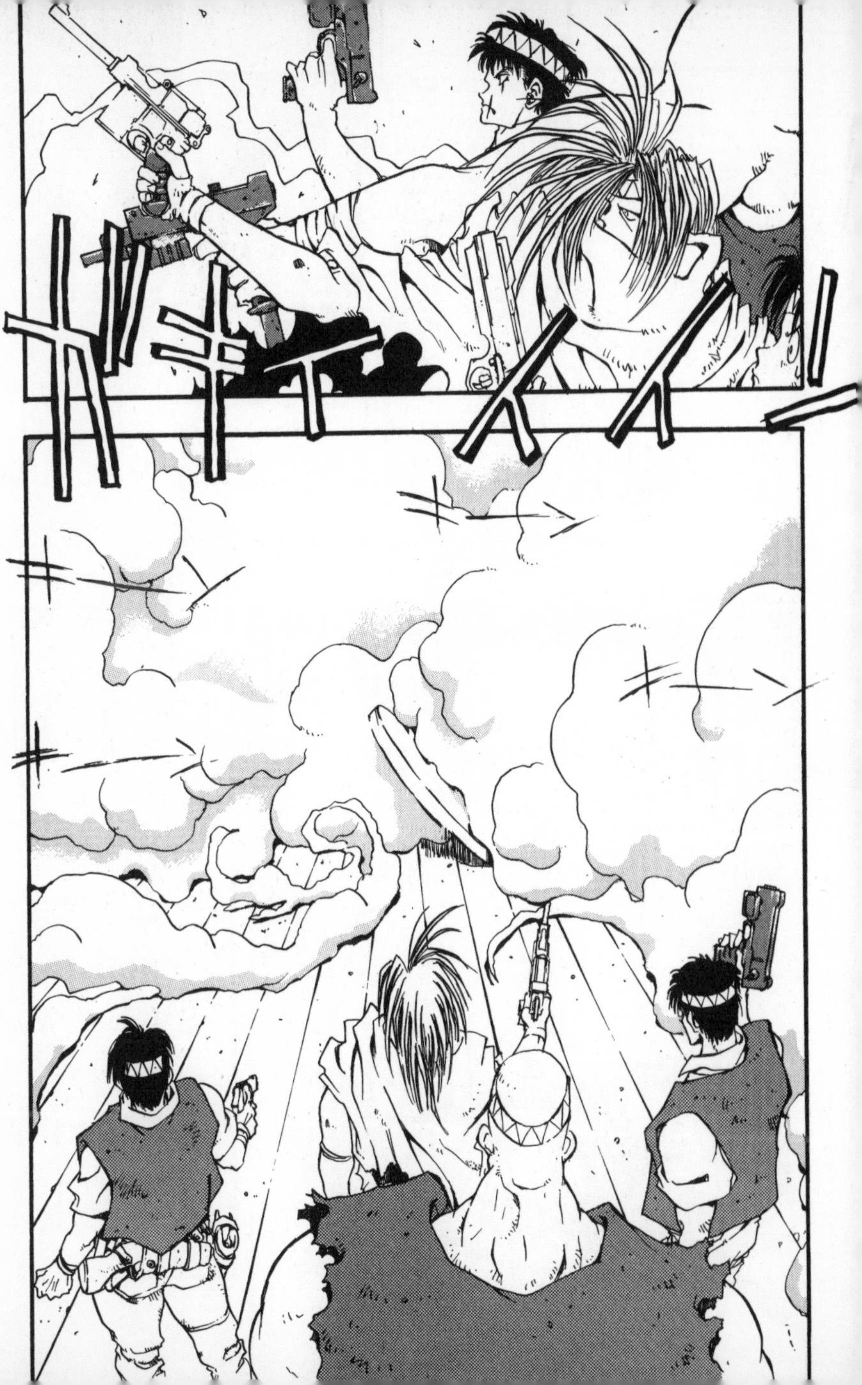

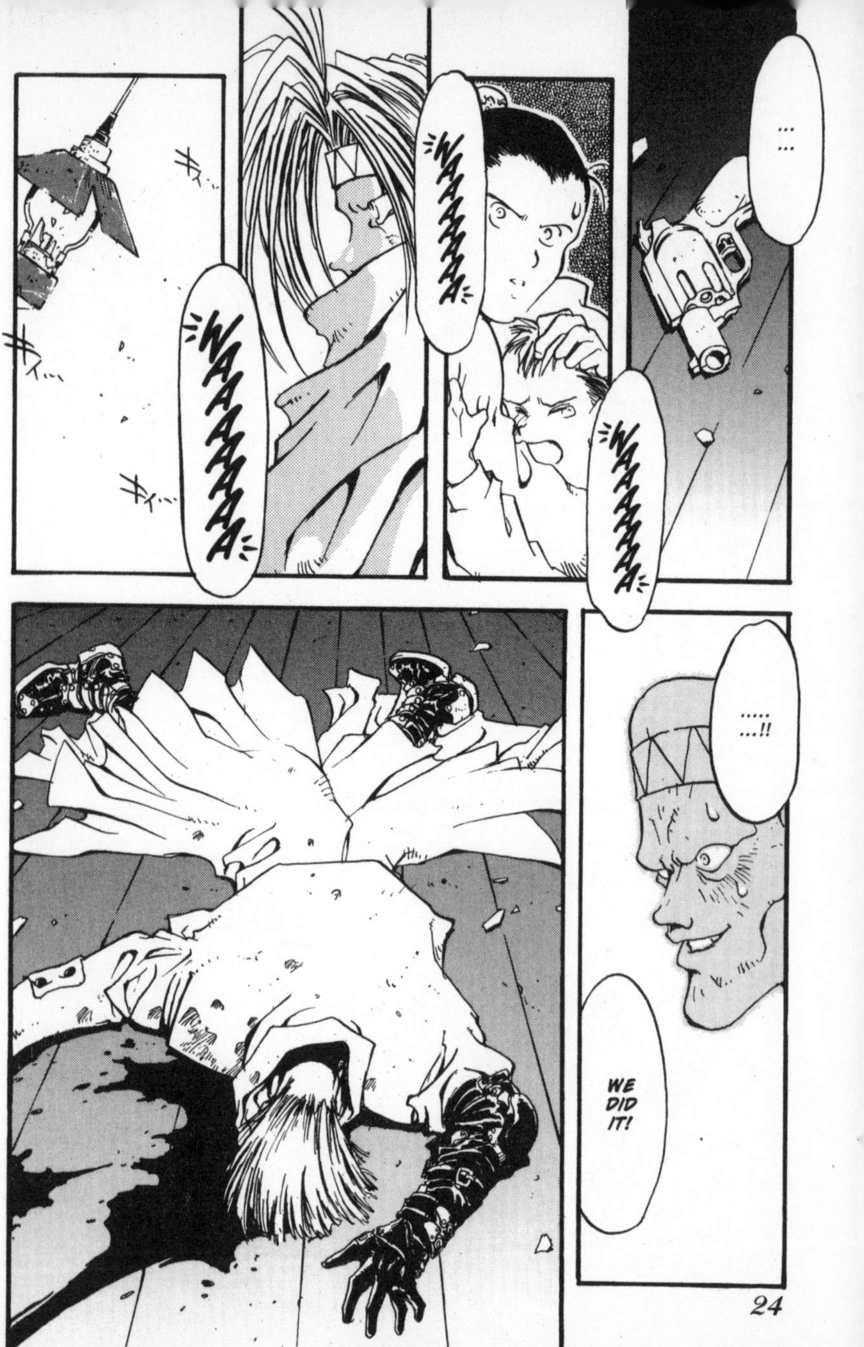
......
WAAAAAAAAA
WAAAAAAAAA
WAAAAAAAAA
......!!
WE DID IT!

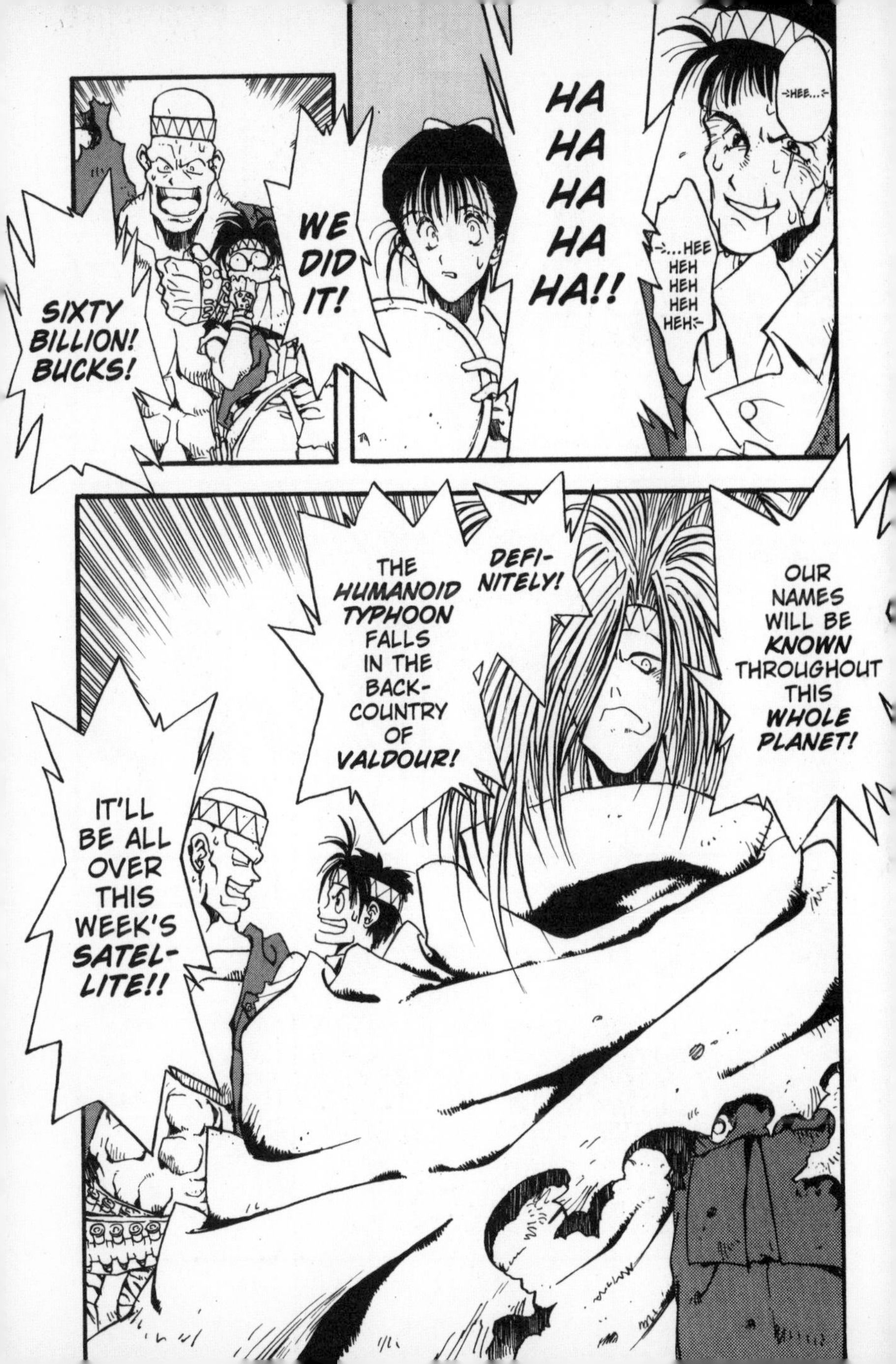

HEE...
HA HA HA HA HA!!
...HEE HEH HEH HEH HEH
WE DID IT!
SIXTY BILLION! BUCKS!
OUR NAMES WILL BE KNOWN THROUGHOUT THIS WHOLE PLANET!
DEFI-NITELY!
THE HUMANOID TYPHOON FALLS IN THE BACK-COUNTRY OF VALDOUR!
IT'LL BE ALL OVER THIS WEEK'S SATEL-LITE!!

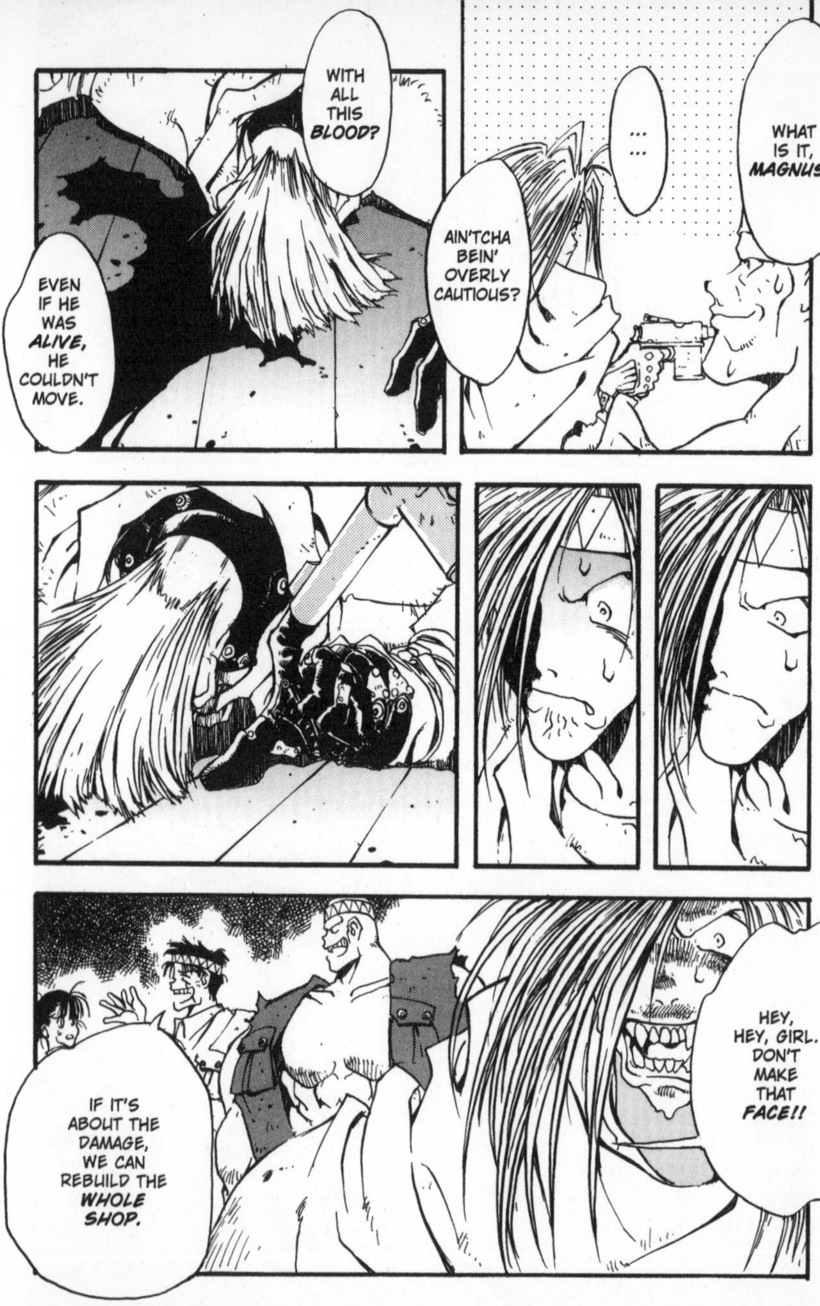
WHAT IS IT, MAGNUS?
... ...
AIN'TCHA BEIN' OVERLY CAUTIOUS?
WITH ALL THIS BLOOD?
EVEN IF HE WAS ALIVE, HE COULDN'T MOVE.
HEY, HEY, GIRL. DON'T MAKE THAT FACE!!
IF IT'S ABOUT THE DAMAGE, WE CAN REBUILD THE WHOLE SHOP.

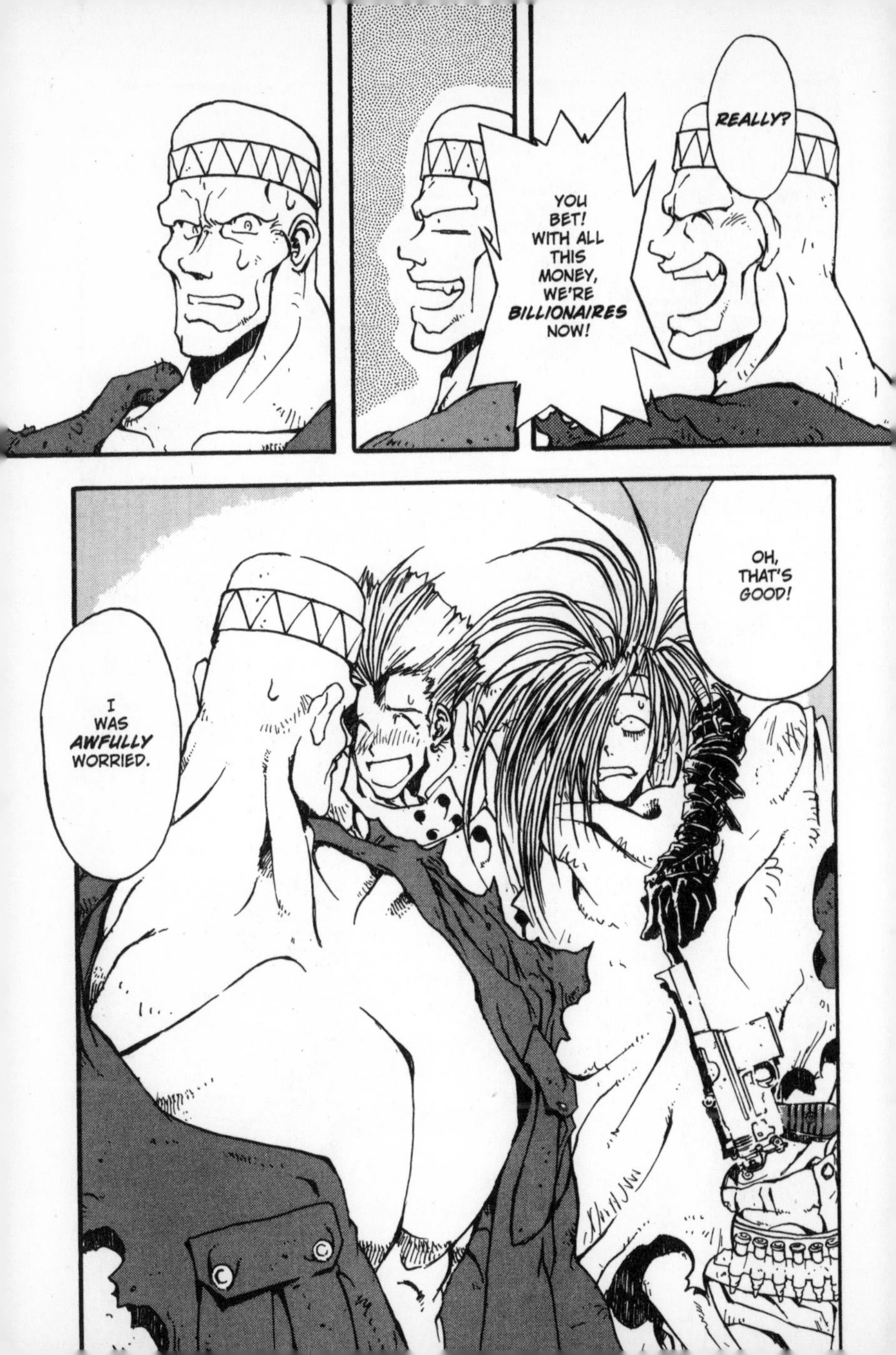
REALLY?
YOU BET! WITH ALL THIS MONEY, WE'RE BILLIONAIRES NOW!
OH, THAT'S GOOD!
I WAS AWFULLY WORRIED.

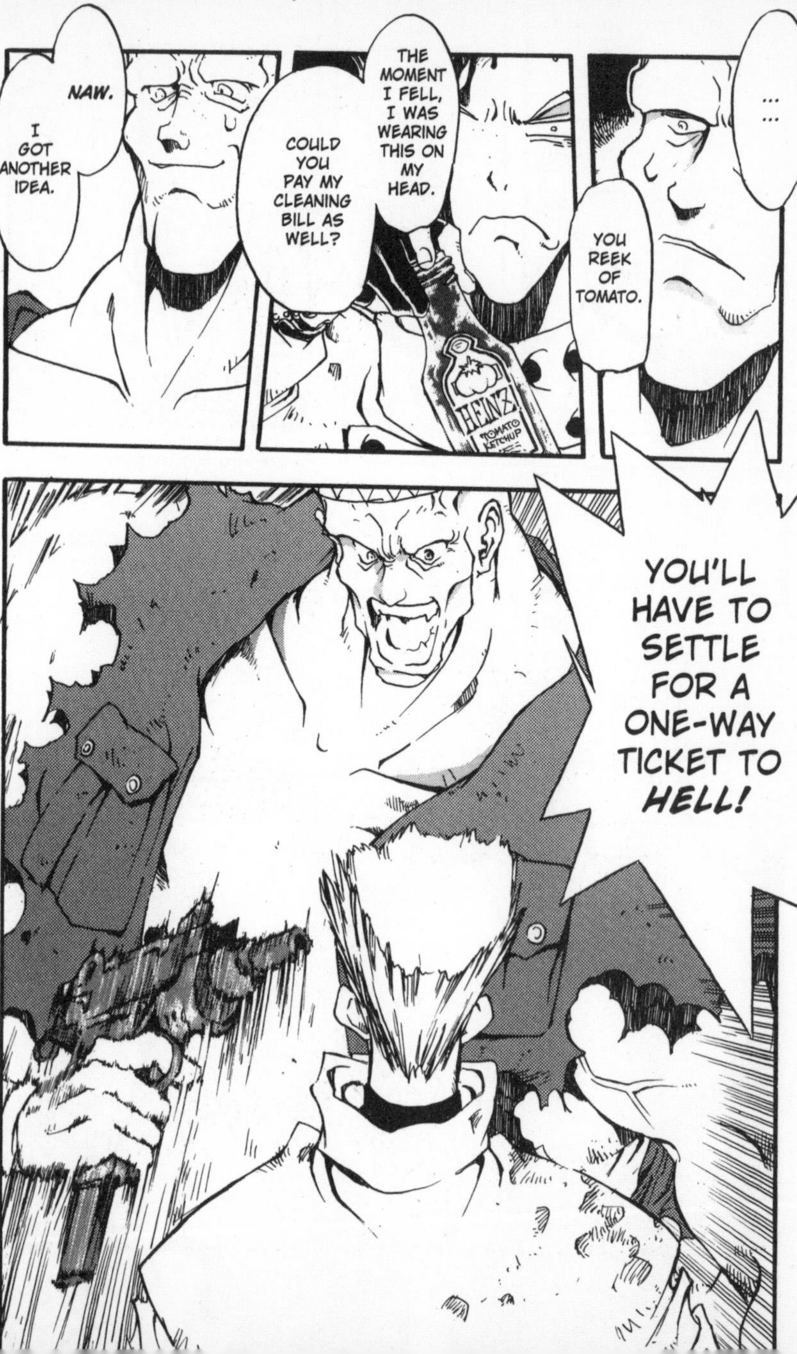
... ...
YOU REEK OF TOMATO.
THE MOMENT I FELL, I WAS WEARING THIS ON MY HEAD.
HEINZ
TOMATO KETCHUP
COULD YOU PAY MY CLEANING BILL AS WELL?
NAW.
I GOT ANOTHER IDEA.
YOU'LL HAVE TO SETTLE FOR A ONE-WAY TICKET TO HELL!

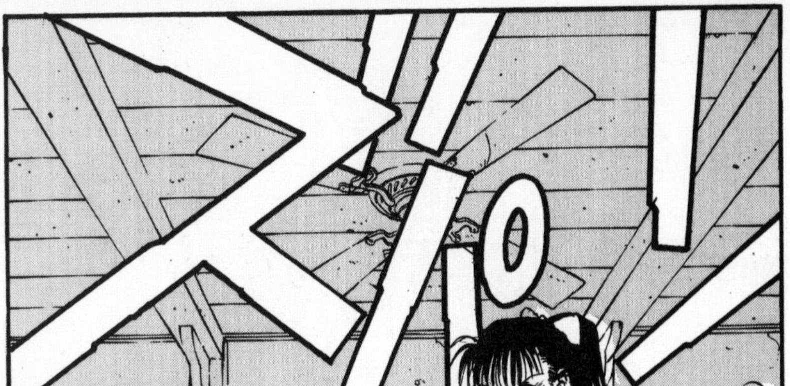

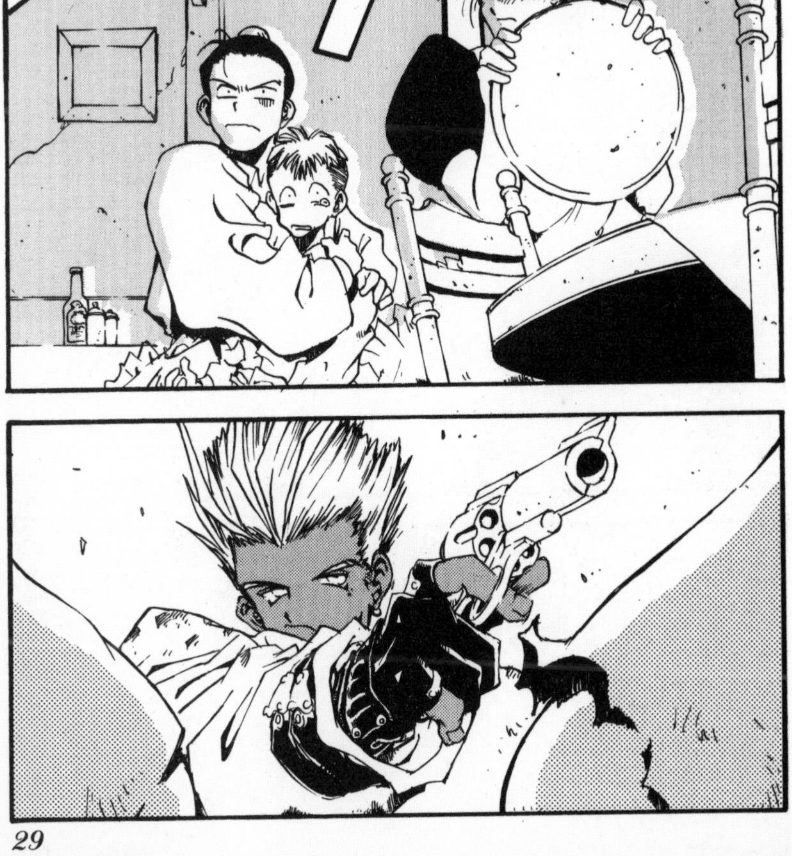

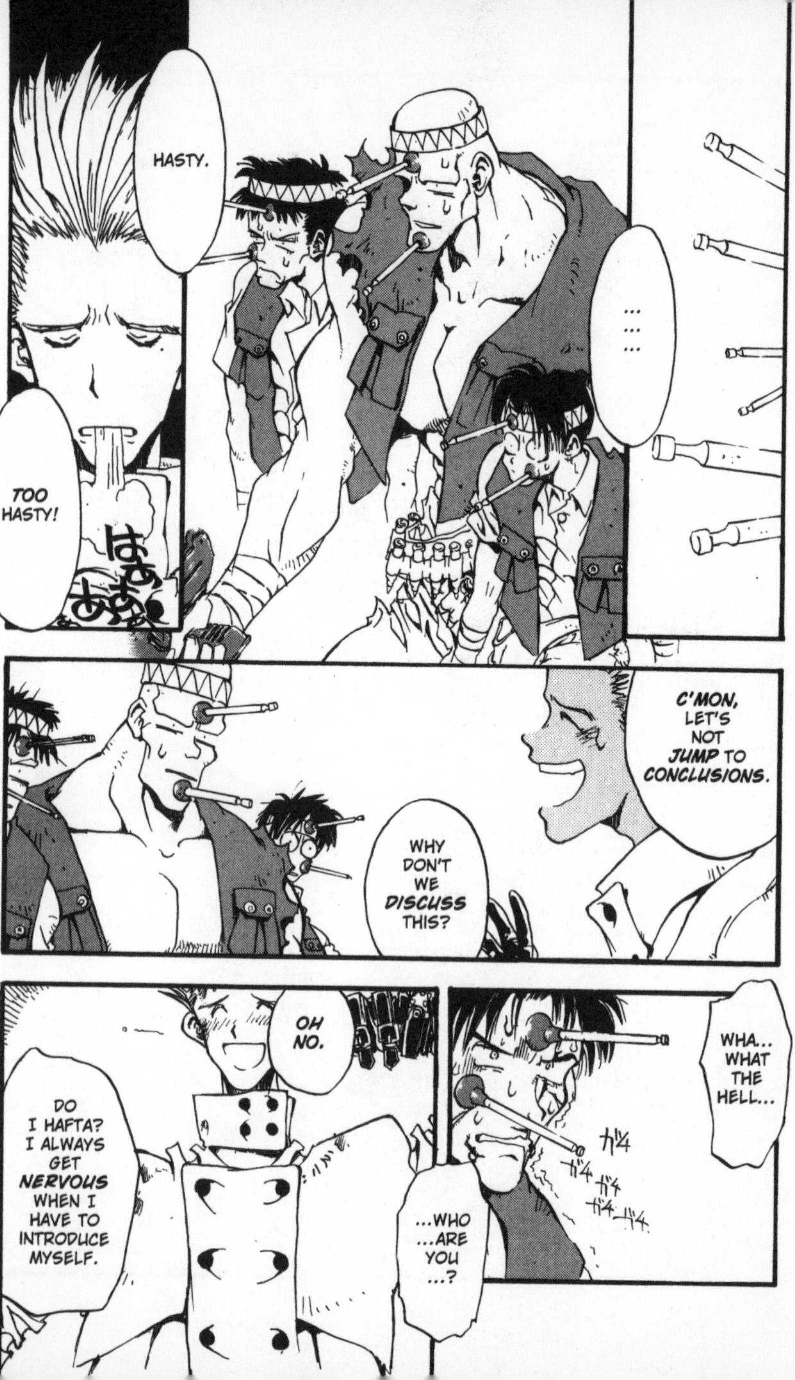
...
...
...
HASTY.
TOO HASTY!
はあああ
C'MON, LET'S NOT JUMP TO CONCLUSIONS.
WHY DON'T WE DISCUSS THIS?
WHA... WHAT THE HELL...
ガタ ガタ ガタ ガタ ガタ
...WHO ...ARE YOU ...?
OH NO.
DO I HAFTA? I ALWAYS GET NERVOUS WHEN I HAVE TO INTRODUCE MYSELF.

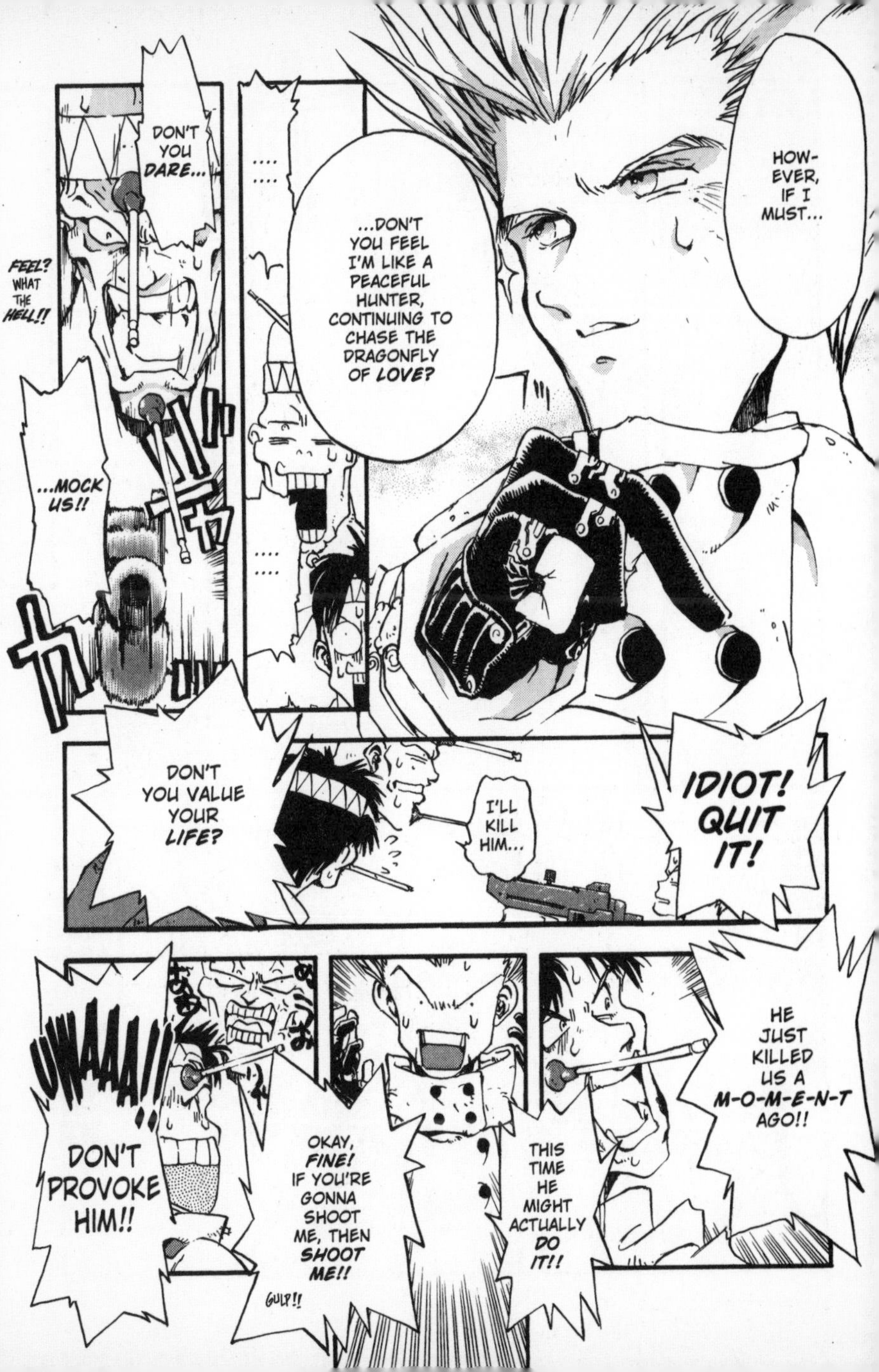
HOW-EVER, IF I MUST...
...DON'T YOU FEEL I'M LIKE A PEACEFUL HUNTER, CONTINUING TO CHASE THE DRAGONFLY OF LOVE?
....
....
DON'T YOU DARE...
...MOCK US!!
FEEL? WHAT THE HELL!!
IDIOT! QUIT IT!
I'LL KILL HIM...
DON'T YOU VALUE YOUR LIFE?
HE JUST KILLED US A M-O-M-E-N-T AGO!!
THIS TIME HE MIGHT ACTUALLY DO IT!!
OKAY, FINE! IF YOU'RE GONNA SHOOT ME, THEN SHOOT ME!!
GULP!!
UWAAA!!
DON'T PROVOKE HIM!!

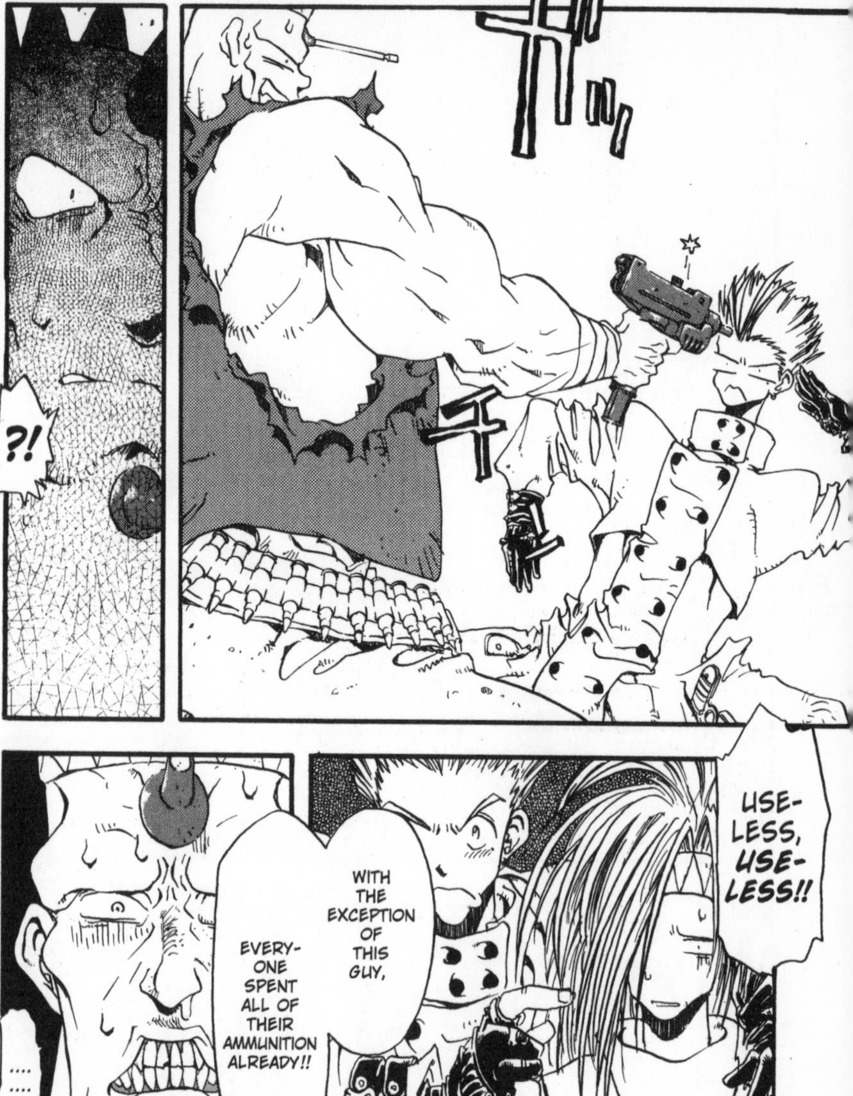
?!
USE-LESS, USE-LESS!!
WITH THE EXCEPTION OF THIS GUY,
EVERY-ONE SPENT ALL OF THEIR AMMUNITION ALREADY!!
....
....

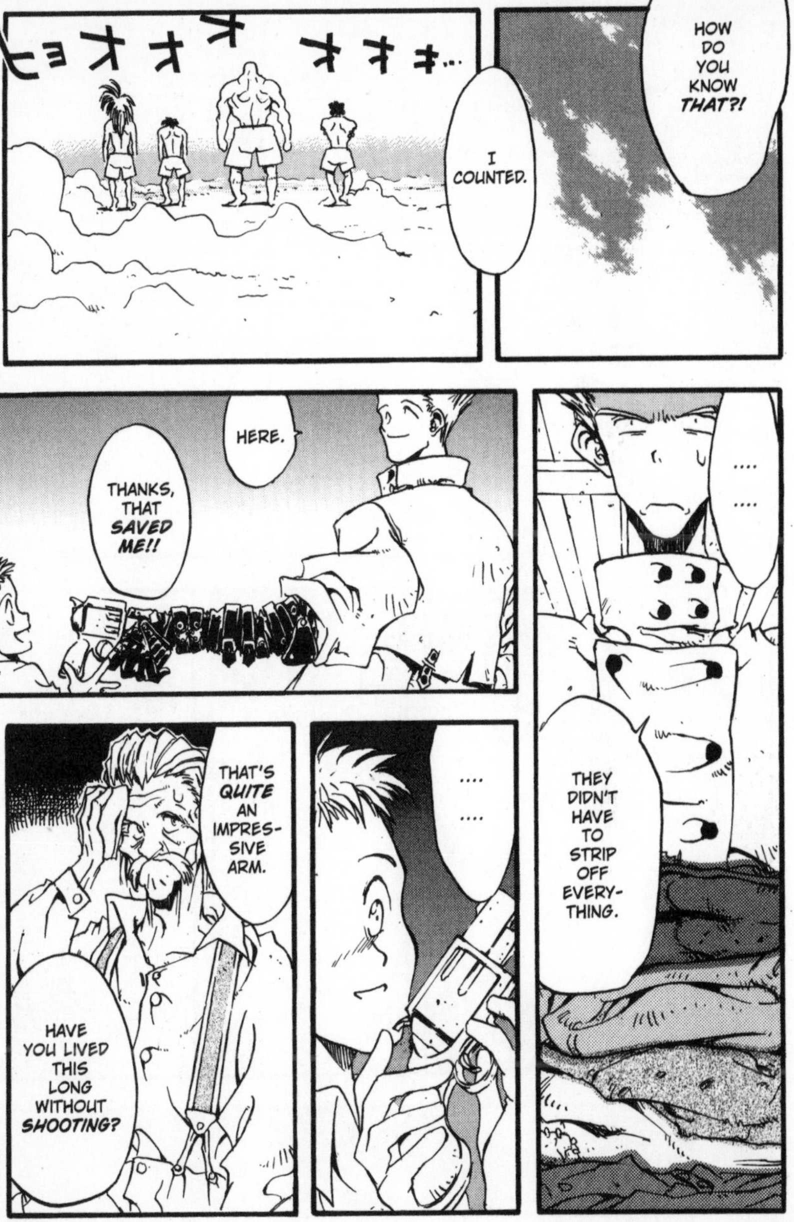
HOW DO YOU KNOW *THAT?!*
I COUNTED.
ヒョオオオ オオオ…
....
....
THEY DIDN'T HAVE TO STRIP OFF EVERYTHING.
HERE.
THANKS, THAT *SAVED ME!!*
....
....
THAT'S *QUITE* AN IMPRES-SIVE ARM.
HAVE YOU LIVED THIS LONG WITHOUT *SHOOTING?*

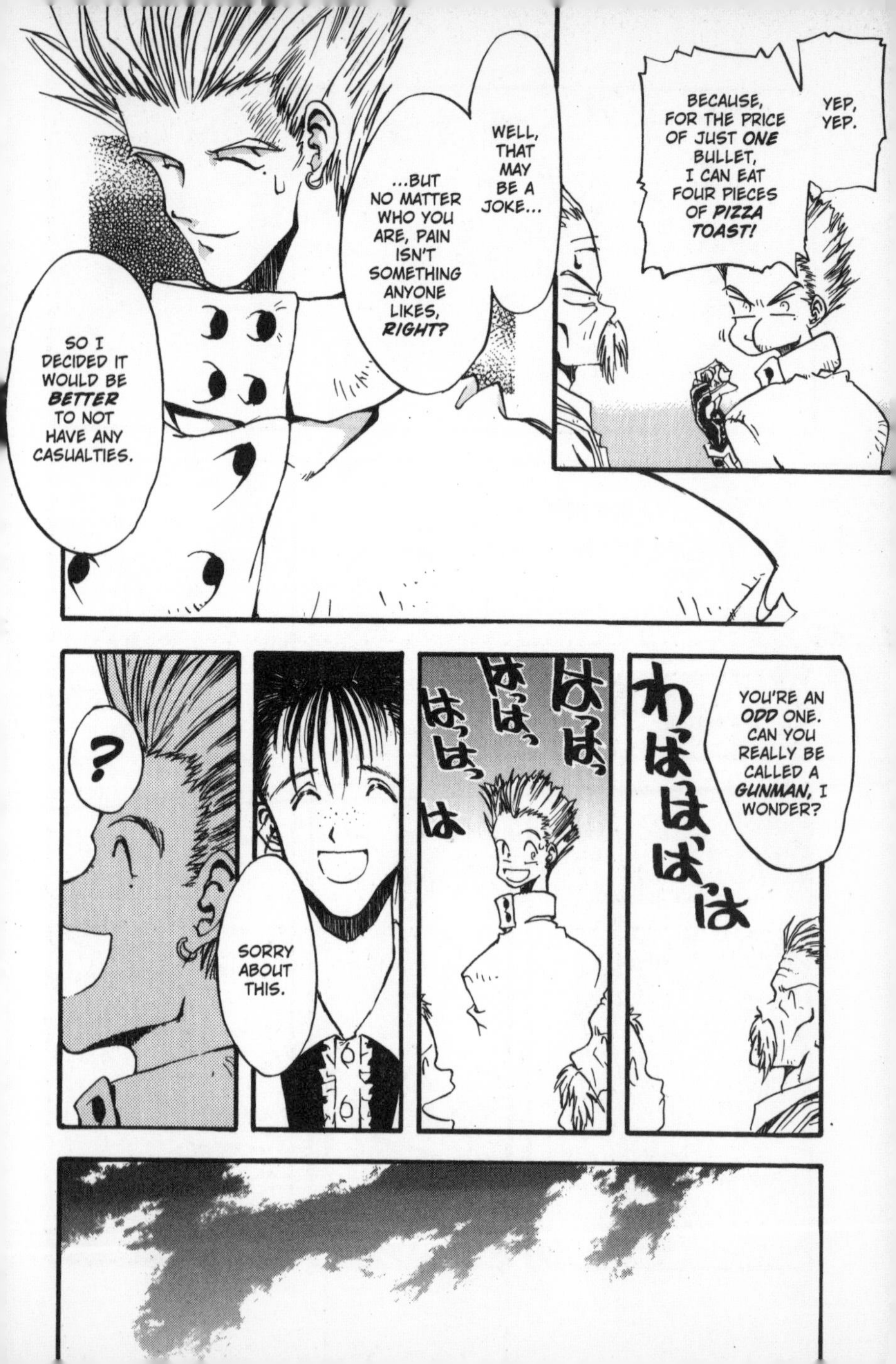
YEP, YEP.
BECAUSE, FOR THE PRICE OF JUST ONE BULLET, I CAN EAT FOUR PIECES OF PIZZA TOAST!
WELL, THAT MAY BE A JOKE...
...BUT NO MATTER WHO YOU ARE, PAIN ISN'T SOMETHING ANYONE LIKES, RIGHT?
SO I DECIDED IT WOULD BE BETTER TO NOT HAVE ANY CASUALTIES.
YOU'RE AN ODD ONE. CAN YOU REALLY BE CALLED A GUNMAN, I WONDER?
わっはははっは
はっはっ
はっはっ
はっはっ
は
SORRY ABOUT THIS.
?

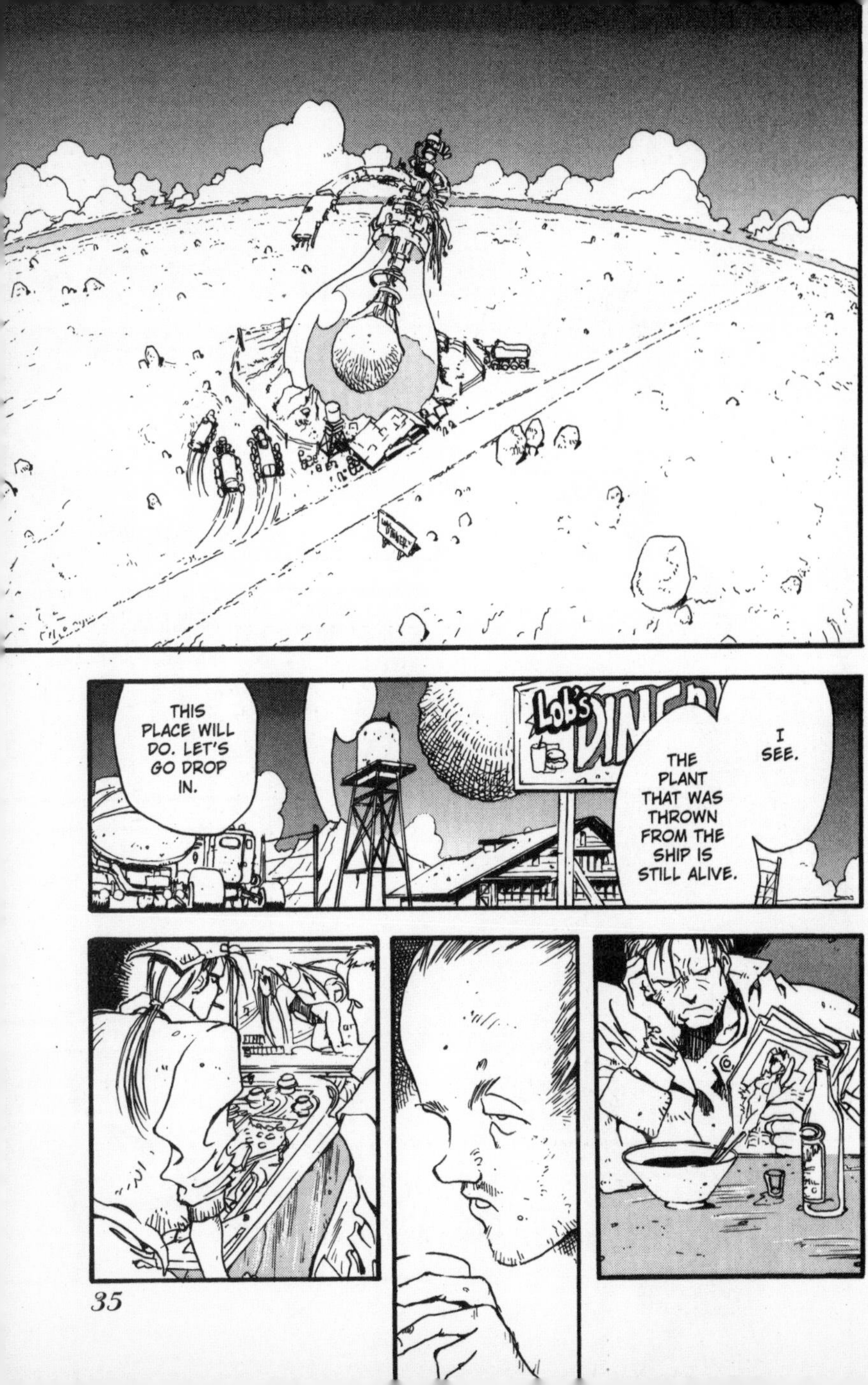
Lob's
I SEE.
THE PLANT THAT WAS THROWN FROM THE SHIP IS STILL ALIVE.
THIS PLACE WILL DO. LET'S GO DROP IN.

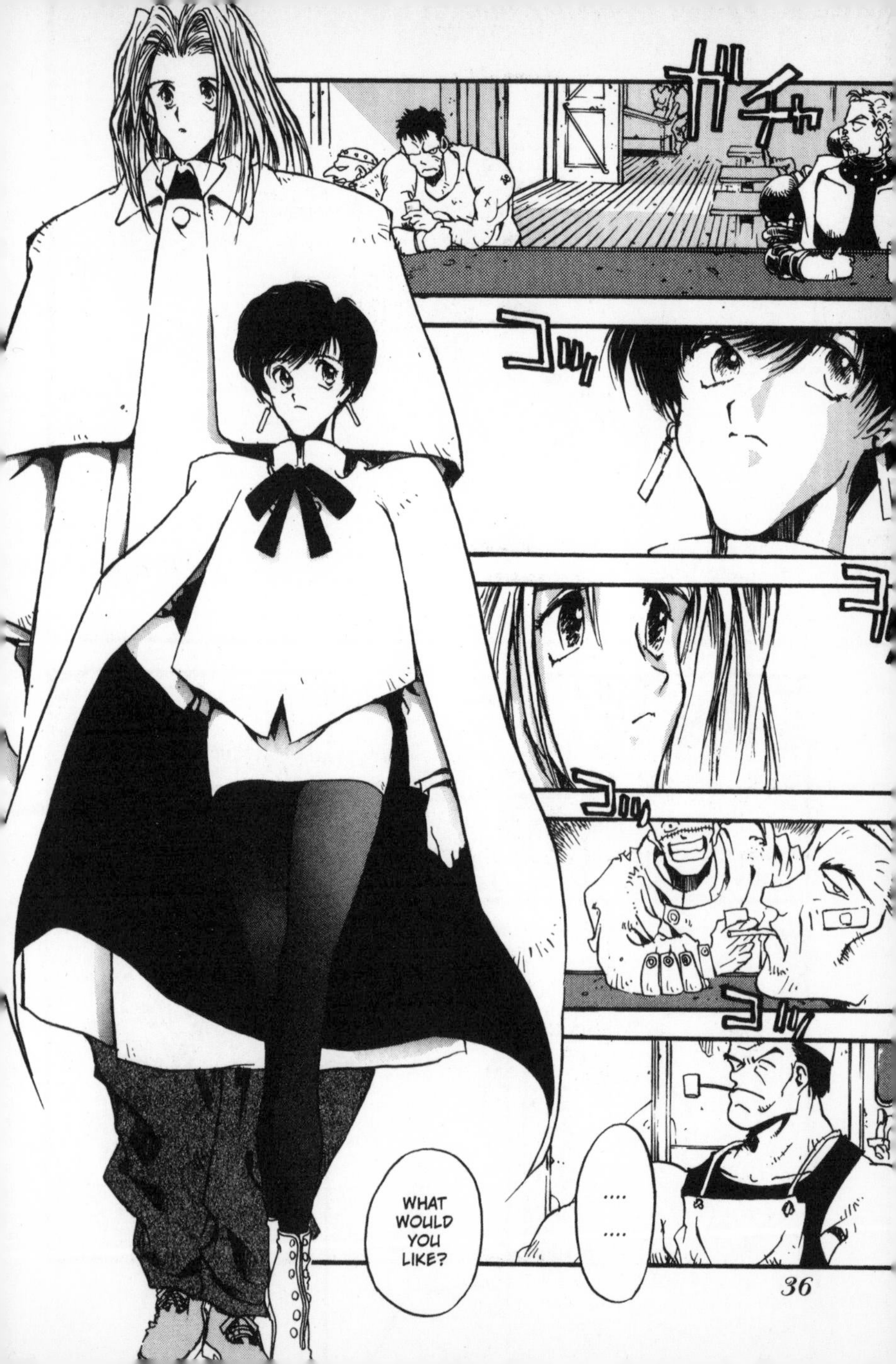
ガチャ
コッ
コッ
コッ
コッ
....
....
WHAT WOULD YOU LIKE?

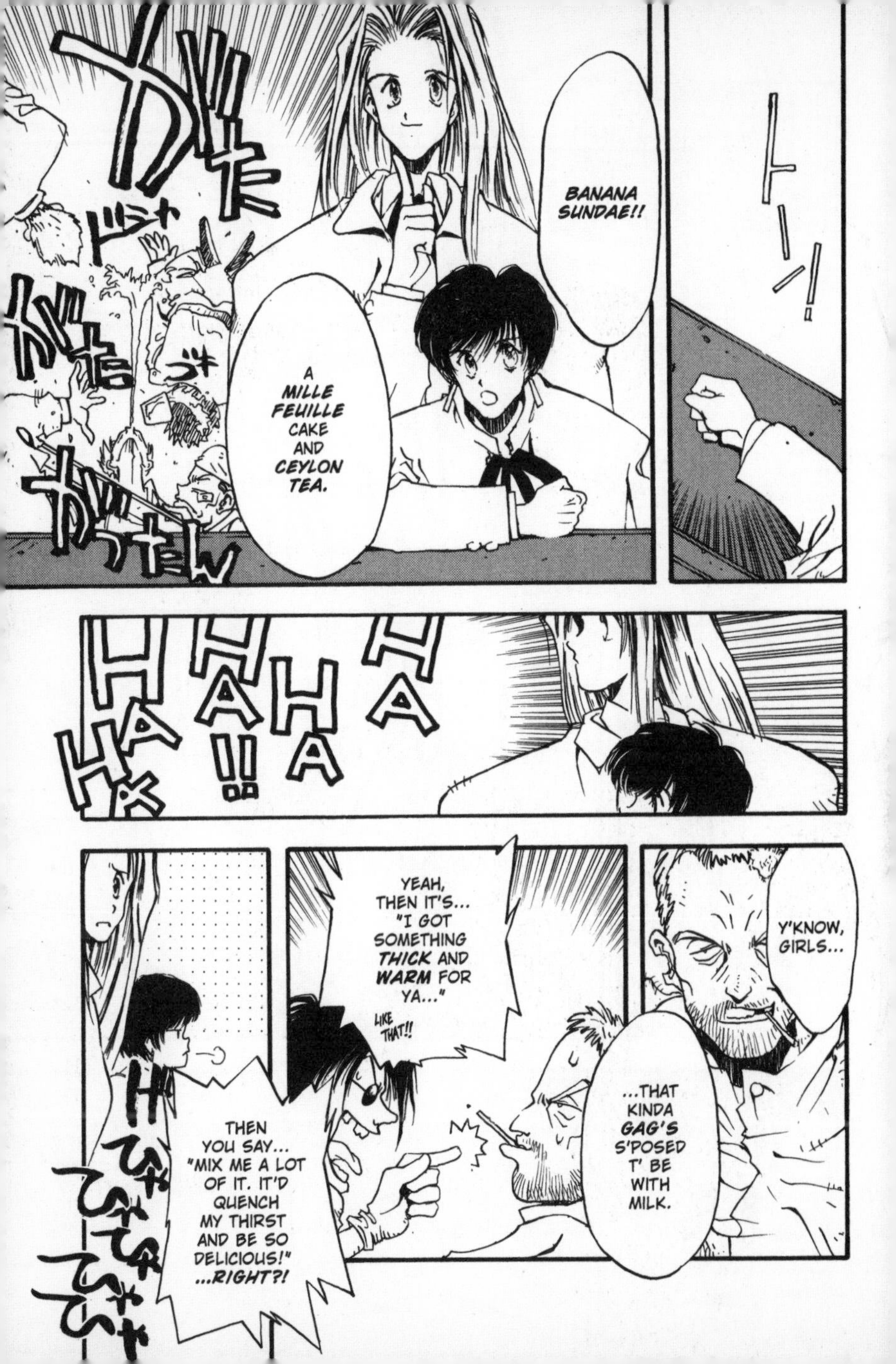
BANANA SUNDAE!!
A MILLE FEUILLE CAKE AND CEYLON TEA.
HAHAHAHA!!
Y'KNOW, GIRLS...
...THAT KINDA GAG'S S'POSED T' BE WITH MILK.
YEAH, THEN IT'S... "I GOT SOMETHING THICK AND WARM FOR YA..."
LIKE THAT!!
THEN YOU SAY... "MIX ME A LOT OF IT. IT'D QUENCH MY THIRST AND BE SO DELICIOUS!" ...RIGHT?!

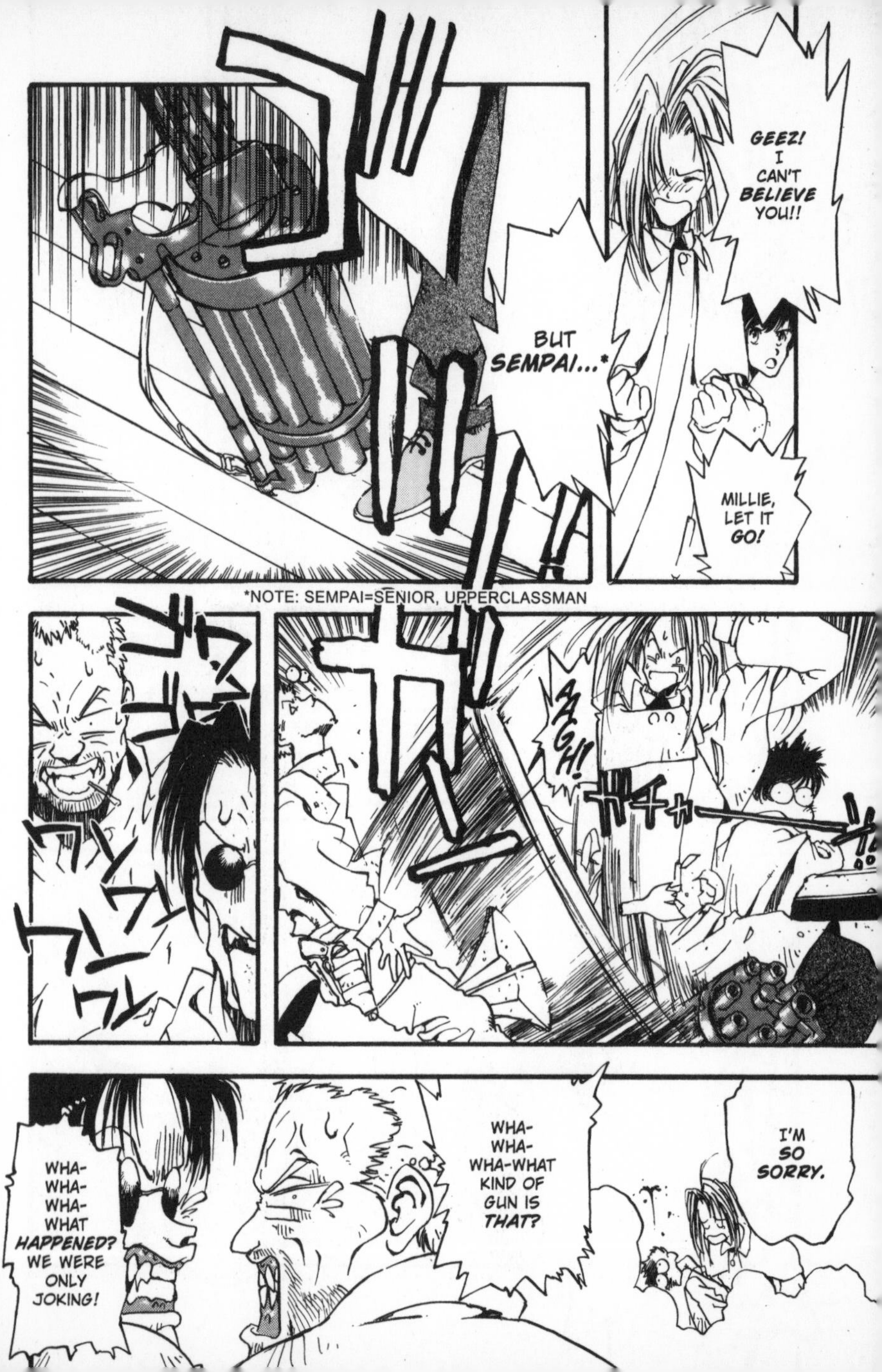
GEEZ! I CAN'T BELIEVE YOU!!
MILLIE, LET IT GO!
BUT SEMPAI...*
*NOTE: SEMPAI=SENIOR, UPPERCLASSMAN
AAAGH!!
I'M SO SORRY.
WHA-WHA-WHA-WHAT KIND OF GUN IS THAT?
WHA-WHA-WHA-WHAT HAPPENED? WE WERE ONLY JOKING!

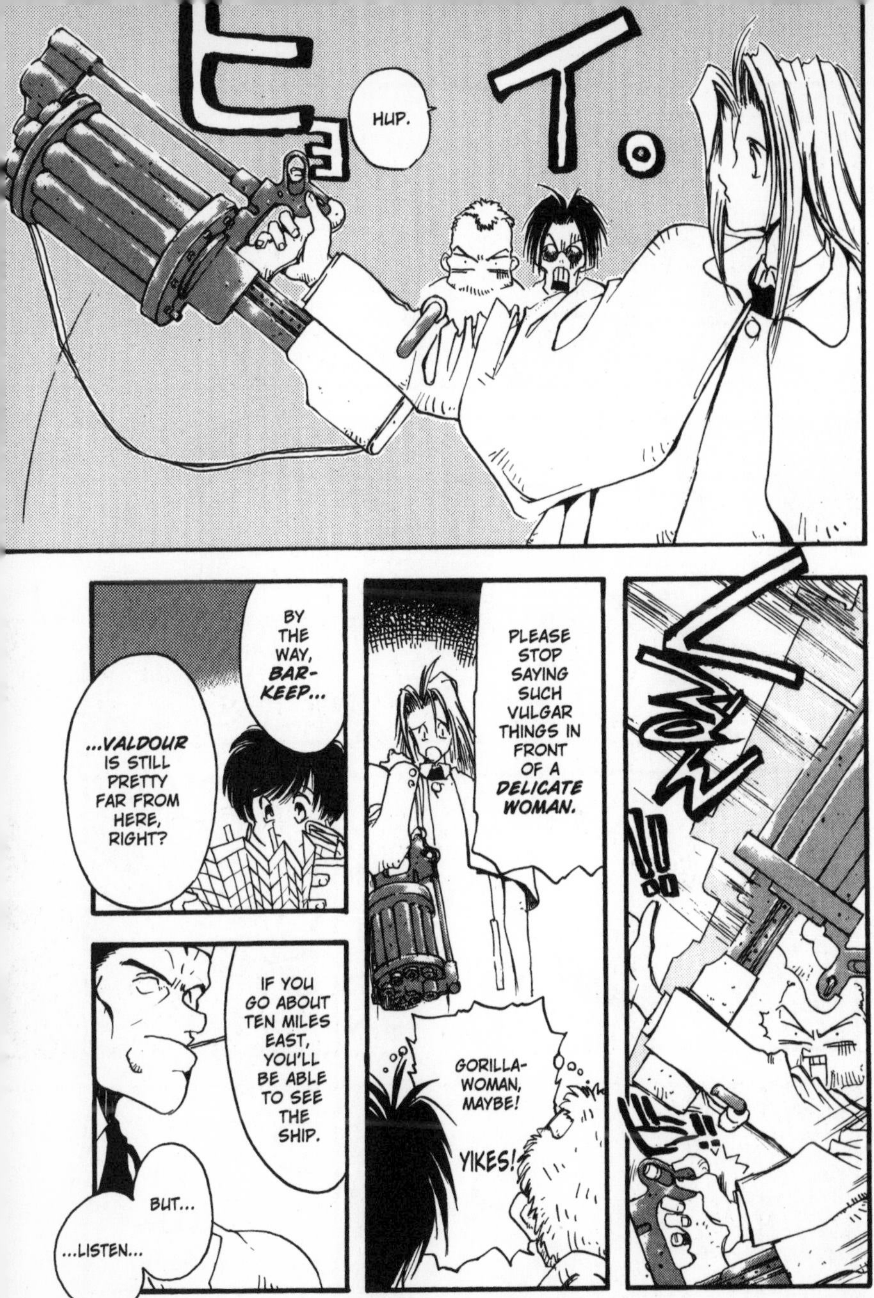
ヒョイ。
HUP.
PLEASE STOP SAYING SUCH VULGAR THINGS IN FRONT OF A *DELICATE WOMAN.*
GORILLA-WOMAN, MAYBE!
YIKES!
BY THE WAY, *BAR-KEEP...*
*...VALDOUR* IS STILL PRETTY FAR FROM HERE, RIGHT?
IF YOU GO ABOUT TEN MILES EAST, YOU'LL BE ABLE TO SEE THE SHIP.
BUT...
...LISTEN...

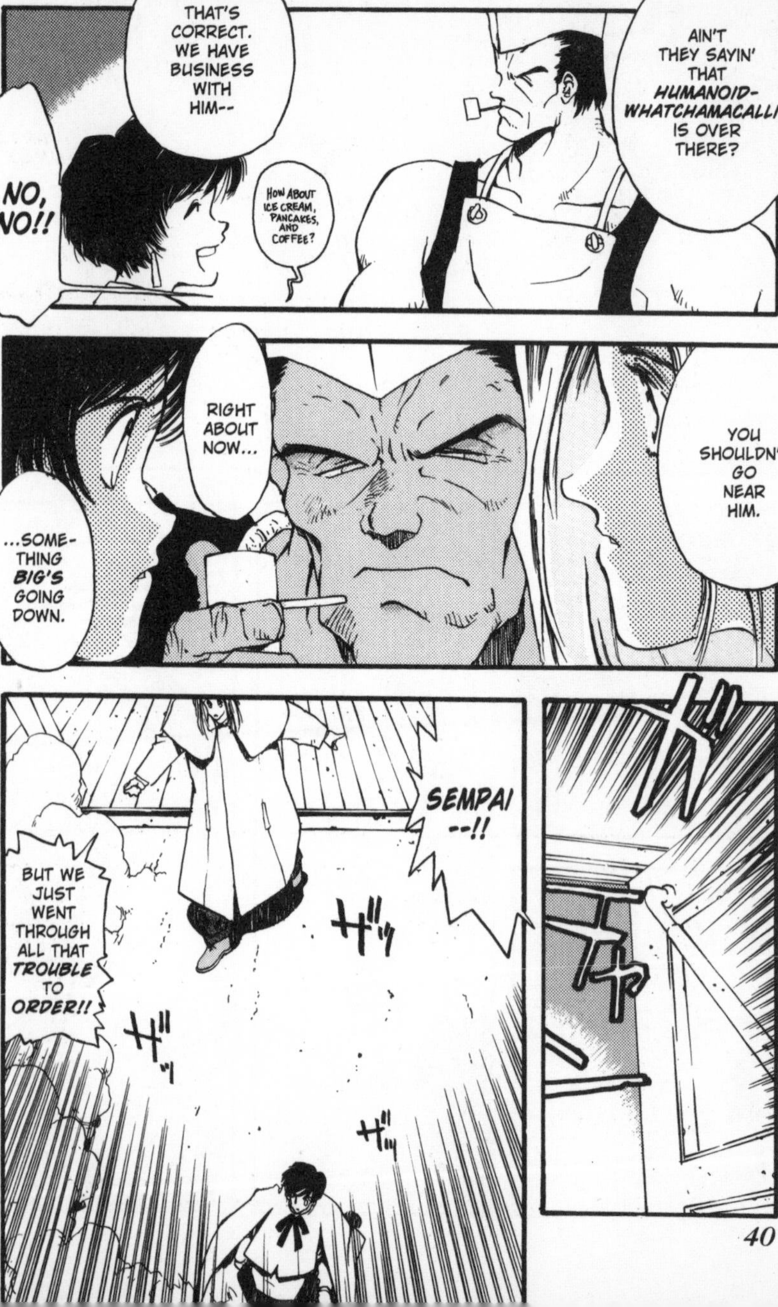
AIN'T THEY SAYIN' THAT HUMANOID-WHATCHAMACALLIT IS OVER THERE?
THAT'S CORRECT. WE HAVE BUSINESS WITH HIM--
HOW ABOUT ICE CREAM, PANCAKES, AND COFFEE?
NO, NO!!
YOU SHOULDN'T GO NEAR HIM.
RIGHT ABOUT NOW...
...SOME-THING BIG'S GOING DOWN.
SEMPAI --!!
BUT WE JUST WENT THROUGH ALL THAT TROUBLE TO ORDER!!

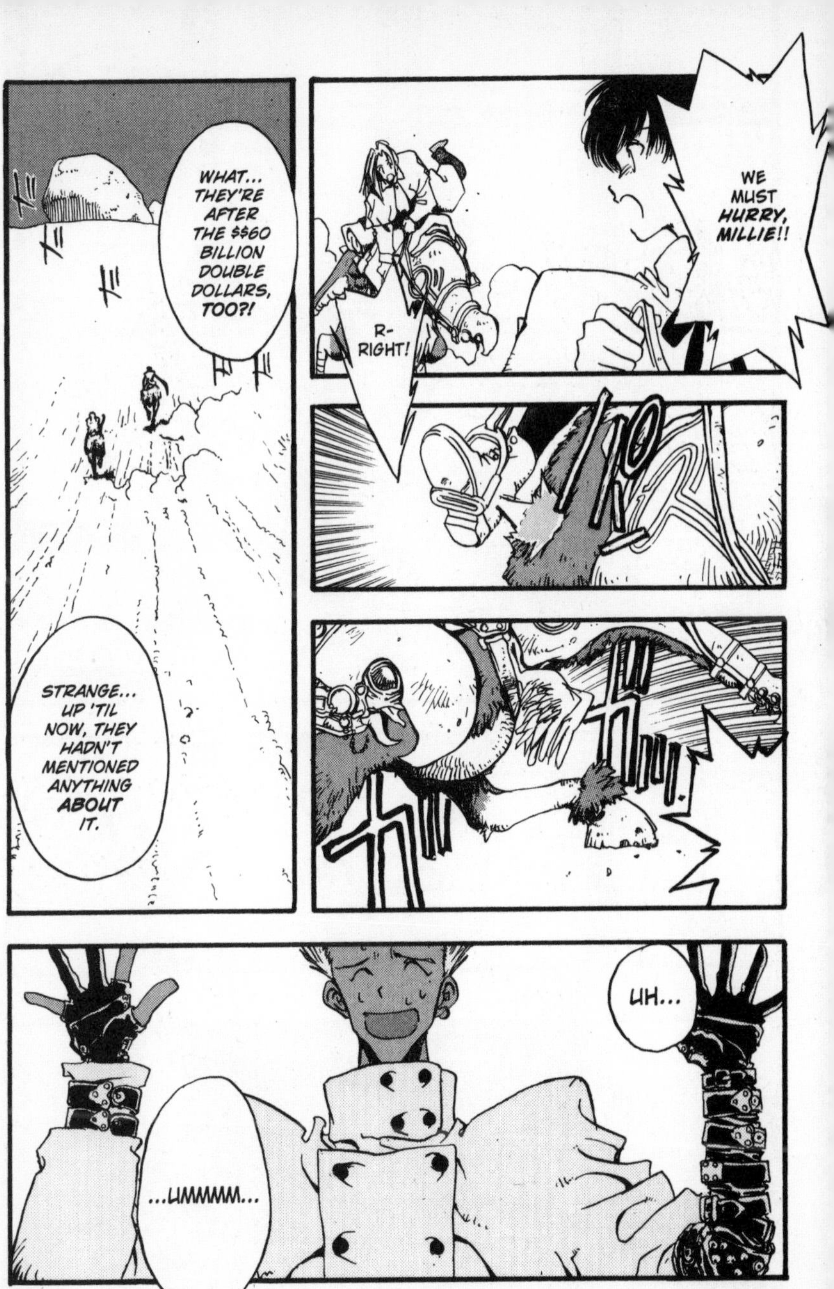
WE MUST HURRY, MILLIE!!
R-RIGHT!
WHAT... THEY'RE AFTER THE $$60 BILLION DOUBLE DOLLARS, TOO?!
STRANGE... UP 'TIL NOW, THEY HADN'T MENTIONED ANYTHING ABOUT IT.
UH...
...UMMMMM...

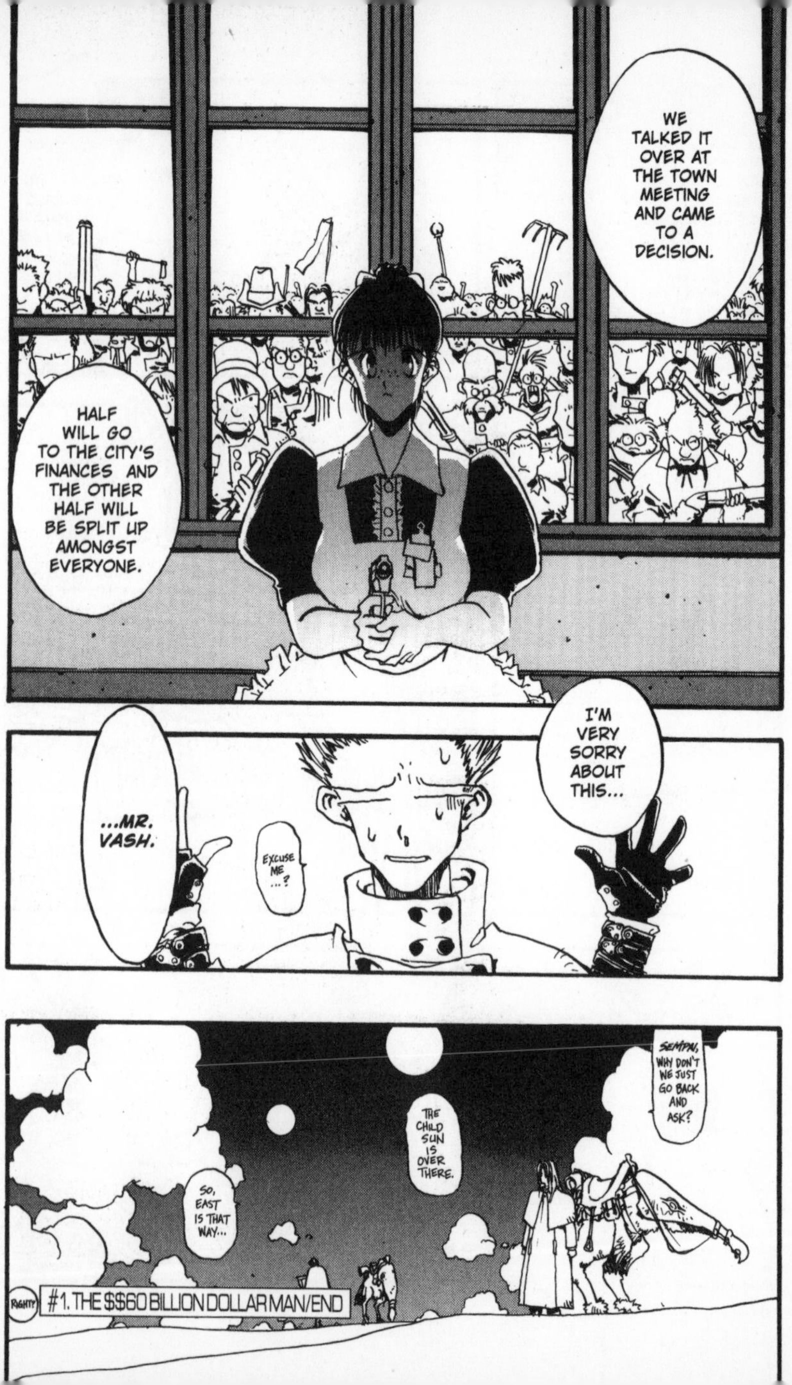
WE TALKED IT OVER AT THE TOWN MEETING AND CAME TO A DECISION.
HALF WILL GO TO THE CITY'S FINANCES AND THE OTHER HALF WILL BE SPLIT UP AMONGST EVERYONE.
I'M VERY SORRY ABOUT THIS...
...MR. VASH.
EXCUSE ME ...?
SEMPAI, WHY DON'T WE JUST GO BACK AND ASK?
THE CHILD SUN IS OVER THERE.
SO, EAST IS THAT WAY...
RIGHTY
#1. THE $$60 BILLION DOLLAR MAN/END

# #2

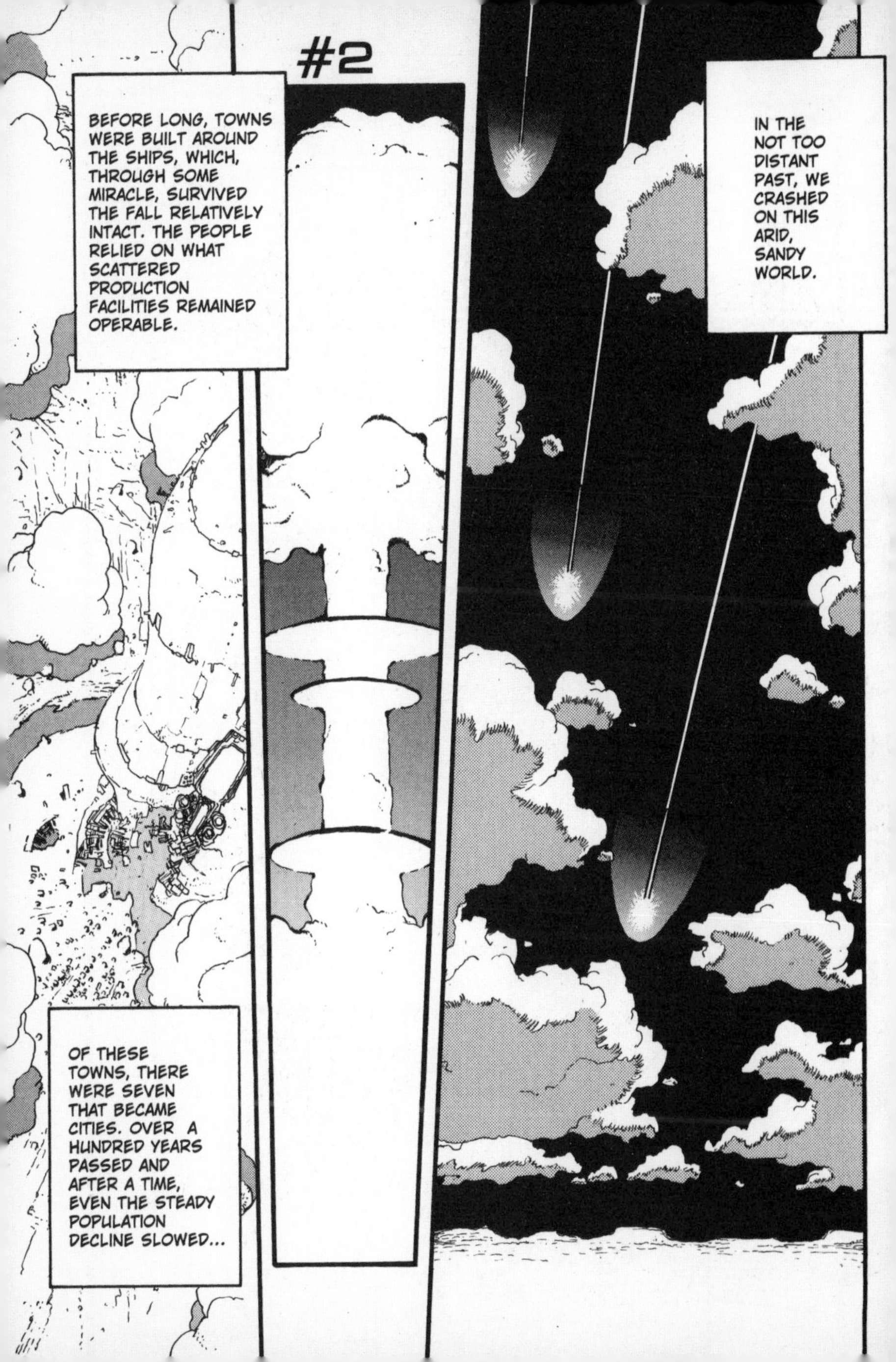
IN THE NOT TOO DISTANT PAST, WE CRASHED ON THIS ARID, SANDY WORLD.
BEFORE LONG, TOWNS WERE BUILT AROUND THE SHIPS, WHICH, THROUGH SOME MIRACLE, SURVIVED THE FALL RELATIVELY INTACT. THE PEOPLE RELIED ON WHAT SCATTERED PRODUCTION FACILITIES REMAINED OPERABLE.
OF THESE TOWNS, THERE WERE SEVEN THAT BECAME CITIES. OVER A HUNDRED YEARS PASSED AND AFTER A TIME, EVEN THE STEADY POPULATION DECLINE SLOWED...

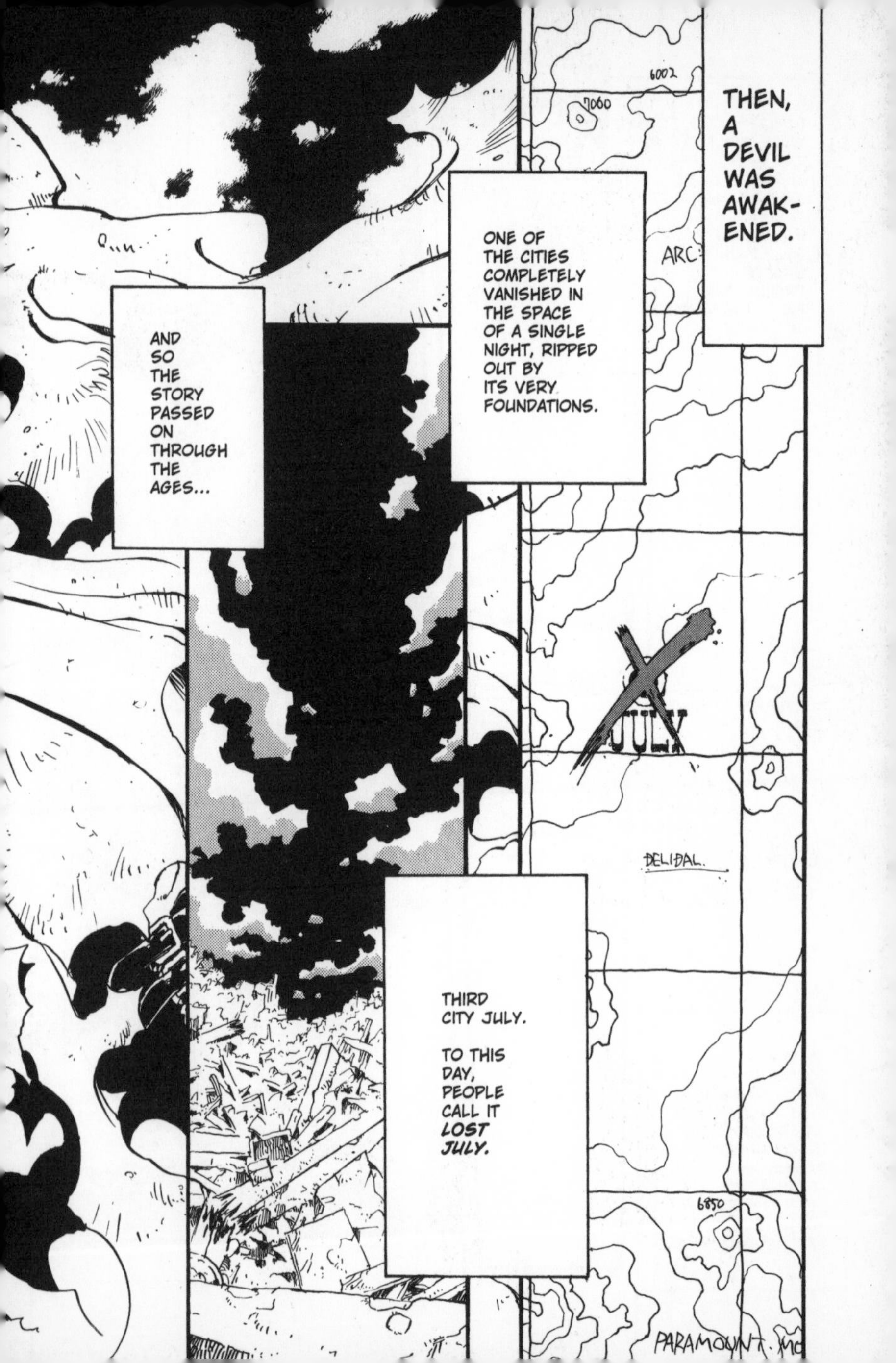
THEN, A DEVIL WAS AWAKENED.
6002
7060
ARC
ONE OF THE CITIES COMPLETELY VANISHED IN THE SPACE OF A SINGLE NIGHT, RIPPED OUT BY ITS VERY FOUNDATIONS.
JULY
DELIDAL.
6850
THIRD CITY JULY.
TO THIS DAY, PEOPLE CALL IT *LOST JULY.*
AND SO THE STORY PASSED ON THROUGH THE AGES...

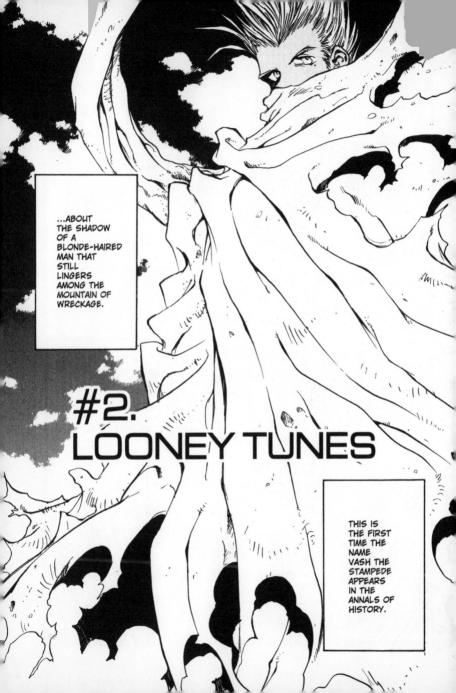

...ABOUT
THE SHADOW
OF A
BLONDE-HAIRED
MAN THAT
STILL
LINGERS
AMONG THE
MOUNTAIN OF
WRECKAGE.

# #2.
# LOONEY TUNES

THIS IS
THE FIRST
TIME THE
NAME
VASH THE
STAMPEDE
APPEARS
IN THE
ANNALS OF
HISTORY.

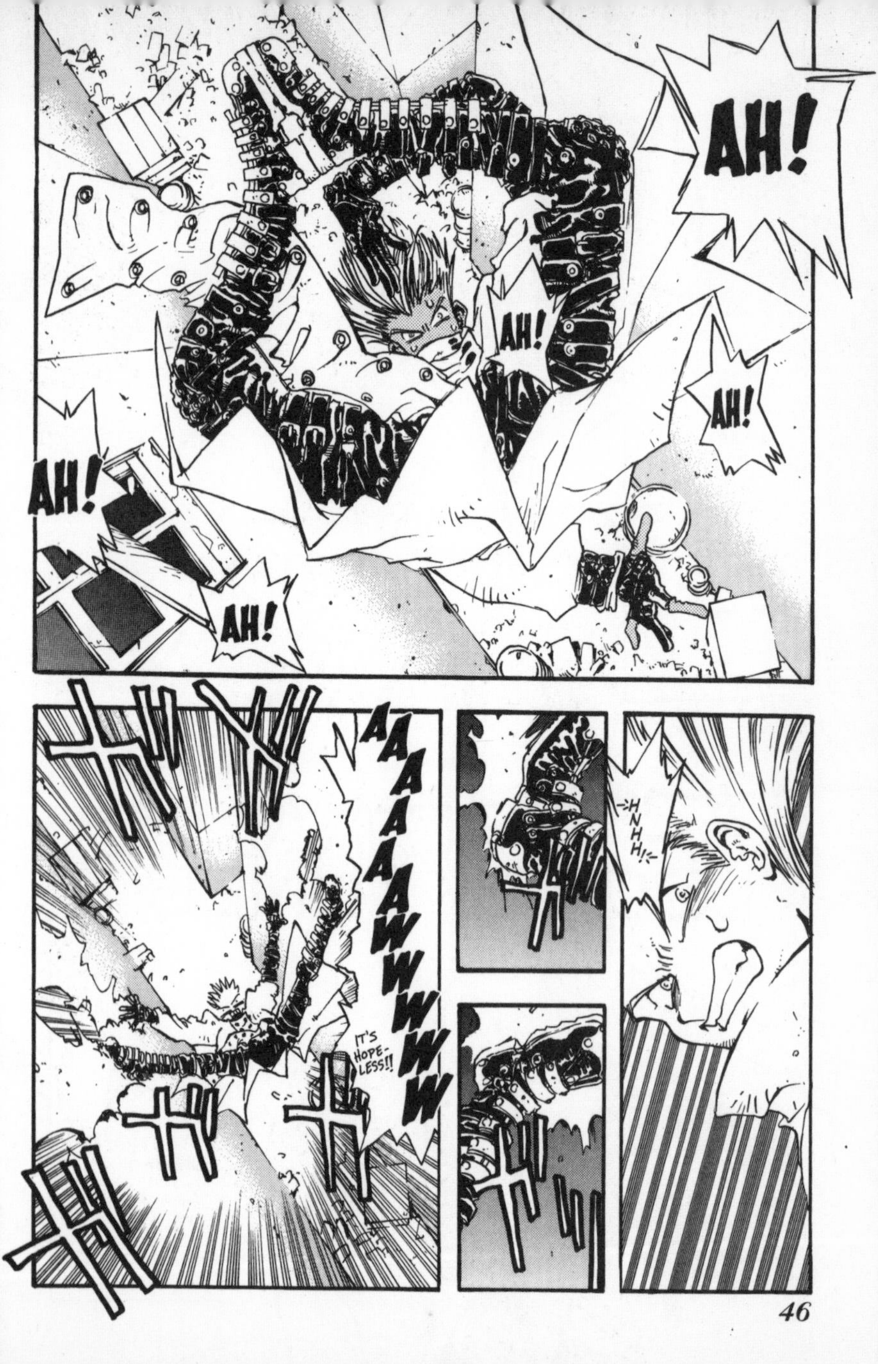
AH!
AH!
AH!
AH!
AH!
HNHH!
AAAAAAWWWWWW
IT'S HOPE-LESS!!

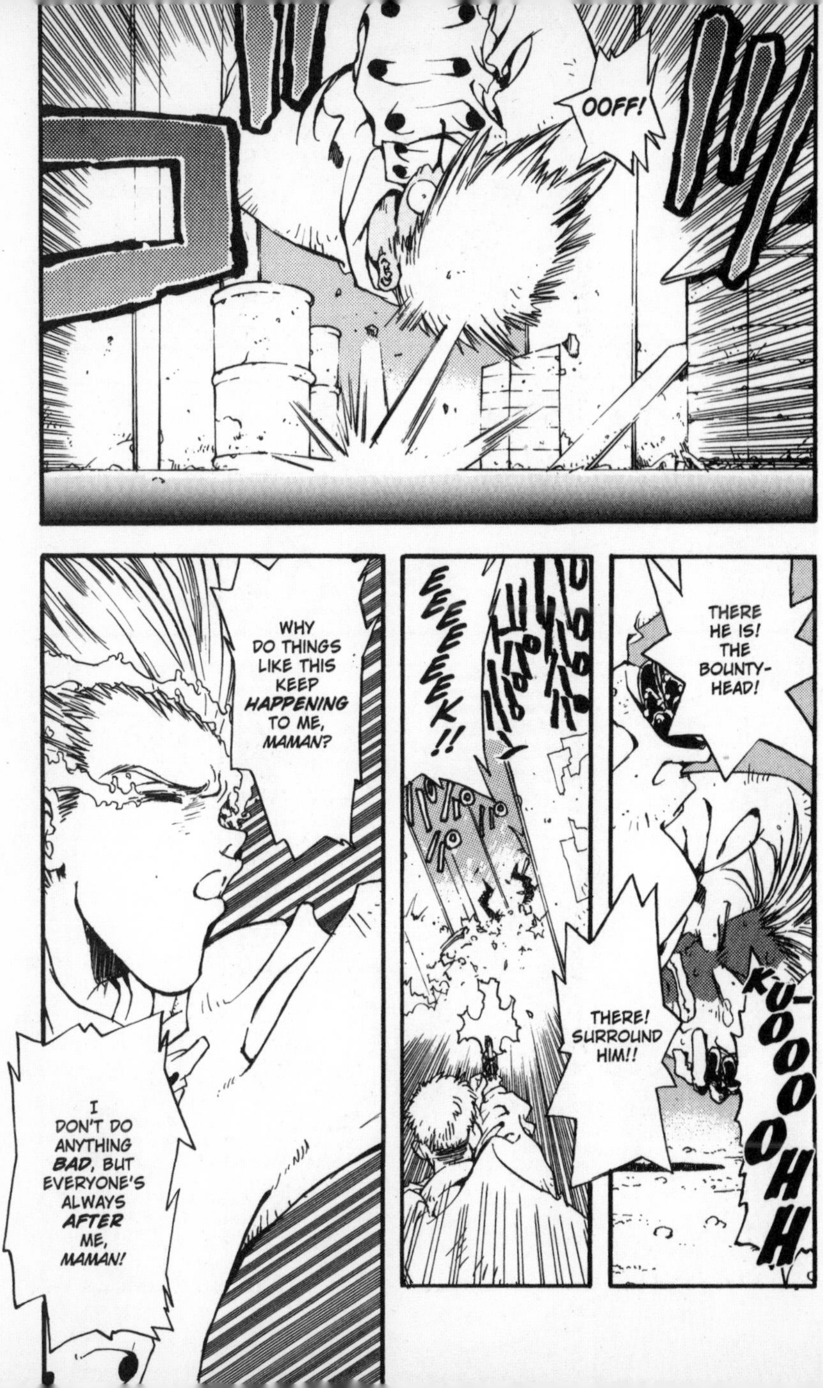
OOFF!
THERE HE IS! THE BOUNTY-HEAD!
KU-OOOOOHH.
EEEEEEK!!
THERE! SURROUND HIM!!
WHY DO THINGS LIKE THIS KEEP **HAPPENING** TO ME, ***MAMAN***?
I DON'T DO ANYTHING **BAD**, BUT EVERYONE'S ALWAYS **AFTER** ME, ***MAMAN***!

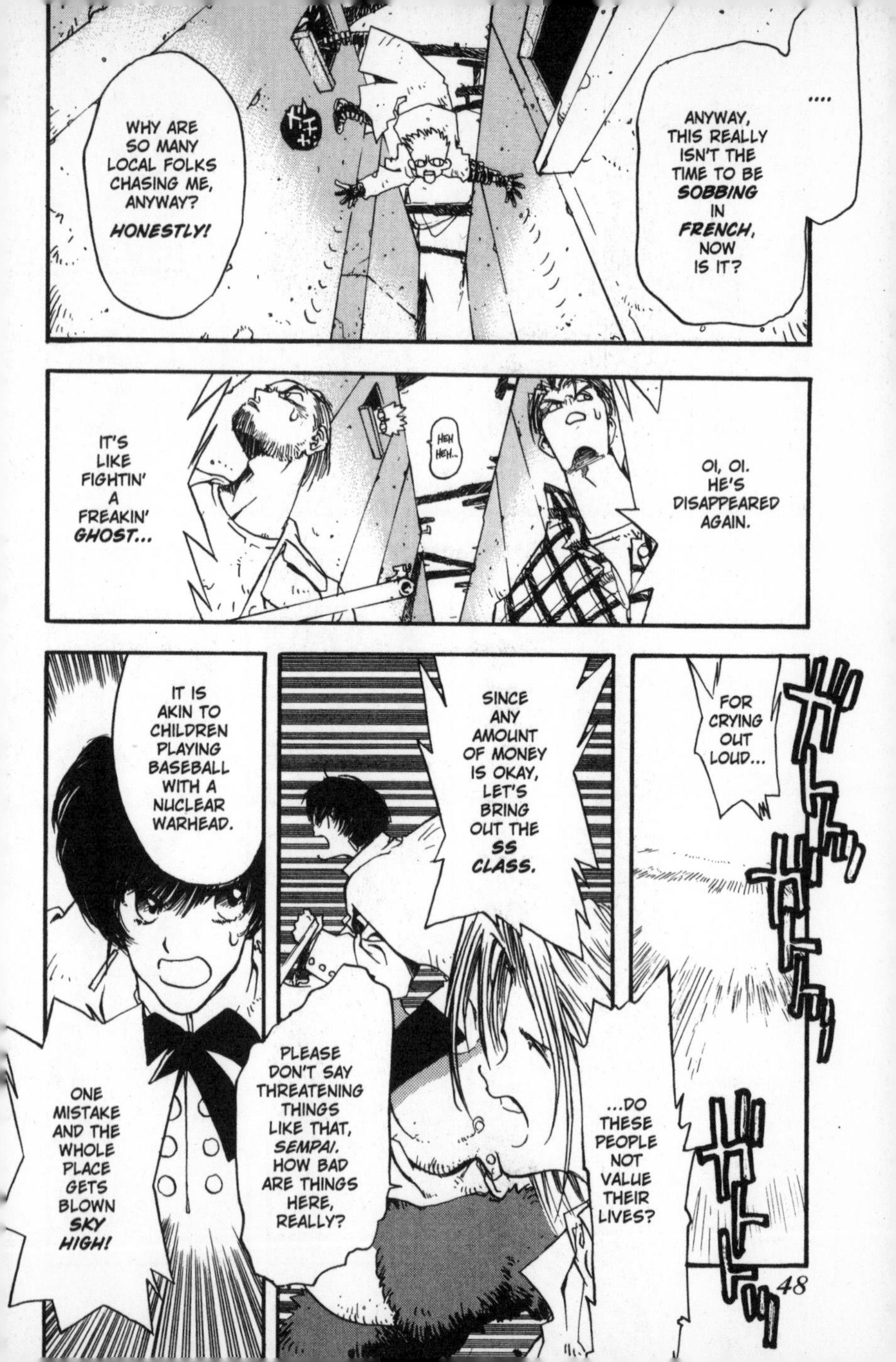
....
ANYWAY, THIS REALLY ISN'T THE TIME TO BE SOBBING IN FRENCH, NOW IS IT?
WHY ARE SO MANY LOCAL FOLKS CHASING ME, ANYWAY? HONESTLY!
OI, OI. HE'S DISAPPEARED AGAIN.
HEH HEH...
IT'S LIKE FIGHTIN' A FREAKIN' GHOST...
FOR CRYING OUT LOUD...
...DO THESE PEOPLE NOT VALUE THEIR LIVES?
SINCE ANY AMOUNT OF MONEY IS OKAY, LET'S BRING OUT THE SS CLASS.
PLEASE DON'T SAY THREATENING THINGS LIKE THAT, SEMPAI. HOW BAD ARE THINGS HERE, REALLY?
IT IS AKIN TO CHILDREN PLAYING BASEBALL WITH A NUCLEAR WARHEAD.
ONE MISTAKE AND THE WHOLE PLACE GETS BLOWN SKY HIGH!

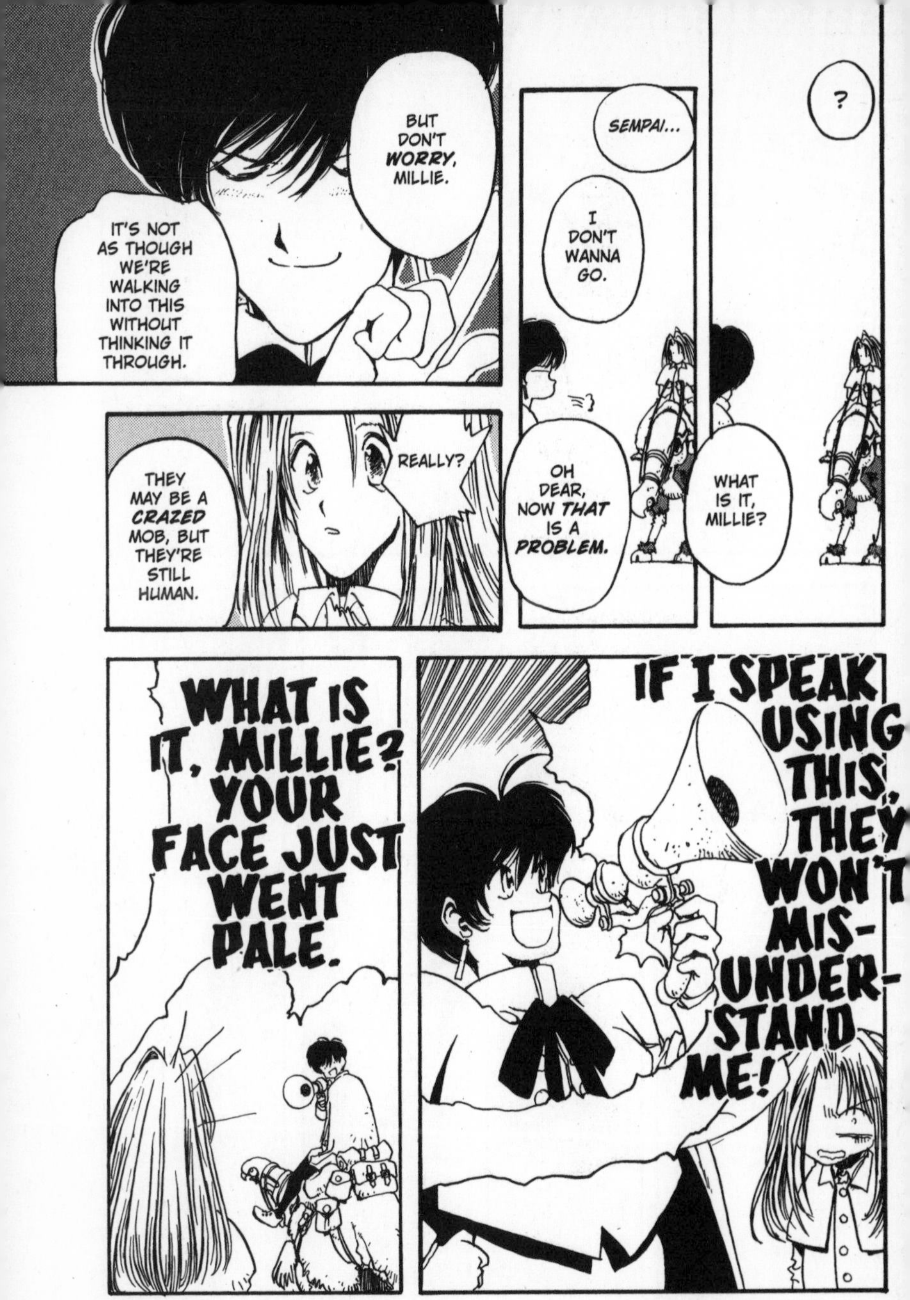
?
WHAT IS IT, MILLIE?
SEMPAI...
I DON'T WANNA GO.
OH DEAR, NOW *THAT* IS A *PROBLEM.*
BUT DON'T *WORRY,* MILLIE.
IT'S NOT AS THOUGH WE'RE WALKING INTO THIS WITHOUT THINKING IT THROUGH.
REALLY?
THEY MAY BE A *CRAZED* MOB, BUT THEY'RE STILL HUMAN.
IF I SPEAK USING THIS, THEY WON'T MIS-UNDER-STAND ME!
WHAT IS IT, MILLIE? YOUR FACE JUST WENT PALE.

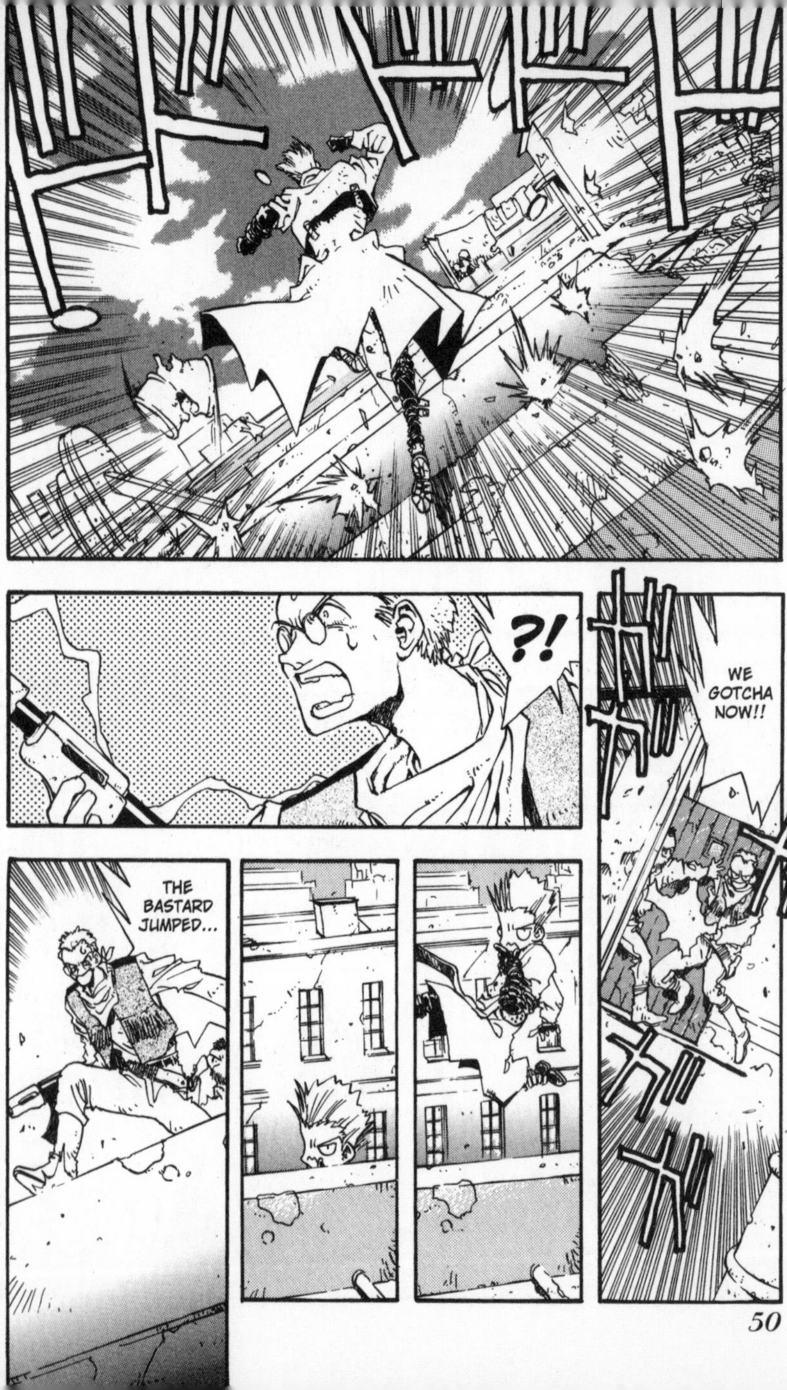
WE GOTCHA NOW!!
?!
THE BASTARD JUMPED...

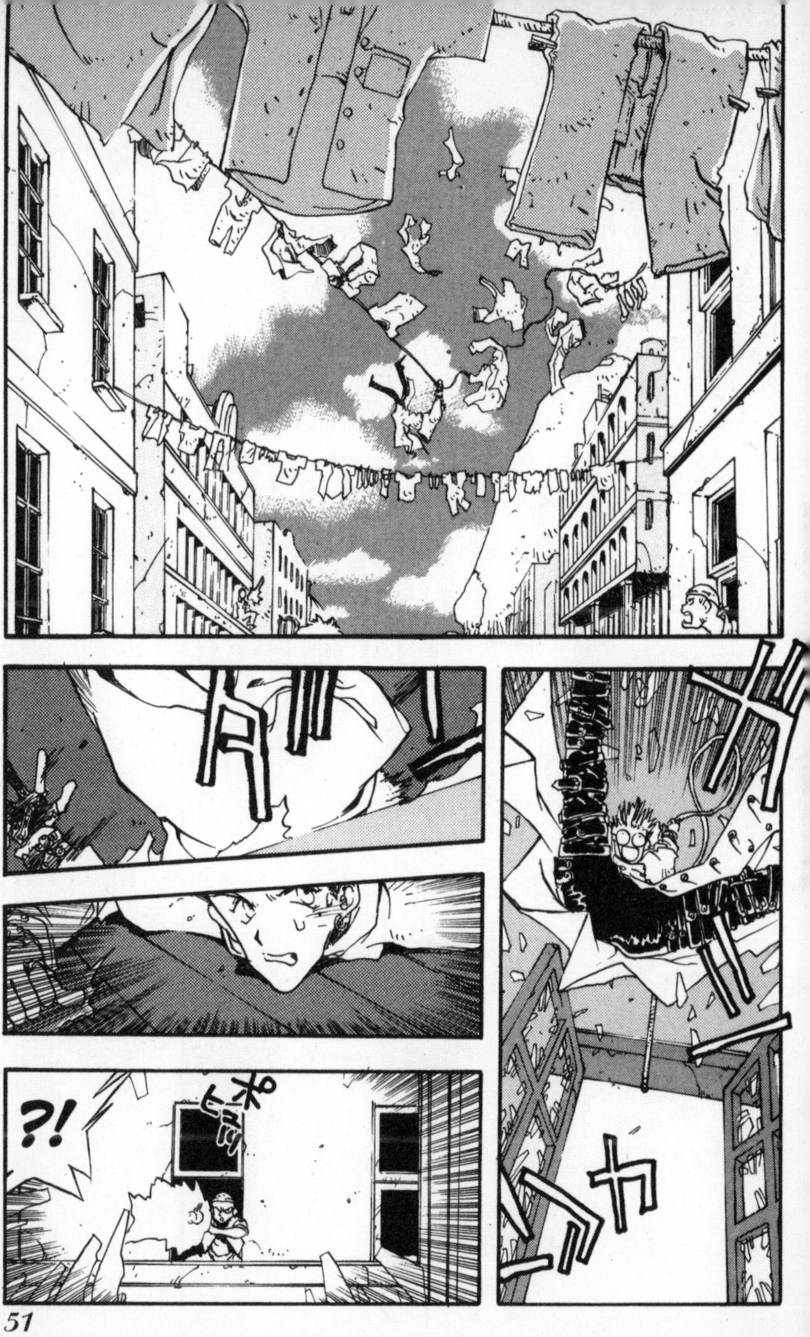
?!

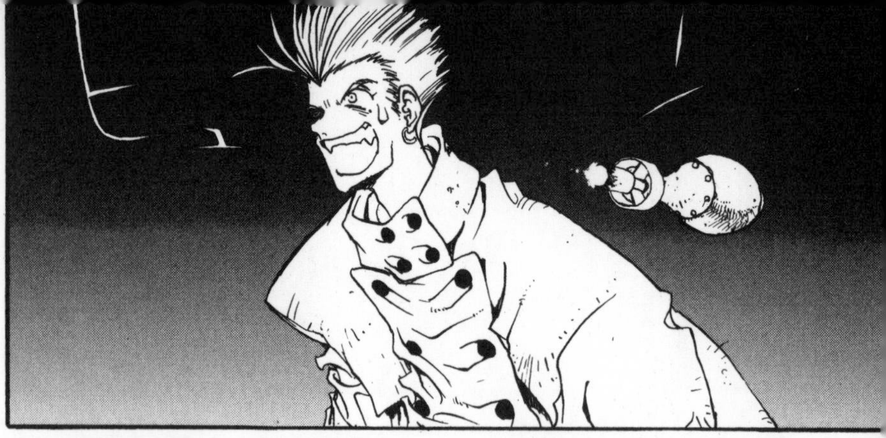

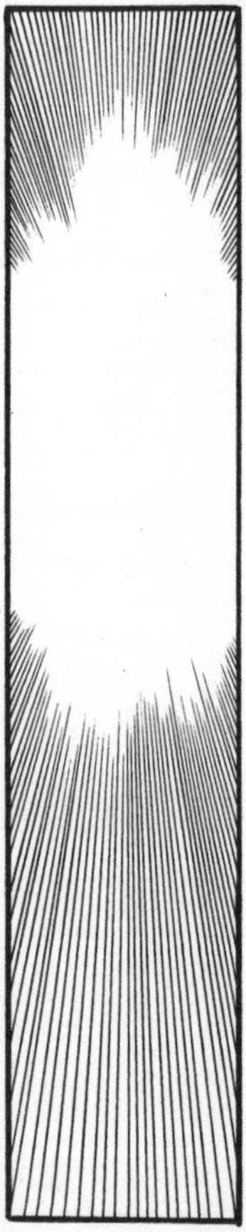

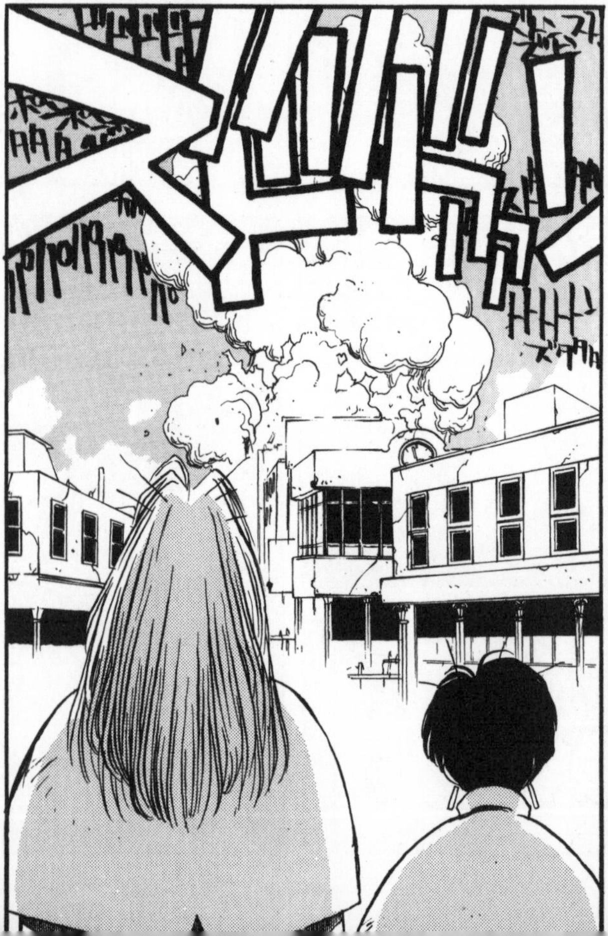

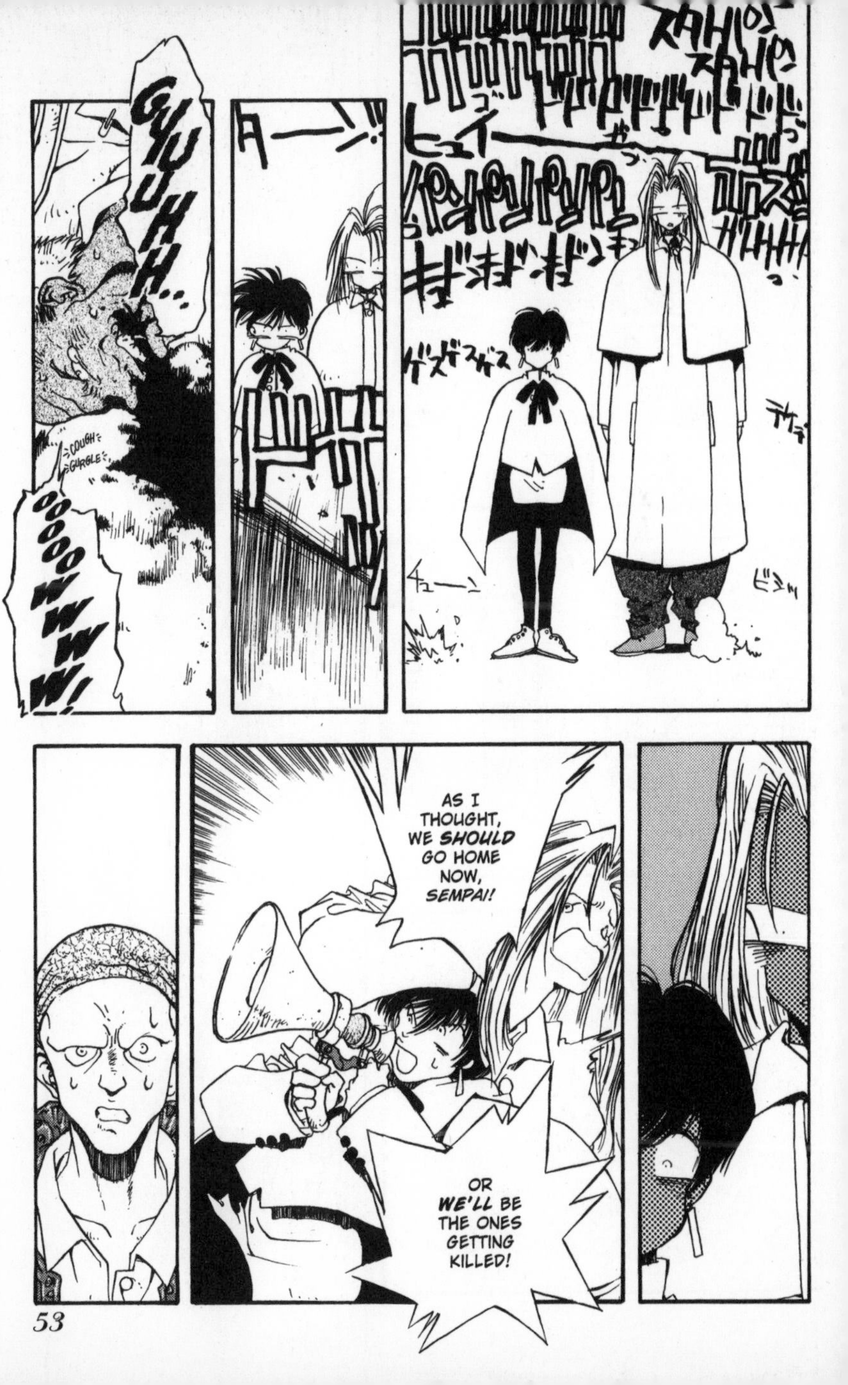
ヒュイー
ターン!!
GYUUHHH...
COUGH
GURGLE
OOOOOWWWWW!
AS I THOUGHT, WE SHOULD GO HOME NOW, SEMPAI!
OR WE'LL BE THE ONES GETTING KILLED!

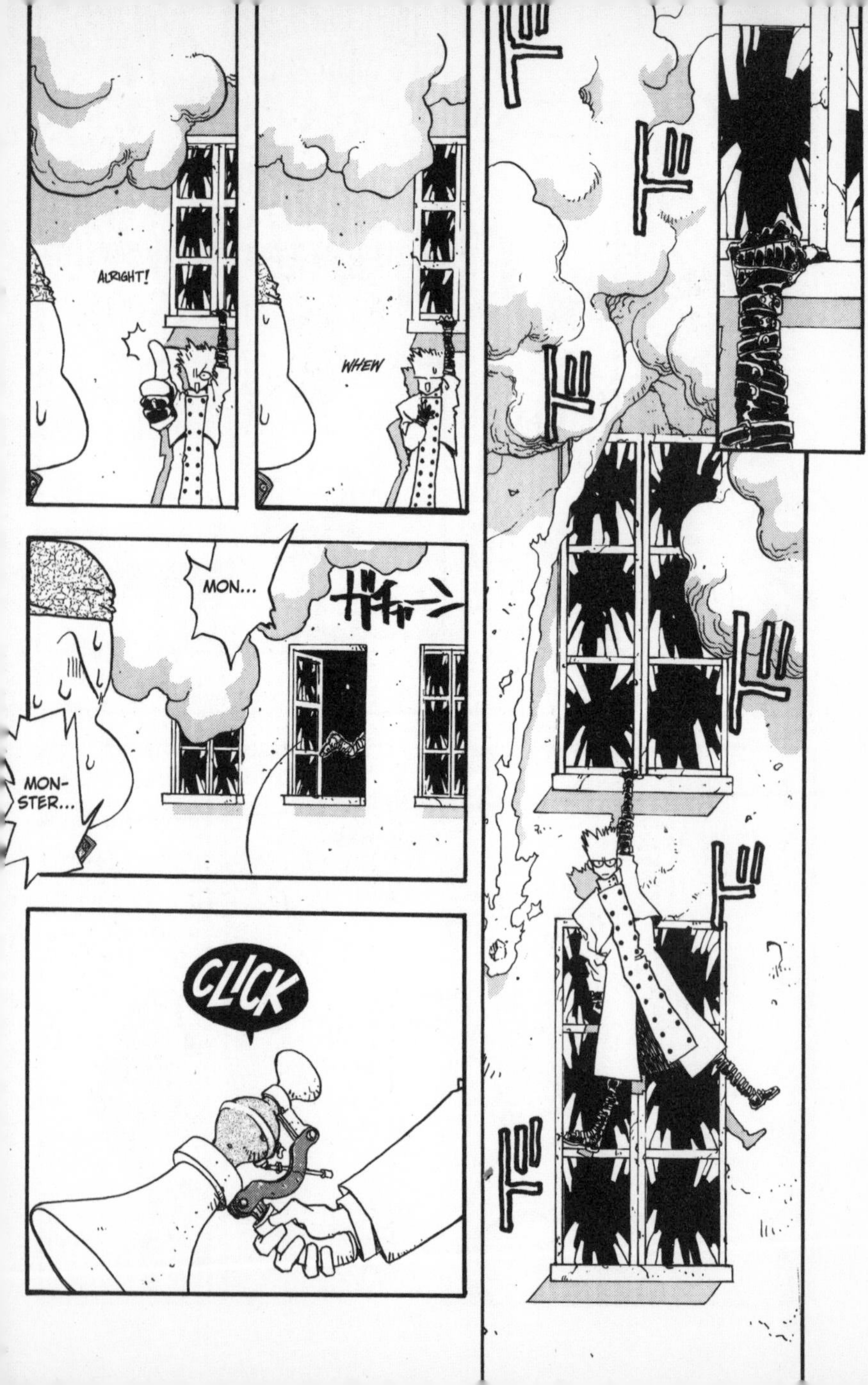
WHEW
ALRIGHT!
ガチャーン
MON...
MON-
STER...
CLICK

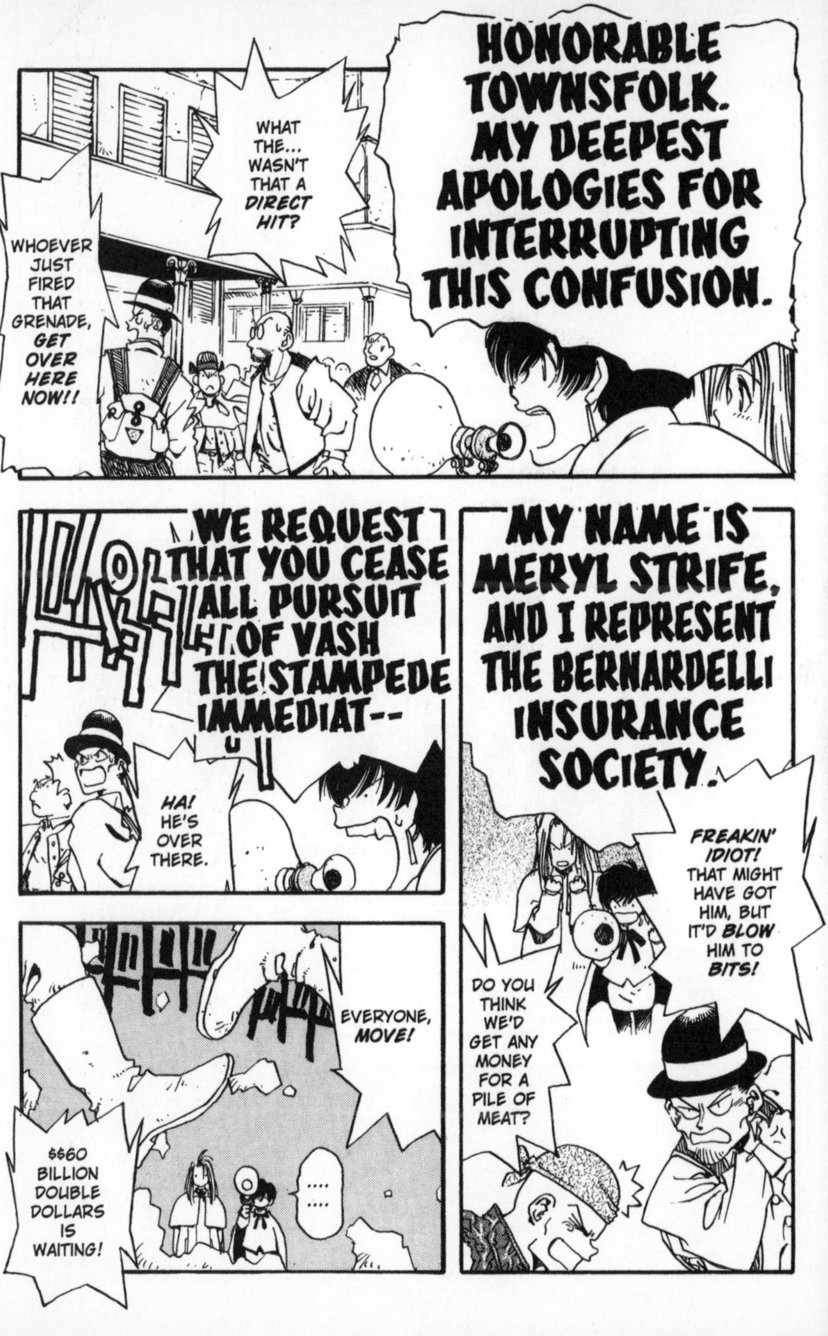
HONORABLE TOWNSFOLK. MY DEEPEST APOLOGIES FOR INTERRUPTING THIS CONFUSION.
WHAT THE... WASN'T THAT A *DIRECT HIT?*
WHOEVER JUST FIRED THAT GRENADE, ***GET OVER HERE NOW!!***
MY NAME IS MERYL STRIFE, AND I REPRESENT THE BERNARDELLI INSURANCE SOCIETY.
*FREAKIN' IDIOT!* THAT MIGHT HAVE GOT HIM, BUT IT'D ***BLOW*** HIM TO ***BITS!***
DO YOU THINK WE'D GET ANY MONEY FOR A PILE OF MEAT?
WE REQUEST THAT YOU CEASE ALL PURSUIT OF VASH THE STAMPEDE IMMEDIAT--
*HA!* HE'S OVER THERE.
EVERYONE, ***MOVE!***
.... ....
$$60 BILLION DOUBLE DOLLARS IS WAITING!

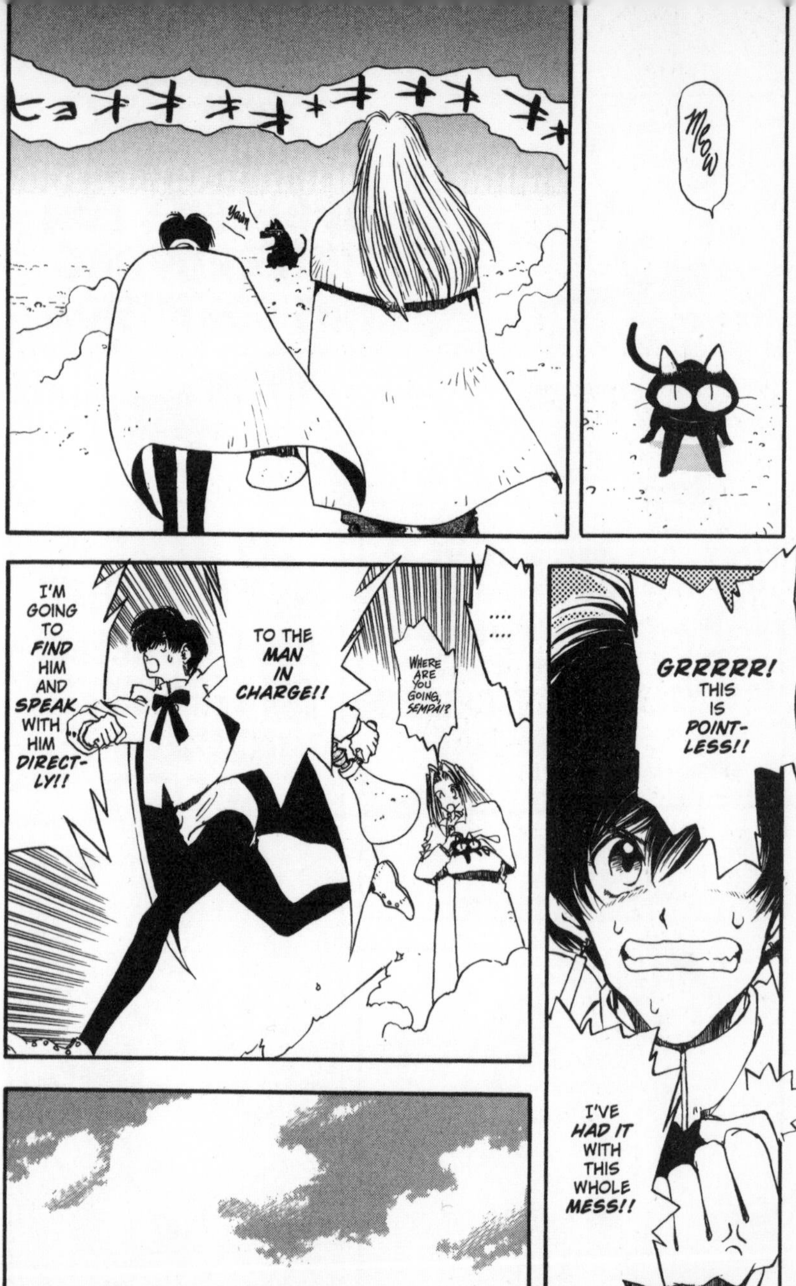
MEOW
ヒョオオオオオオオオ
YAWN
GRRRRR! THIS IS POINTLESS!!
I'VE HAD IT WITH THIS WHOLE MESS!!
....
....
WHERE ARE YOU GOING, SEMPAI!?
TO THE MAN IN CHARGE!!
I'M GOING TO FIND HIM AND SPEAK WITH HIM DIRECTLY!!

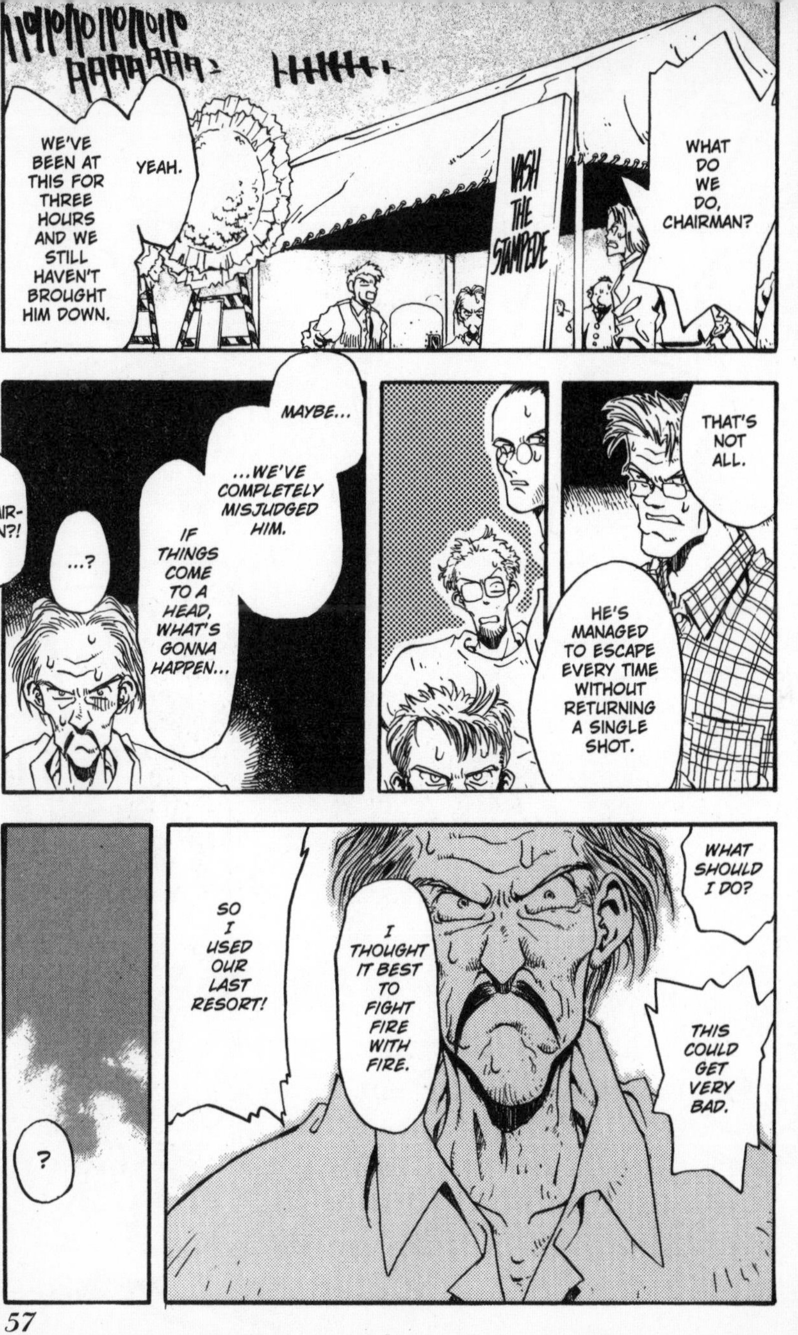
WHAT DO WE DO, CHAIRMAN?
WE'VE BEEN AT THIS FOR THREE HOURS AND WE STILL HAVEN'T BROUGHT HIM DOWN.
YEAH.
VASH THE STAMPEDE
THAT'S NOT ALL.
HE'S MANAGED TO ESCAPE EVERY TIME WITHOUT RETURNING A SINGLE SHOT.
MAYBE...
...WE'VE COMPLETELY MISJUDGED HIM.
IF THINGS COME TO A HEAD, WHAT'S GONNA HAPPEN...
...?
CHAIR-MAN?!
WHAT SHOULD I DO?
THIS COULD GET VERY BAD.
I THOUGHT IT BEST TO FIGHT FIRE WITH FIRE.
SO I USED OUR LAST RESORT!
?

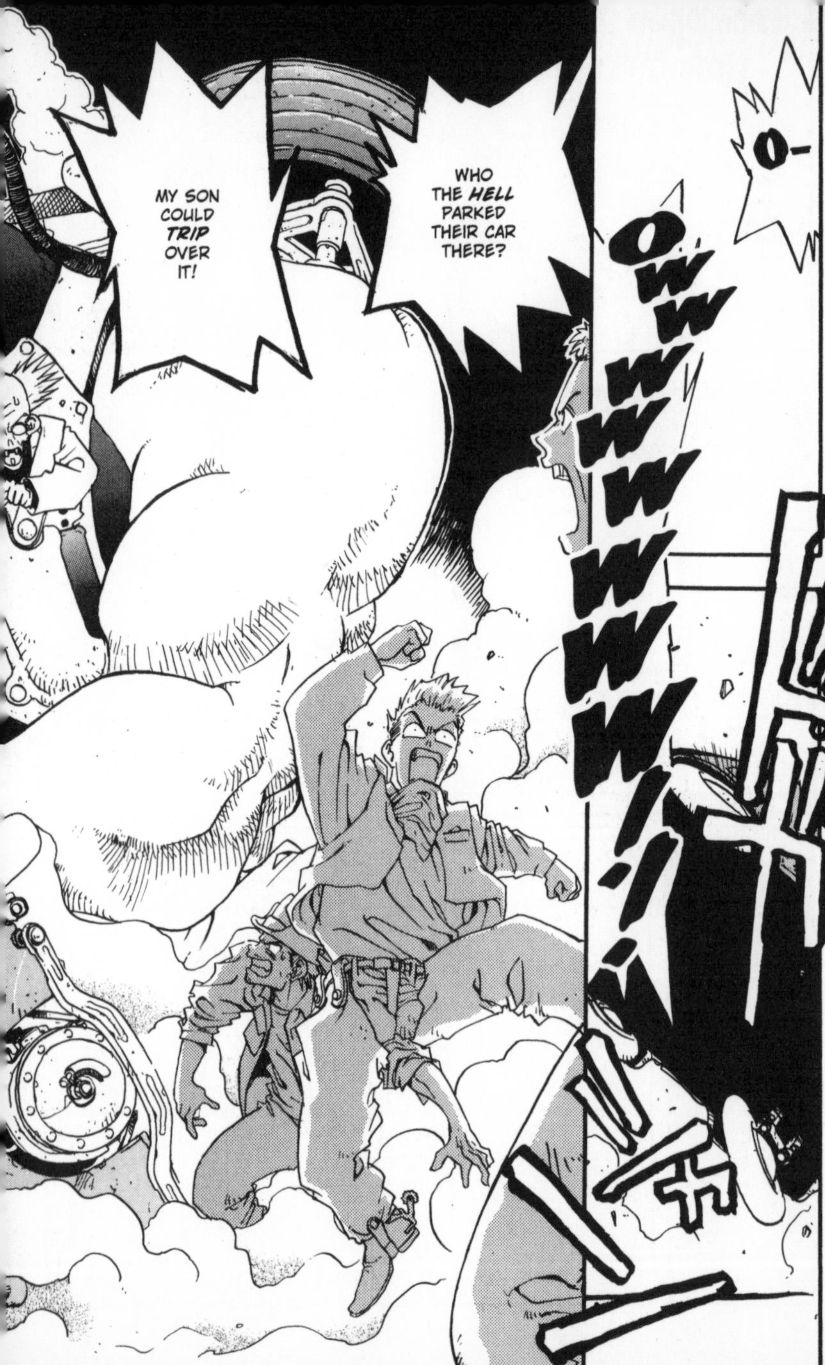
O-
OWWWWWWWWWWWW--!!
WHO THE *HELL* PARKED THEIR CAR THERE?
MY SON COULD *TRIP* OVER IT!

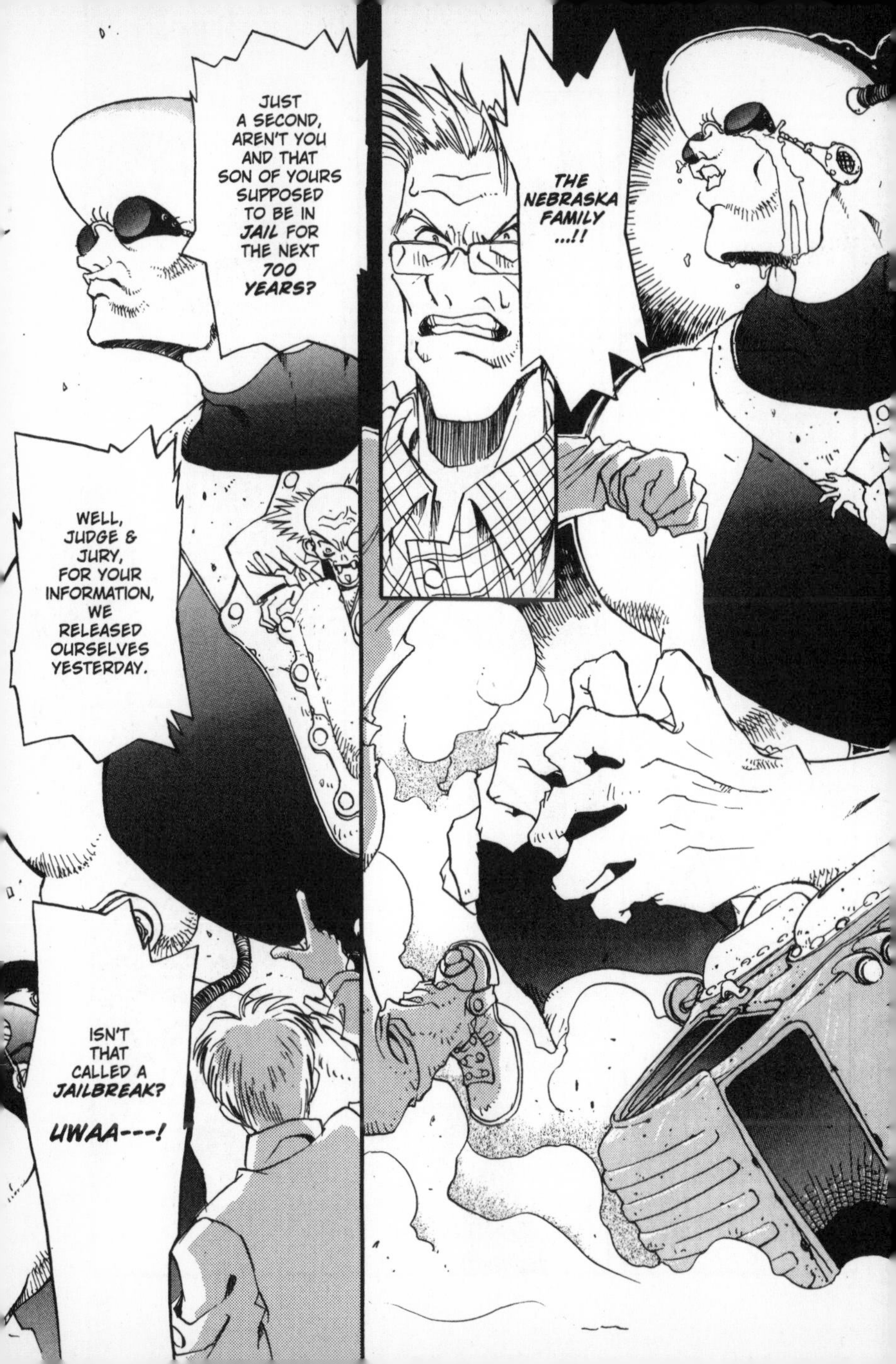
THE NEBRASKA FAMILY ...!!
JUST A SECOND, AREN'T YOU AND THAT SON OF YOURS SUPPOSED TO BE IN JAIL FOR THE NEXT 700 YEARS?
WELL, JUDGE & JURY, FOR YOUR INFORMATION, WE RELEASED OURSELVES YESTERDAY.
ISN'T THAT CALLED A JAILBREAK?
UWAA---!

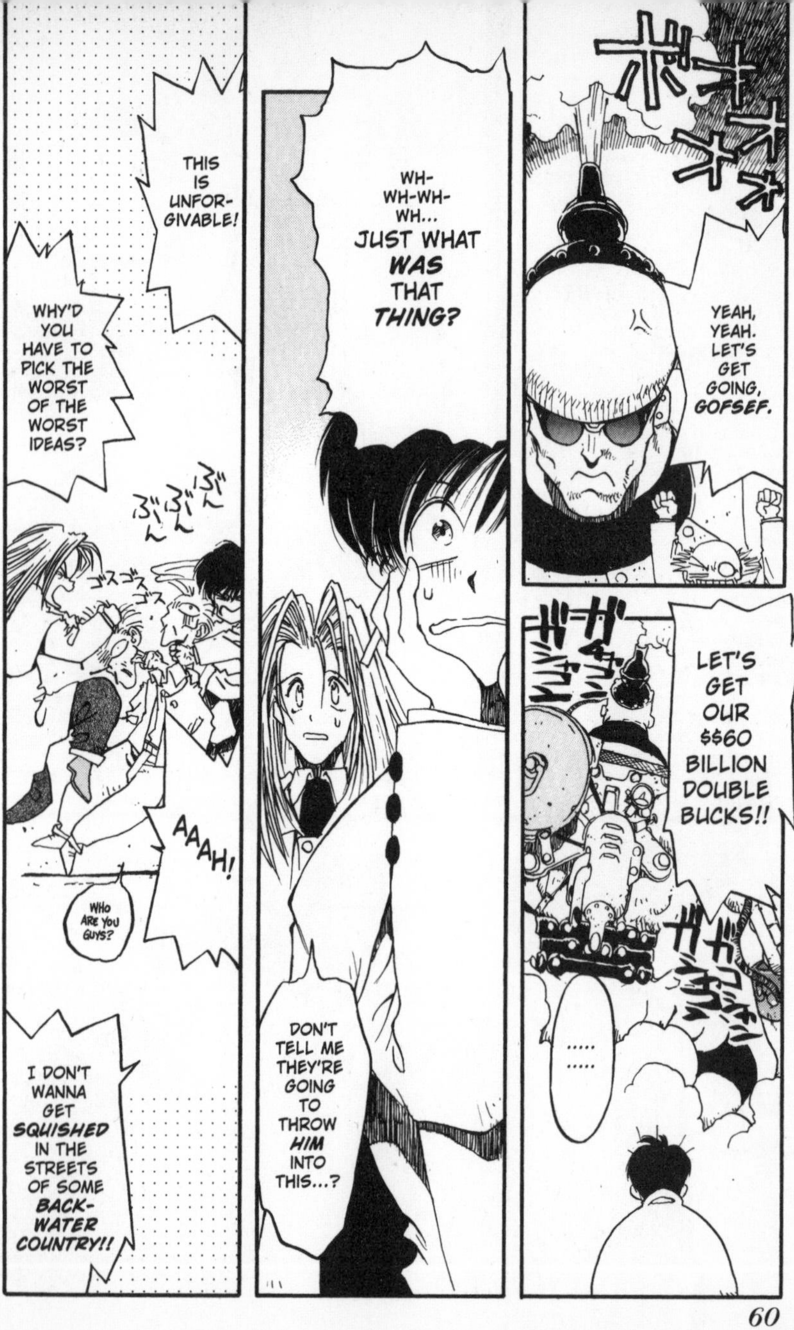
YEAH, YEAH. LET'S GET GOING, GOFSEF.
LET'S GET OUR $$60 BILLION DOUBLE BUCKS!!
.....
.....
WH- WH-WH- WH... JUST WHAT WAS THAT THING?
DON'T TELL ME THEY'RE GOING TO THROW HIM INTO THIS...?
THIS IS UNFORGIVABLE!
WHY'D YOU HAVE TO PICK THE WORST OF THE WORST IDEAS?
ぶん ぶん ぶん
ゴスゴス ゴス
AAAH!
WHO ARE YOU GUYS?
I DON'T WANNA GET SQUISHED IN THE STREETS OF SOME BACKWATER COUNTRY!!

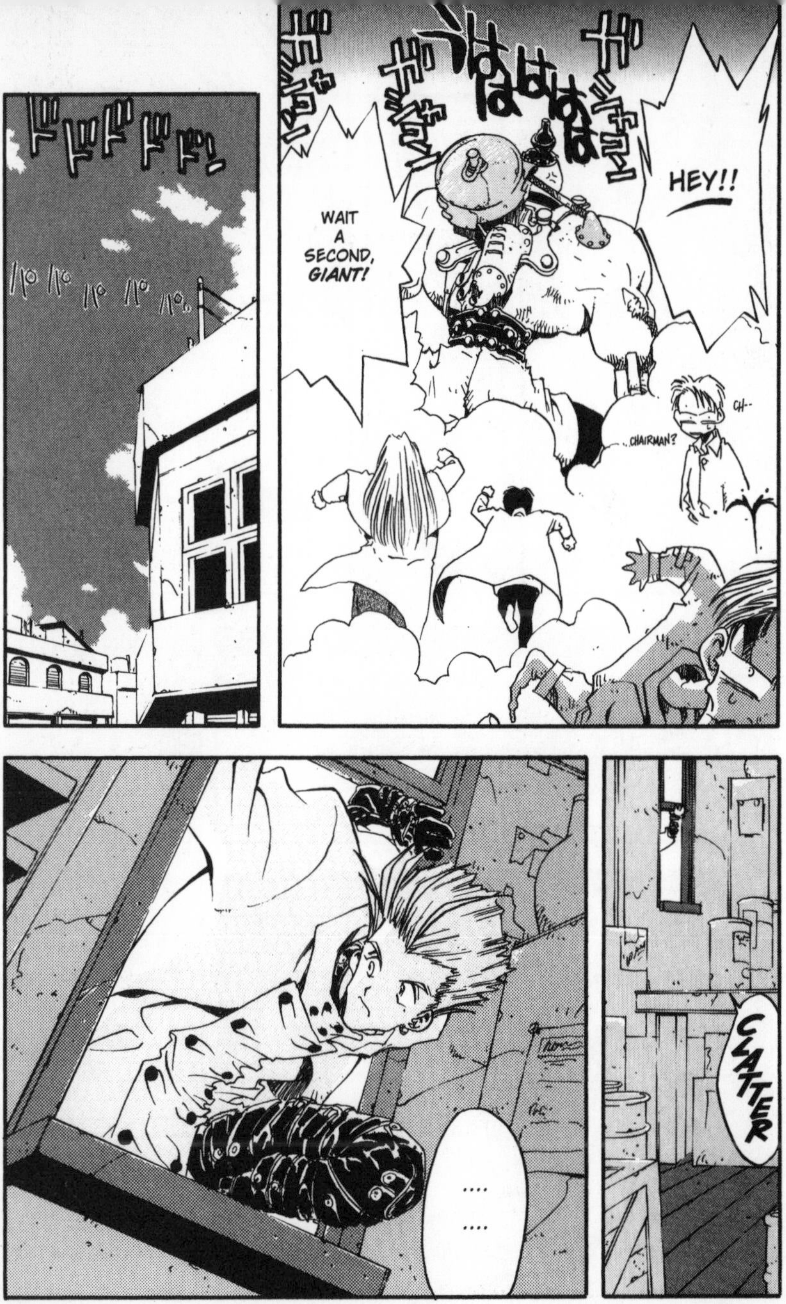

うははははは
HEY!!
WAIT A SECOND, GIANT!
CH--
...CHAIRMAN?
ドドドドド
パパパパパ
CLATTER
....
....

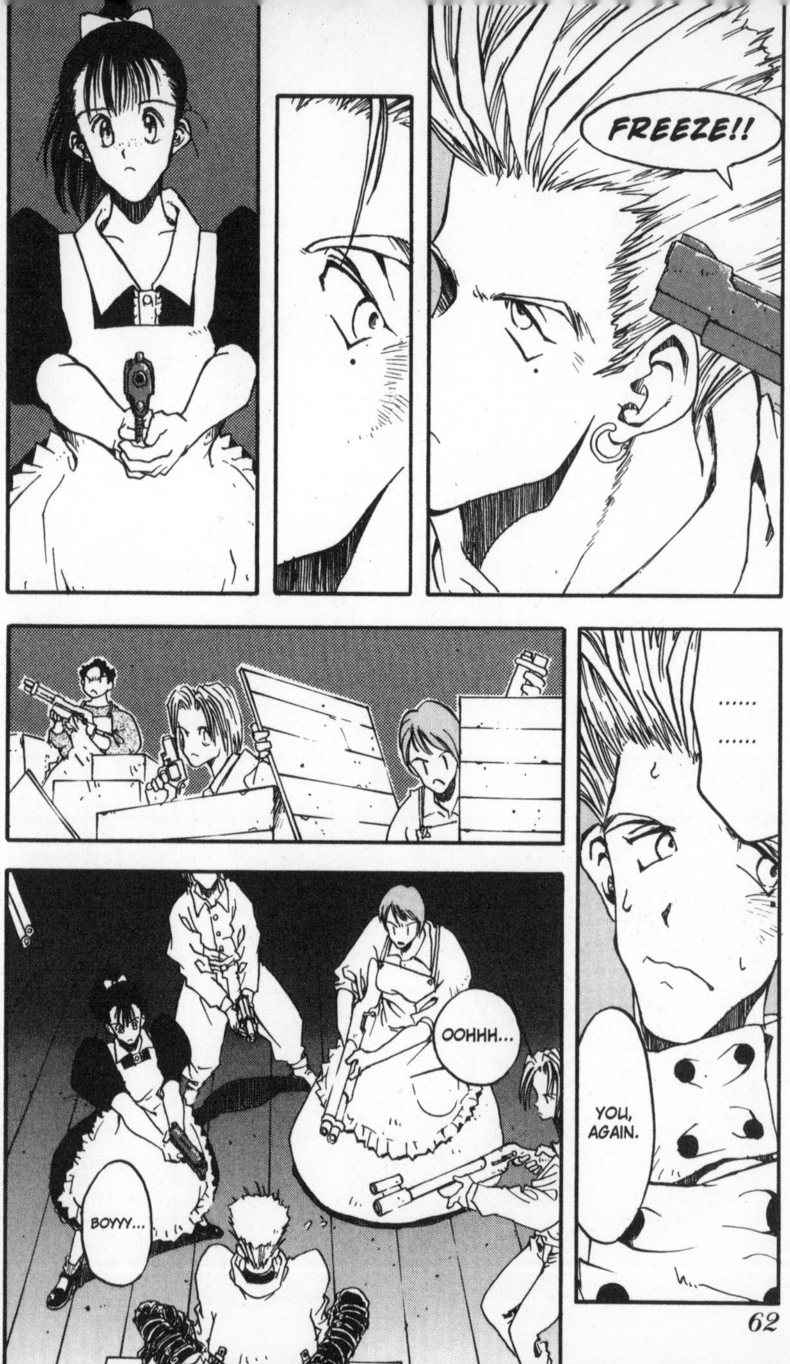
FREEZE!!
......
......
YOU, AGAIN.
OOHHH...
BOYYY...

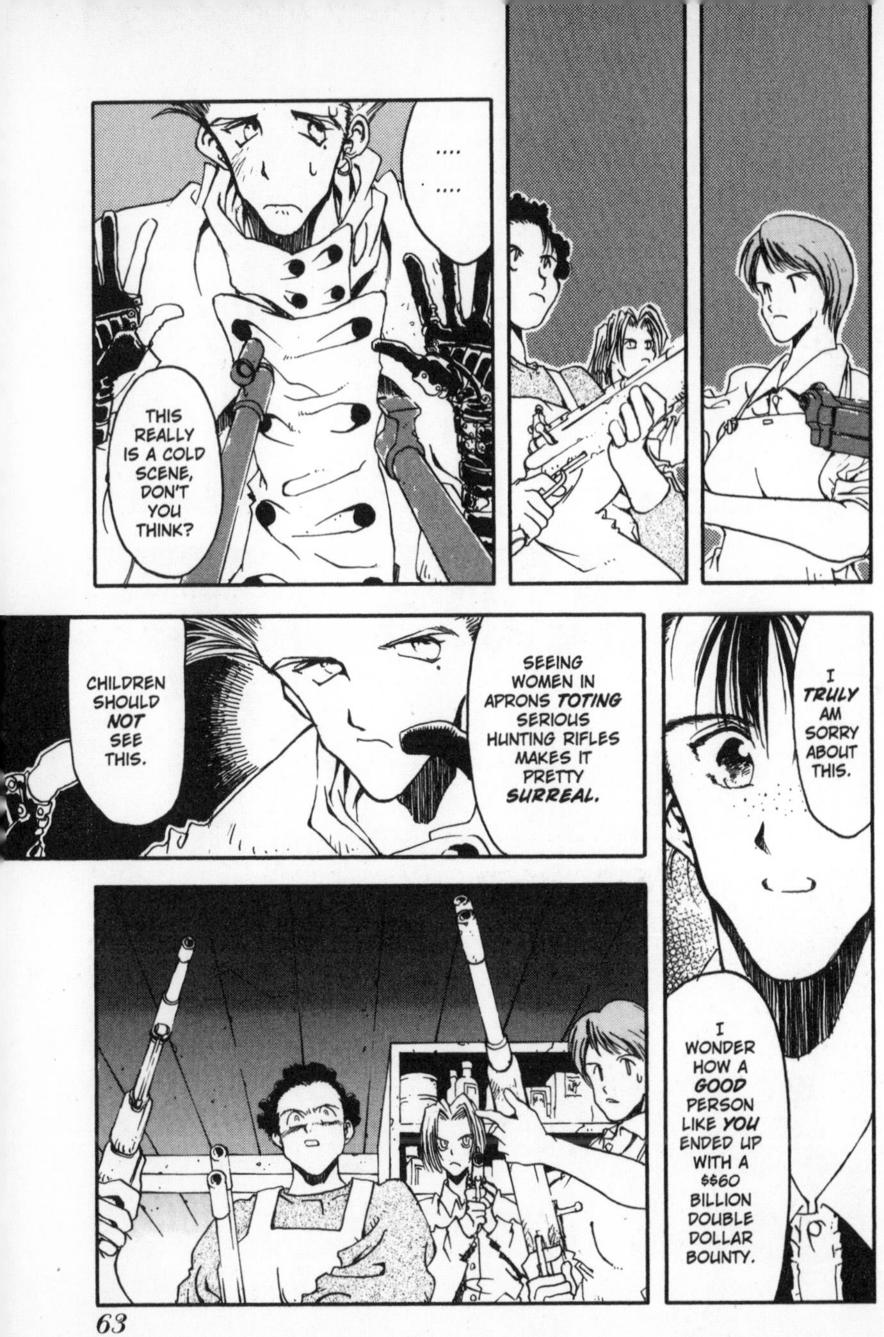

....
....
THIS REALLY IS A COLD SCENE, DON'T YOU THINK?
I TRULY AM SORRY ABOUT THIS.
I WONDER HOW A GOOD PERSON LIKE YOU ENDED UP WITH A $$60 BILLION DOUBLE DOLLAR BOUNTY.
SEEING WOMEN IN APRONS TOTING SERIOUS HUNTING RIFLES MAKES IT PRETTY SURREAL.
CHILDREN SHOULD NOT SEE THIS.

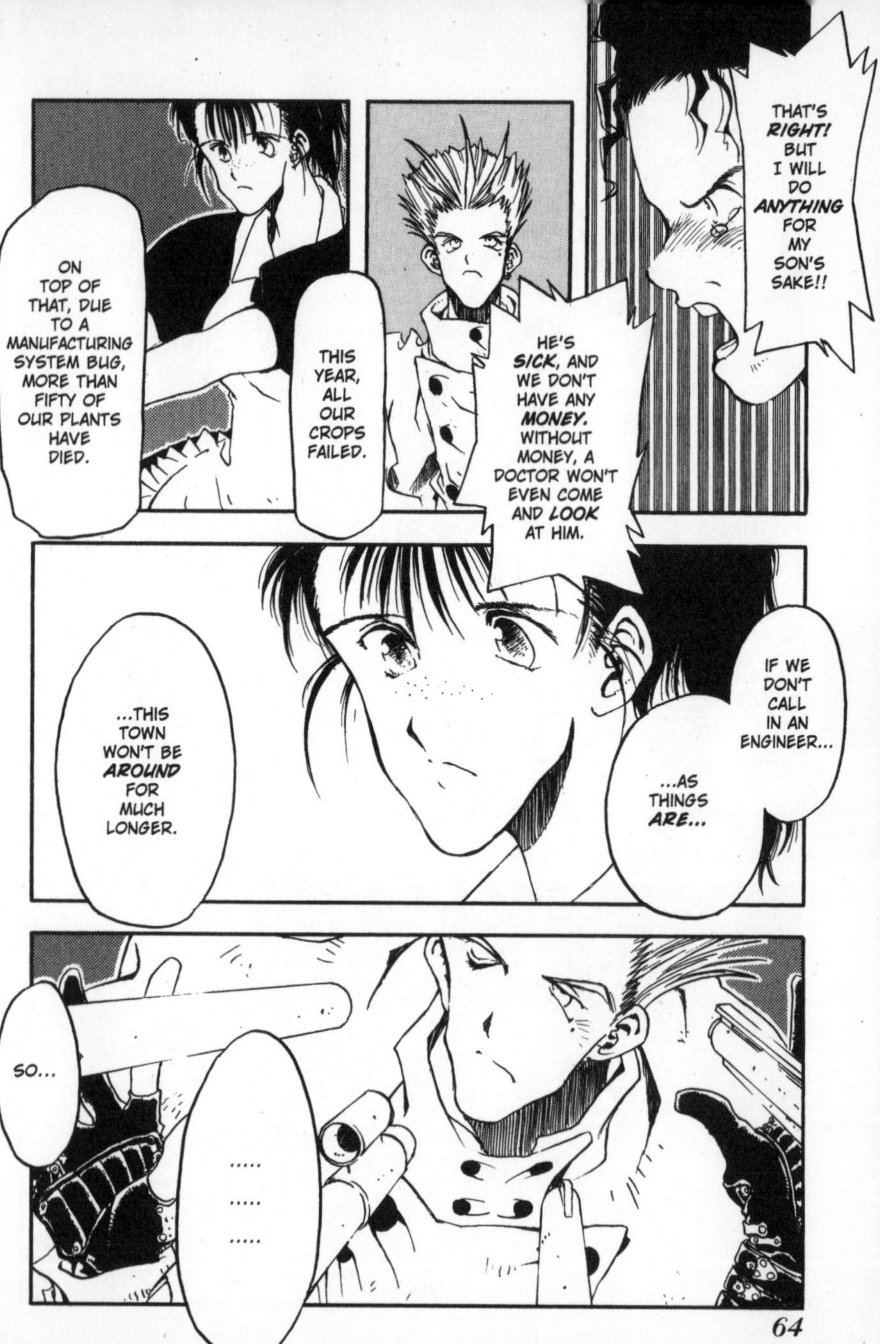
THAT'S RIGHT! BUT I WILL DO ANYTHING FOR MY SON'S SAKE!!
HE'S SICK, AND WE DON'T HAVE ANY MONEY. WITHOUT MONEY, A DOCTOR WON'T EVEN COME AND LOOK AT HIM.
THIS YEAR, ALL OUR CROPS FAILED.
ON TOP OF THAT, DUE TO A MANUFACTURING SYSTEM BUG, MORE THAN FIFTY OF OUR PLANTS HAVE DIED.
IF WE DON'T CALL IN AN ENGINEER...
...AS THINGS ARE...
...THIS TOWN WON'T BE AROUND FOR MUCH LONGER.
..... ..... .....
SO...

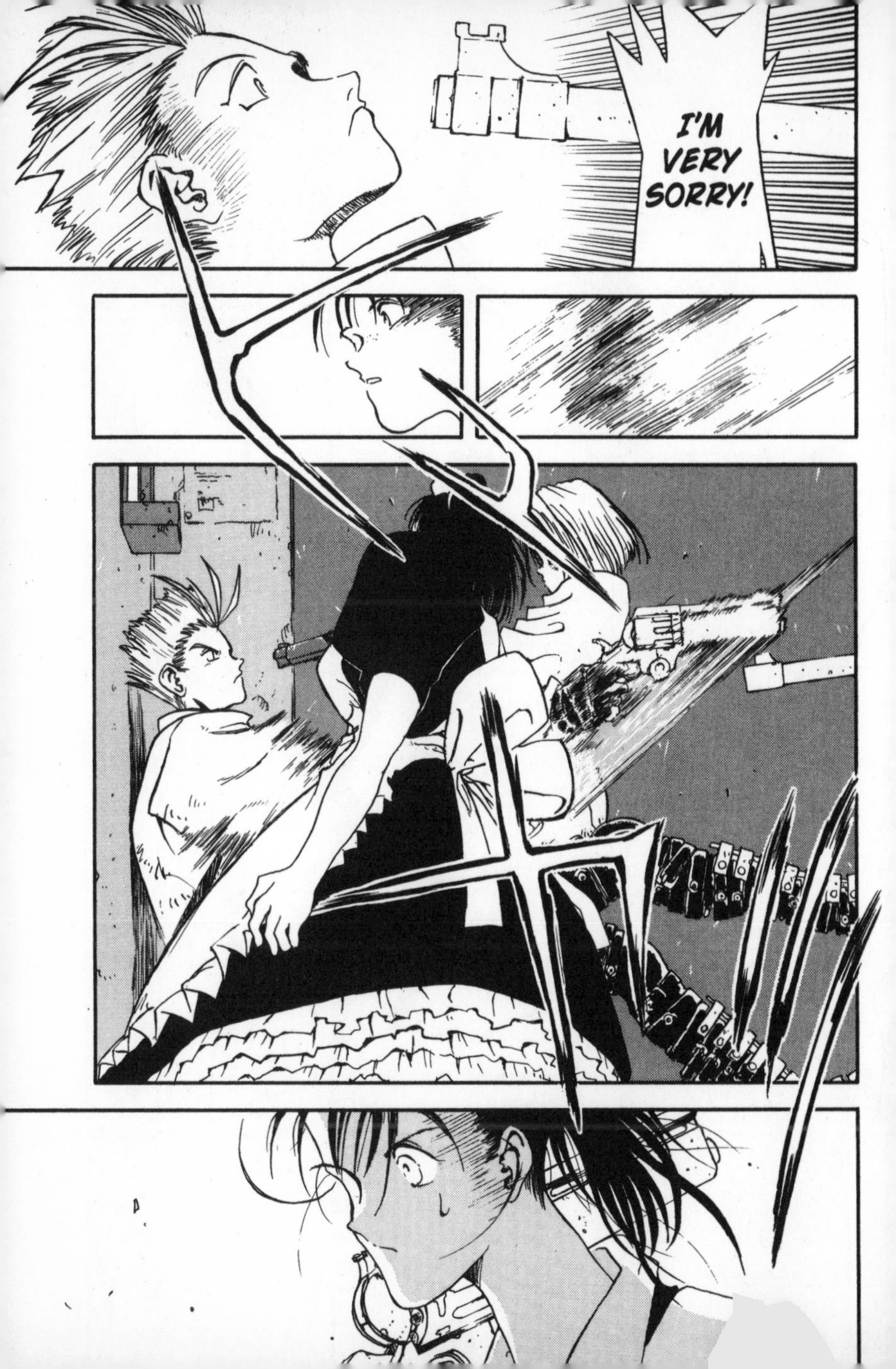
I'M VERY SORRY!

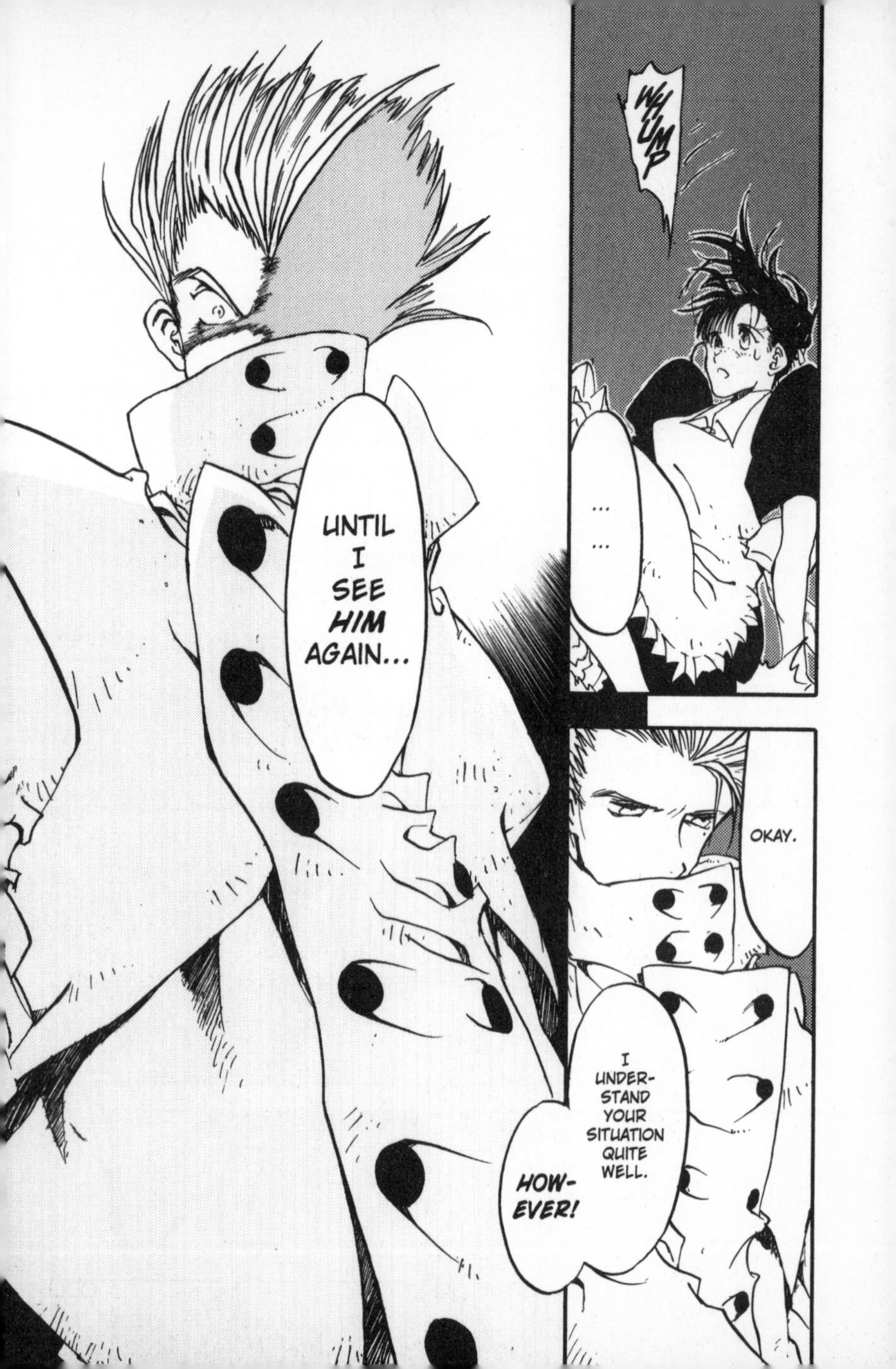
WHUMP
... ...
OKAY.
I UNDER-STAND YOUR SITUATION QUITE WELL.
HOW-EVER!
UNTIL I SEE HIM AGAIN...

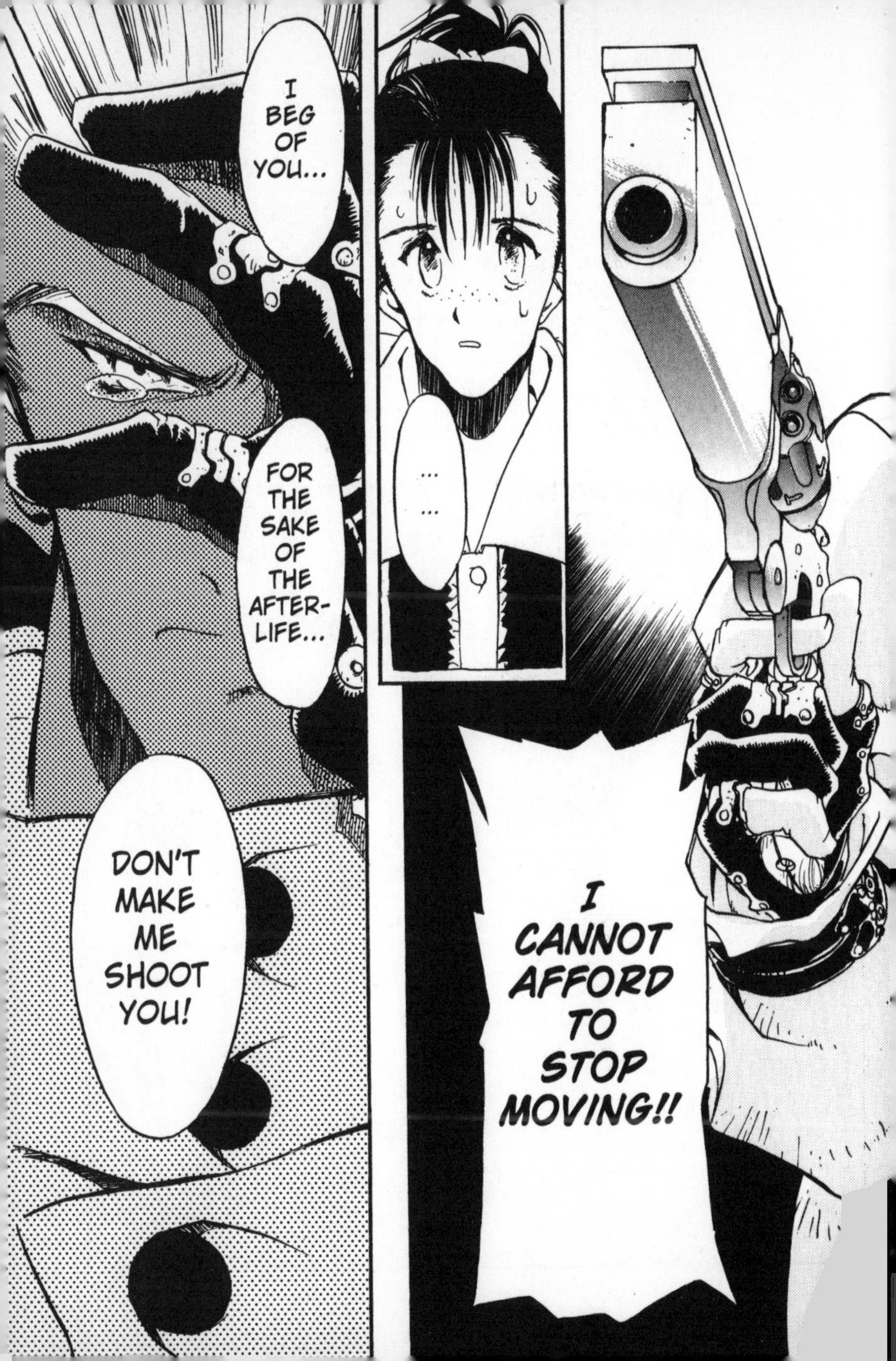

......
I CANNOT AFFORD TO STOP MOVING!!
I BEG OF YOU...
FOR THE SAKE OF THE AFTER-LIFE...
DON'T MAKE ME SHOOT YOU!

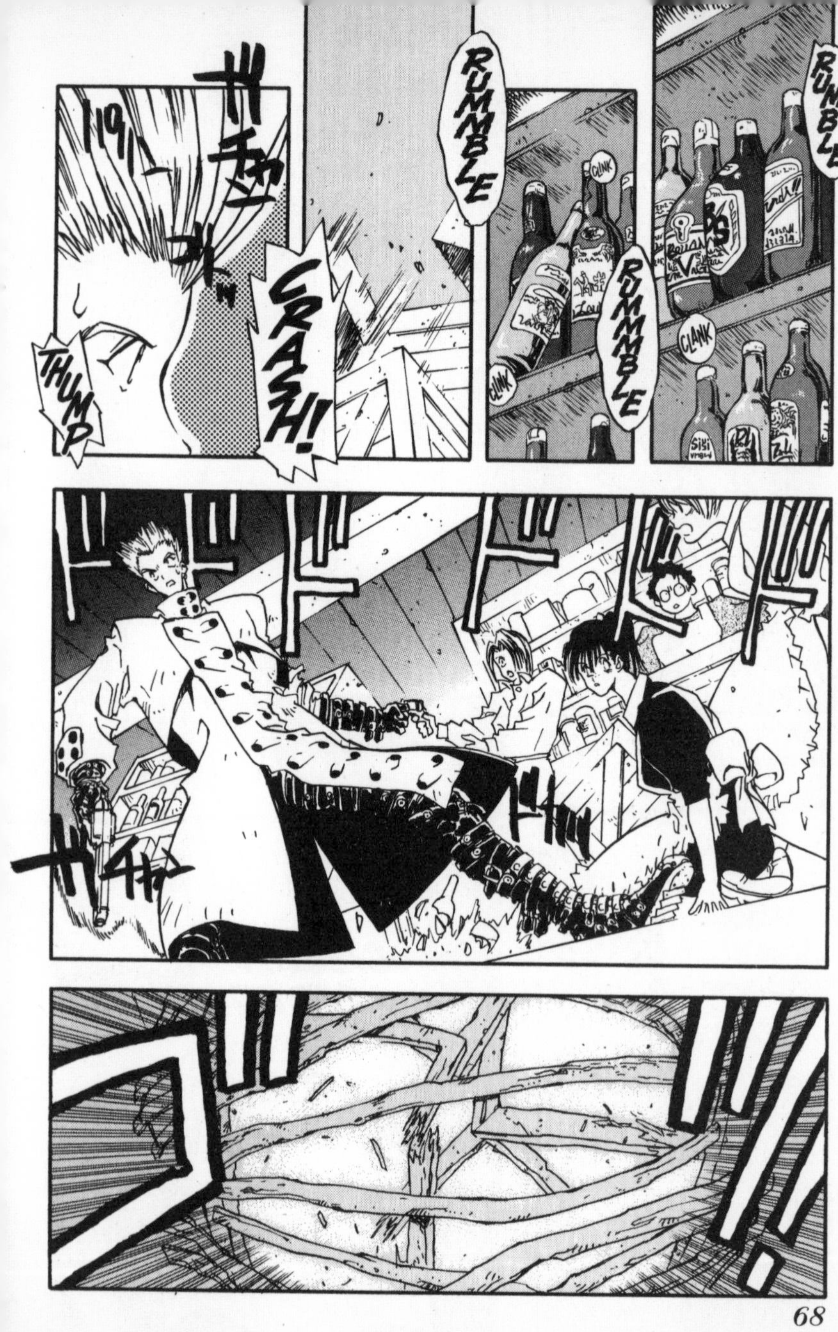
RUMBLE
CLANK
RUMMBLE
CLINK
CLINK
RUMMMBLE
CRASH!
THUMP

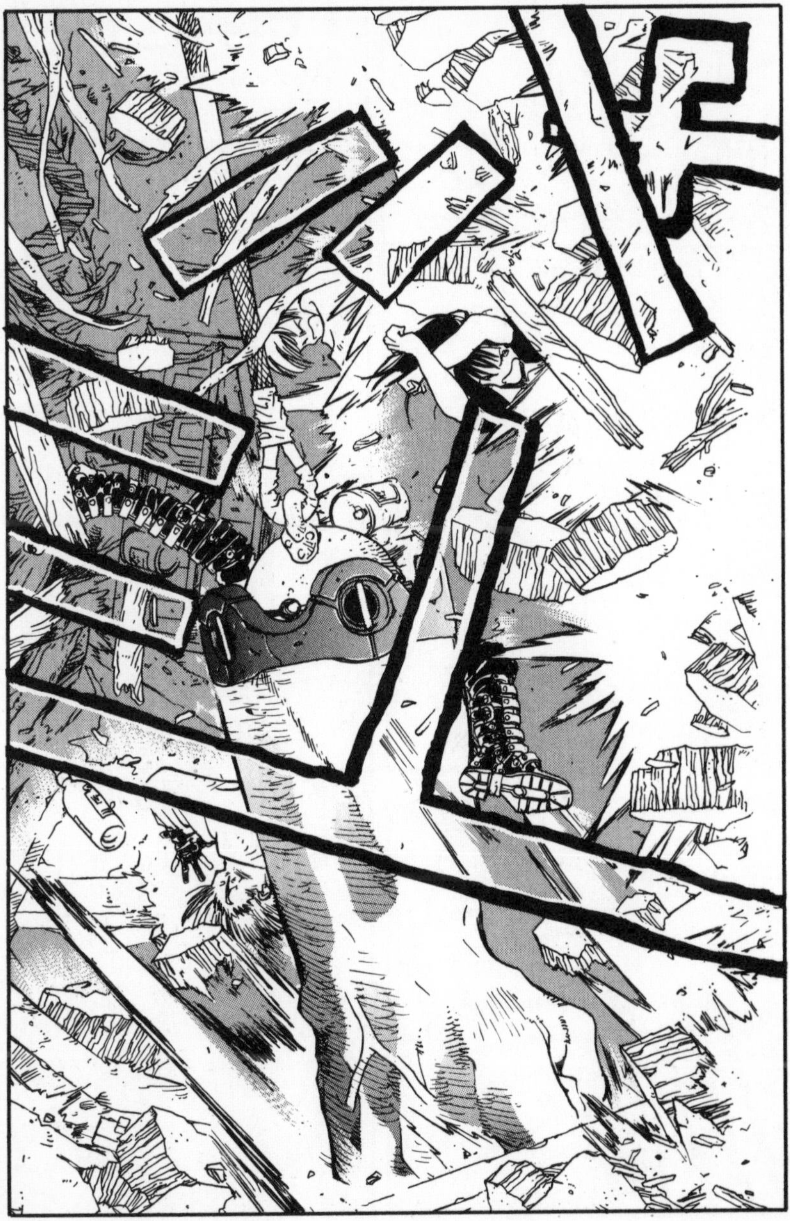

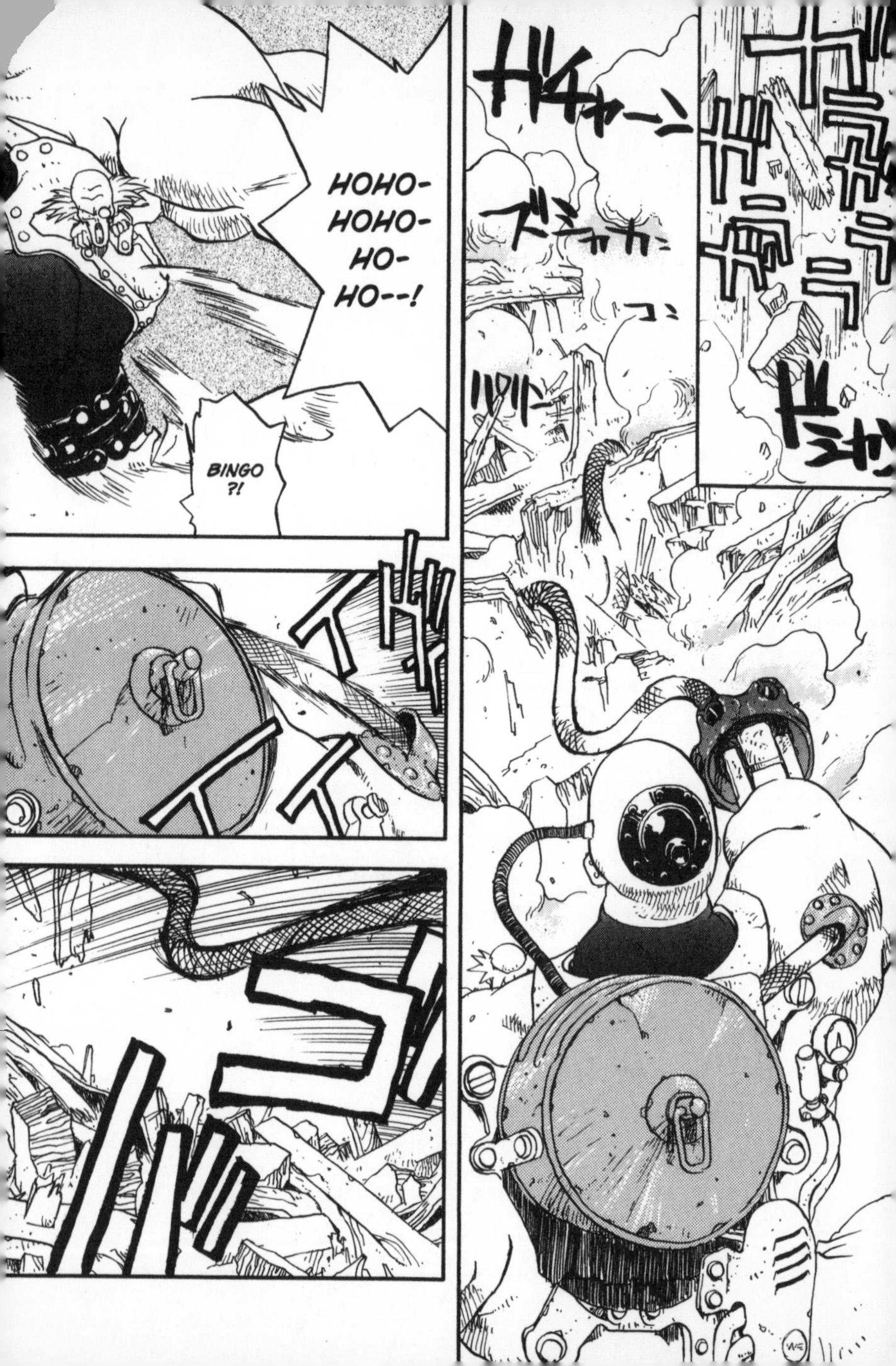
HOHO-HOHO-HO-HO--!
BINGO ?!

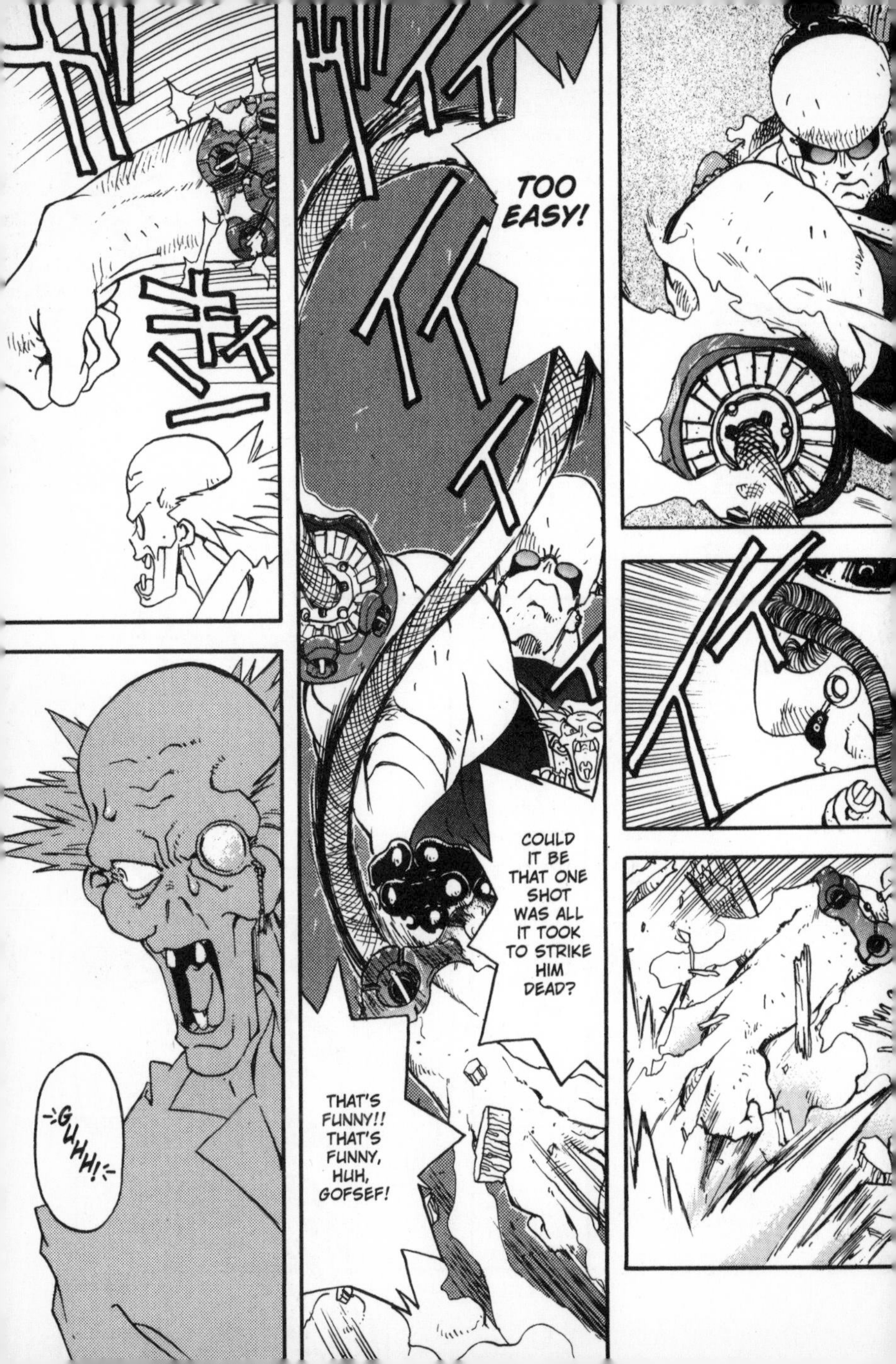
TOO EASY!
COULD IT BE THAT ONE SHOT WAS ALL IT TOOK TO STRIKE HIM DEAD?
THAT'S FUNNY!! THAT'S FUNNY, HUH, GOFSEF!
GUHH!

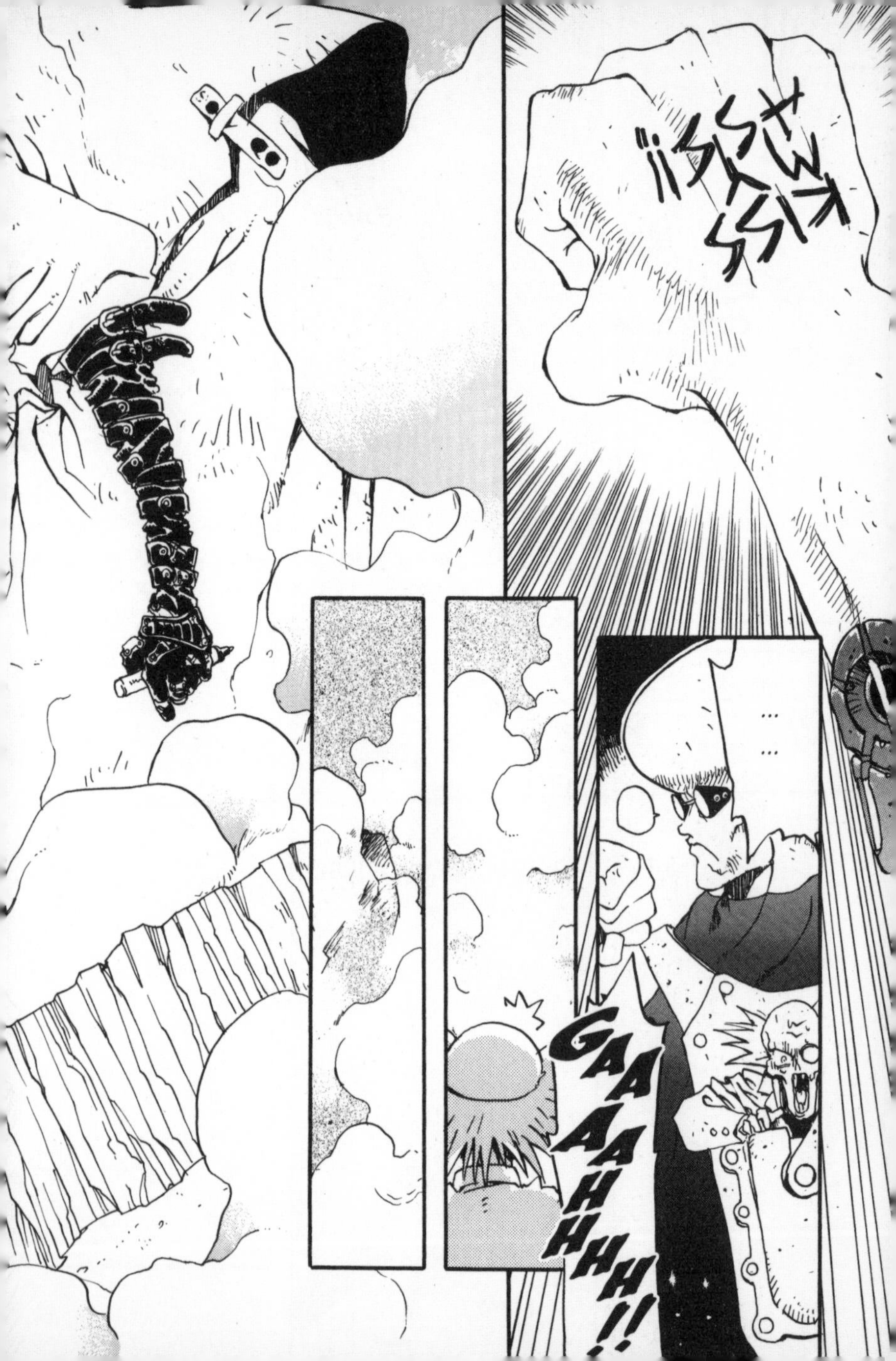
...
...
GAAAAHHHHH!!

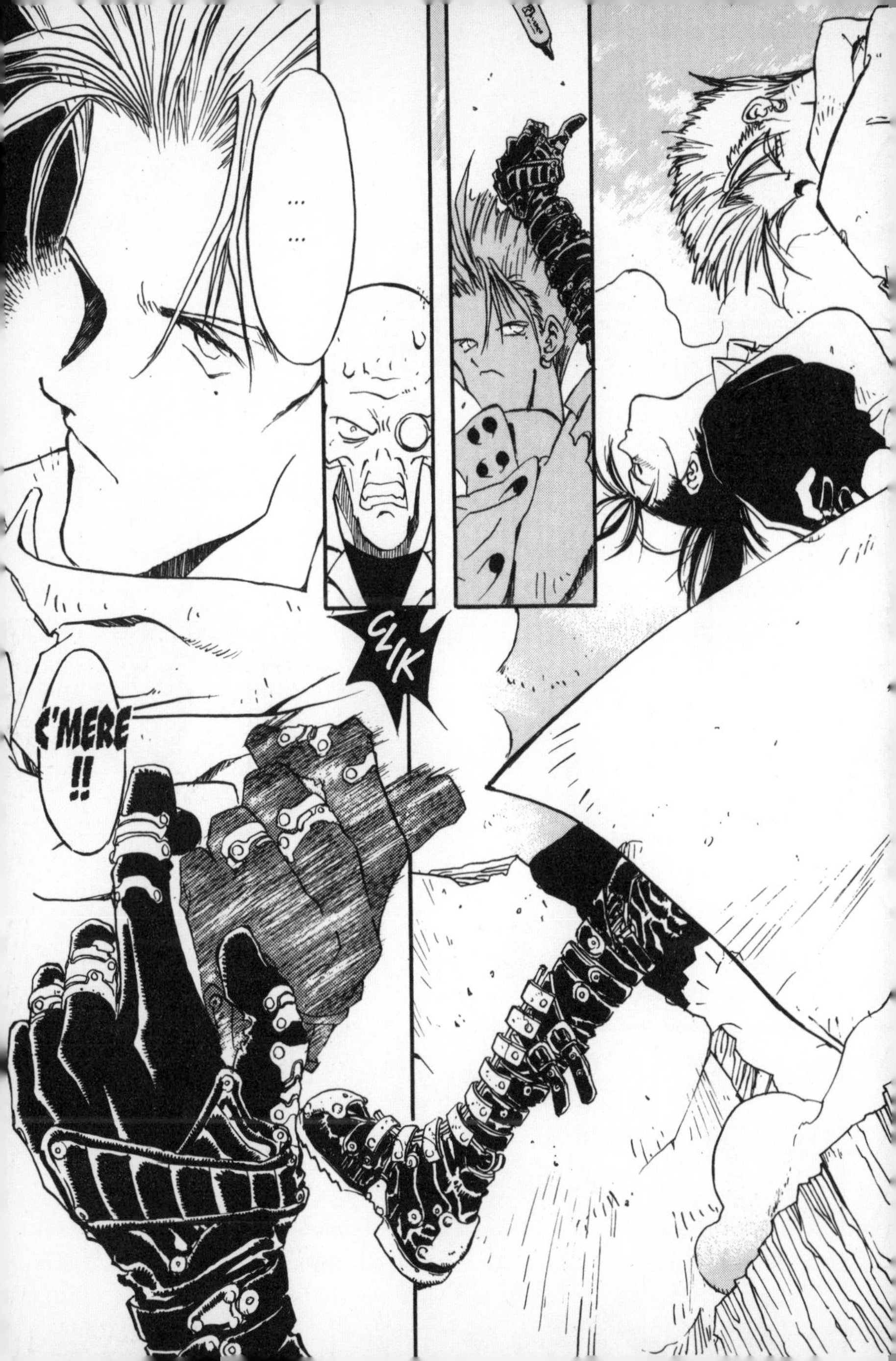
......
CLIK
C'MERE !!

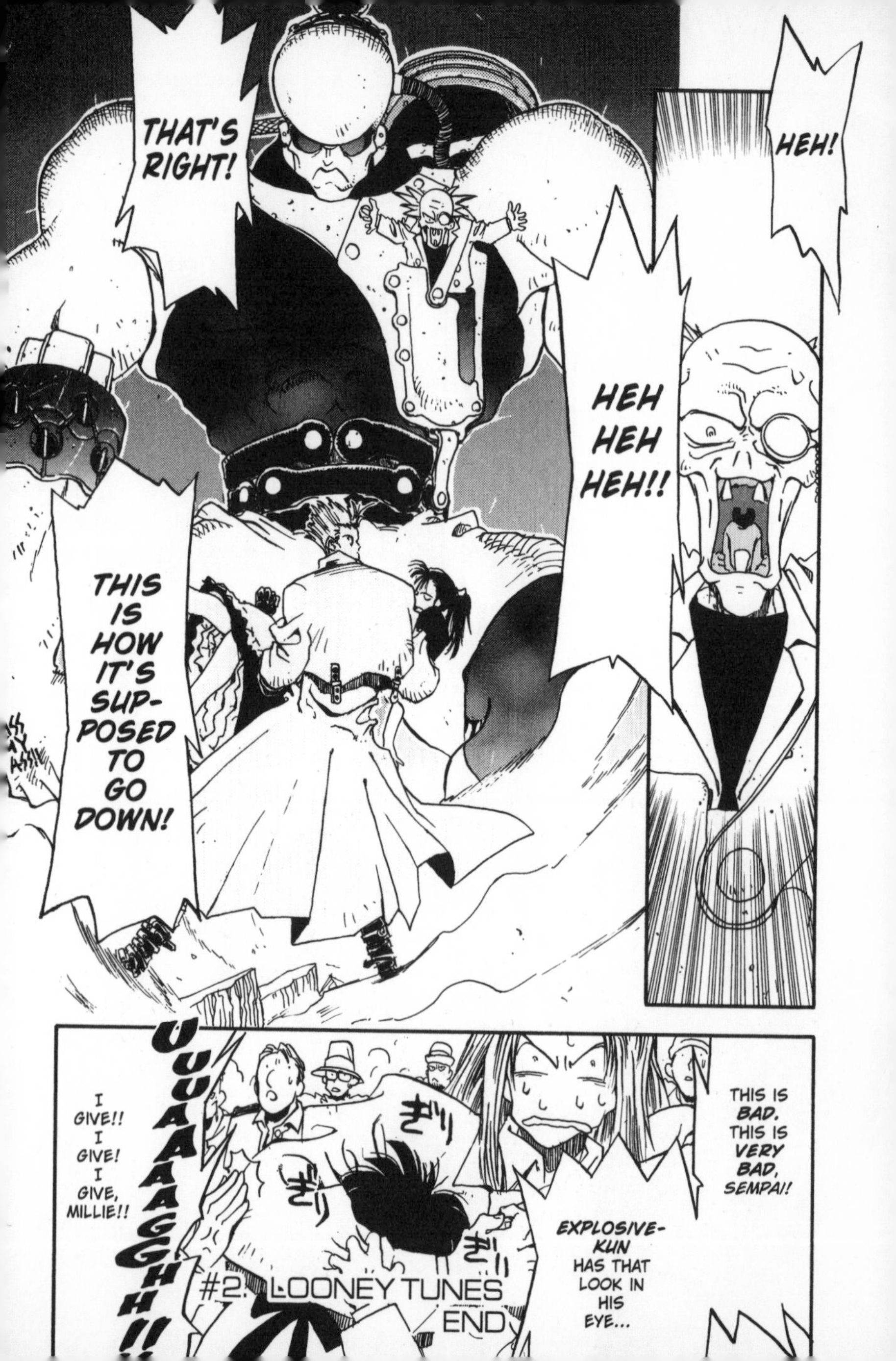
HEH!
HEH HEH HEH!!
THAT'S RIGHT!
THIS IS HOW IT'S SUPPOSED TO GO DOWN!
THIS IS BAD. THIS IS VERY BAD, SEMPAI!
EXPLOSIVE-KUN HAS THAT LOOK IN HIS EYE...
ぎり
ぎり
ぎり
I GIVE!! I GIVE! I GIVE, MILLIE!!
UUUAAAAAGGHH!!
#2. LOONEY TUNES END

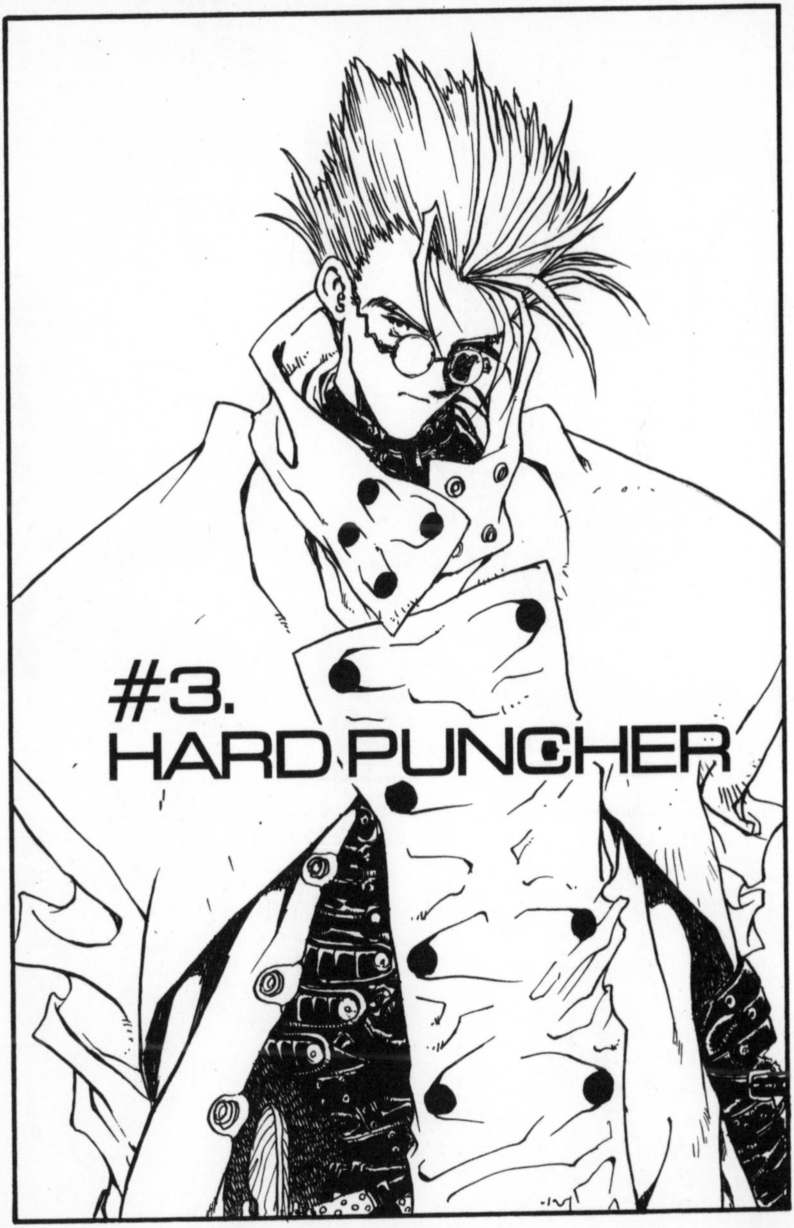
#3.
HARD PUNCHER

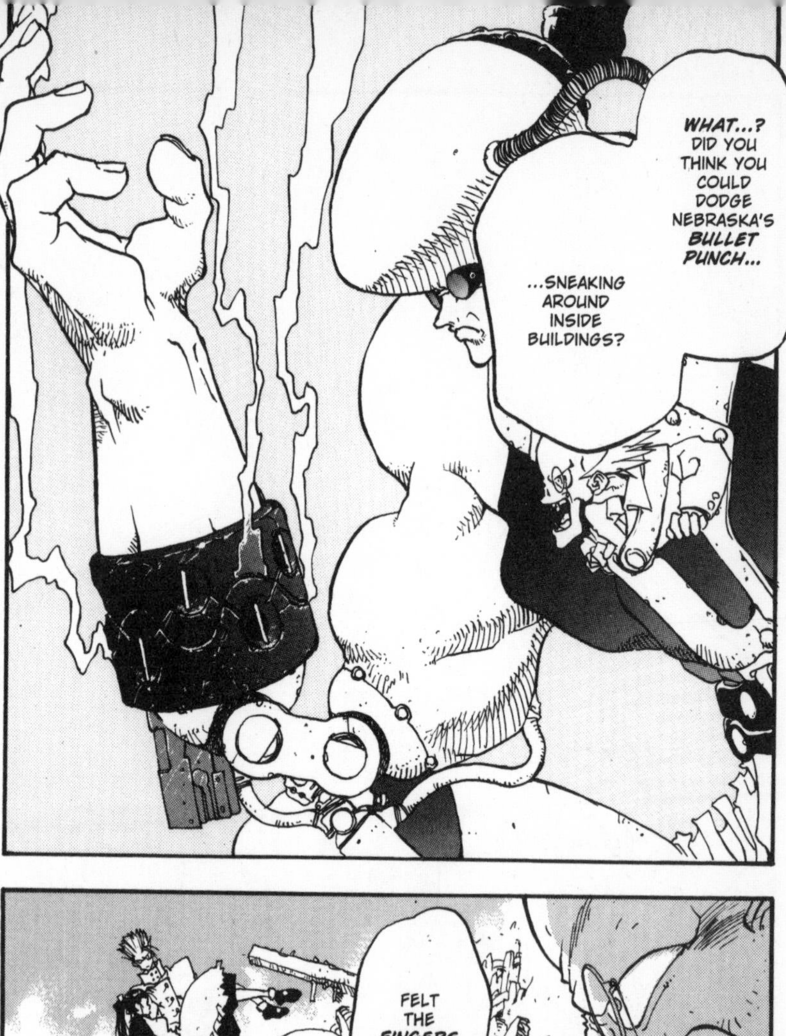
WHAT...? DID YOU THINK YOU COULD DODGE NEBRASKA'S BULLET PUNCH...
...SNEAKING AROUND INSIDE BUILDINGS?

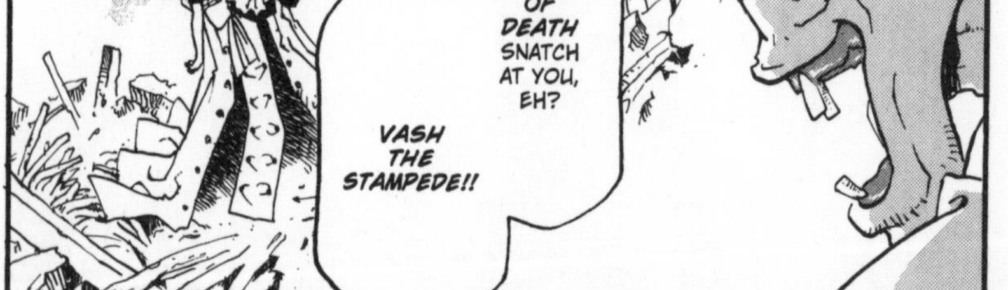
FELT THE FINGERS OF DEATH SNATCH AT YOU, EH?
VASH THE STAMPEDE!!

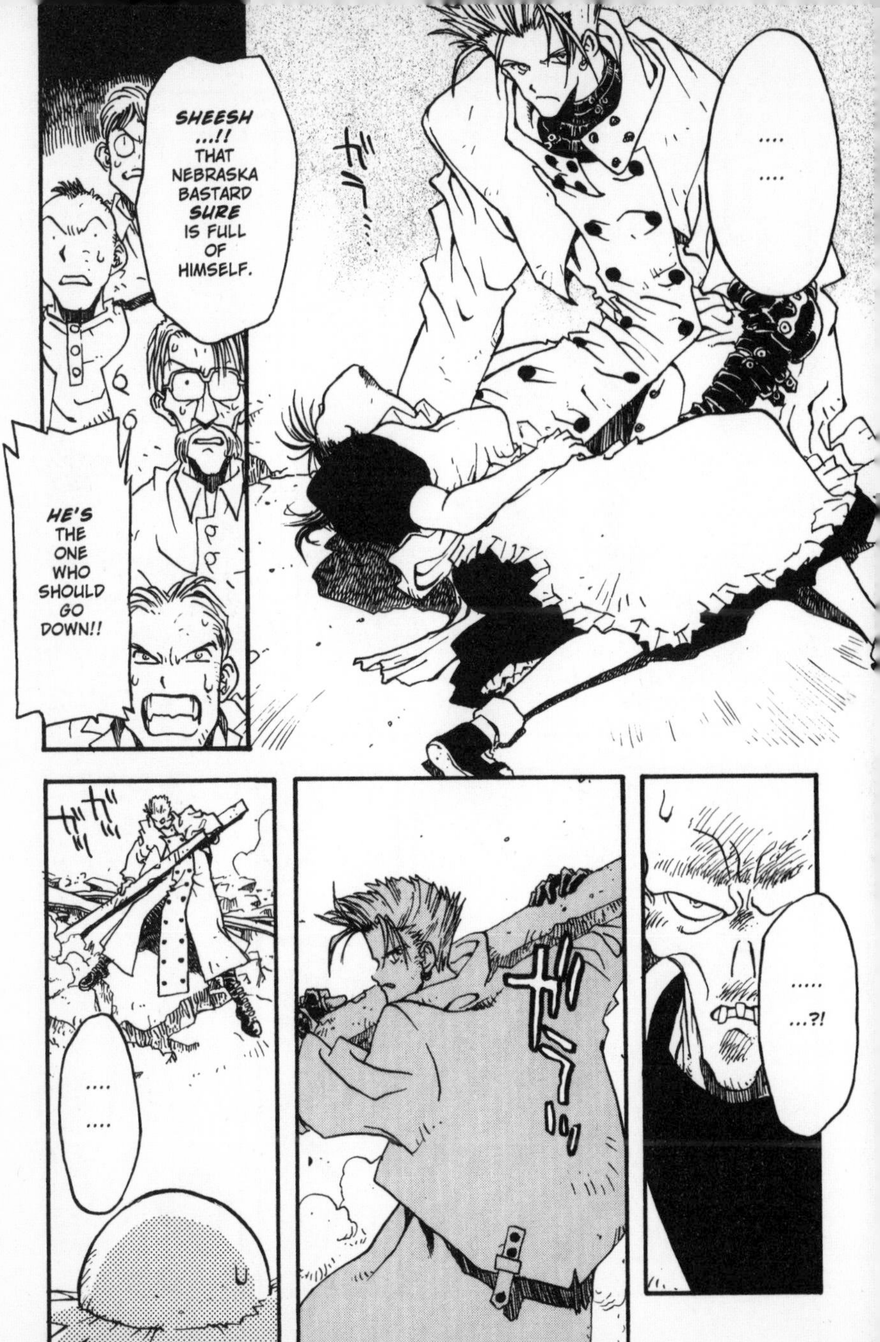
.... ....
SHEESH ...!! THAT NEBRASKA BASTARD SURE IS FULL OF HIMSELF.
HE'S THE ONE WHO SHOULD GO DOWN!!
..... ...?!
.... ....

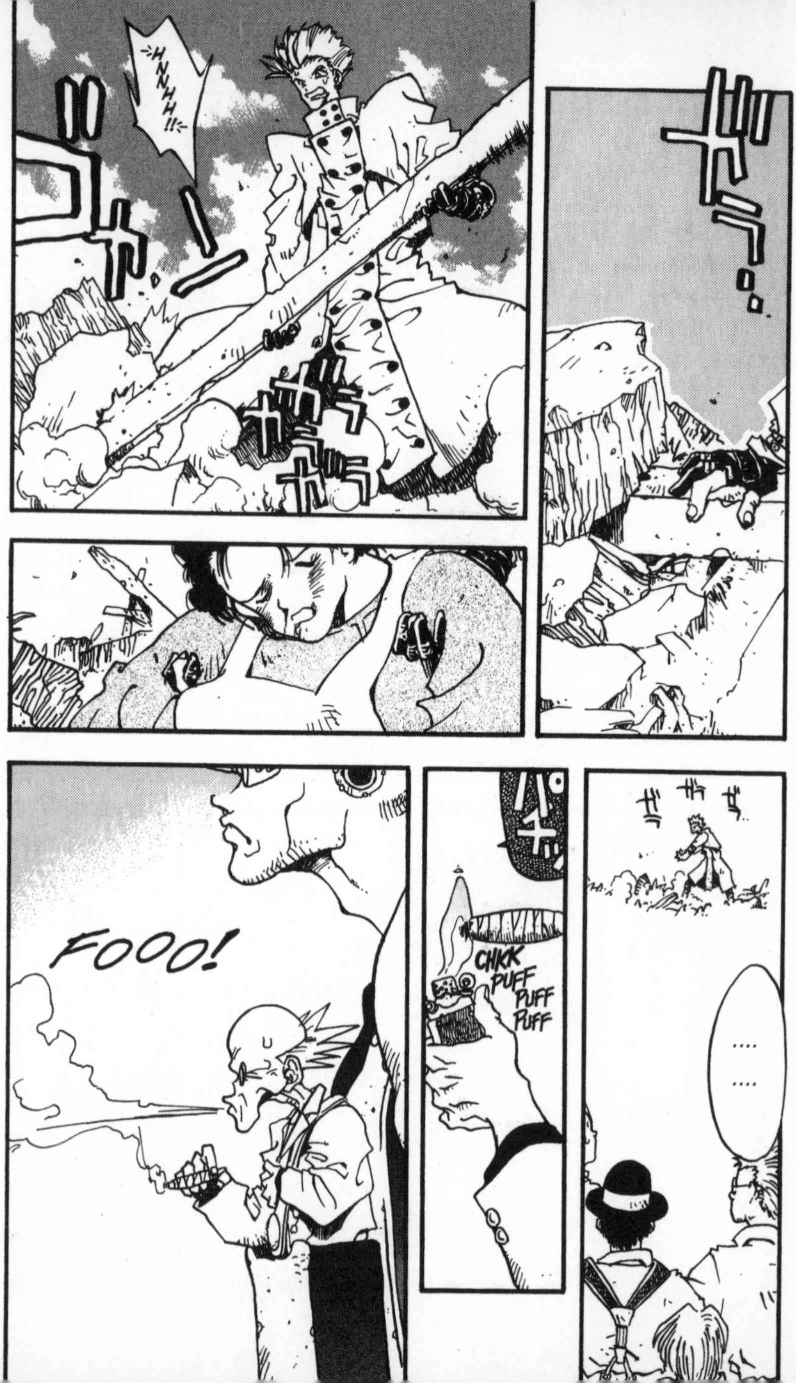
HNNNH!!
....
....
CHKK
PUFF
PUFF
PUFF
FOOO!

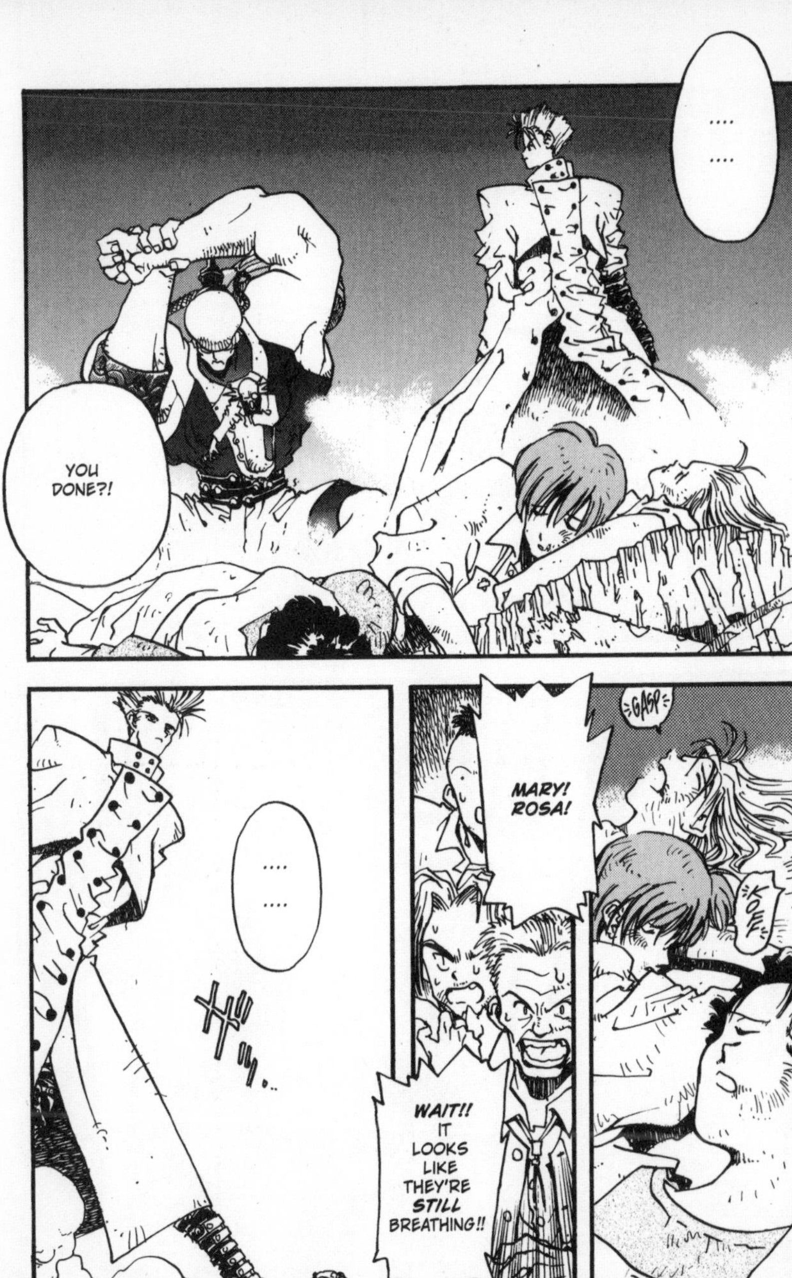

....
....
YOU DONE?!
GASP
MARY! ROSA!
KOFF
WAIT!! IT LOOKS LIKE THEY'RE STILL BREATHING!!
....
....

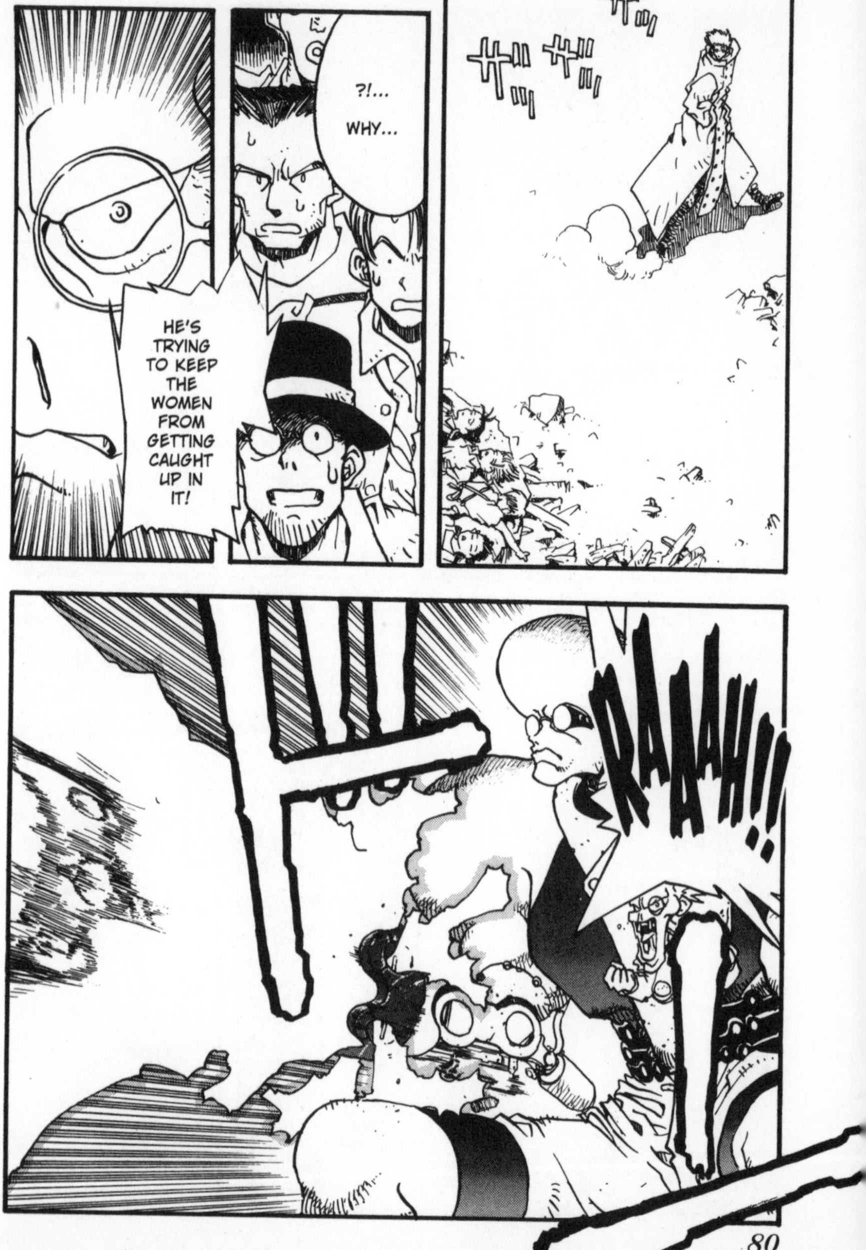
?!...
WHY...
HE'S TRYING TO KEEP THE WOMEN FROM GETTING CAUGHT UP IN IT!
RAAAH!!!

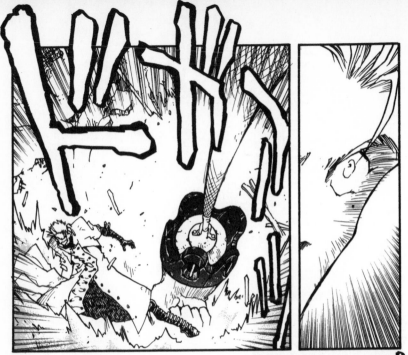

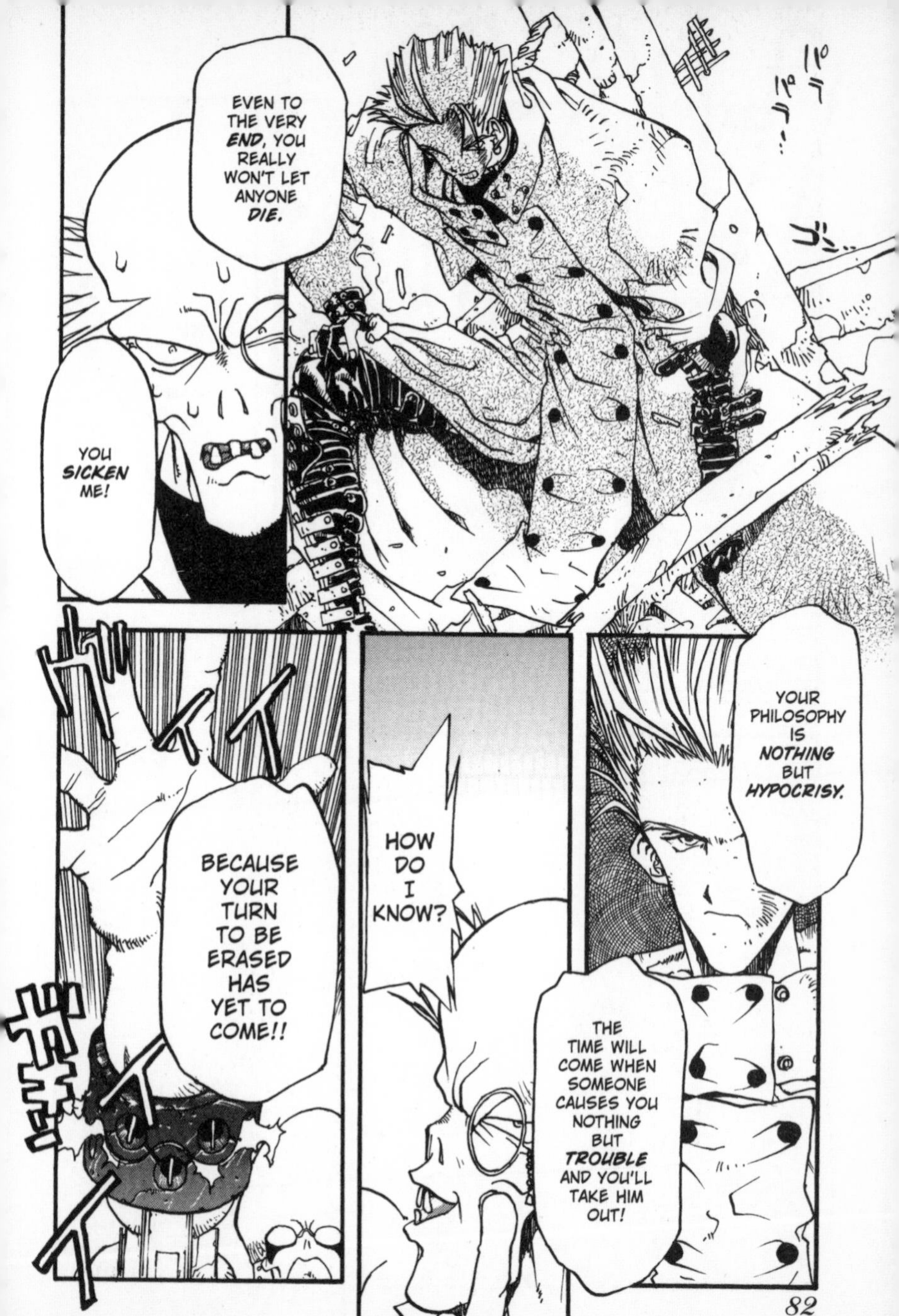

EVEN TO THE VERY END, YOU REALLY WON'T LET ANYONE DIE.
YOU SICKEN ME!
YOUR PHILOSOPHY IS NOTHING BUT HYPOCRISY.
THE TIME WILL COME WHEN SOMEONE CAUSES YOU NOTHING BUT TROUBLE AND YOU'LL TAKE HIM OUT!
HOW DO I KNOW?
BECAUSE YOUR TURN TO BE ERASED HAS YET TO COME!!

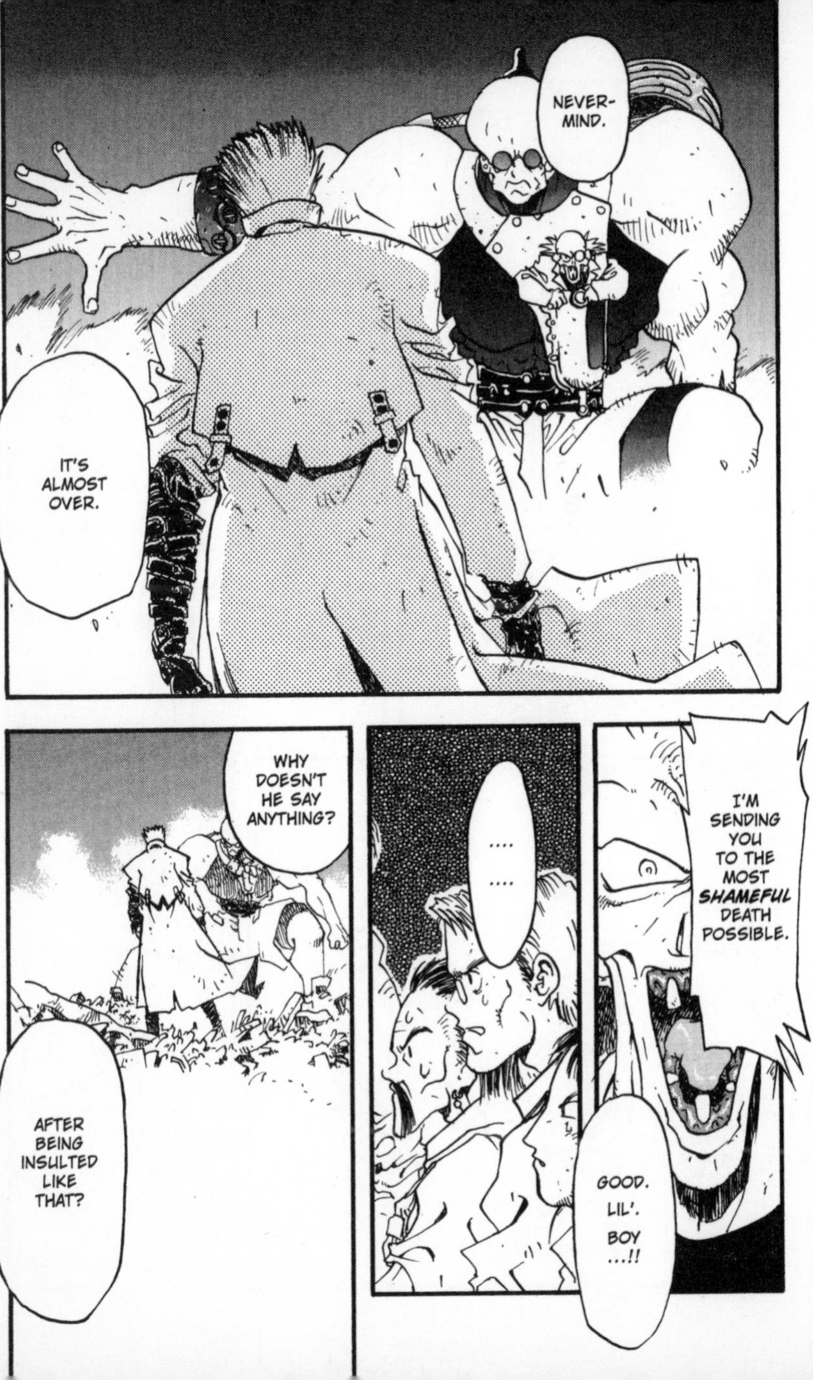
NEVER-MIND.
IT'S ALMOST OVER.
I'M SENDING YOU TO THE MOST ***SHAMEFUL*** DEATH POSSIBLE.
GOOD. LIL'. BOY ...!!
.... ....
WHY DOESN'T HE SAY ANYTHING?
AFTER BEING INSULTED LIKE THAT?

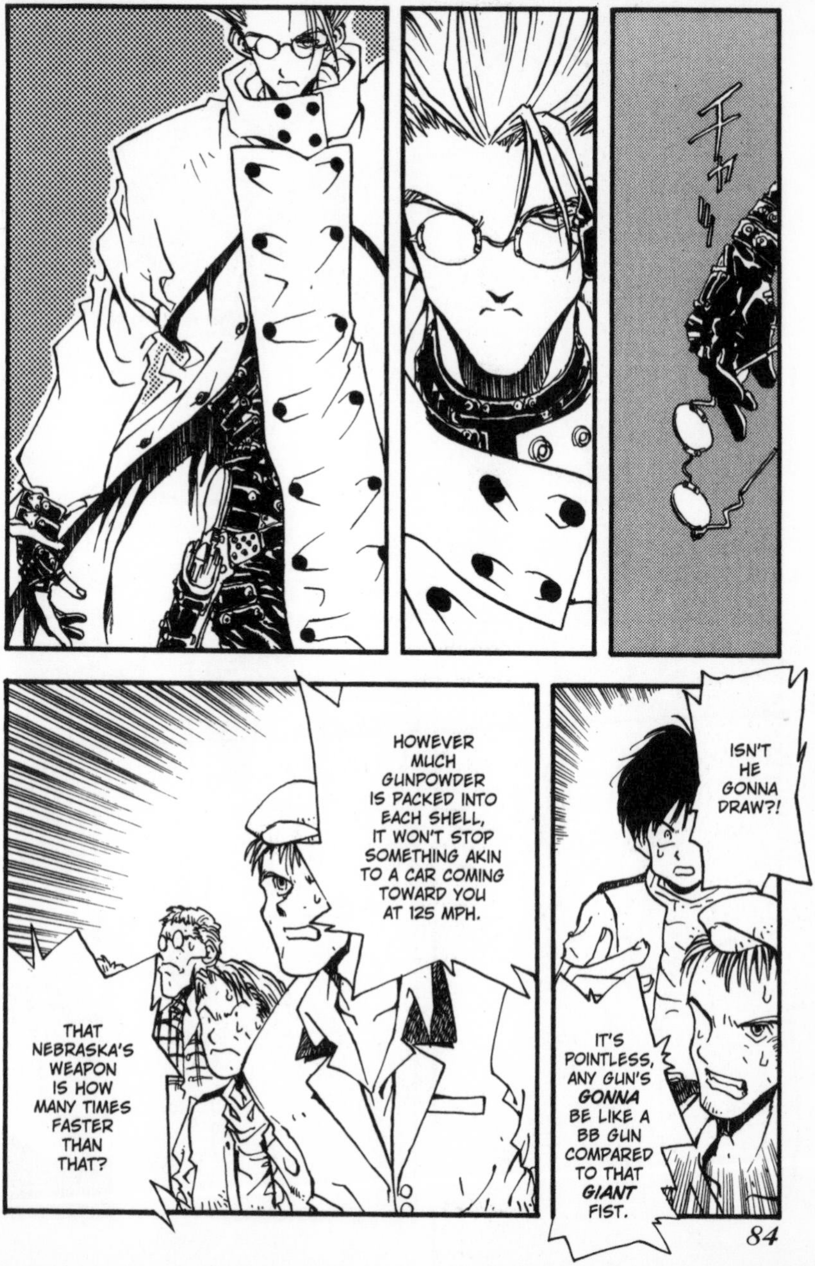
ISN'T HE GONNA DRAW?!
IT'S POINTLESS, ANY GUN'S ***GONNA*** BE LIKE A BB GUN COMPARED TO THAT ***GIANT*** FIST.
HOWEVER MUCH GUNPOWDER IS PACKED INTO EACH SHELL, IT WON'T STOP SOMETHING AKIN TO A CAR COMING TOWARD YOU AT 125 MPH.
THAT NEBRASKA'S WEAPON IS HOW MANY TIMES FASTER THAN THAT?

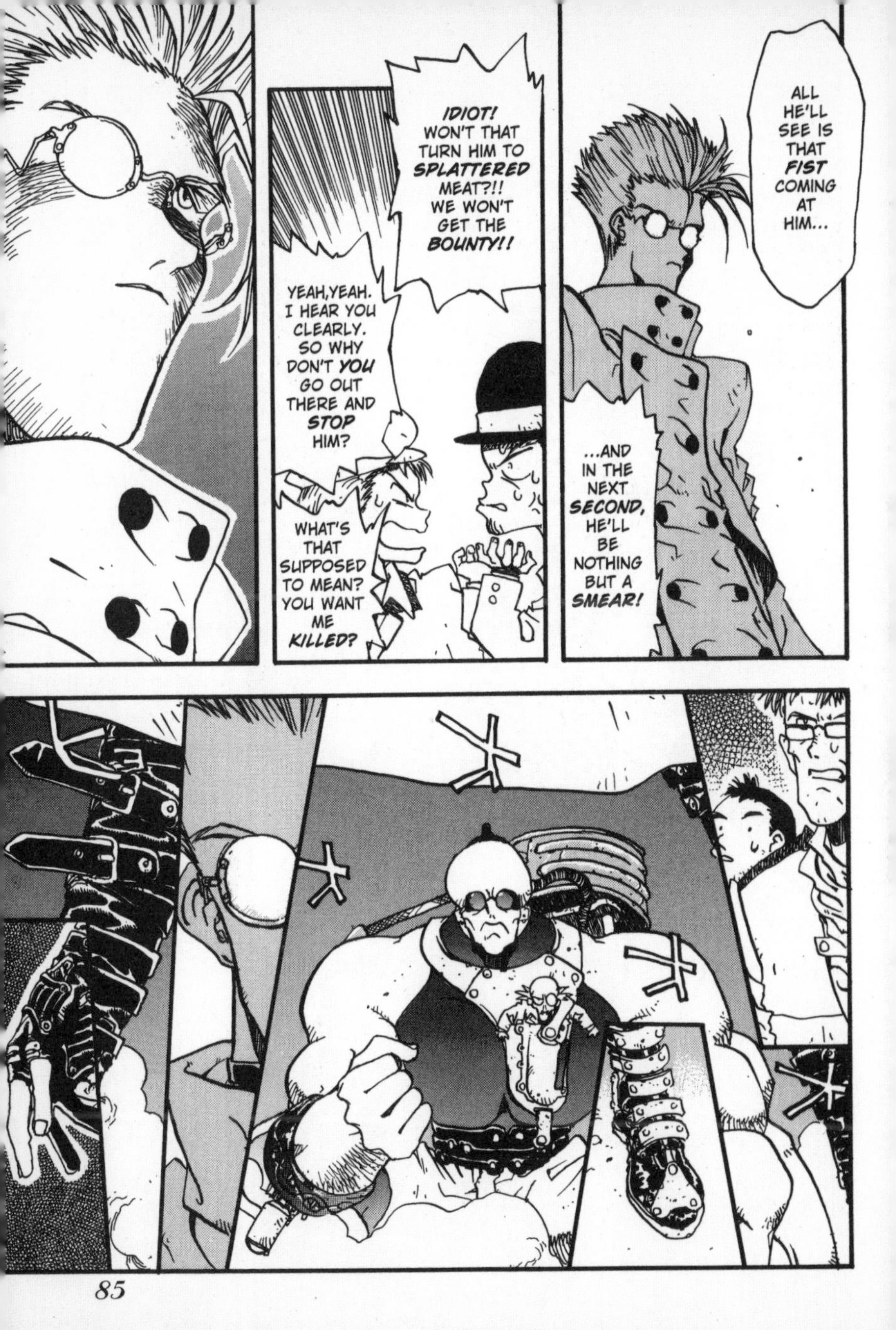
ALL HE'LL SEE IS THAT FIST COMING AT HIM...
...AND IN THE NEXT SECOND, HE'LL BE NOTHING BUT A SMEAR!
IDIOT! WON'T THAT TURN HIM TO SPLATTERED MEAT?!! WE WON'T GET THE BOUNTY!!
YEAH,YEAH. I HEAR YOU CLEARLY. SO WHY DON'T YOU GO OUT THERE AND STOP HIM?
WHAT'S THAT SUPPOSED TO MEAN? YOU WANT ME KILLED?

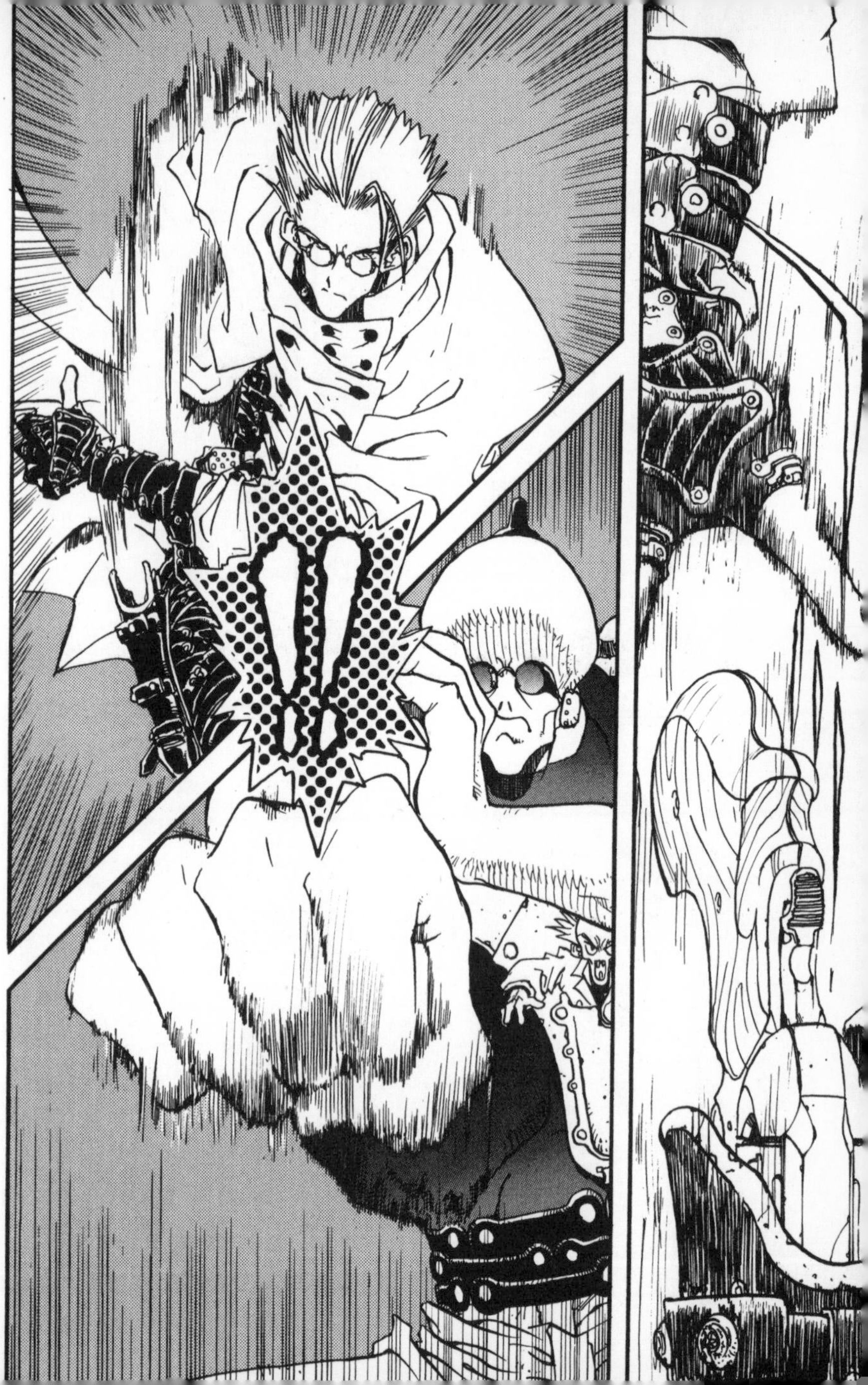
!!

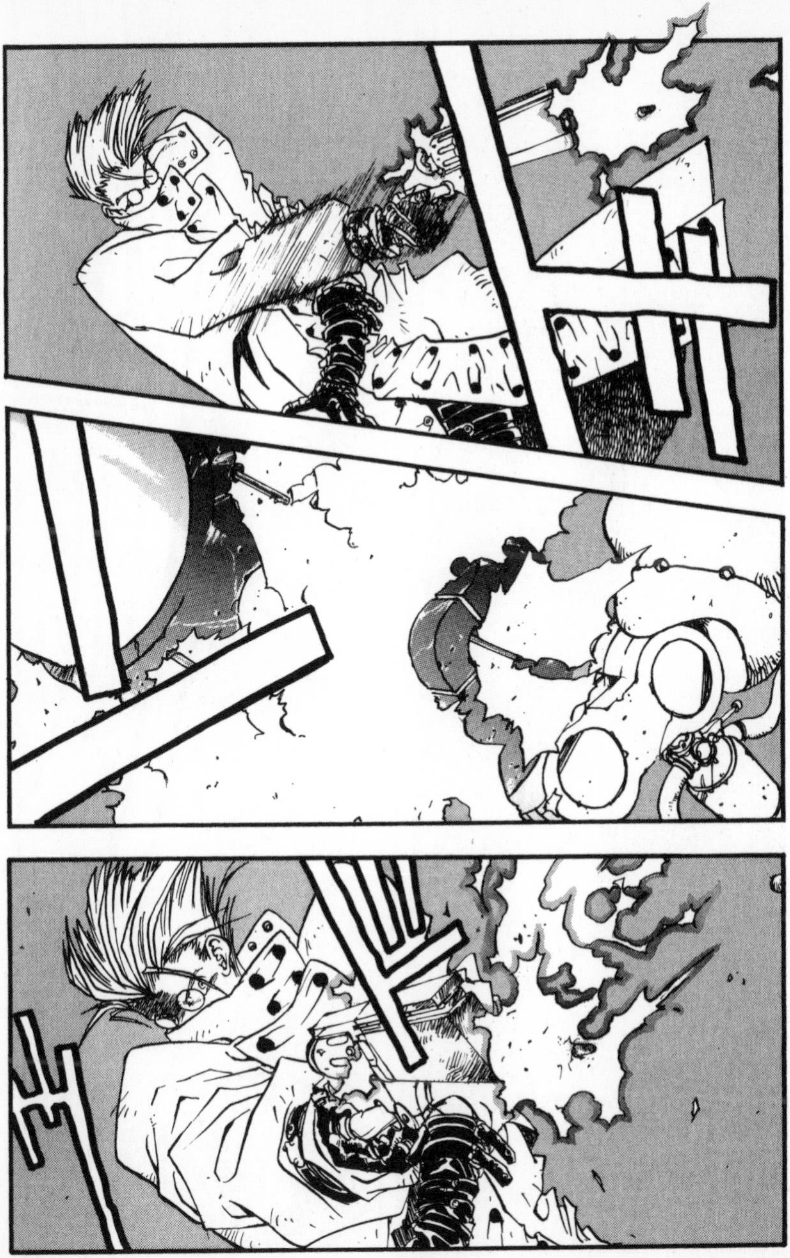

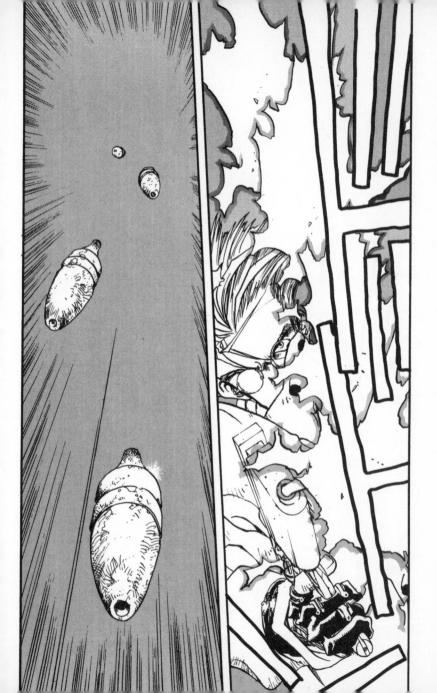

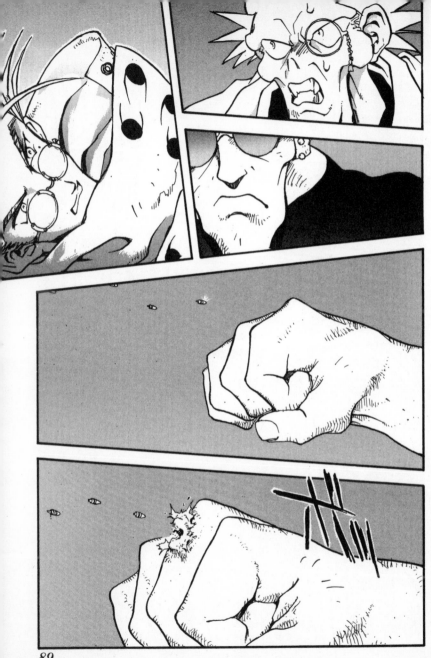

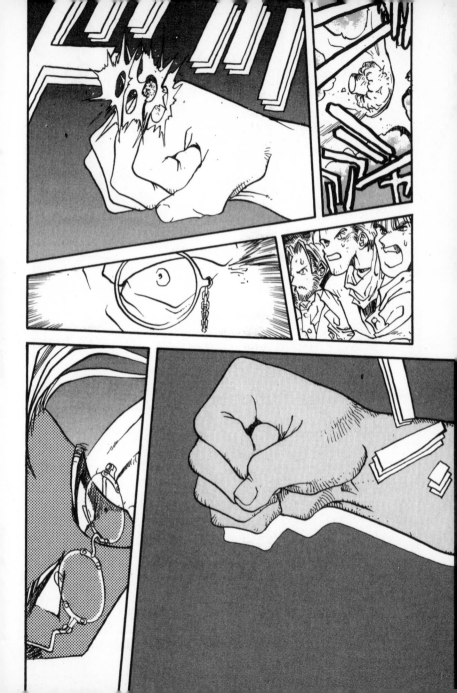

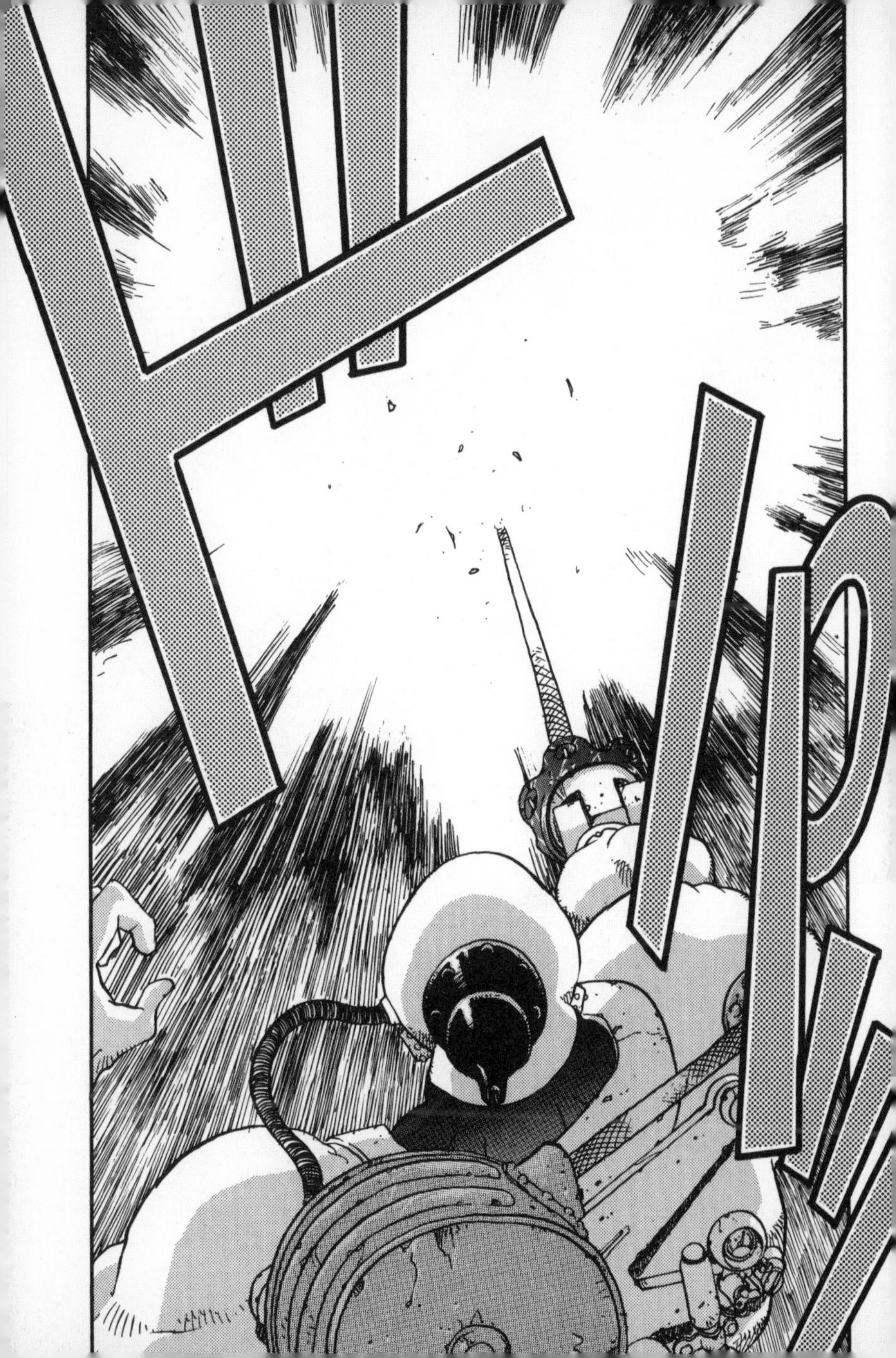

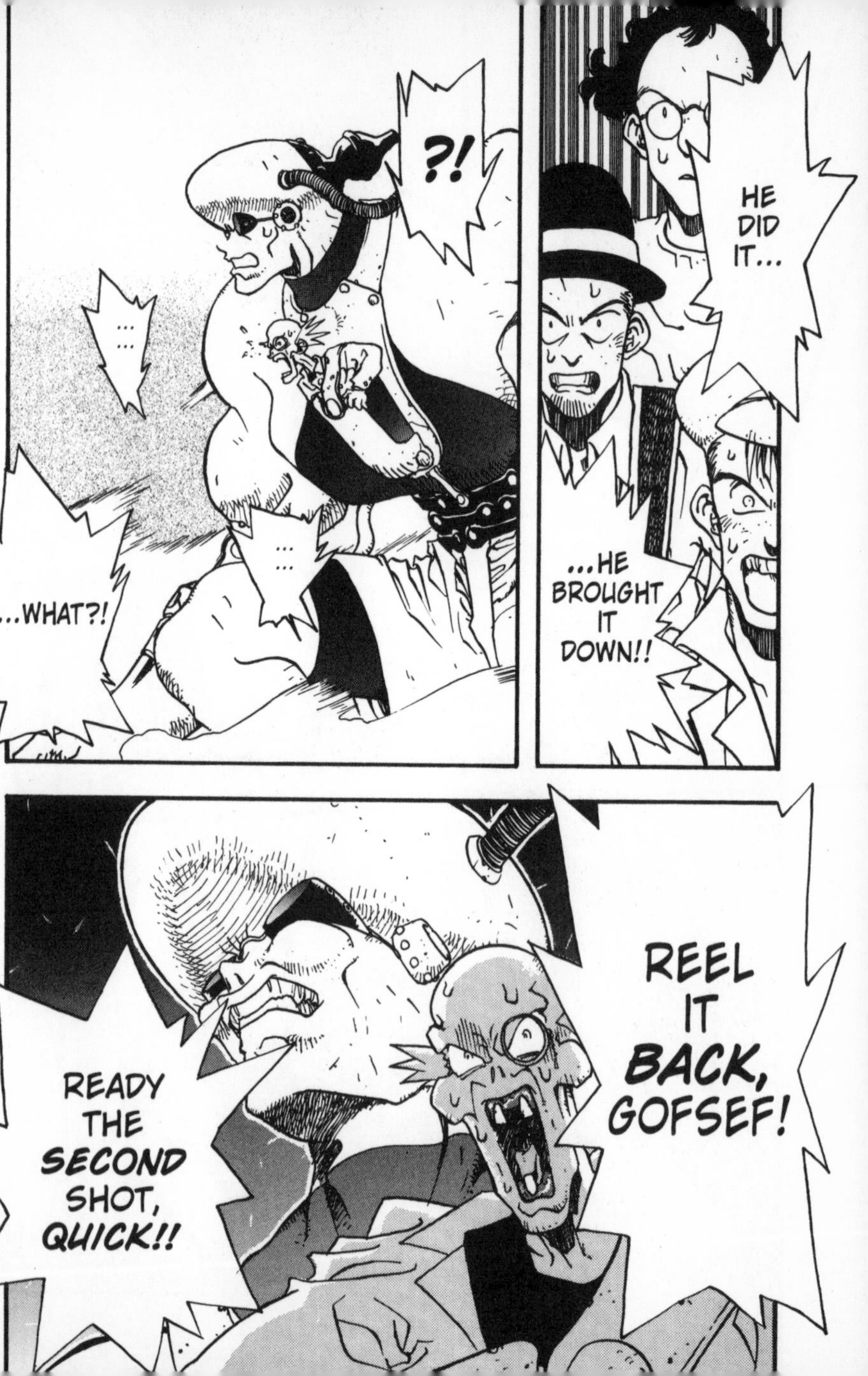
HE DID IT...
...HE BROUGHT IT DOWN!!
?!
...
...
...
...
...WHAT?!
REEL IT BACK, GOFSEF!
READY THE SECOND SHOT, QUICK!!

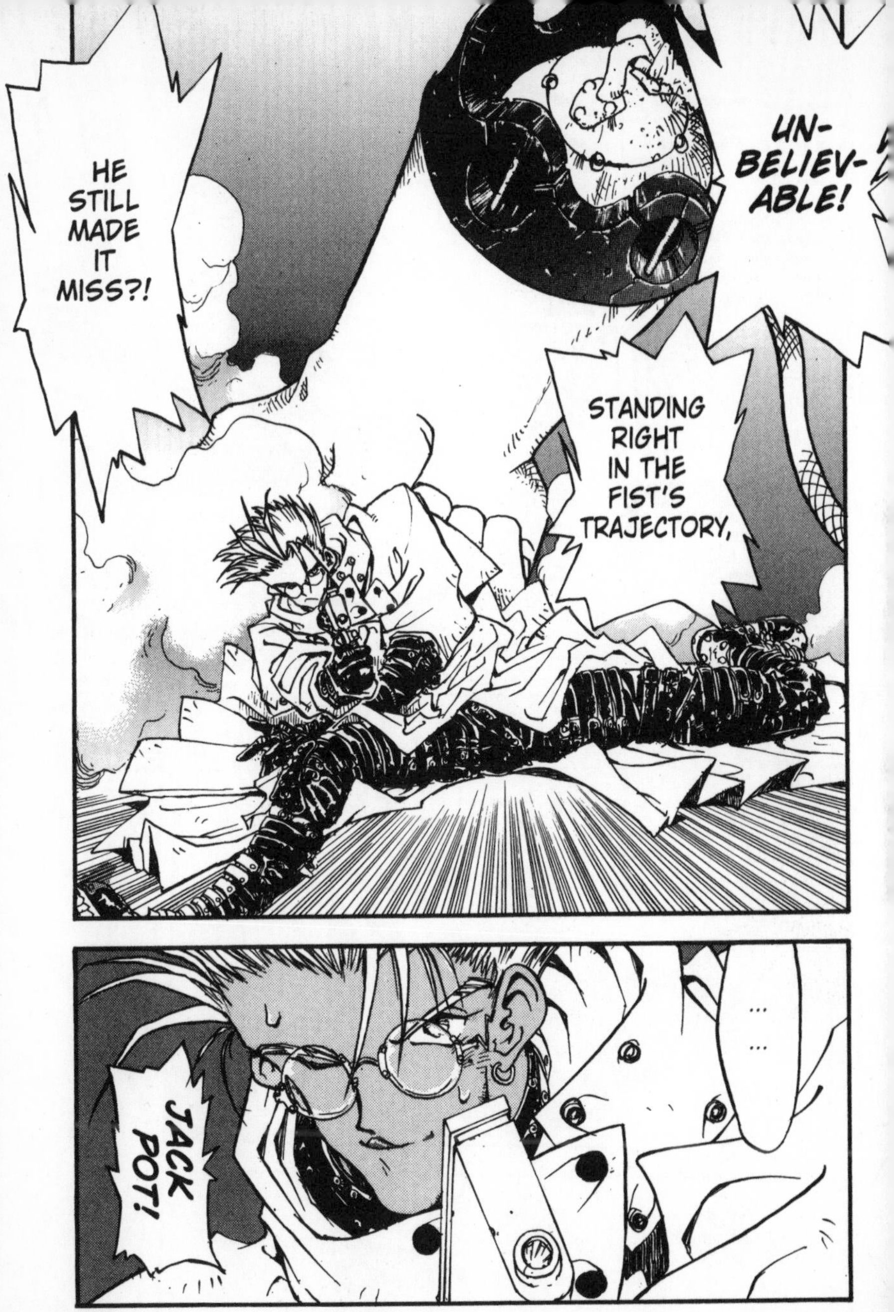
UN-BELIEV-ABLE!
HE STILL MADE IT MISS?!
STANDING RIGHT IN THE FIST'S TRAJECTORY,
... ...
JACK POT!

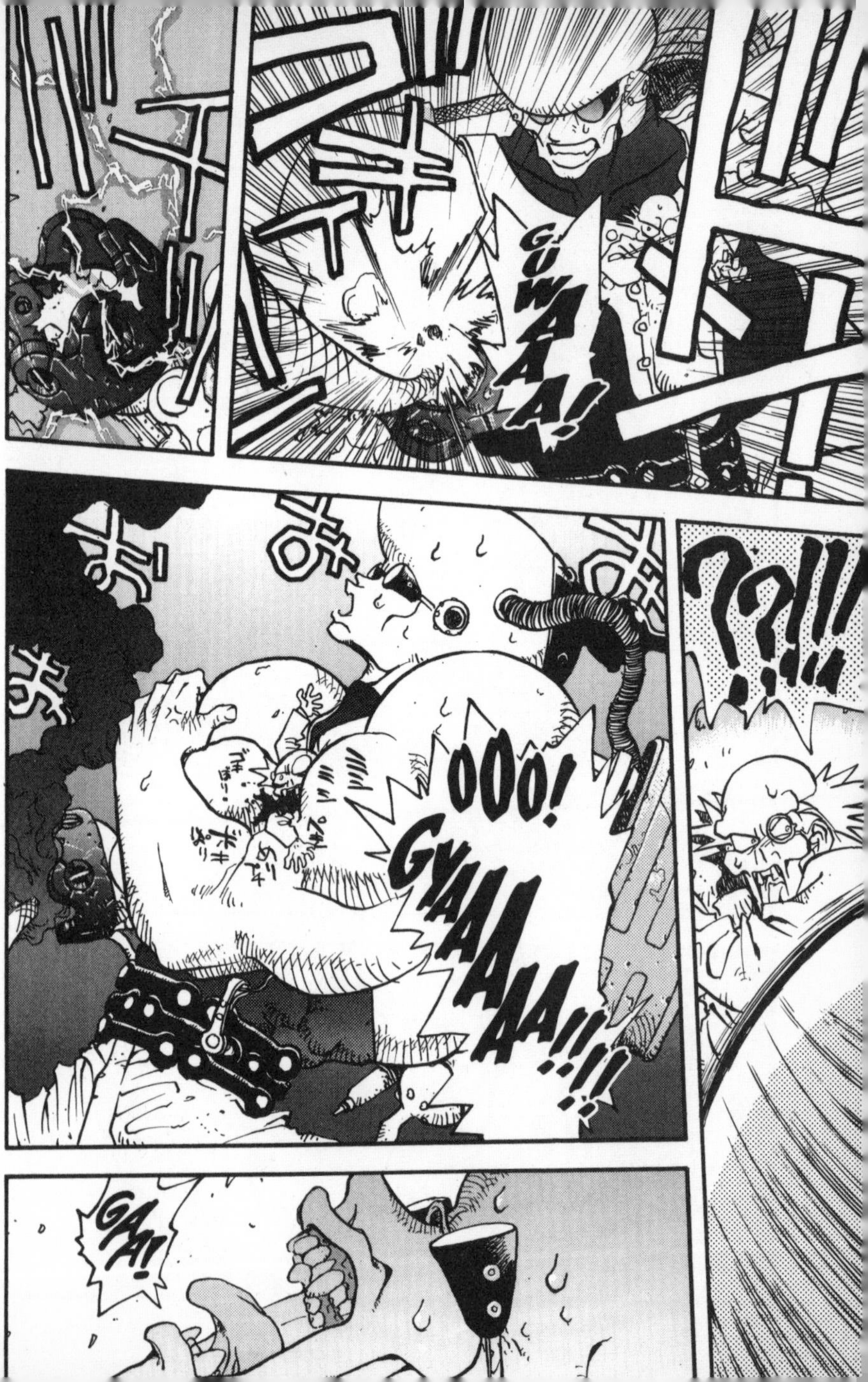

GUWAAAA!
??!!
OOO!
GYAAAAAA!!!!
GAA!

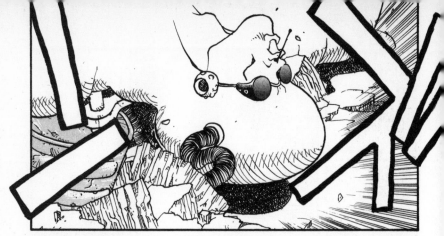

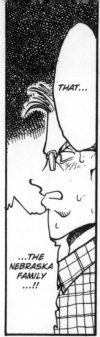

THAT...

...THE NEBRASKA FAMILY ...!!

HE...

...HE DID IT...

SUDDENLY IT MAKES SENSE TO ME.

WHY THAT MAN IS CALLED THE HUMANOID TYPHOON!!

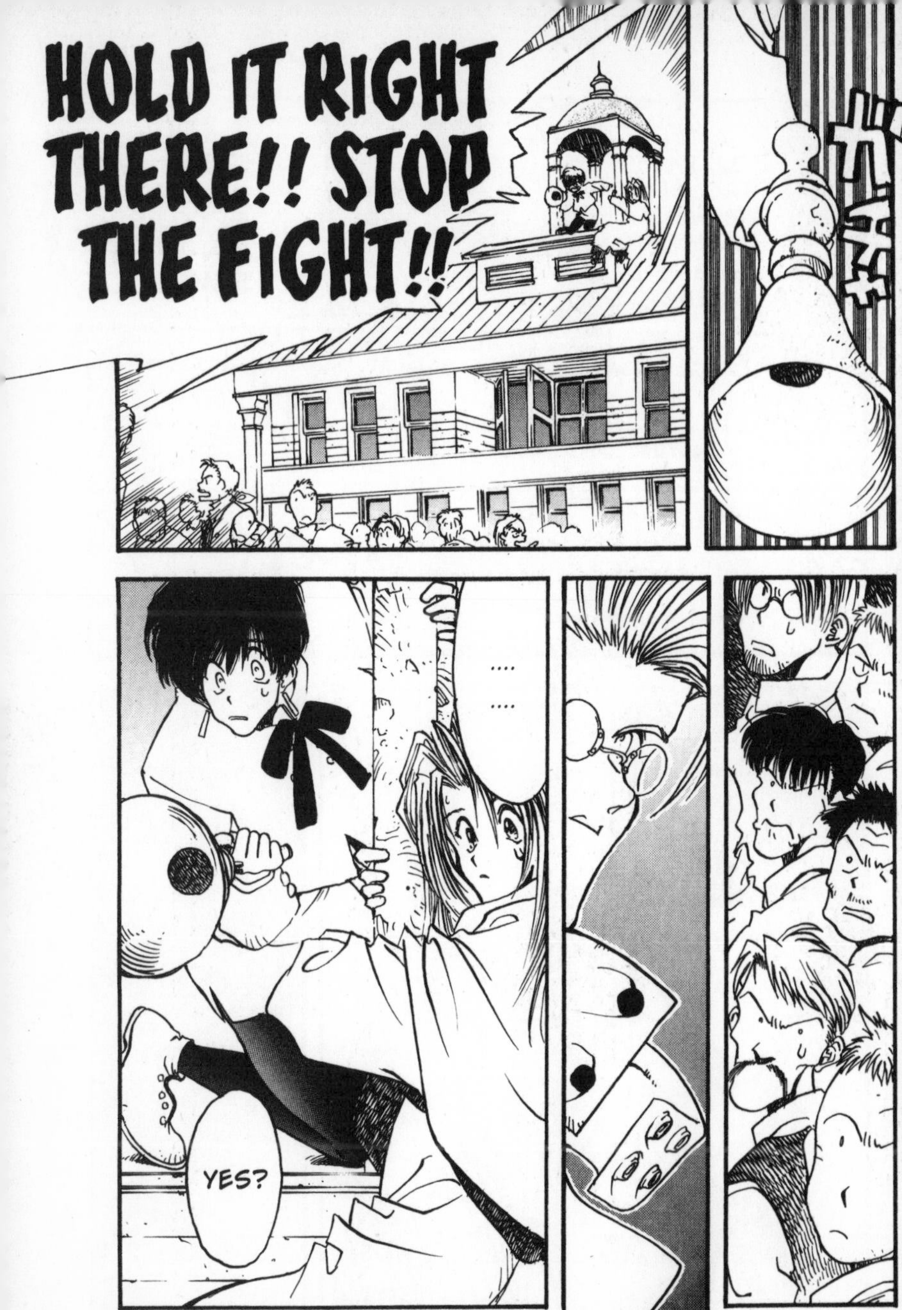
HOLD IT RIGHT THERE!! STOP THE FIGHT!!
....
....
YES?

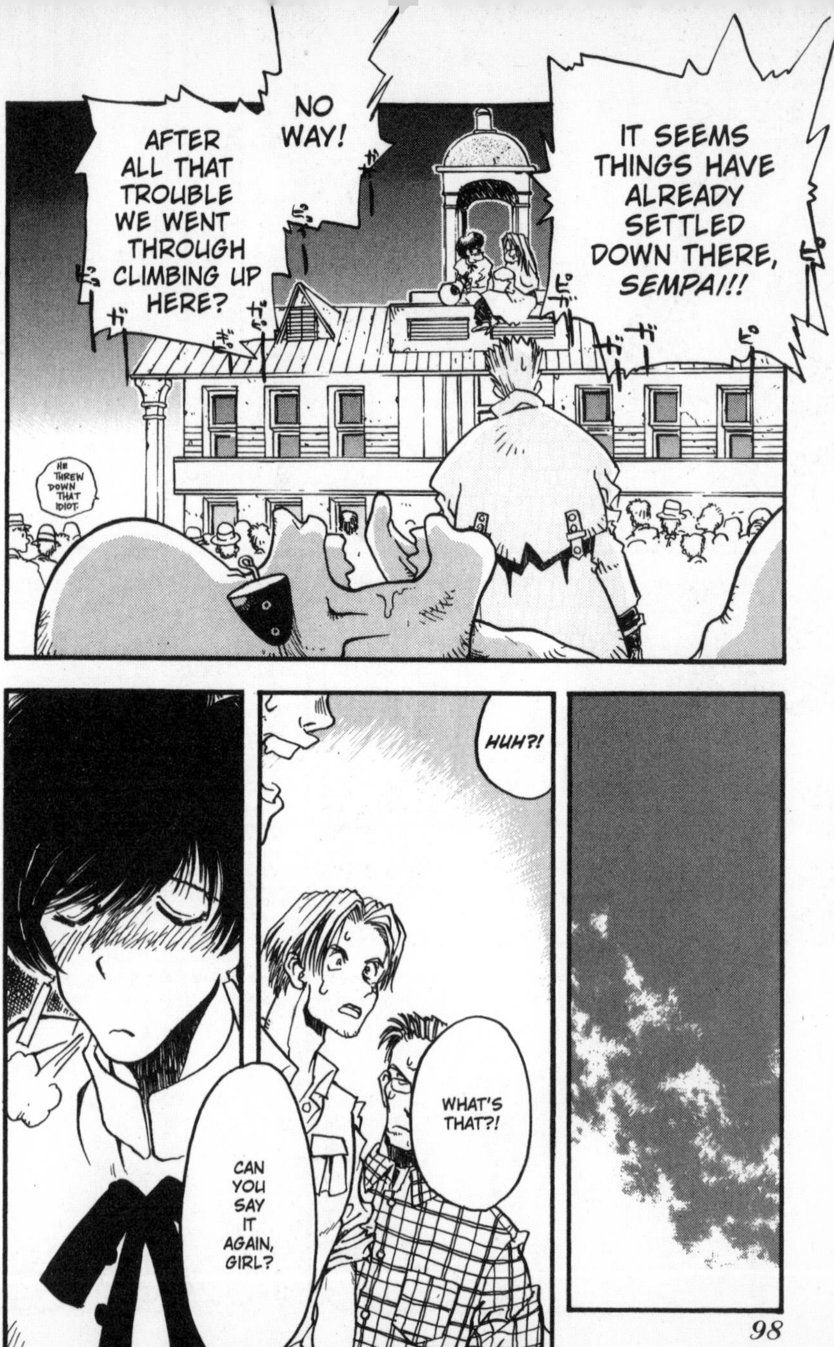
IT SEEMS THINGS HAVE ALREADY SETTLED DOWN THERE, SEMPAI!!
NO WAY!
AFTER ALL THAT TROUBLE WE WENT THROUGH CLIMBING UP HERE?
HE THREW DOWN THAT IDIOT.
HUH?!
WHAT'S THAT?!
CAN YOU SAY IT AGAIN, GIRL?

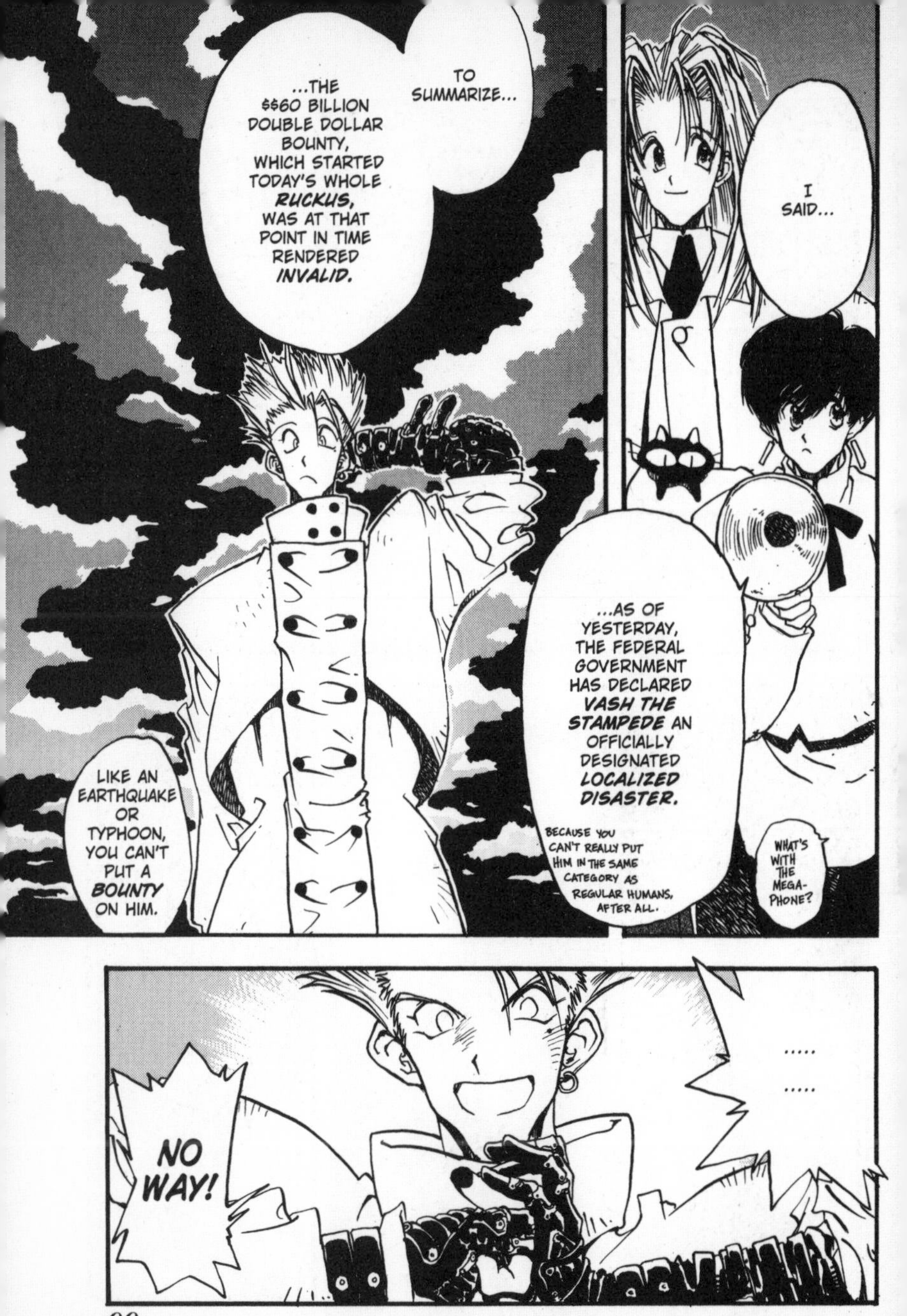
I SAID...
...AS OF YESTERDAY, THE FEDERAL GOVERNMENT HAS DECLARED VASH THE STAMPEDE AN OFFICIALLY DESIGNATED LOCALIZED DISASTER.
BECAUSE YOU CAN'T REALLY PUT HIM IN THE SAME CATEGORY AS REGULAR HUMANS, AFTER ALL.
WHAT'S WITH THE MEGA-PHONE?
TO SUMMARIZE...
...THE $$60 BILLION DOUBLE DOLLAR BOUNTY, WHICH STARTED TODAY'S WHOLE RUCKUS, WAS AT THAT POINT IN TIME RENDERED INVALID.
LIKE AN EARTHQUAKE OR TYPHOON, YOU CAN'T PUT A BOUNTY ON HIM.
.....
.....
NO WAY!

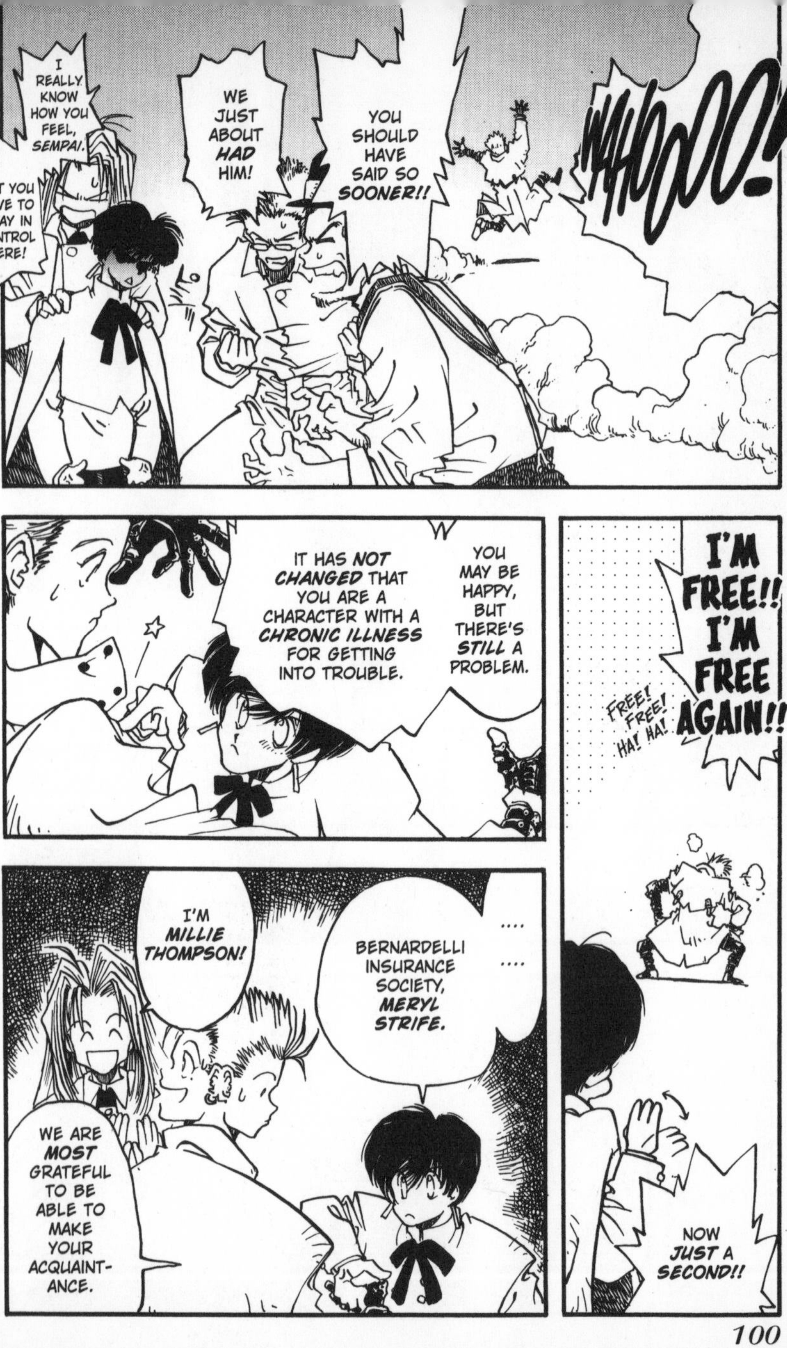
WAHOOOO!
YOU SHOULD HAVE SAID SO SOONER!!
WE JUST ABOUT HAD HIM!
I REALLY KNOW HOW YOU FEEL, SEMPAI.
BUT YOU HAVE TO STAY IN CONTROL HERE!
I'M FREE!! I'M FREE AGAIN!!
FREE! FREE! HA! HA!
NOW JUST A SECOND!!
YOU MAY BE HAPPY, BUT THERE'S STILL A PROBLEM.
IT HAS NOT CHANGED THAT YOU ARE A CHARACTER WITH A CHRONIC ILLNESS FOR GETTING INTO TROUBLE.
....
....
BERNARDELLI INSURANCE SOCIETY, MERYL STRIFE.
I'M MILLIE THOMPSON!
WE ARE MOST GRATEFUL TO BE ABLE TO MAKE YOUR ACQUAINT-ANCE.

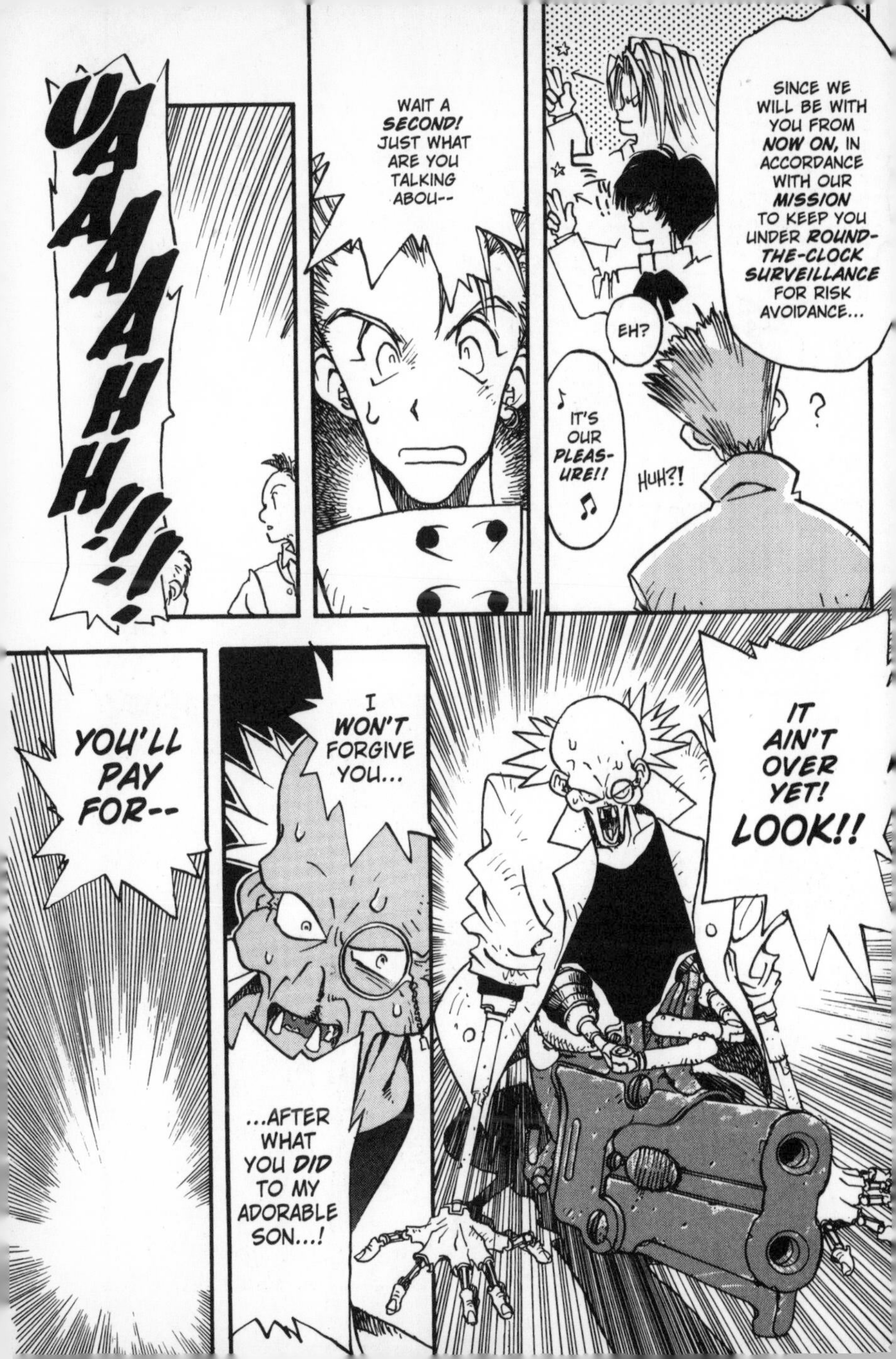
SINCE WE WILL BE WITH YOU FROM NOW ON, IN ACCORDANCE WITH OUR MISSION TO KEEP YOU UNDER ROUND-THE-CLOCK SURVEILLANCE FOR RISK AVOIDANCE...
EH?
?
IT'S OUR PLEASURE!! ♪ ♫
HUH?!
WAIT A SECOND! JUST WHAT ARE YOU TALKING ABOU--
UAAAAAHH!!!!!
IT AIN'T OVER YET! LOOK!!
I WON'T FORGIVE YOU...
...AFTER WHAT YOU DID TO MY ADORABLE SON...!
YOU'LL PAY FOR--

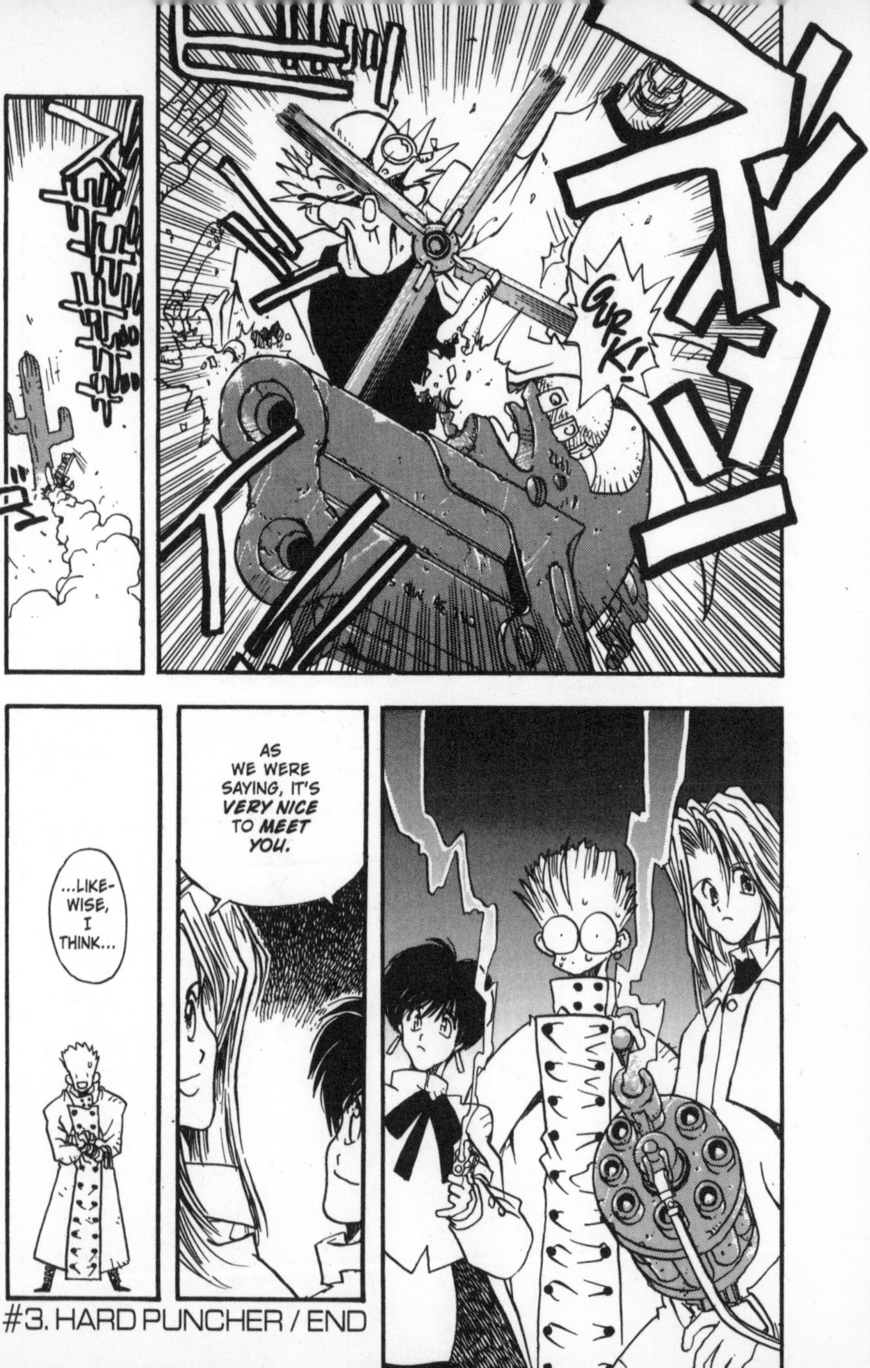
GURK!
AS WE WERE SAYING, IT'S *VERY NICE* TO *MEET* *YOU.*
...LIKE-WISE, I THINK...

#3. HARD PUNCHER / END

#4

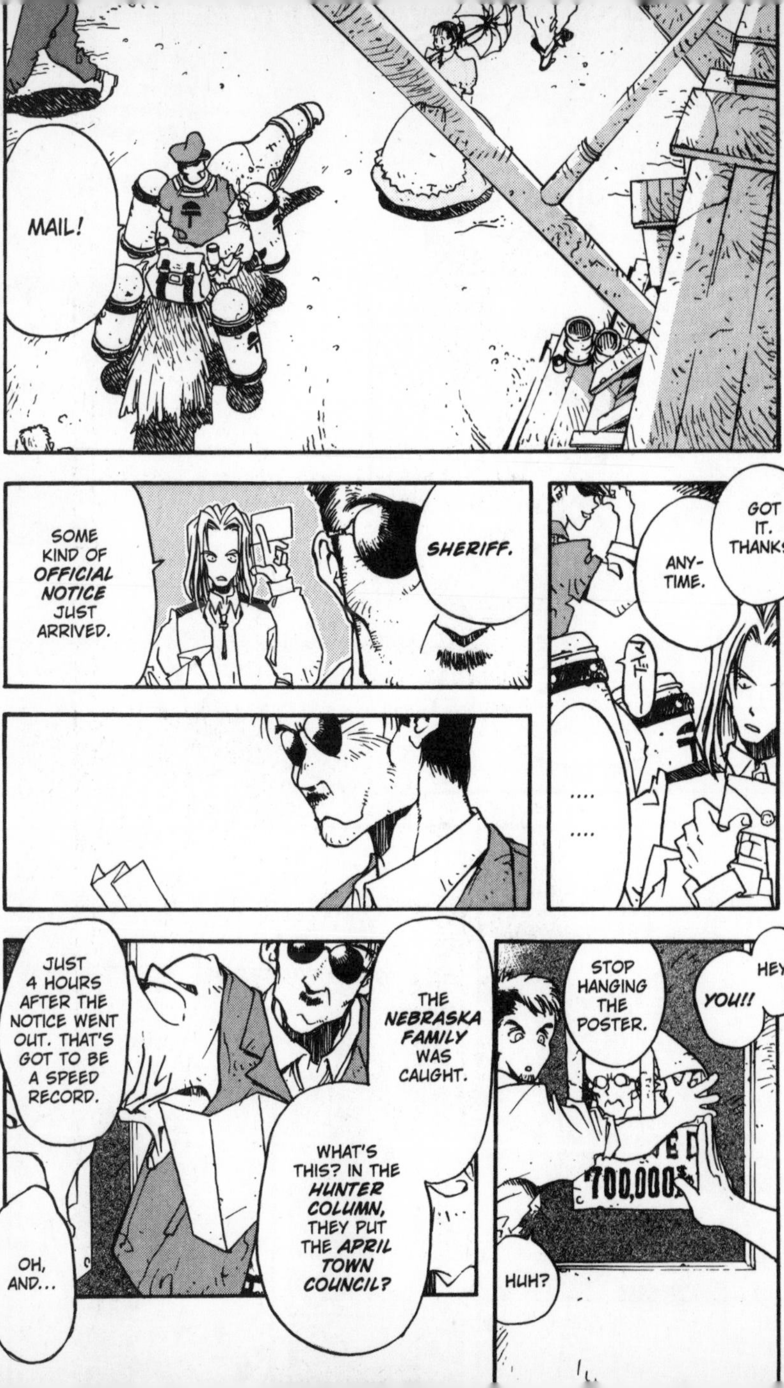
MAIL!
GOT IT. THANKS.
ANY-TIME.
....
....
SHERIFF.
SOME KIND OF OFFICIAL NOTICE JUST ARRIVED.
HEY!
YOU!!
STOP HANGING THE POSTER.
700,000$
HUH?
THE NEBRASKA FAMILY WAS CAUGHT.
JUST 4 HOURS AFTER THE NOTICE WENT OUT. THAT'S GOT TO BE A SPEED RECORD.
WHAT'S THIS? IN THE HUNTER COLUMN, THEY PUT THE APRIL TOWN COUNCIL?
OH, AND...

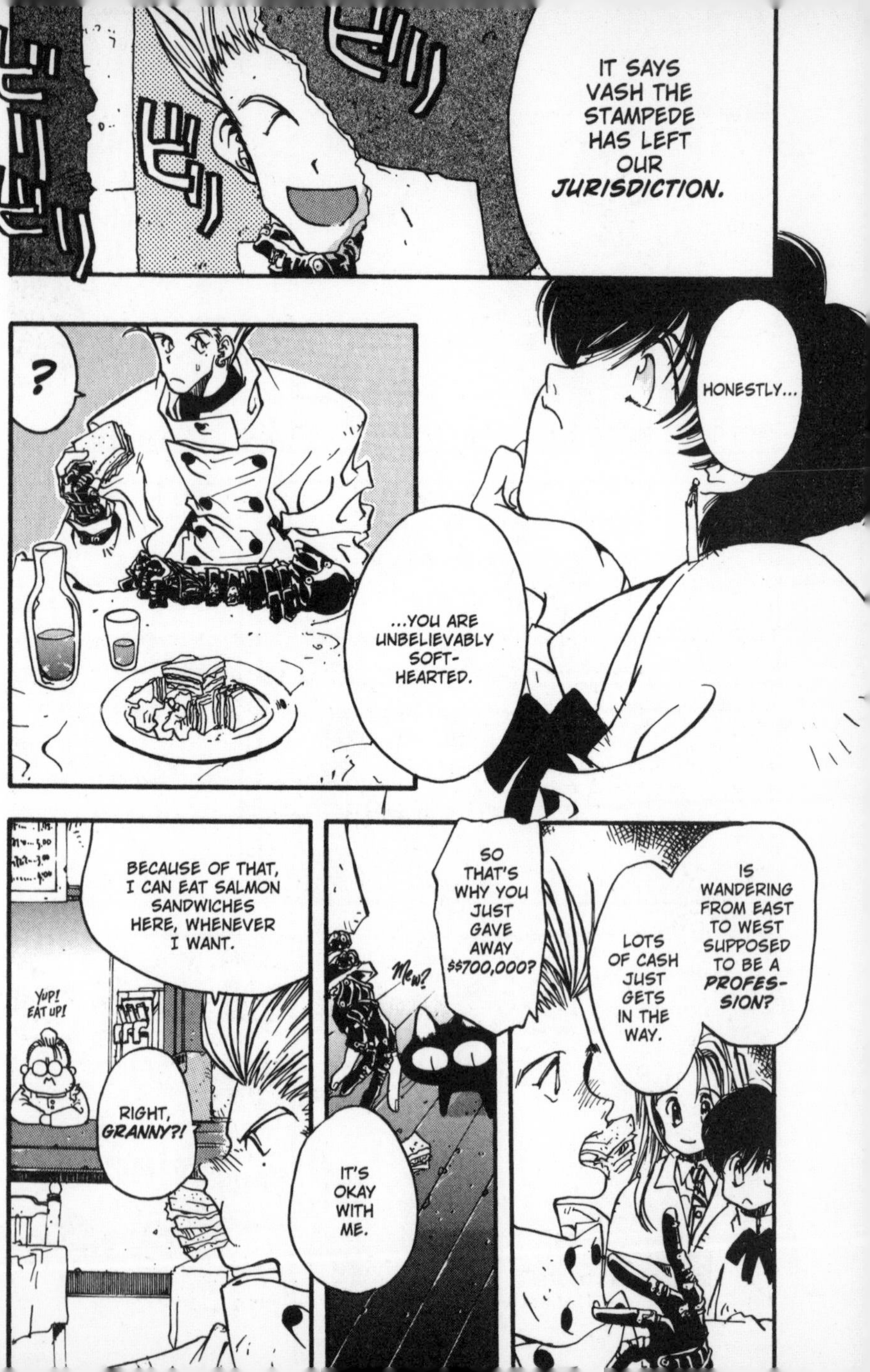
IT SAYS VASH THE STAMPEDE HAS LEFT OUR JURISDICTION.
HONESTLY...
...YOU ARE UNBELIEVABLY SOFT-HEARTED.
?
SO THAT'S WHY YOU JUST GAVE AWAY $$700,000?
LOTS OF CASH JUST GETS IN THE WAY.
IS WANDERING FROM EAST TO WEST SUPPOSED TO BE A PROFESSION?
MEW?
IT'S OKAY WITH ME.
BECAUSE OF THAT, I CAN EAT SALMON SANDWICHES HERE, WHENEVER I WANT.
RIGHT, GRANNY?!
YUP! EAT UP!

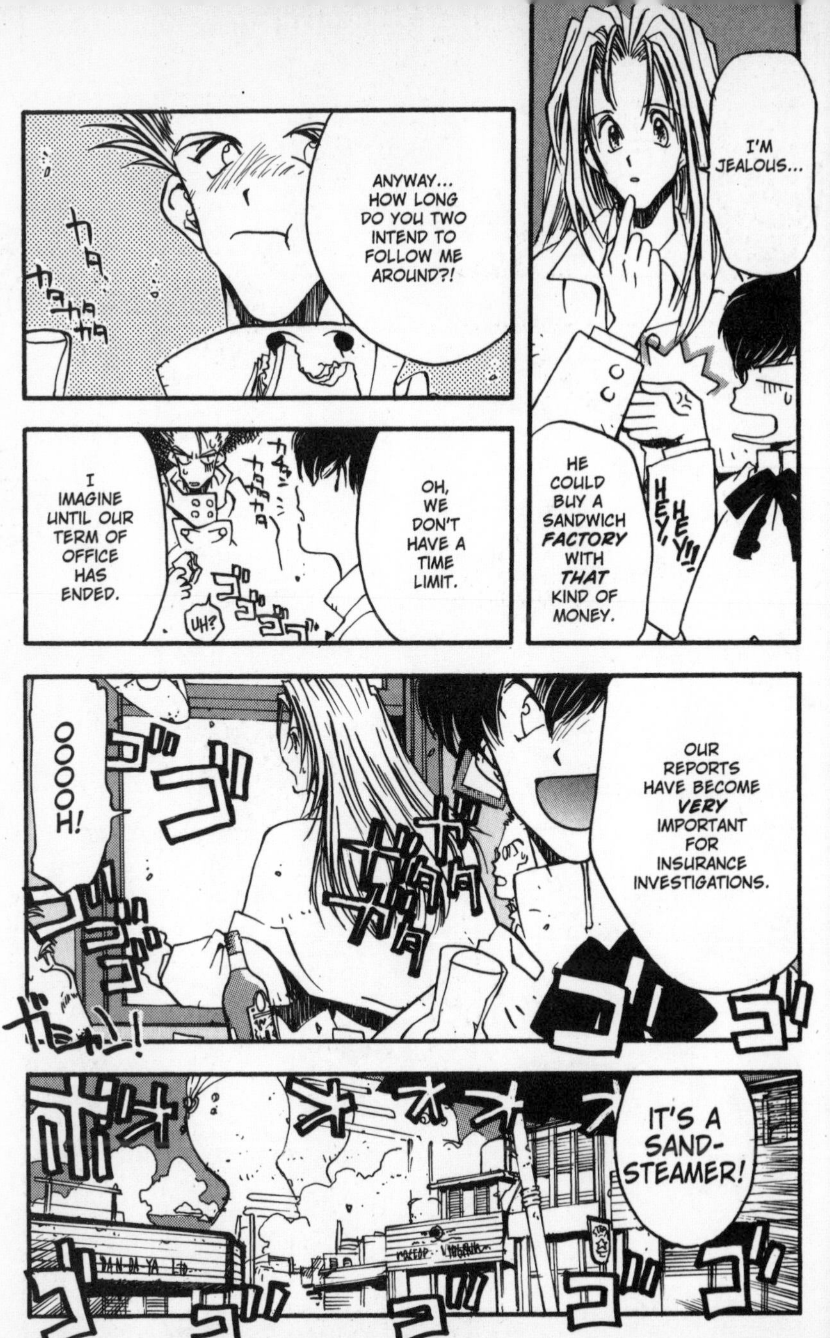
I'M JEALOUS...
HE COULD BUY A SANDWICH *FACTORY* WITH *THAT* KIND OF MONEY.
HEY, HEY!!!
ANYWAY... HOW LONG DO YOU TWO INTEND TO FOLLOW ME AROUND?!
OH, WE DON'T HAVE A TIME LIMIT.
I IMAGINE UNTIL OUR TERM OF OFFICE HAS ENDED.
UH?
OUR REPORTS HAVE BECOME *VERY* IMPORTANT FOR INSURANCE INVESTIGATIONS.
OOOOOH!
IT'S A SAND-STEAMER!

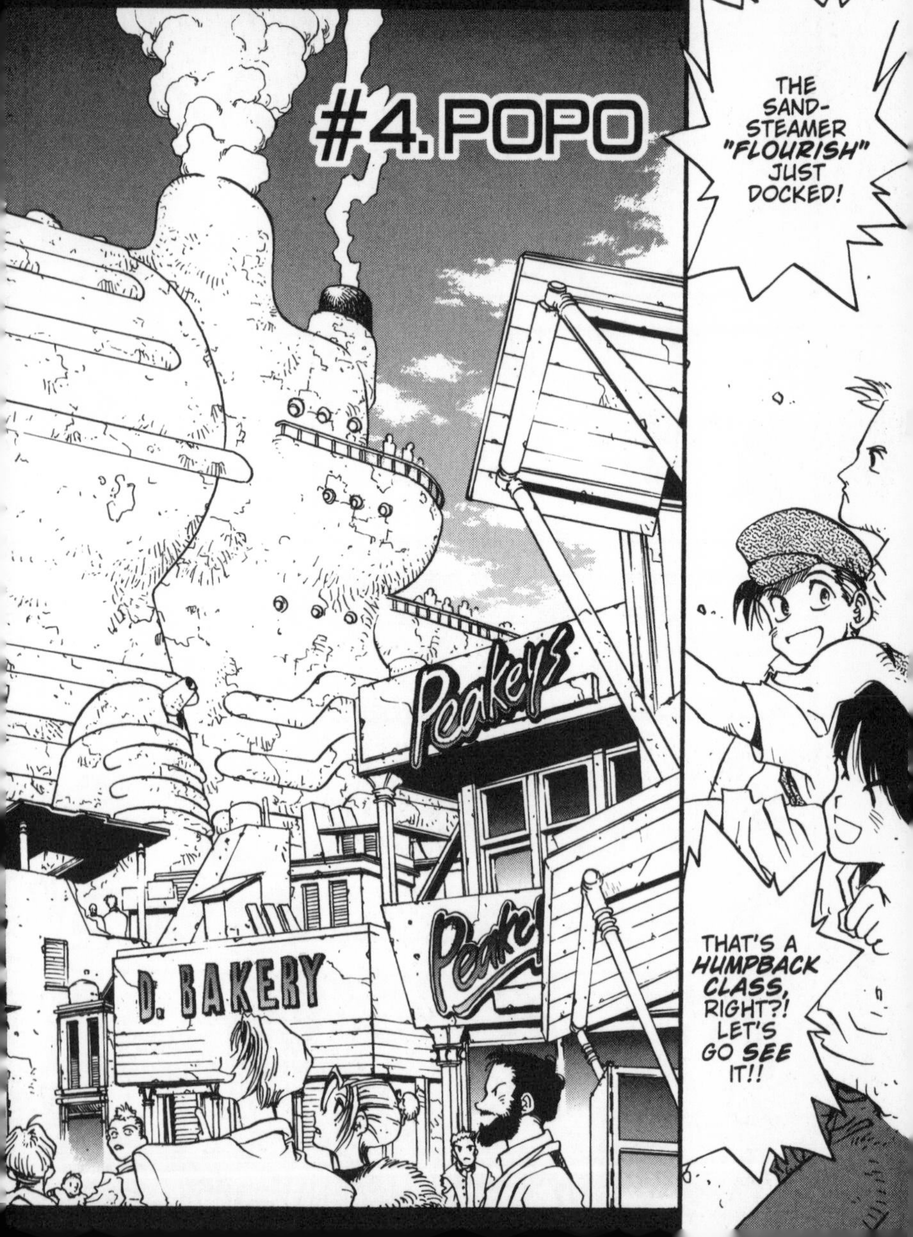
#4. POPO
THE SAND-STEAMER "FLOURISH" JUST DOCKED!
THAT'S A HUMPBACK CLASS, RIGHT?! LET'S GO SEE IT!!
Peakeys
D. BAKERY
Peakeys

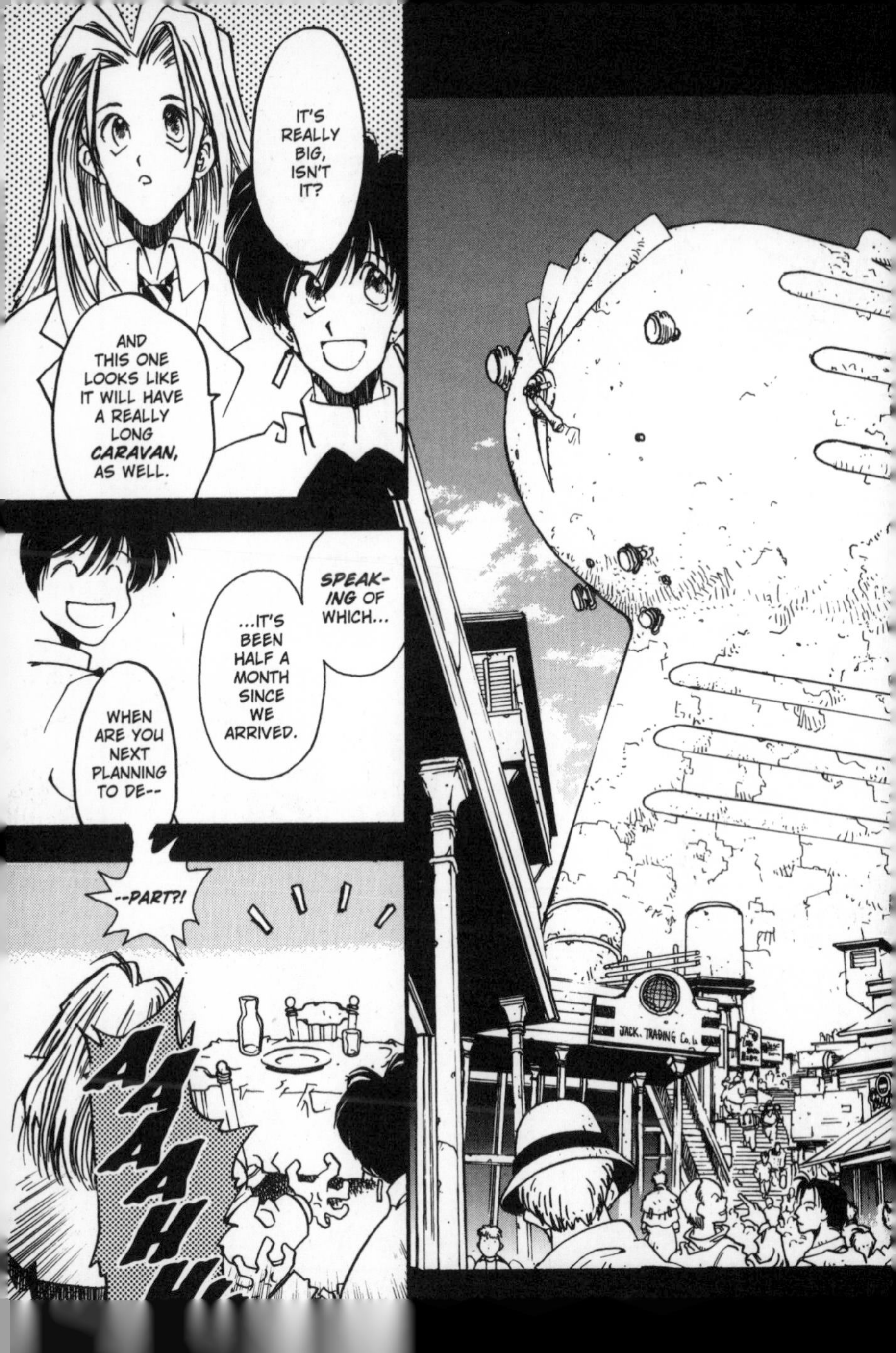
JACK. TRADING Co.
IT'S REALLY BIG, ISN'T IT?
AND THIS ONE LOOKS LIKE IT WILL HAVE A REALLY LONG *CARAVAN,* AS WELL.
*SPEAKING* OF WHICH...
...IT'S BEEN HALF A MONTH SINCE WE ARRIVED.
WHEN ARE YOU NEXT PLANNING TO DE--
--PART?!
AAAAAH

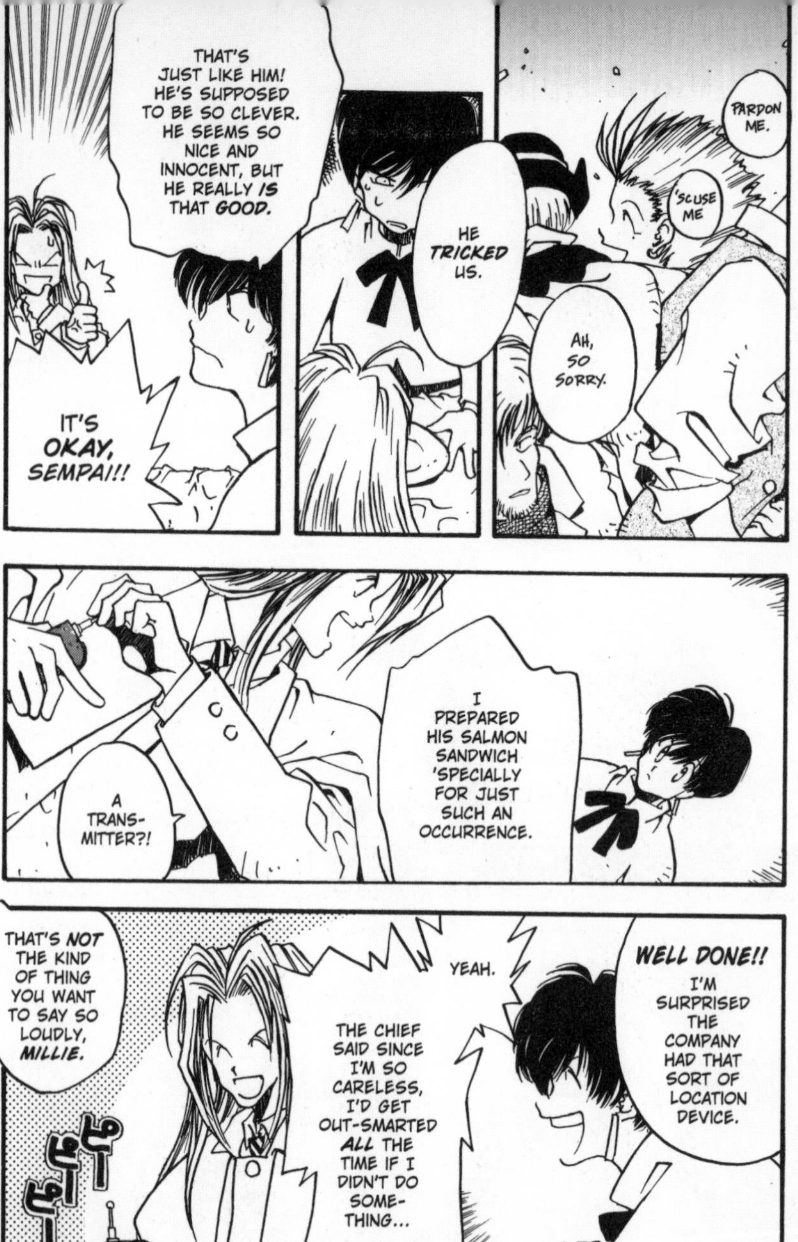
PARDON ME.
'SCUSE ME
AH, SO SORRY.
HE TRICKED US.
THAT'S JUST LIKE HIM! HE'S SUPPOSED TO BE SO CLEVER. HE SEEMS SO NICE AND INNOCENT, BUT HE REALLY IS THAT GOOD.
IT'S OKAY, SEMPAI!!
I PREPARED HIS SALMON SANDWICH 'SPECIALLY FOR JUST SUCH AN OCCURRENCE.
A TRANS-MITTER?!
WELL DONE!! I'M SURPRISED THE COMPANY HAD THAT SORT OF LOCATION DEVICE.
YEAH.
THE CHIEF SAID SINCE I'M SO CARELESS, I'D GET OUT-SMARTED ALL THE TIME IF I DIDN'T DO SOME-THING...
THAT'S NOT THE KIND OF THING YOU WANT TO SAY SO LOUDLY, MILLIE.
ピー ピー ピー

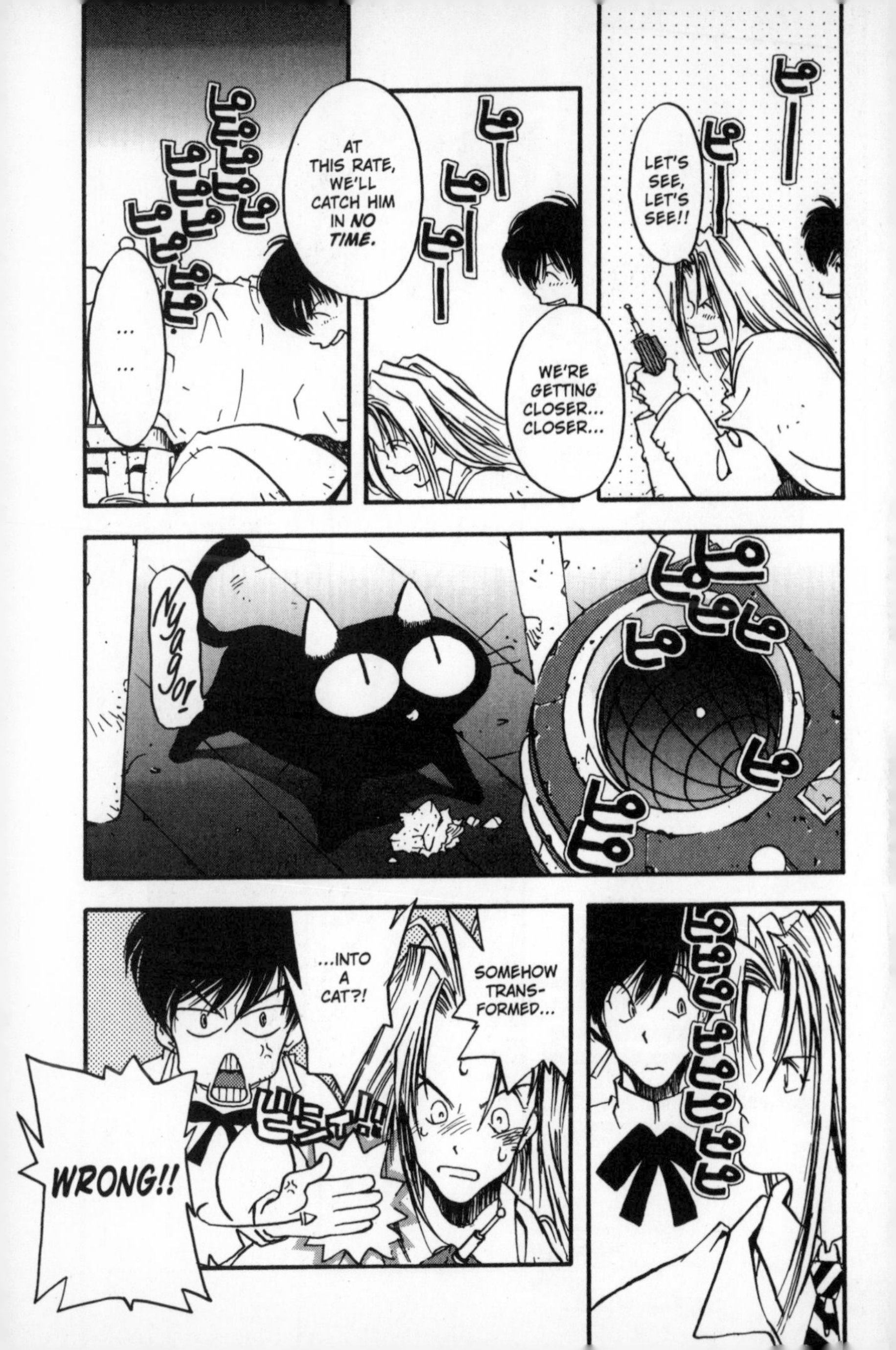
LET'S SEE, LET'S SEE!!
WE'RE GETTING CLOSER... CLOSER...
AT THIS RATE, WE'LL CATCH HIM IN *NO TIME.*
... ...
Nyago!
SOMEHOW TRANS-FORMED...
...INTO A CAT?!
WRONG!!

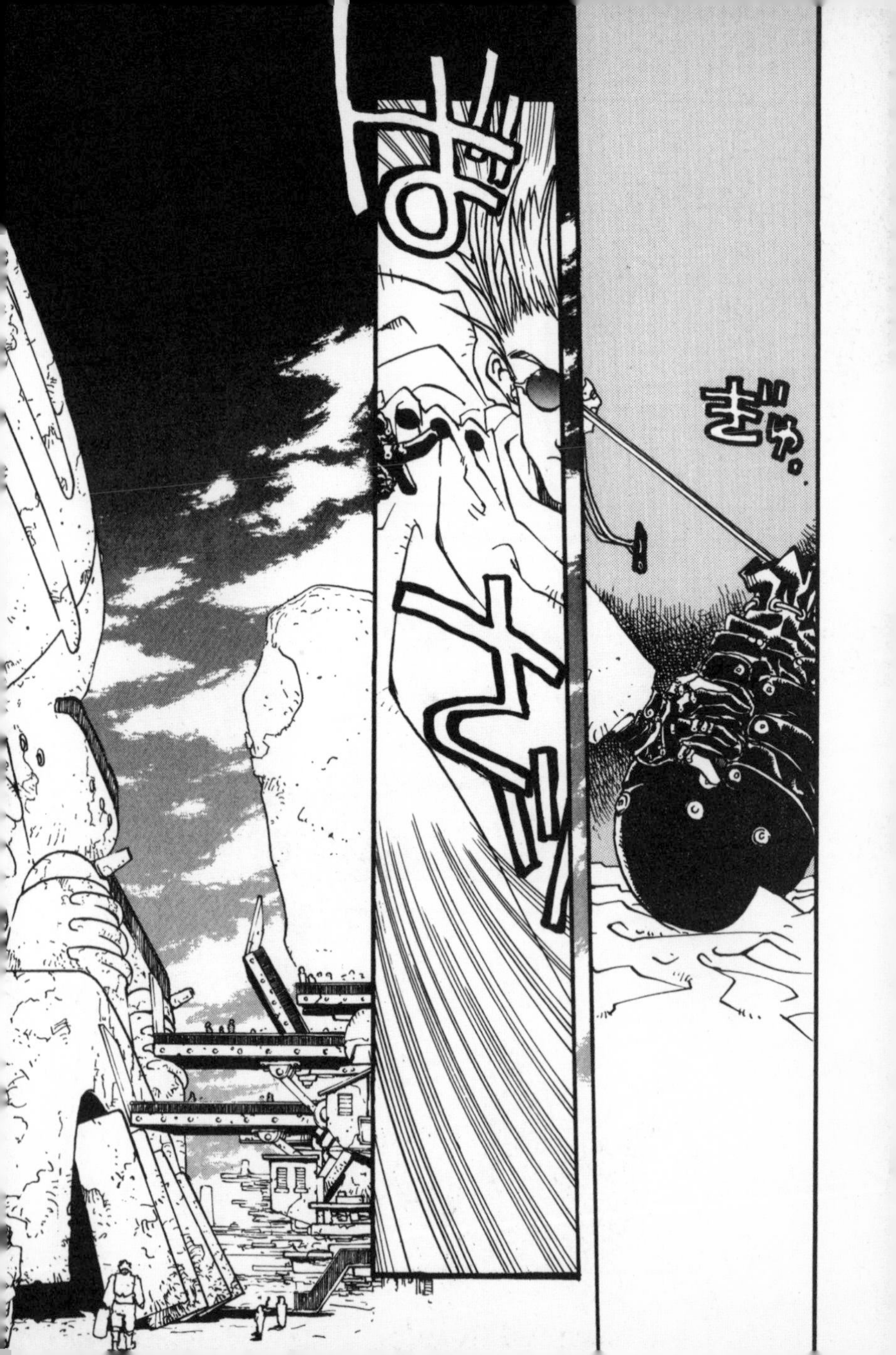
ぎゅ。
ぼ

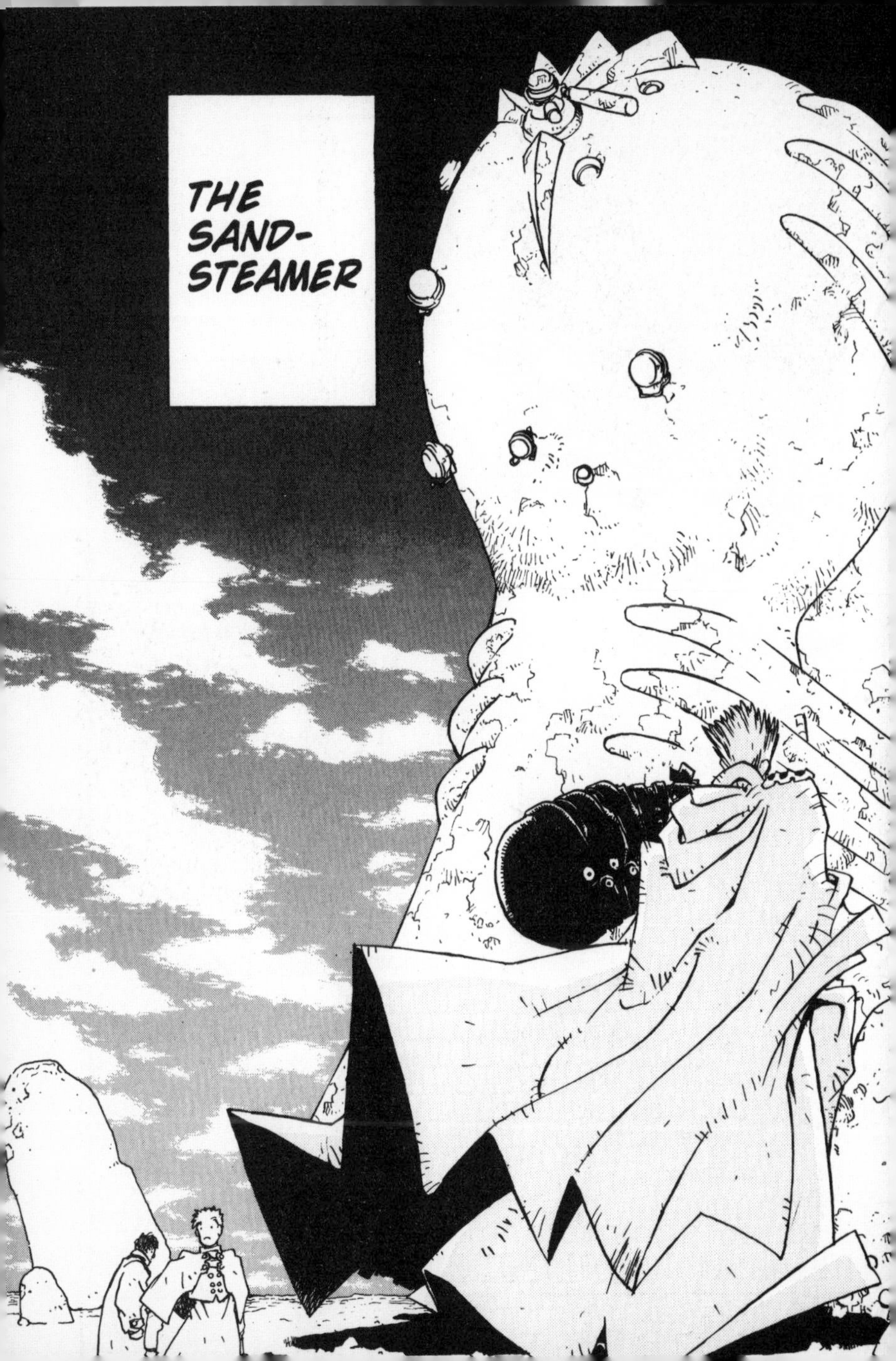
THE SAND-STEAMER

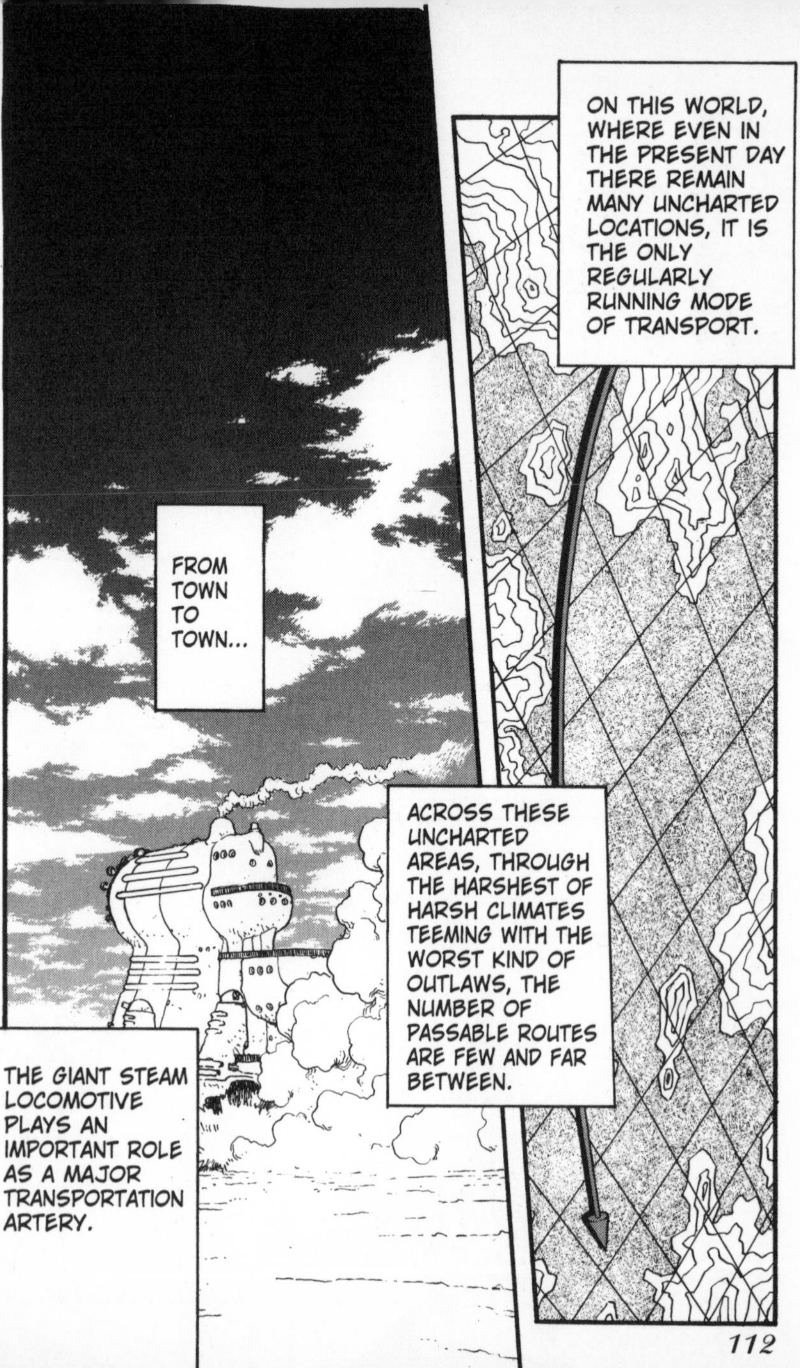
ON THIS WORLD, WHERE EVEN IN THE PRESENT DAY THERE REMAIN MANY UNCHARTED LOCATIONS, IT IS THE ONLY REGULARLY RUNNING MODE OF TRANSPORT.
ACROSS THESE UNCHARTED AREAS, THROUGH THE HARSHEST OF HARSH CLIMATES TEEMING WITH THE WORST KIND OF OUTLAWS, THE NUMBER OF PASSABLE ROUTES ARE FEW AND FAR BETWEEN.
FROM TOWN TO TOWN...
THE GIANT STEAM LOCOMOTIVE PLAYS AN IMPORTANT ROLE AS A MAJOR TRANSPORTATION ARTERY.

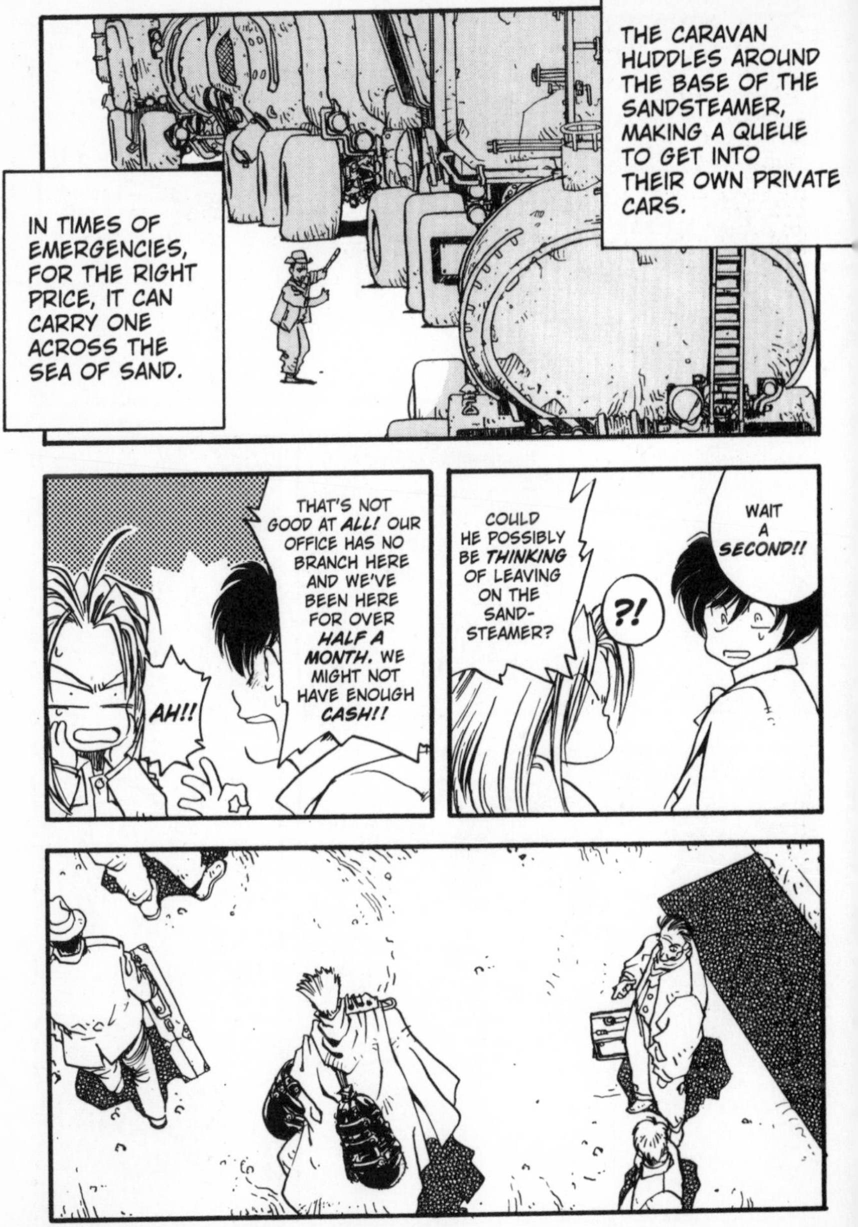
THE CARAVAN HUDDLES AROUND THE BASE OF THE SANDSTEAMER, MAKING A QUEUE TO GET INTO THEIR OWN PRIVATE CARS.
IN TIMES OF EMERGENCIES, FOR THE RIGHT PRICE, IT CAN CARRY ONE ACROSS THE SEA OF SAND.
WAIT A SECOND!!
?!
COULD HE POSSIBLY BE THINKING OF LEAVING ON THE SAND-STEAMER?
THAT'S NOT GOOD AT ALL! OUR OFFICE HAS NO BRANCH HERE AND WE'VE BEEN HERE FOR OVER HALF A MONTH. WE MIGHT NOT HAVE ENOUGH CASH!!
AH!!

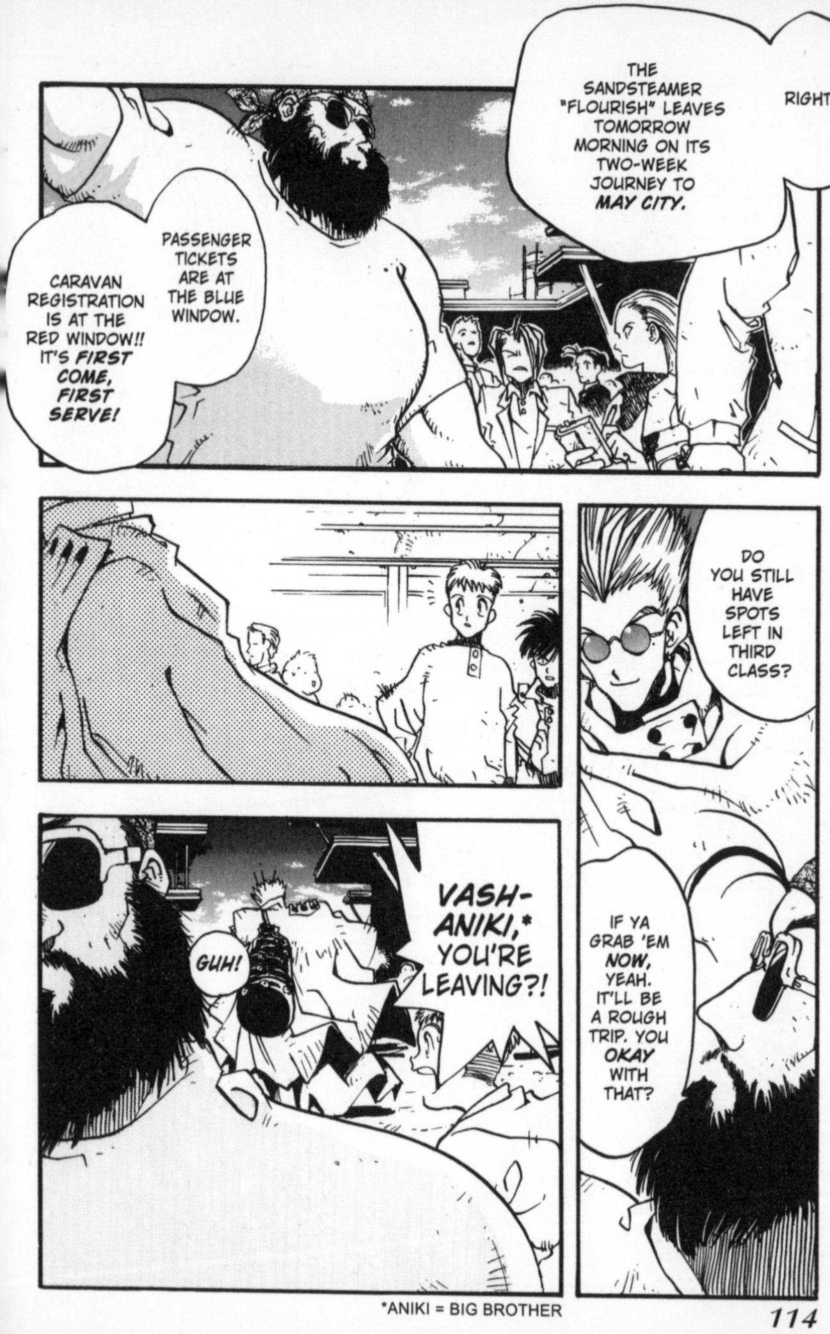
RIGHT!
THE SANDSTEAMER "FLOURISH" LEAVES TOMORROW MORNING ON ITS TWO-WEEK JOURNEY TO **MAY CITY.**
PASSENGER TICKETS ARE AT THE BLUE WINDOW.
CARAVAN REGISTRATION IS AT THE RED WINDOW!! IT'S ***FIRST COME, FIRST SERVE!***
DO YOU STILL HAVE SPOTS LEFT IN THIRD CLASS?
IF YA GRAB 'EM ***NOW,*** YEAH. IT'LL BE A ROUGH TRIP. YOU ***OKAY*** WITH THAT?
***VASH-ANIKI,**** YOU'RE LEAVING?!
GUH!

*ANIKI = BIG BROTHER

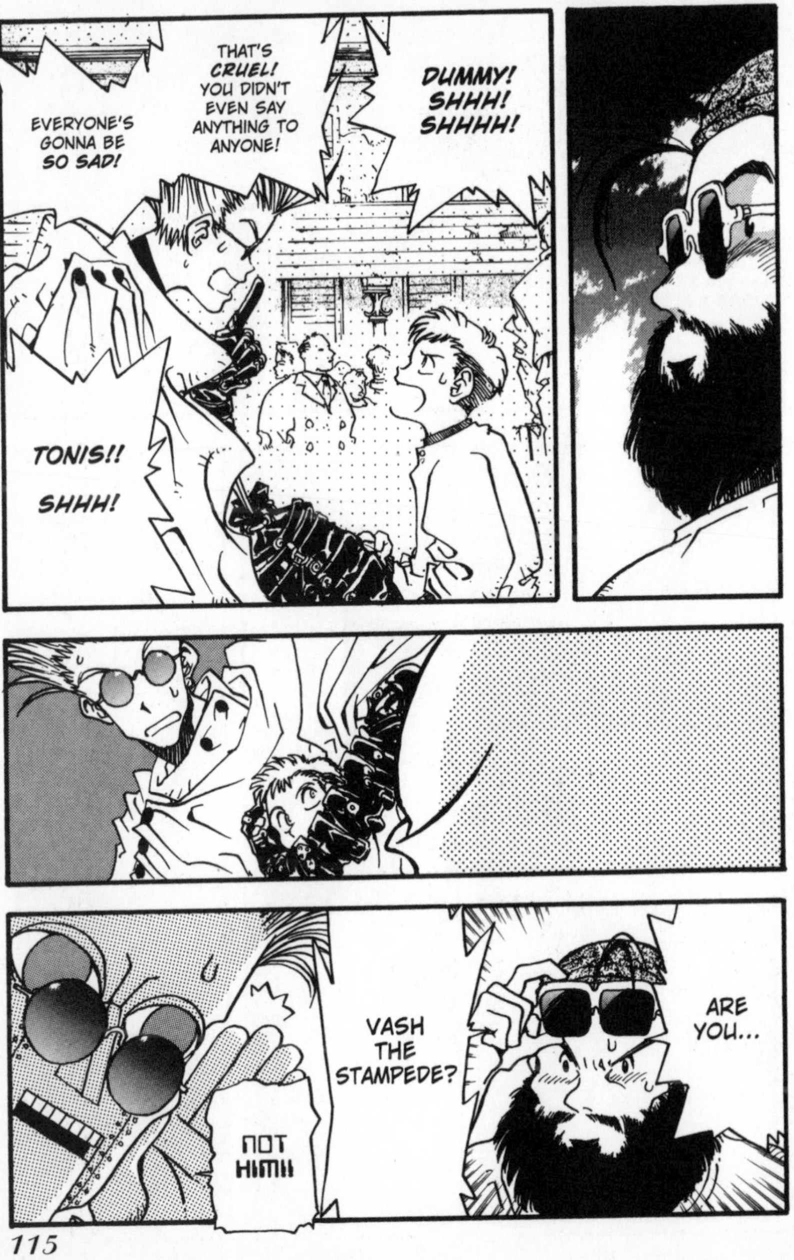
DUMMY! SHHH! SHHHH!
THAT'S CRUEL! YOU DIDN'T EVEN SAY ANYTHING TO ANYONE!
EVERYONE'S GONNA BE SO SAD!
TONIS!!
SHHH!
ARE YOU...
VASH THE STAMPEDE?
NOT HIM!!

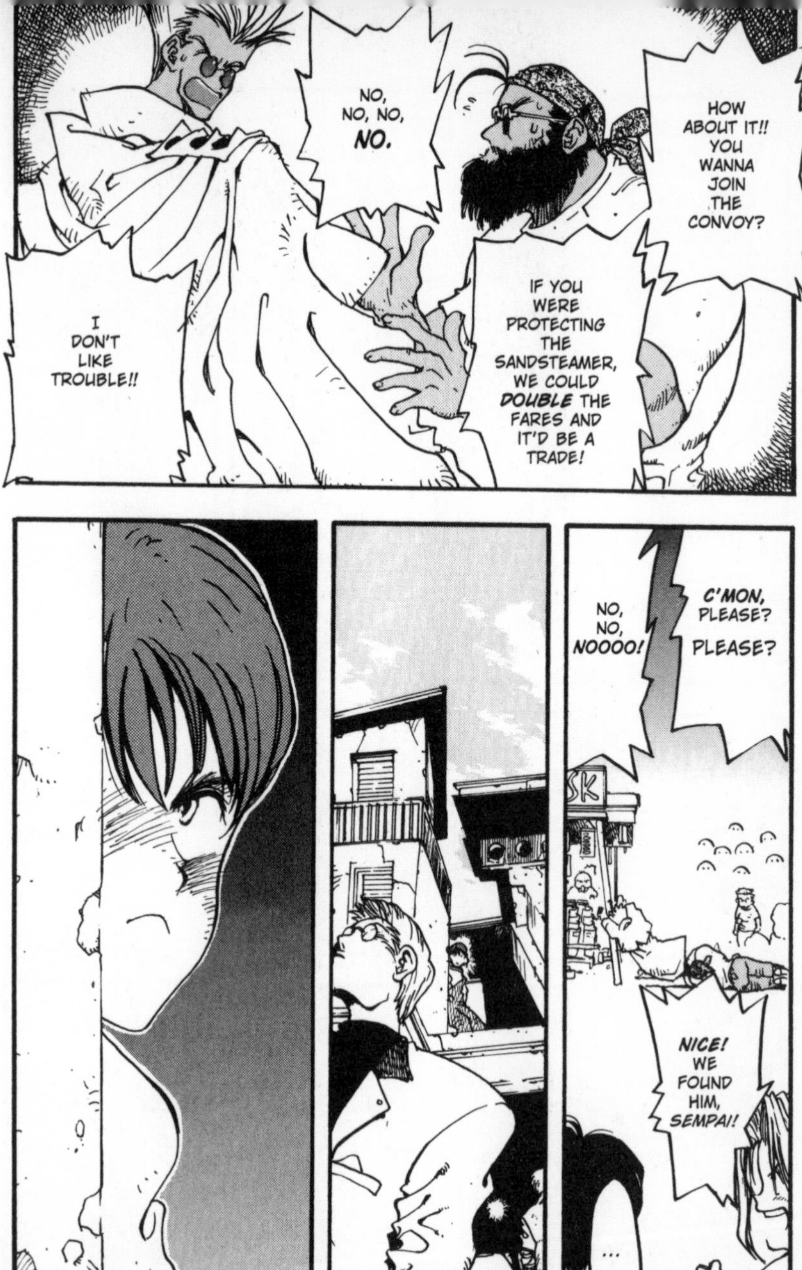
HOW ABOUT IT!! YOU WANNA JOIN THE CONVOY?
NO, NO, NO, NO.
IF YOU WERE PROTECTING THE SANDSTEAMER, WE COULD DOUBLE THE FARES AND IT'D BE A TRADE!
I DON'T LIKE TROUBLE!!
C'MON, PLEASE? PLEASE?
NO, NO, NOOOO!
NICE! WE FOUND HIM, SEMPAI!
...

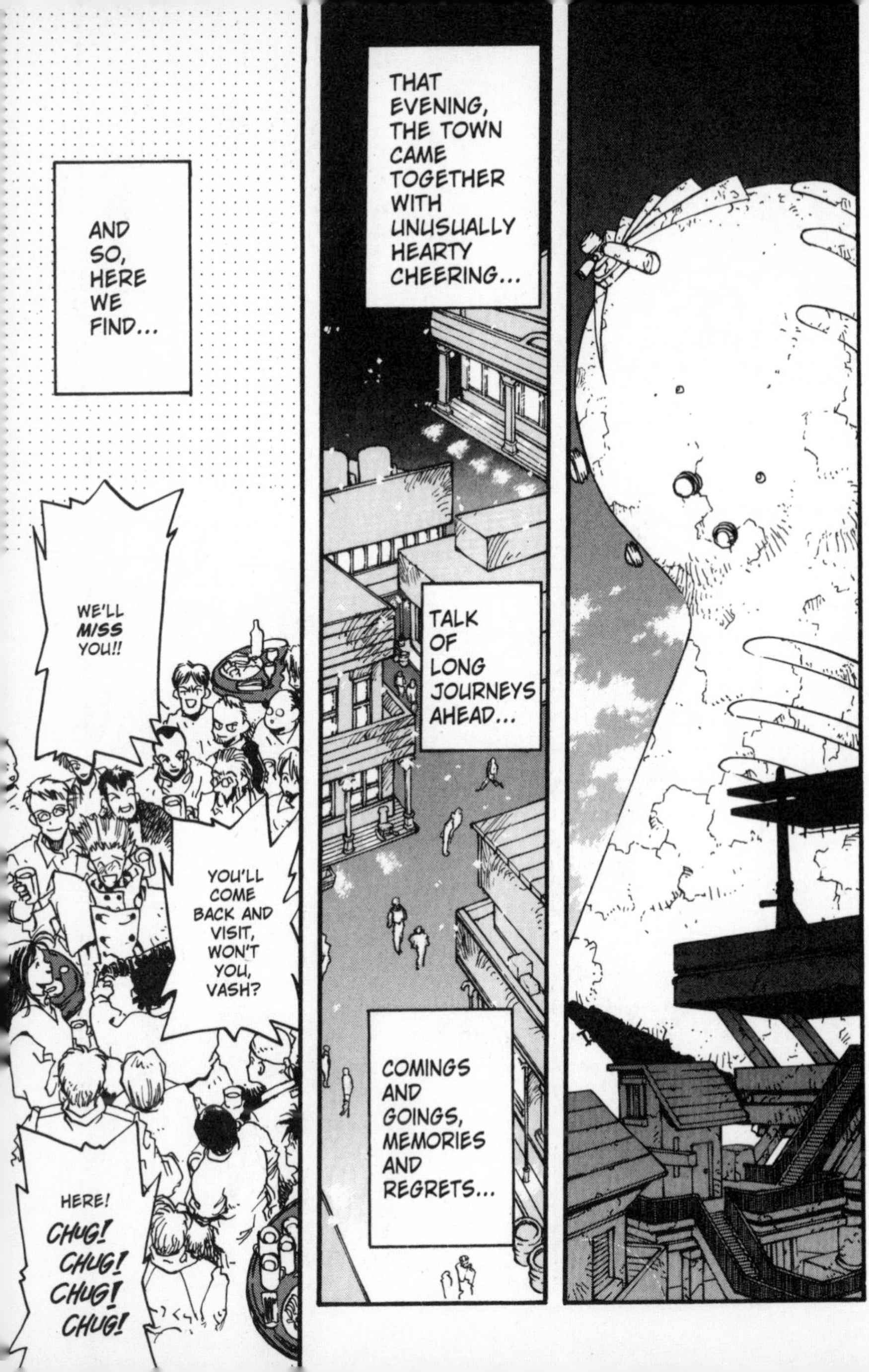
THAT EVENING, THE TOWN CAME TOGETHER WITH UNUSUALLY HEARTY CHEERING...
TALK OF LONG JOURNEYS AHEAD...
COMINGS AND GOINGS, MEMORIES AND REGRETS...
AND SO, HERE WE FIND...
WE'LL *MISS* YOU!!
YOU'LL COME BACK AND VISIT, WON'T YOU, VASH?
HERE! *CHUG! CHUG! CHUG! CHUG!*

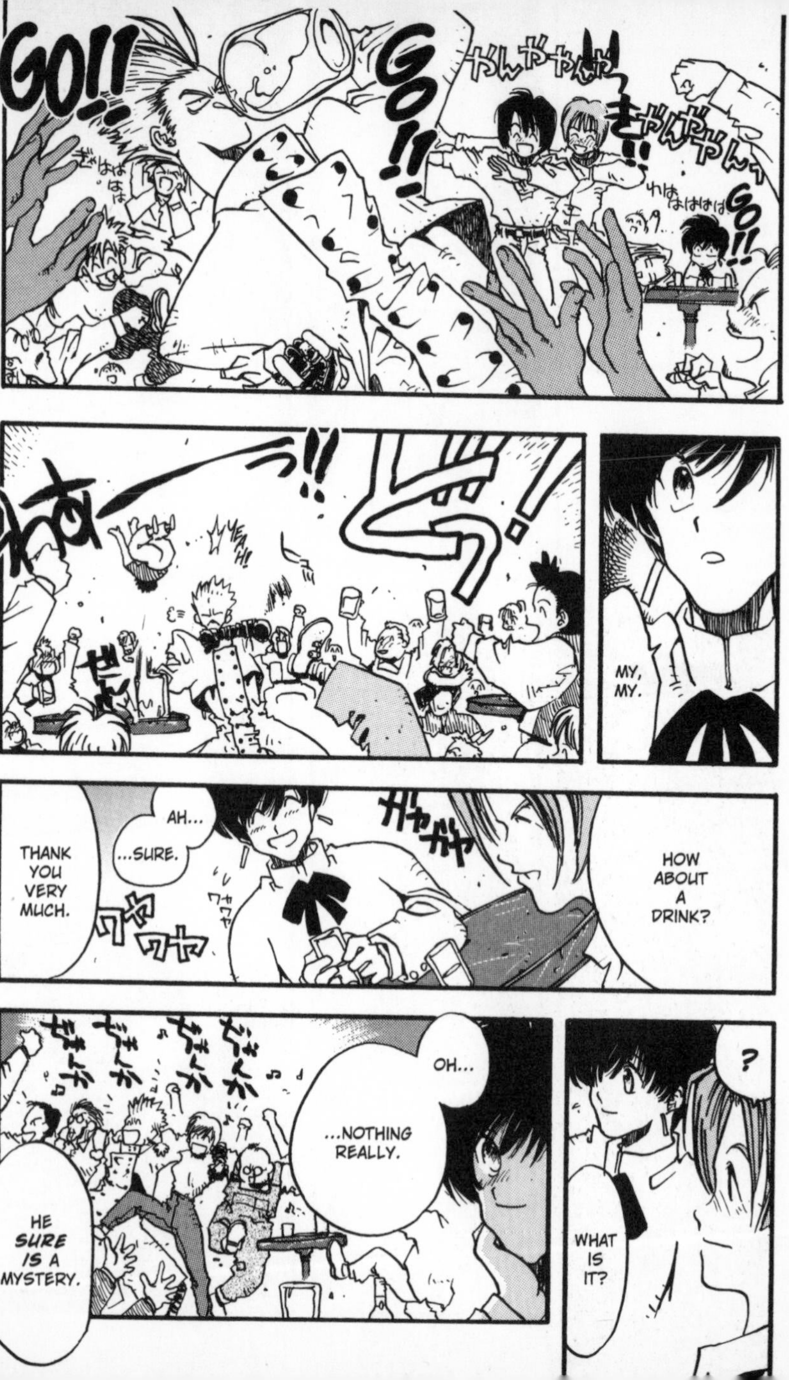
GO!!
GO!!
GO!!
MY, MY.
HOW ABOUT A DRINK?
AH...
...SURE.
THANK YOU VERY MUCH.
?
WHAT IS IT?
OH...
...NOTHING REALLY.
HE *SURE IS* A MYSTERY.

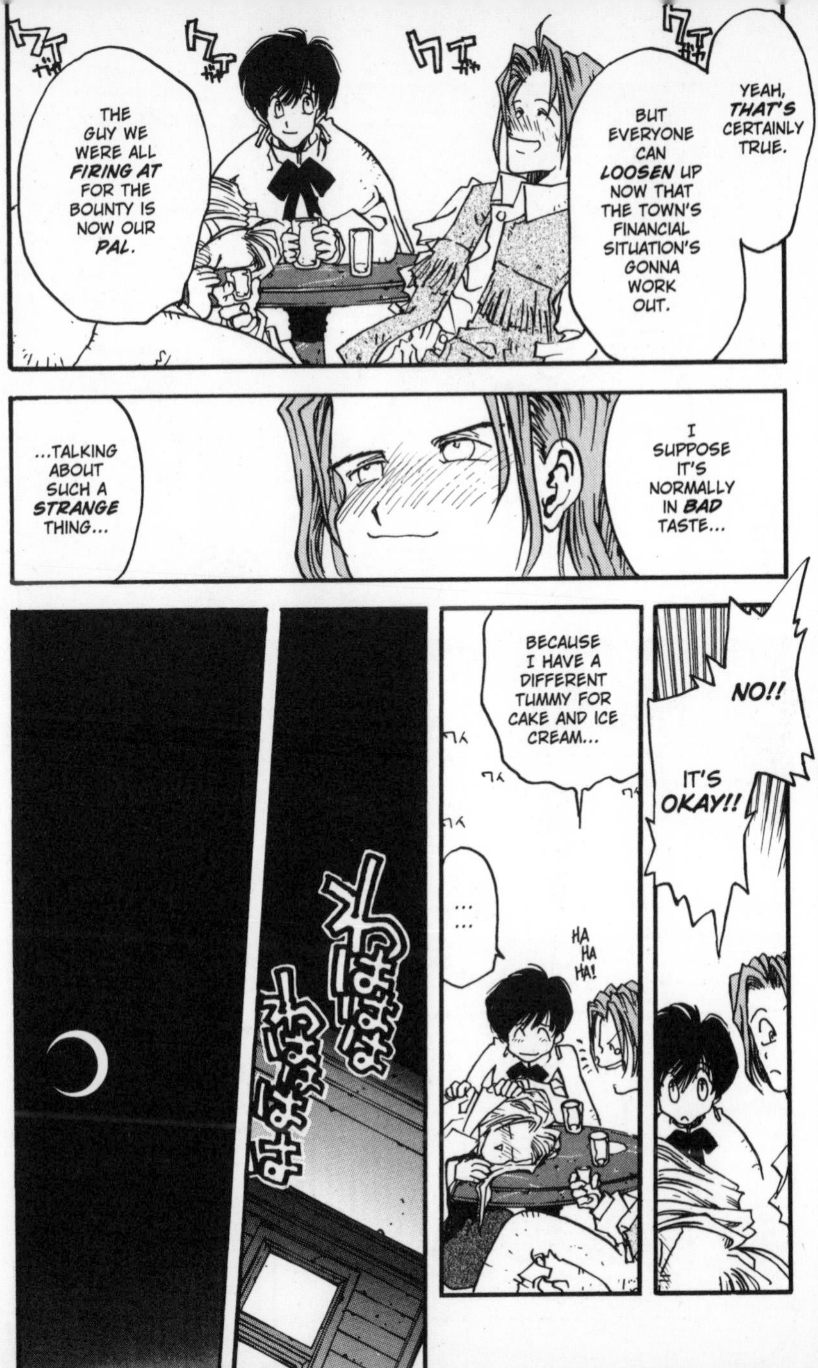
YEAH, THAT'S CERTAINLY TRUE.
BUT EVERYONE CAN LOOSEN UP NOW THAT THE TOWN'S FINANCIAL SITUATION'S GONNA WORK OUT.
THE GUY WE WERE ALL FIRING AT FOR THE BOUNTY IS NOW OUR PAL.
I SUPPOSE IT'S NORMALLY IN BAD TASTE...
...TALKING ABOUT SUCH A STRANGE THING...
NO!!
IT'S OKAY!!
BECAUSE I HAVE A DIFFERENT TUMMY FOR CAKE AND ICE CREAM...
......
HA HA HA!

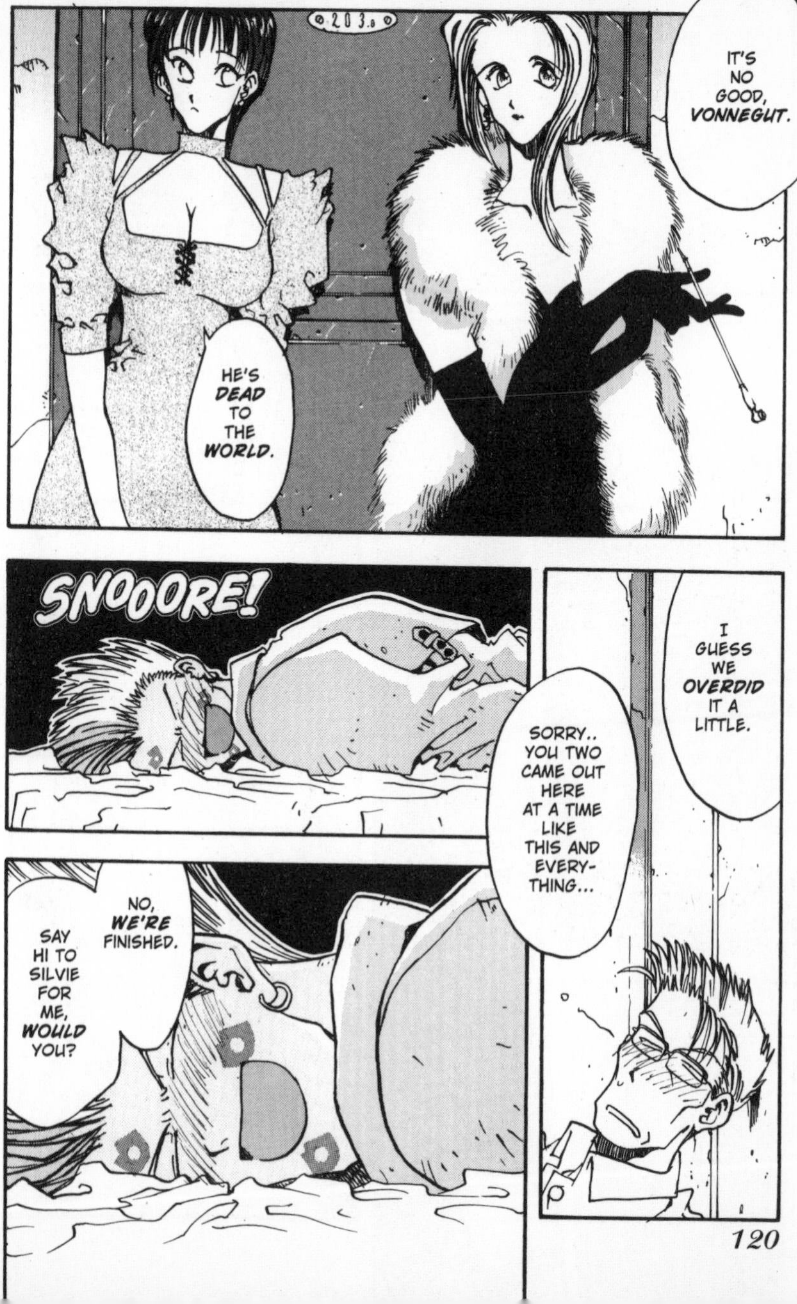
IT'S NO GOOD, VONNEGUT.
HE'S DEAD TO THE WORLD.
I GUESS WE OVERDID IT A LITTLE.
SORRY.. YOU TWO CAME OUT HERE AT A TIME LIKE THIS AND EVERYTHING...
SNOOORE!
NO, WE'RE FINISHED.
SAY HI TO SILVIE FOR ME, WOULD YOU?

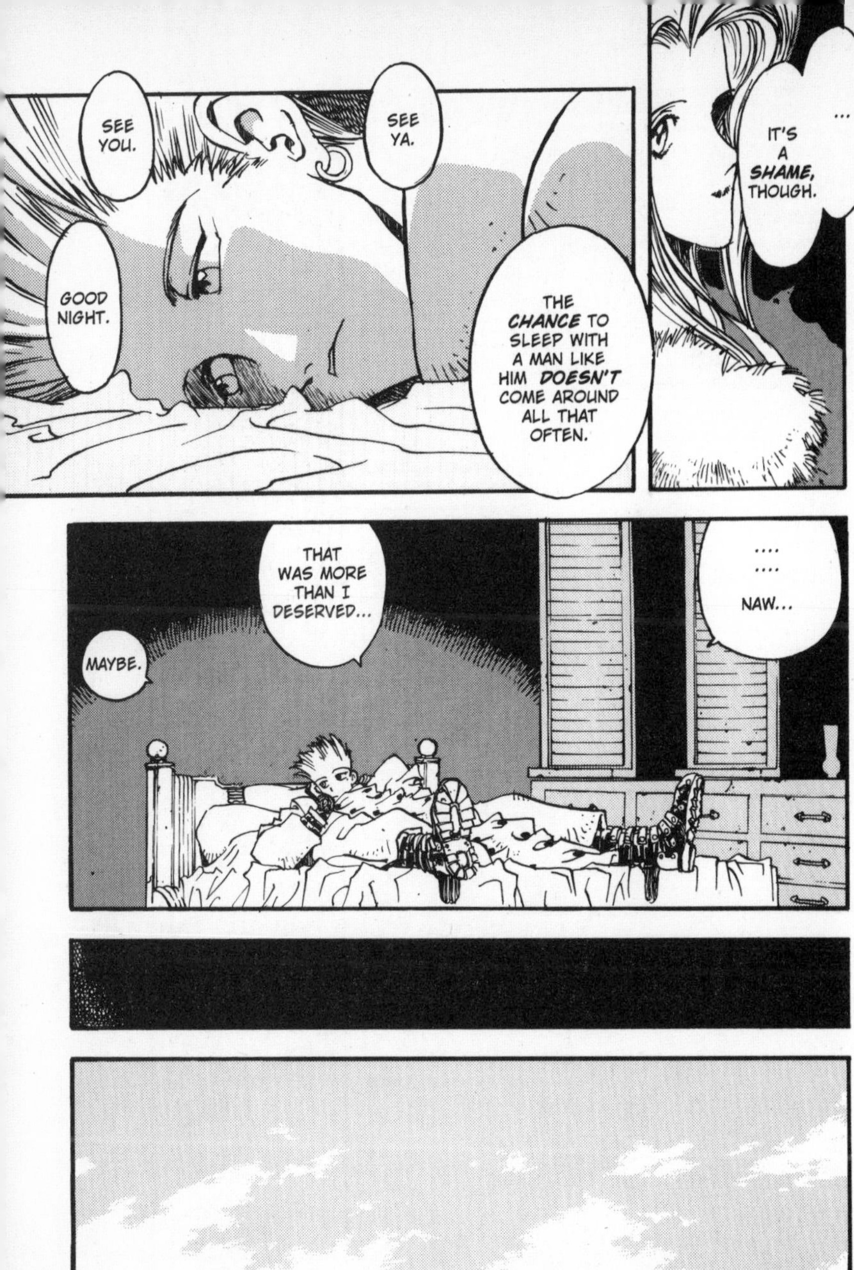
...
IT'S A SHAME, THOUGH.
THE CHANCE TO SLEEP WITH A MAN LIKE HIM DOESN'T COME AROUND ALL THAT OFTEN.
SEE YA.
SEE YOU.
GOOD NIGHT.
.... .... NAW...
THAT WAS MORE THAN I DESERVED...
MAYBE.

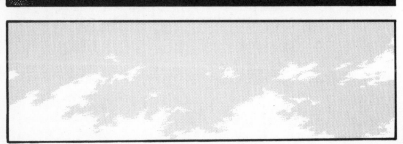

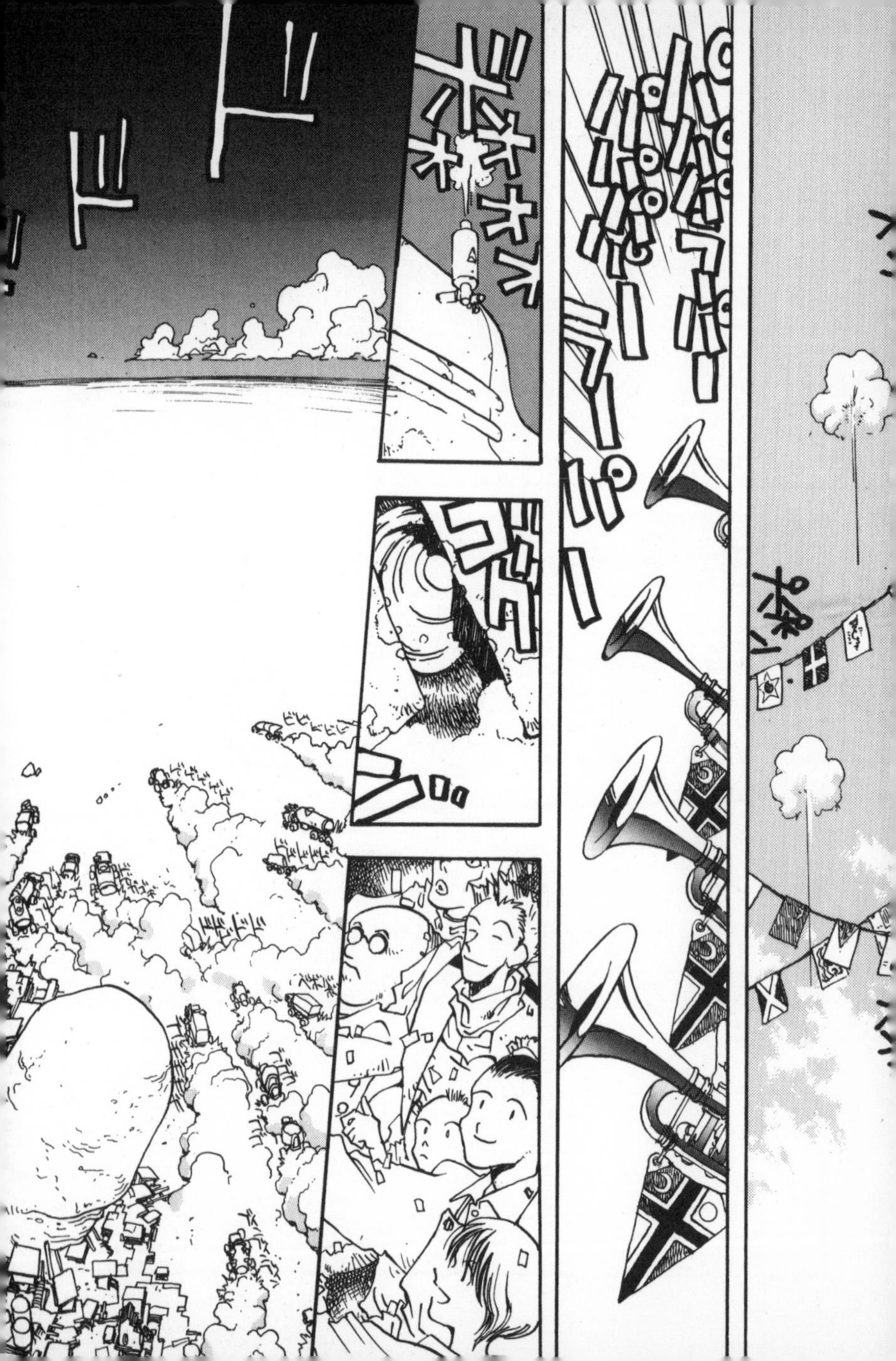

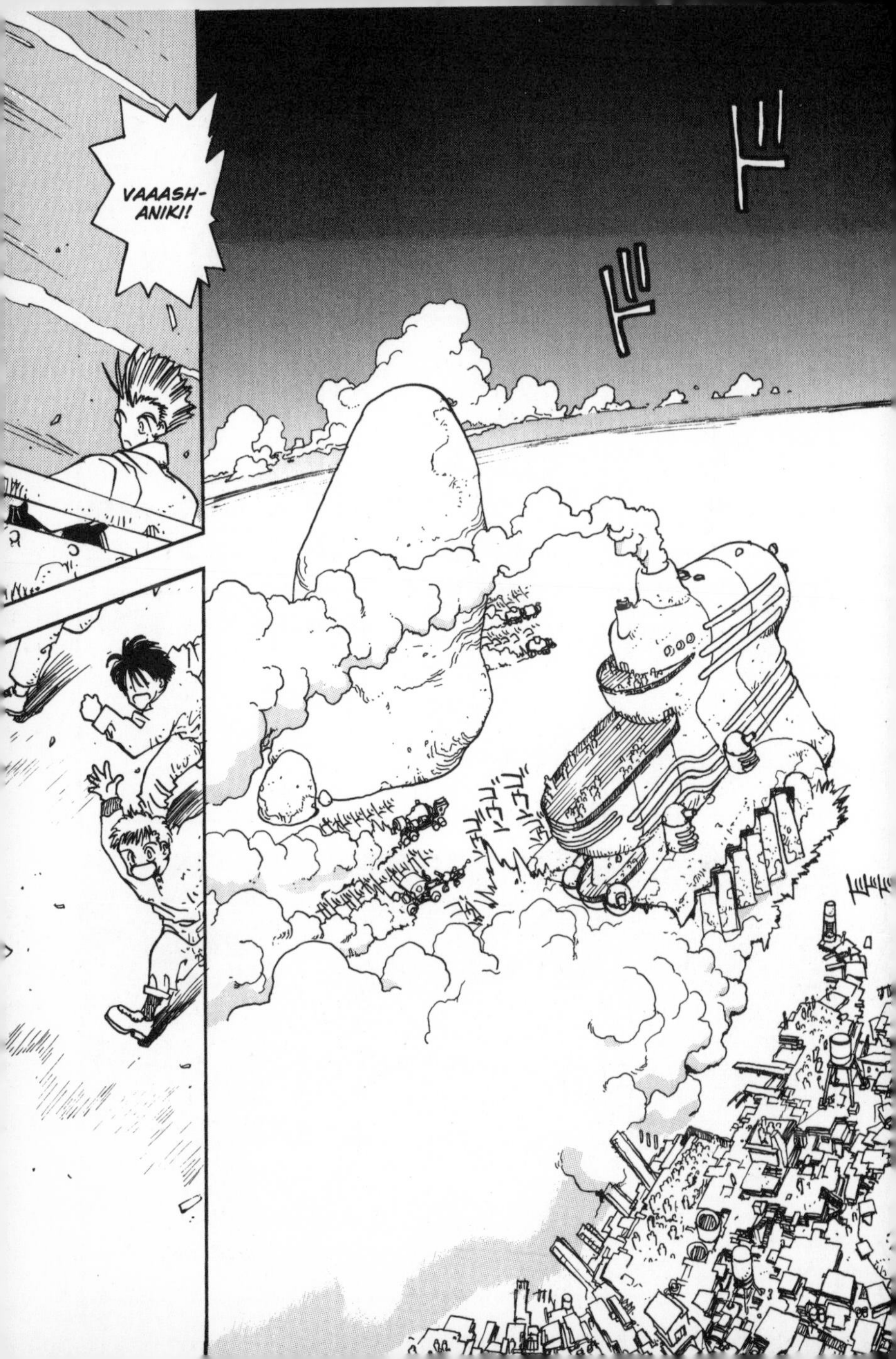
ド
ド
VAAASH-ANIKI!

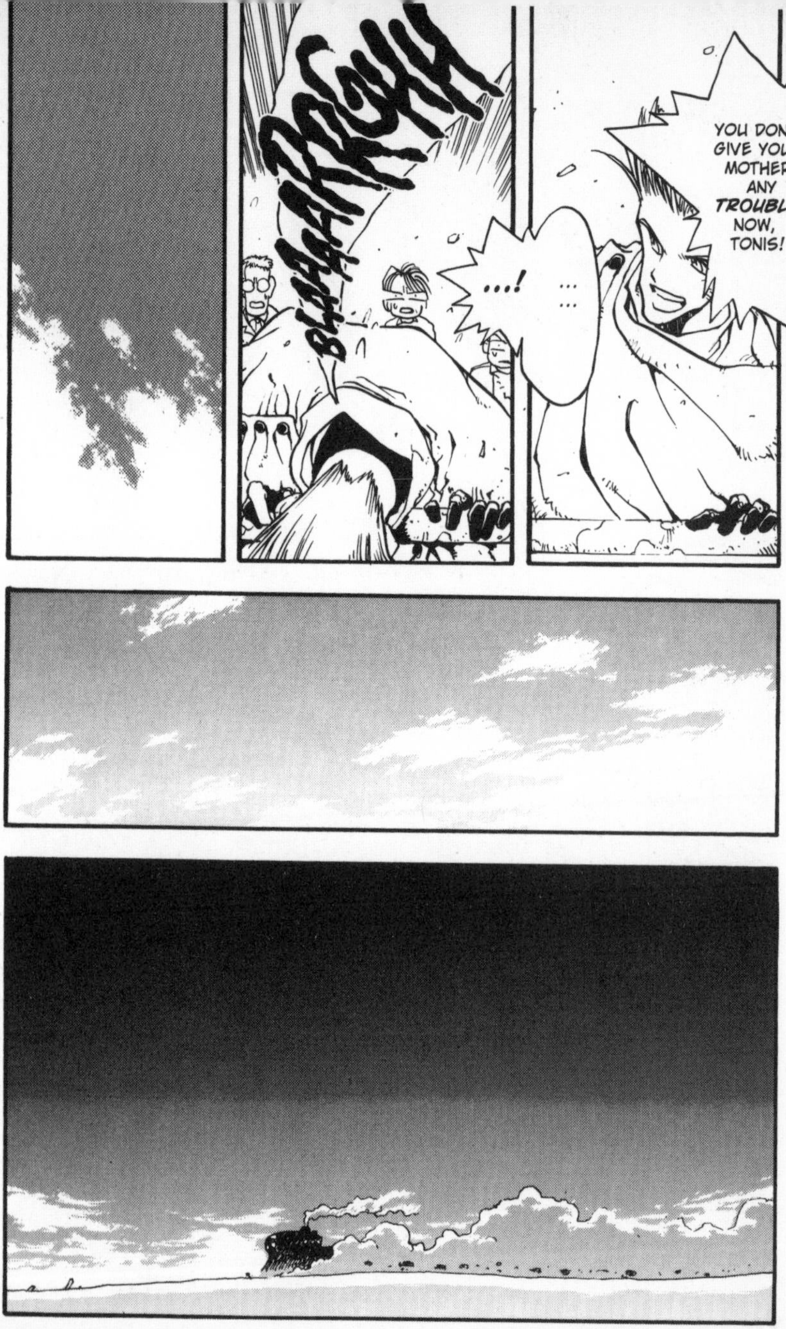
YOU DON'T GIVE YOUR MOTHER ANY TROUBLE NOW, TONIS!
...!
...
...
BLUAAAHRGHA

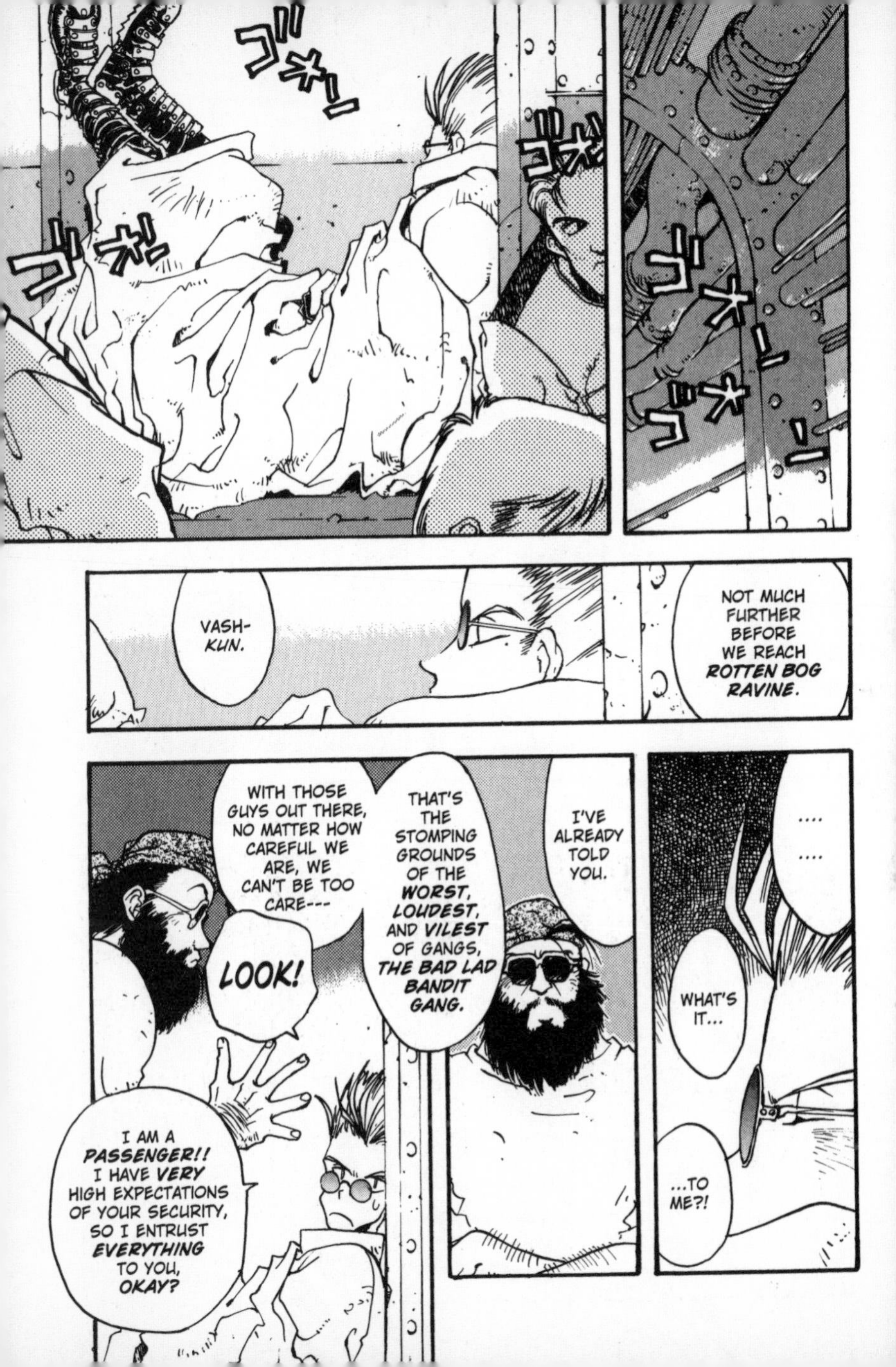
NOT MUCH FURTHER BEFORE WE REACH ROTTEN BOG RAVINE.
VASH-KUN.
....
....
WHAT'S IT...
...TO ME?!
I'VE ALREADY TOLD YOU.
THAT'S THE STOMPING GROUNDS OF THE WORST, LOUDEST, AND VILEST OF GANGS, THE BAD LAD BANDIT GANG.
WITH THOSE GUYS OUT THERE, NO MATTER HOW CAREFUL WE ARE, WE CAN'T BE TOO CARE---
LOOK!
I AM A PASSENGER!! I HAVE VERY HIGH EXPECTATIONS OF YOUR SECURITY, SO I ENTRUST EVERYTHING TO YOU, OKAY?

-SIGH!-

THOSE TWO INSURANCE GIRLS WERE ENOUGH...

I WAS HOPING FOR A NICE, QUIET TRIP.

....

JEEZ!

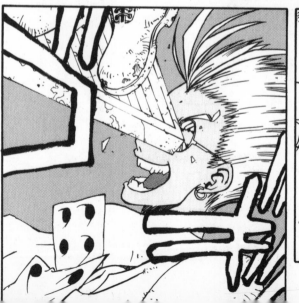

RIGHT, THEN!!

IT'S NAP-TIME AGAIN!!

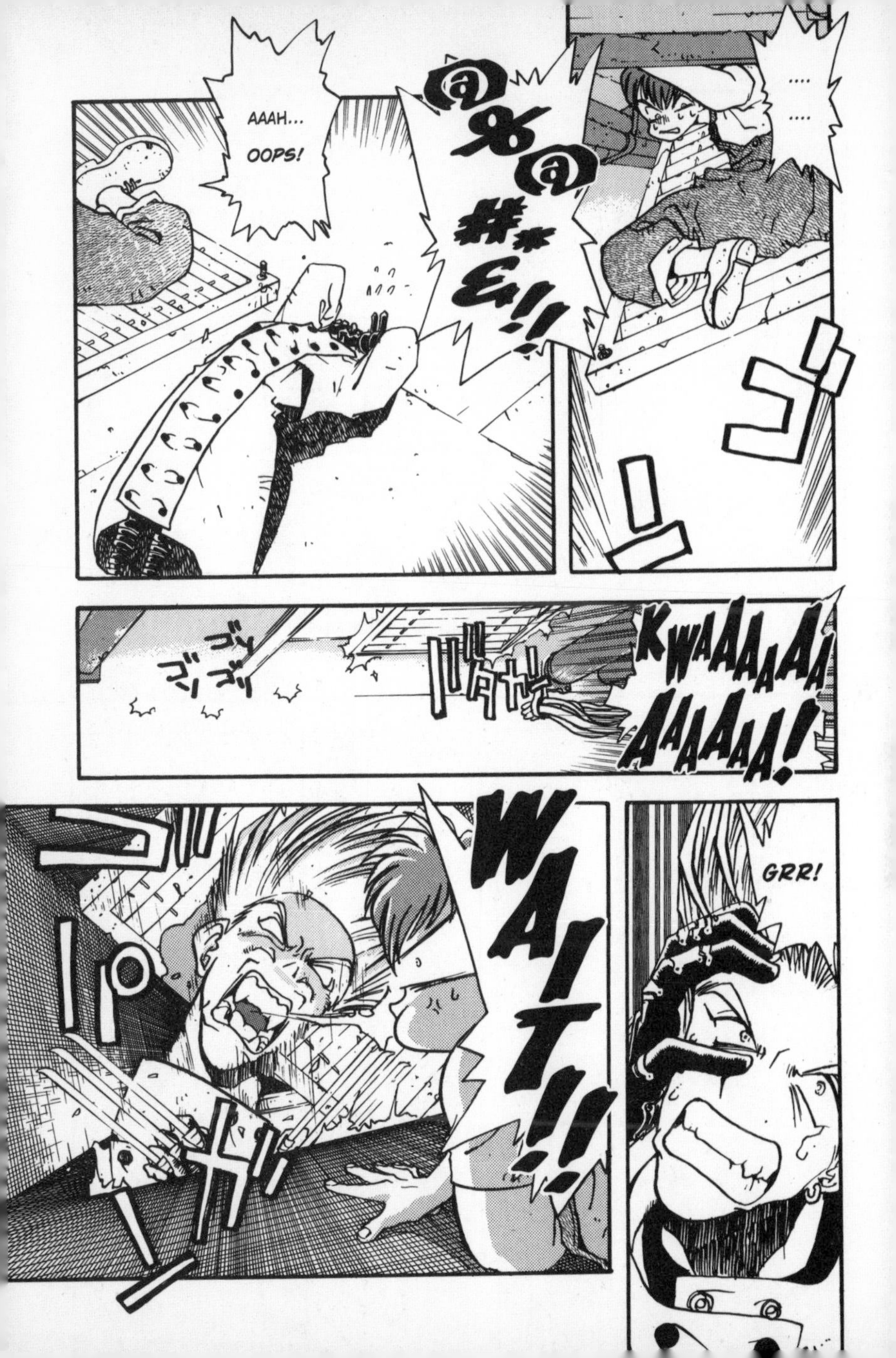
....
....
@%@#*&!!
AAAH...
OOPS!
KWAAAAAA
AAAAAAA!
GRR!
WAIT!!!

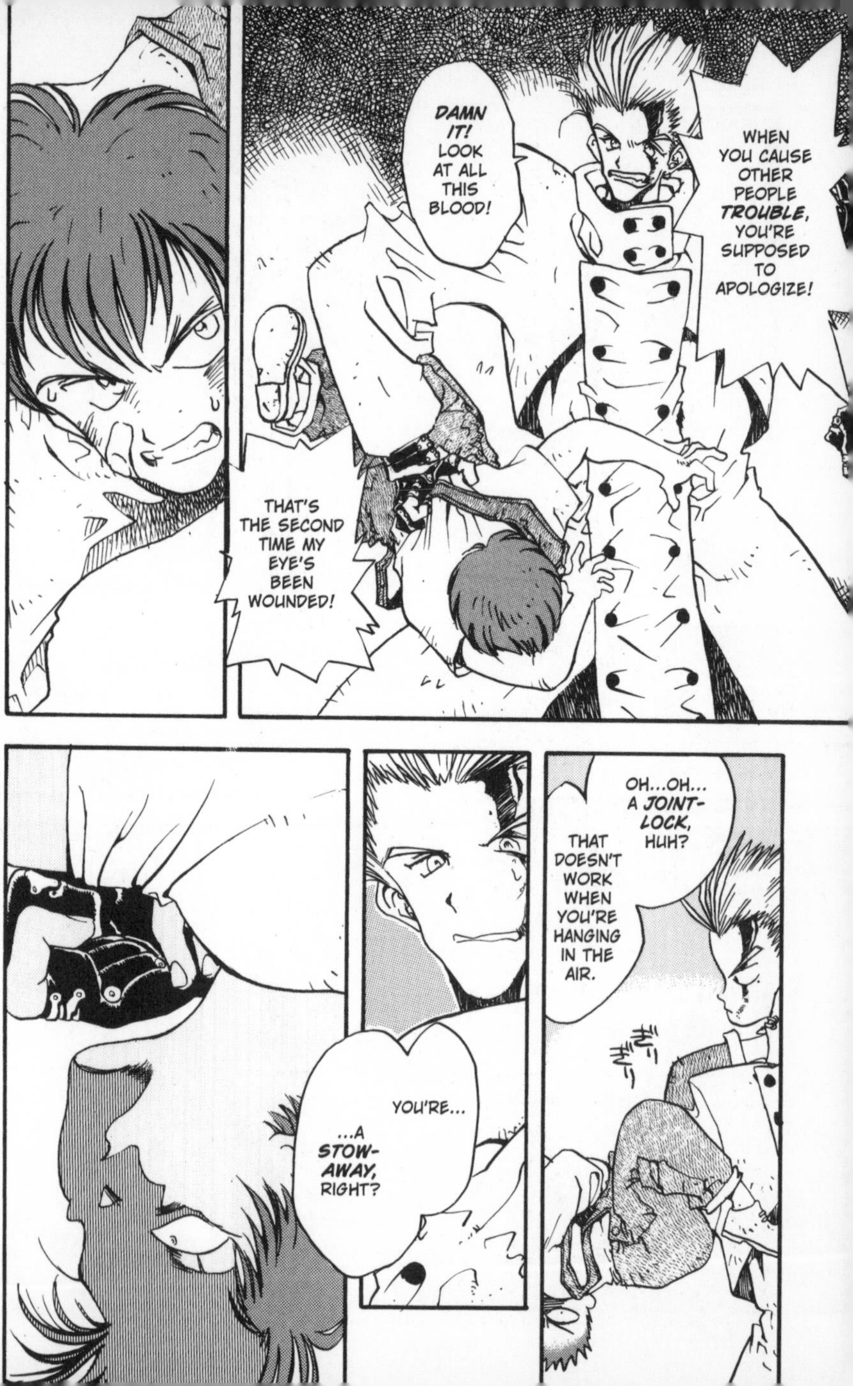
WHEN YOU CAUSE OTHER PEOPLE TROUBLE, YOU'RE SUPPOSED TO APOLOGIZE!
DAMN IT! LOOK AT ALL THIS BLOOD!
THAT'S THE SECOND TIME MY EYE'S BEEN WOUNDED!
OH...OH... A JOINT-LOCK, HUH?
THAT DOESN'T WORK WHEN YOU'RE HANGING IN THE AIR.
YOU'RE...
...A STOW-AWAY, RIGHT?

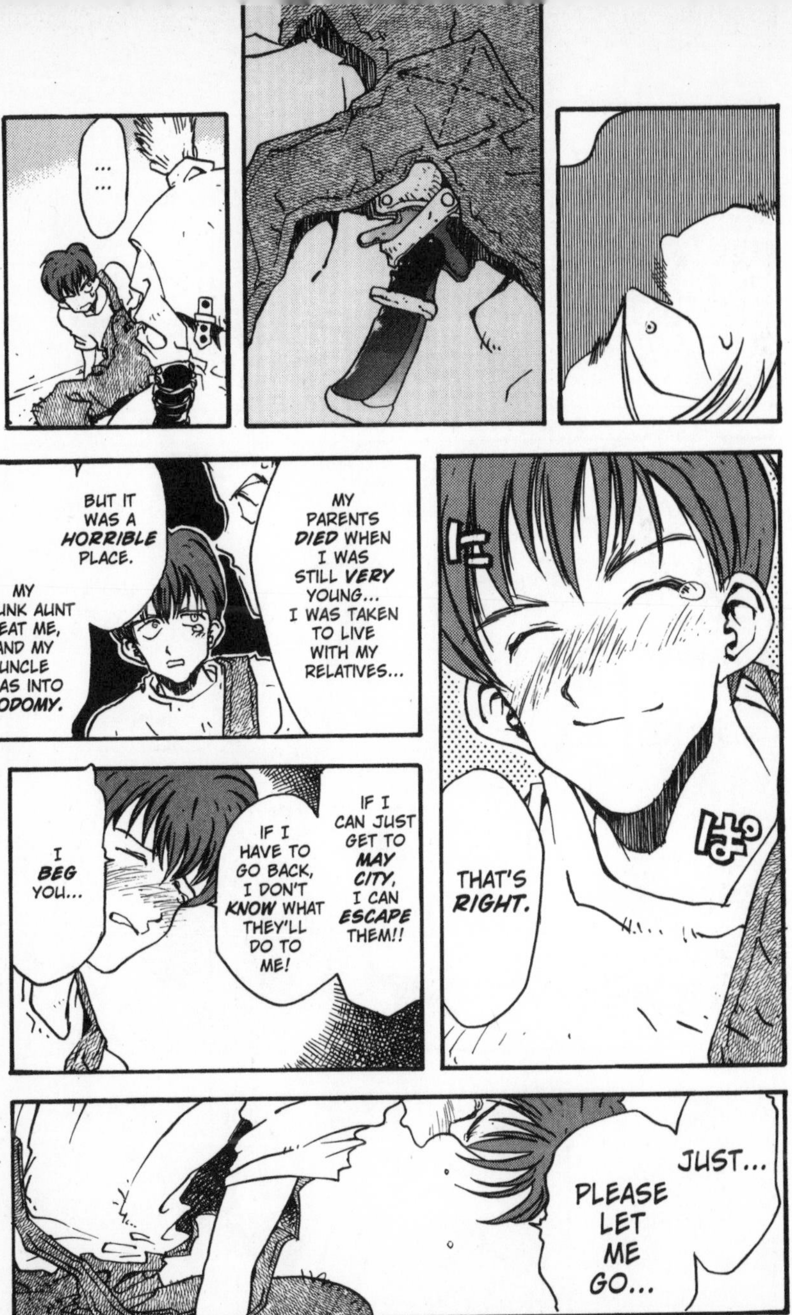
... ...
THAT'S RIGHT.
に
ぱ
MY PARENTS DIED WHEN I WAS STILL VERY YOUNG... I WAS TAKEN TO LIVE WITH MY RELATIVES...
BUT IT WAS A HORRIBLE PLACE.
MY DRUNK AUNT BEAT ME, AND MY UNCLE WAS INTO SODOMY.
IF I CAN JUST GET TO MAY CITY, I CAN ESCAPE THEM!!
IF I HAVE TO GO BACK, I DON'T KNOW WHAT THEY'LL DO TO ME!
I BEG YOU...
JUST...
PLEASE LET ME GO...

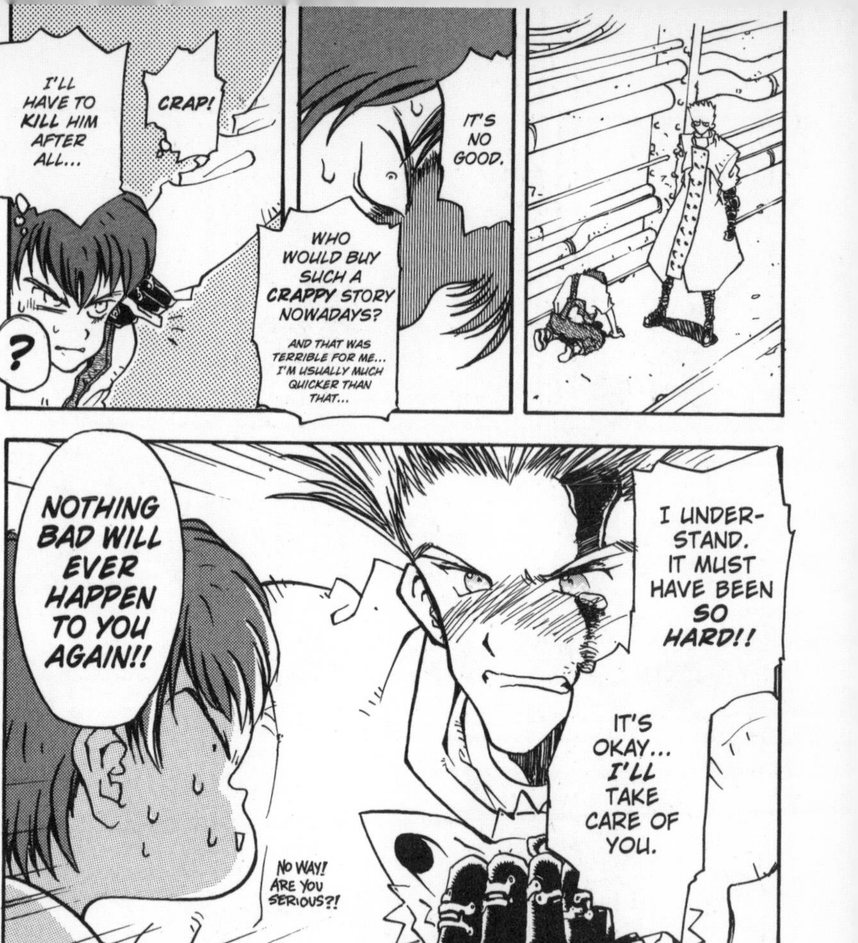
IT'S NO GOOD.
WHO WOULD BUY SUCH A CRAPPY STORY NOWADAYS?
AND THAT WAS TERRIBLE FOR ME... I'M USUALLY MUCH QUICKER THAN THAT...
I'LL HAVE TO KILL HIM AFTER ALL...
CRAP!
?
I UNDER-STAND. IT MUST HAVE BEEN SO HARD!!
IT'S OKAY... I'LL TAKE CARE OF YOU.
NOTHING BAD WILL EVER HAPPEN TO YOU AGAIN!!
NO WAY! ARE YOU SERIOUS?!

MEANWHILE, MERYL AND MILLIE ...

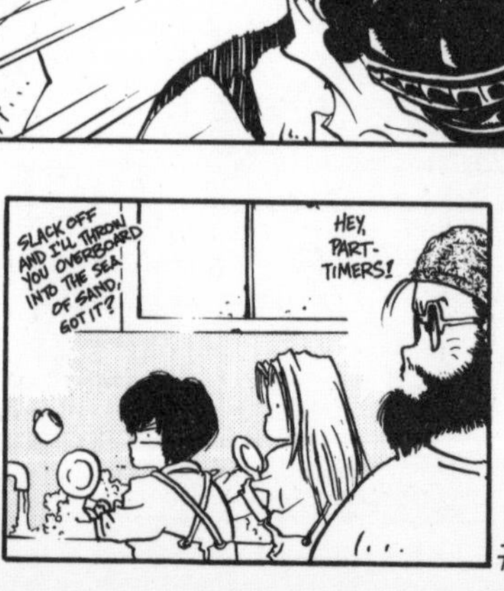
HEY, PART-TIMERS!
SLACK OFF AND I'LL THROW YOU OVERBOARD INTO THE SEA OF SAND, GOT IT?
!...

...ARE WORKING IN THE GALLEY OF THE "FLOURISH."

#4. POPO / END

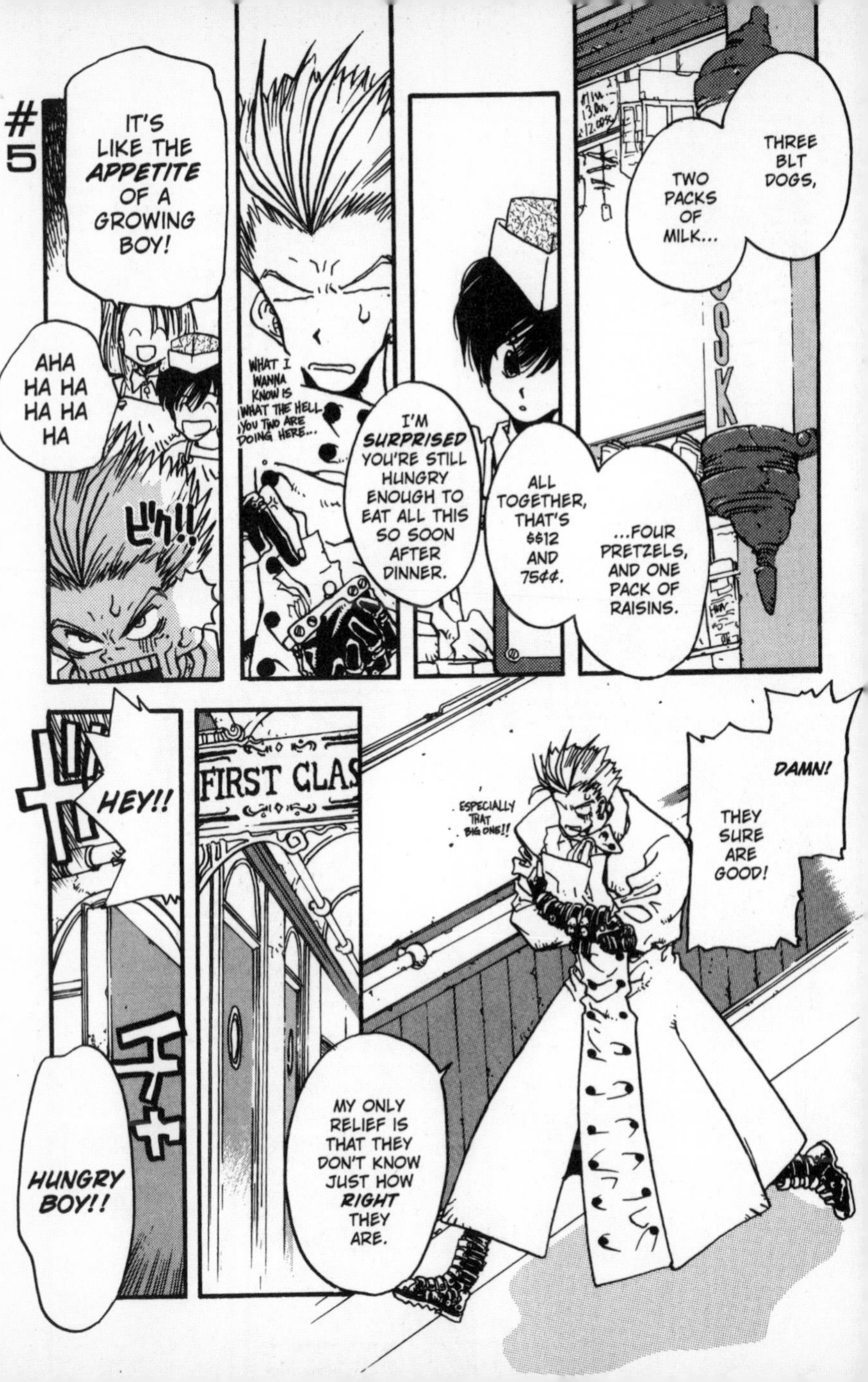

THREE BLT DOGS,
TWO PACKS OF MILK...
...FOUR PRETZELS, AND ONE PACK OF RAISINS.
ALL TOGETHER, THAT'S $$12 AND 75¢¢.
I'M **SURPRISED** YOU'RE STILL HUNGRY ENOUGH TO EAT ALL THIS SO SOON AFTER DINNER.
WHAT I WANNA KNOW IS WHAT THE HELL YOU TWO ARE DOING HERE...
#5
IT'S LIKE THE ***APPETITE*** OF A GROWING BOY!
AHA HA HA HA HA HA
ビク!!
DAMN!
THEY SURE ARE GOOD!
ESPECIALLY THAT BIG ONE!!
MY ONLY RELIEF IS THAT THEY DON'T KNOW JUST HOW ***RIGHT*** THEY ARE.
FIRST CLAS
HEY!!
HUNGRY BOY!!

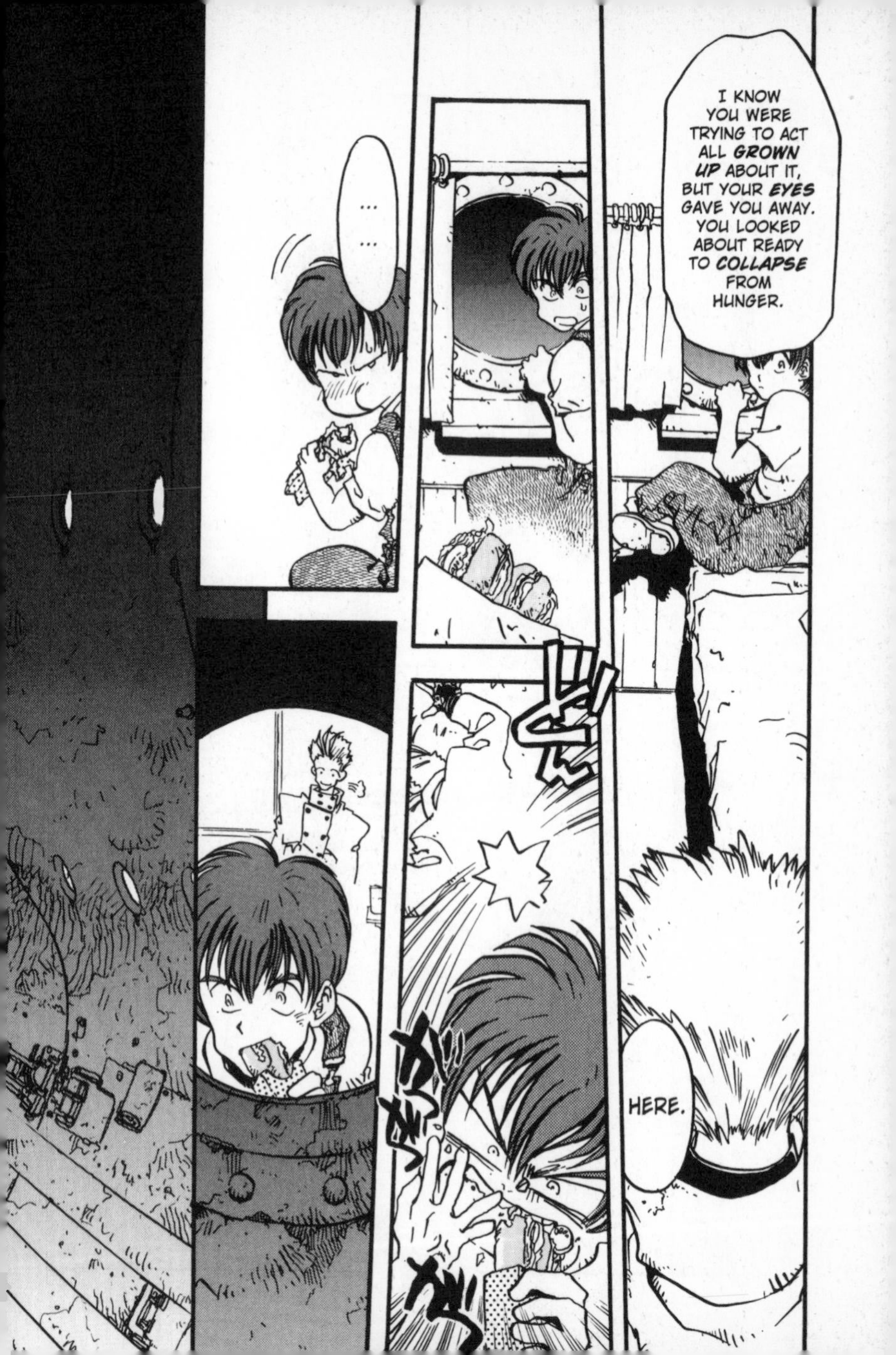
I KNOW YOU WERE TRYING TO ACT ALL GROWN UP ABOUT IT, BUT YOUR EYES GAVE YOU AWAY. YOU LOOKED ABOUT READY TO COLLAPSE FROM HUNGER.
... ...
HERE.

# #5. ASSAULT

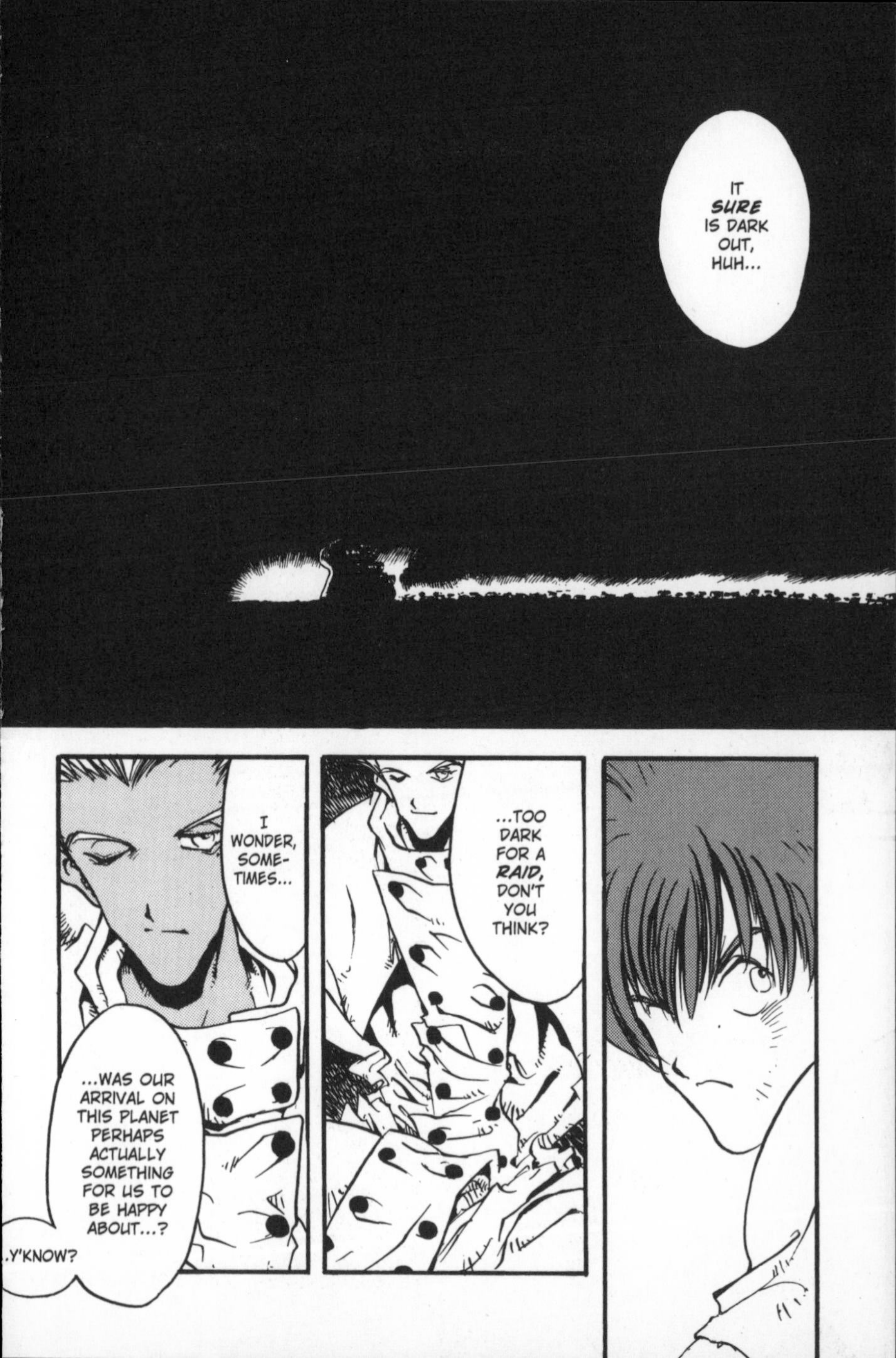
IT SURE IS DARK OUT, HUH...
...TOO DARK FOR A RAID, DON'T YOU THINK?
I WONDER, SOME-TIMES...
...WAS OUR ARRIVAL ON THIS PLANET PERHAPS ACTUALLY SOMETHING FOR US TO BE HAPPY ABOUT...?
.Y'KNOW?

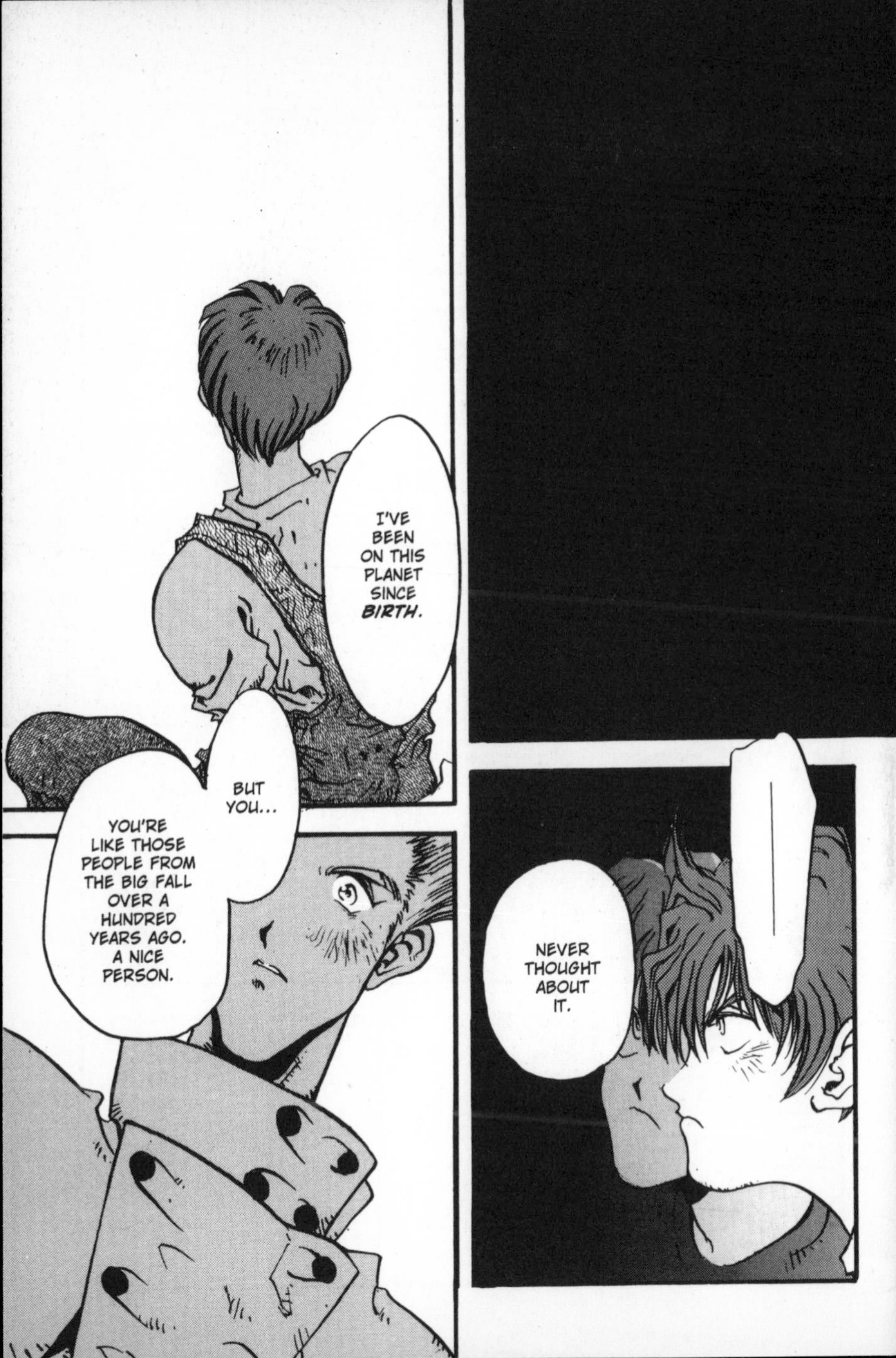

I'VE BEEN ON THIS PLANET SINCE *BIRTH*.
BUT YOU...
YOU'RE LIKE THOSE PEOPLE FROM THE BIG FALL OVER A HUNDRED YEARS AGO. A NICE PERSON.
—
NEVER THOUGHT ABOUT IT.

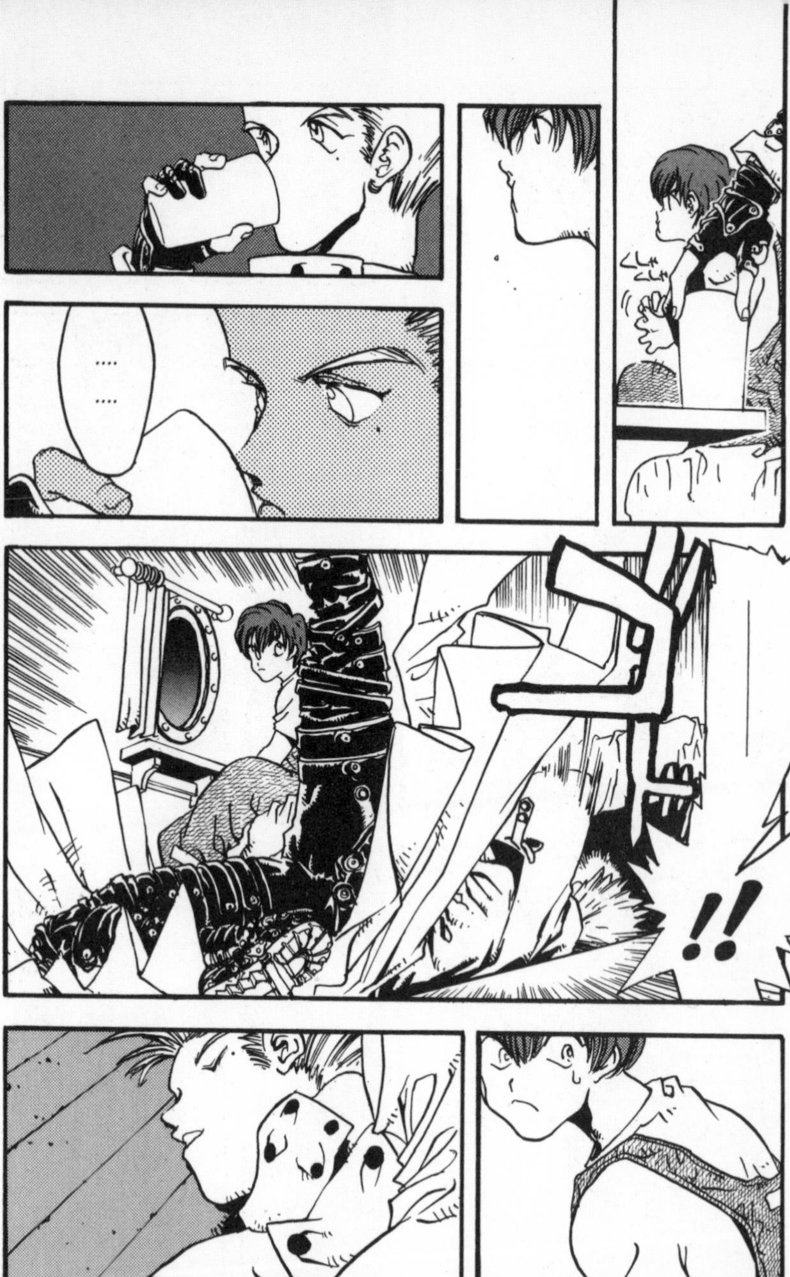
くしゃ
くしゃ
....
....
!!

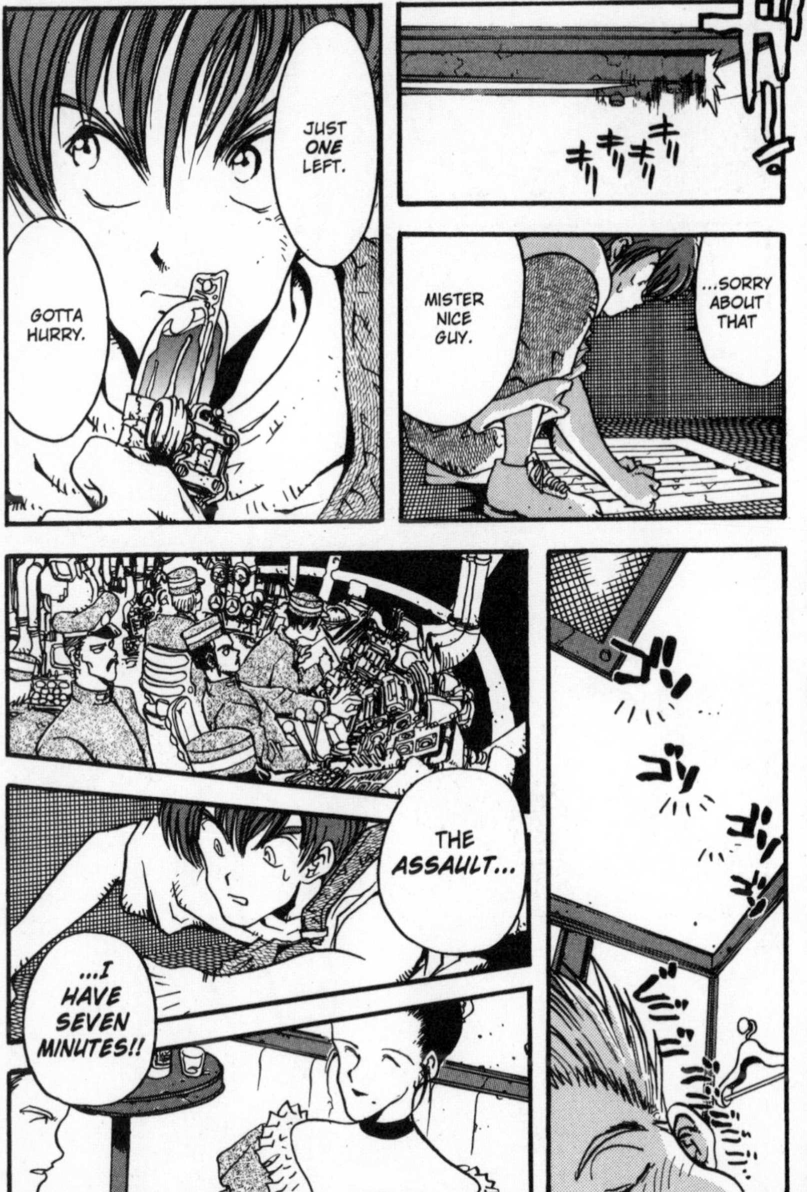
キリキリキリキリ
...SORRY ABOUT THAT
MISTER NICE GUY.
JUST ONE LEFT.
GOTTA HURRY.
ゴッ
ゴッ
ゴッ
THE ASSAULT...
...I HAVE SEVEN MINUTES!!

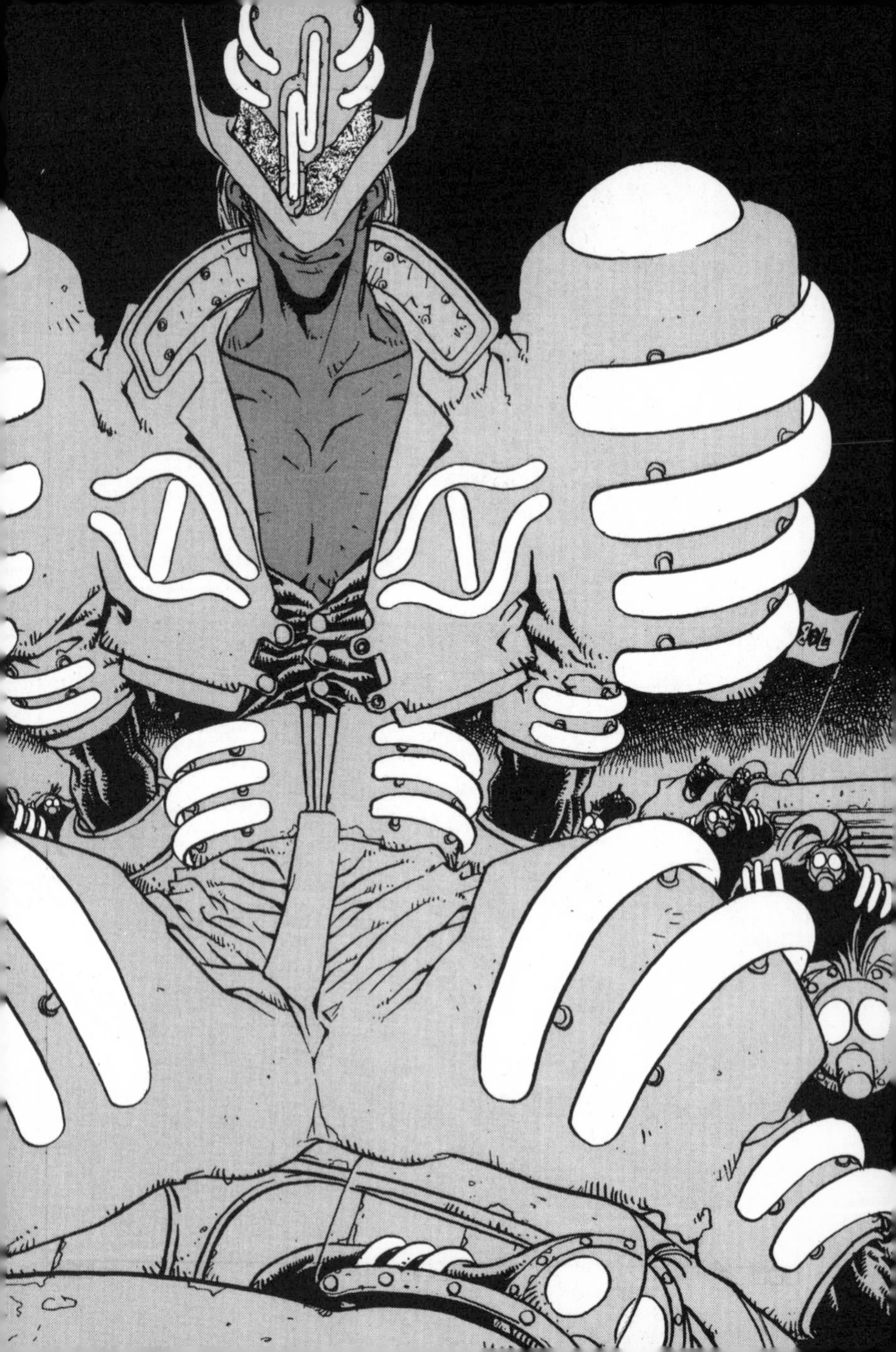

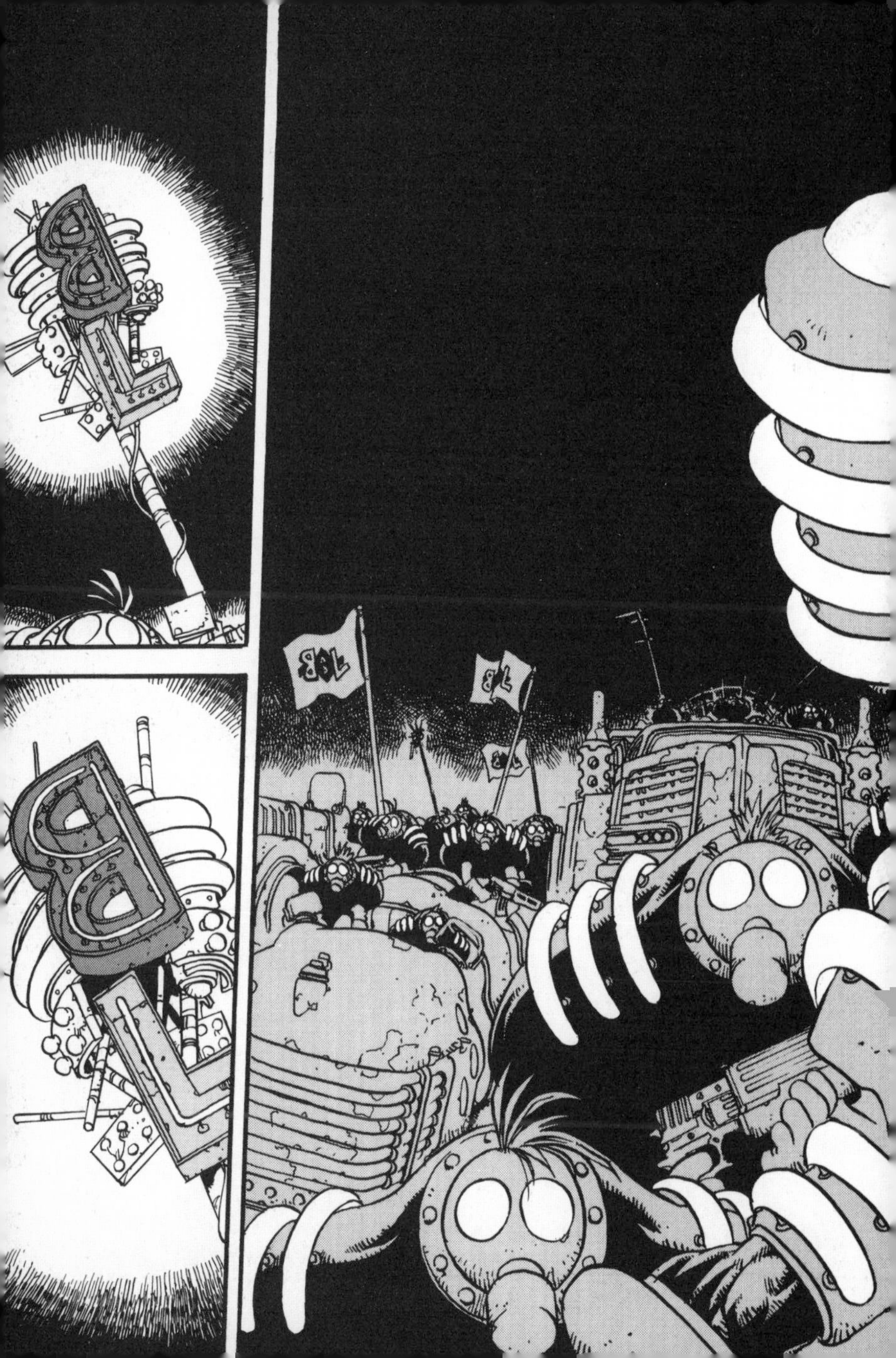

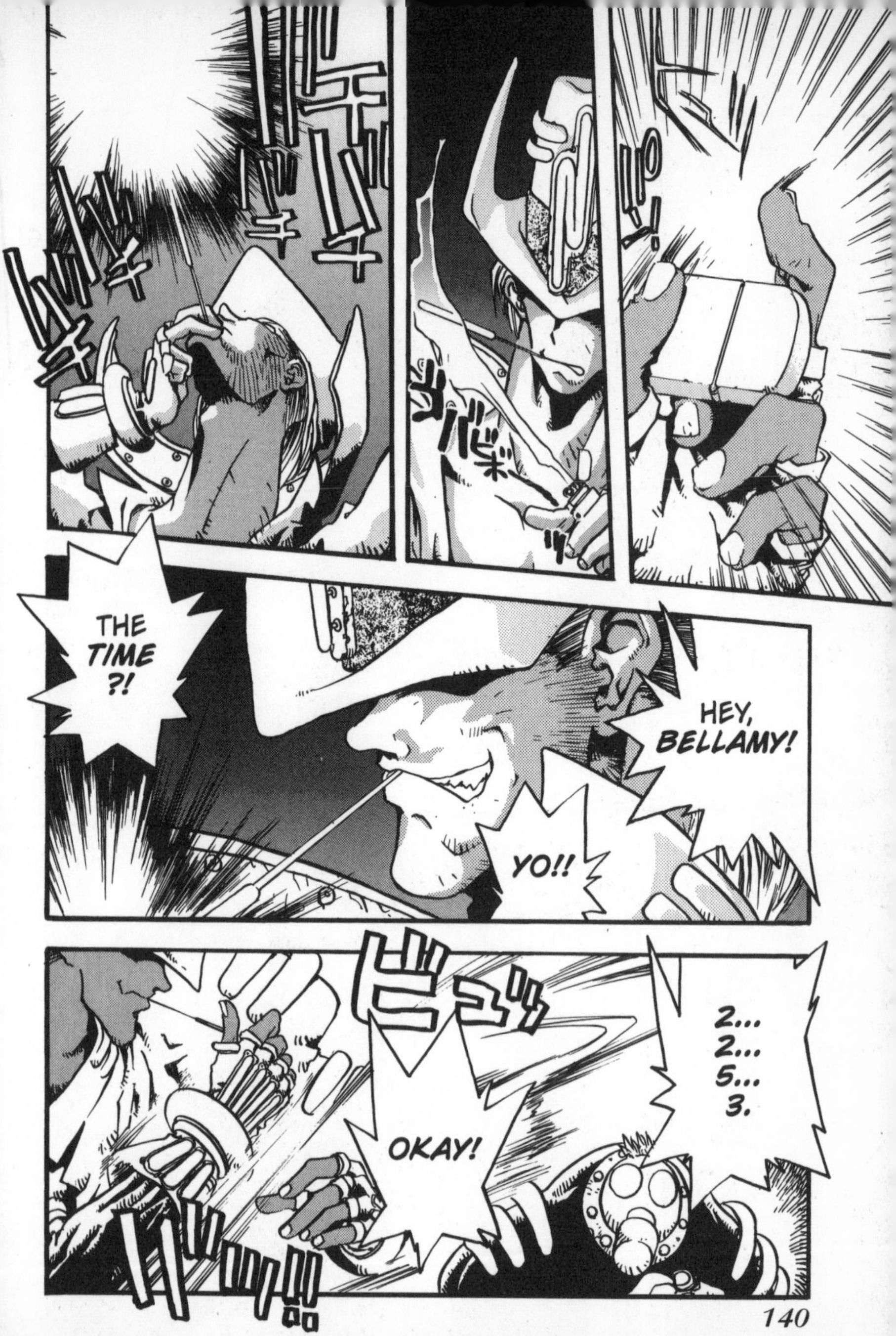
HEY, BELLAMY!
YO!!
THE TIME?!
2... 2... 5... 3.
OKAY!

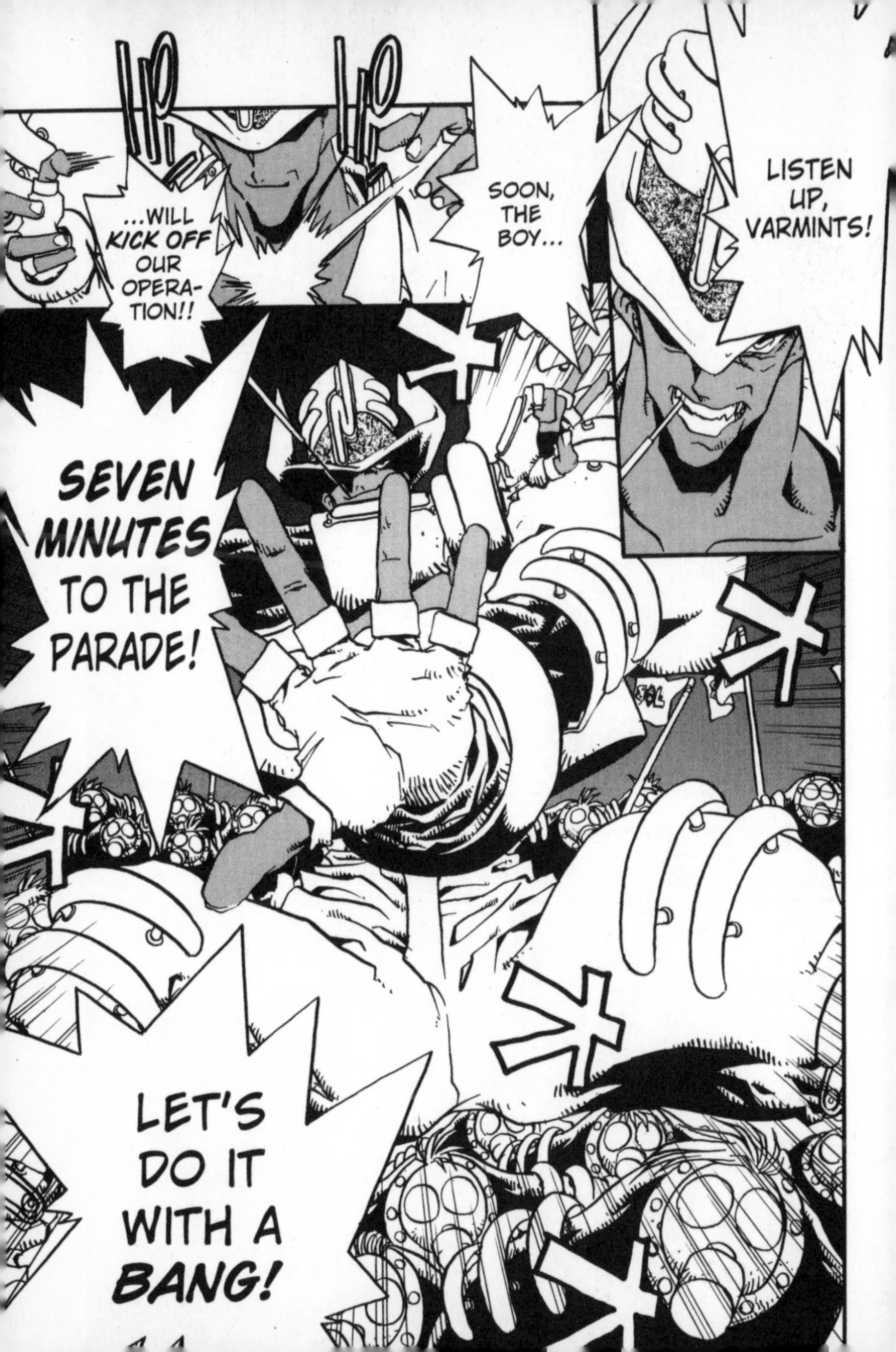
LISTEN UP, VARMINTS!
SOON, THE BOY...
...WILL KICK OFF OUR OPERATION!!
SEVEN MINUTES TO THE PARADE!
LET'S DO IT WITH A BANG!

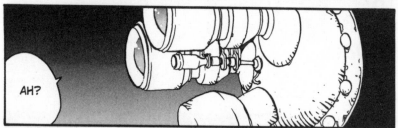

AH?

HERE WE GOOOO!!

THE PURPLE FLARE...

RIGHT ON TIME...

YO!

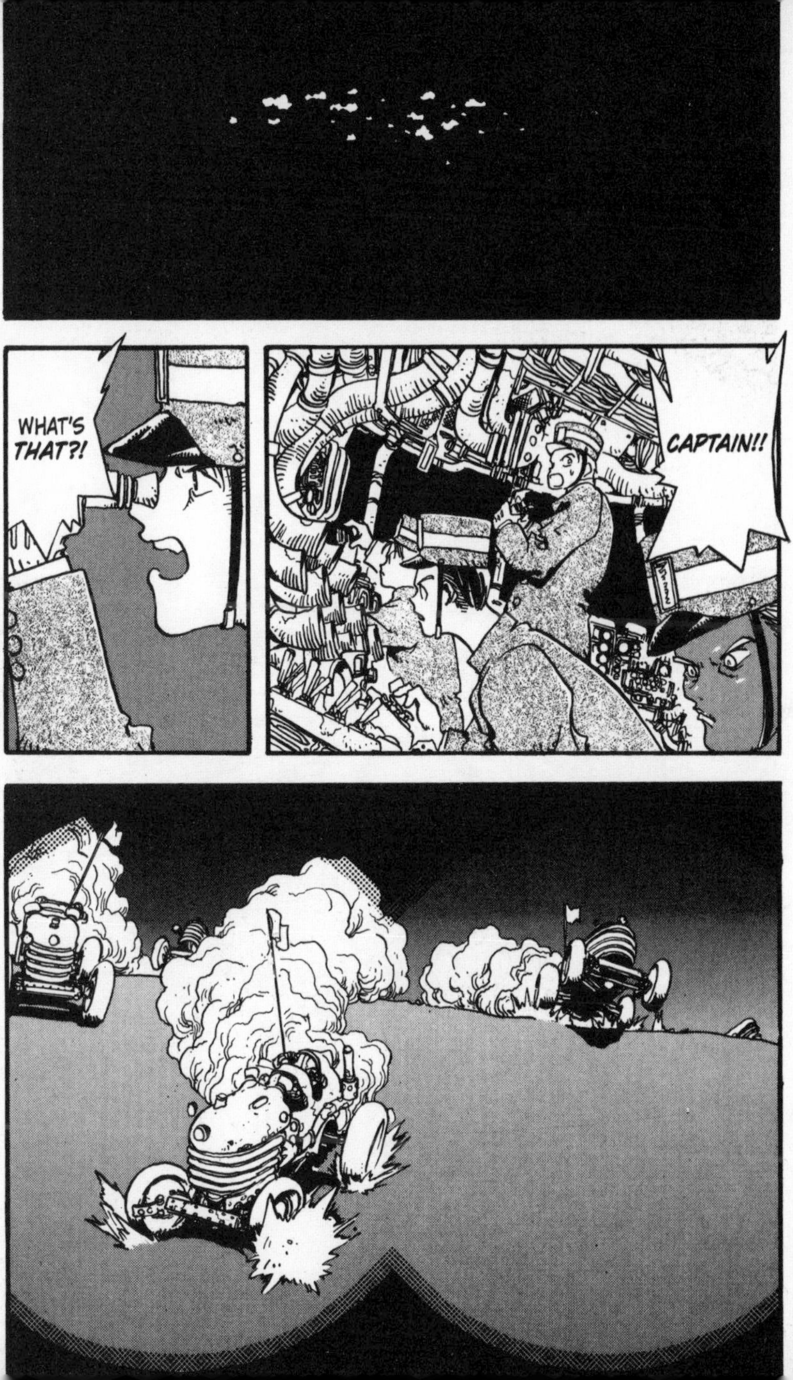
CAPTAIN!!
WHAT'S THAT?!

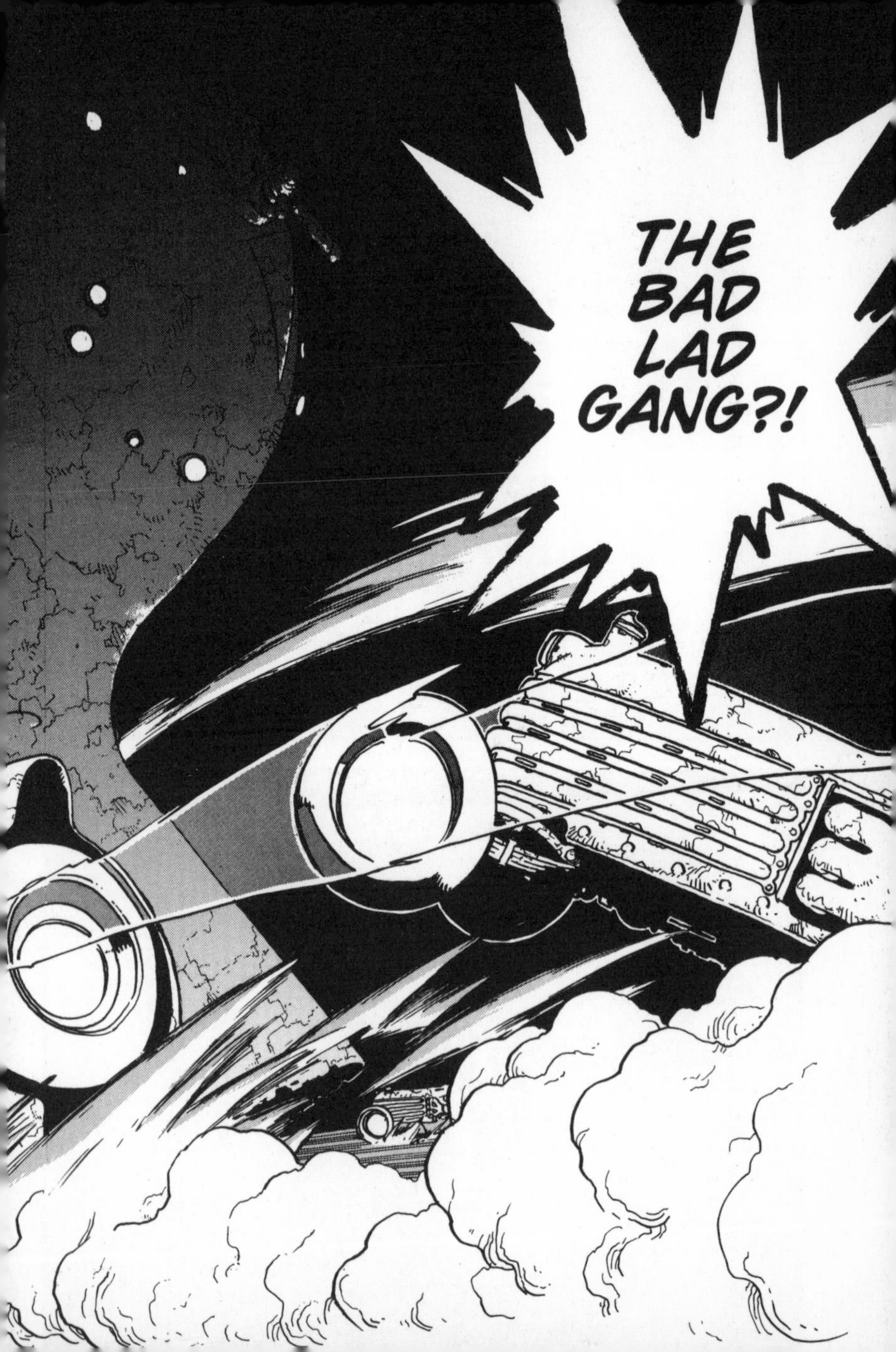
THE BAD LAD GANG?!

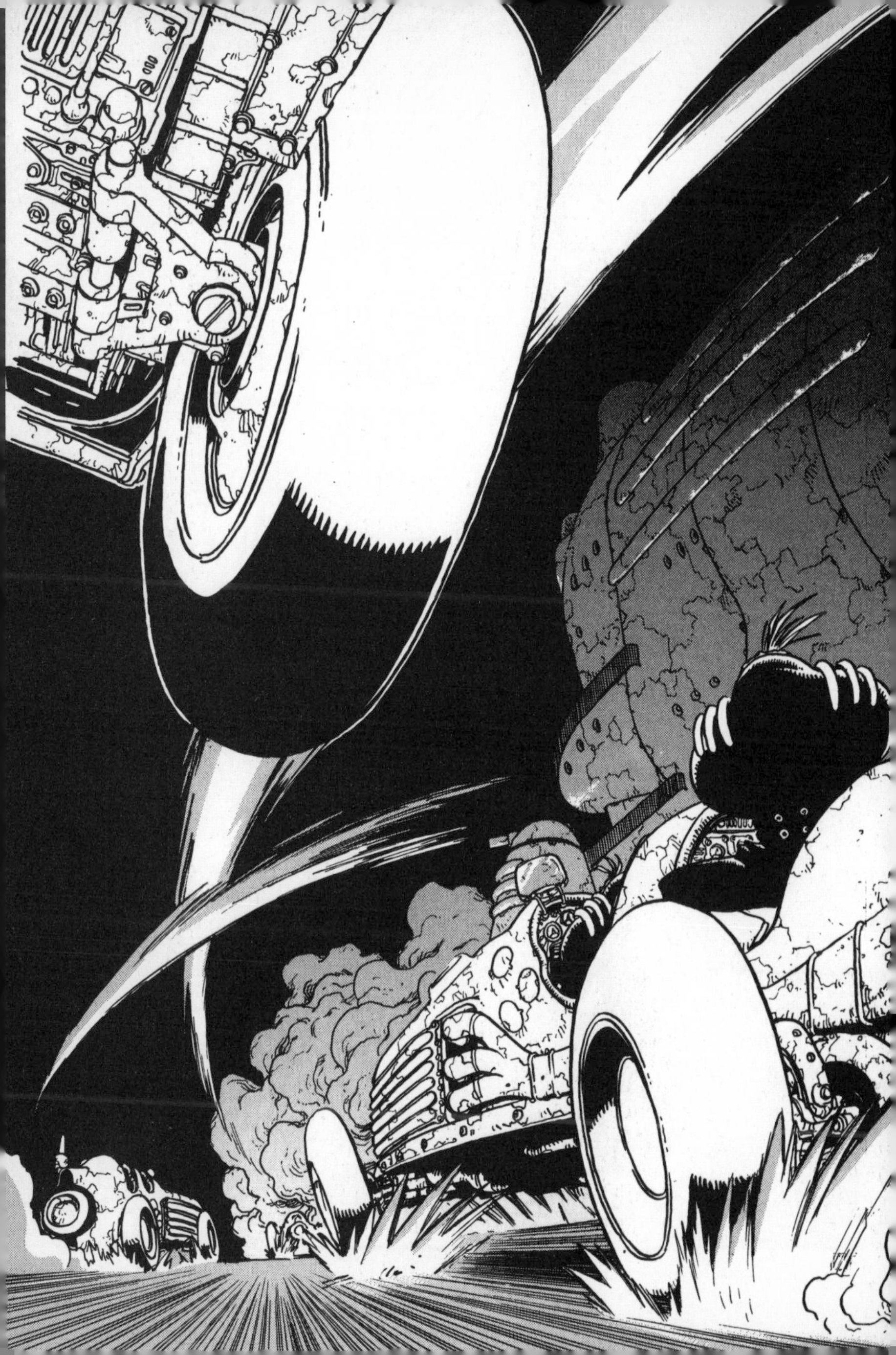

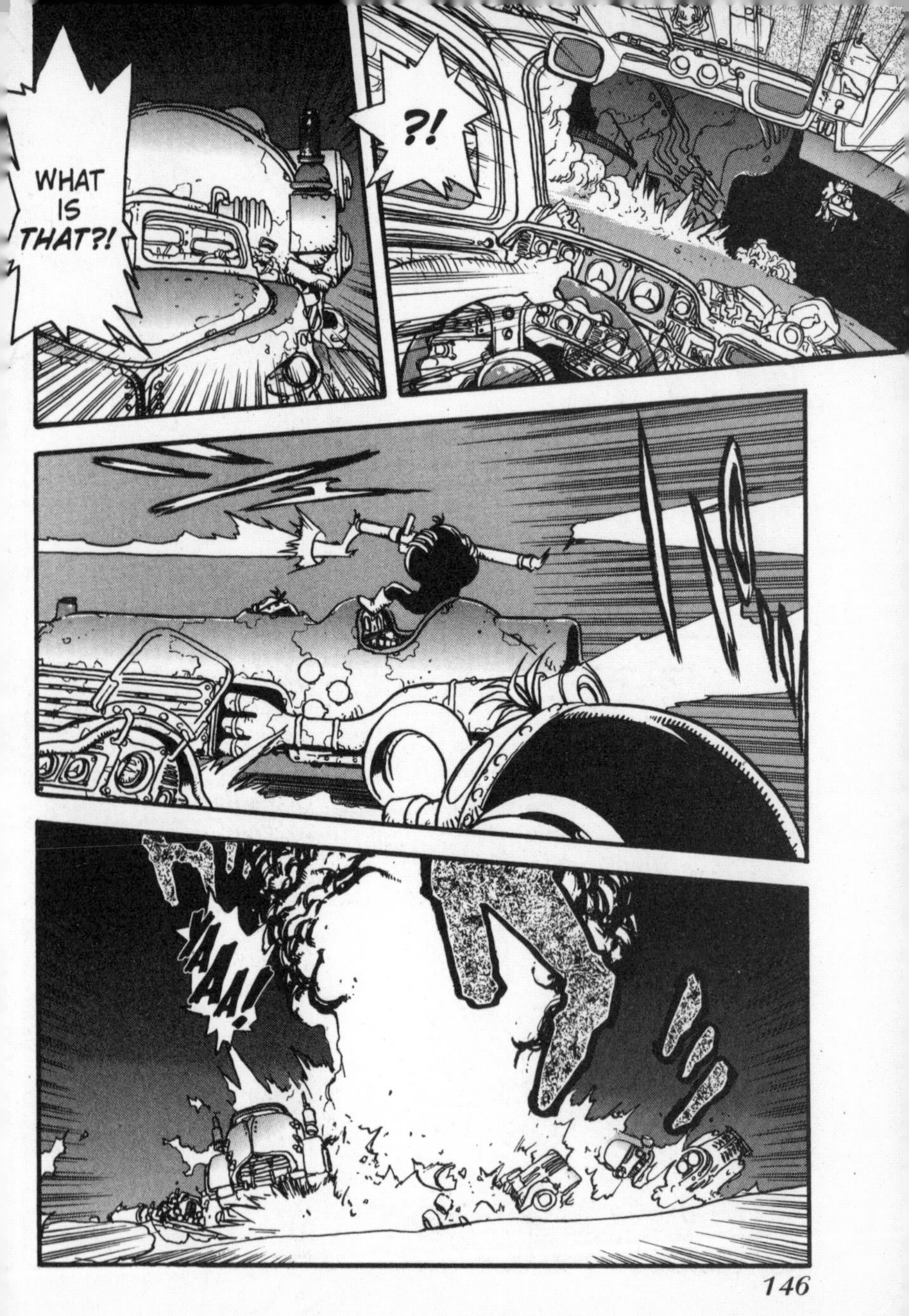
?!
WHAT IS THAT?!
YAAAA!

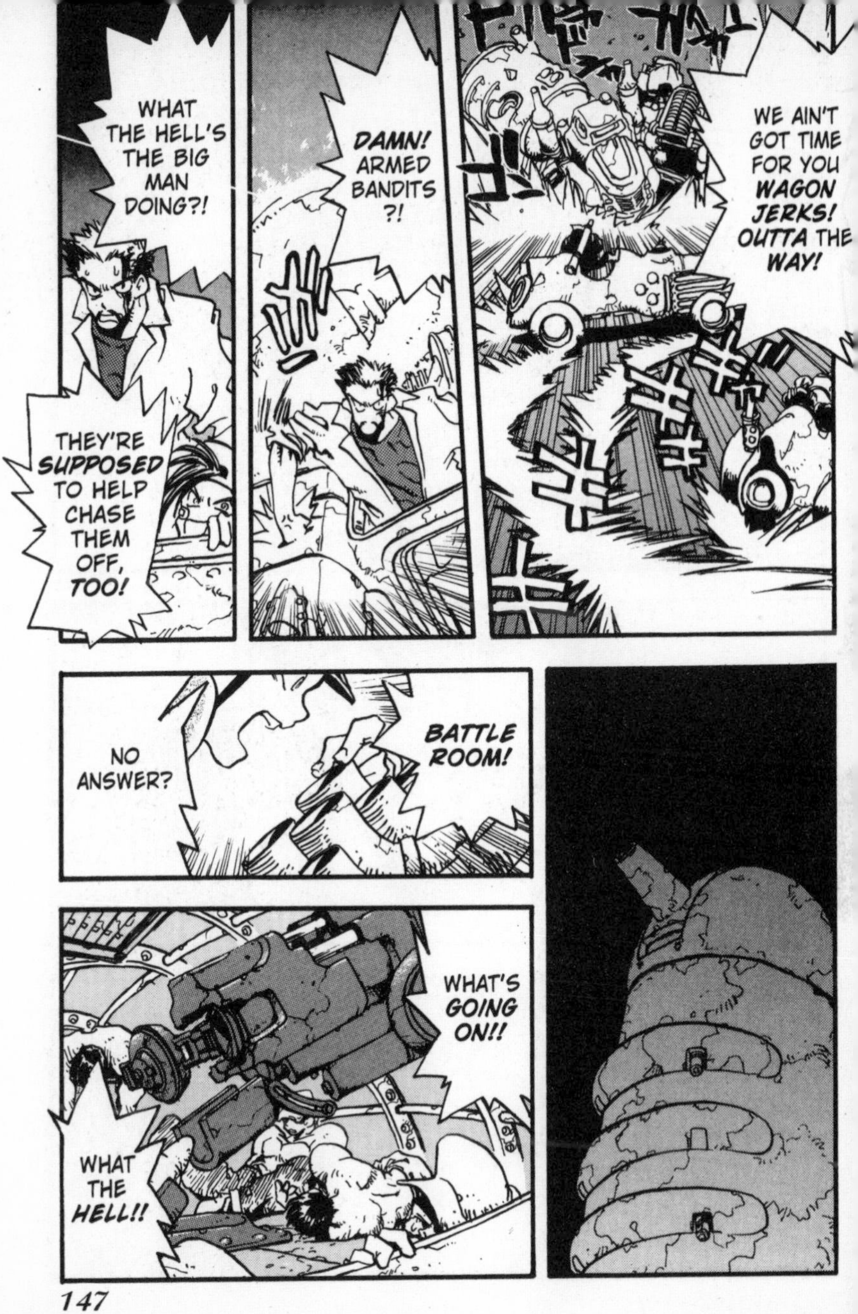
WE AIN'T GOT TIME FOR YOU WAGON JERKS! OUTTA THE WAY!
DAMN! ARMED BANDITS ?!
WHAT THE HELL'S THE BIG MAN DOING?!
THEY'RE SUPPOSED TO HELP CHASE THEM OFF, TOO!
BATTLE ROOM!
NO ANSWER?
WHAT'S GOING ON!!
WHAT THE HELL!!

HUH ?!

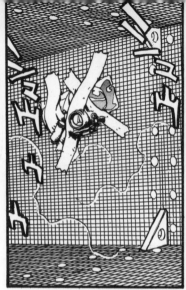

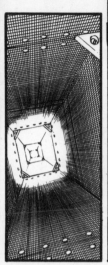

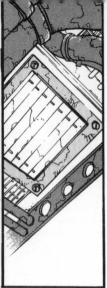

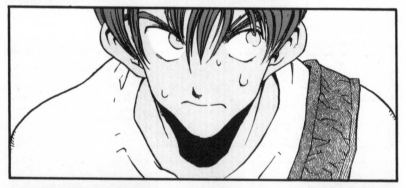

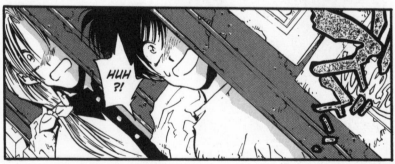

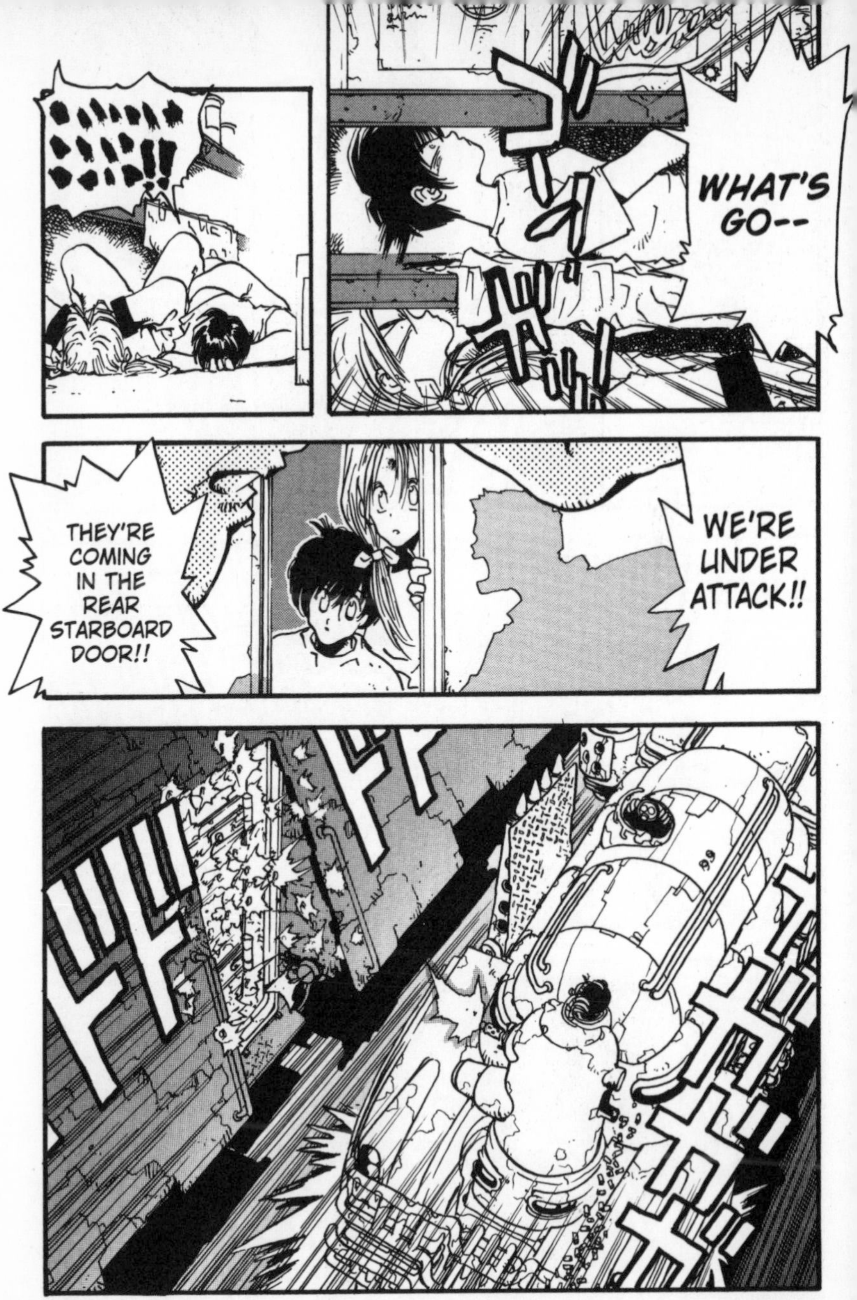
WHAT'S GO--
WE'RE UNDER ATTACK!!
THEY'RE COMING IN THE REAR STARBOARD DOOR!!

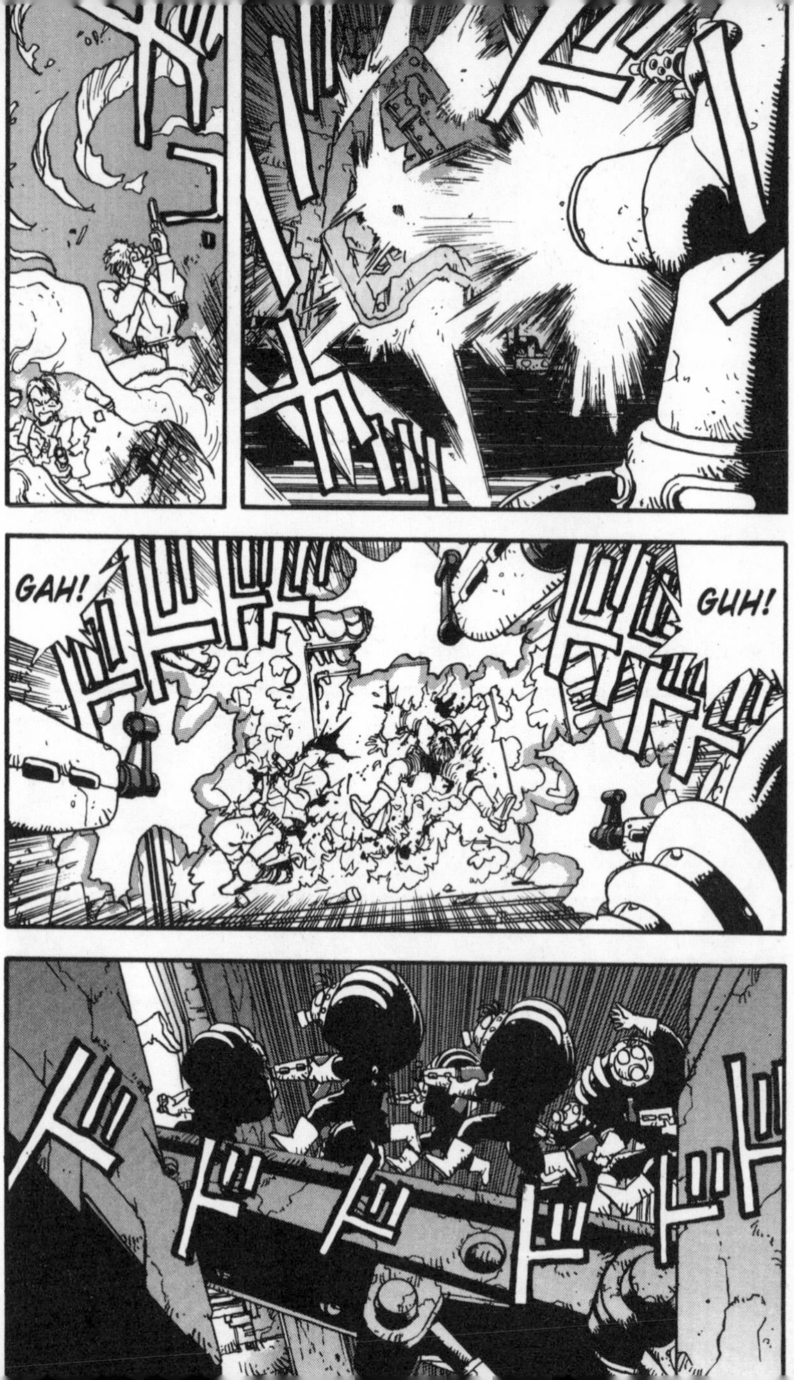
GUH!
GAH!

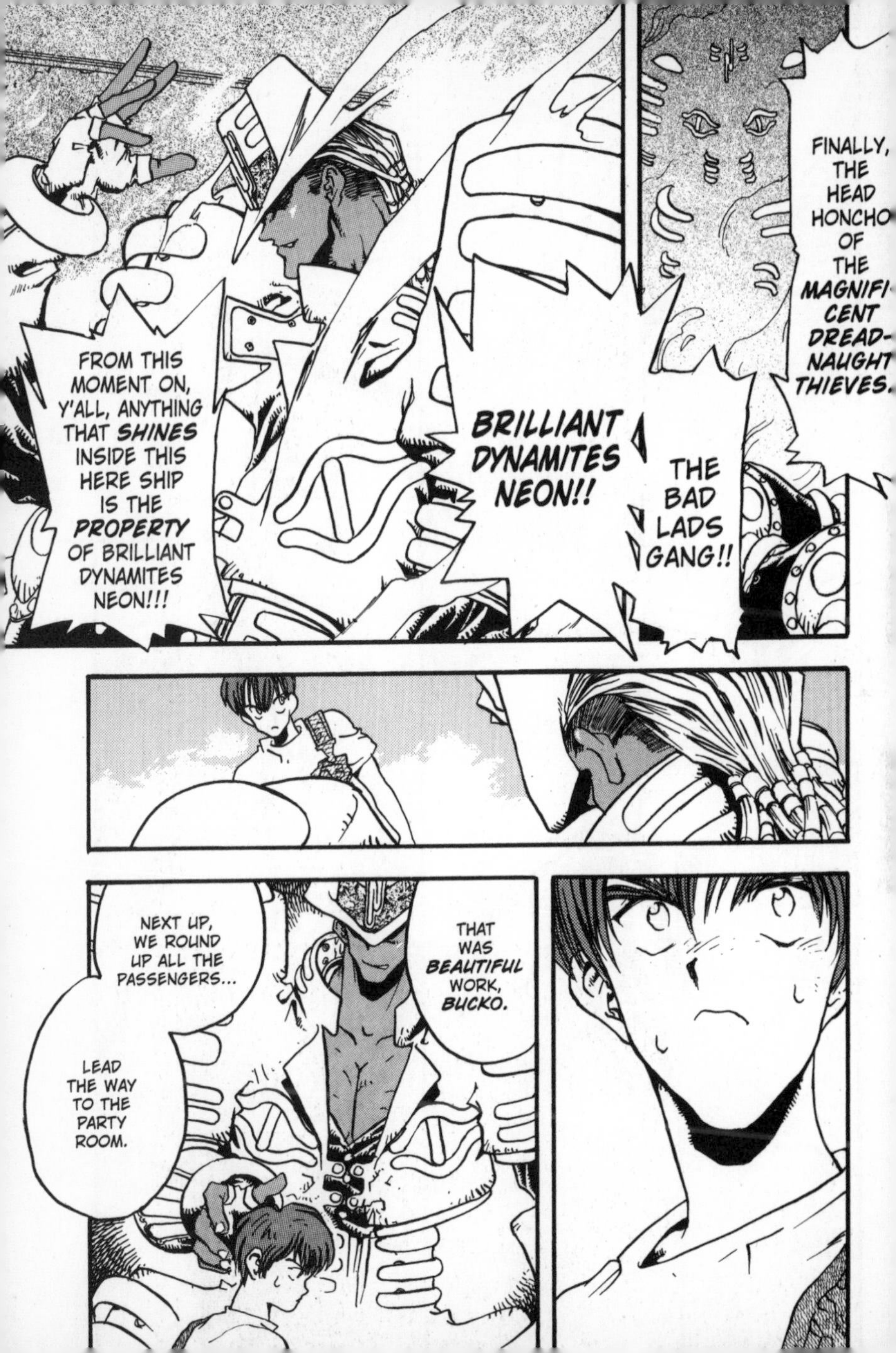

FINALLY, THE HEAD HONCHO OF THE *MAGNIFICENT DREADNAUGHT THIEVES.*
THE BAD LADS GANG!!
*BRILLIANT DYNAMITES NEON!!*
FROM THIS MOMENT ON, Y'ALL, ANYTHING THAT ***SHINES*** INSIDE THIS HERE SHIP IS THE ***PROPERTY*** OF BRILLIANT DYNAMITES NEON!!!
THAT WAS ***BEAUTIFUL*** WORK, ***BUCKO.***
NEXT UP, WE ROUND UP ALL THE PASSENGERS...
LEAD THE WAY TO THE PARTY ROOM.

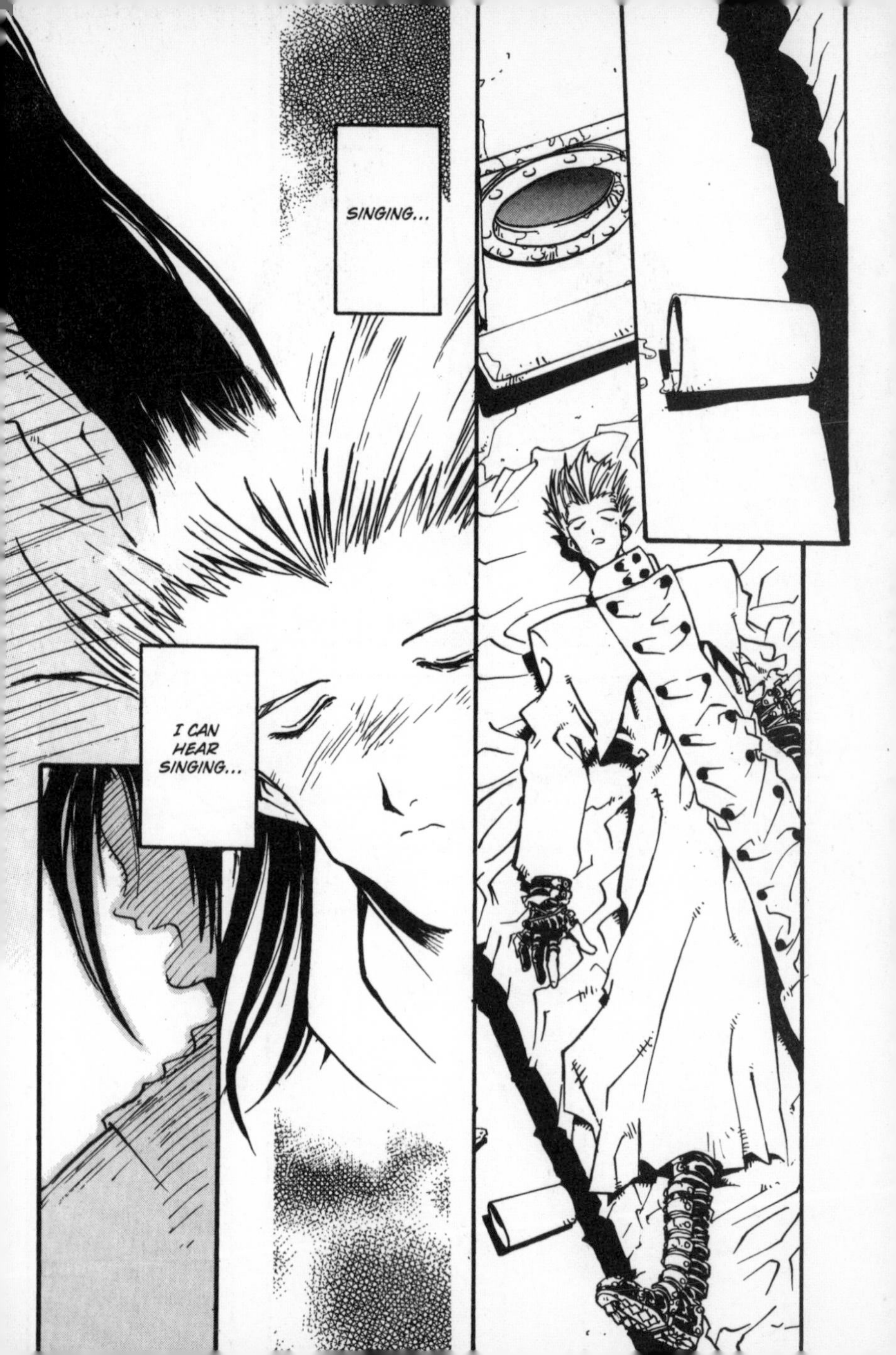
SINGING...
I CAN HEAR SINGING...

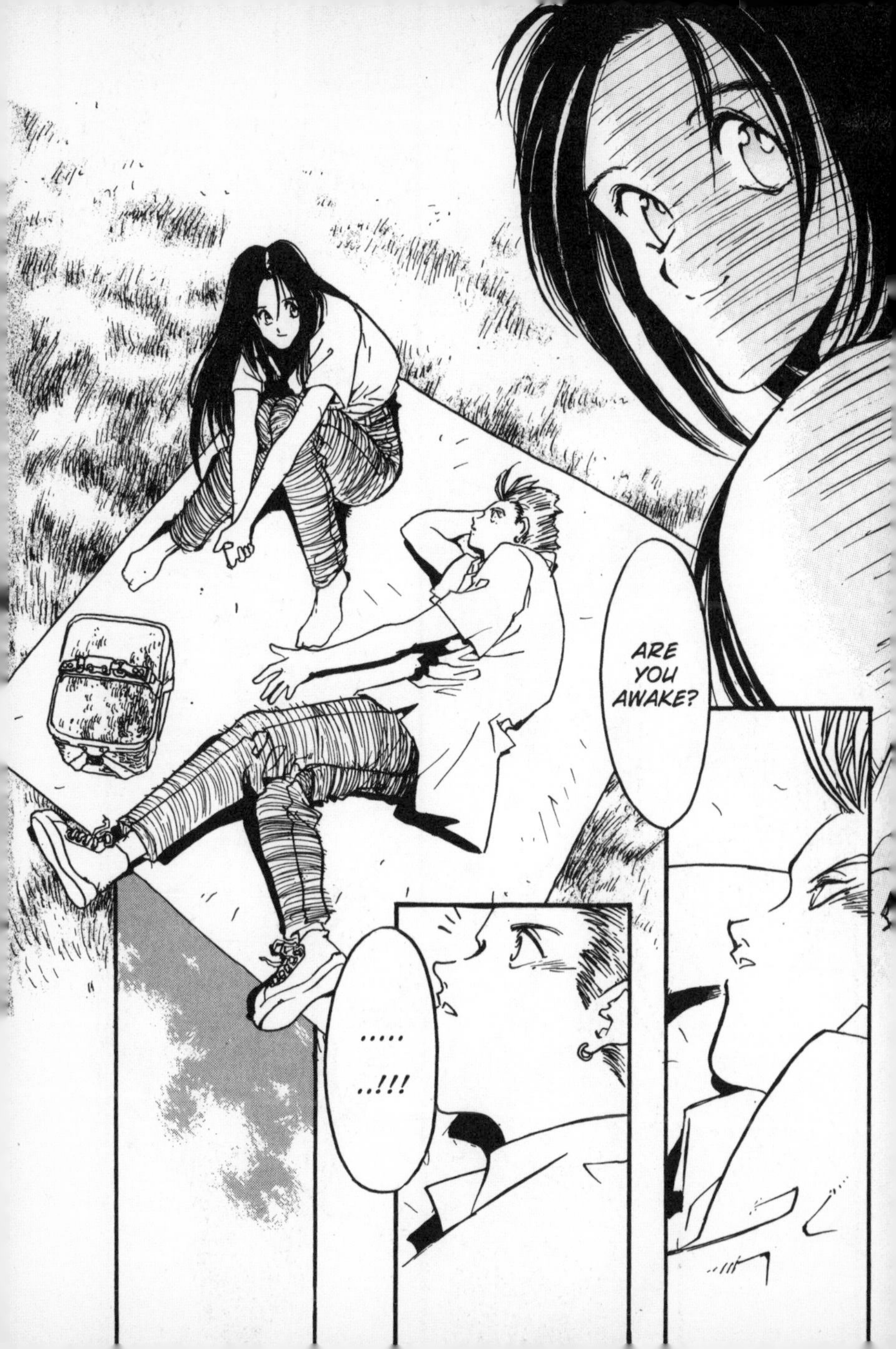
ARE YOU AWAKE?
.....
..!!!

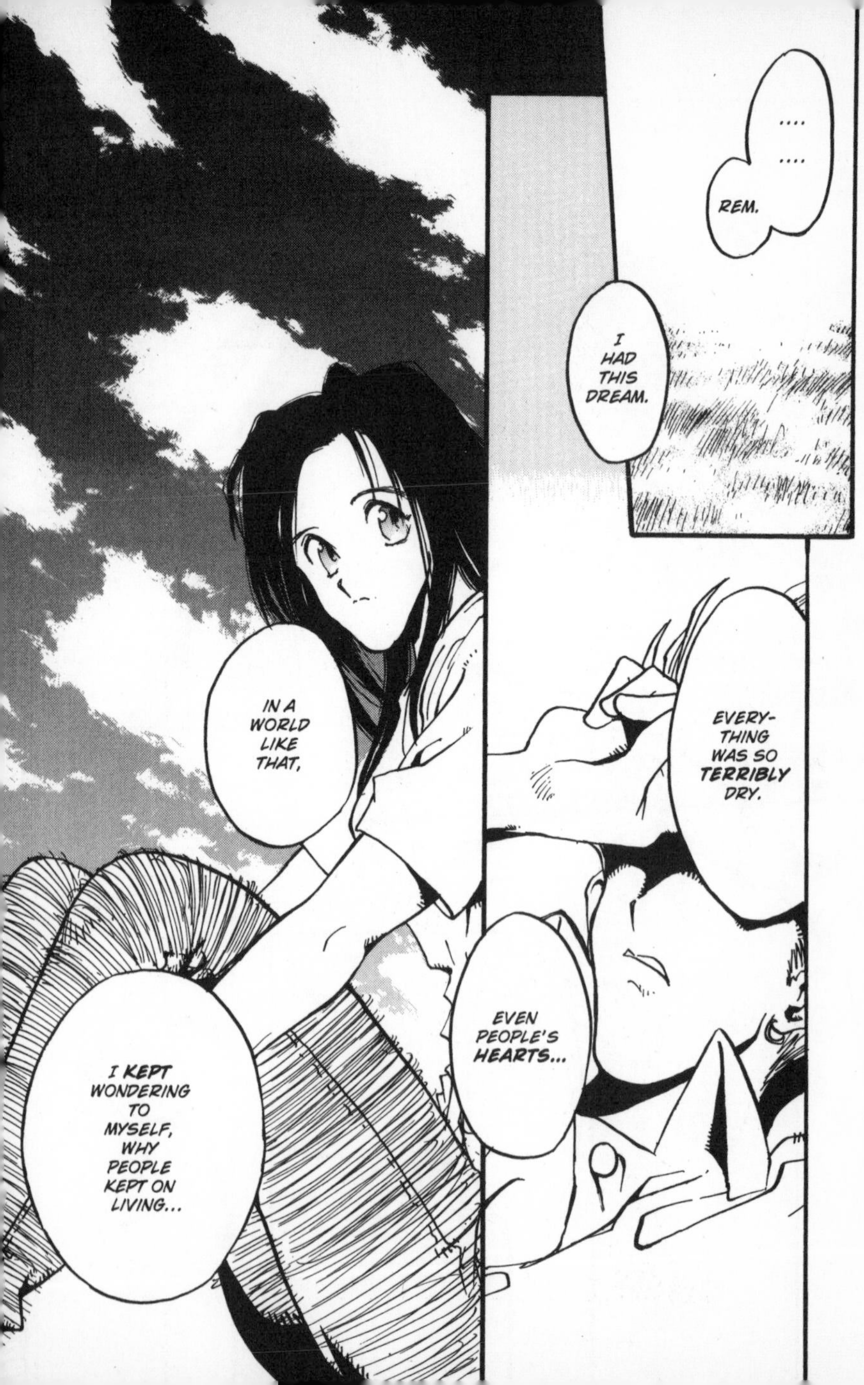
....
....
REM.
I HAD THIS DREAM.
EVERY-THING WAS SO TERRIBLY DRY.
EVEN PEOPLE'S HEARTS...
IN A WORLD LIKE THAT,
I KEPT WONDERING TO MYSELF, WHY PEOPLE KEPT ON LIVING...

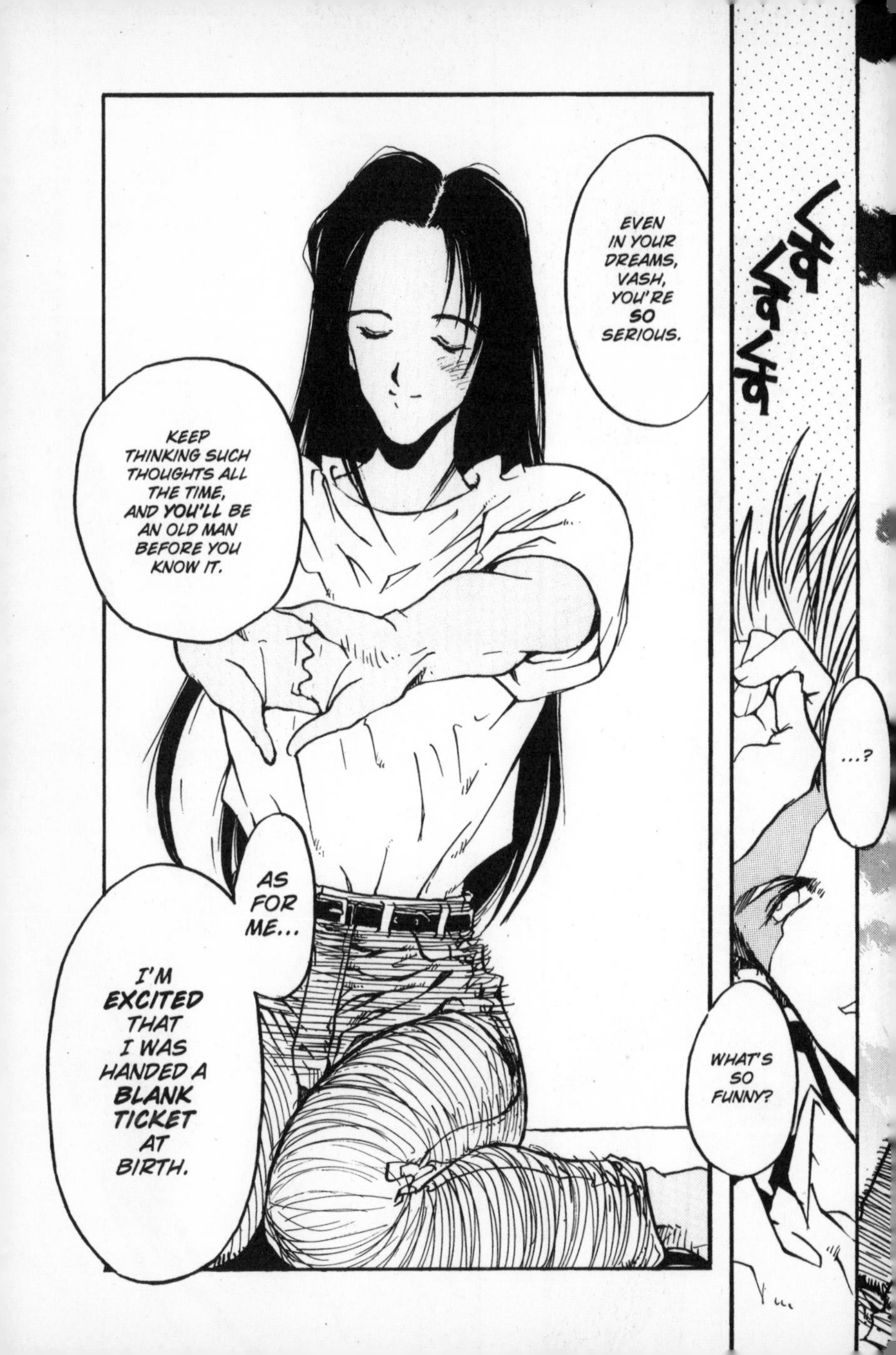
...?
WHAT'S SO FUNNY?
EVEN IN YOUR DREAMS, VASH, YOU'RE SO SERIOUS.
KEEP THINKING SUCH THOUGHTS ALL THE TIME, AND YOU'LL BE AN OLD MAN BEFORE YOU KNOW IT.
AS FOR ME...
I'M EXCITED THAT I WAS HANDED A BLANK TICKET AT BIRTH.

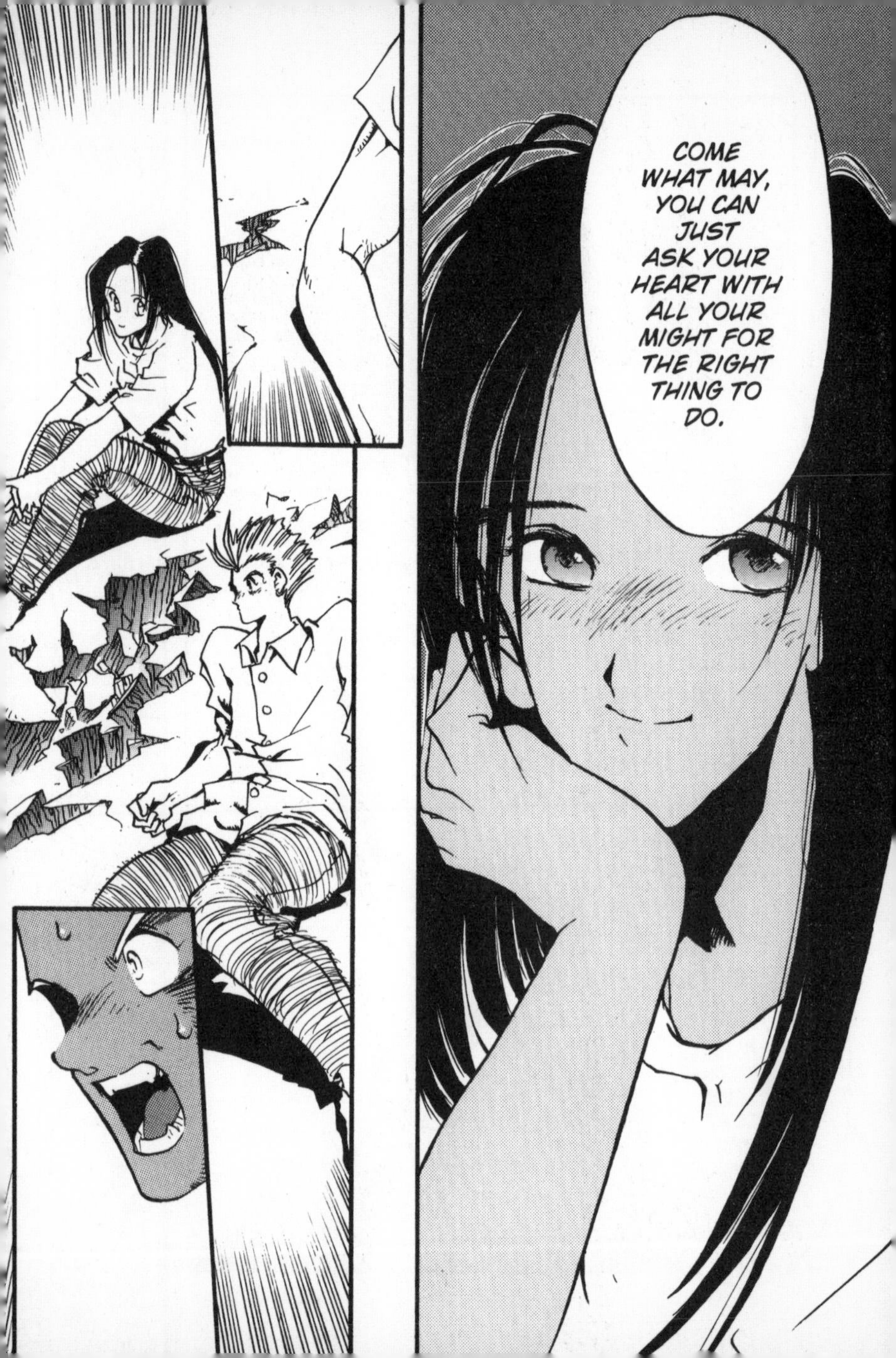
COME WHAT MAY, YOU CAN JUST ASK YOUR HEART WITH ALL YOUR MIGHT FOR THE RIGHT THING TO DO.

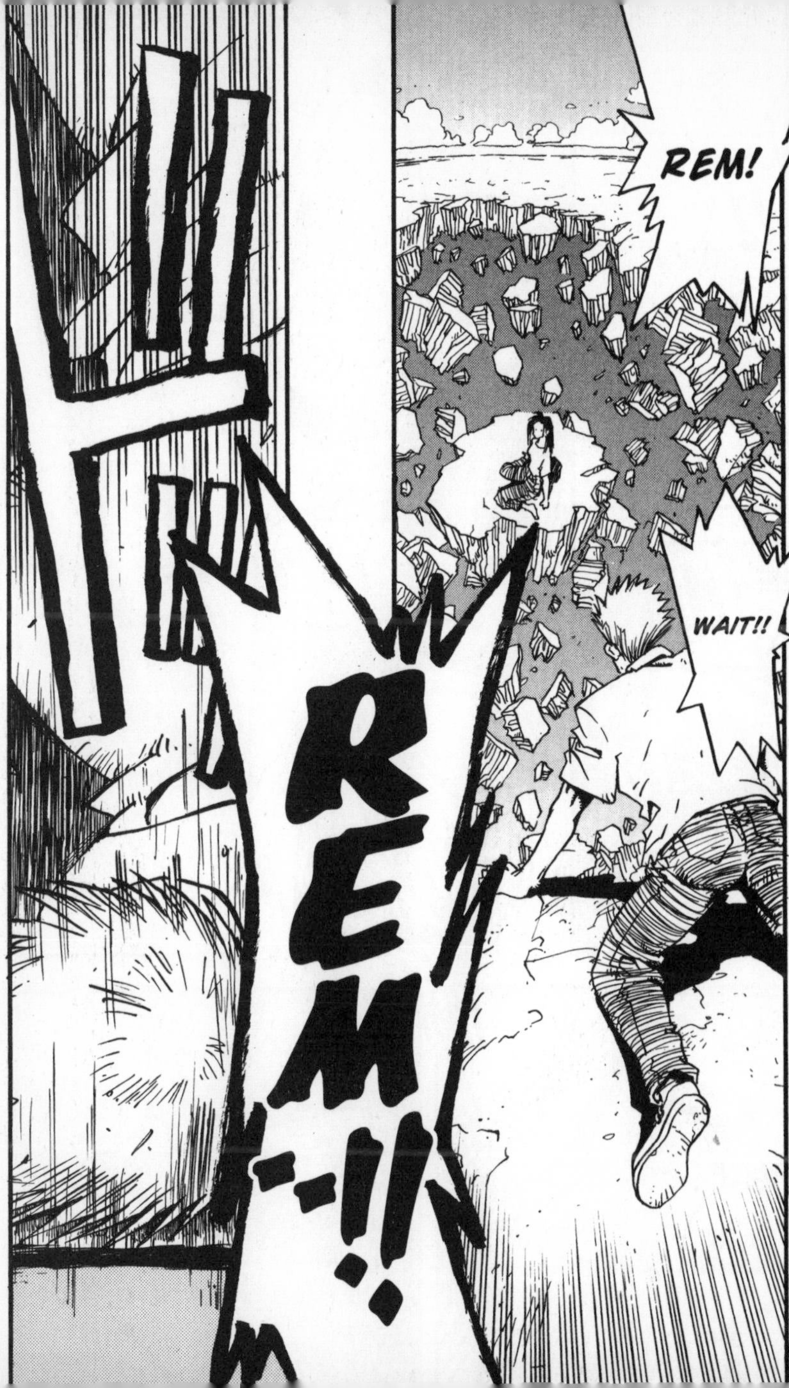
REM!
WAIT!!
REM--!!

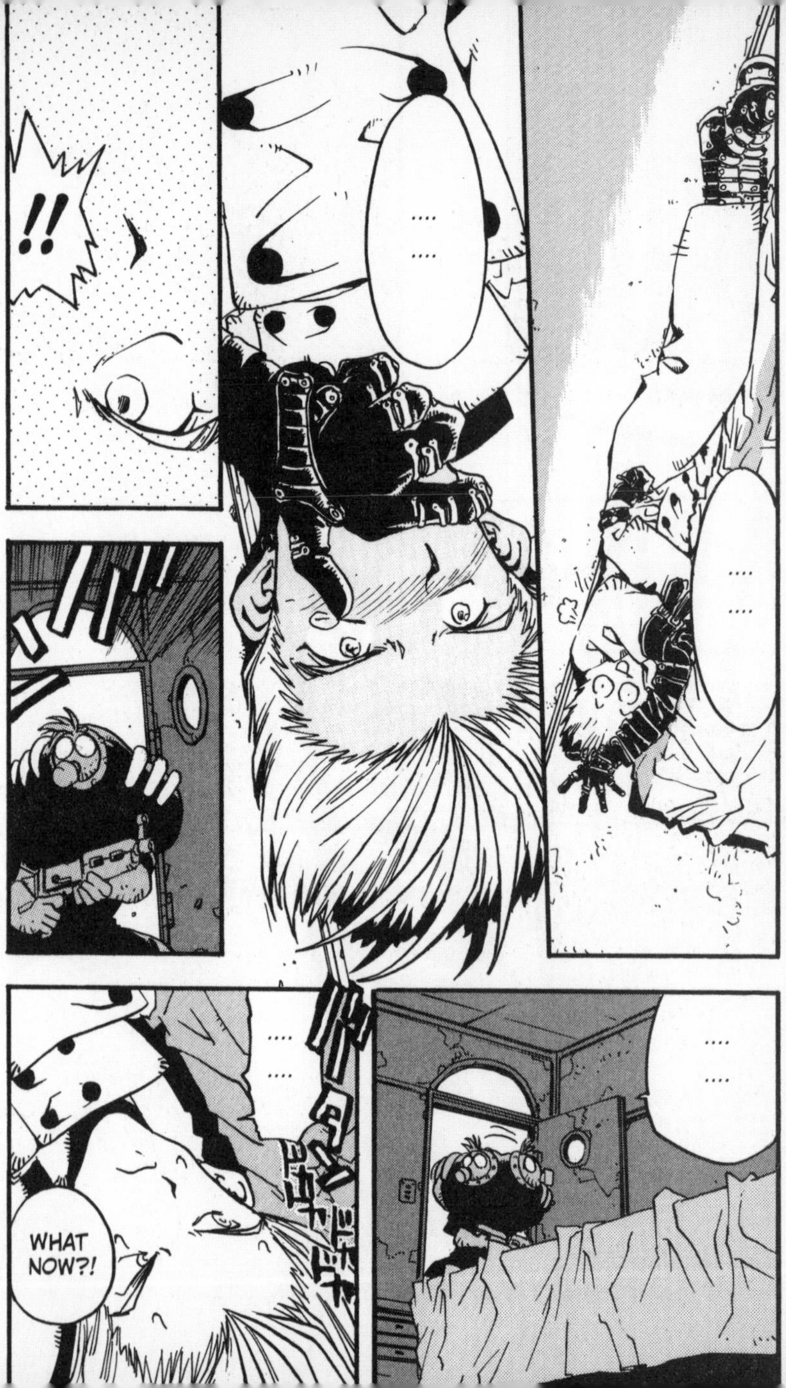

....
....
....
....
!!
....
....
....
....
WHAT NOW?!

BOSS!

?!

UGH!

IS THIS ALL? PATHETIC, BROKE VARMINTS!

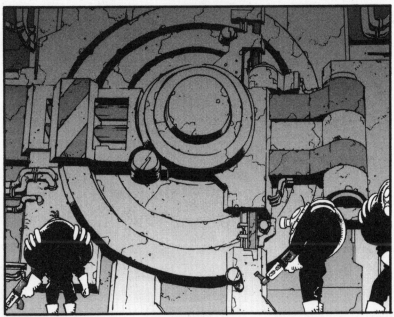

159

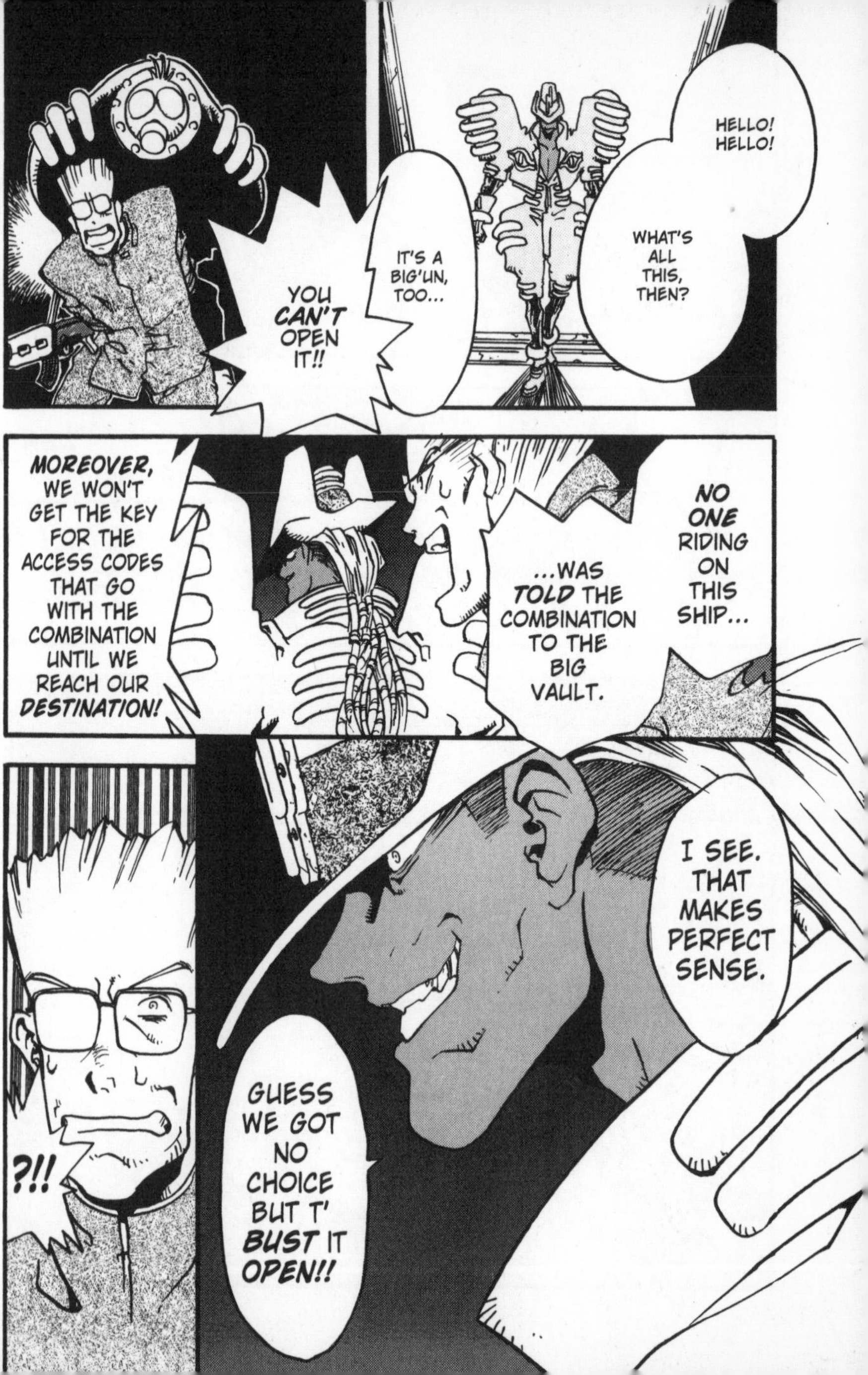
HELLO! HELLO!
WHAT'S ALL THIS, THEN?
IT'S A BIG'UN, TOO...
YOU *CAN'T* OPEN IT!!
*NO ONE* RIDING ON THIS SHIP...
...WAS *TOLD* THE COMBINATION TO THE BIG VAULT.
*MOREOVER,* WE WON'T GET THE KEY FOR THE ACCESS CODES THAT GO WITH THE COMBINATION UNTIL WE REACH OUR *DESTINATION!*
I SEE. THAT MAKES PERFECT SENSE.
GUESS WE GOT NO CHOICE BUT T' *BUST* IT *OPEN!!*
?!!

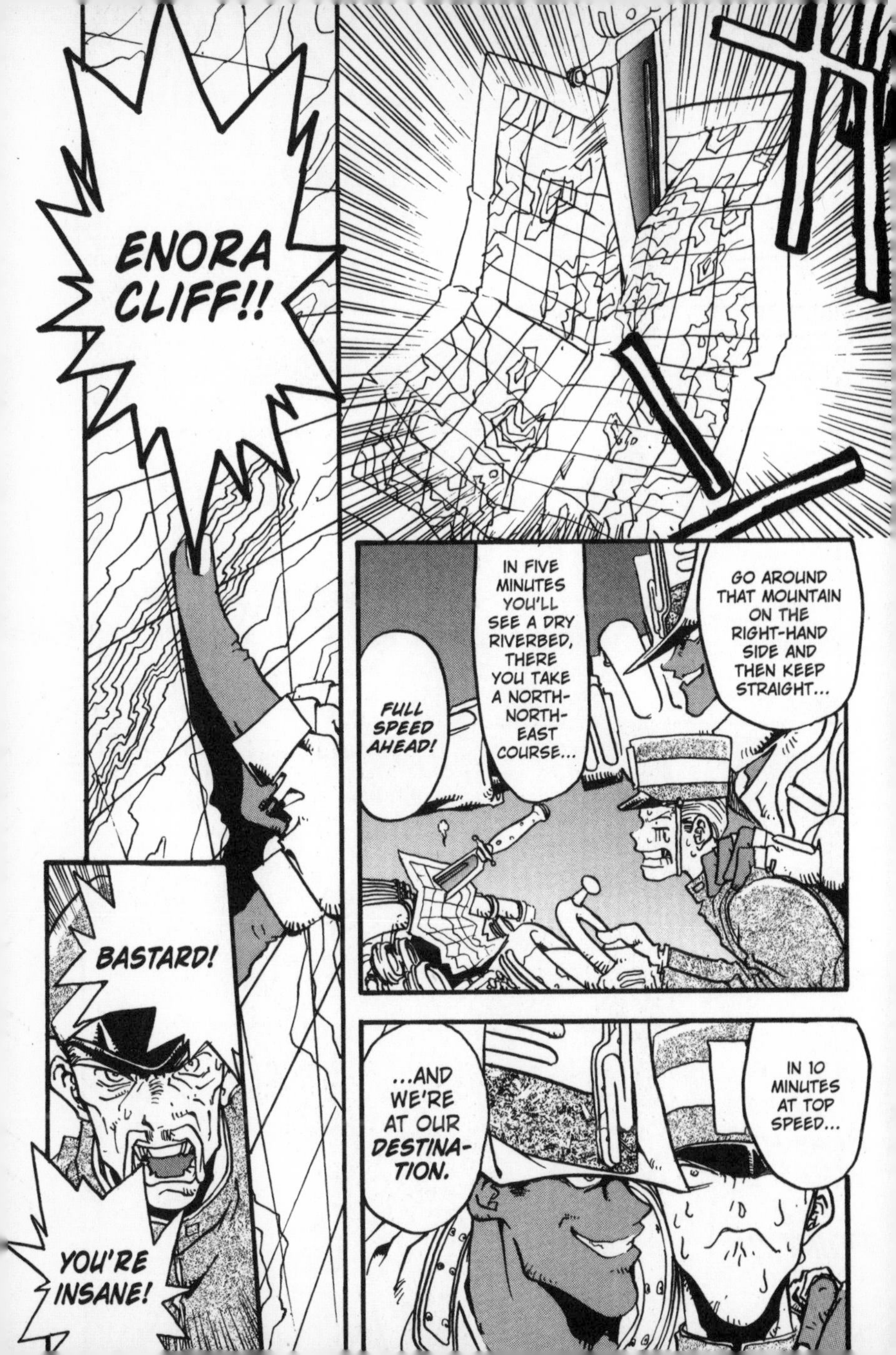
GO AROUND THAT MOUNTAIN ON THE RIGHT-HAND SIDE AND THEN KEEP STRAIGHT...
IN FIVE MINUTES YOU'LL SEE A DRY RIVERBED, THERE YOU TAKE A NORTH-NORTH-EAST COURSE...
FULL SPEED AHEAD!
IN 10 MINUTES AT TOP SPEED...
...AND WE'RE AT OUR DESTINATION.
ENORA CLIFF!!
BASTARD!
YOU'RE INSANE!

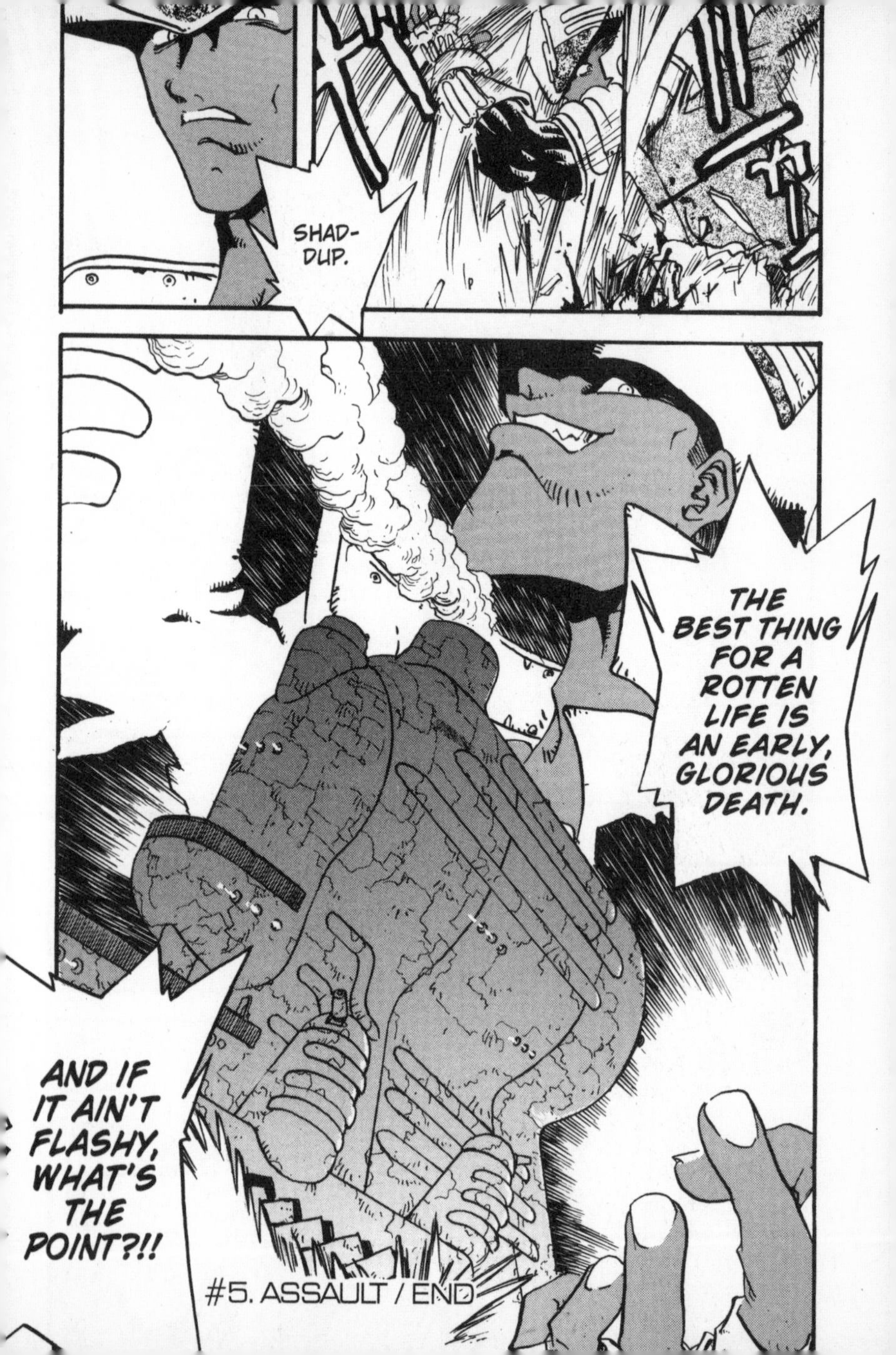
SHAD-DUP.
THE BEST THING FOR A ROTTEN LIFE IS AN EARLY, GLORIOUS DEATH.
AND IF IT AIN'T FLASHY, WHAT'S THE POINT?!!
#5. ASSAULT / END

#6

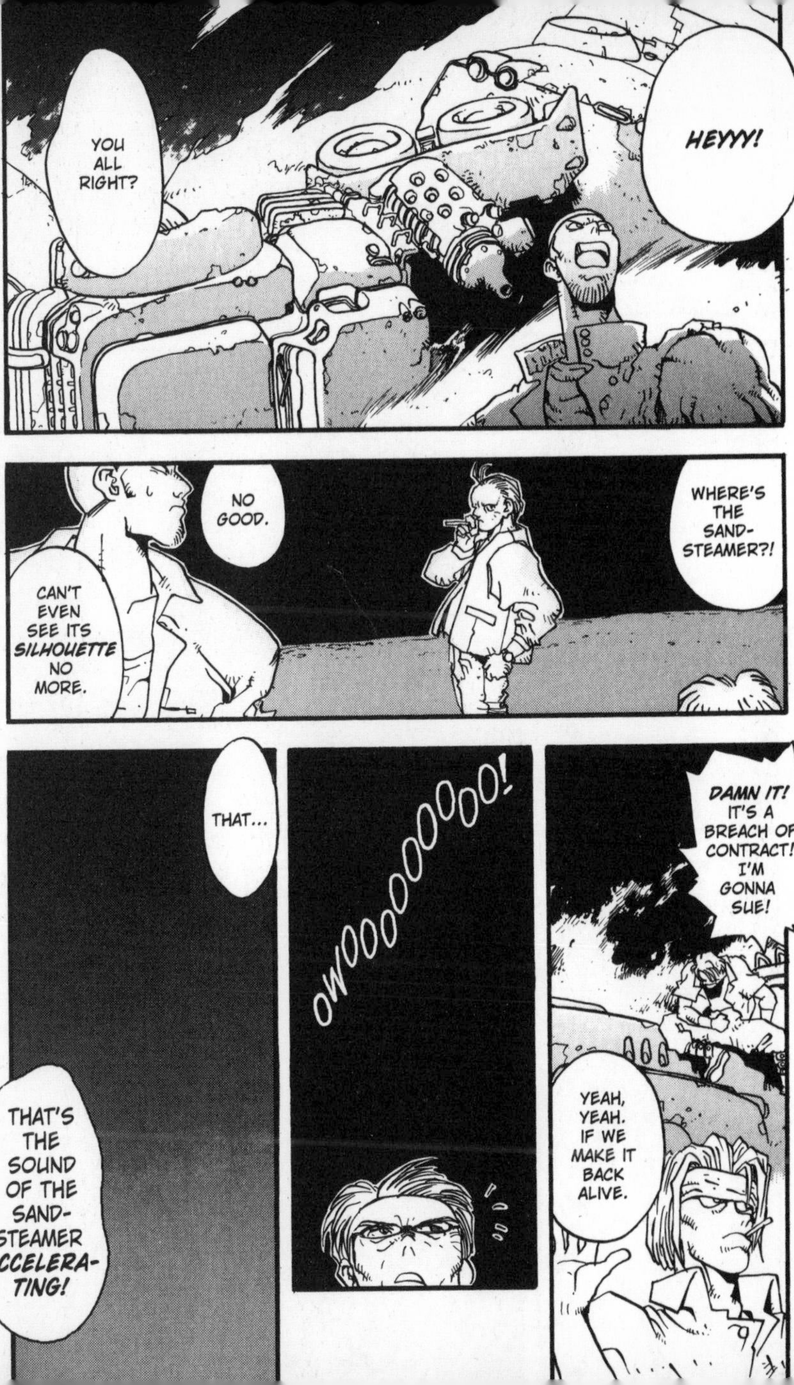
HEYYY!
YOU ALL RIGHT?
WHERE'S THE SAND-STEAMER?!
NO GOOD.
CAN'T EVEN SEE ITS SILHOUETTE NO MORE.
DAMN IT! IT'S A BREACH OF CONTRACT! I'M GONNA SUE!
YEAH, YEAH. IF WE MAKE IT BACK ALIVE.
THAT...
OWOOOOOOOOOOOO!
THAT'S THE SOUND OF THE SAND-STEAMER ACCELERATING!

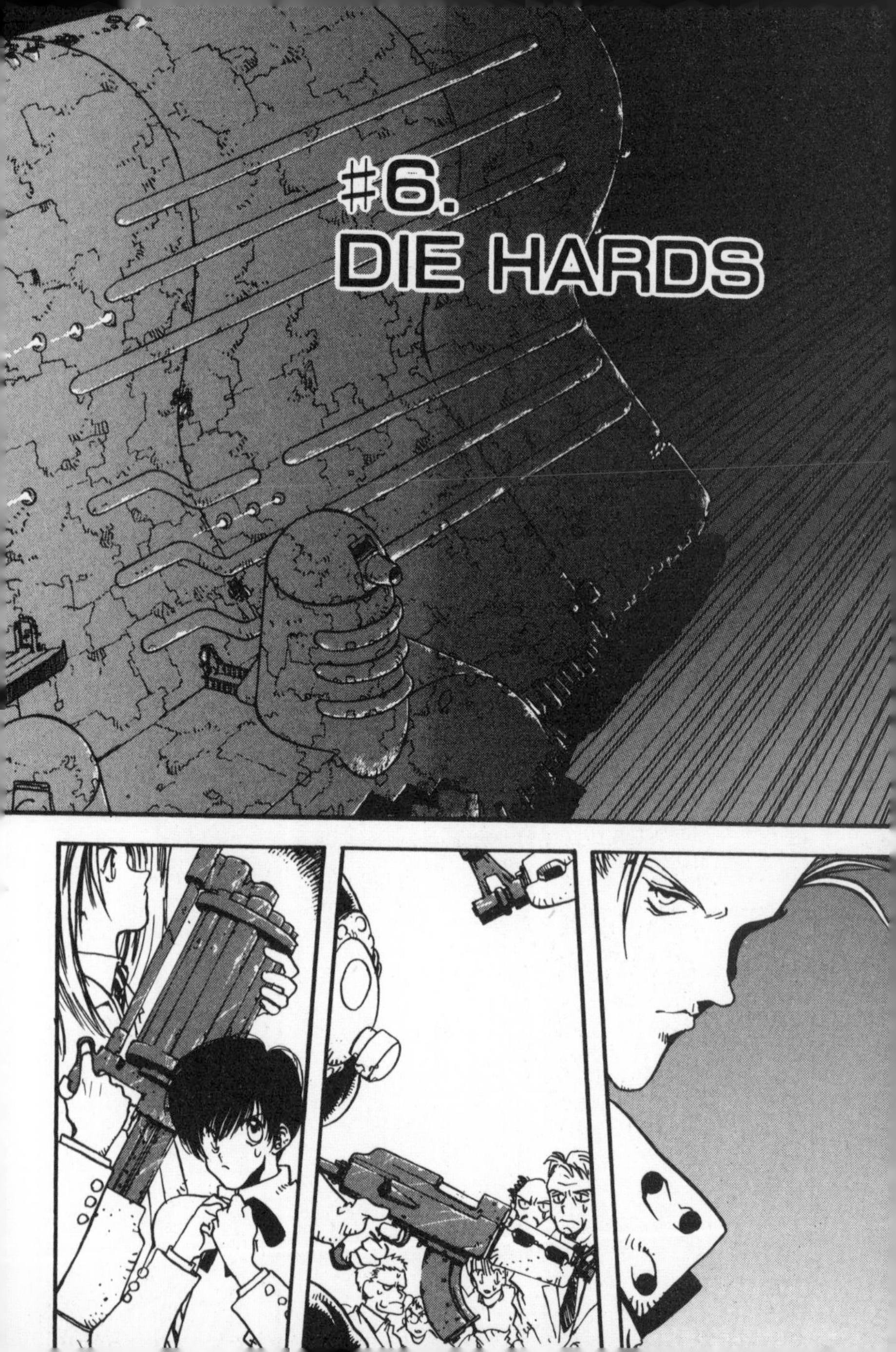
#6.
DIE HARDS

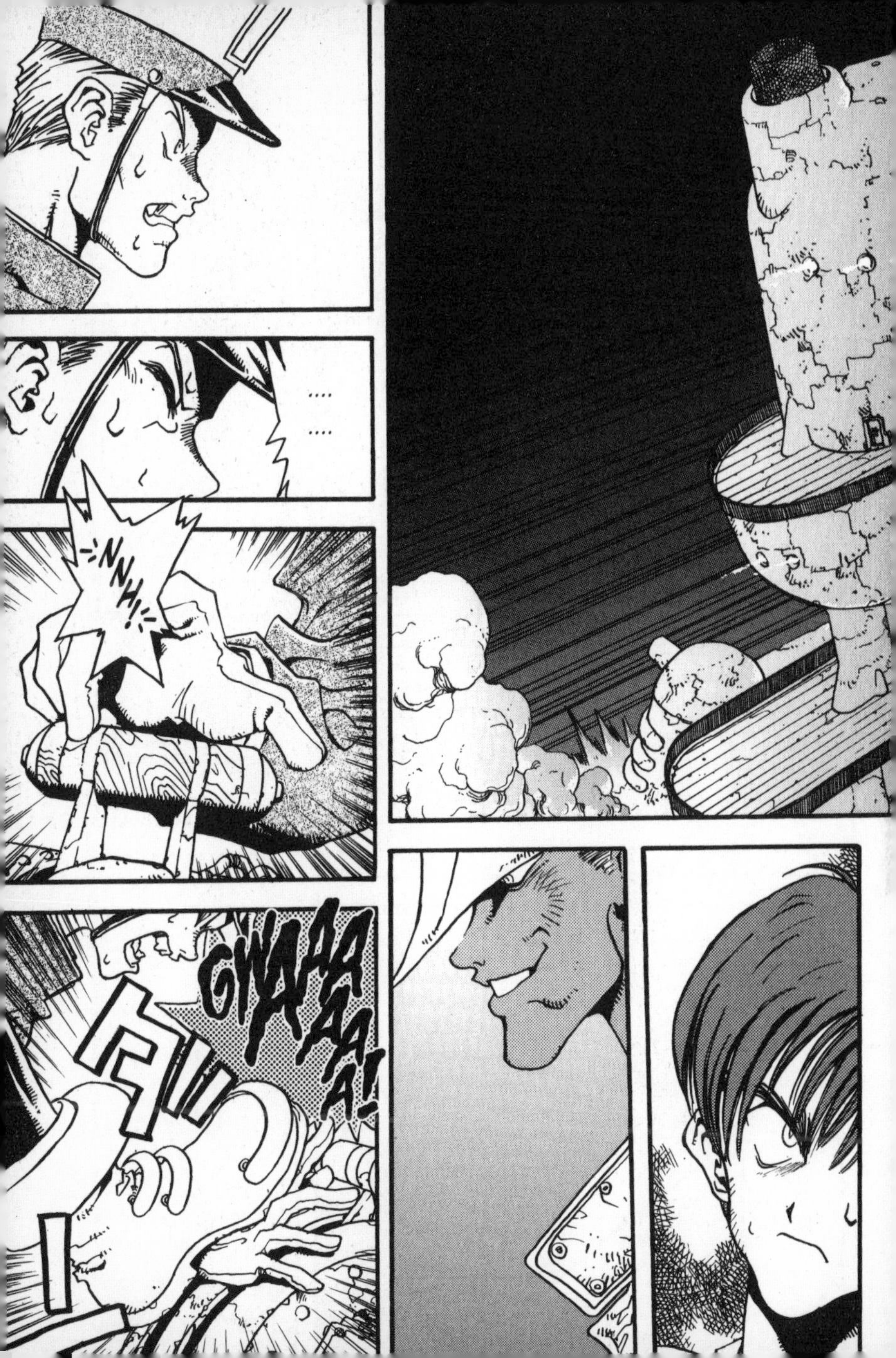
....
....
NNH!!
GWAAAAAA!!

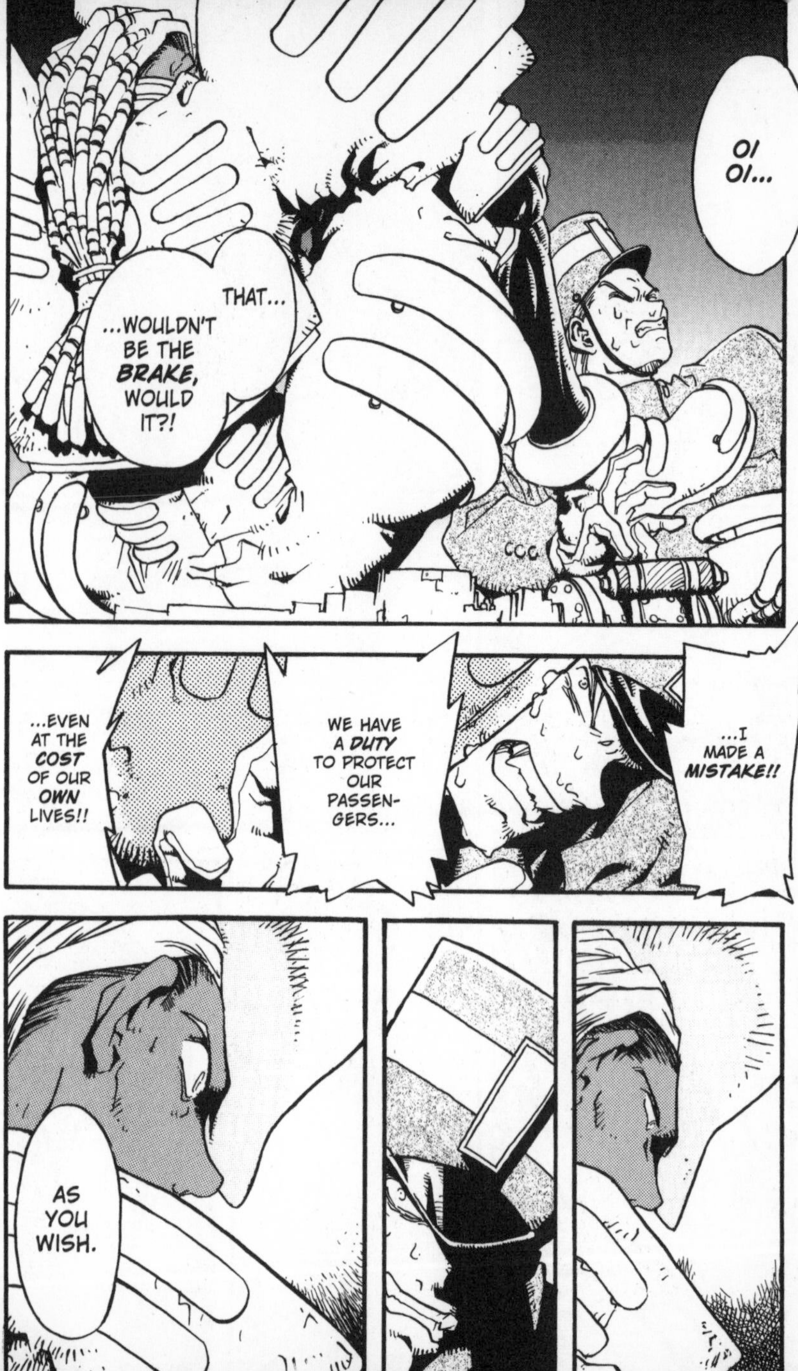
OI OI...
THAT...
...WOULDN'T BE THE BRAKE, WOULD IT?!
...I MADE A MISTAKE!!
WE HAVE A DUTY TO PROTECT OUR PASSENGERS...
...EVEN AT THE COST OF OUR OWN LIVES!!
AS YOU WISH.

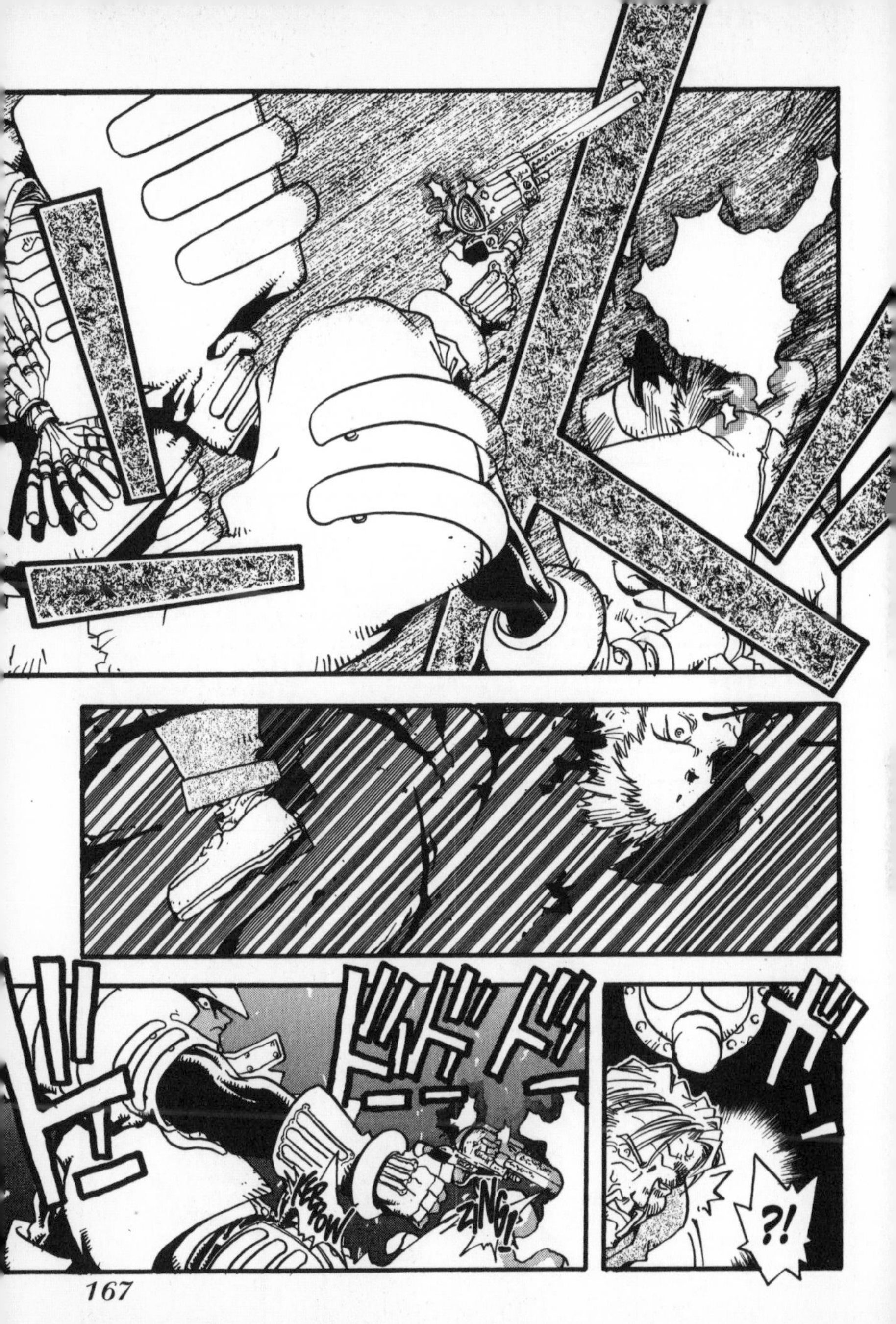
?!
ZING!
KERPOW!

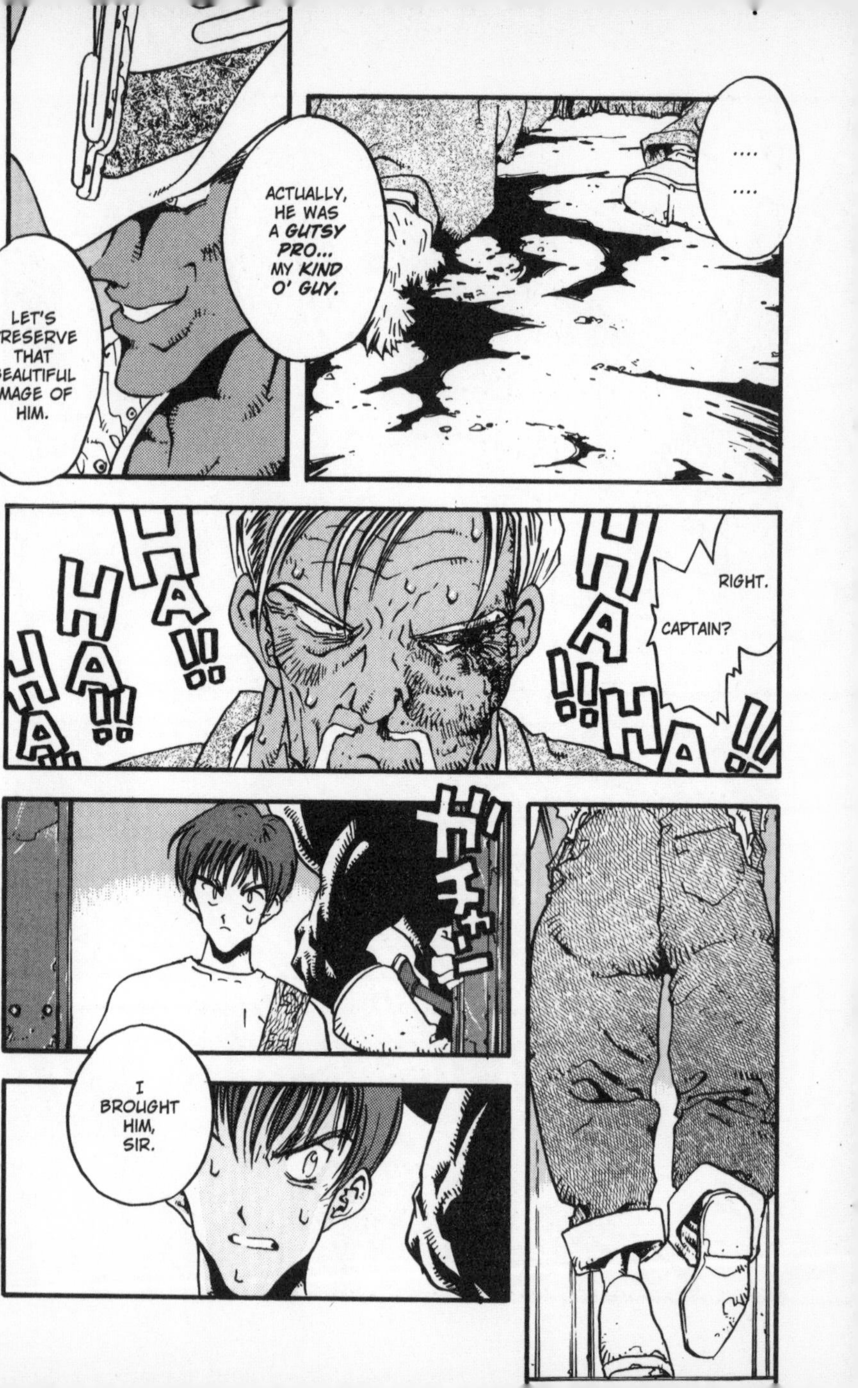
....
....
ACTUALLY, HE WAS A GUTSY PRO... MY KIND O' GUY.
LET'S PRESERVE THAT BEAUTIFUL IMAGE OF HIM.
RIGHT.
CAPTAIN?
HA!! HA!!
HA!! HA!! HA!! HA...
ガチャー
I BROUGHT HIM, SIR.

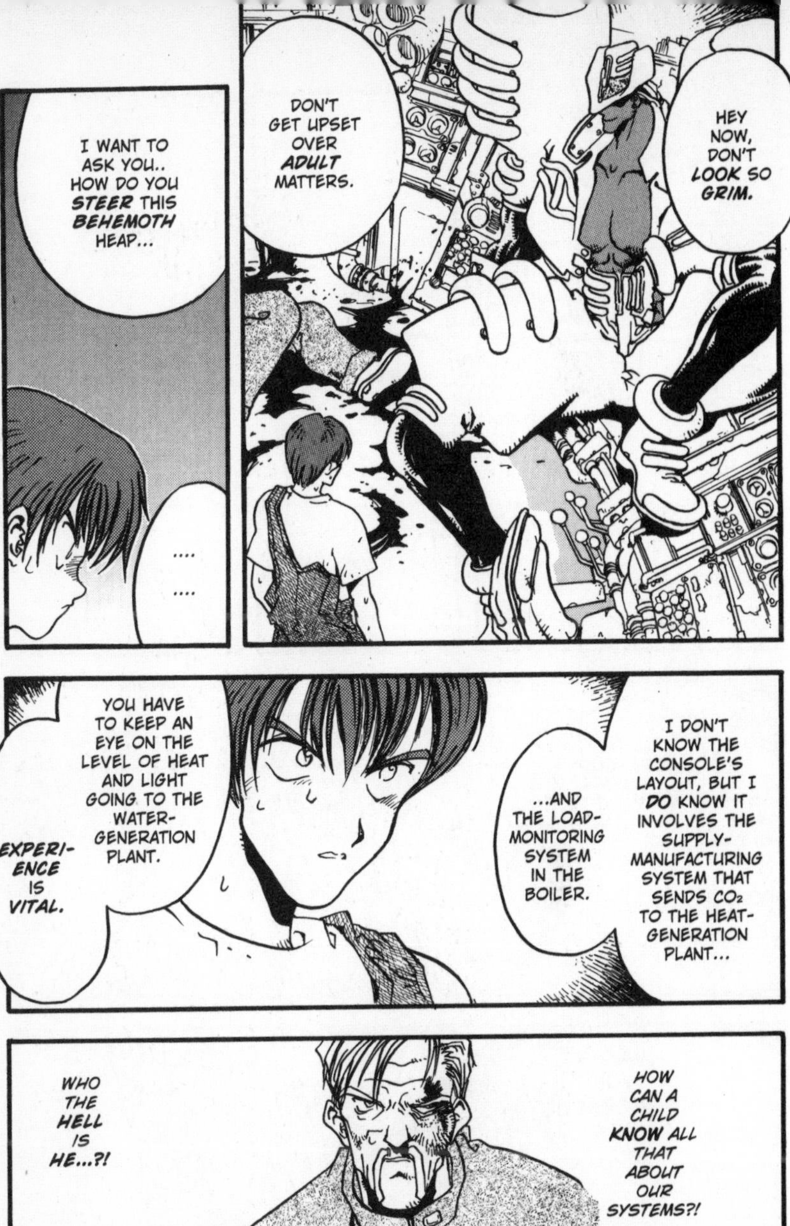
HEY NOW, DON'T LOOK SO GRIM.
DON'T GET UPSET OVER ADULT MATTERS.
I WANT TO ASK YOU.. HOW DO YOU STEER THIS BEHEMOTH HEAP...
....
....
I DON'T KNOW THE CONSOLE'S LAYOUT, BUT I DO KNOW IT INVOLVES THE SUPPLY-MANUFACTURING SYSTEM THAT SENDS $CO_2$ TO THE HEAT-GENERATION PLANT...
...AND THE LOAD-MONITORING SYSTEM IN THE BOILER.
YOU HAVE TO KEEP AN EYE ON THE LEVEL OF HEAT AND LIGHT GOING TO THE WATER-GENERATION PLANT.
EXPERIENCE IS VITAL.
HOW CAN A CHILD KNOW ALL THAT ABOUT OUR SYSTEMS?!
WHO THE HELL IS HE...?!

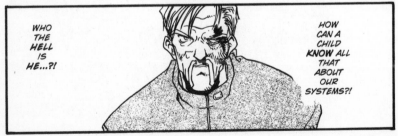

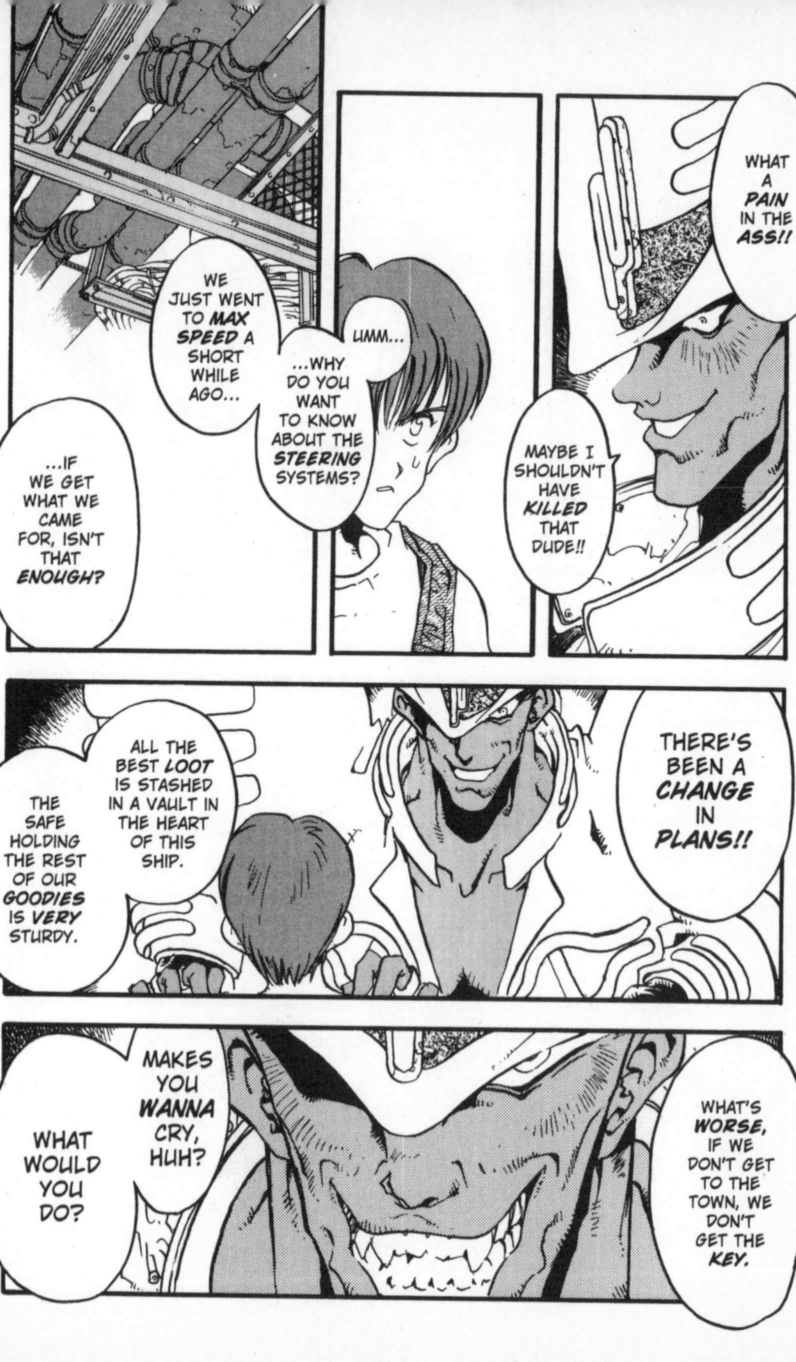
WHAT A PAIN IN THE ASS!!
MAYBE I SHOULDN'T HAVE KILLED THAT DUDE!!
UMM...
...WHY DO YOU WANT TO KNOW ABOUT THE STEERING SYSTEMS?
WE JUST WENT TO MAX SPEED A SHORT WHILE AGO...
...IF WE GET WHAT WE CAME FOR, ISN'T THAT ENOUGH?
THERE'S BEEN A CHANGE IN PLANS!!
ALL THE BEST LOOT IS STASHED IN A VAULT IN THE HEART OF THIS SHIP.
THE SAFE HOLDING THE REST OF OUR GOODIES IS VERY STURDY.
WHAT'S WORSE, IF WE DON'T GET TO THE TOWN, WE DON'T GET THE KEY.
MAKES YOU WANNA CRY, HUH?
WHAT WOULD YOU DO?

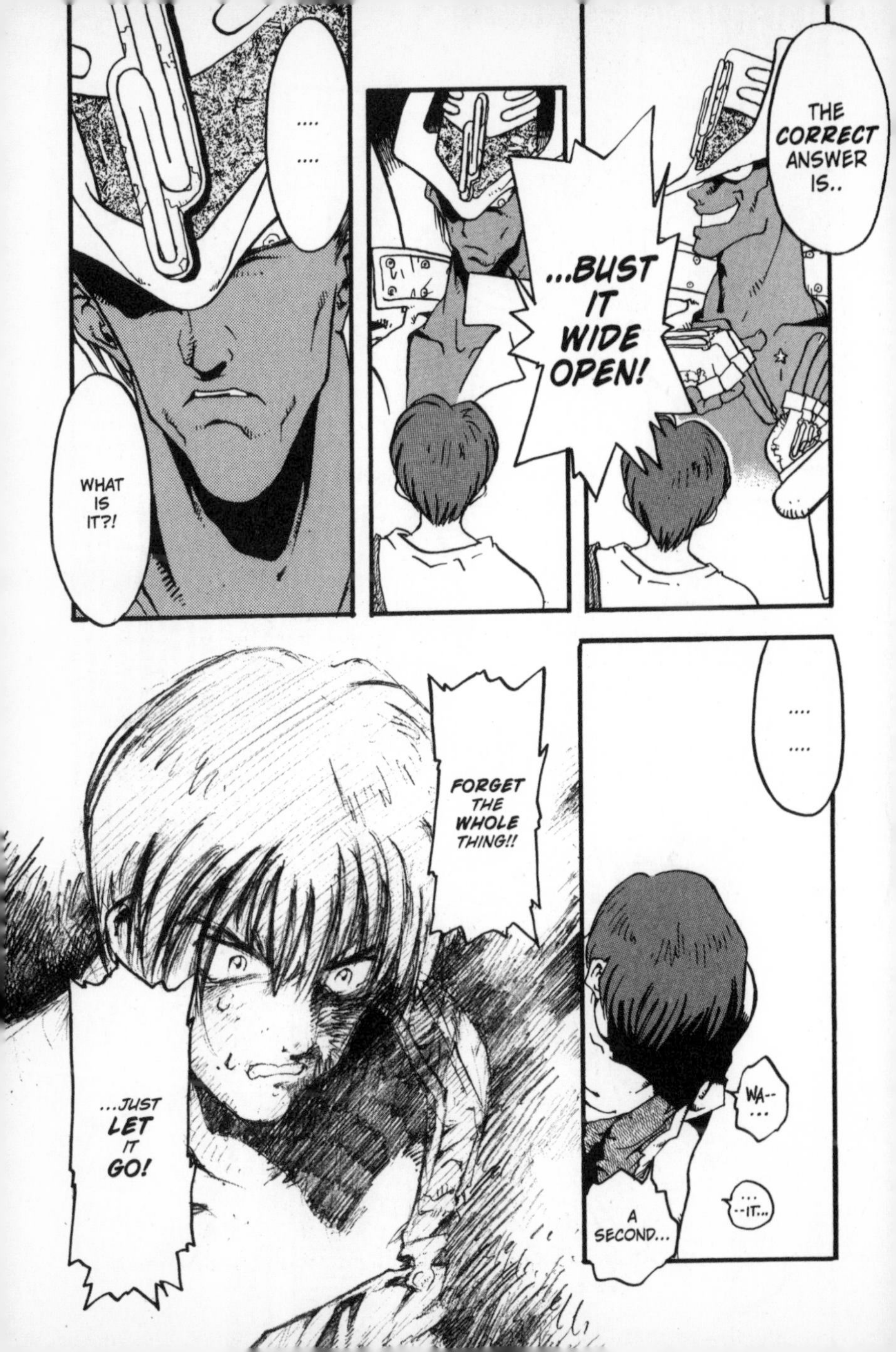
THE CORRECT ANSWER IS..
...BUST IT WIDE OPEN!
....
....
WHAT IS IT?!
....
....
WA-- ...
... --IT...
A SECOND...
FORGET THE WHOLE THING!!
...JUST LET IT GO!

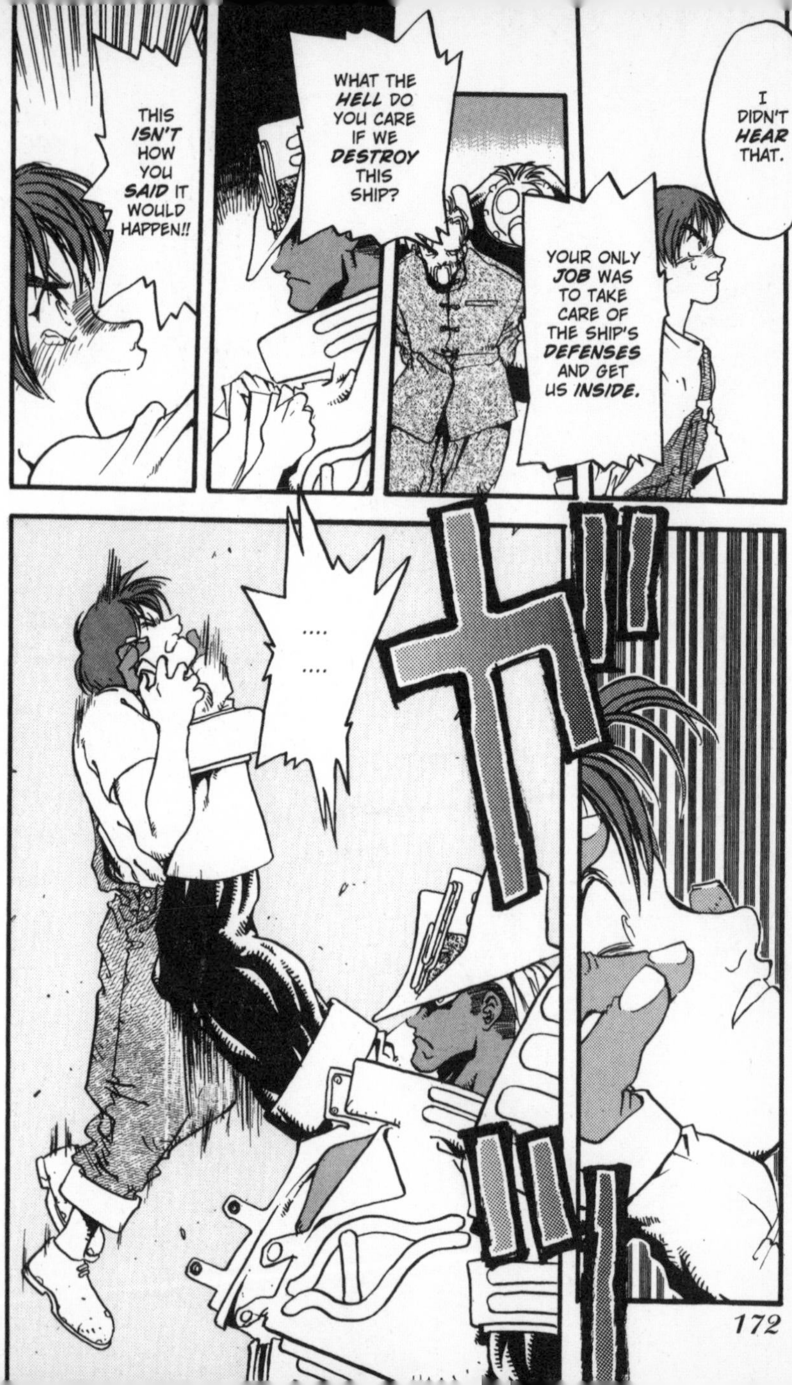
I DIDN'T HEAR THAT.
YOUR ONLY JOB WAS TO TAKE CARE OF THE SHIP'S DEFENSES AND GET US INSIDE.
WHAT THE HELL DO YOU CARE IF WE DESTROY THIS SHIP?
THIS ISN'T HOW YOU SAID IT WOULD HAPPEN!!
....
....

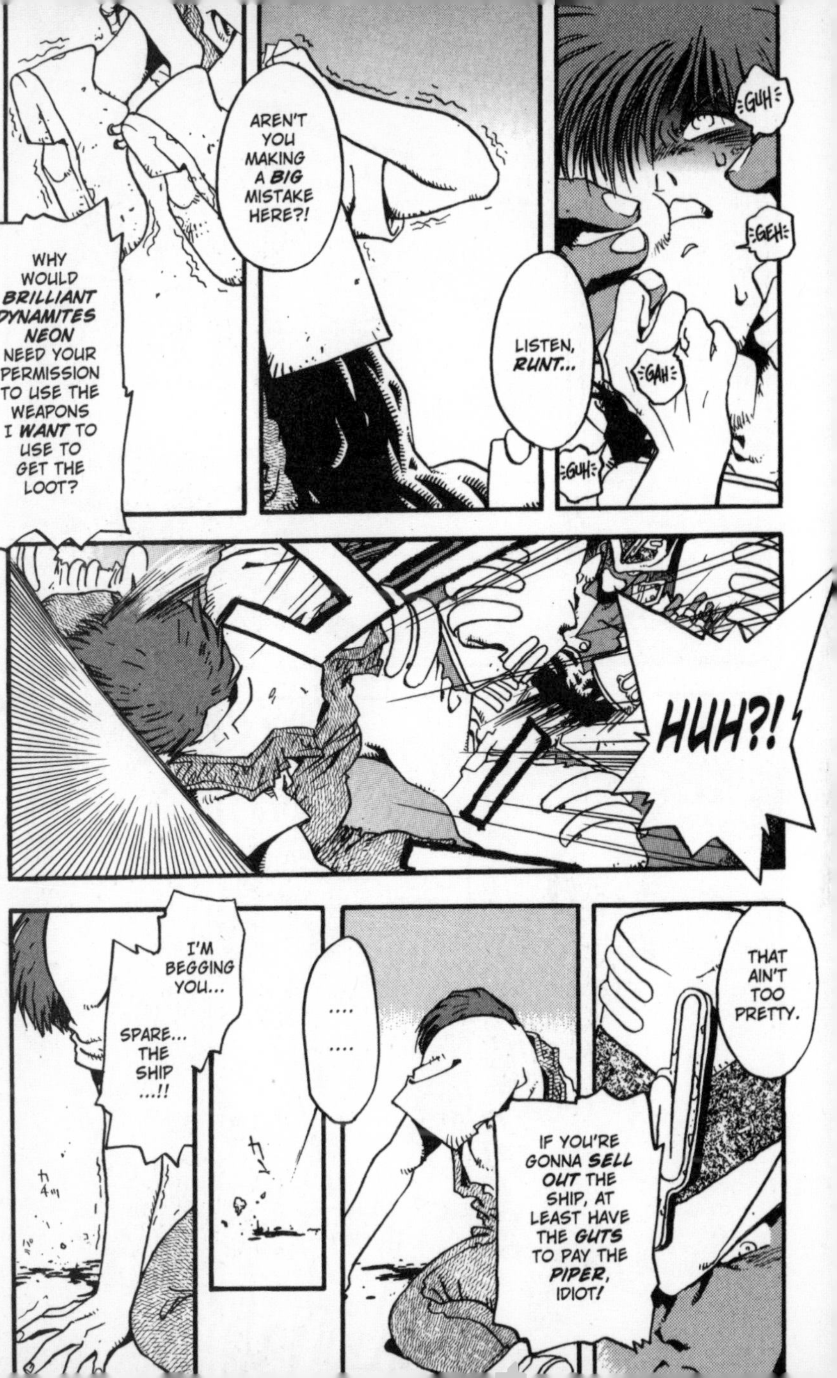
GUH
GEH
GAH
GUH
LISTEN, RUNT...
AREN'T YOU MAKING A BIG MISTAKE HERE?!
WHY WOULD BRILLIANT DYNAMITES NEON NEED YOUR PERMISSION TO USE THE WEAPONS I WANT TO USE TO GET THE LOOT?
HUH?!
THAT AIN'T TOO PRETTY.
IF YOU'RE GONNA SELL OUT THE SHIP, AT LEAST HAVE THE GUTS TO PAY THE PIPER, IDIOT!
....
....
I'M BEGGING YOU...
SPARE... THE SHIP ...!!

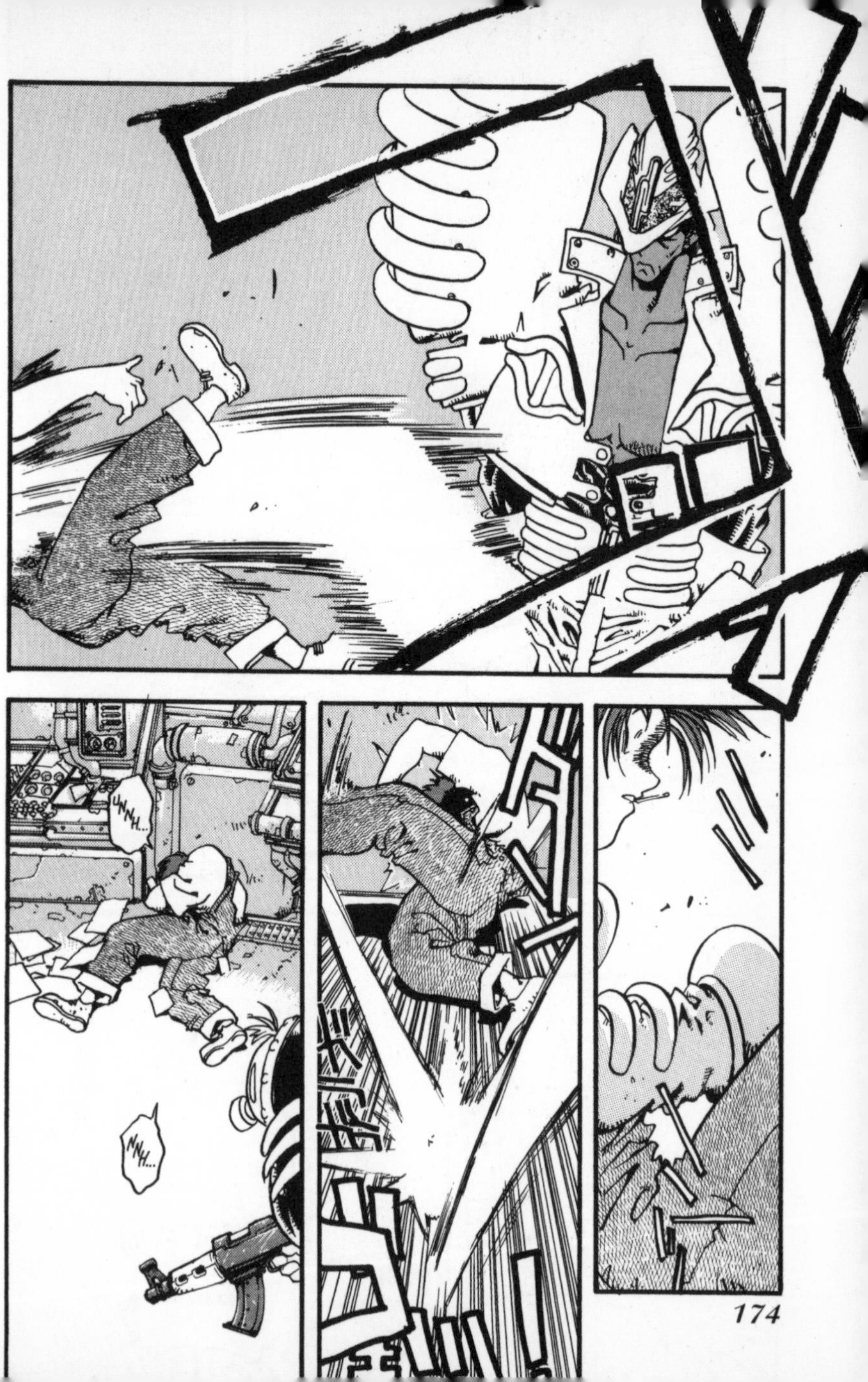
UNNH...
NNH...

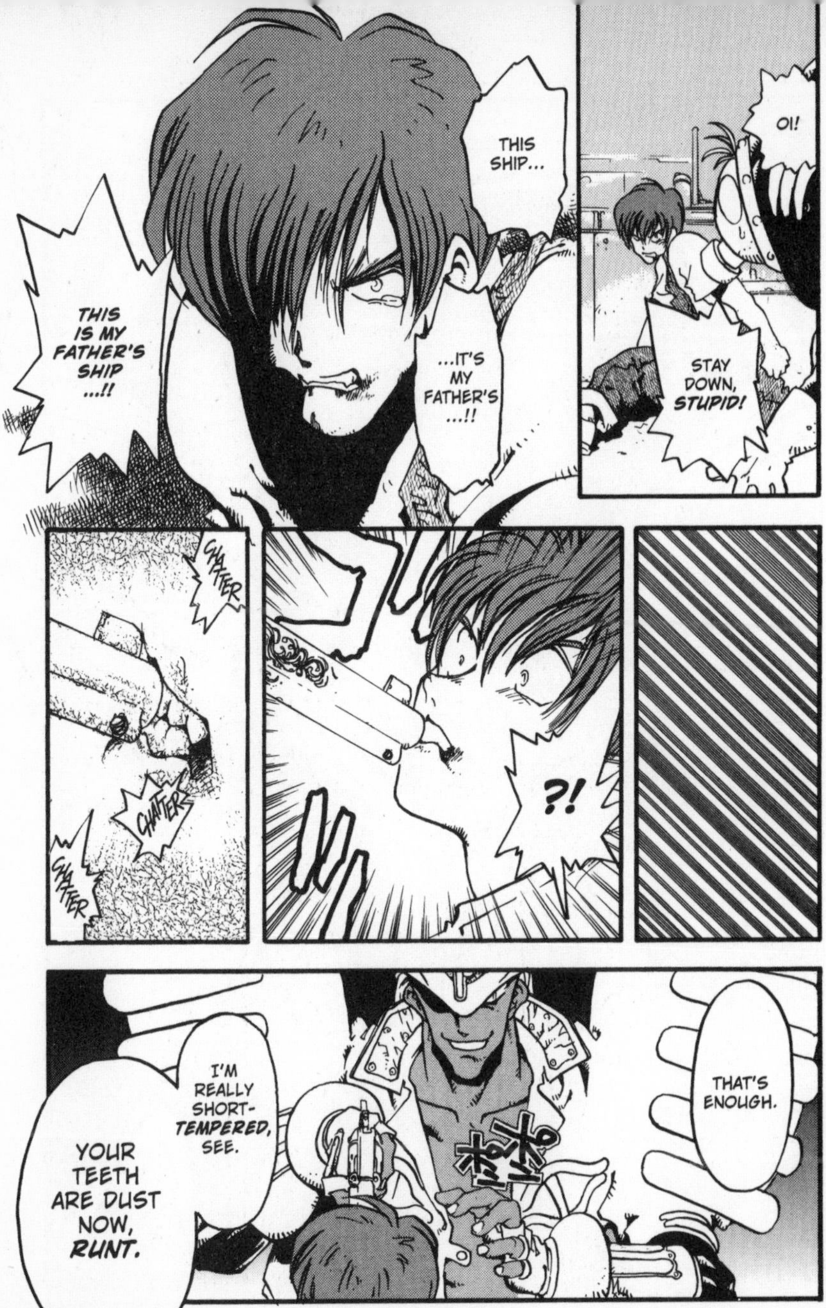
OI!
STAY DOWN, STUPID!
THIS SHIP...
...IT'S MY FATHER'S ...!!
THIS IS MY FATHER'S SHIP ...!!
?!
CHATTER
CHATTER
CHATTER
THAT'S ENOUGH.
I'M REALLY SHORT-TEMPERED, SEE.
YOUR TEETH ARE DUST NOW, RUNT.

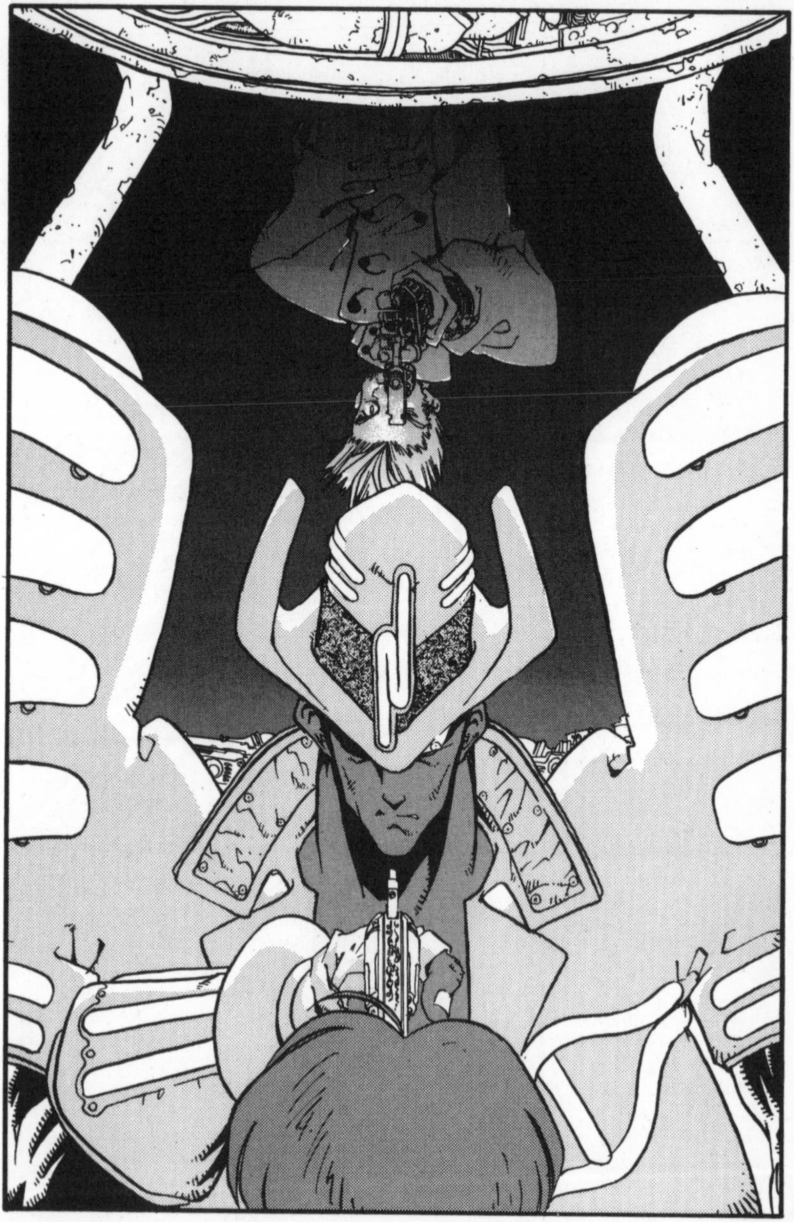

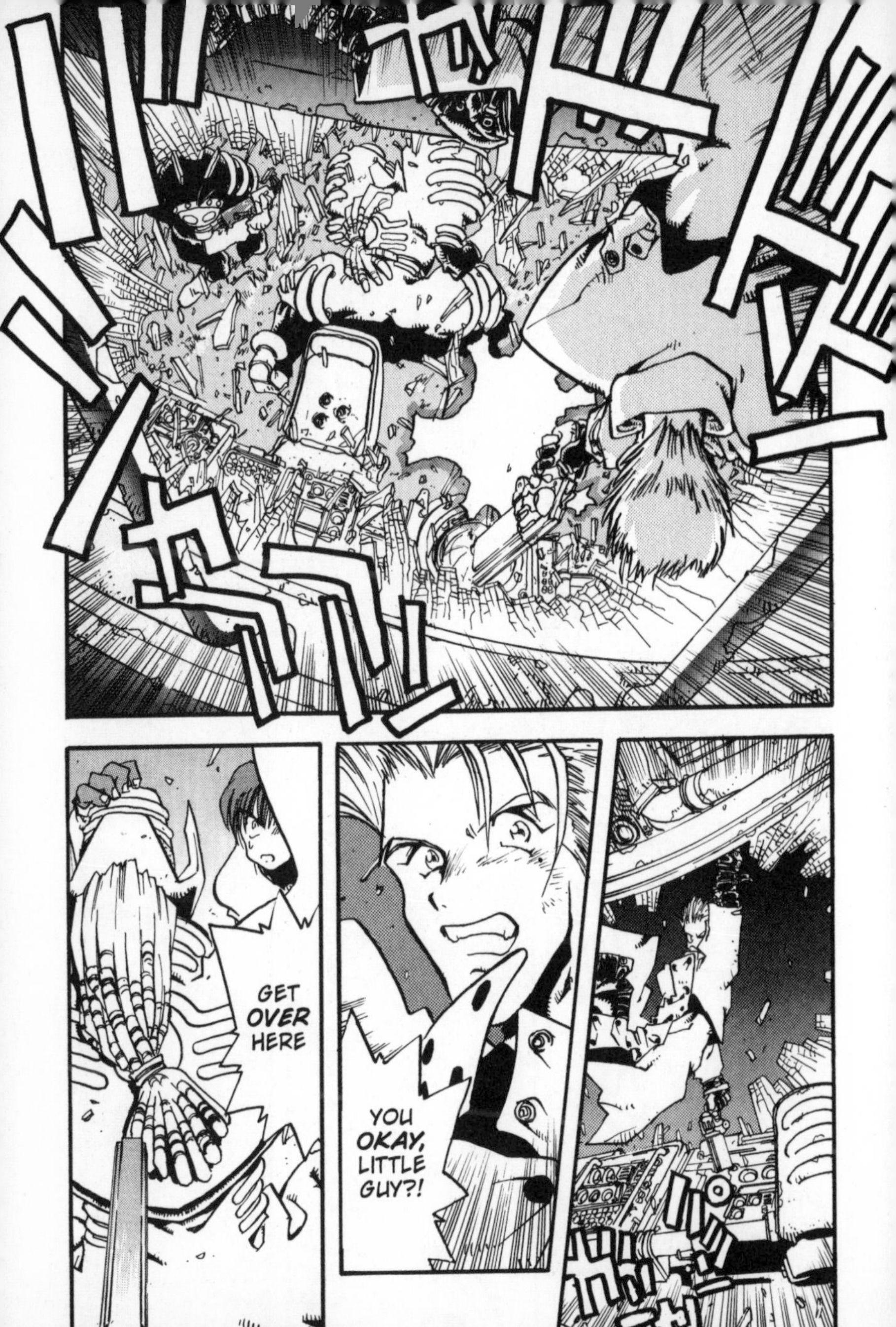
YOU OKAY, LITTLE GUY?!
GET OVER HERE

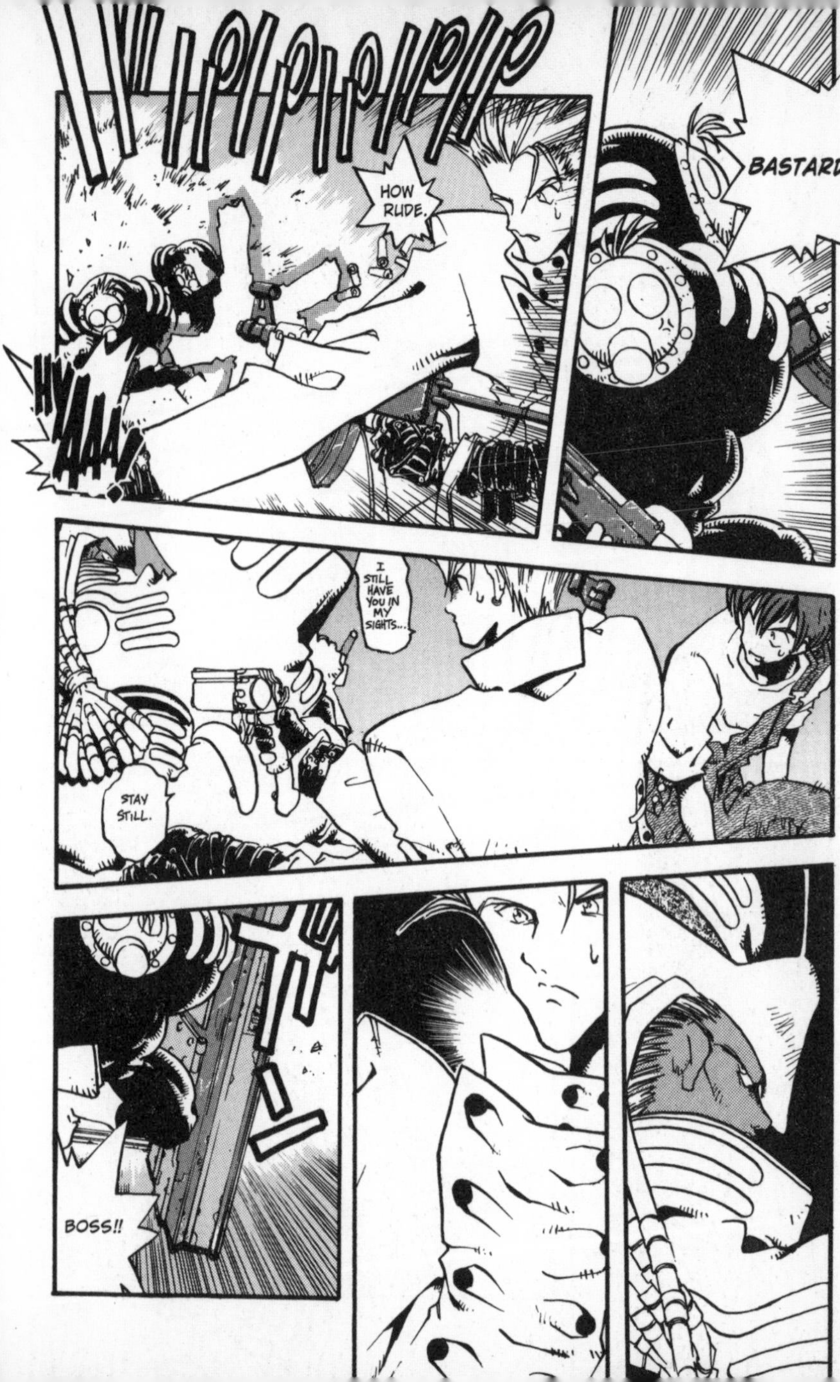
BASTARD!
HOW RUDE.
HYAAAA!
I STILL HAVE YOU IN MY SIGHTS...
STAY STILL.
BOSS!!

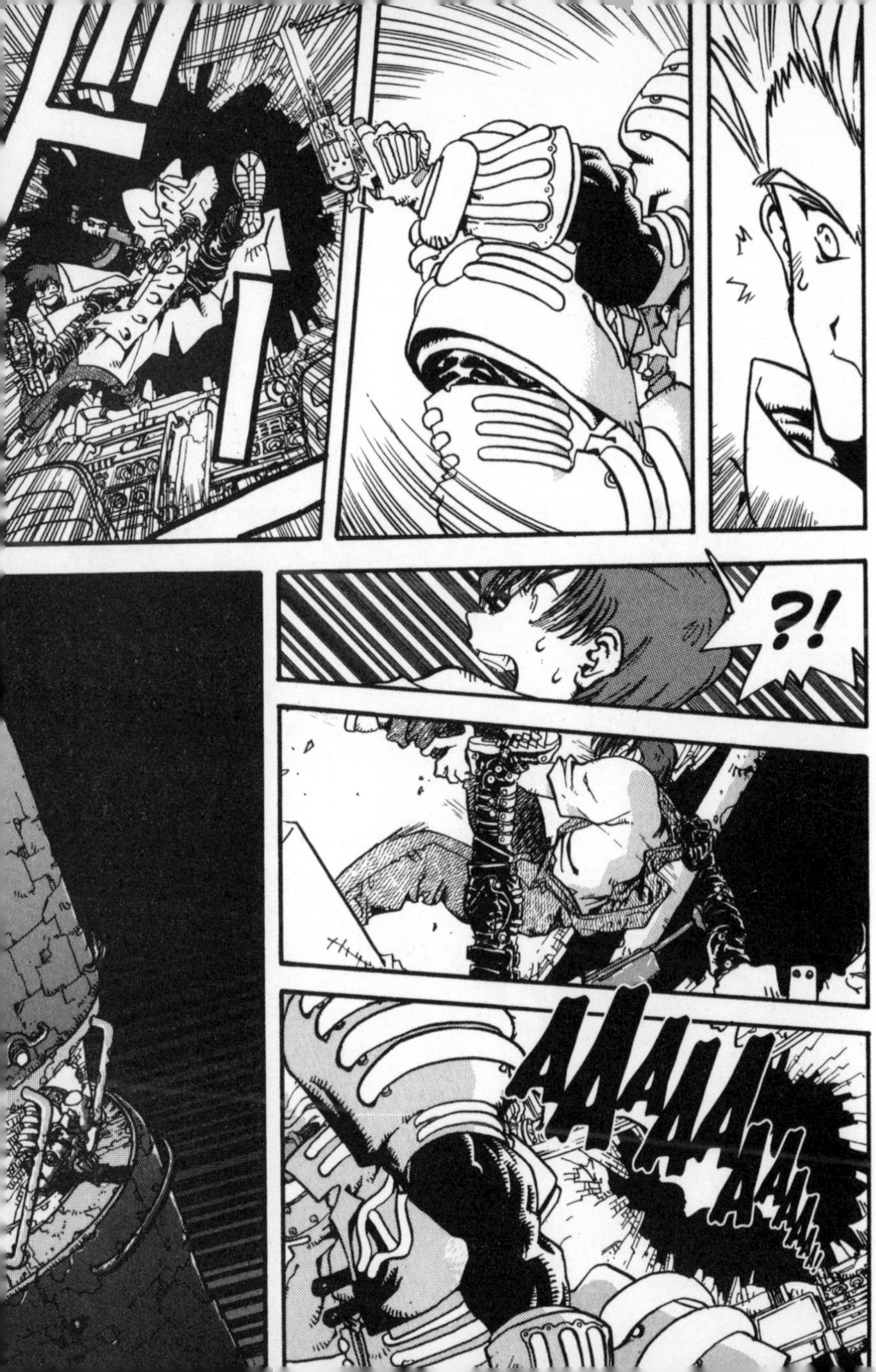
?!
AAAAAAAAA

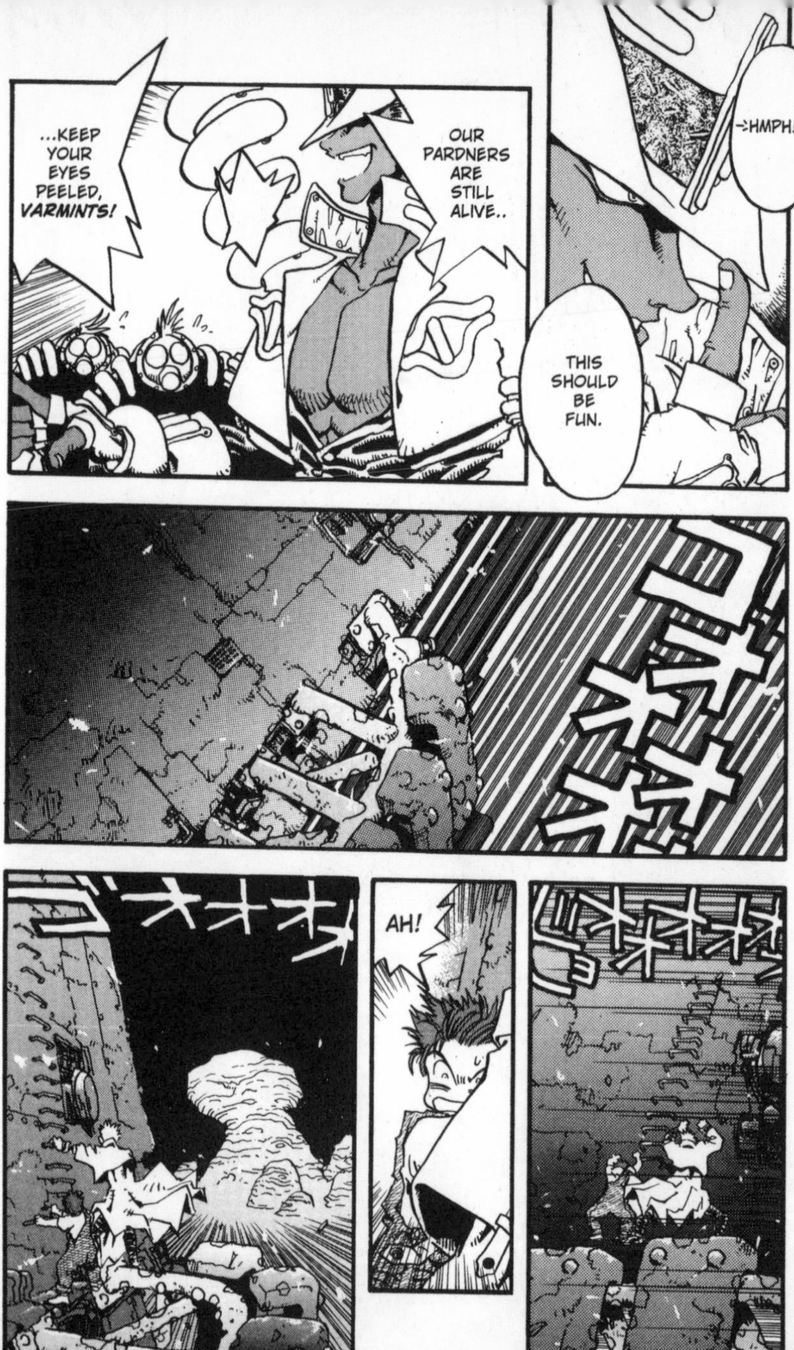
-HMPH!-
THIS SHOULD BE FUN.
OUR PARDNERS ARE STILL ALIVE..
...KEEP YOUR EYES PEELED, VARMINTS!
AH!

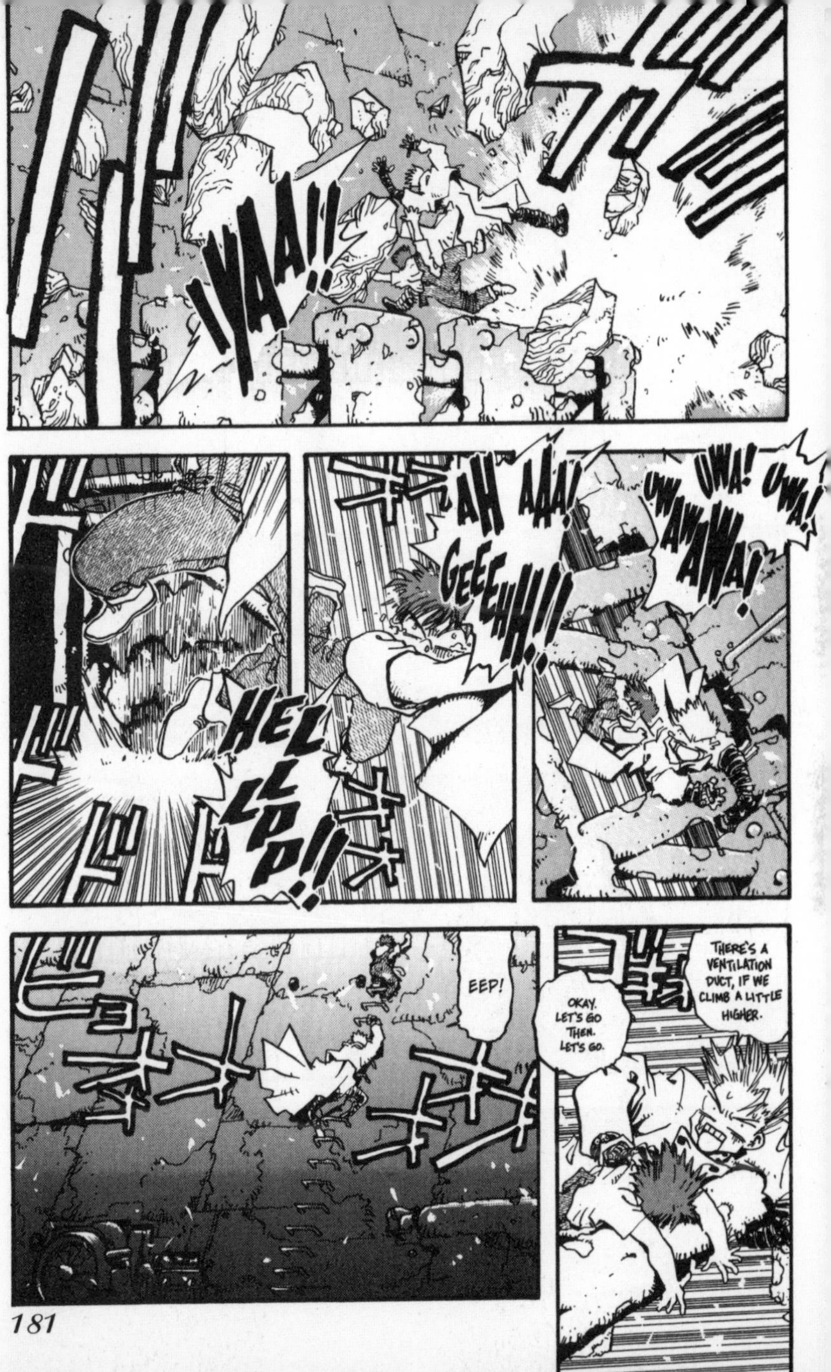
¡YAA!!
UWA! UWA!
UWAWAWA AWA!
AH AAA!
GEEEHH!!
HELLLPP!!
THERE'S A VENTILATION DUCT, IF WE CLIMB A LITTLE HIGHER.
OKAY. LET'S GO THEN. LET'S GO.
EEP!

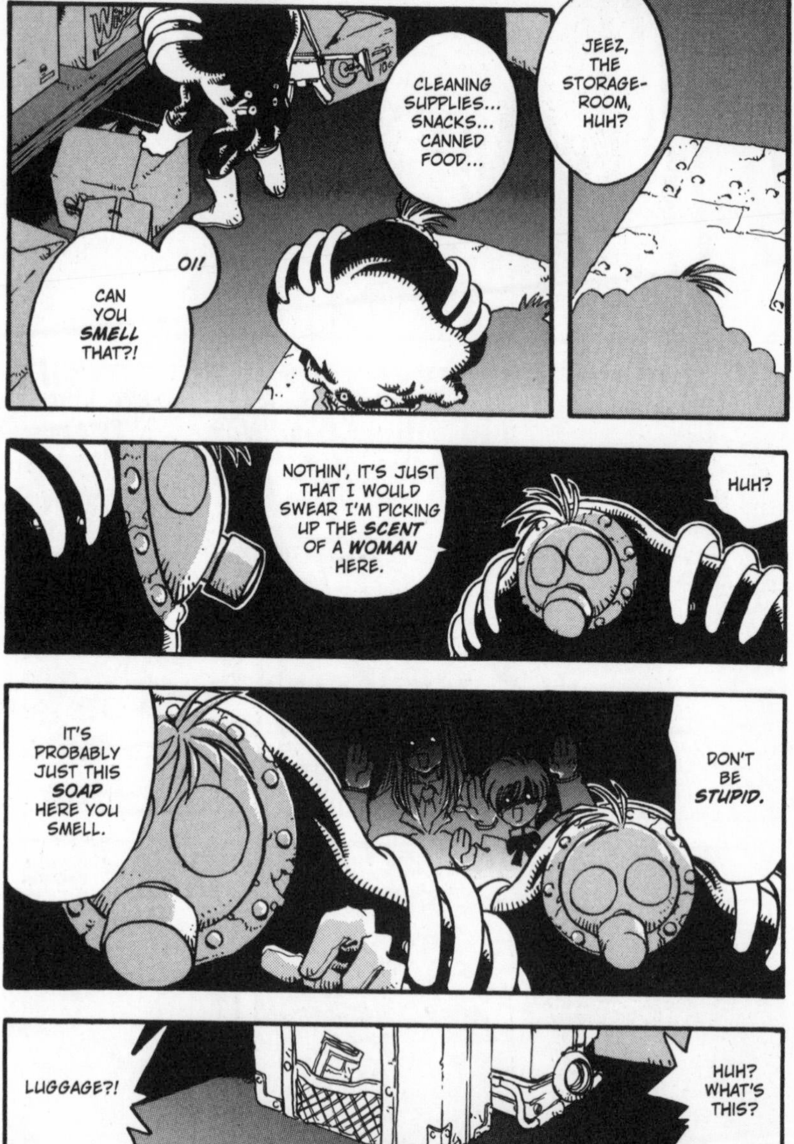
JEEZ, THE STORAGE-ROOM, HUH?
CLEANING SUPPLIES... SNACKS... CANNED FOOD...
OI!
CAN YOU SMELL THAT?!
HUH?
NOTHIN', IT'S JUST THAT I WOULD SWEAR I'M PICKING UP THE SCENT OF A WOMAN HERE.
DON'T BE STUPID.
IT'S PROBABLY JUST THIS SOAP HERE YOU SMELL.
HUH? WHAT'S THIS?
LUGGAGE?!

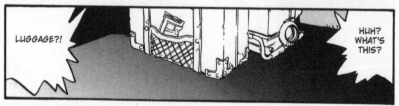

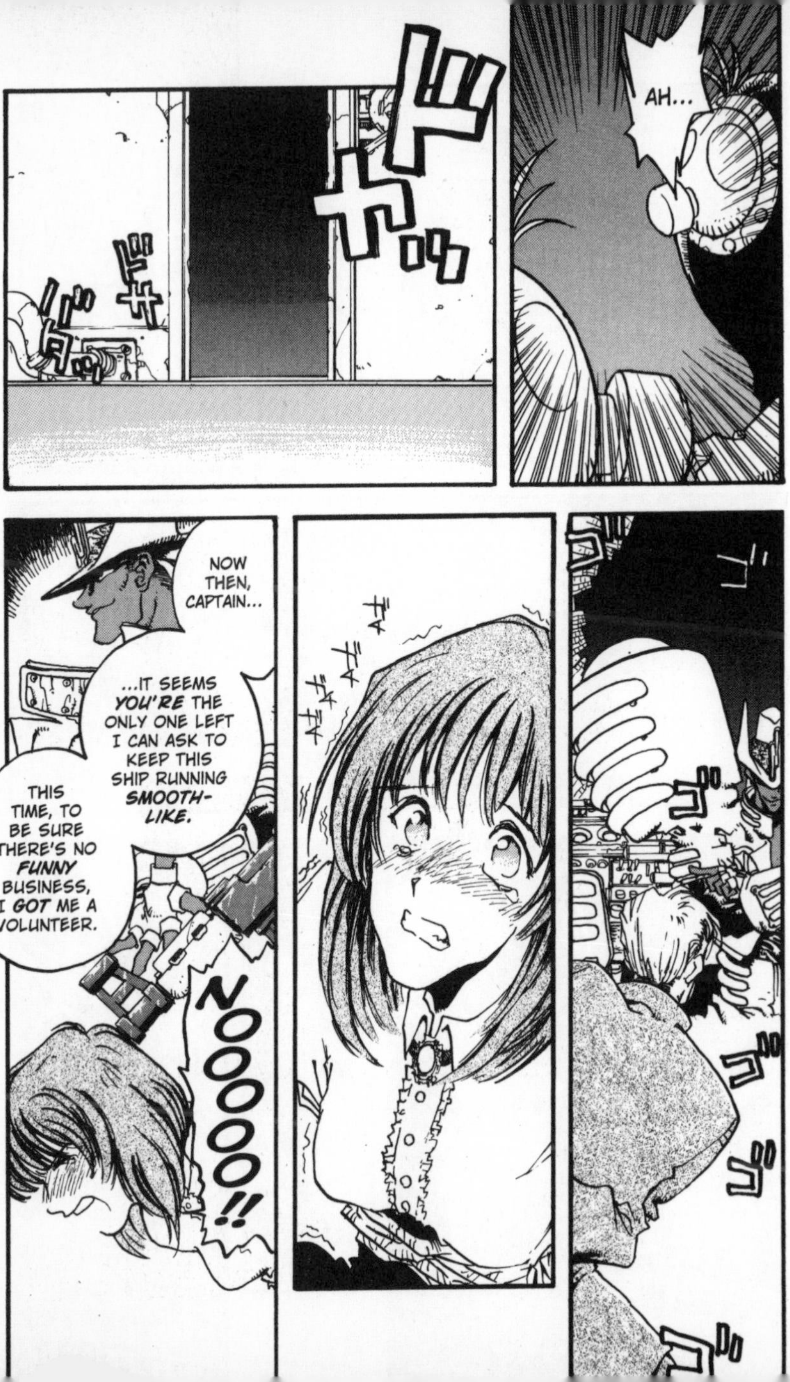
AH...
NOW THEN, CAPTAIN...
...IT SEEMS *YOU'RE* THE ONLY ONE LEFT I CAN ASK TO KEEP THIS SHIP RUNNING *SMOOTH-LIKE.*
THIS TIME, TO BE SURE THERE'S NO *FUNNY* BUSINESS, I *GOT* ME A VOLUNTEER.
NOOOOOO!!

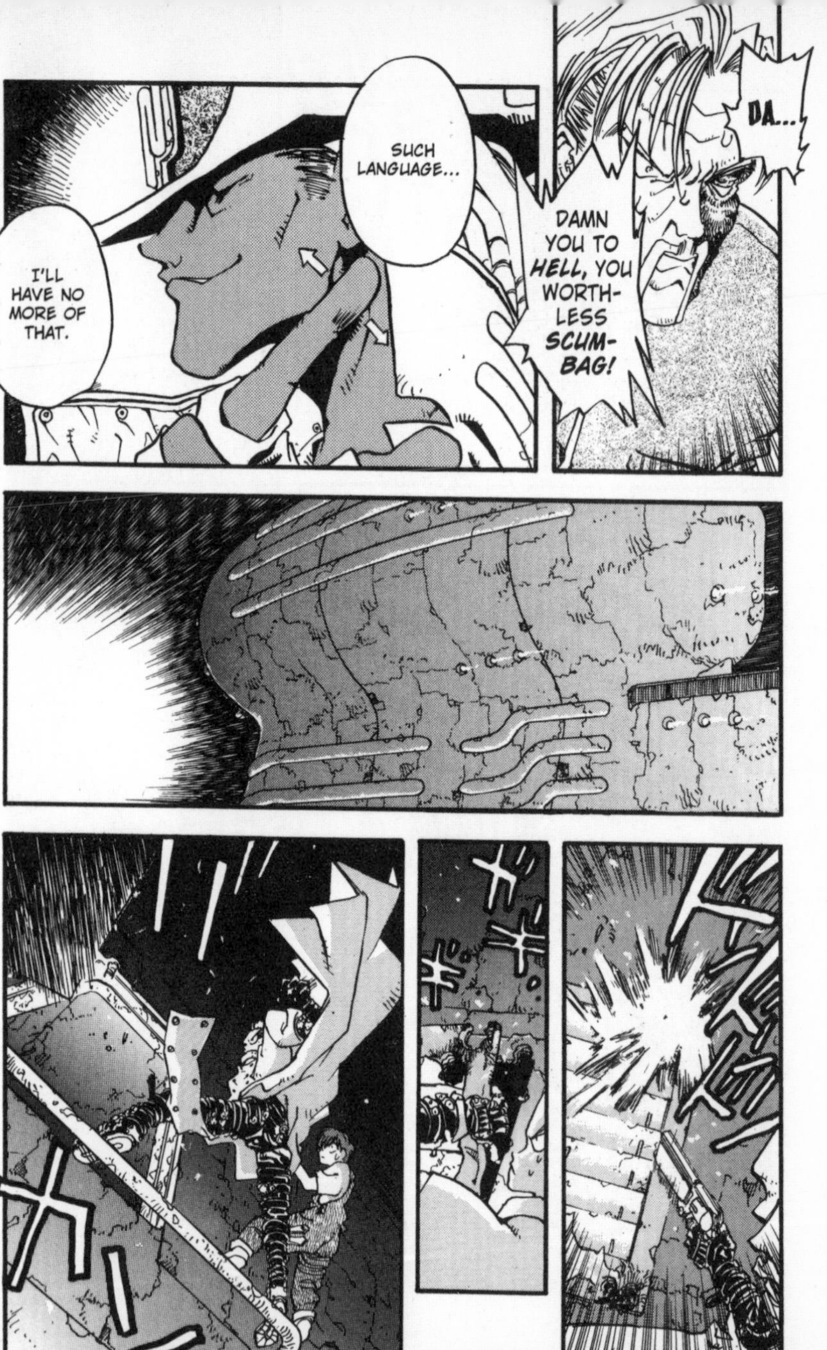
DA...
DAMN YOU TO HELL, YOU WORTHLESS SCUMBAG!
SUCH LANGUAGE...
I'LL HAVE NO MORE OF THAT.

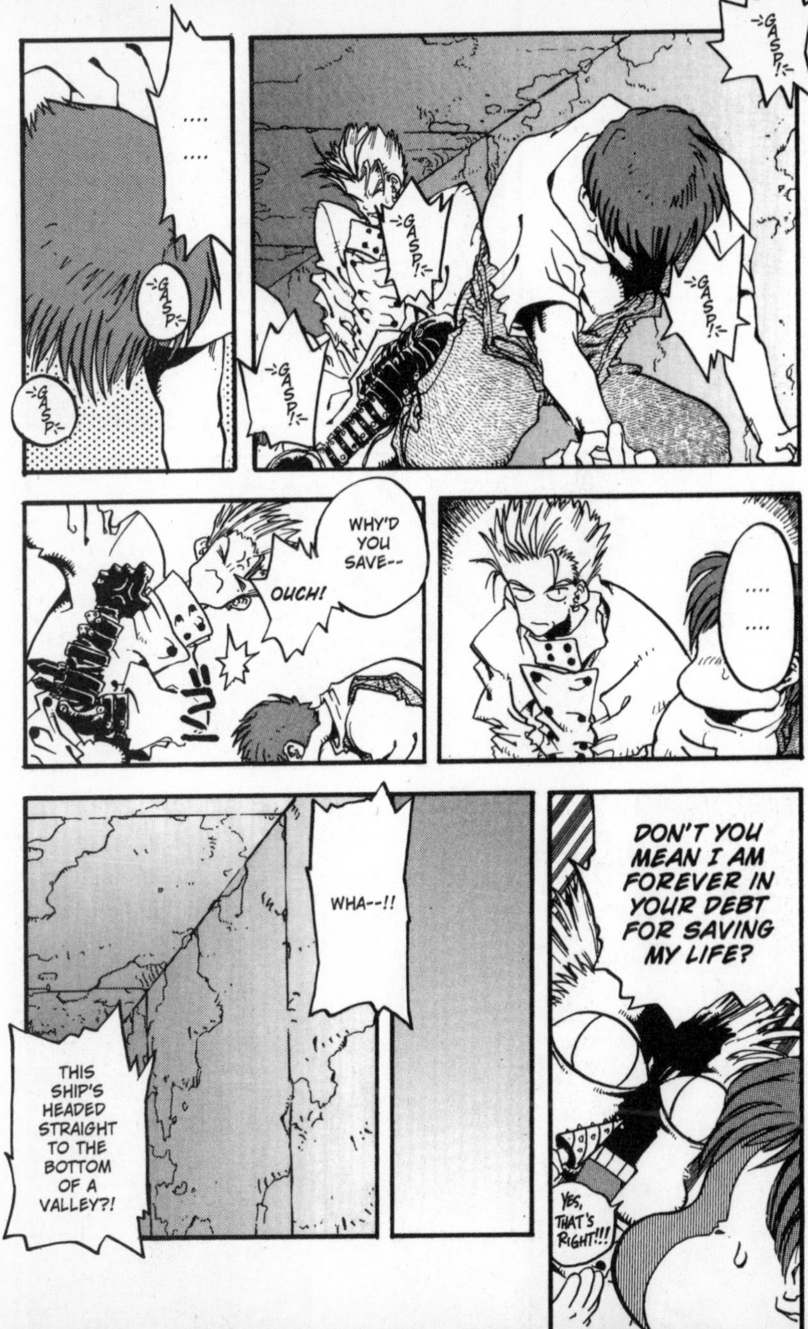GASP!
GASP!
GASP!
GASP!
....
....
GASP
GASP
....
....
WHY'D YOU SAVE--
OUCH!
DON'T YOU MEAN I AM FOREVER IN YOUR DEBT FOR SAVING MY LIFE?
YES, THAT'S RIGHT!!!
WHA--!!
THIS SHIP'S HEADED STRAIGHT TO THE BOTTOM OF A VALLEY?!

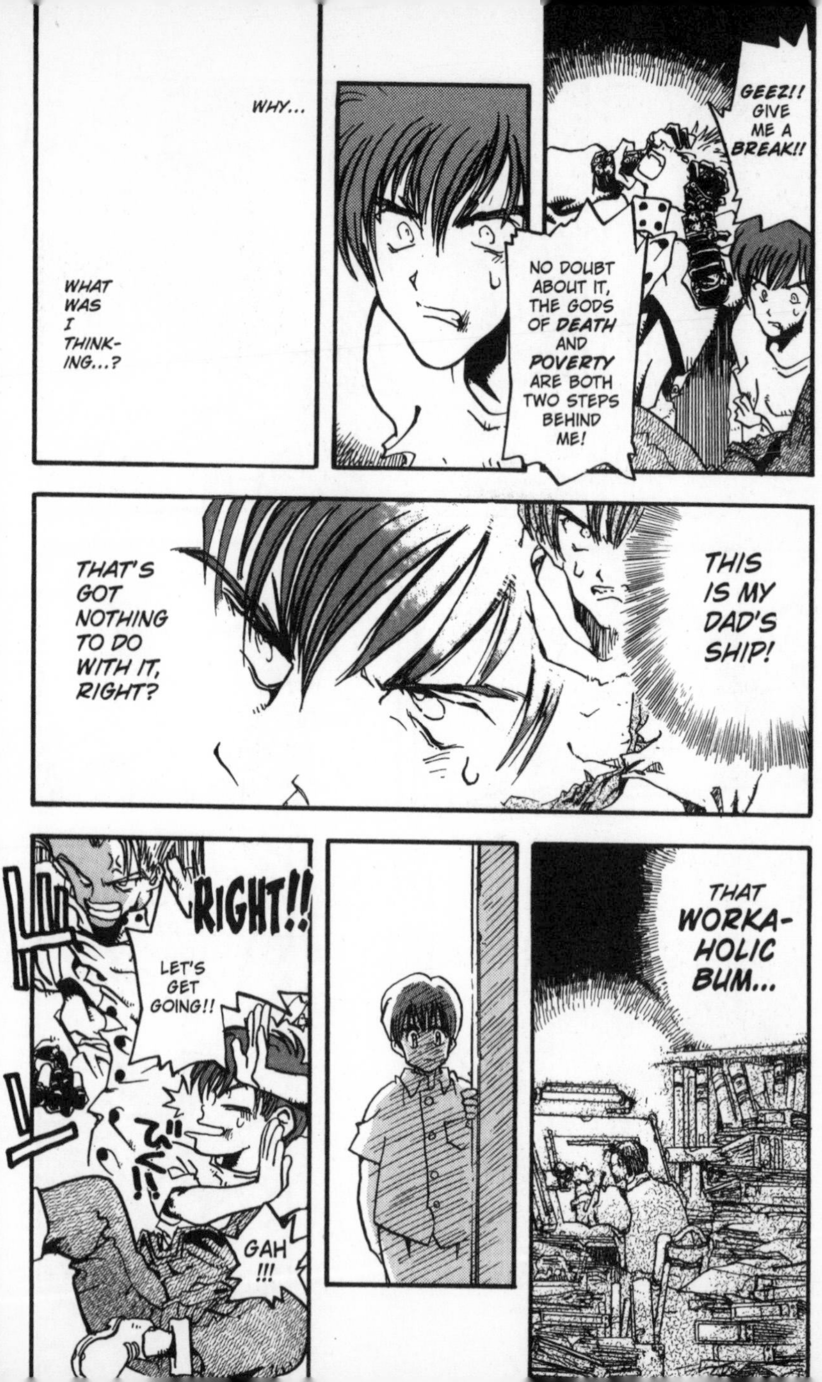
GEEZ!! GIVE ME A BREAK!!
NO DOUBT ABOUT IT, THE GODS OF DEATH AND POVERTY ARE BOTH TWO STEPS BEHIND ME!
WHY...
WHAT WAS I THINKING...?
THIS IS MY DAD'S SHIP!
THAT'S GOT NOTHING TO DO WITH IT, RIGHT?
THAT WORKAHOLIC BUM...
RIGHT!!
LET'S GET GOING!!
びく!!
GAH!!!

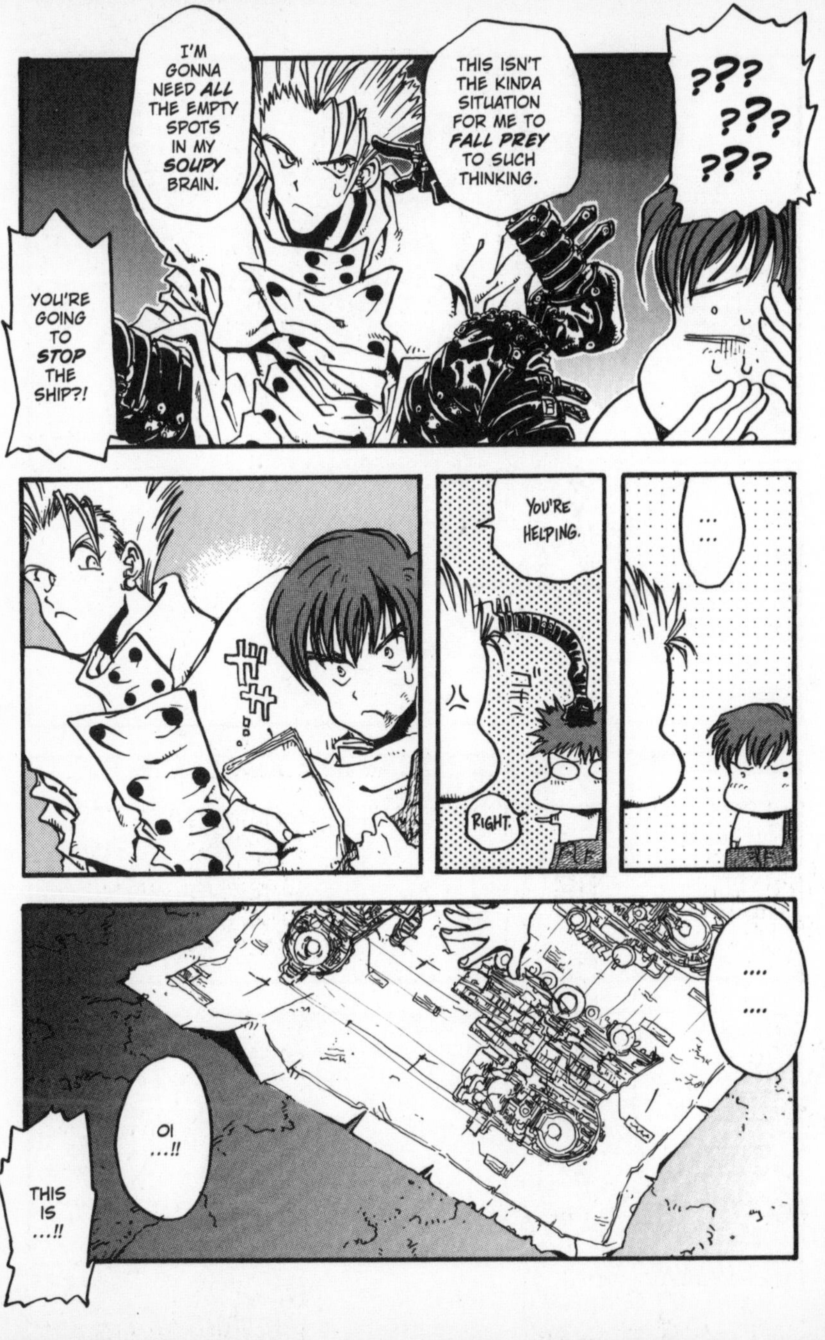
???
???
???
THIS ISN'T THE KINDA SITUATION FOR ME TO FALL PREY TO SUCH THINKING.
I'M GONNA NEED ALL THE EMPTY SPOTS IN MY SOUPY BRAIN.
YOU'RE GOING TO STOP THE SHIP?!
...
...
YOU'RE HELPING.
RIGHT.
....
....
OI ...!!
THIS IS ...!!

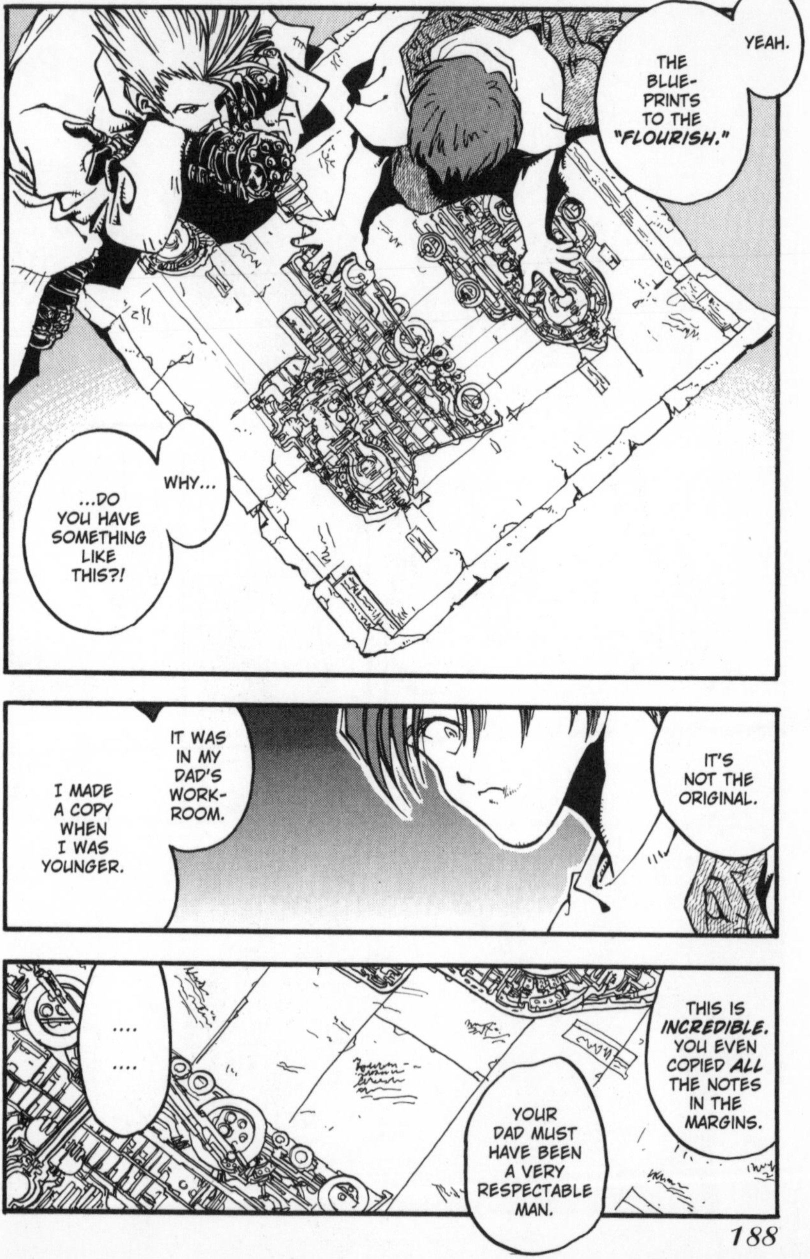
YEAH.
THE BLUE-PRINTS TO THE "FLOURISH."
WHY...
...DO YOU HAVE SOMETHING LIKE THIS?!
IT'S NOT THE ORIGINAL.
IT WAS IN MY DAD'S WORK-ROOM.
I MADE A COPY WHEN I WAS YOUNGER.
THIS IS INCREDIBLE. YOU EVEN COPIED ALL THE NOTES IN THE MARGINS.
YOUR DAD MUST HAVE BEEN A VERY RESPECTABLE MAN.
....
....

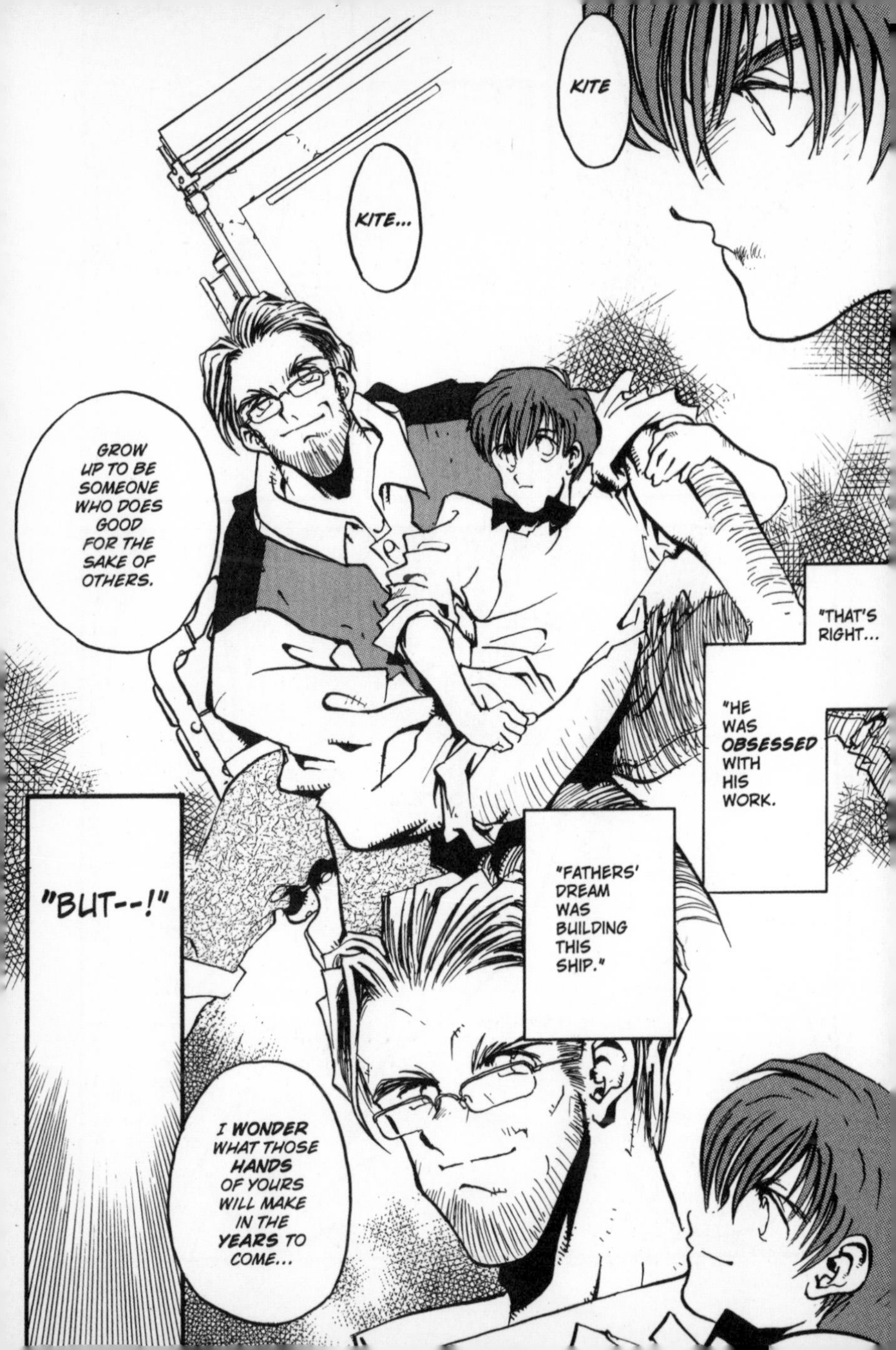
KITE
KITE...
GROW UP TO BE SOMEONE WHO DOES GOOD FOR THE SAKE OF OTHERS.
"THAT'S RIGHT...
"HE WAS OBSESSED WITH HIS WORK.
"FATHERS' DREAM WAS BUILDING THIS SHIP."
I WONDER WHAT THOSE HANDS OF YOURS WILL MAKE IN THE YEARS TO COME...
"BUT--!"

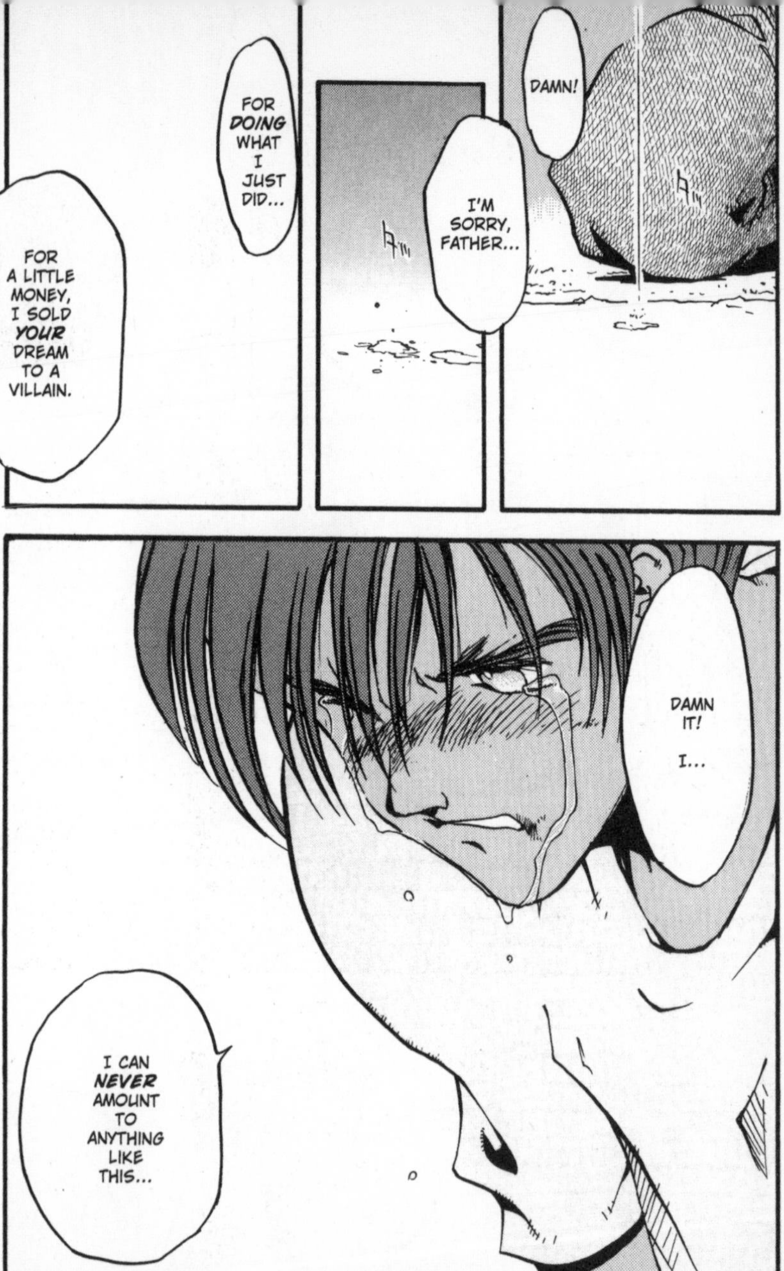
DAMN!
I'M SORRY, FATHER...
FOR DOING WHAT I JUST DID...
FOR A LITTLE MONEY, I SOLD YOUR DREAM TO A VILLAIN.
DAMN IT!
I...
I CAN NEVER AMOUNT TO ANYTHING LIKE THIS...

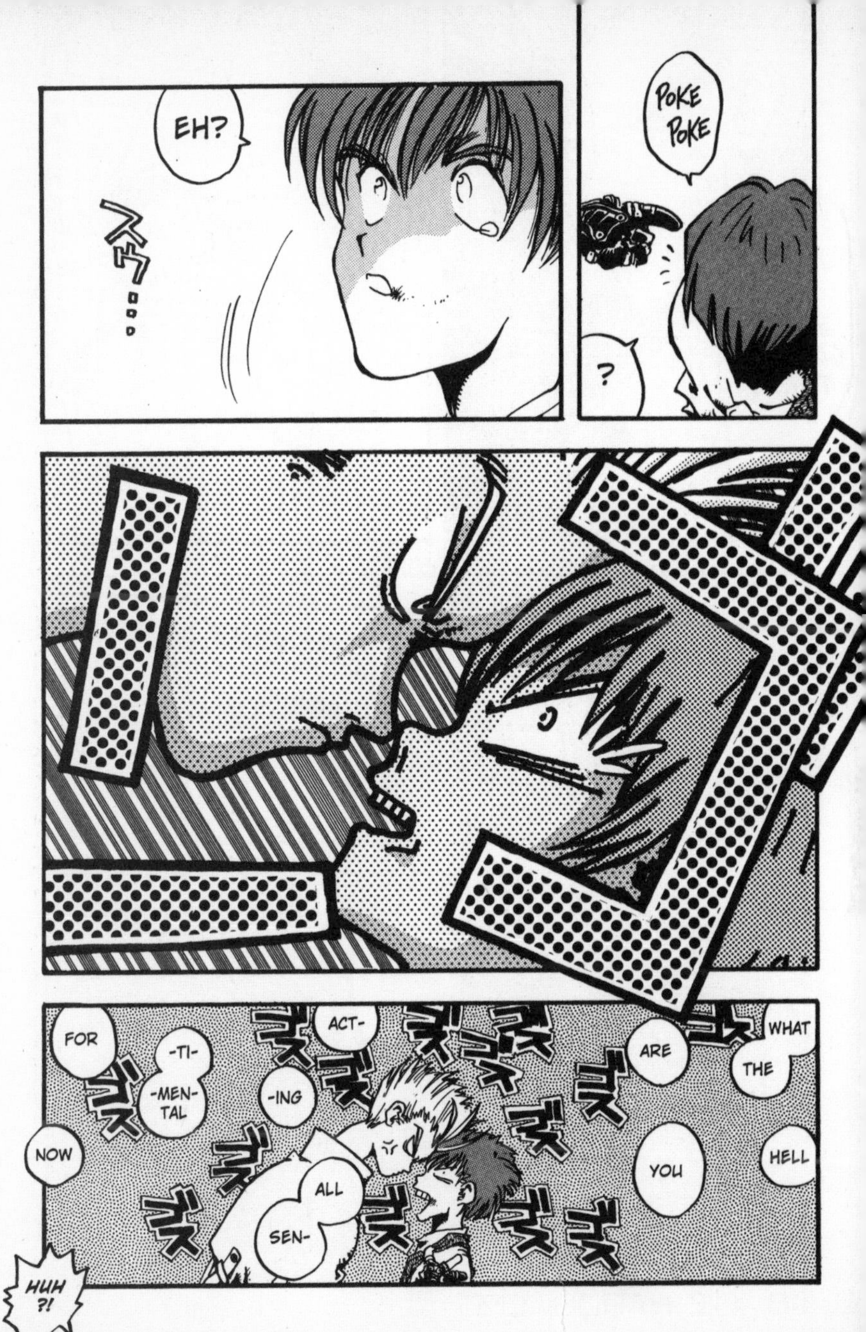
POKE POKE
?
EH?
スウ…
WHAT
THE
HELL
ARE
YOU
ACT-
-ING
ALL
SEN-
-TI-
-MENTAL
FOR
NOW
HUH?!

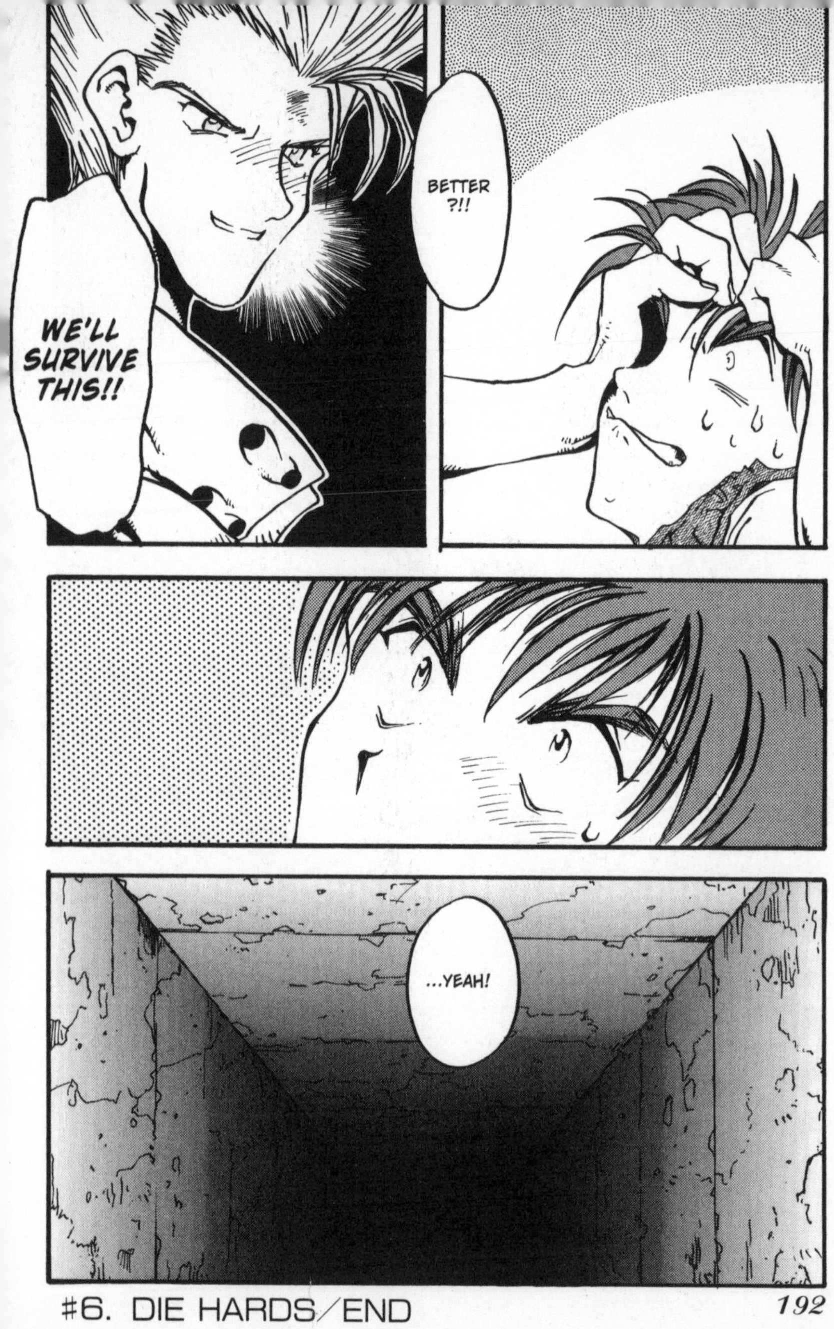
BETTER ?!!
WE'LL SURVIVE THIS!!
...YEAH!

#6. DIE HARDS/END

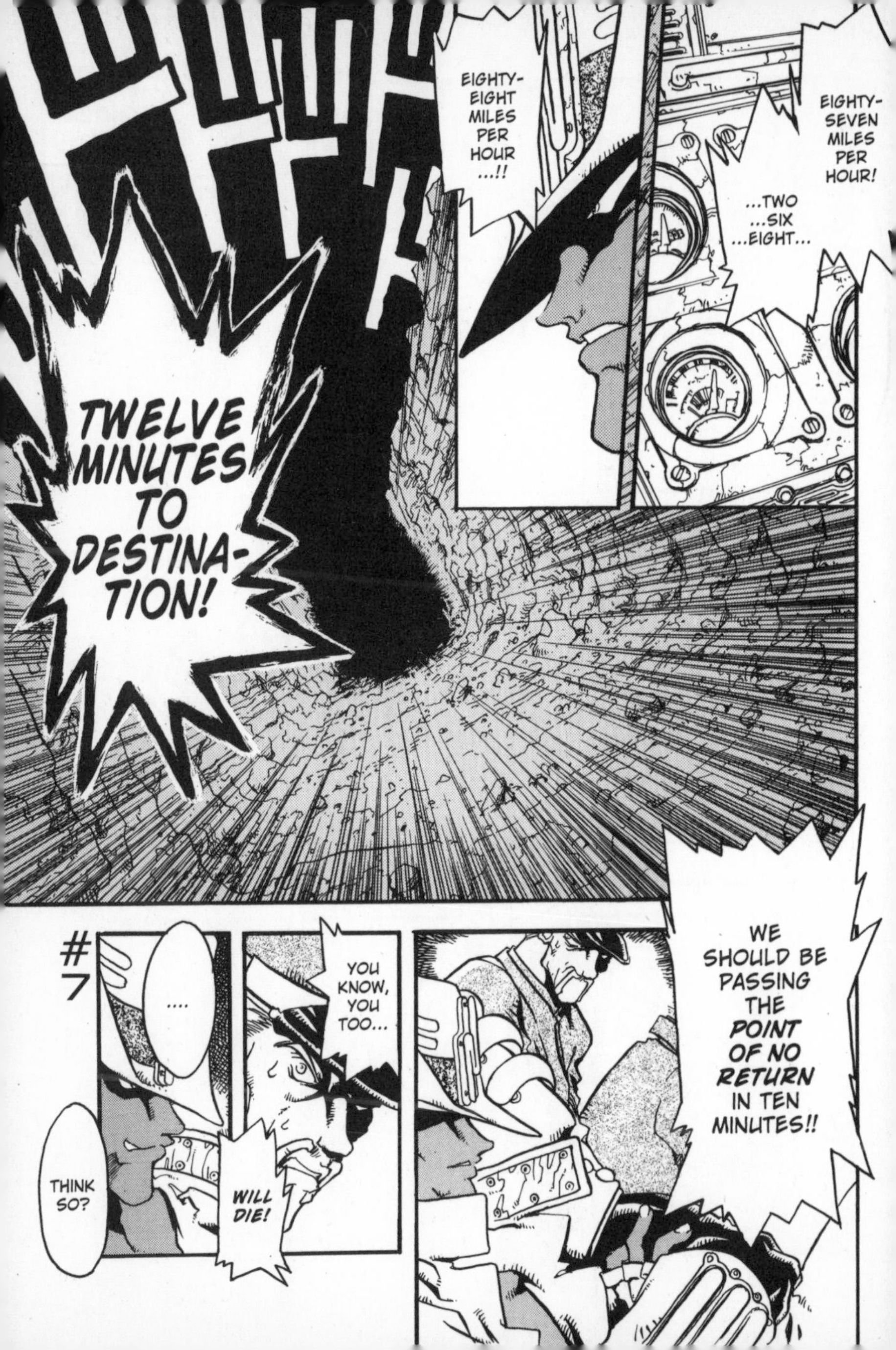
EIGHTY-SEVEN MILES PER HOUR!
...TWO ...SIX ...EIGHT...
EIGHTY-EIGHT MILES PER HOUR ...!!
TWELVE MINUTES TO DESTINATION!
WE SHOULD BE PASSING THE POINT OF NO RETURN IN TEN MINUTES!!
YOU KNOW, YOU TOO...
WILL DIE!
#7
....
THINK SO?

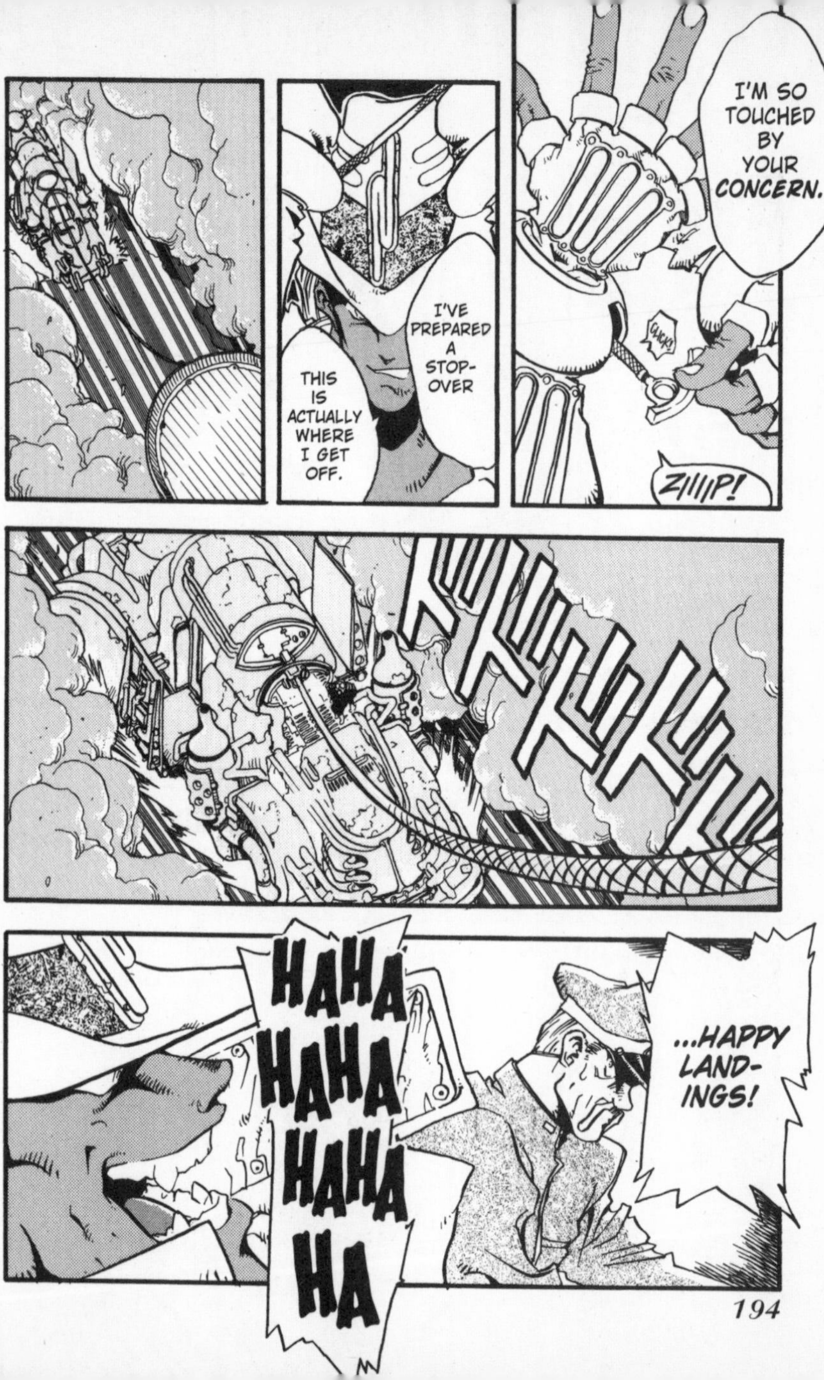

I'M SO TOUCHED BY YOUR CONCERN.
CLICK!
ZIIIP!
I'VE PREPARED A STOP-OVER
THIS IS ACTUALLY WHERE I GET OFF.
...HAPPY LAND-INGS!
HAHA HAHA HAHA HAHA HAHA HA

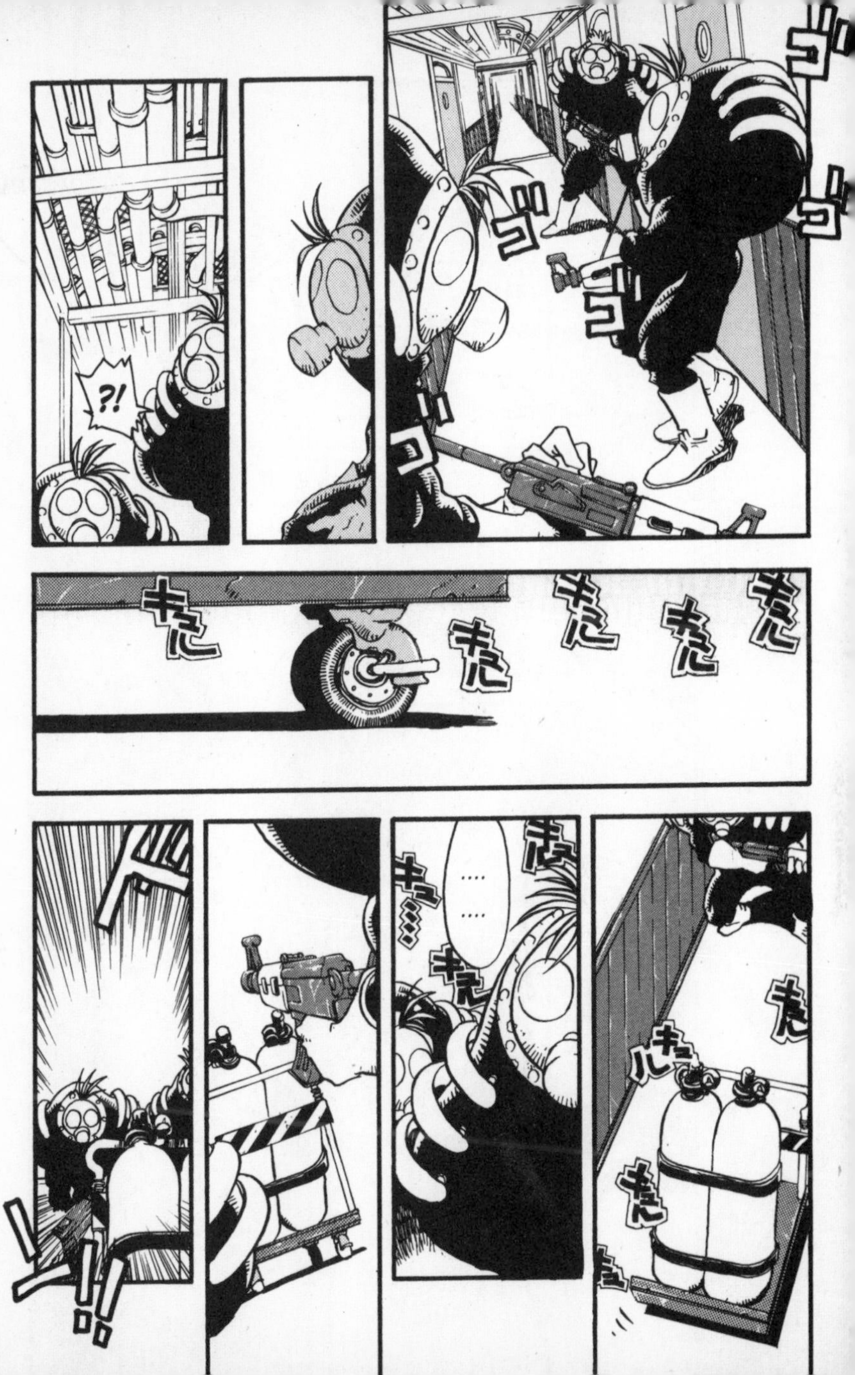
?!
....
....
!!

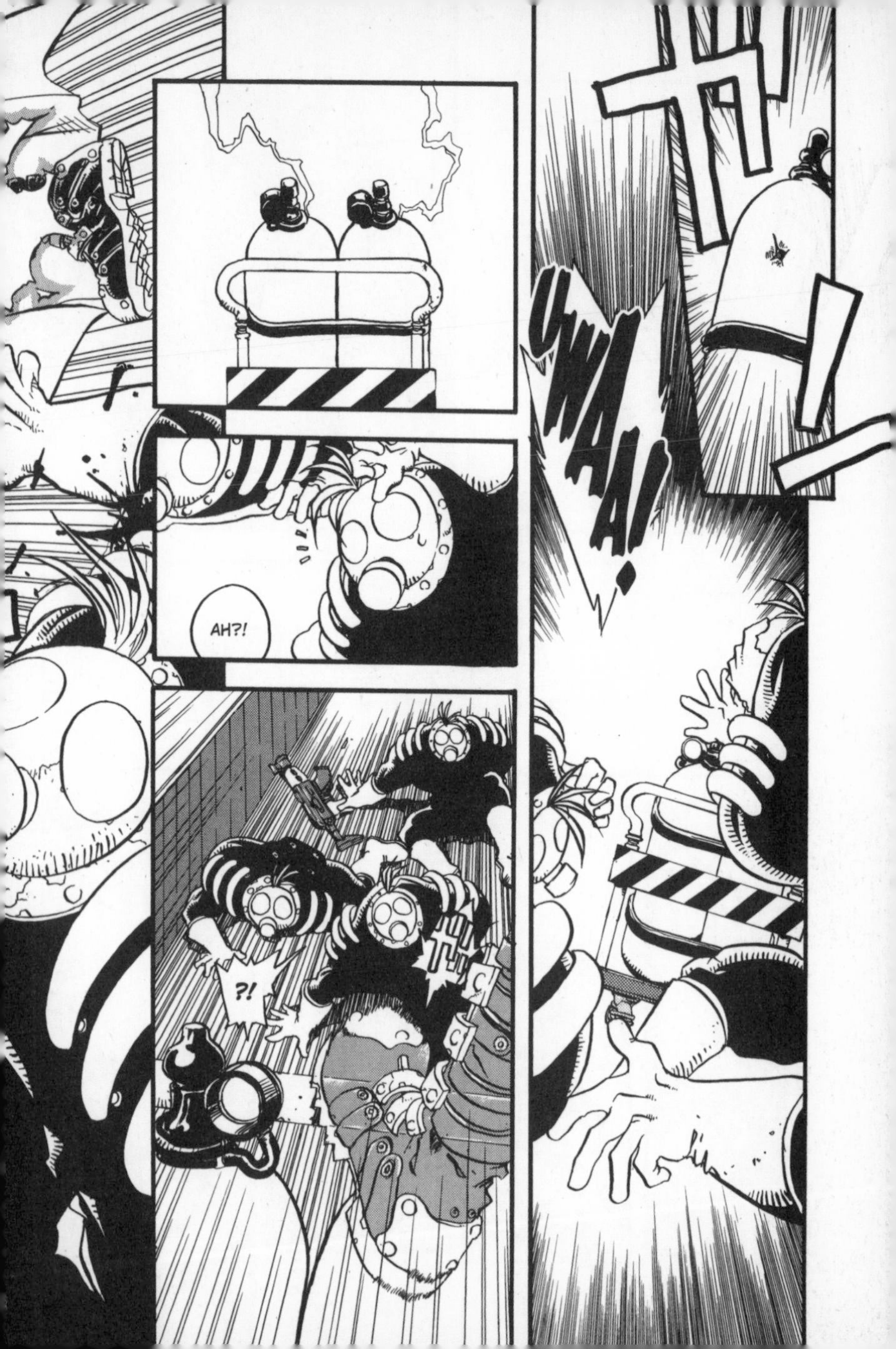
UWAAA!
AH?!
?!

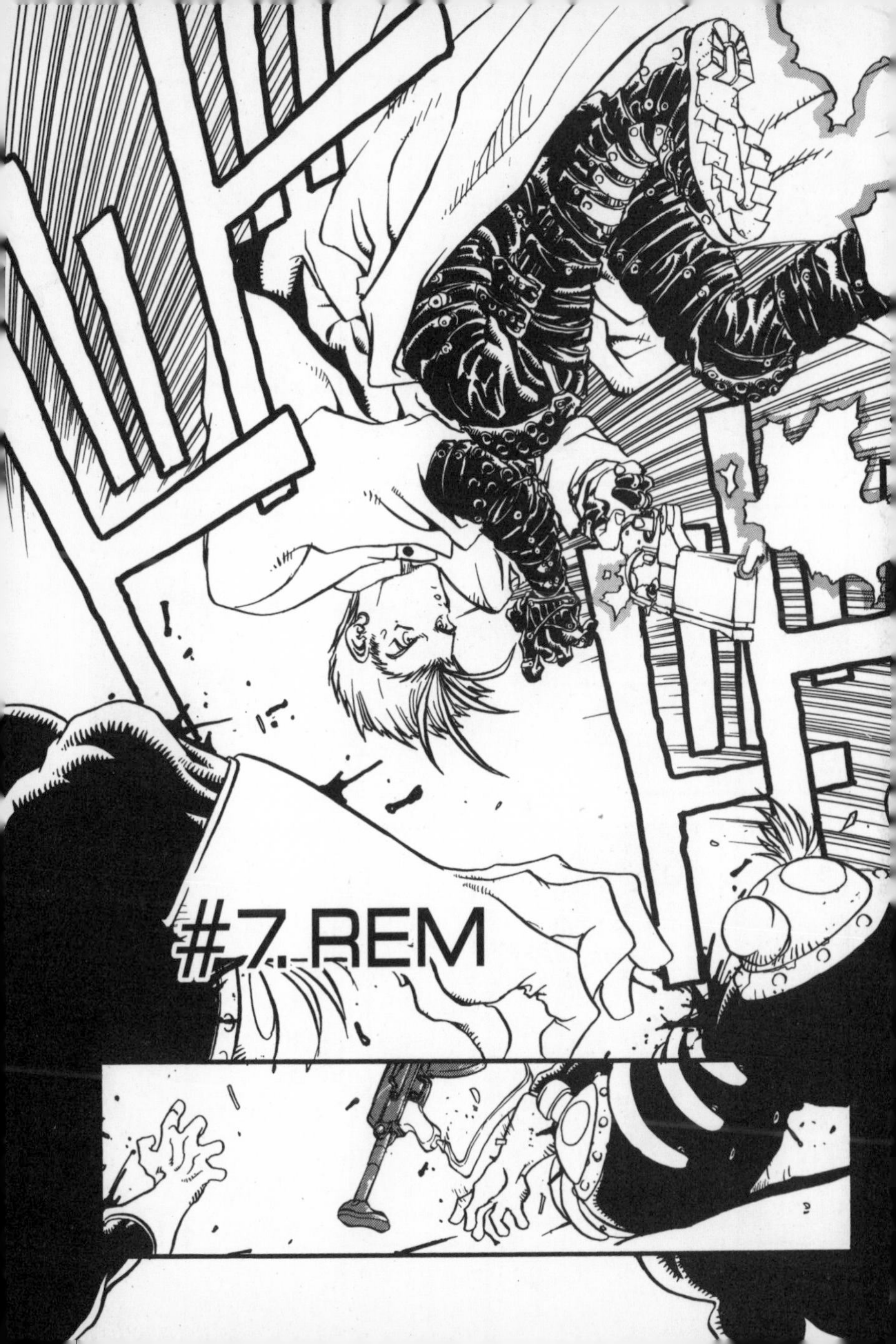
#7. REM

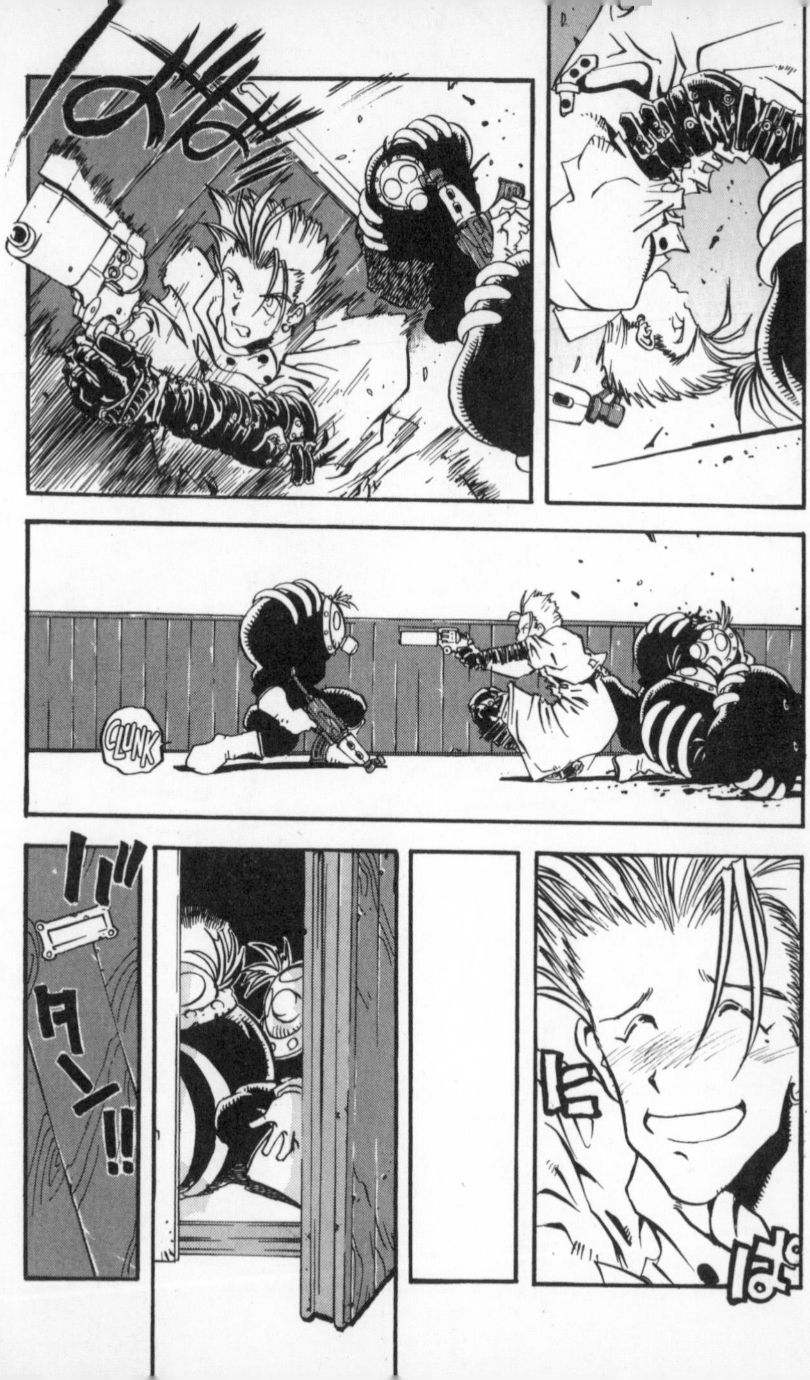
CLUNK
にぱ
ダーン!!

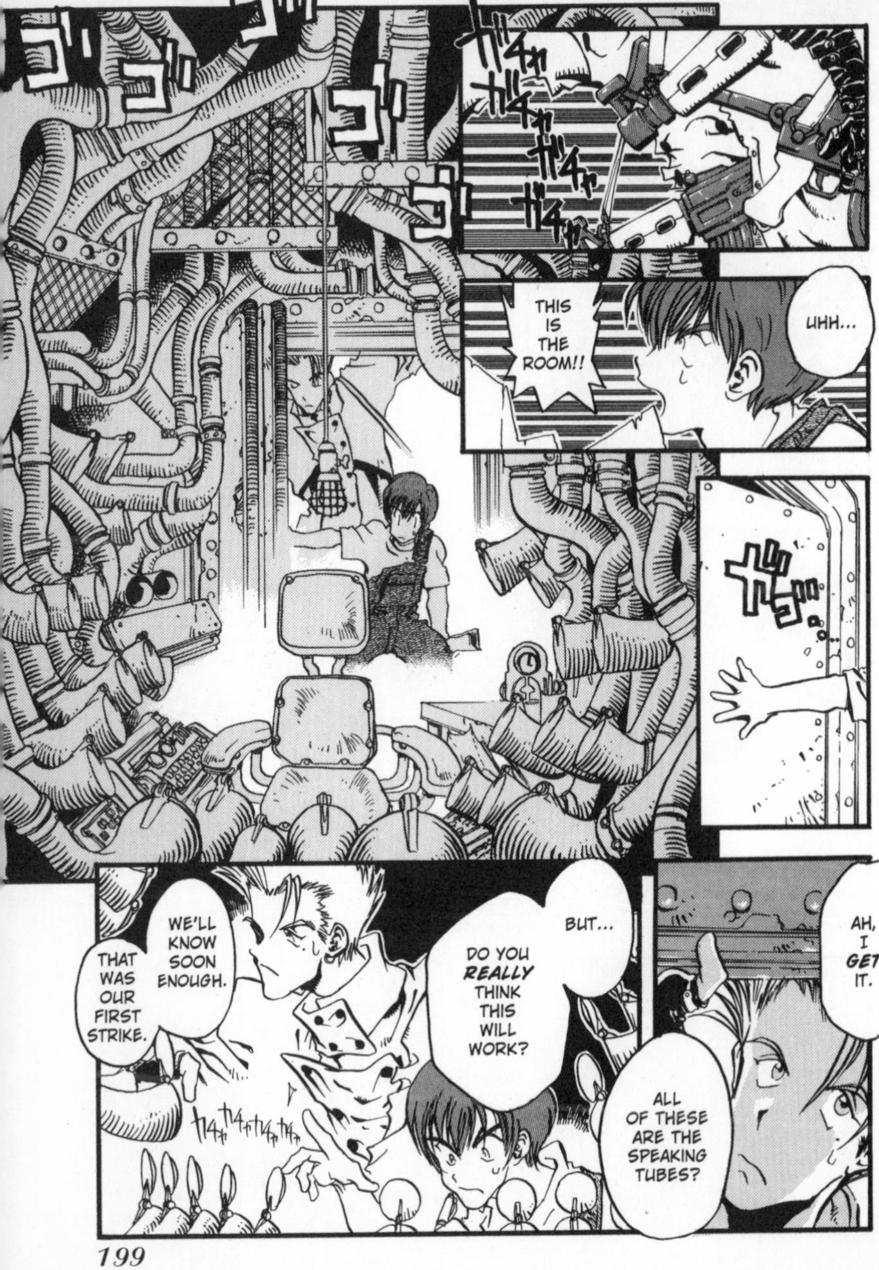

UHH...
THIS IS THE ROOM!!
AH, I GET IT.
ALL OF THESE ARE THE SPEAKING TUBES?
BUT...
DO YOU REALLY THINK THIS WILL WORK?
WE'LL KNOW SOON ENOUGH.
THAT WAS OUR FIRST STRIKE.

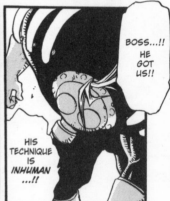

BOSS...!! HE GOT US!!

HIS TECHNIQUE IS *INHUMAN* ...!!

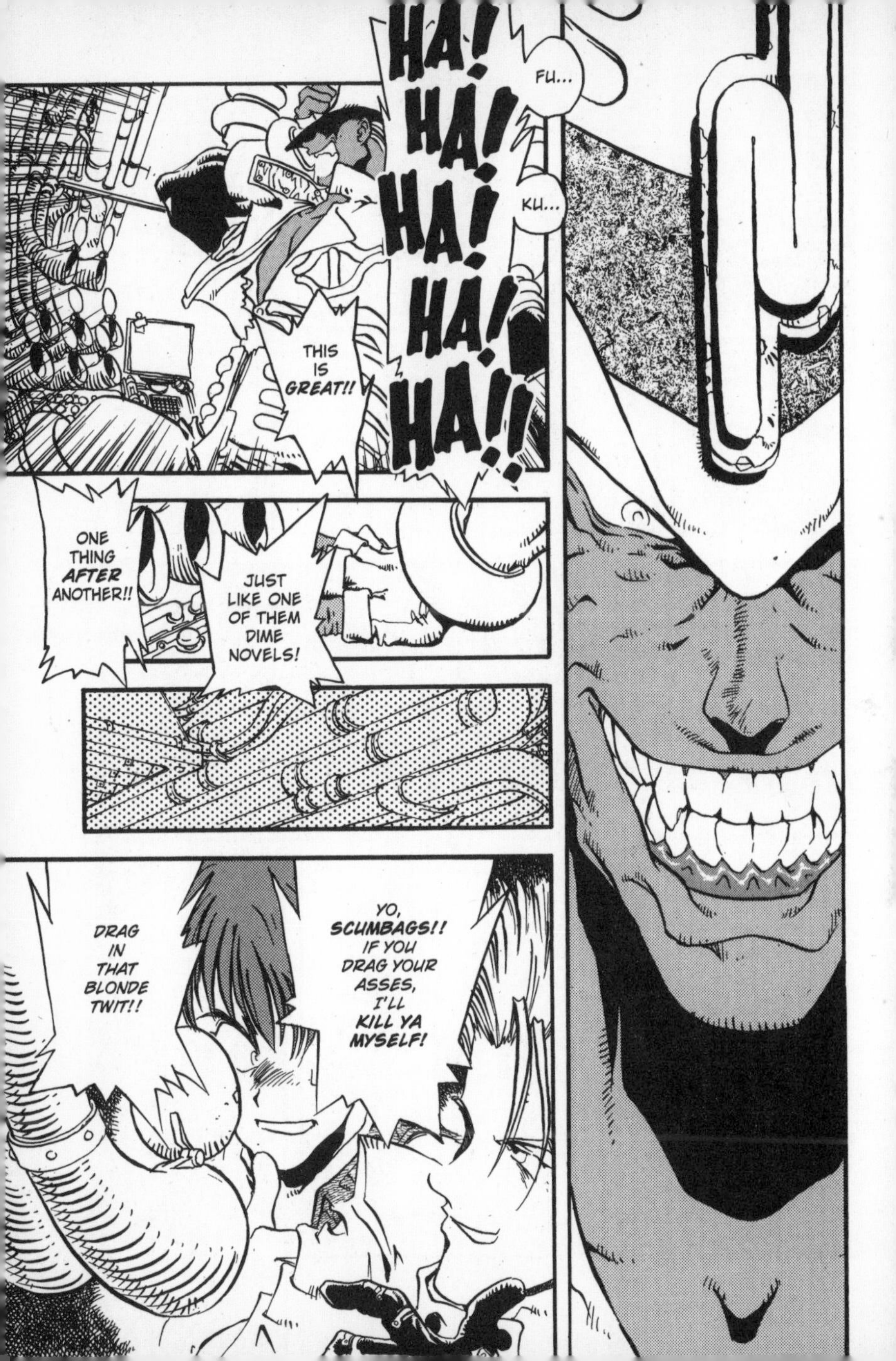
FU...
KU...
HA! HA! HA! HA! HA!!
THIS IS GREAT!!
ONE THING AFTER ANOTHER!!
JUST LIKE ONE OF THEM DIME NOVELS!
YO, SCUMBAGS!! IF YOU DRAG YOUR ASSES, I'LL KILL YA MYSELF!
DRAG IN THAT BLONDE TWIT!!

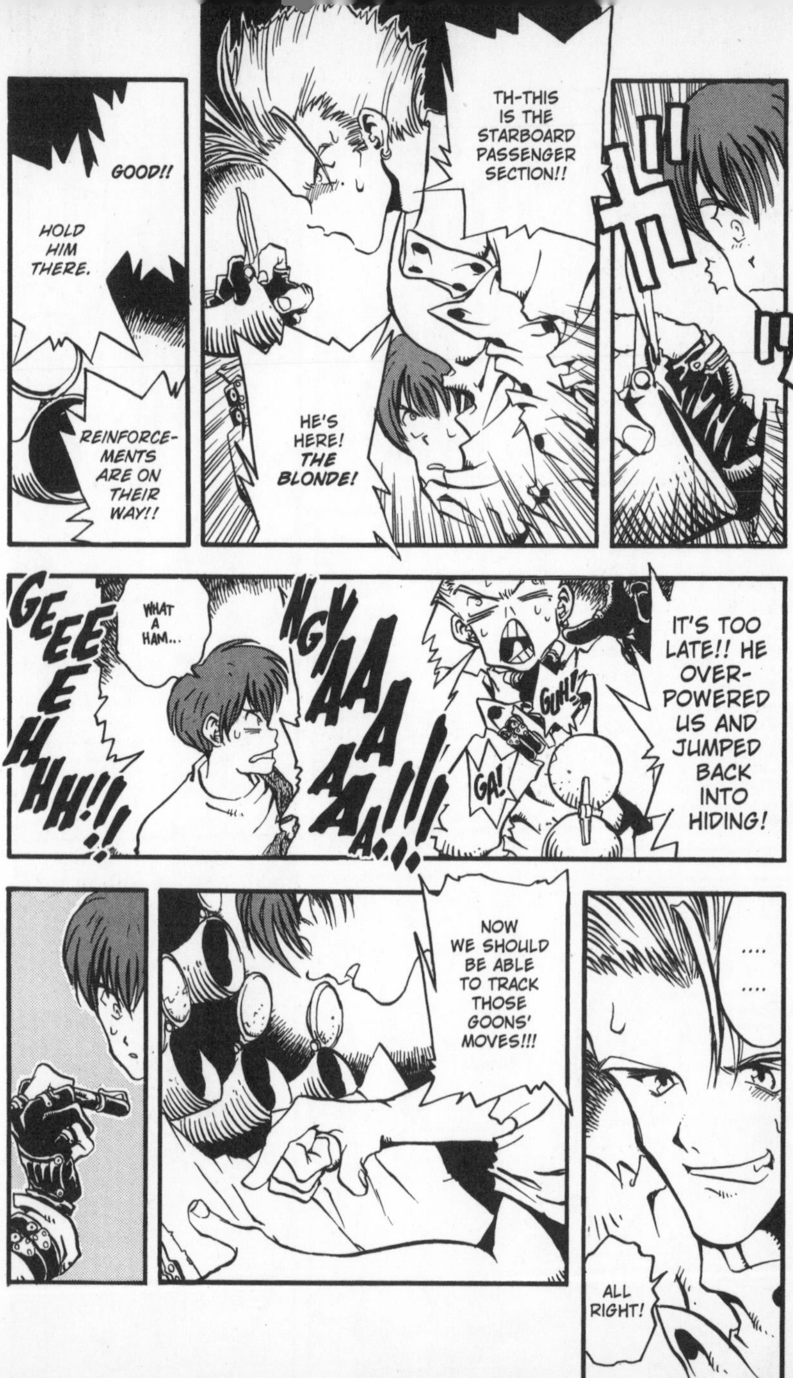
TH-THIS IS THE STARBOARD PASSENGER SECTION!!
HE'S HERE! THE BLONDE!
GOOD!!
HOLD HIM THERE.
REINFORCE-MENTS ARE ON THEIR WAY!!
IT'S TOO LATE!! HE OVER-POWERED US AND JUMPED BACK INTO HIDING!
GUH!
GA!
NGYAAAAAAA...!!!
WHAT A HAM...
GEEEEEHHH!!!
....
....
ALL RIGHT!
NOW WE SHOULD BE ABLE TO TRACK THOSE GOONS' MOVES!!!

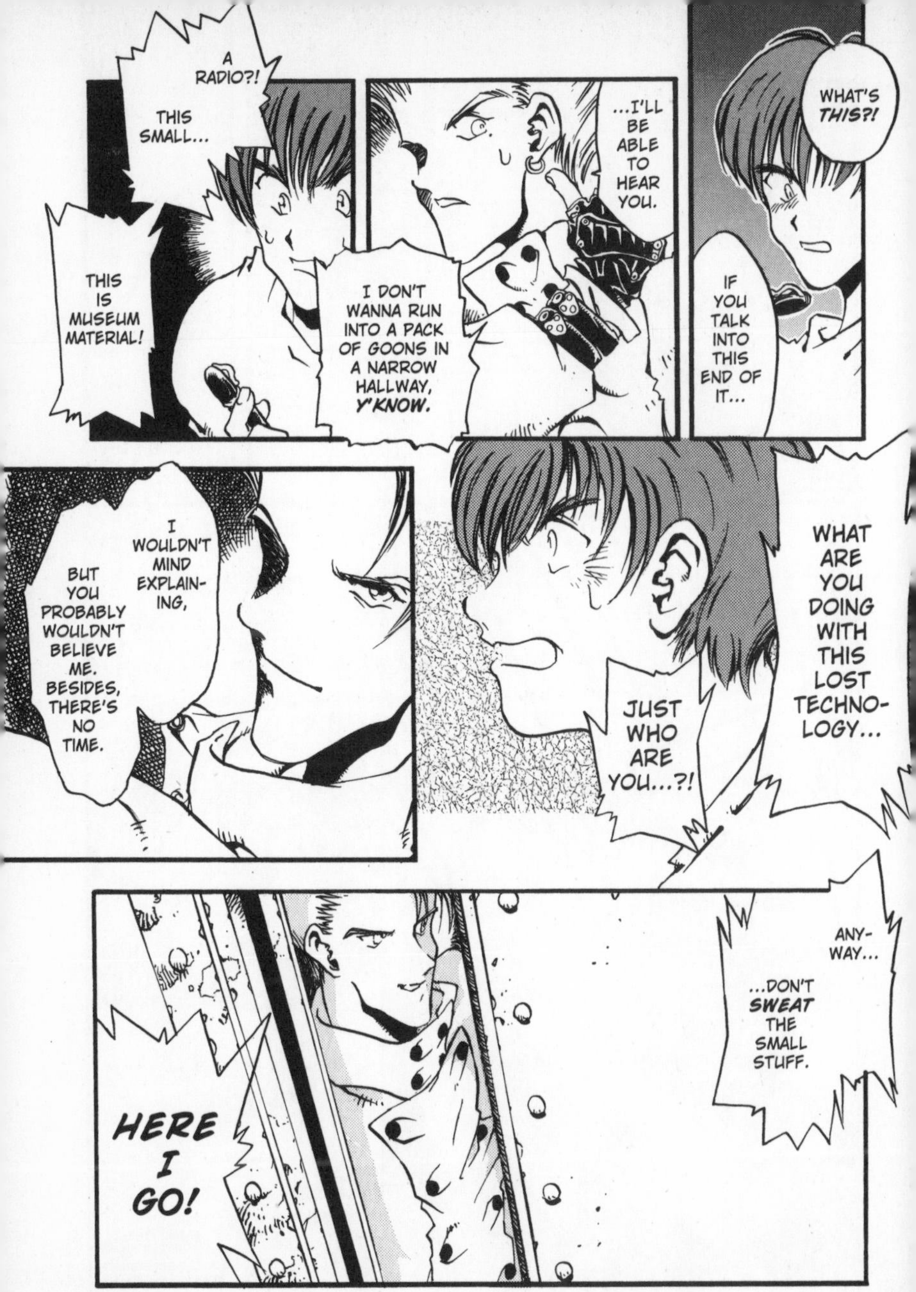
WHAT'S *THIS?!*
IF YOU TALK INTO THIS END OF IT...
...I'LL BE ABLE TO HEAR YOU.
I DON'T WANNA RUN INTO A PACK OF GOONS IN A NARROW HALLWAY, *Y'KNOW.*
A RADIO?!
THIS SMALL...
THIS IS MUSEUM MATERIAL!
WHAT ARE YOU DOING WITH THIS LOST TECHNOLOGY...
JUST WHO ARE YOU...?!
I WOULDN'T MIND EXPLAINING,
BUT YOU PROBABLY WOULDN'T BELIEVE ME. BESIDES, THERE'S NO TIME.
ANY-WAY...
...DON'T ***SWEAT*** THE SMALL STUFF.
***HERE I GO!***

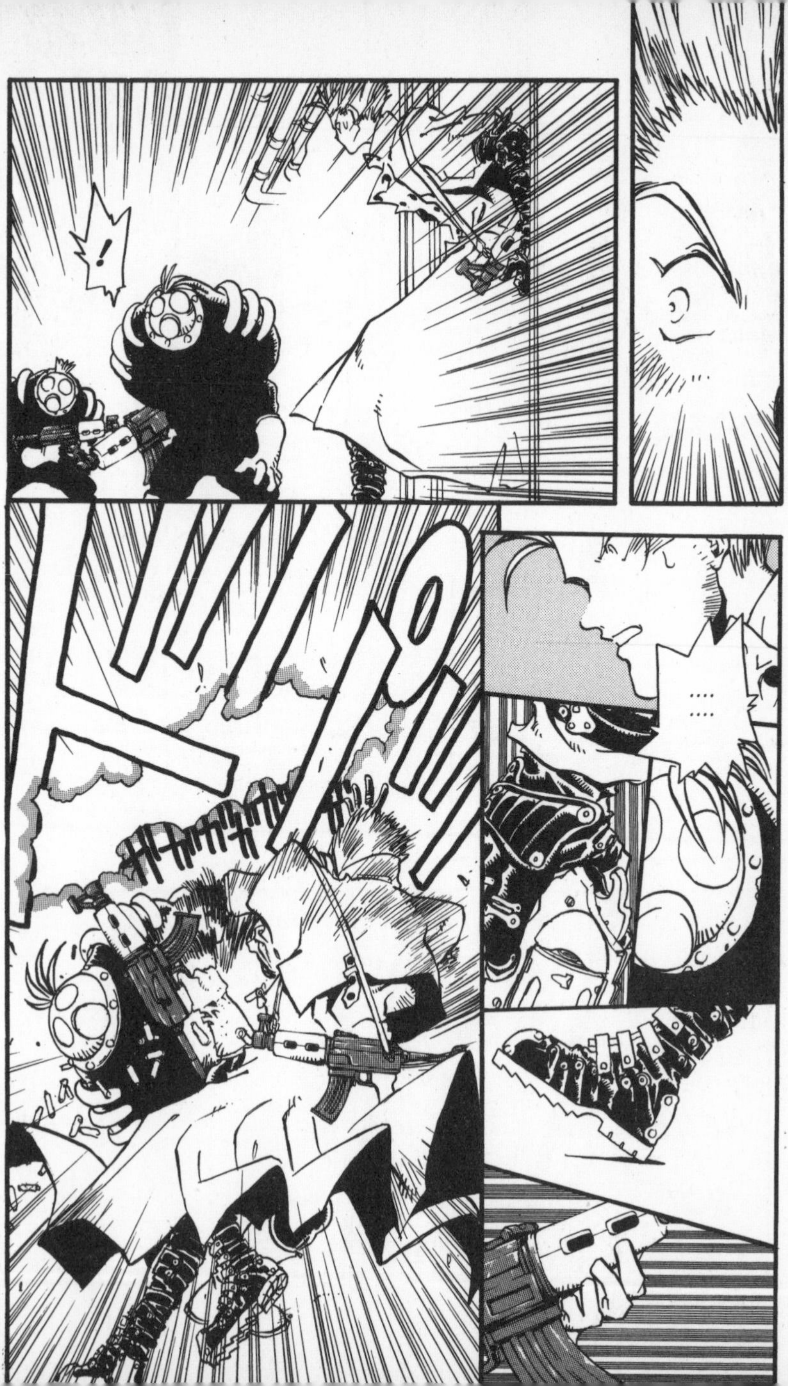
!
....
....

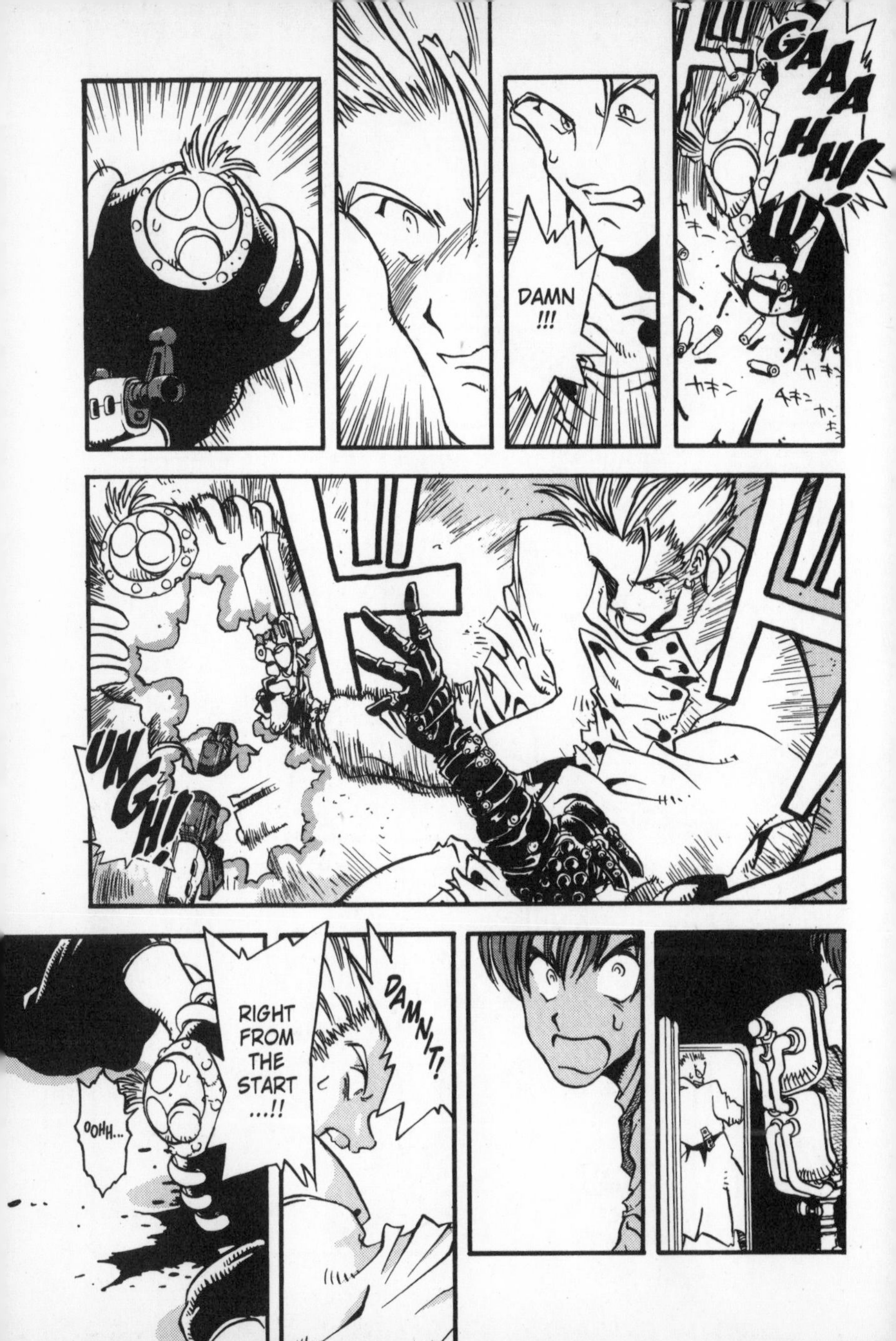
GAAAHHH!
DAMN !!!
UNGH!!
DAMNIT!
RIGHT FROM THE START ...!!
OOHH...

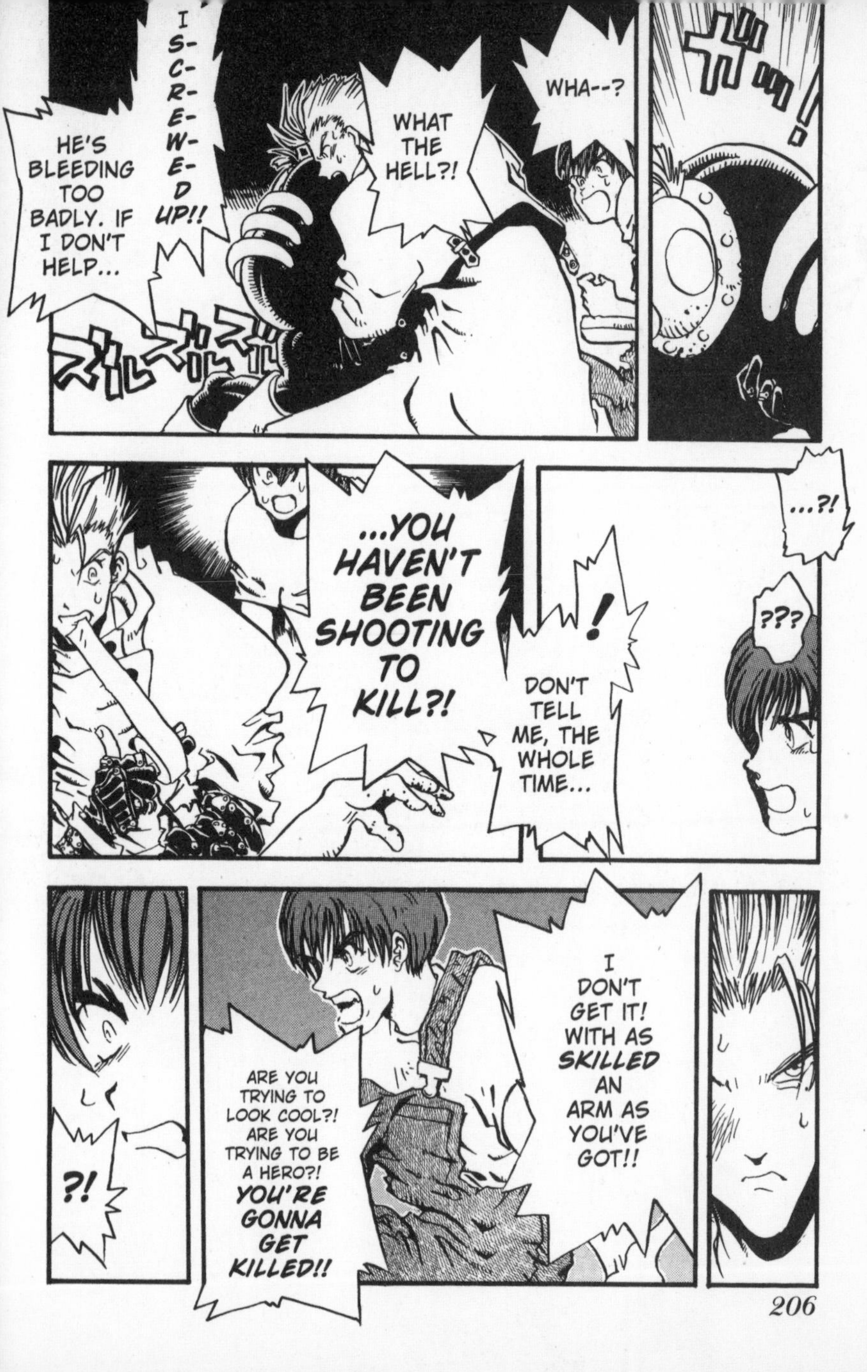

ガッ!
WHA--?
WHAT THE HELL?!
I S-C-R-E-W-E-D UP!!
HE'S BLEEDING TOO BADLY. IF I DON'T HELP...
...?!
???
!
DON'T TELL ME, THE WHOLE TIME...
...YOU HAVEN'T BEEN SHOOTING TO KILL?!
I DON'T GET IT! WITH AS SKILLED AN ARM AS YOU'VE GOT!!
ARE YOU TRYING TO LOOK COOL?! ARE YOU TRYING TO BE A HERO?! YOU'RE GONNA GET KILLED!!
?!

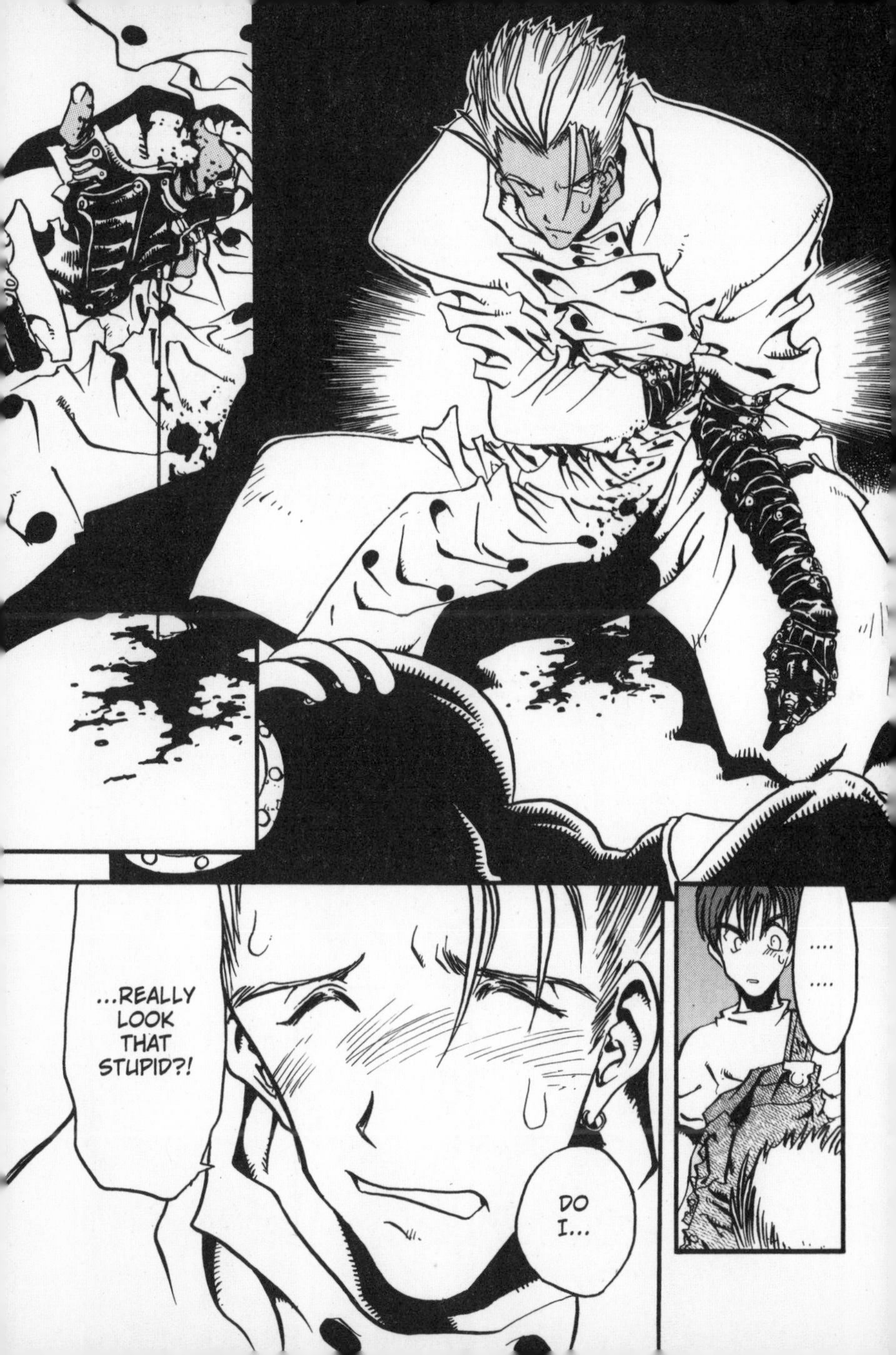
....
....
DO I...
...REALLY LOOK THAT STUPID?!

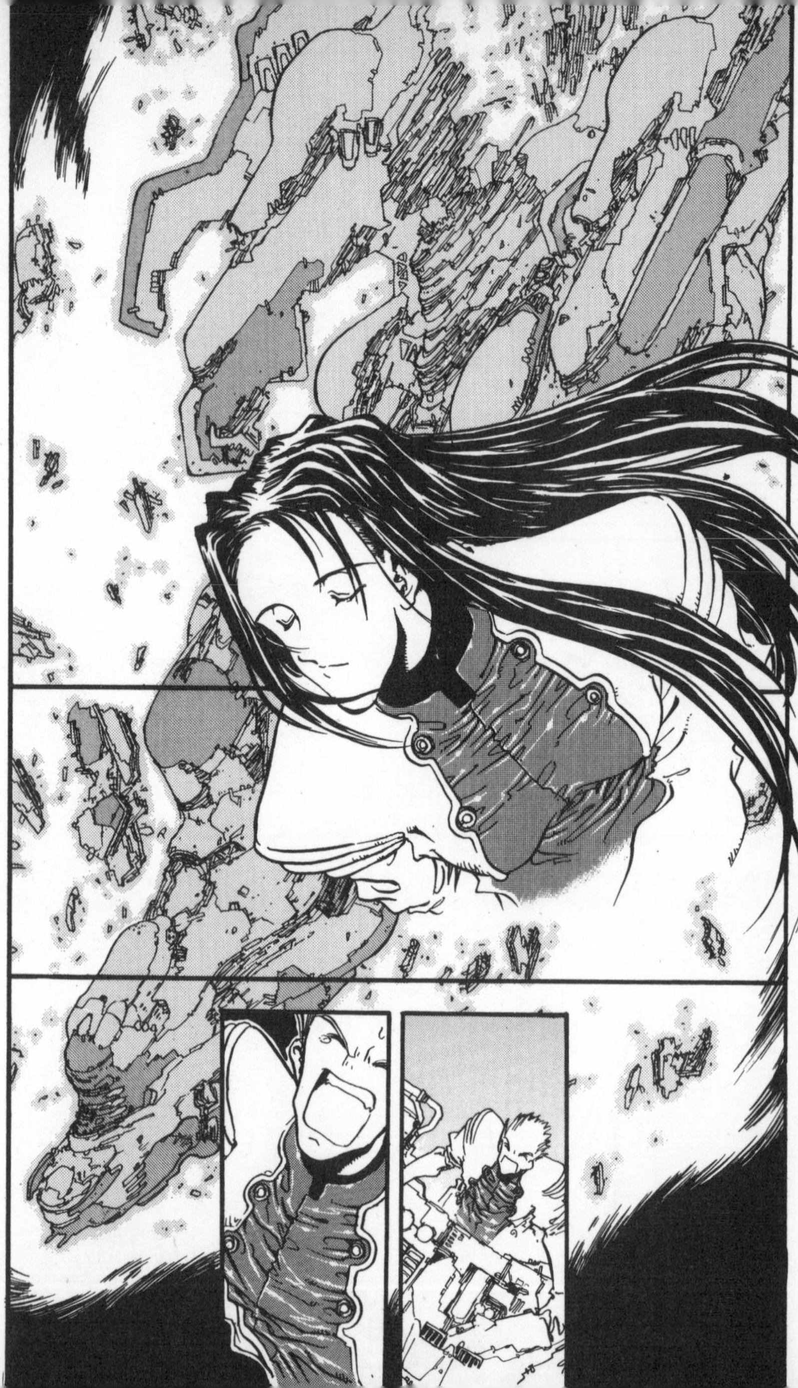

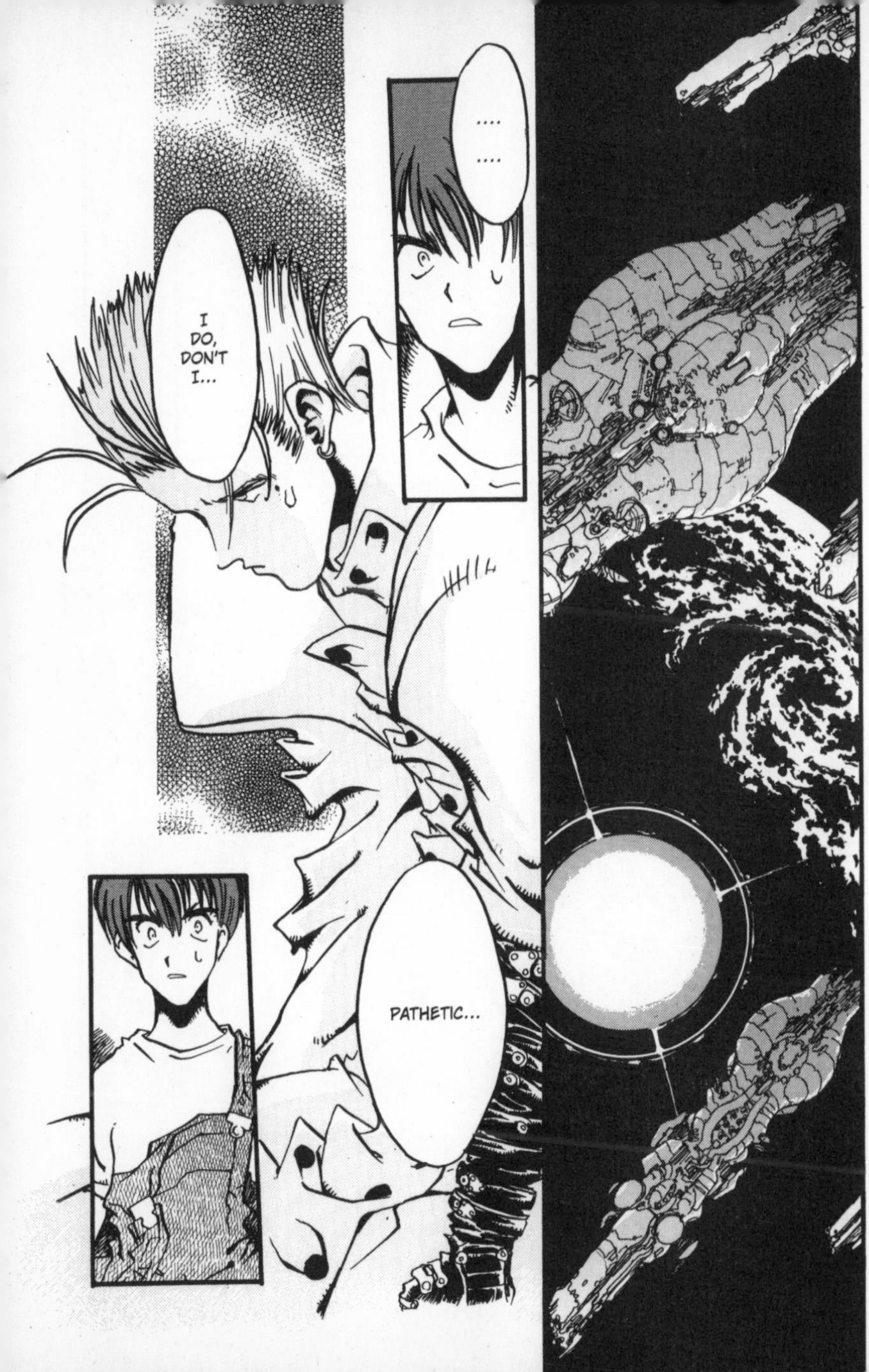
....
....
I DO, DON'T I...
PATHETIC...

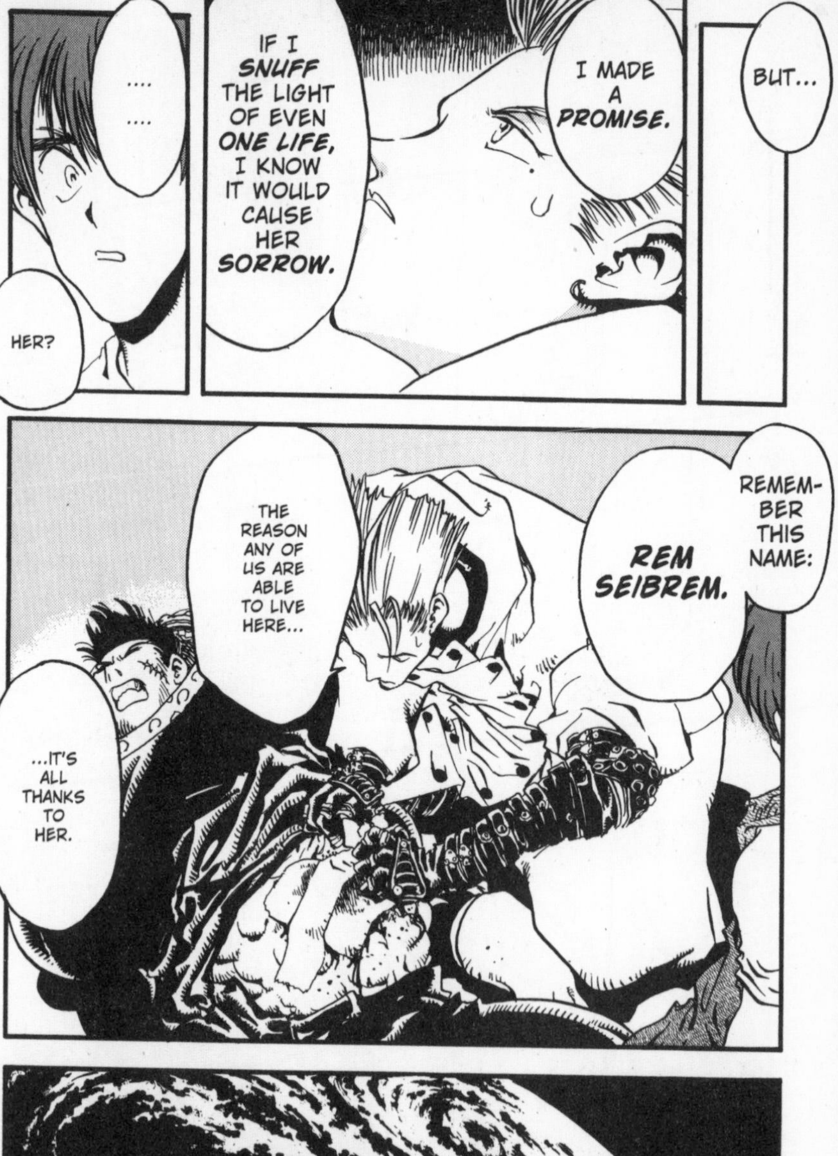
BUT...
I MADE A PROMISE.
IF I SNUFF THE LIGHT OF EVEN ONE LIFE, I KNOW IT WOULD CAUSE HER SORROW.
....
....
HER?
REMEM-BER THIS NAME:
REM SEIBREM.
THE REASON ANY OF US ARE ABLE TO LIVE HERE...
...IT'S ALL THANKS TO HER.

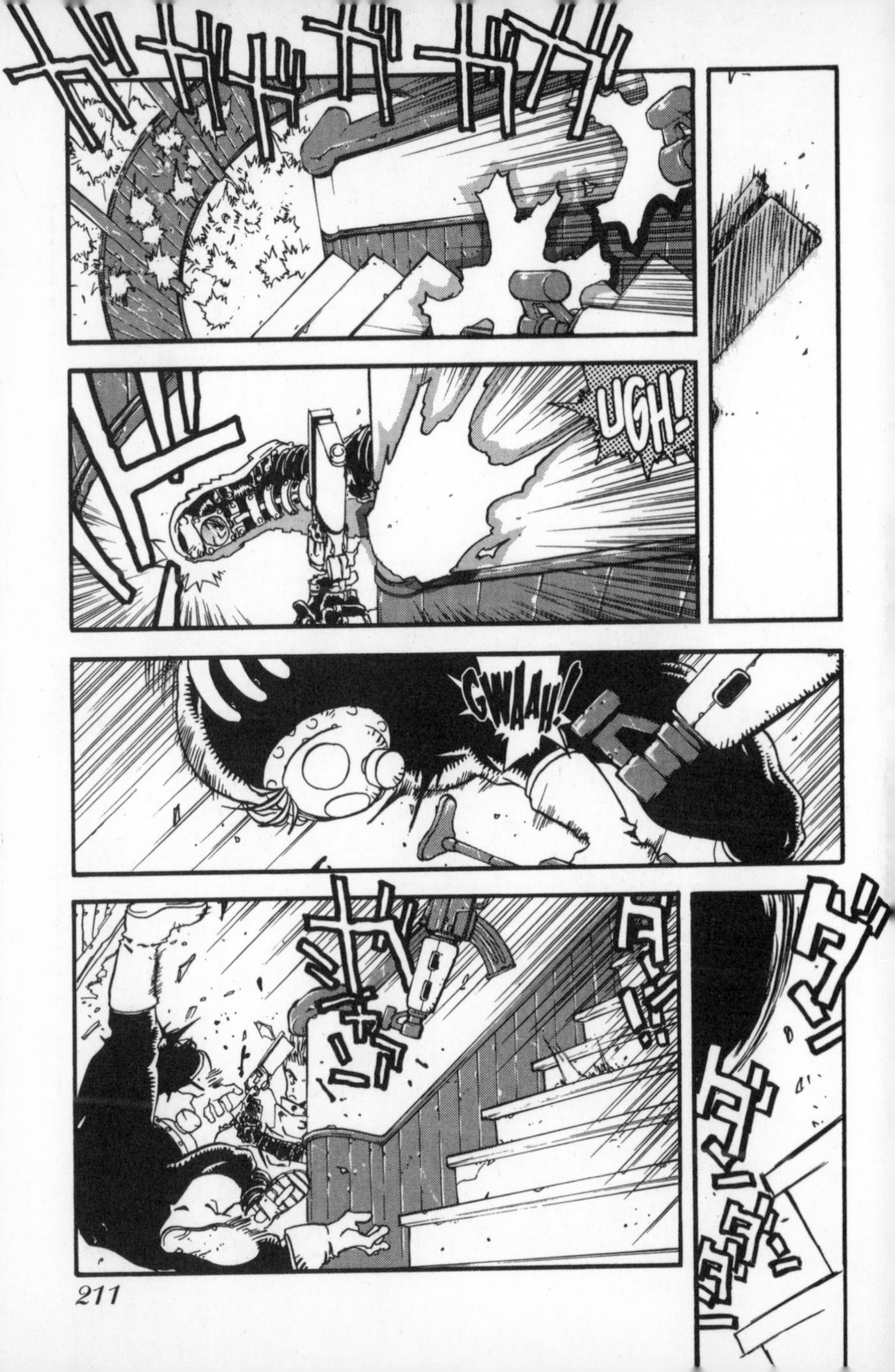
UGH!
GWAAH!!

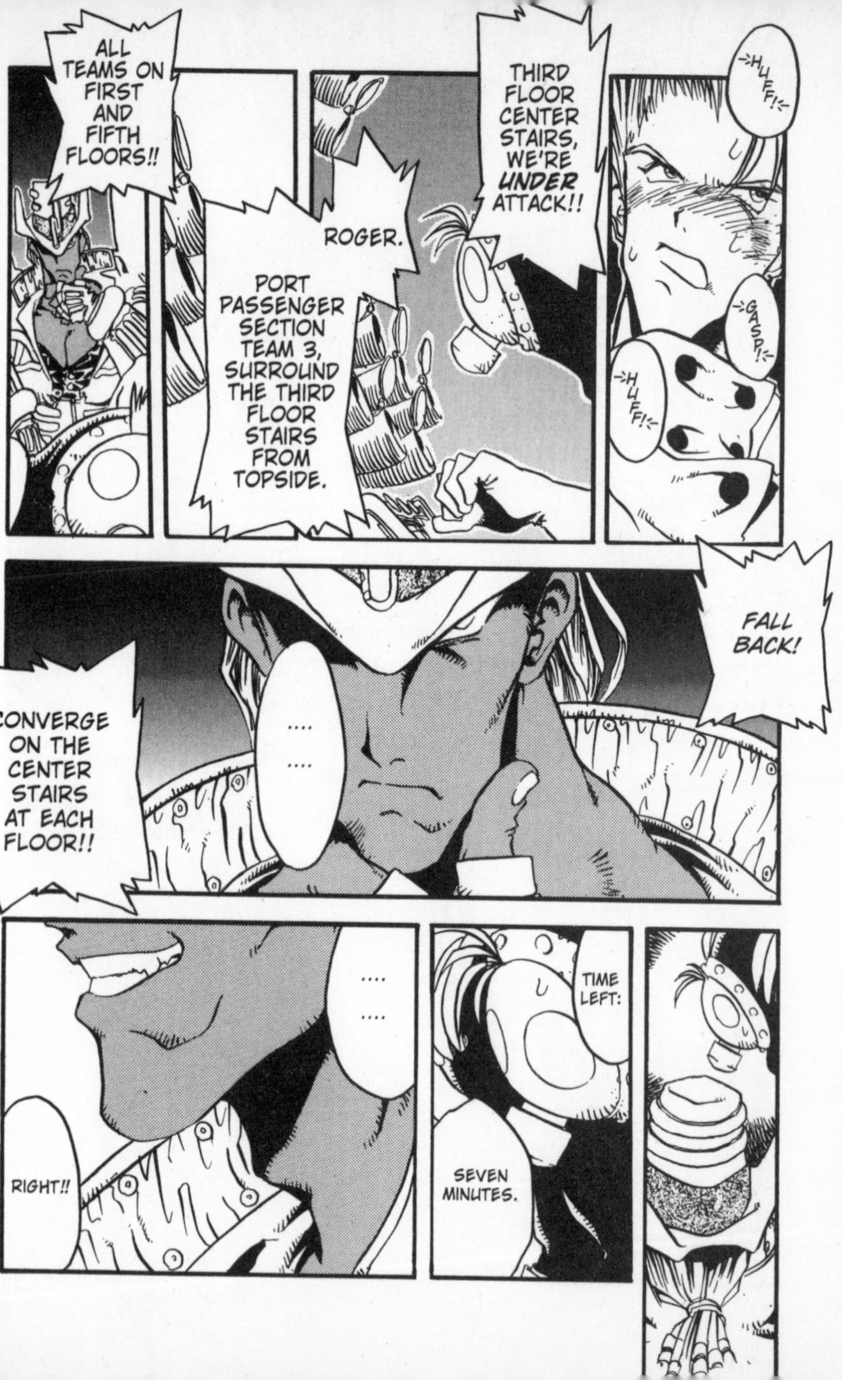
THIRD FLOOR CENTER STAIRS, WE'RE *UNDER* ATTACK!!
HUFF!
GASP!
HUFF!
ROGER.
PORT PASSENGER SECTION TEAM 3, SURROUND THE THIRD FLOOR STAIRS FROM TOPSIDE.
ALL TEAMS ON FIRST AND FIFTH FLOORS!!
FALL BACK!
.... ....
CONVERGE ON THE CENTER STAIRS AT EACH FLOOR!!
TIME LEFT:
SEVEN MINUTES.
.... ....
RIGHT!!

.....
.....

ROGER
THAT.

YOU
SHOULD
CUT
STRAIGHT
ACROSS
THERE.

THEY'RE
WAITING
*ABOVE*
AND
*BELOW*
YOU.

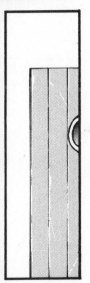

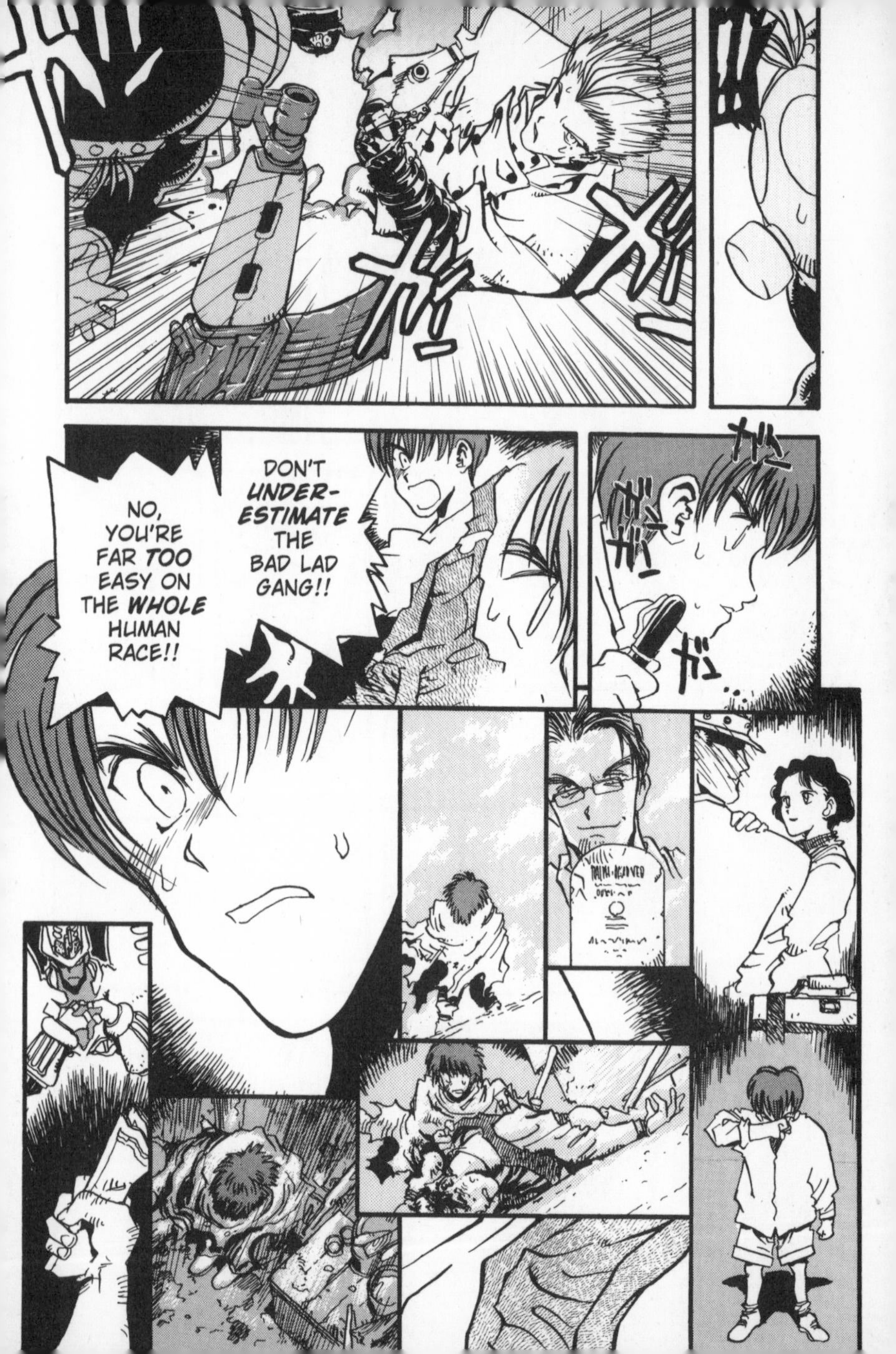
DON'T UNDER-ESTIMATE THE BAD LAD GANG!!
NO, YOU'RE FAR TOO EASY ON THE WHOLE HUMAN RACE!!

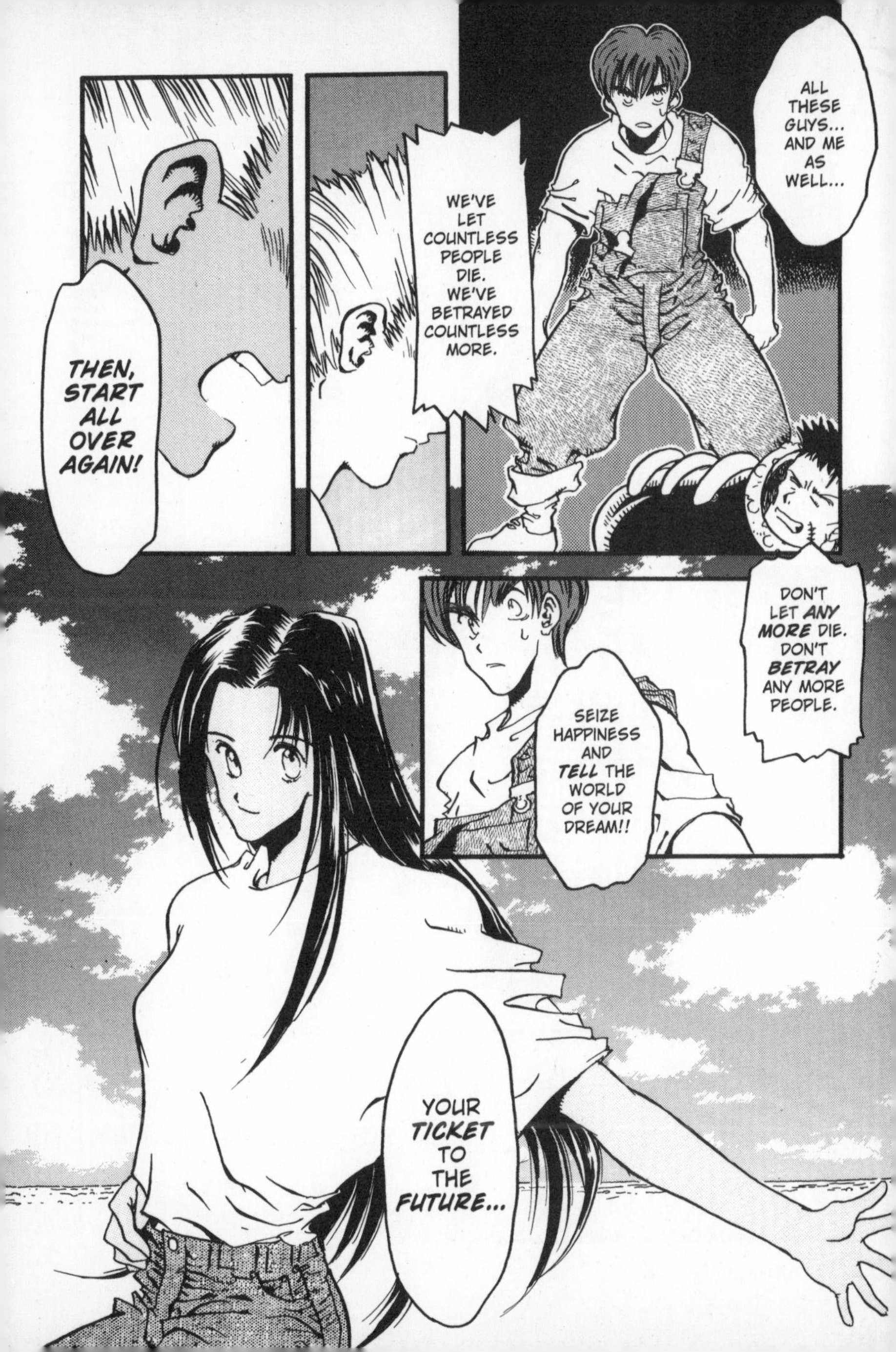
ALL THESE GUYS... AND ME AS WELL...
WE'VE LET COUNTLESS PEOPLE DIE. WE'VE BETRAYED COUNTLESS MORE.
THEN, START ALL OVER AGAIN!
DON'T LET ANY MORE DIE. DON'T BETRAY ANY MORE PEOPLE.
SEIZE HAPPINESS AND TELL THE WORLD OF YOUR DREAM!!
YOUR TICKET TO THE FUTURE...

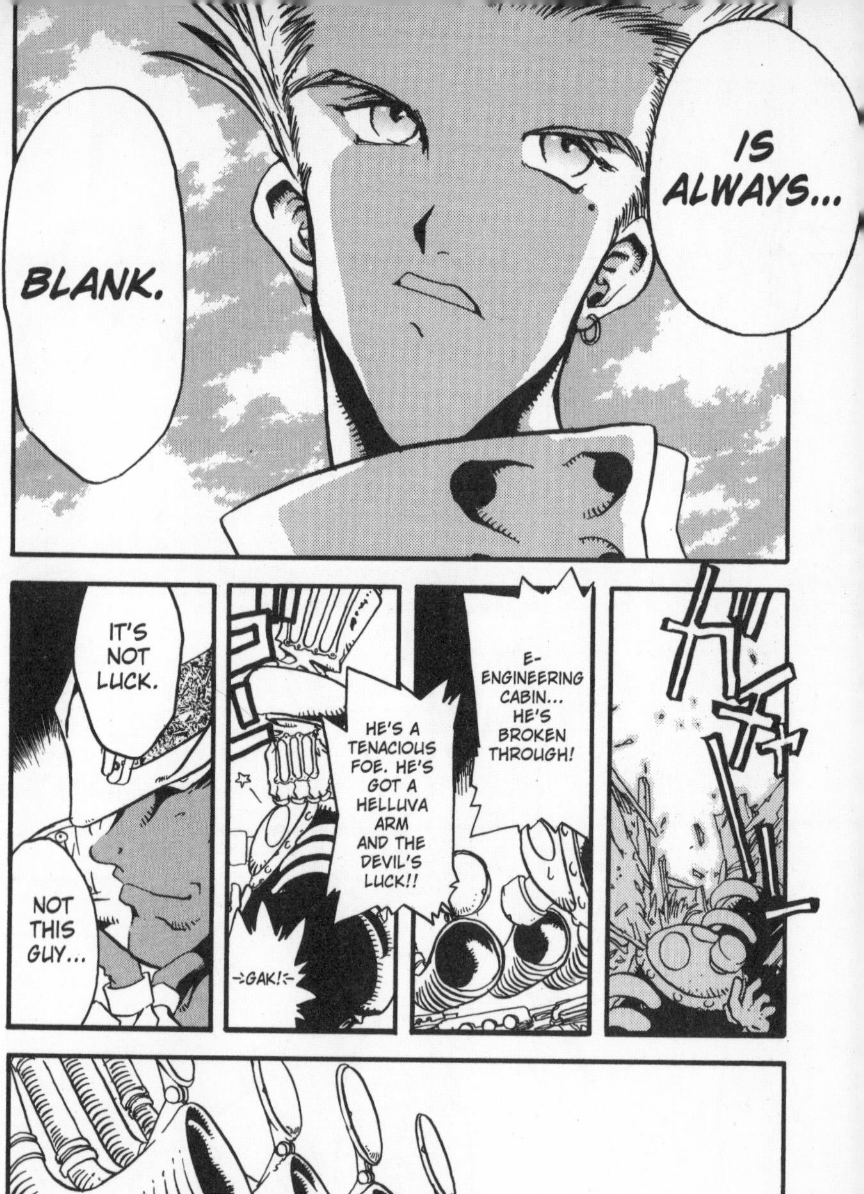
IS ALWAYS...
BLANK.
E-ENGINEERING CABIN... HE'S BROKEN THROUGH!
HE'S A TENACIOUS FOE. HE'S GOT A HELLUVA ARM AND THE DEVIL'S LUCK!!
GAK!
IT'S NOT LUCK.
NOT THIS GUY...

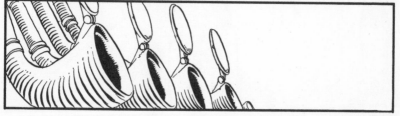

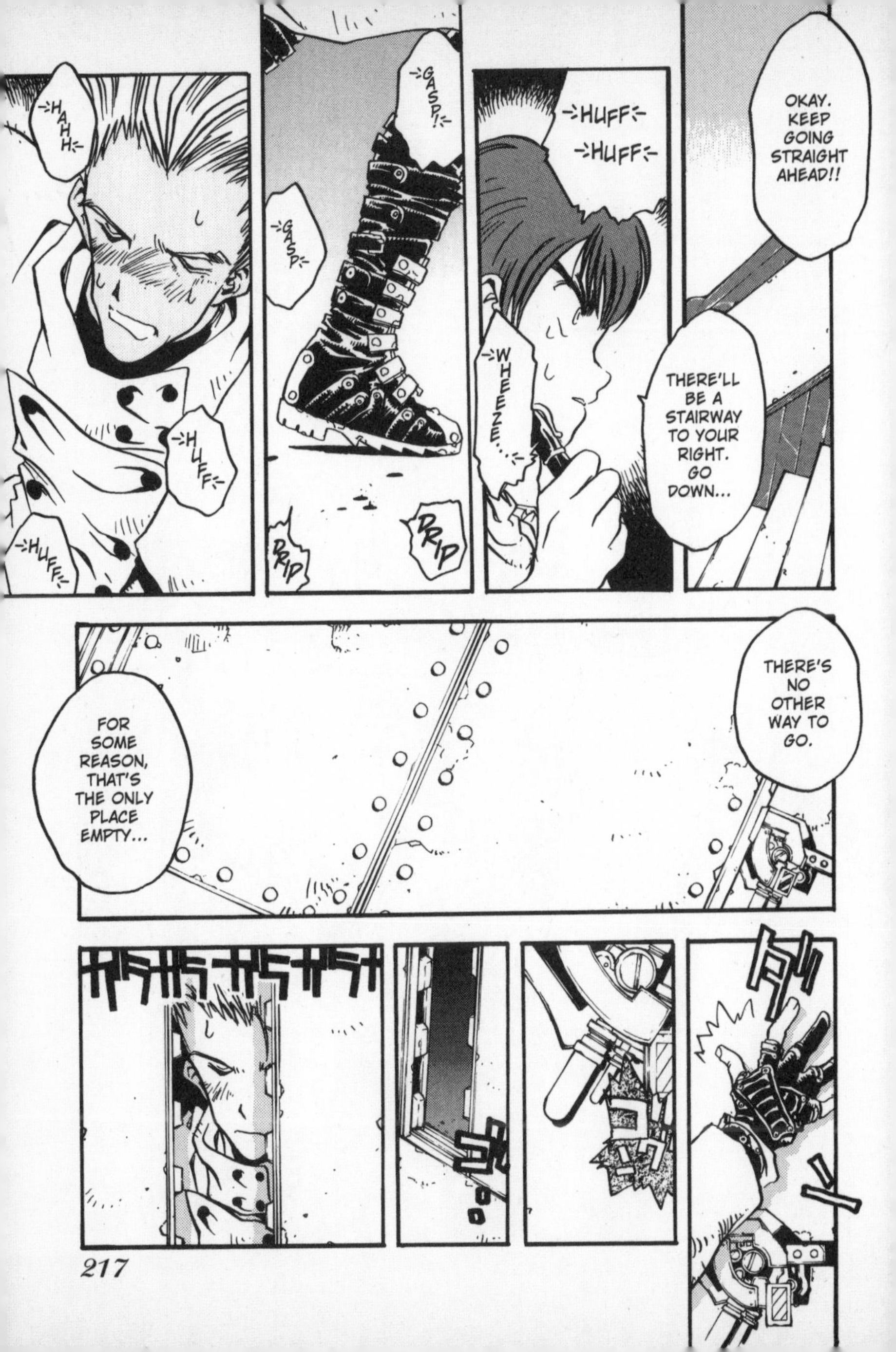
OKAY. KEEP GOING STRAIGHT AHEAD!!
THERE'LL BE A STAIRWAY TO YOUR RIGHT. GO DOWN...
HUFF
HUFF
WHEEZE...
GASP!
GASP
DRIP
DRIP
HAHH
HUFF
HUFF
THERE'S NO OTHER WAY TO GO.
FOR SOME REASON, THAT'S THE ONLY PLACE EMPTY...

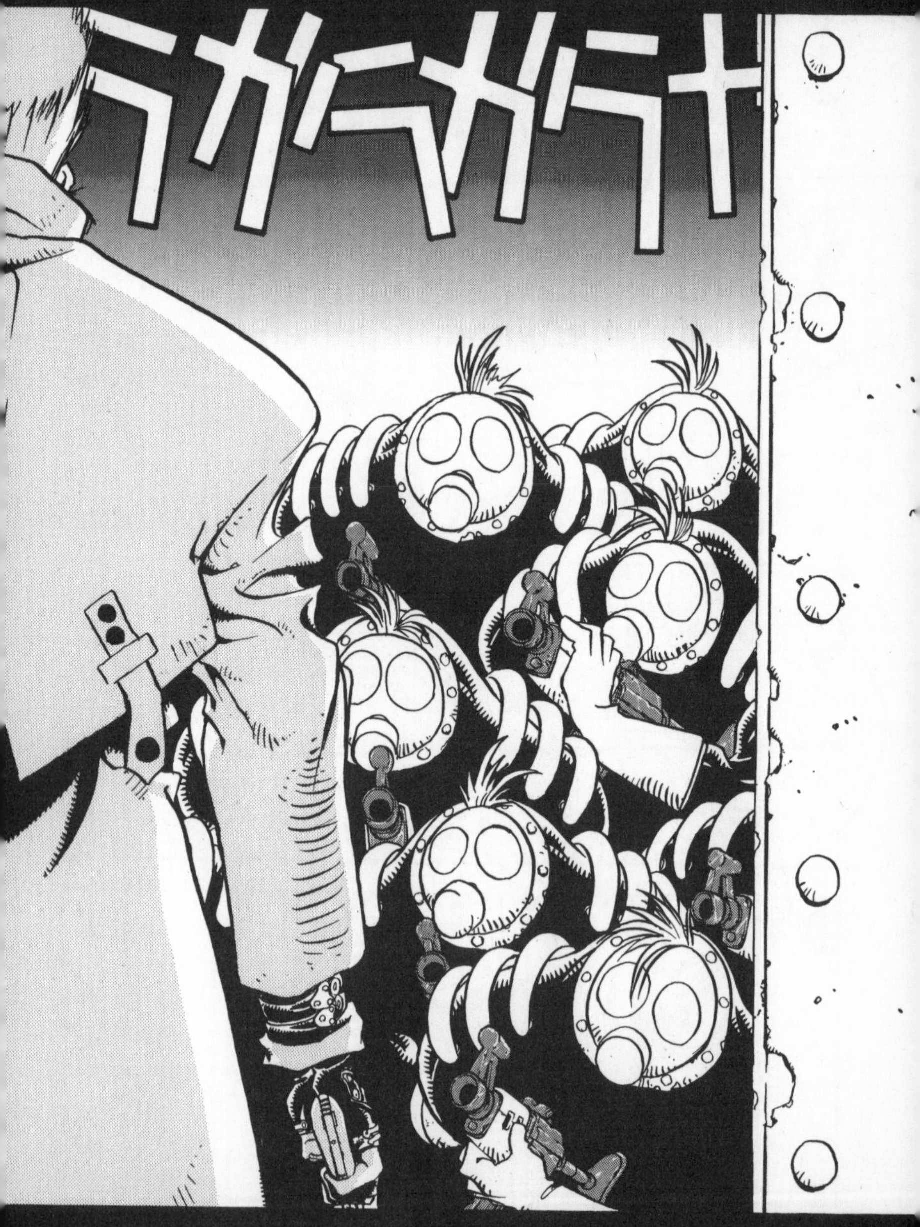
ラガラガラガ

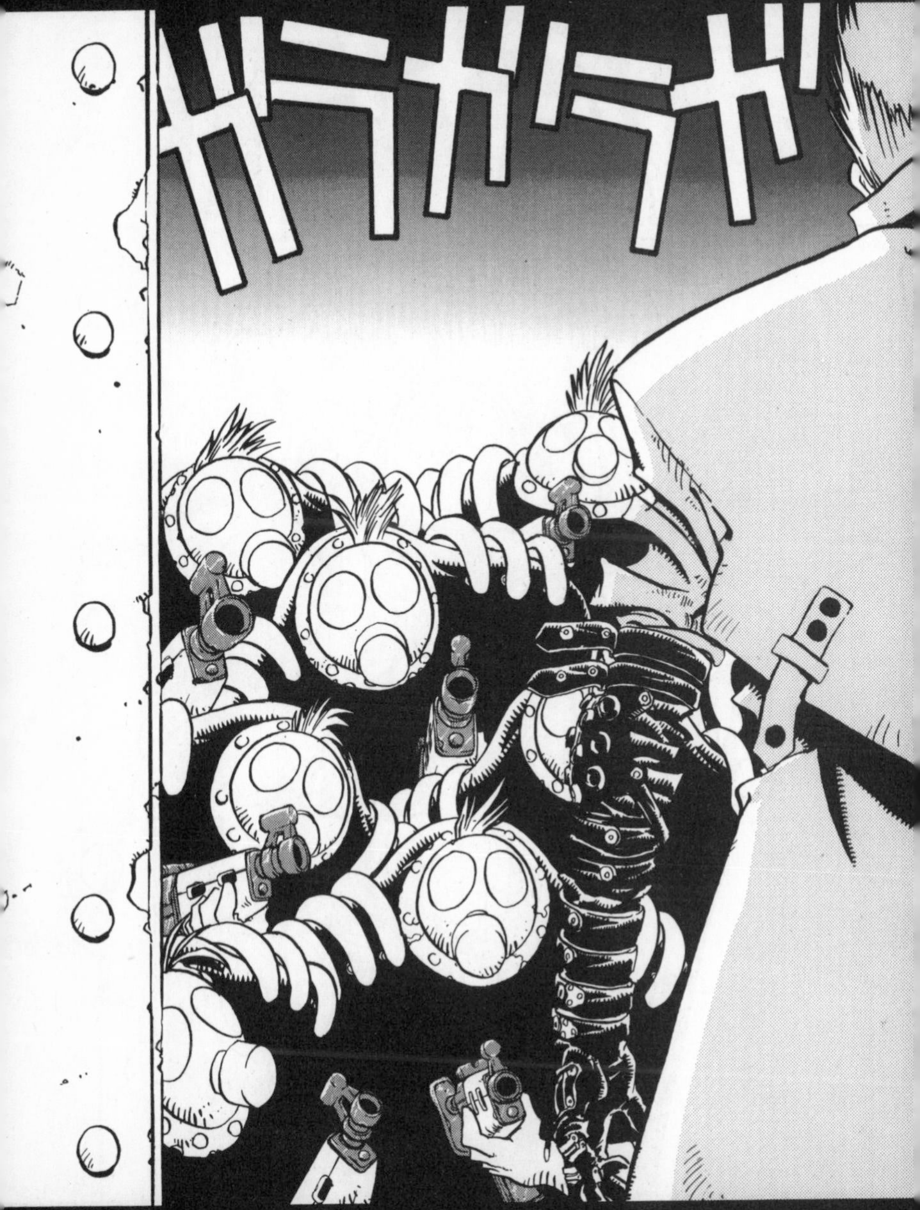
ガラガラガ

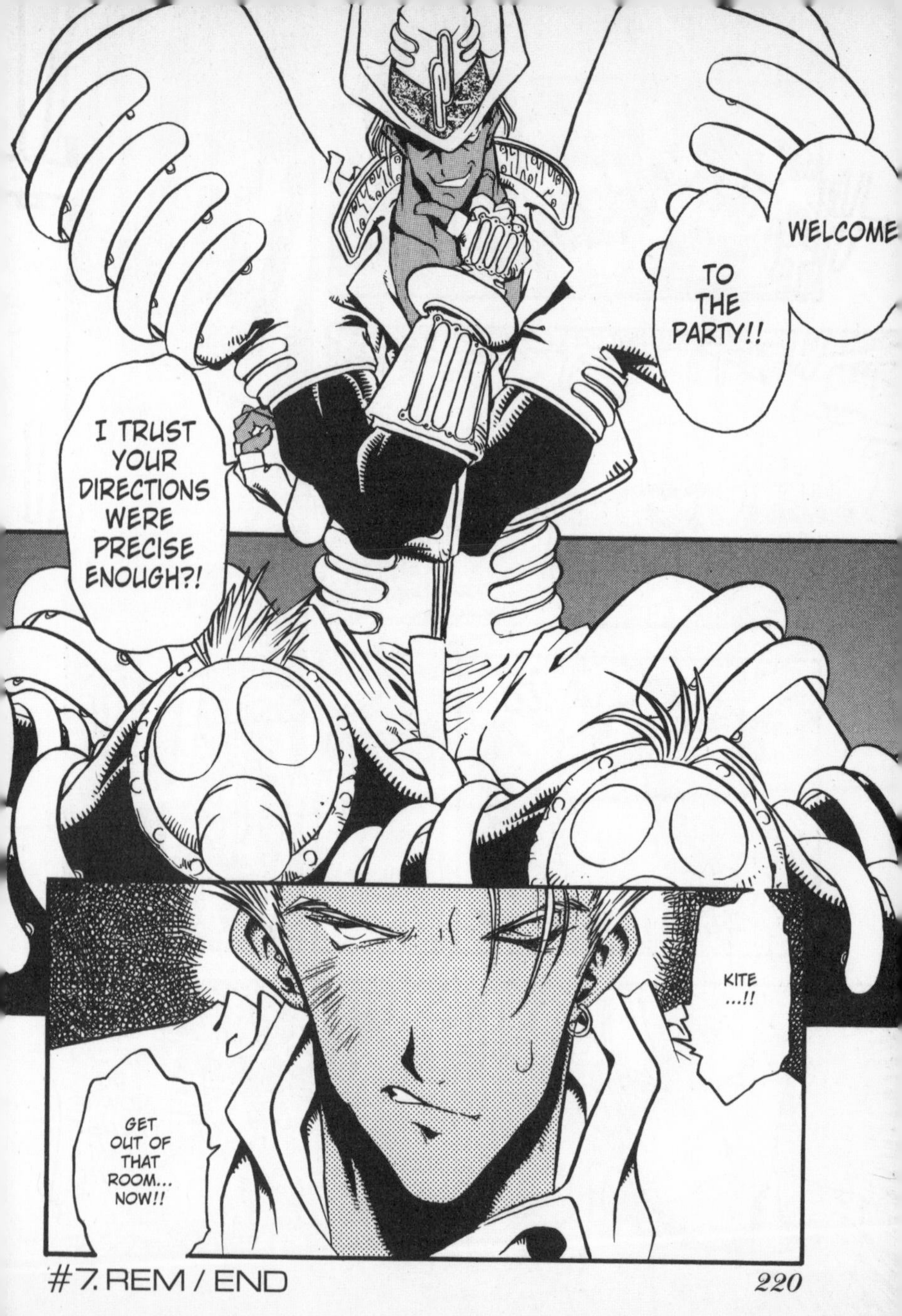
WELCOME TO THE PARTY!!
I TRUST YOUR DIRECTIONS WERE PRECISE ENOUGH?!
KITE ...!!
GET OUT OF THAT ROOM... NOW!!

#7. REM / END

#8

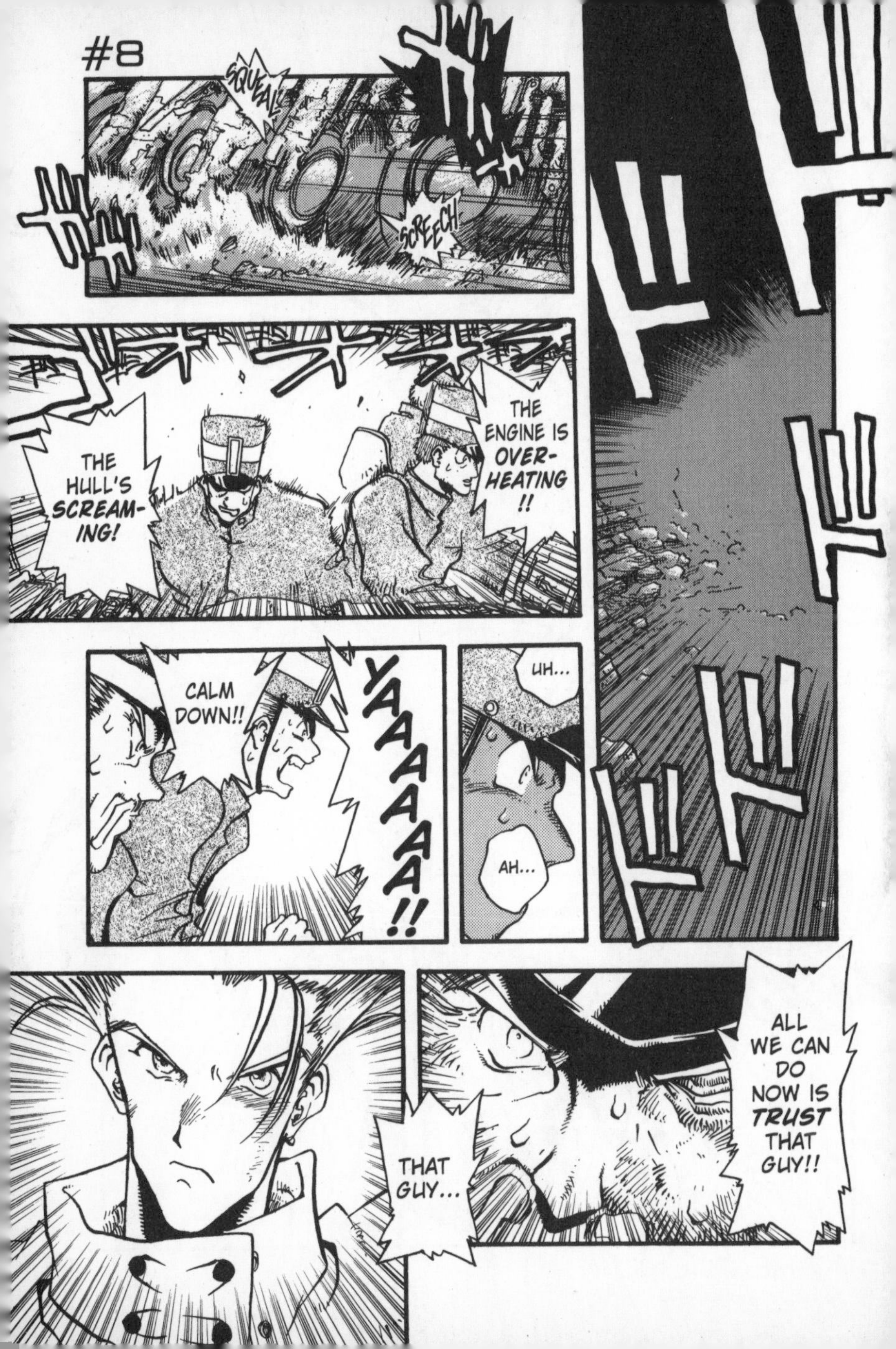

SQUEAL!
SCREECH!
THE ENGINE IS OVER-HEATING!!
THE HULL'S SCREAMING!
UH...
AH...
YAAAAAA!!
CALM DOWN!!
ALL WE CAN DO NOW IS TRUST THAT GUY!!
THAT GUY...

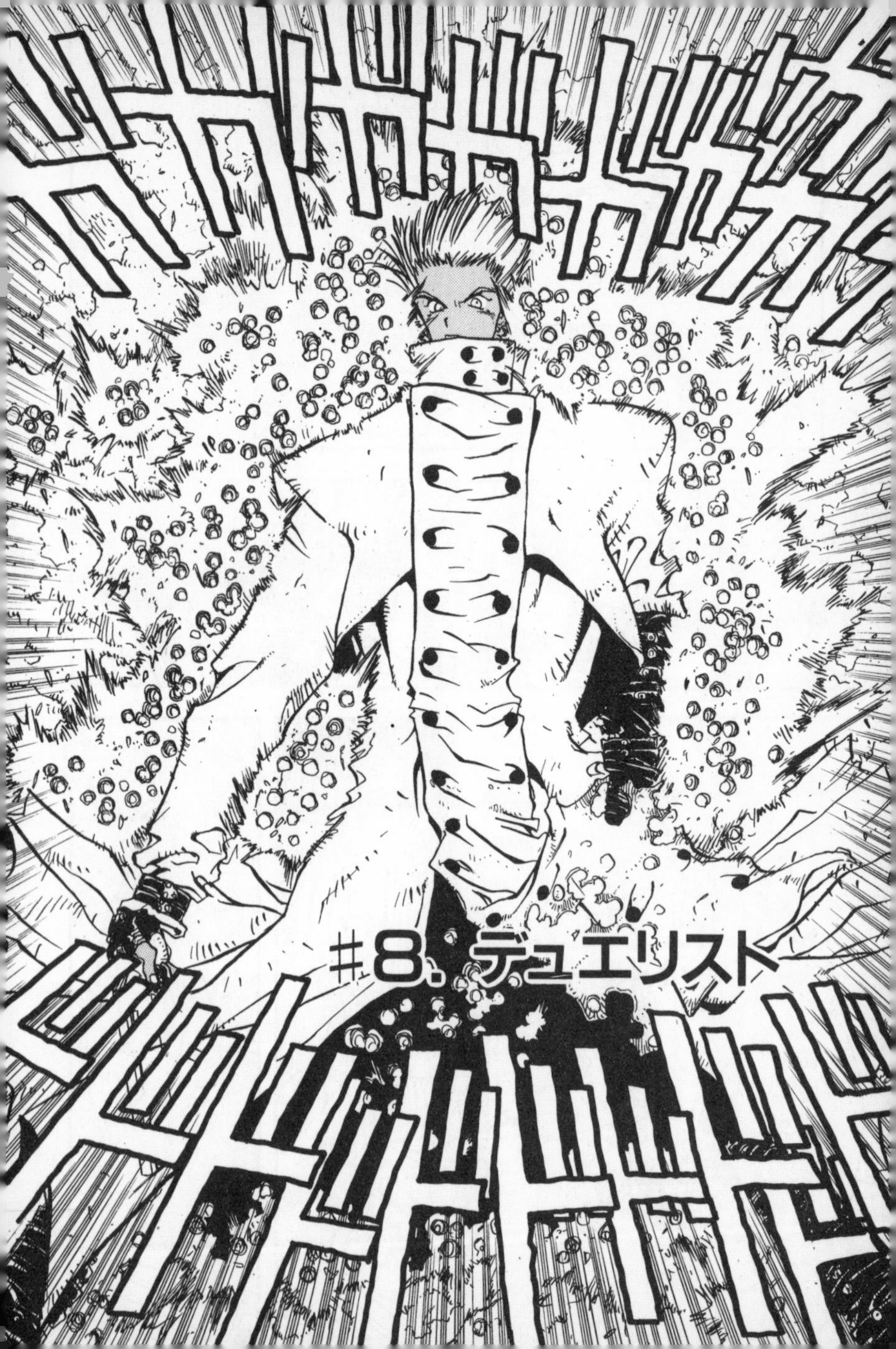
#8. デュエリスト

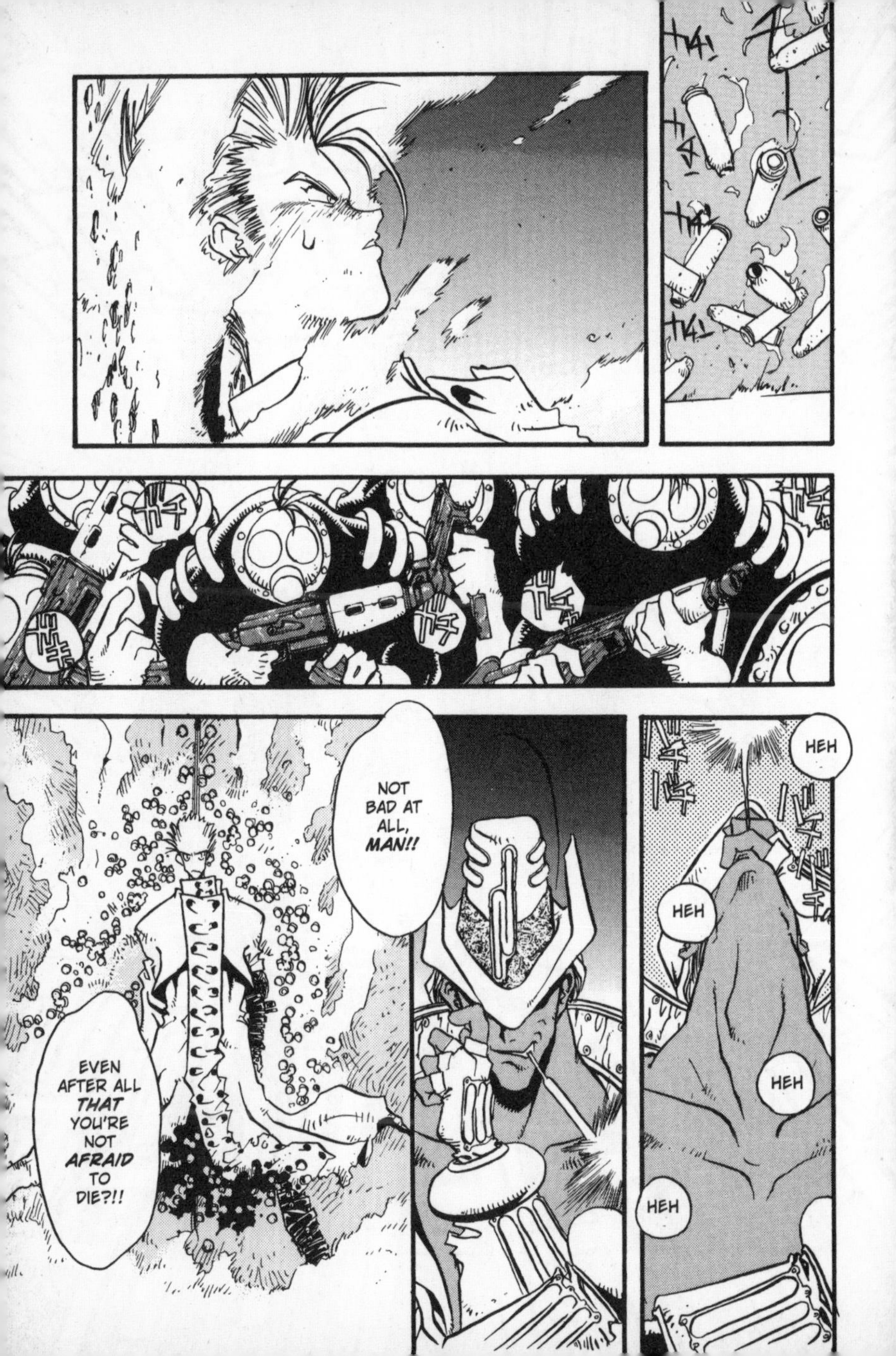
HEH
HEH
HEH
HEH
NOT BAD AT ALL, *MAN!!*
EVEN AFTER ALL *THAT* YOU'RE NOT *AFRAID* TO DIE?!!

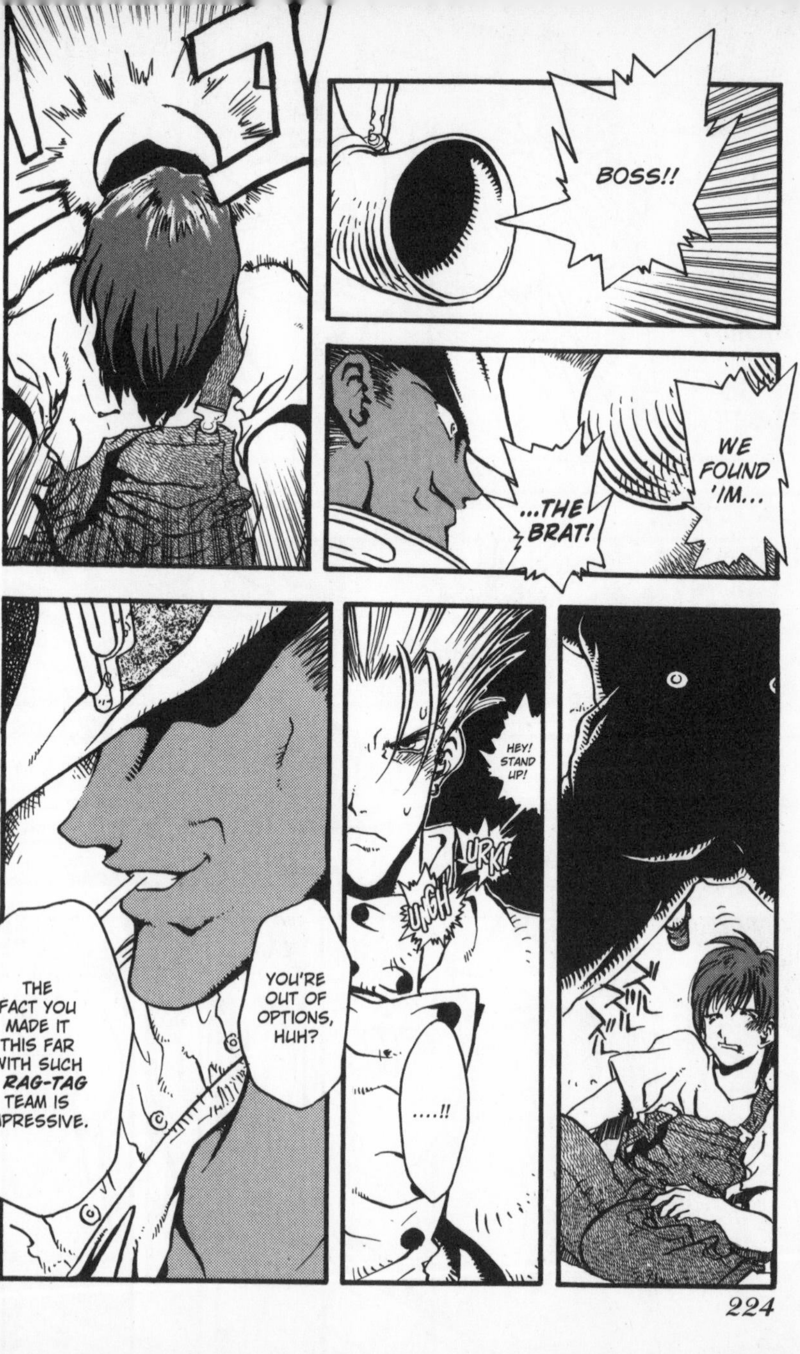
BOSS!!
WE FOUND 'IM...
...THE BRAT!
HEY! STAND UP!
URK!
UNGH
....!!
YOU'RE OUT OF OPTIONS, HUH?
THE FACT YOU MADE IT THIS FAR WITH SUCH A *RAG-TAG* TEAM IS IMPRESSIVE.

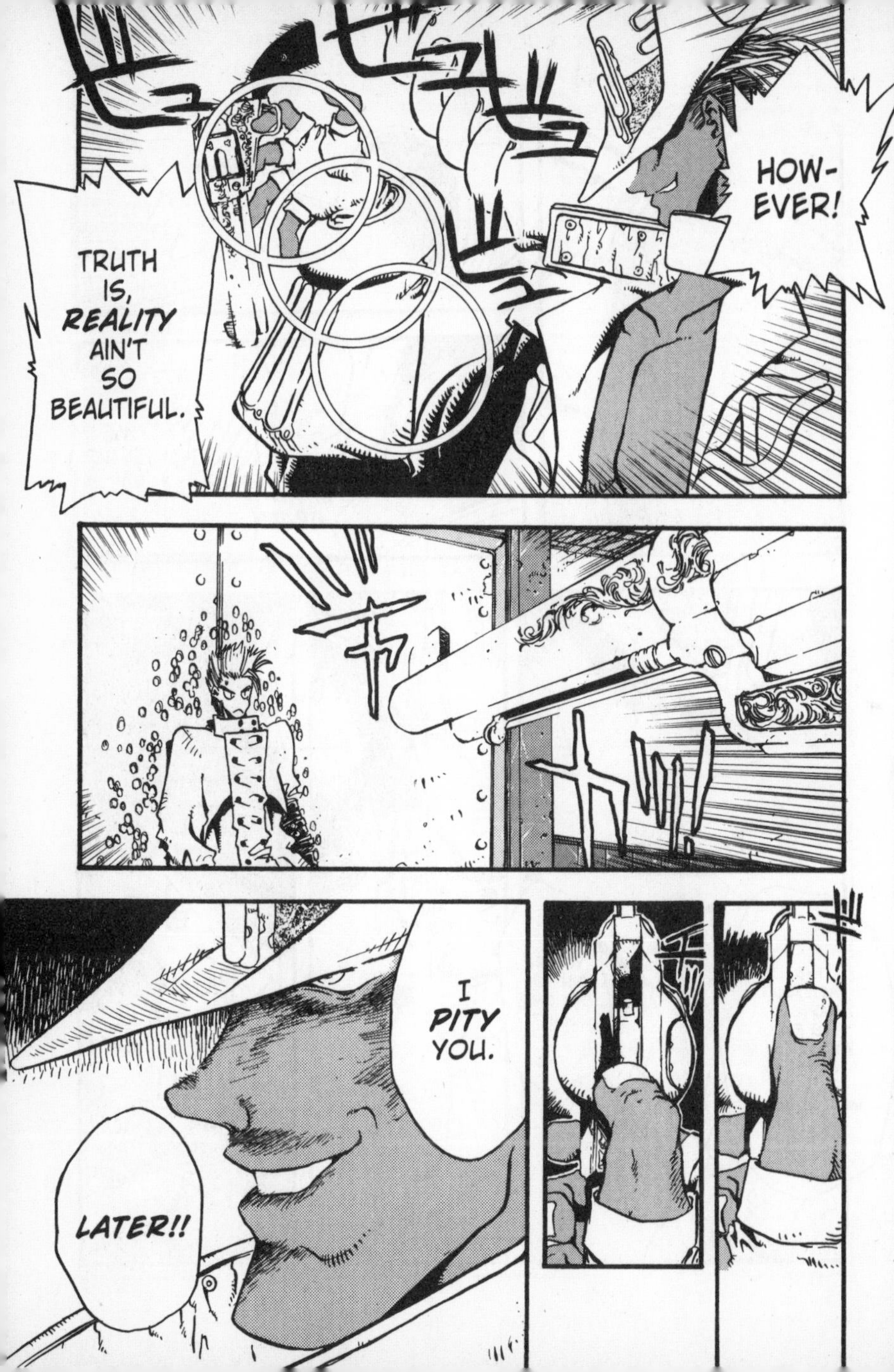
HOW-EVER!
TRUTH IS, *REALITY* AIN'T SO BEAUTIFUL.
I *PITY* YOU.
*LATER!!*

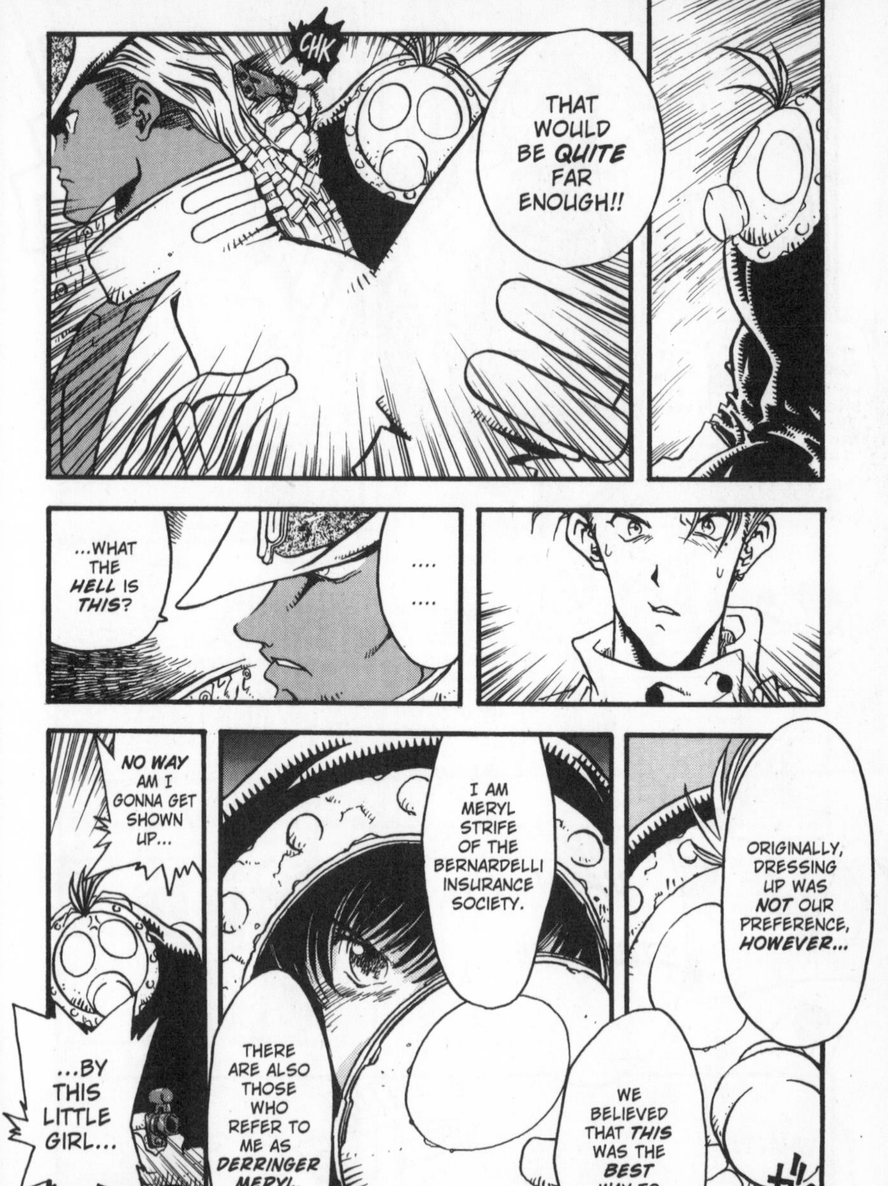
CHK
THAT WOULD BE QUITE FAR ENOUGH!!
...WHAT THE HELL IS THIS?
....
....
ORIGINALLY, DRESSING UP WAS NOT OUR PREFERENCE, HOWEVER...
WE BELIEVED THAT THIS WAS THE BEST WAY TO GET PAST YOU.
I AM MERYL STRIFE OF THE BERNARDELLI INSURANCE SOCIETY.
THERE ARE ALSO THOSE WHO REFER TO ME AS DERRINGER MERYL.
NO WAY AM I GONNA GET SHOWN UP...
...BY THIS LITTLE GIRL...

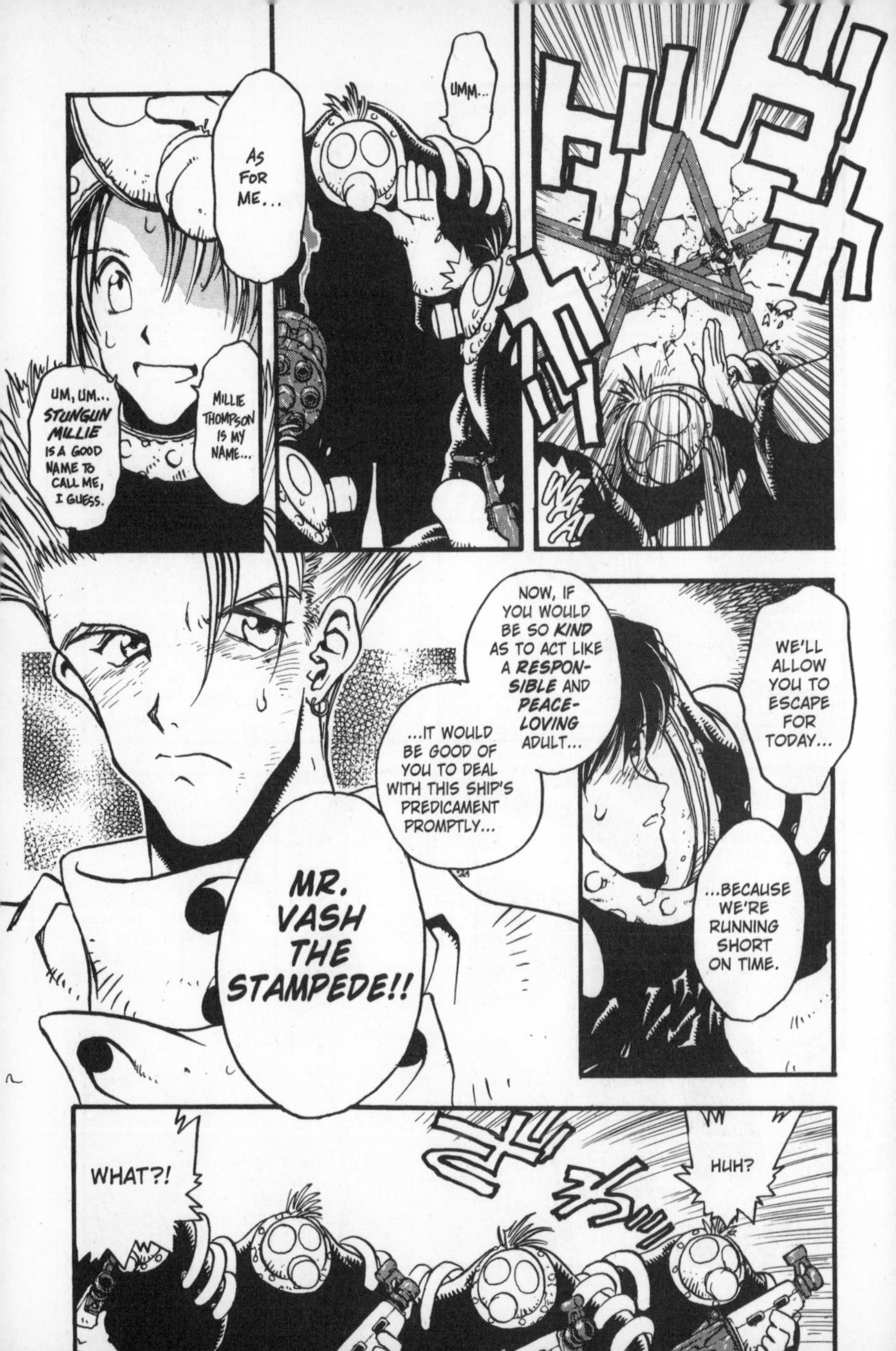
WAA
UMM...
AS FOR ME...
MILLIE THOMPSON IS MY NAME...
UM, UM... **STUNGUN MILLIE** IS A GOOD NAME TO CALL ME, I GUESS.
WE'LL ALLOW YOU TO ESCAPE FOR TODAY...
...BECAUSE WE'RE RUNNING SHORT ON TIME.
NOW, IF YOU WOULD BE SO **KIND** AS TO ACT LIKE A **RESPONSIBLE** AND **PEACE-LOVING** ADULT...
...IT WOULD BE GOOD OF YOU TO DEAL WITH THIS SHIP'S PREDICAMENT PROMPTLY...
**MR. VASH THE STAMPEDE!!**
HUH?
WHAT?!

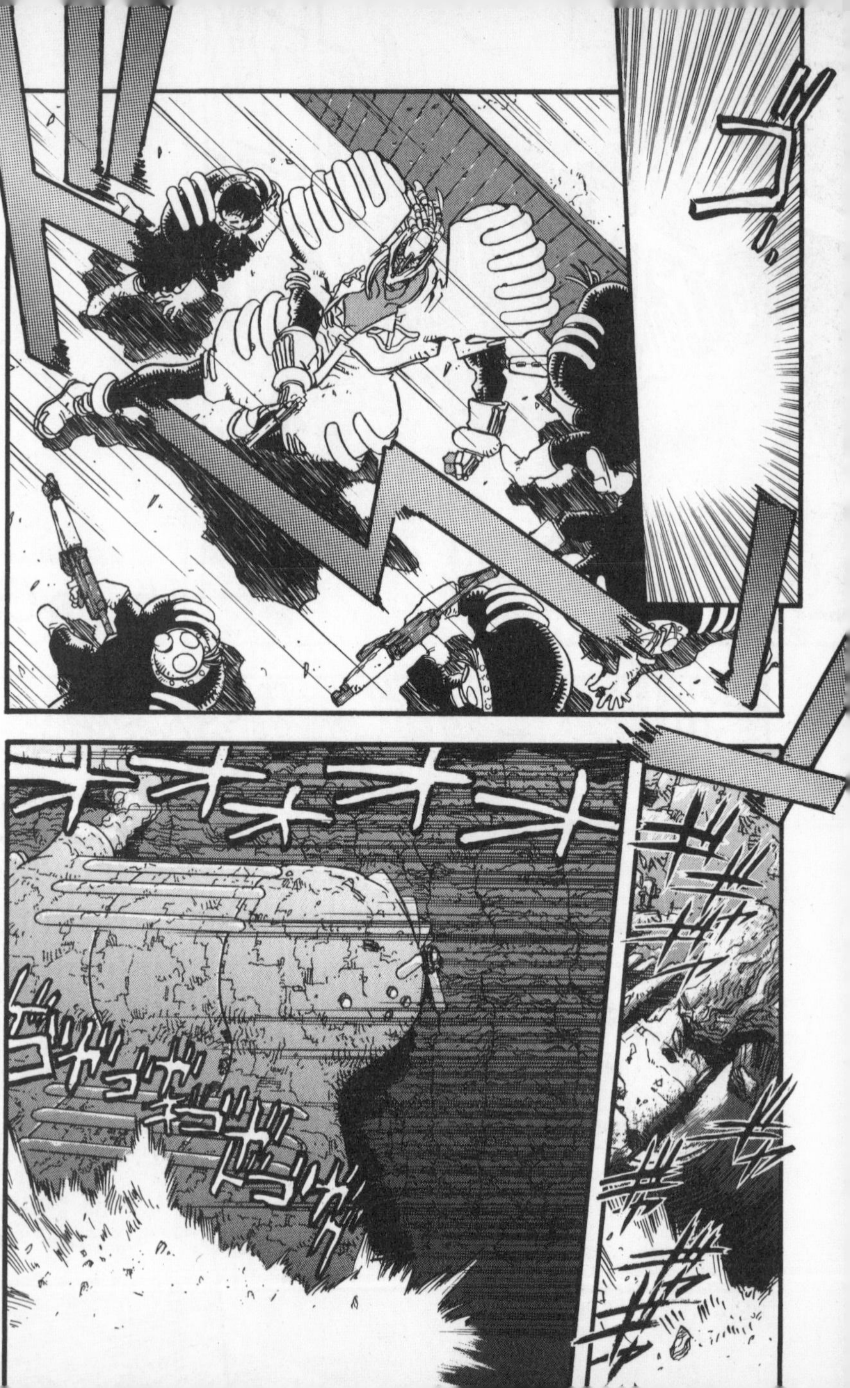

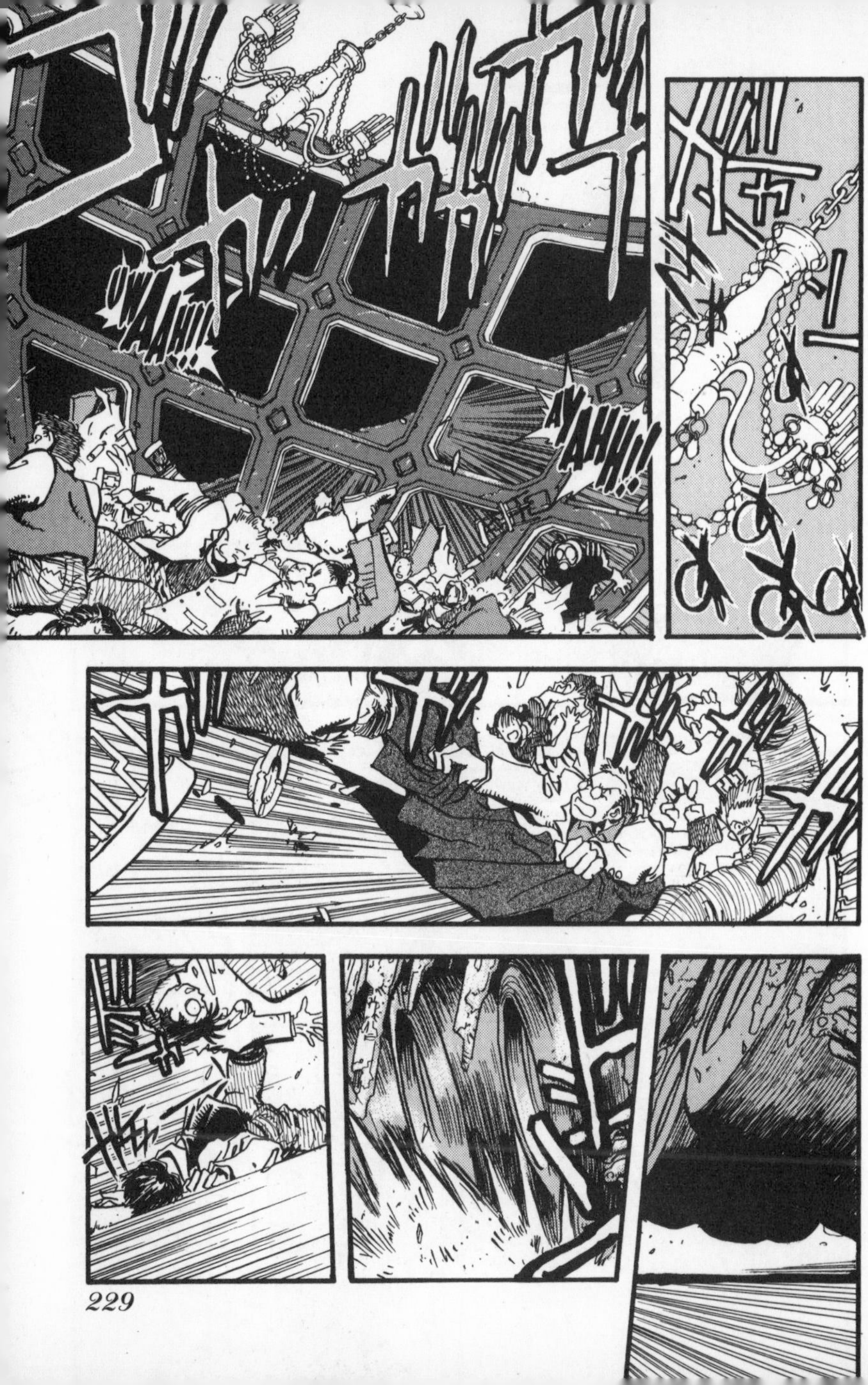
AYAAHH!!
OWAAAH!!

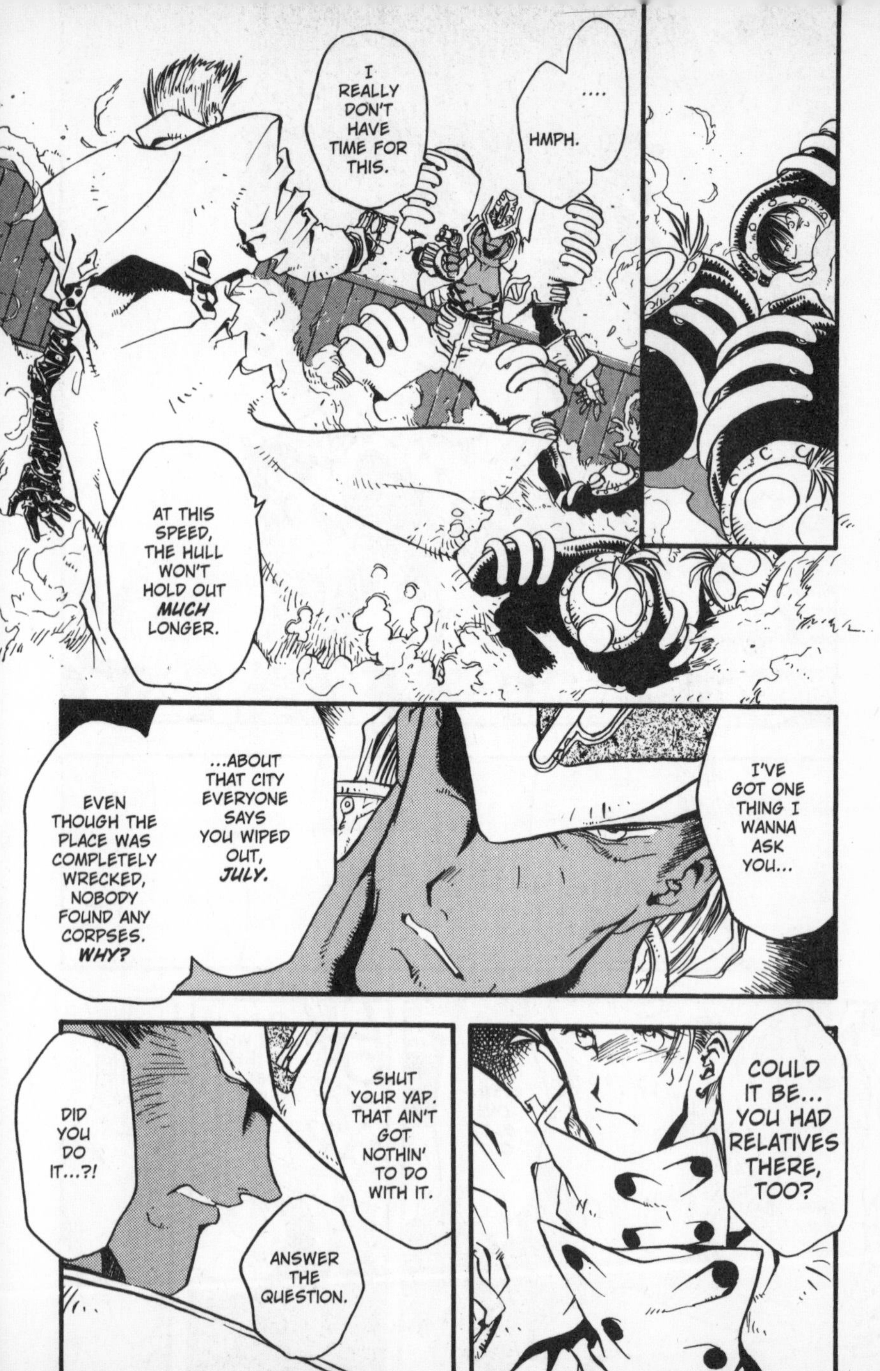
....
HMPH.
I REALLY DON'T HAVE TIME FOR THIS.
AT THIS SPEED, THE HULL WON'T HOLD OUT *MUCH* LONGER.
I'VE GOT ONE THING I WANNA ASK YOU...
...ABOUT THAT CITY EVERYONE SAYS YOU WIPED OUT, *JULY.*
EVEN THOUGH THE PLACE WAS COMPLETELY WRECKED, NOBODY FOUND ANY CORPSES. *WHY?*
COULD IT BE... YOU HAD RELATIVES THERE, TOO?
SHUT YOUR YAP. THAT AIN'T GOT NOTHIN' TO DO WITH IT.
DID YOU DO IT...?!
ANSWER THE QUESTION.

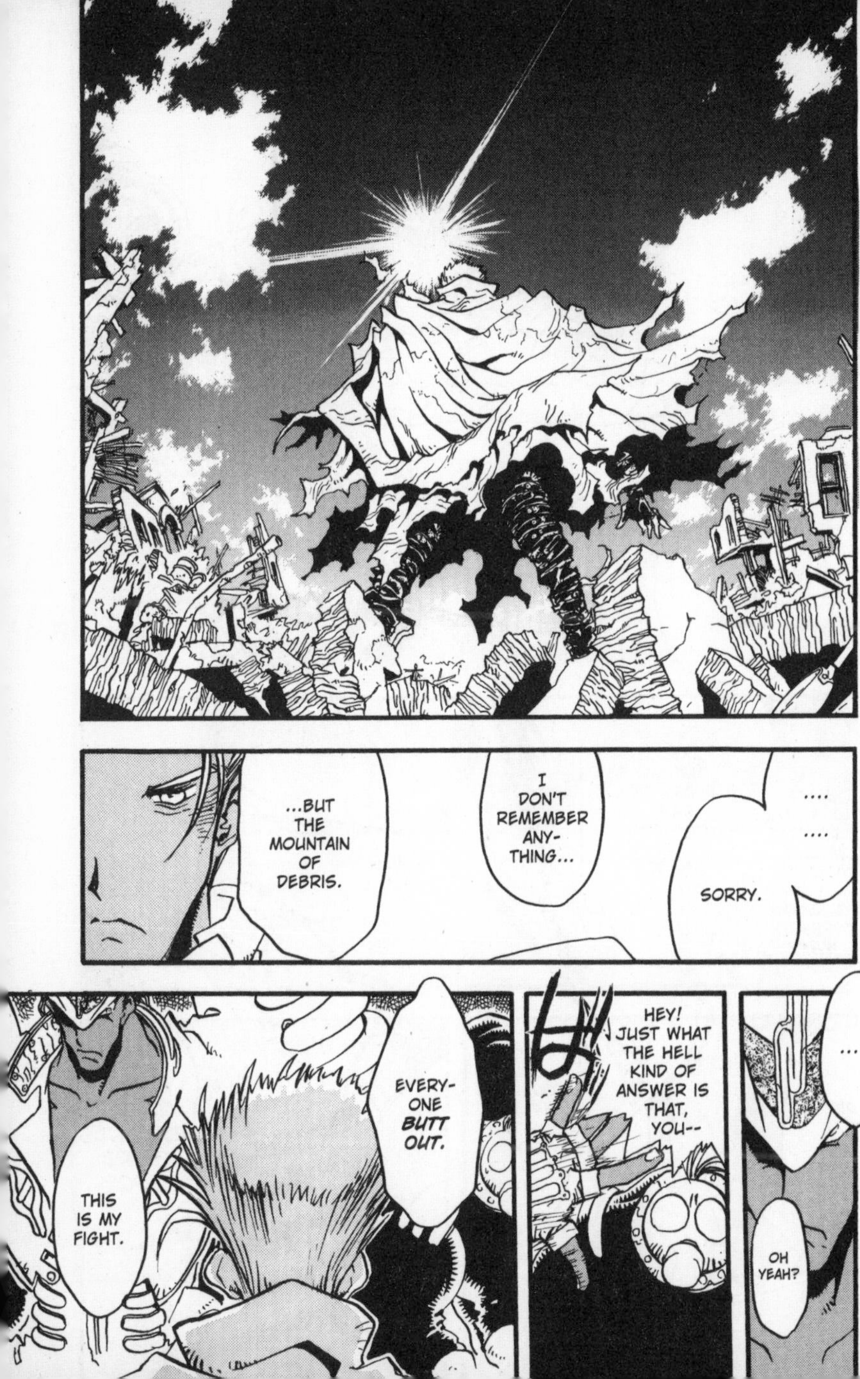
....
....
SORRY.
I DON'T REMEMBER ANY-THING...
...BUT THE MOUNTAIN OF DEBRIS.
....
OH YEAH?
HEY! JUST WHAT THE HELL KIND OF ANSWER IS THAT, YOU--
EVERY-ONE *BUTT* OUT.
THIS IS MY FIGHT.

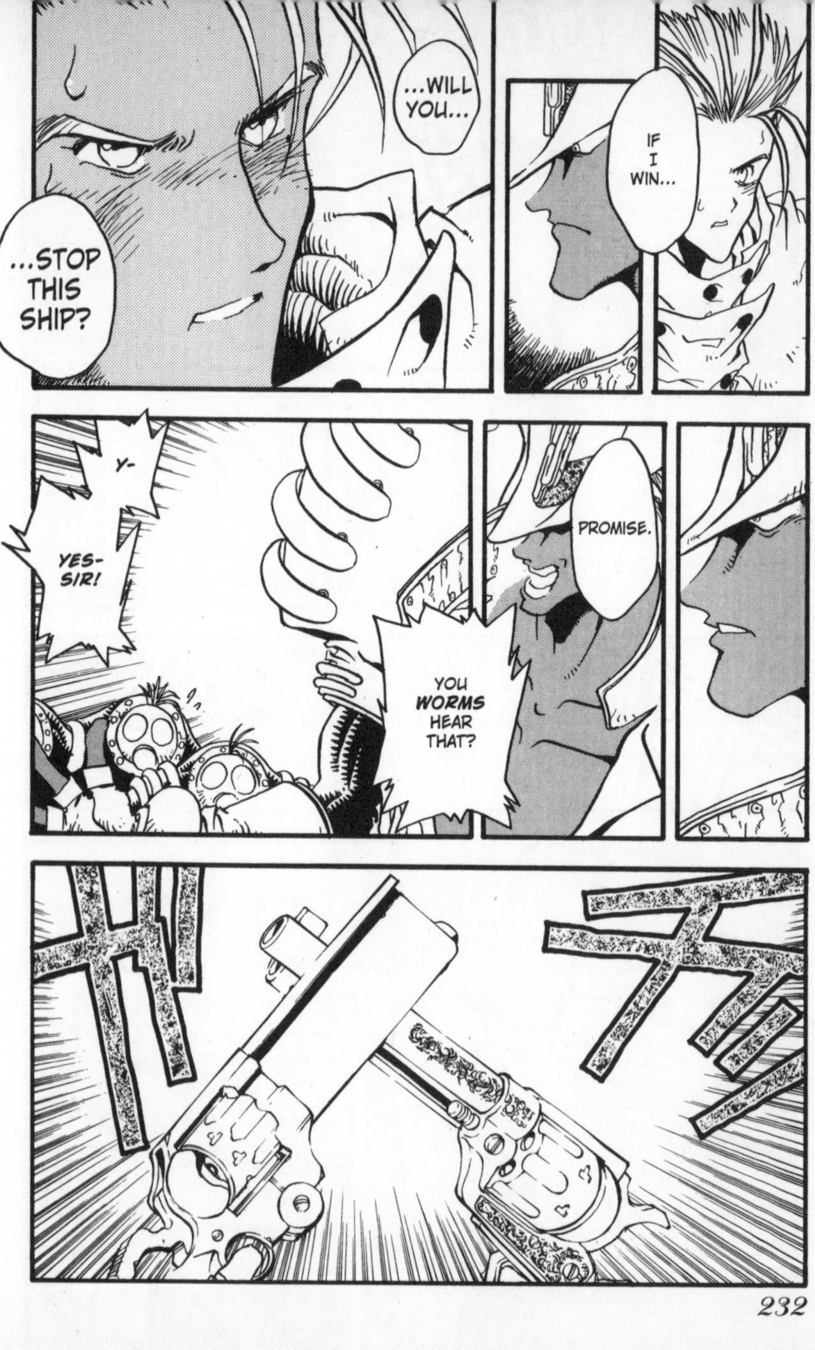
IF I WIN...
...WILL YOU...
...STOP THIS SHIP?
PROMISE.
YOU **WORMS** HEAR THAT?
Y-
*YES-SIR!*

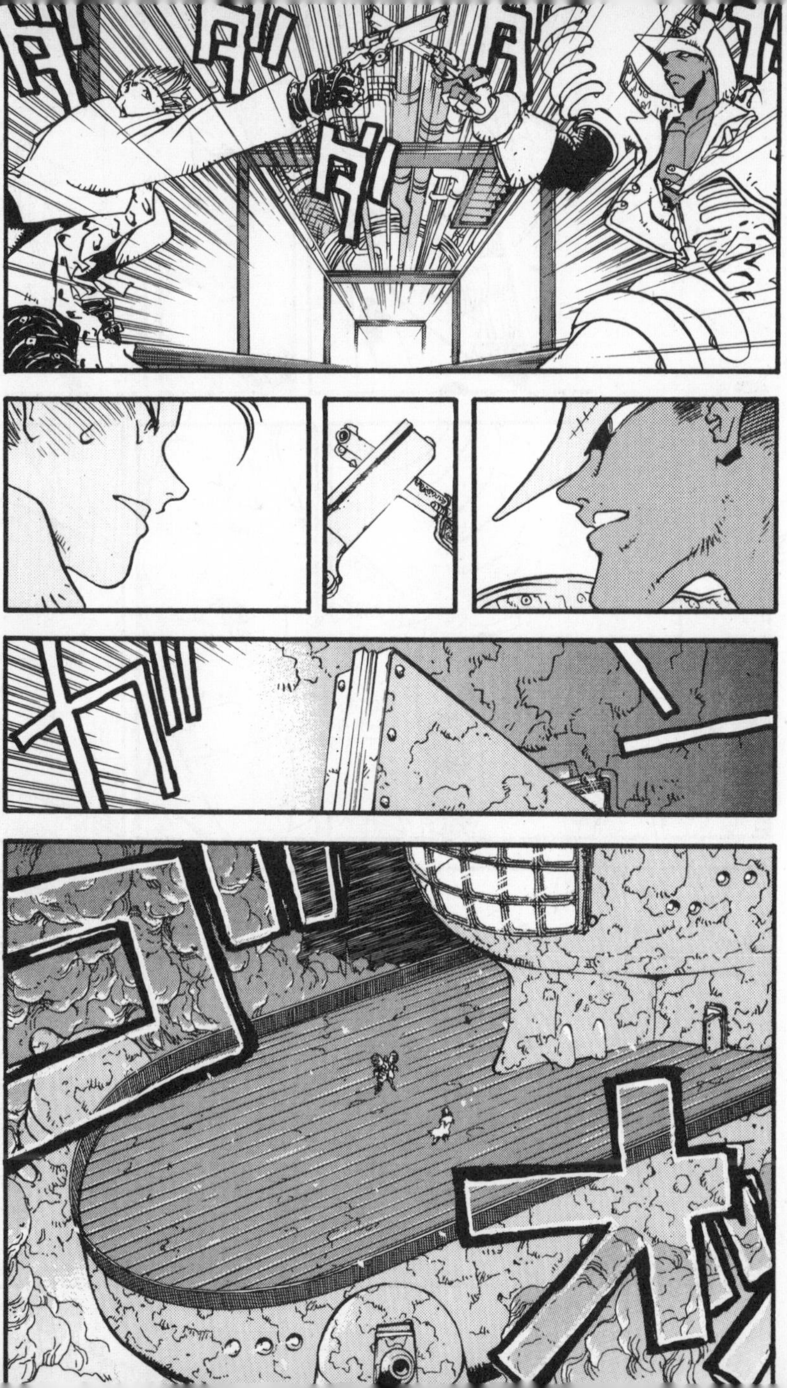

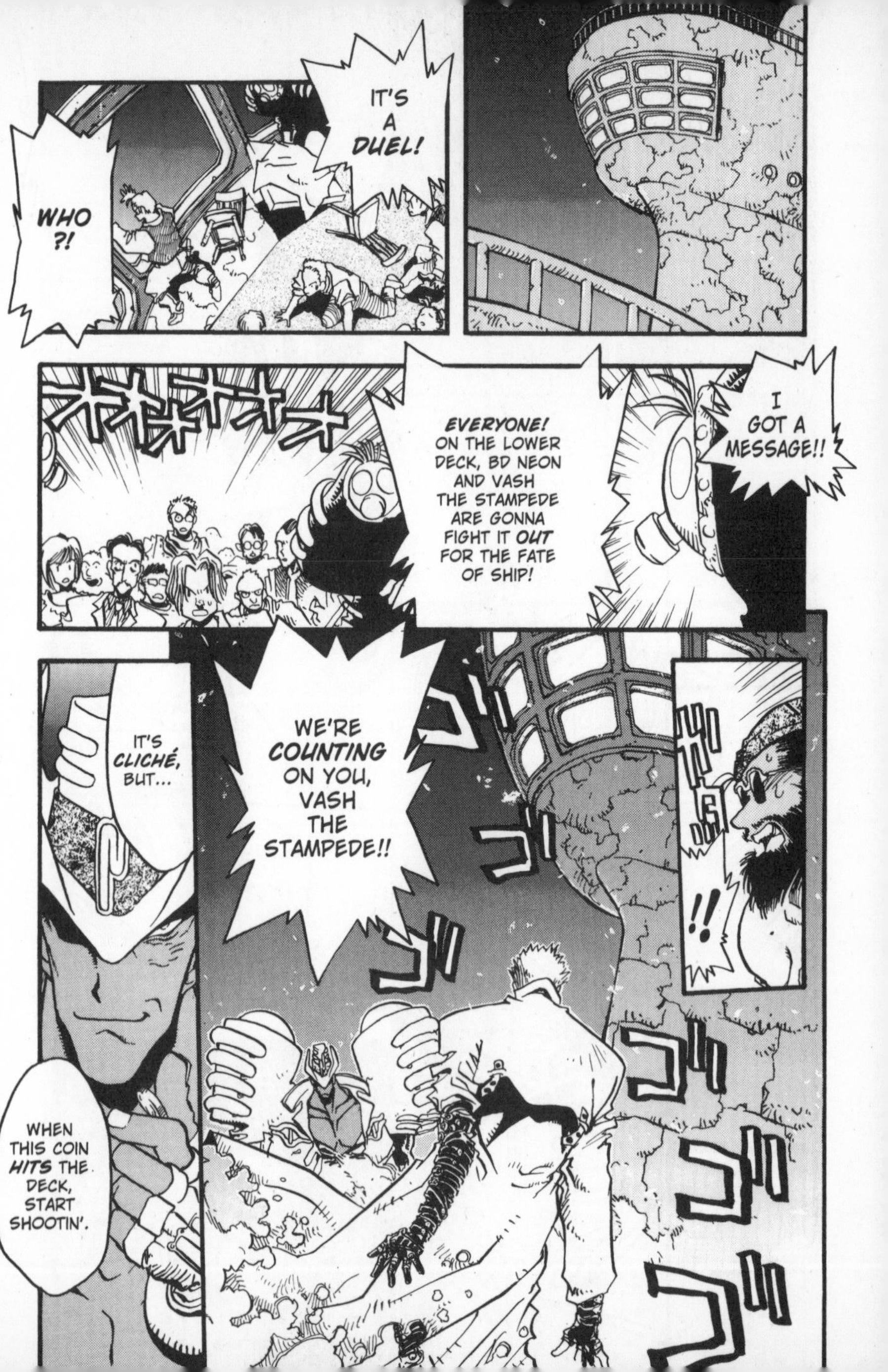
IT'S A DUEL!
WHO ?!
I GOT A MESSAGE!!
EVERYONE! ON THE LOWER DECK, BD NEON AND VASH THE STAMPEDE ARE GONNA FIGHT IT OUT FOR THE FATE OF SHIP!
!!
WE'RE COUNTING ON YOU, VASH THE STAMPEDE!!
IT'S CLICHÉ, BUT...
WHEN THIS COIN HITS THE DECK, START SHOOTIN'.

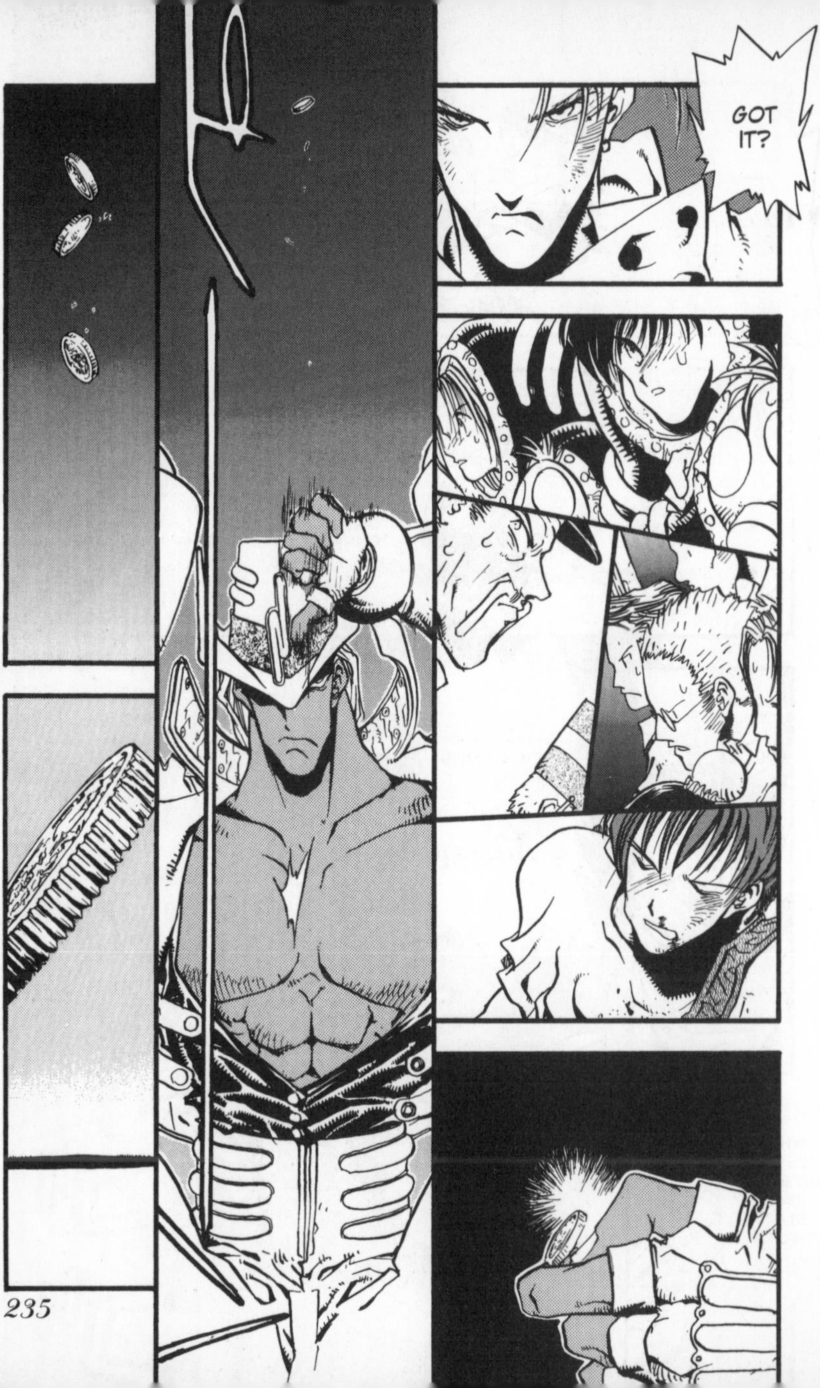
GOT IT?

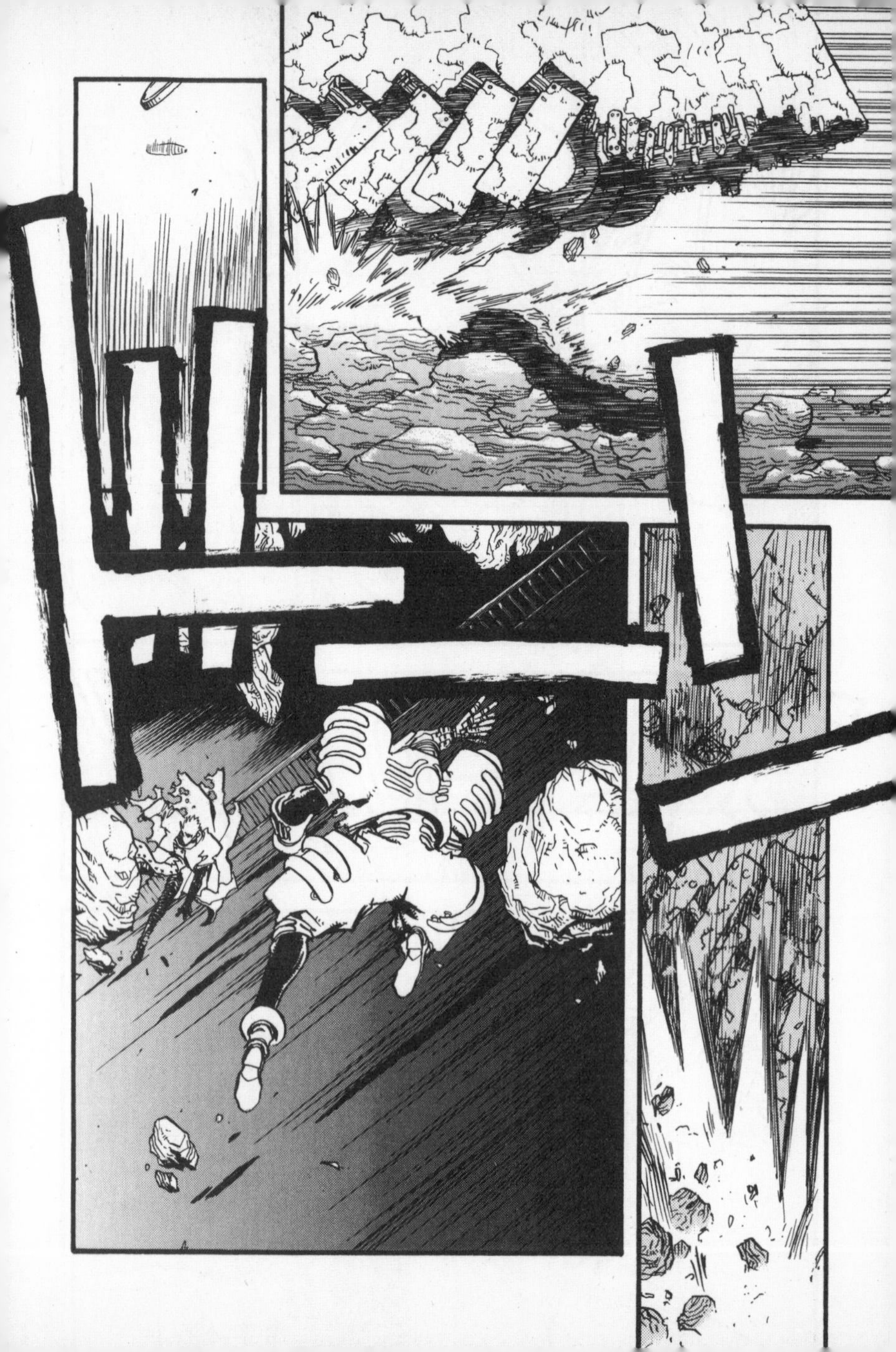

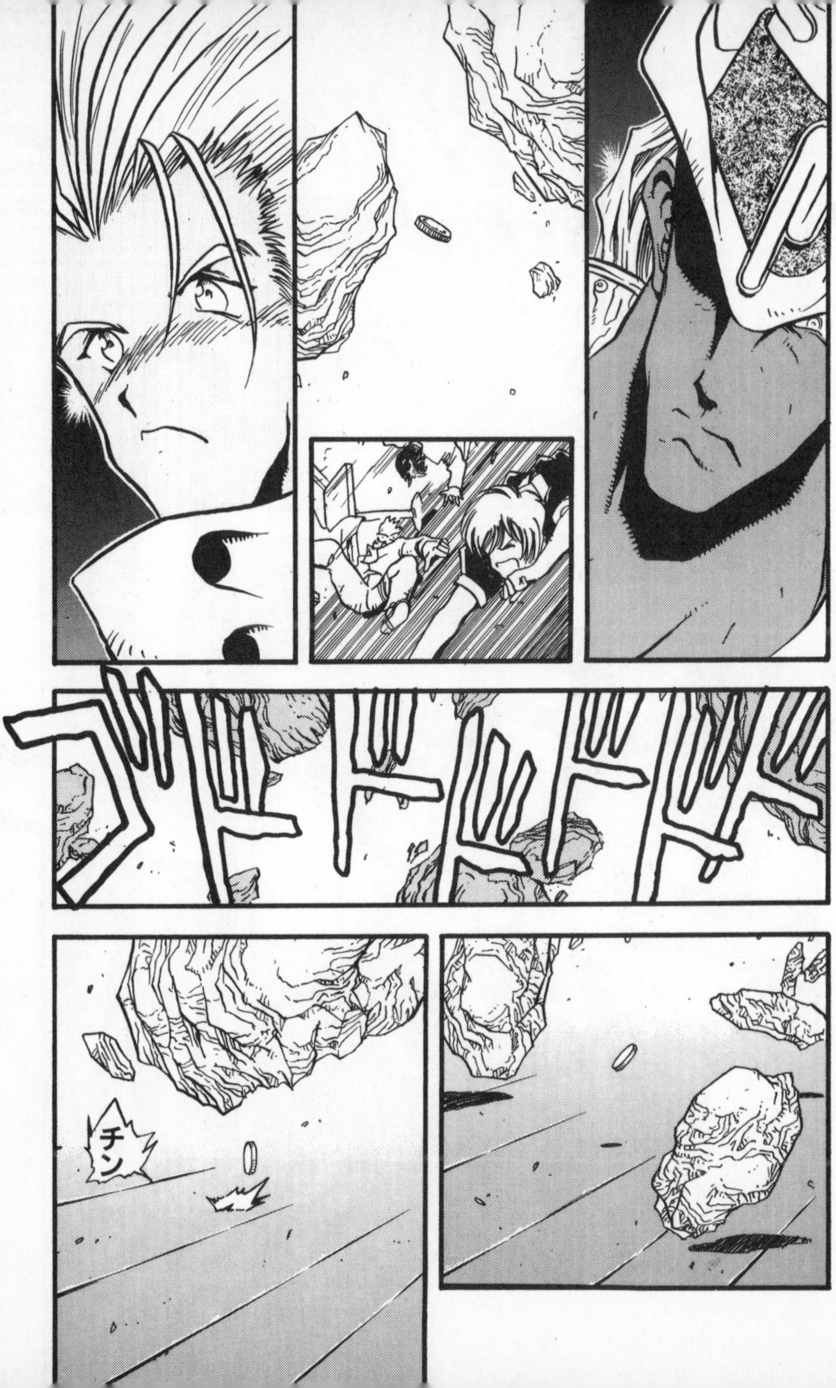
ゴドドドドド
チン

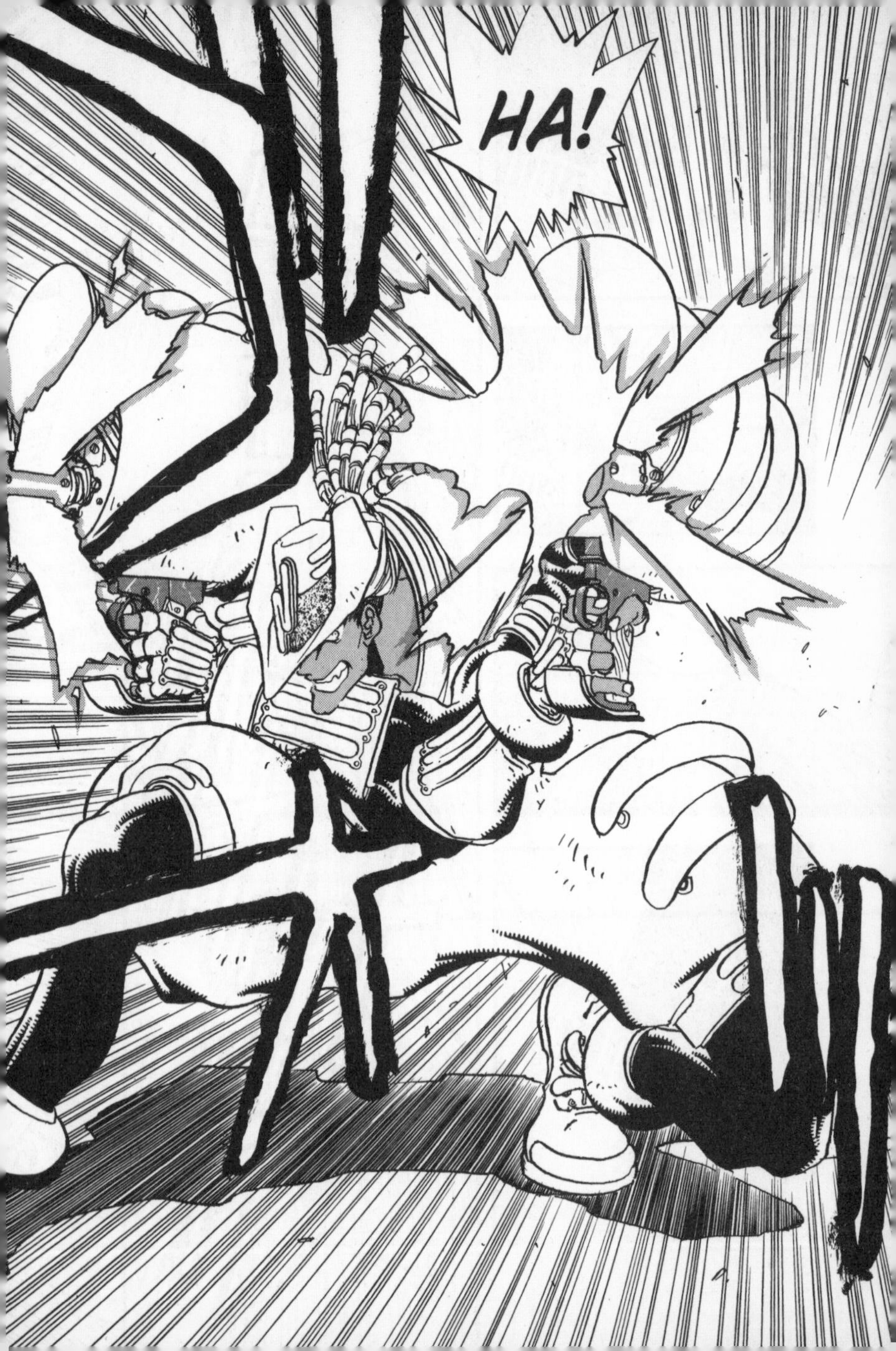
HA!

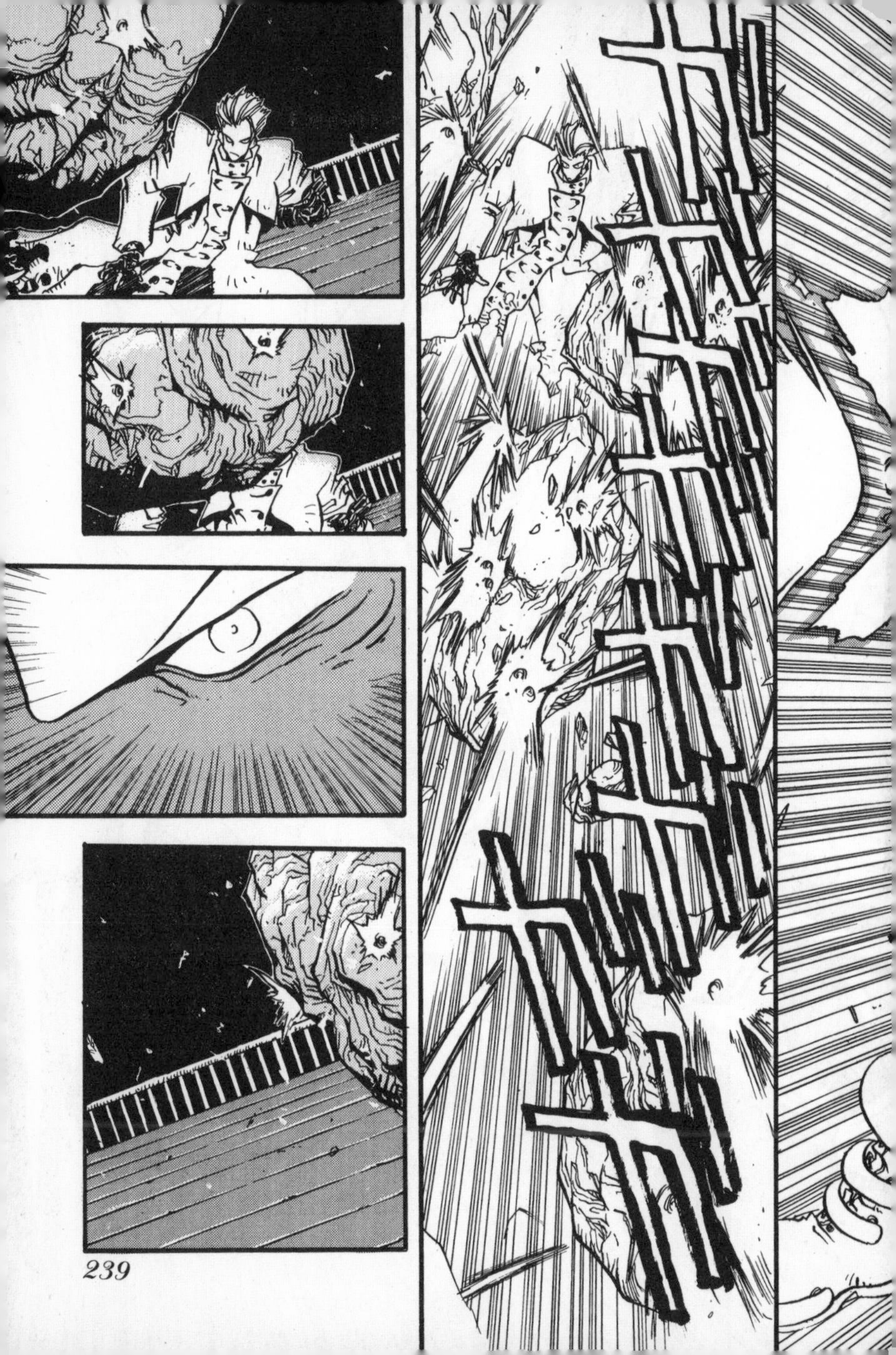

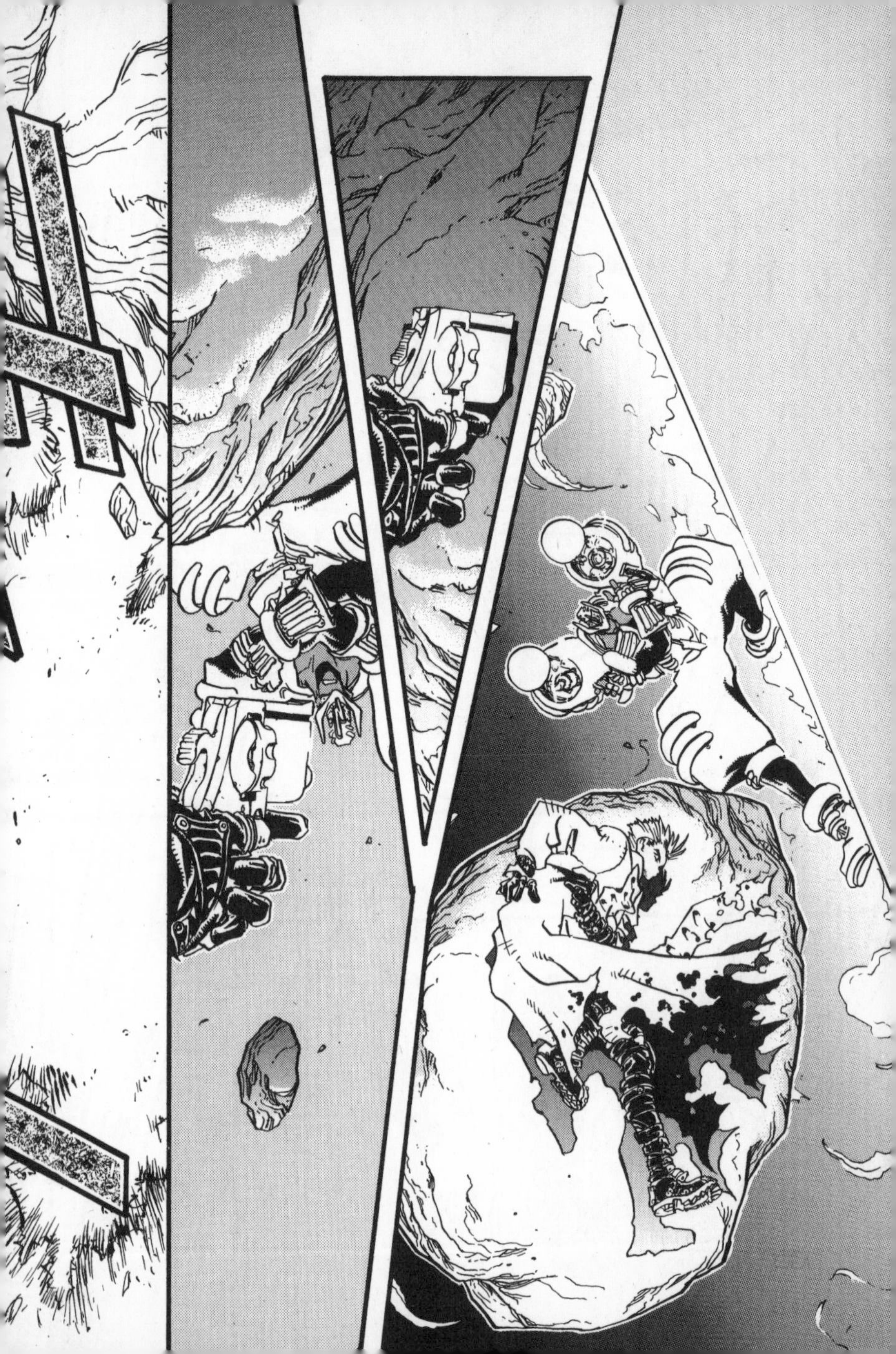

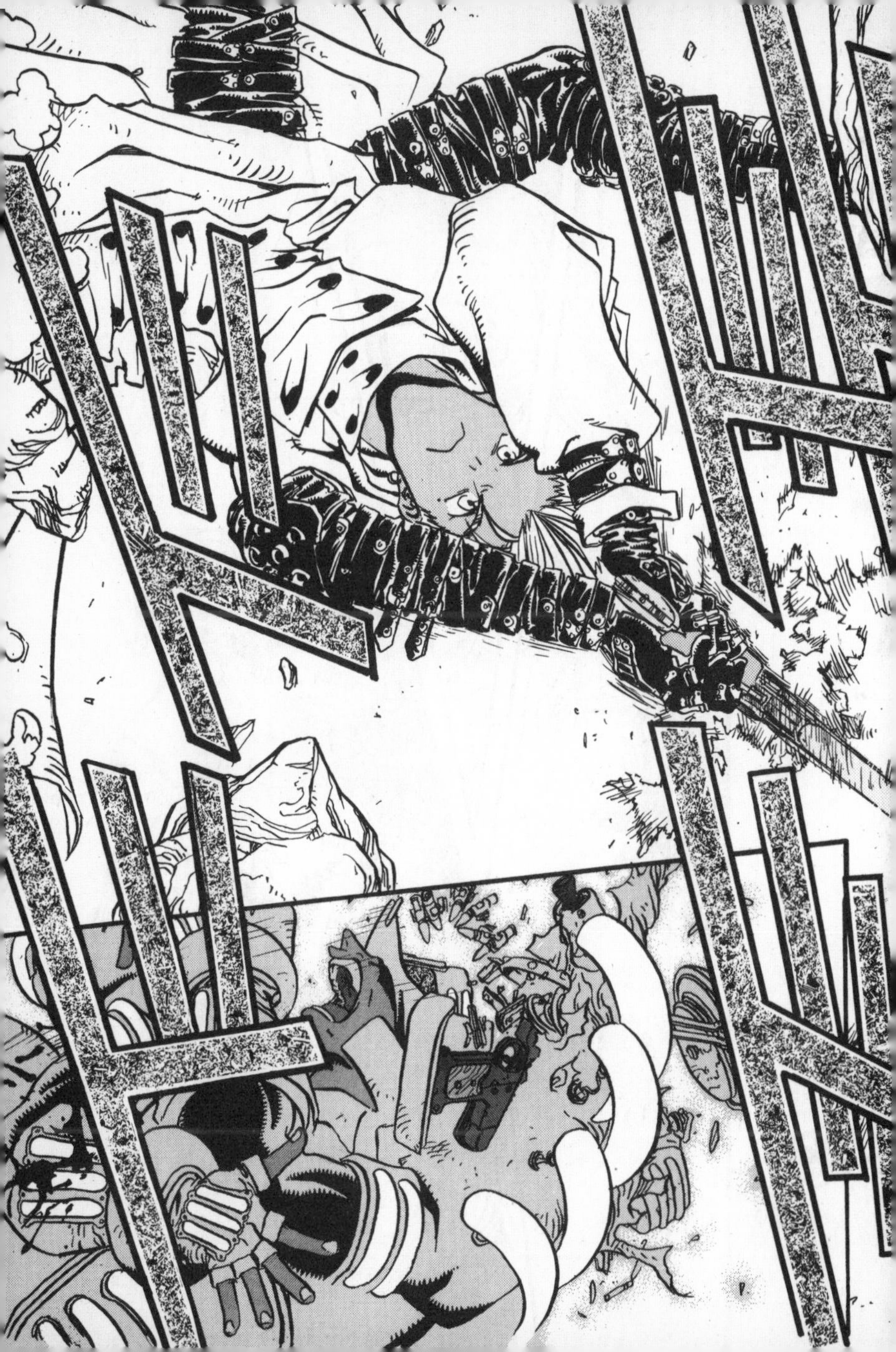

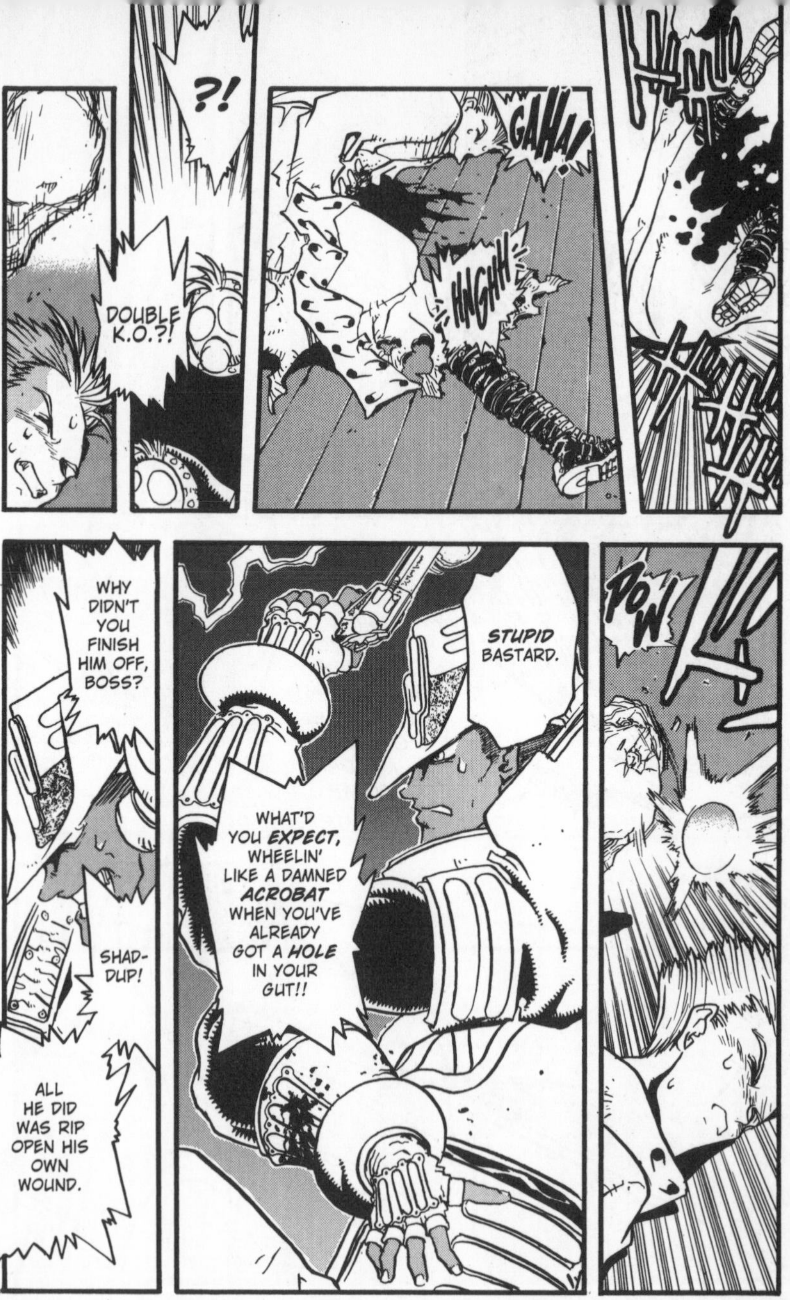
GAHA!
HNGHH
?!
DOUBLE K.O.?!
POW
STUPID BASTARD.
WHAT'D YOU EXPECT, WHEELIN' LIKE A DAMNED ACROBAT WHEN YOU'VE ALREADY GOT A HOLE IN YOUR GUT!!
WHY DIDN'T YOU FINISH HIM OFF, BOSS?
SHAD-DUP!
ALL HE DID WAS RIP OPEN HIS OWN WOUND.

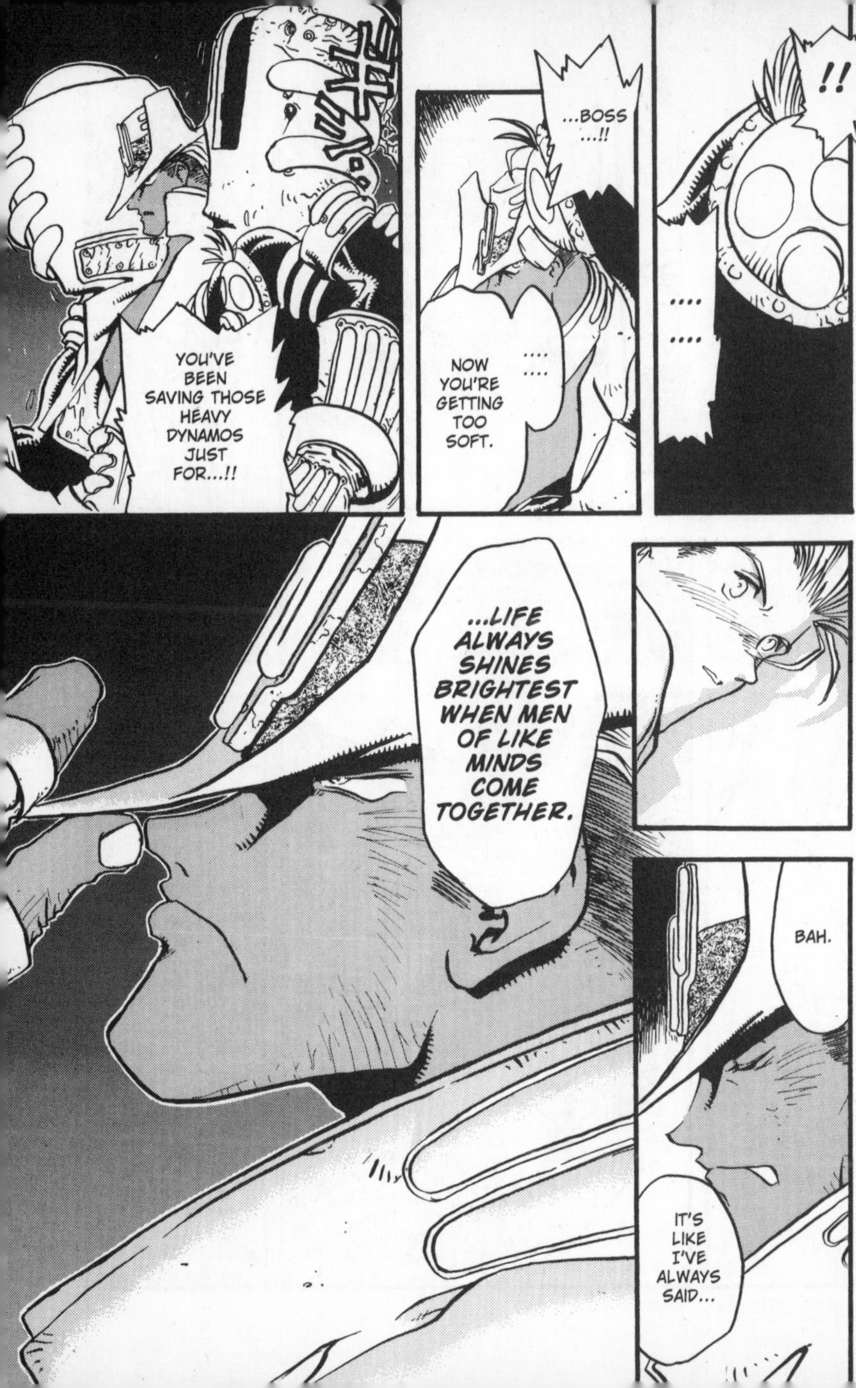
!!
....
....
...BOSS ...!!
.... ....
NOW YOU'RE GETTING TOO SOFT.
YOU'VE BEEN SAVING THOSE HEAVY DYNAMOS JUST FOR...!!
BAH.
IT'S LIKE I'VE ALWAYS SAID...
...LIFE ALWAYS SHINES BRIGHTEST WHEN MEN OF LIKE MINDS COME TOGETHER.

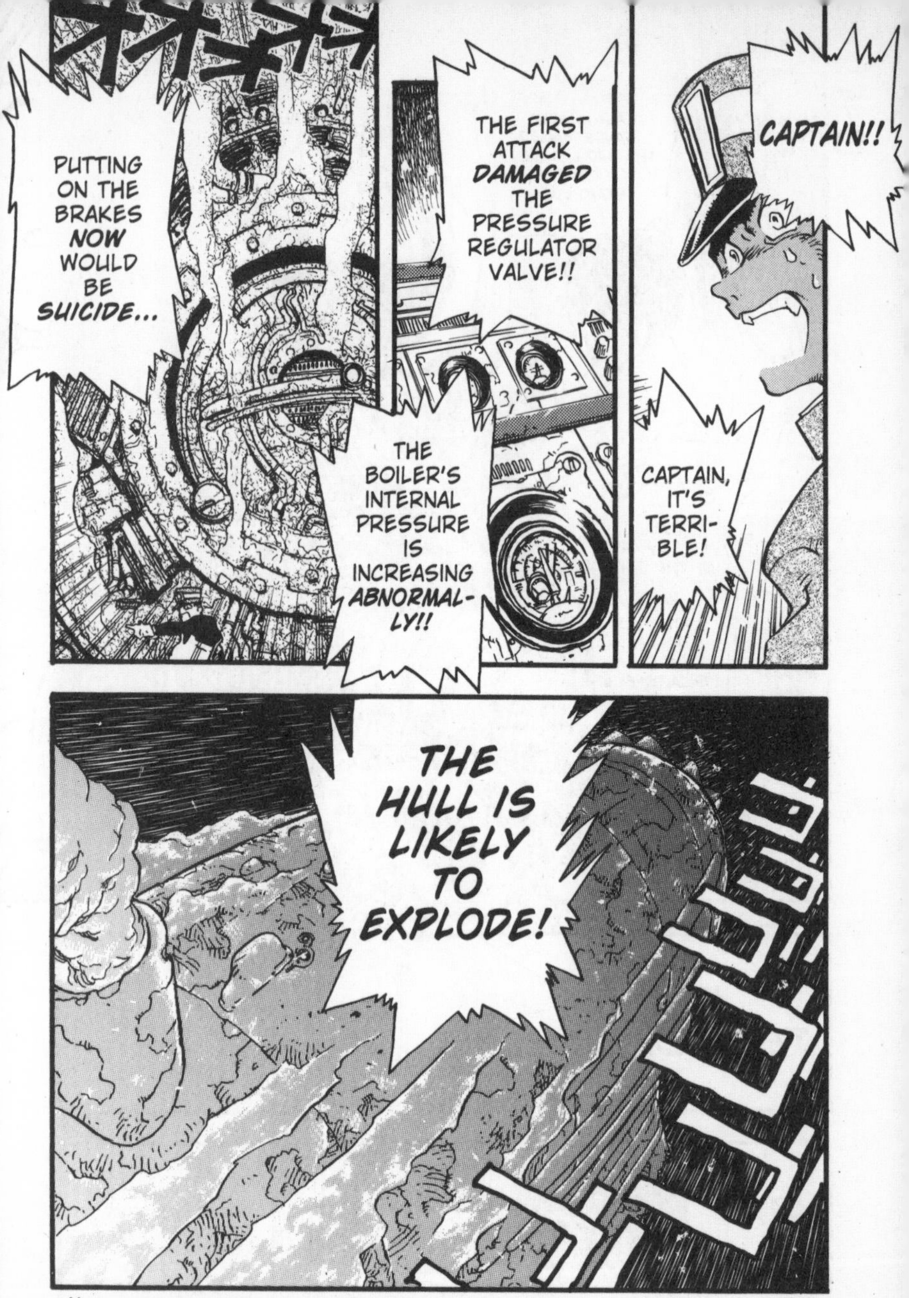
CAPTAIN!!
CAPTAIN, IT'S TERRIBLE!
THE FIRST ATTACK DAMAGED THE PRESSURE REGULATOR VALVE!!
THE BOILER'S INTERNAL PRESSURE IS INCREASING ABNORMALLY!!
PUTTING ON THE BRAKES NOW WOULD BE SUICIDE...
THE HULL IS LIKELY TO EXPLODE!

#8. DUELIST / END

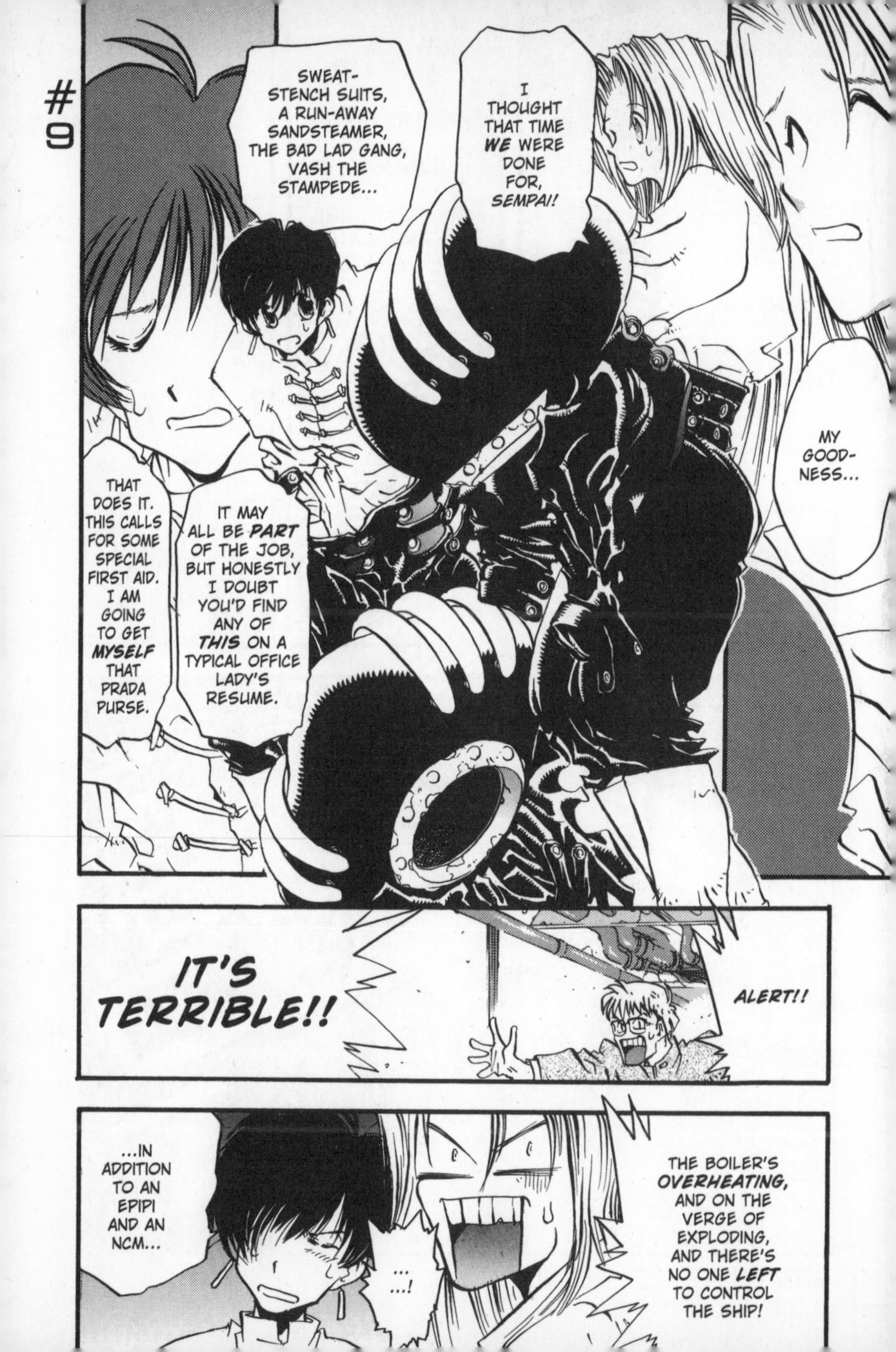
#9
I THOUGHT THAT TIME *WE* WERE DONE FOR, *SEMPAI!*
SWEAT-STENCH SUITS, A RUN-AWAY SANDSTEAMER, THE BAD LAD GANG, VASH THE STAMPEDE...
MY GOODNESS...
IT MAY ALL BE *PART* OF THE JOB, BUT HONESTLY I DOUBT YOU'D FIND ANY OF *THIS* ON A TYPICAL OFFICE LADY'S RESUME.
THAT DOES IT. THIS CALLS FOR SOME SPECIAL FIRST AID. I AM GOING TO GET *MYSELF* THAT PRADA PURSE.
ALERT!!
IT'S TERRIBLE!!
THE BOILER'S *OVERHEATING,* AND ON THE VERGE OF EXPLODING, AND THERE'S NO ONE *LEFT* TO CONTROL THE SHIP!
...
...!
...IN ADDITION TO AN EPIPI AND AN NCM...

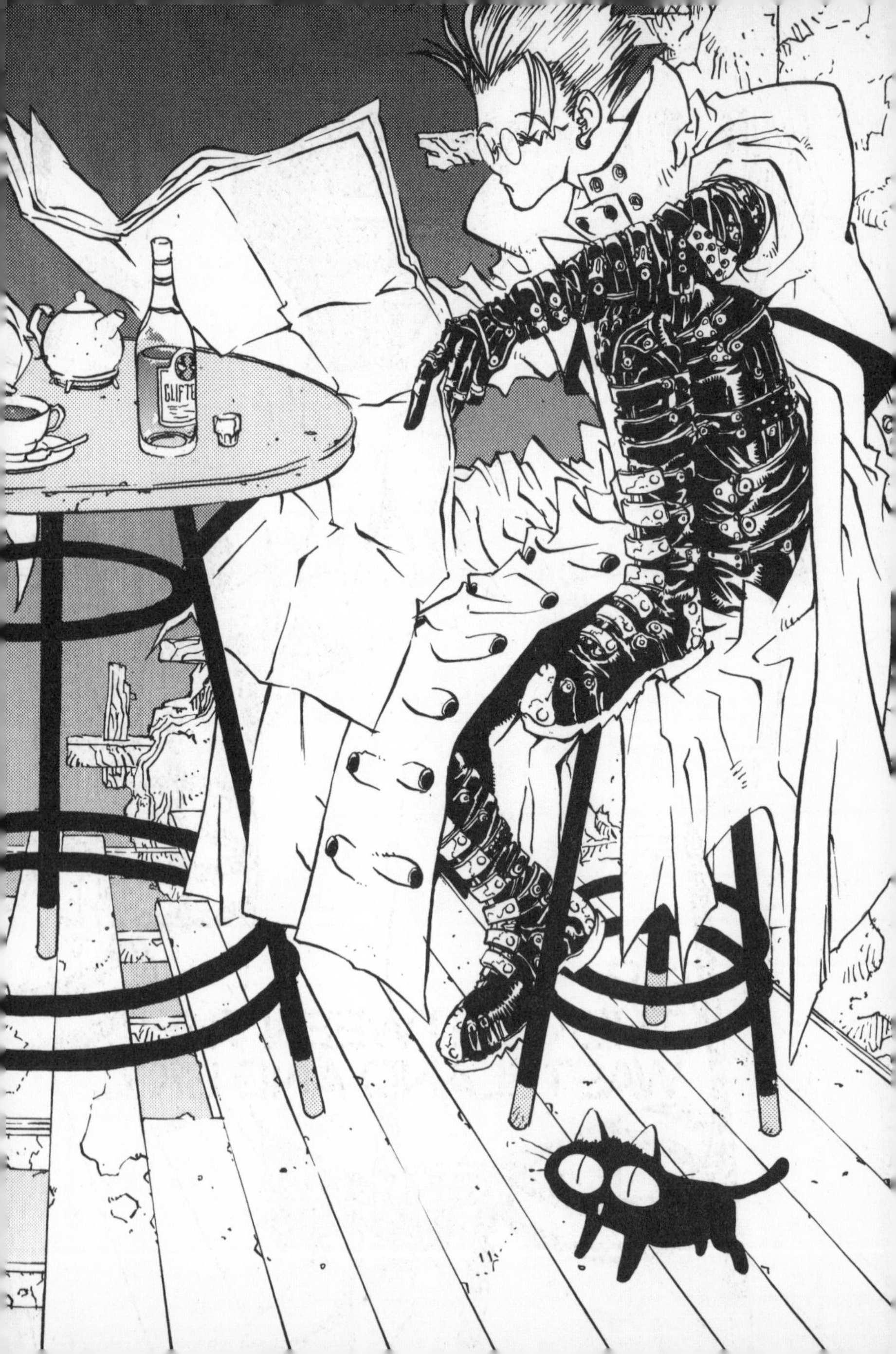

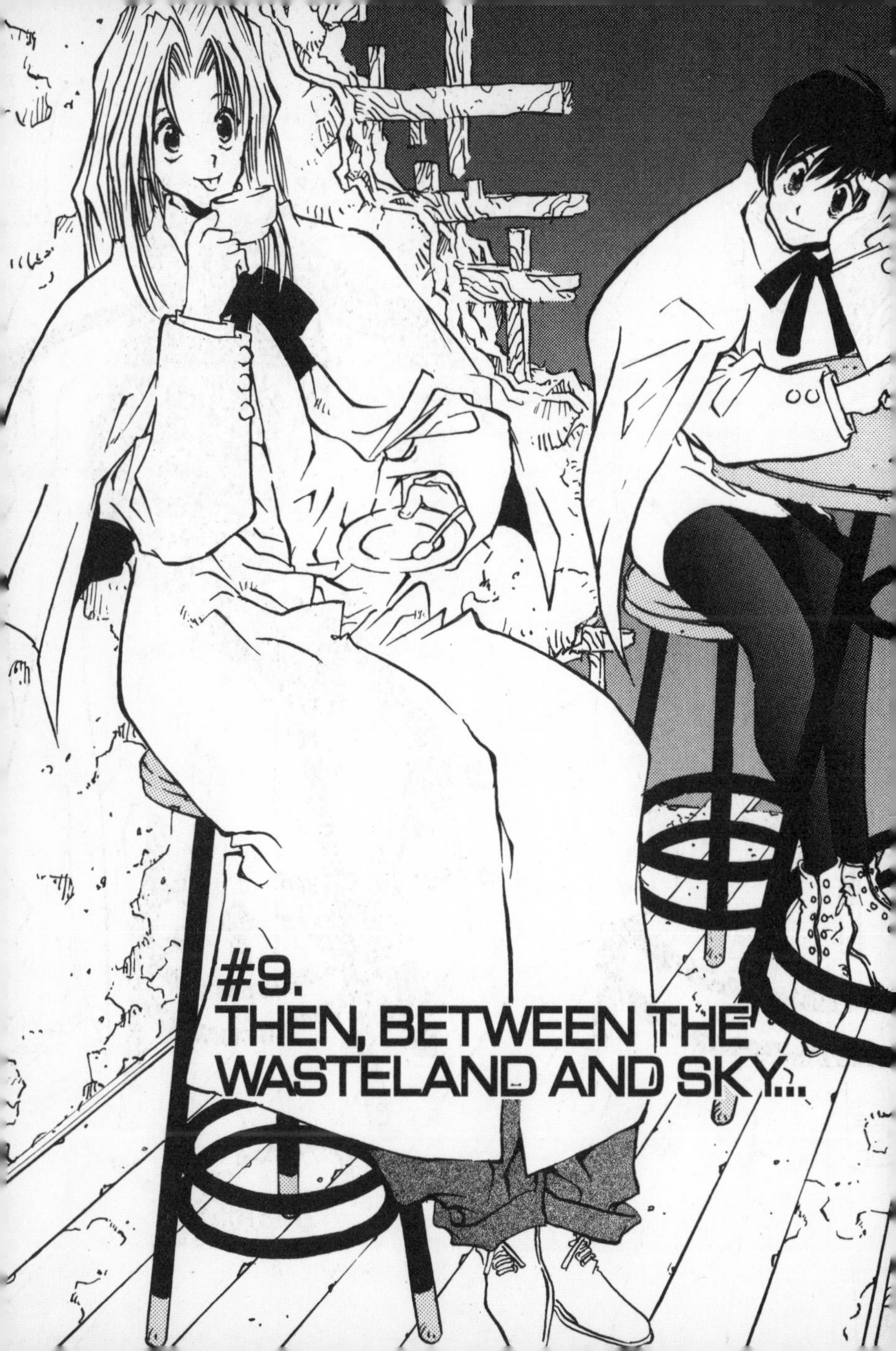
#9.
THEN, BETWEEN THE WASTELAND AND SKY...

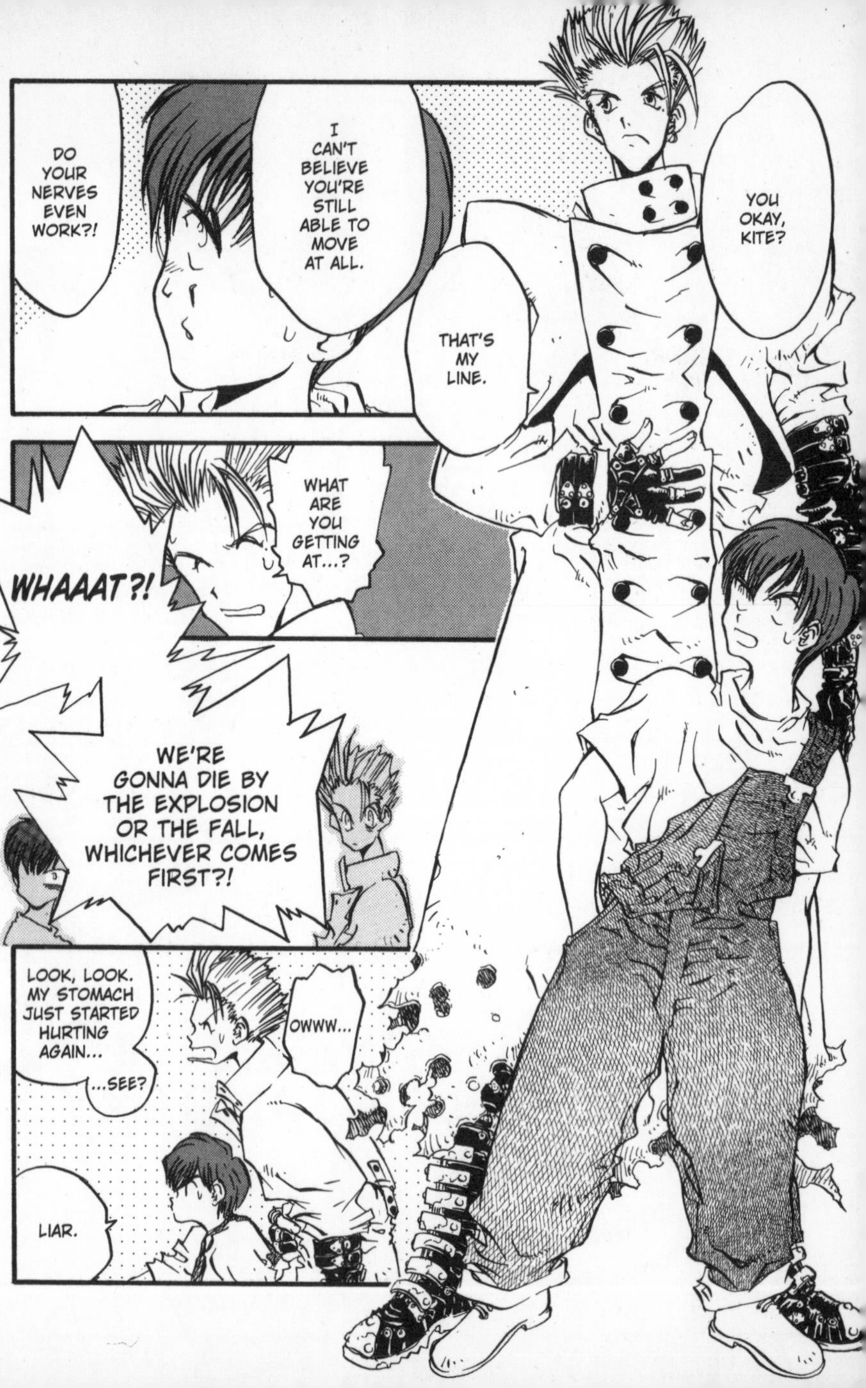
YOU OKAY, KITE?
THAT'S MY LINE.
I CAN'T BELIEVE YOU'RE STILL ABLE TO MOVE AT ALL.
DO YOUR NERVES EVEN WORK?!
WHAT ARE YOU GETTING AT...?
WHAAAT?!
WE'RE GONNA DIE BY THE EXPLOSION OR THE FALL, WHICHEVER COMES FIRST?!
OWWW...
LOOK, LOOK. MY STOMACH JUST STARTED HURTING AGAIN...
...SEE?
LIAR.

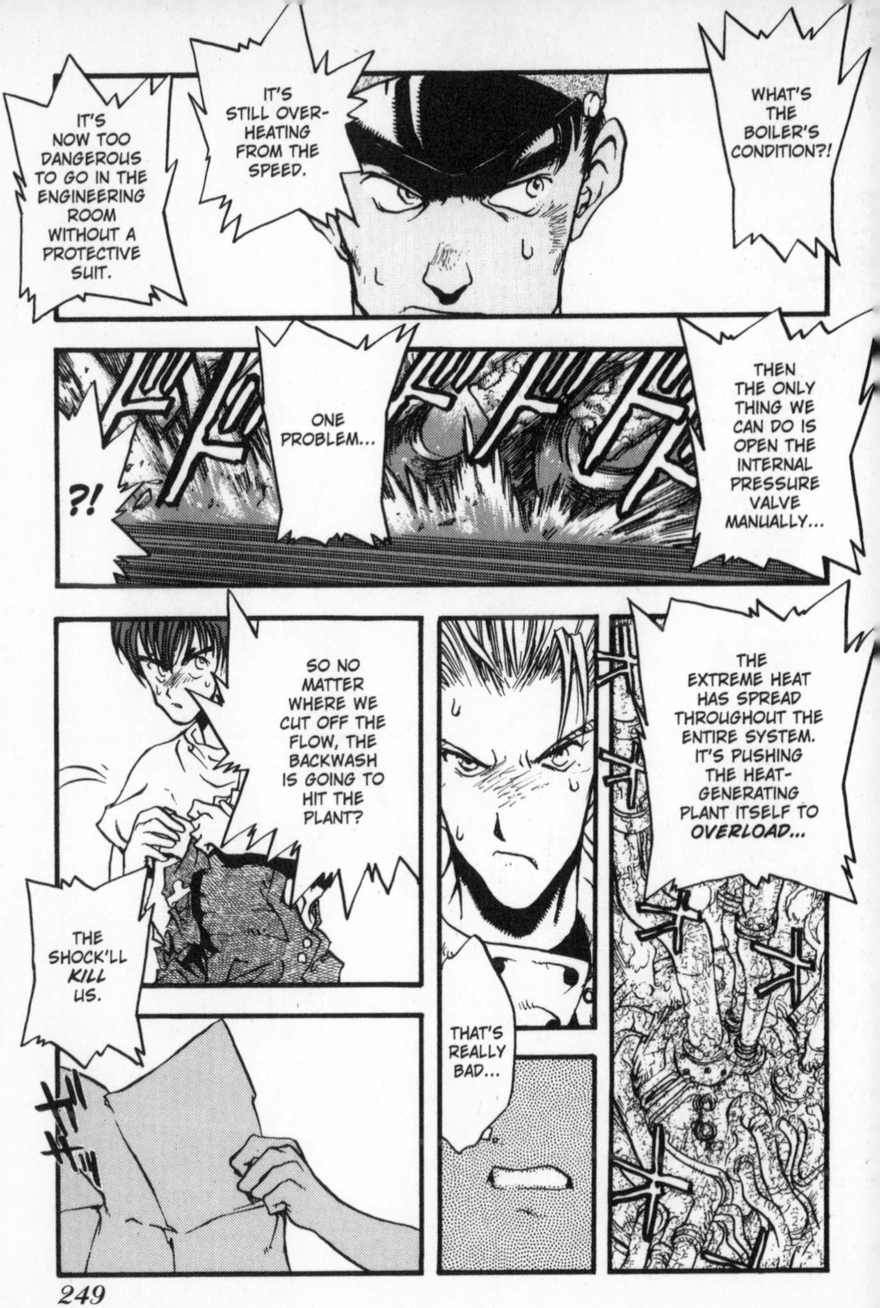
WHAT'S THE BOILER'S CONDITION?!
IT'S STILL OVER-HEATING FROM THE SPEED.
IT'S NOW TOO DANGEROUS TO GO IN THE ENGINEERING ROOM WITHOUT A PROTECTIVE SUIT.
THEN THE ONLY THING WE CAN DO IS OPEN THE INTERNAL PRESSURE VALVE MANUALLY...
ONE PROBLEM...
?!
THE EXTREME HEAT HAS SPREAD THROUGHOUT THE ENTIRE SYSTEM. IT'S PUSHING THE HEAT-GENERATING PLANT ITSELF TO OVERLOAD...
THAT'S REALLY BAD...
SO NO MATTER WHERE WE CUT OFF THE FLOW, THE BACKWASH IS GOING TO HIT THE PLANT?
THE SHOCK'LL KILL US.

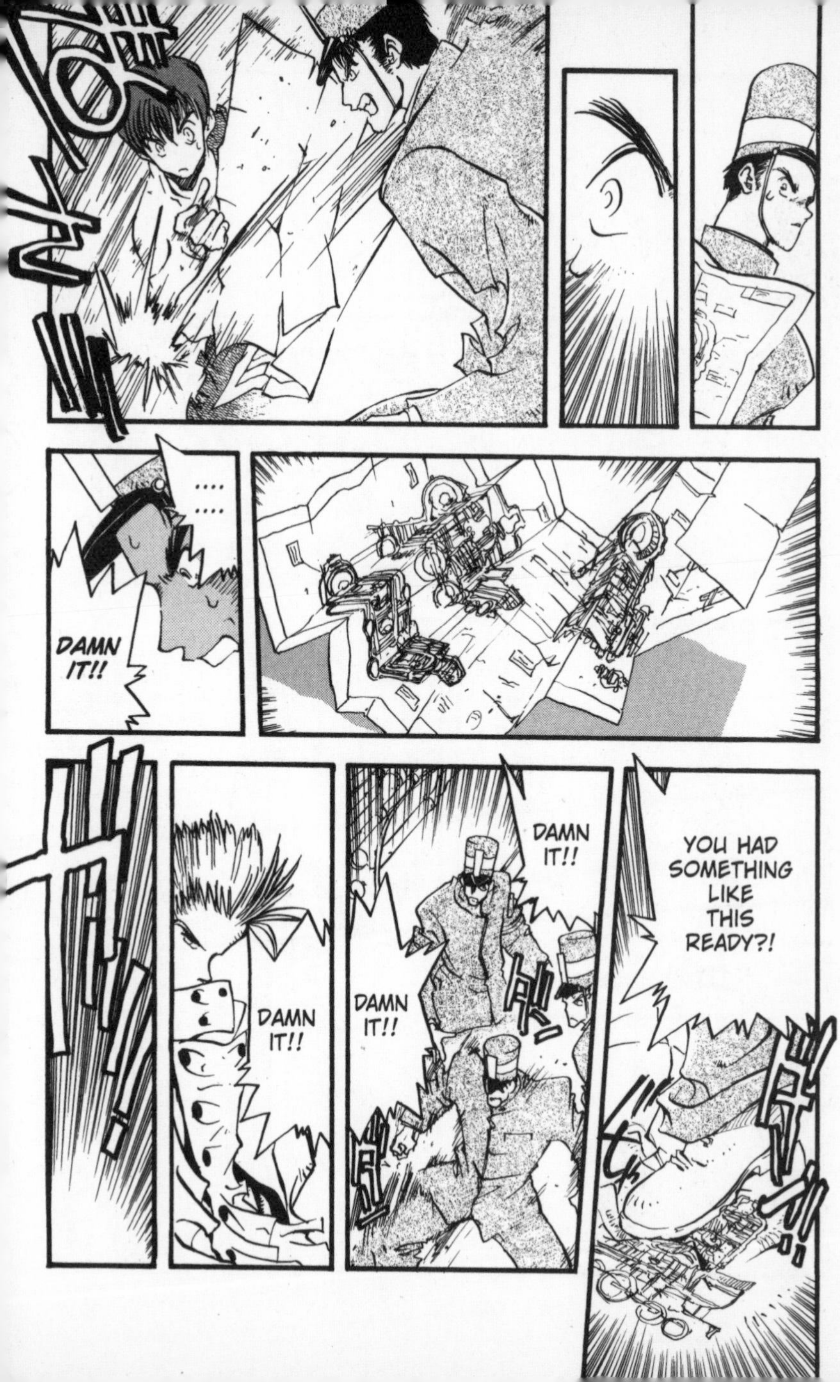
....
....
DAMN IT!!
YOU HAD SOMETHING LIKE THIS READY?!
DAMN IT!!
DAMN IT!!
DAMN IT!!

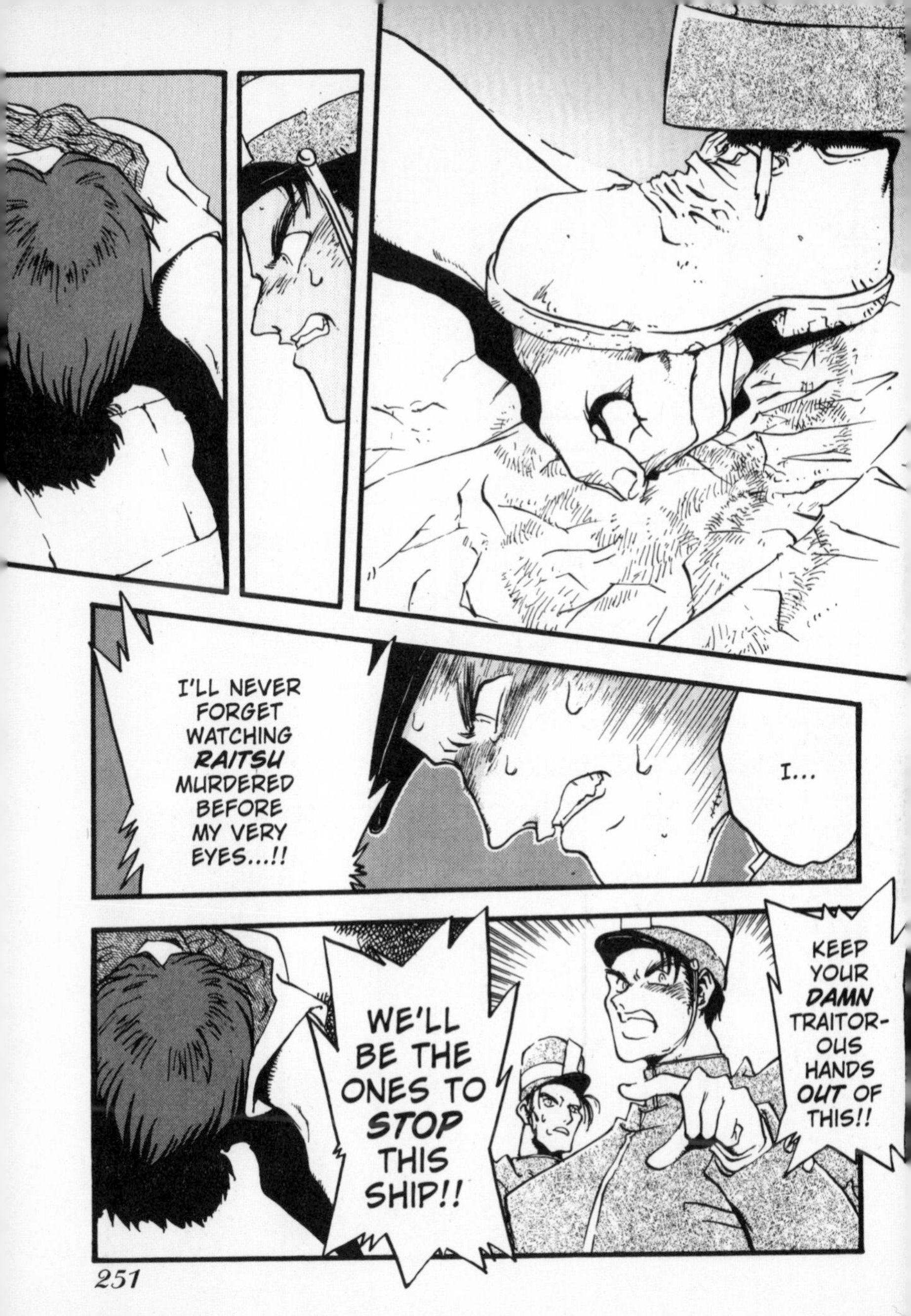
I...
I'LL NEVER FORGET WATCHING ***RAITSU*** MURDERED BEFORE MY VERY EYES...!!
KEEP YOUR ***DAMN*** TRAITOR-OUS HANDS ***OUT*** OF THIS!!
WE'LL BE THE ONES TO ***STOP*** THIS SHIP!!

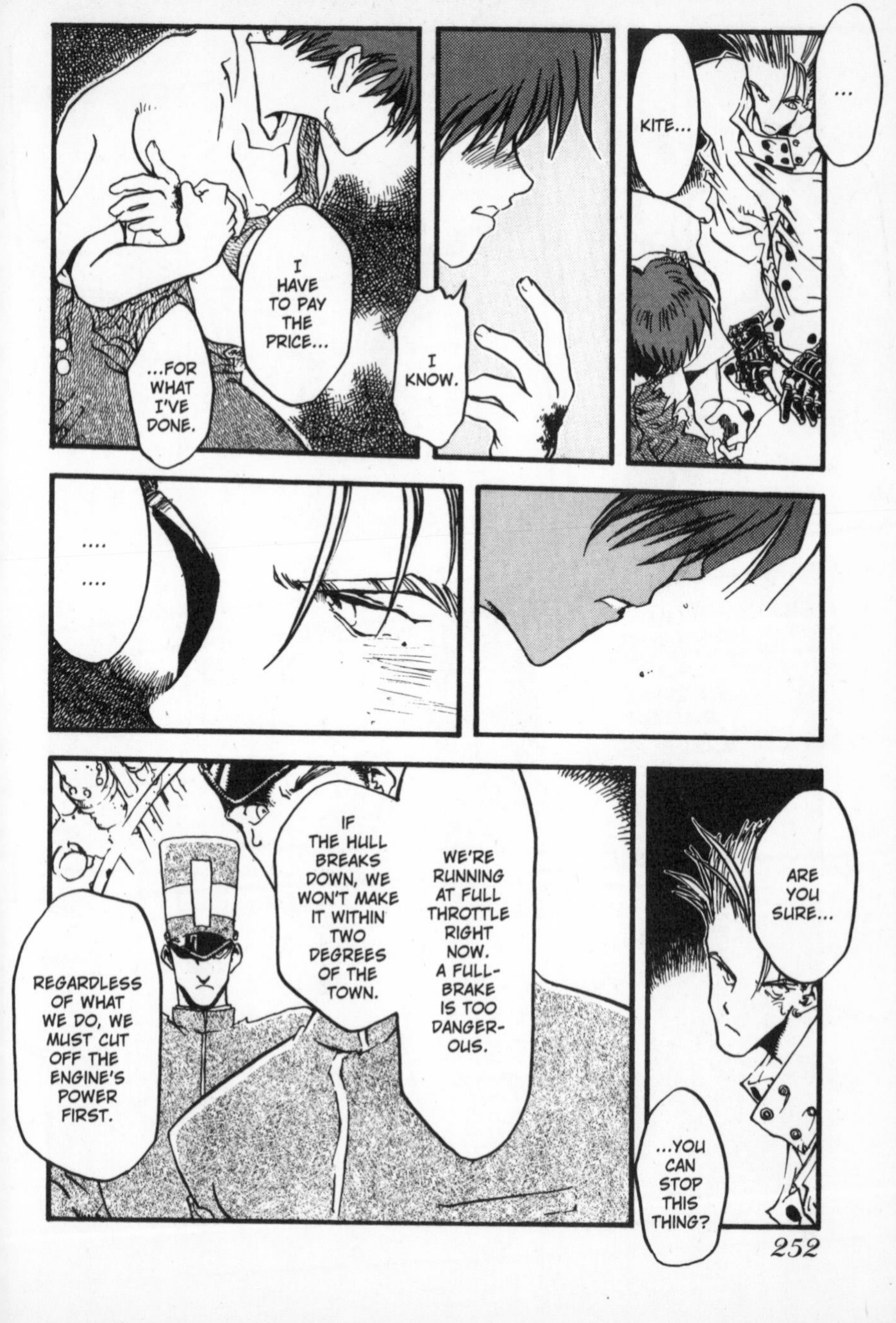
...
KITE...
I KNOW.
I HAVE TO PAY THE PRICE...
...FOR WHAT I'VE DONE.
....
....
ARE YOU SURE...
...YOU CAN STOP THIS THING?
WE'RE RUNNING AT FULL THROTTLE RIGHT NOW. A FULL-BRAKE IS TOO DANGEROUS.
IF THE HULL BREAKS DOWN, WE WON'T MAKE IT WITHIN TWO DEGREES OF THE TOWN.
REGARDLESS OF WHAT WE DO, WE MUST CUT OFF THE ENGINE'S POWER FIRST.

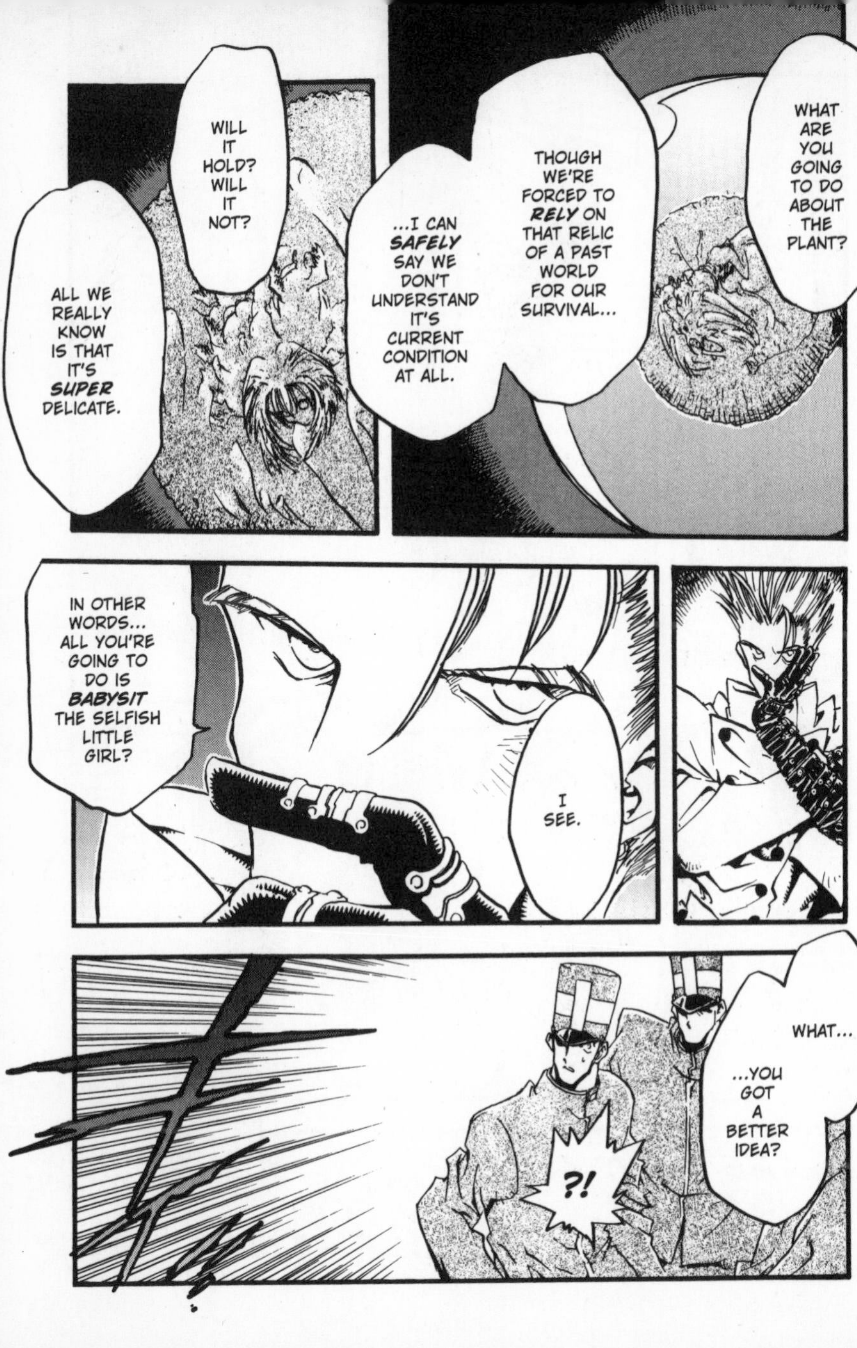
WHAT ARE YOU GOING TO DO ABOUT THE PLANT?
THOUGH WE'RE FORCED TO **RELY** ON THAT RELIC OF A PAST WORLD FOR OUR SURVIVAL...
...I CAN **SAFELY** SAY WE DON'T UNDERSTAND IT'S CURRENT CONDITION AT ALL.
WILL IT HOLD? WILL IT NOT?
ALL WE REALLY KNOW IS THAT IT'S **SUPER** DELICATE.
I SEE.
IN OTHER WORDS... ALL YOU'RE GOING TO DO IS **BABYSIT** THE SELFISH LITTLE GIRL?
WHAT...
...YOU GOT A BETTER IDEA?
?!

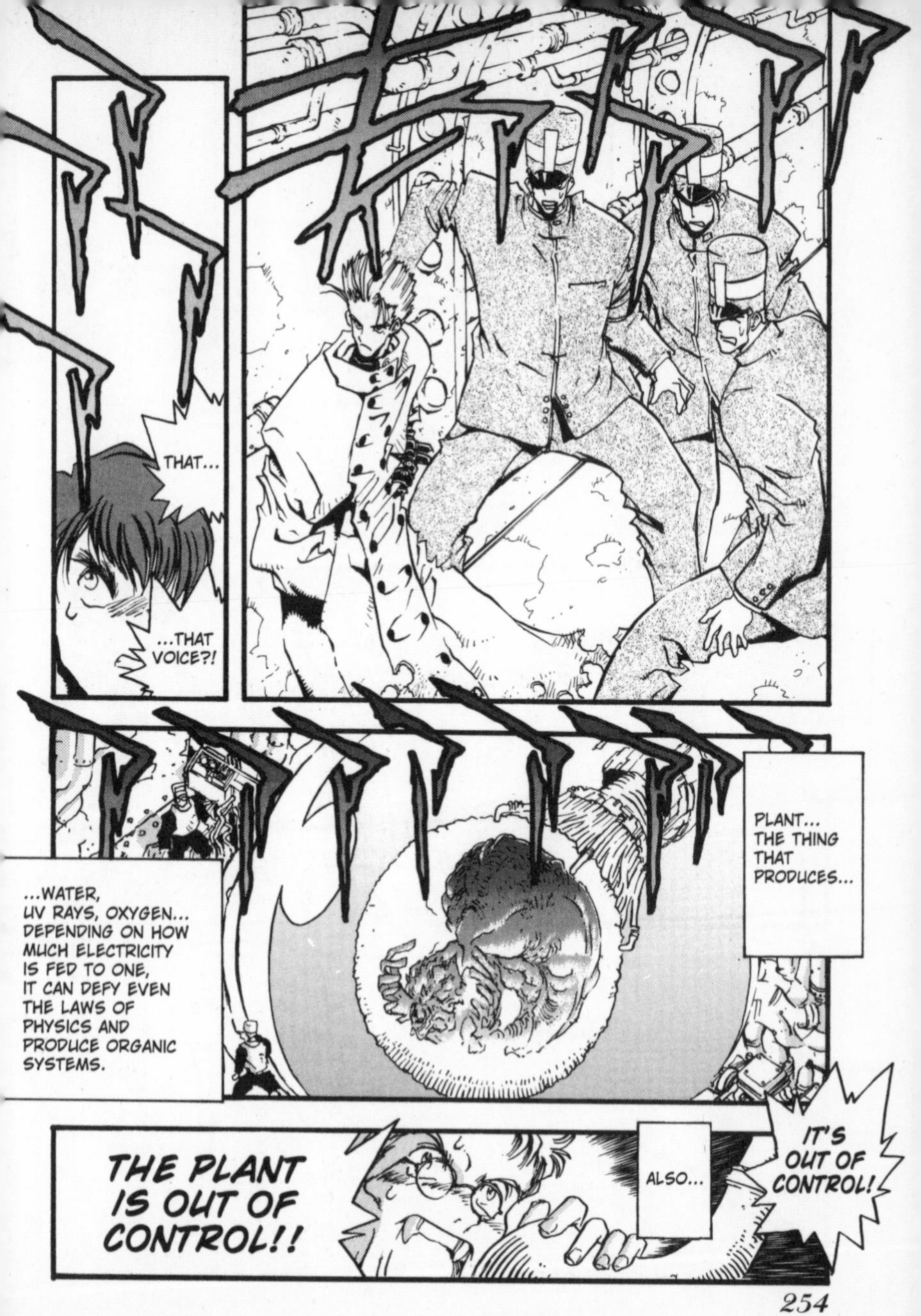
THAT...
...THAT VOICE?!
PLANT... THE THING THAT PRODUCES...
...WATER, UV RAYS, OXYGEN... DEPENDING ON HOW MUCH ELECTRICITY IS FED TO ONE, IT CAN DEFY EVEN THE LAWS OF PHYSICS AND PRODUCE ORGANIC SYSTEMS.
IT'S OUT OF CONTROL!
ALSO...
THE PLANT IS OUT OF CONTROL!!

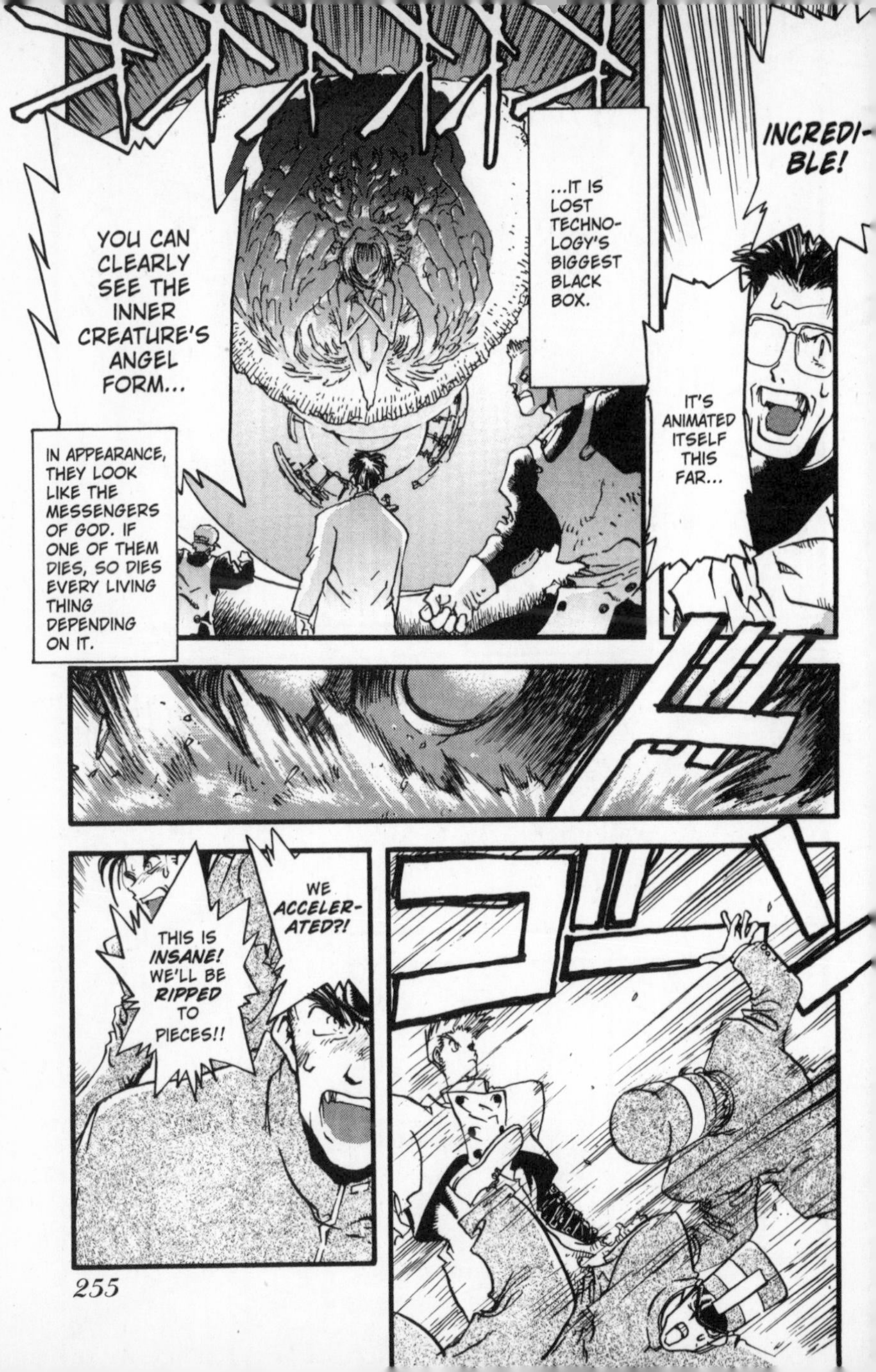
INCREDI-BLE!
IT'S ANIMATED ITSELF THIS FAR...
...IT IS LOST TECHNO-LOGY'S BIGGEST BLACK BOX.
YOU CAN CLEARLY SEE THE INNER CREATURE'S ANGEL FORM...
IN APPEARANCE, THEY LOOK LIKE THE MESSENGERS OF GOD. IF ONE OF THEM DIES, SO DIES EVERY LIVING THING DEPENDING ON IT.
WE ACCELER-ATED?!
THIS IS *INSANE!* WE'LL BE *RIPPED* TO PIECES!!

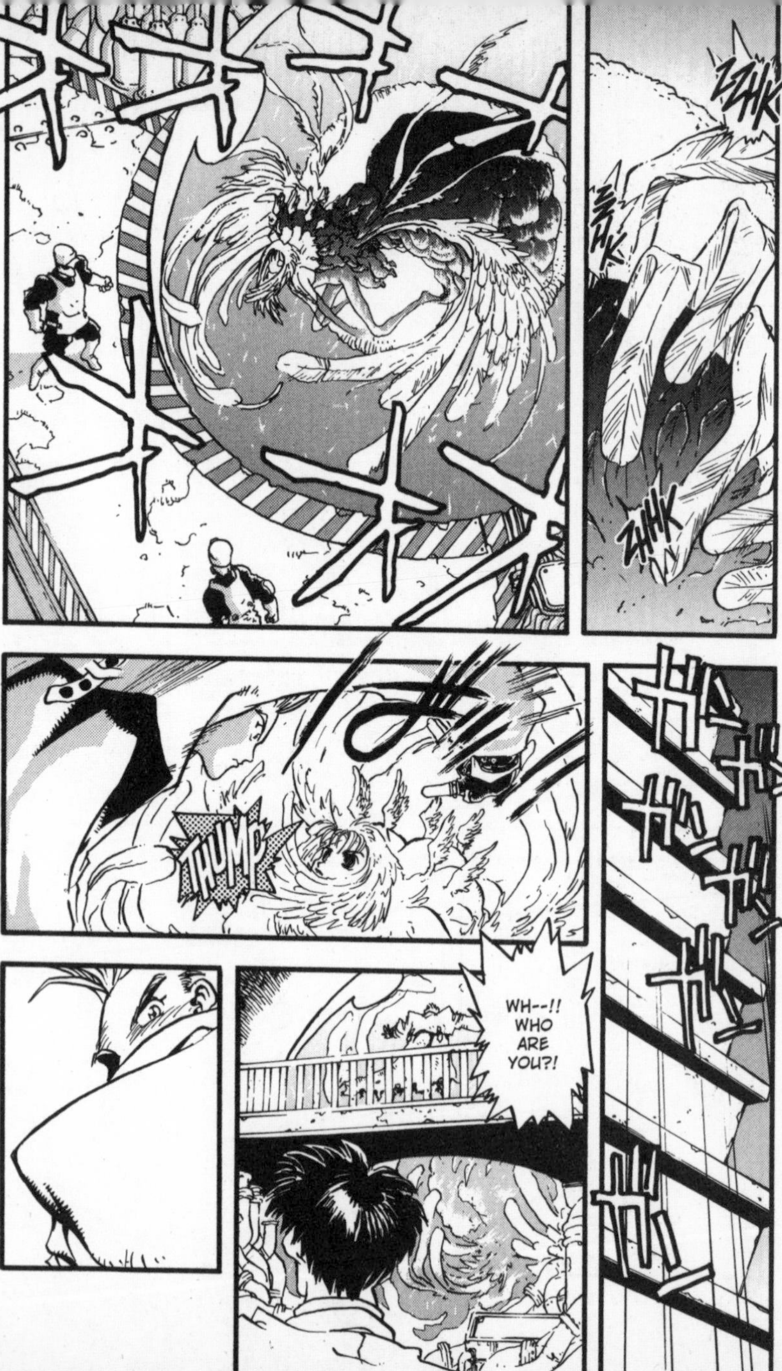
ZZHK
ZZHK
ZHHK
THUMP
WH--!! WHO ARE YOU?!

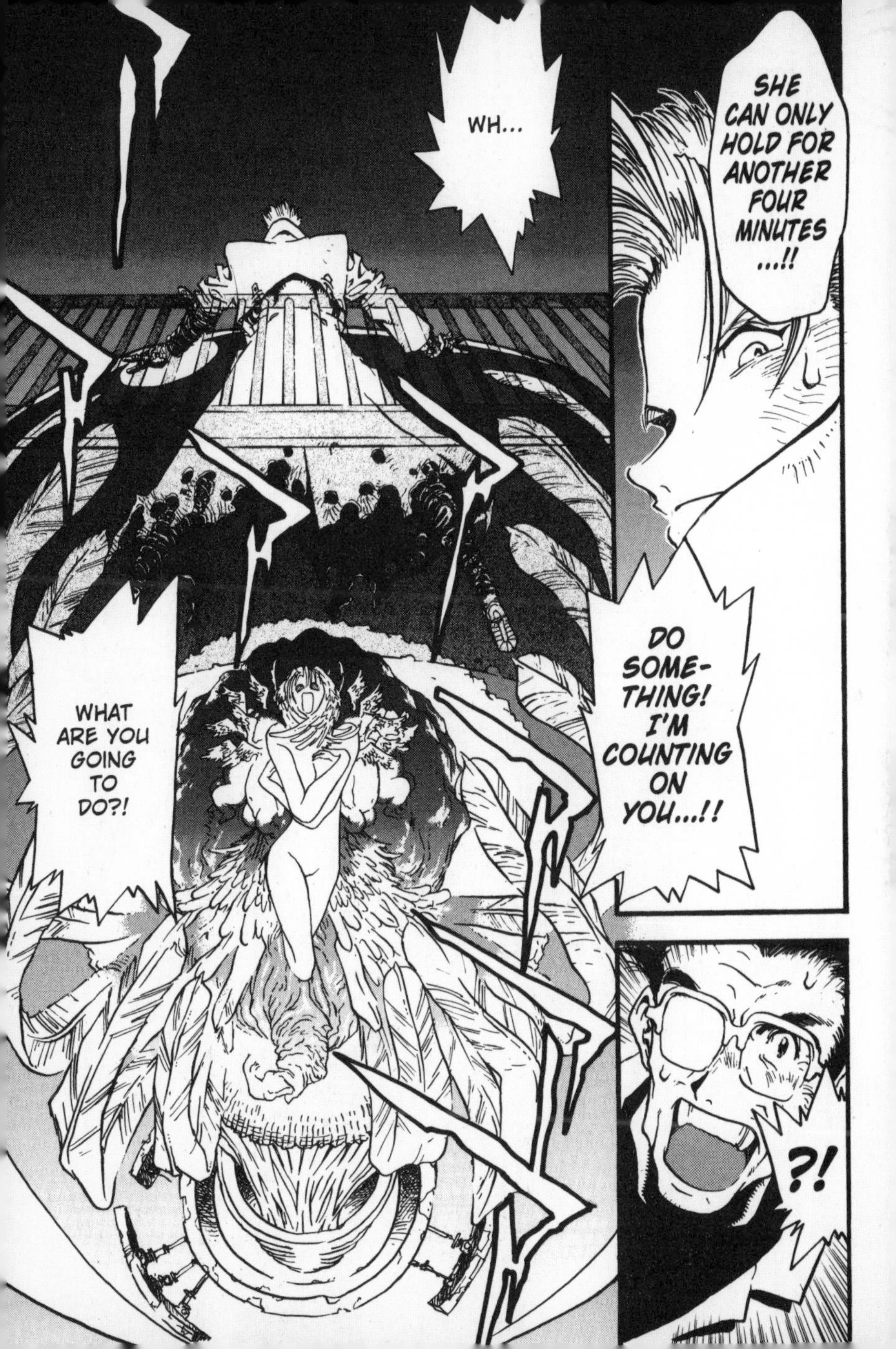
SHE CAN ONLY HOLD FOR ANOTHER FOUR MINUTES ...!!
DO SOME-THING! I'M COUNTING ON YOU...!!
?!
WH...
WHAT ARE YOU GOING TO DO?!

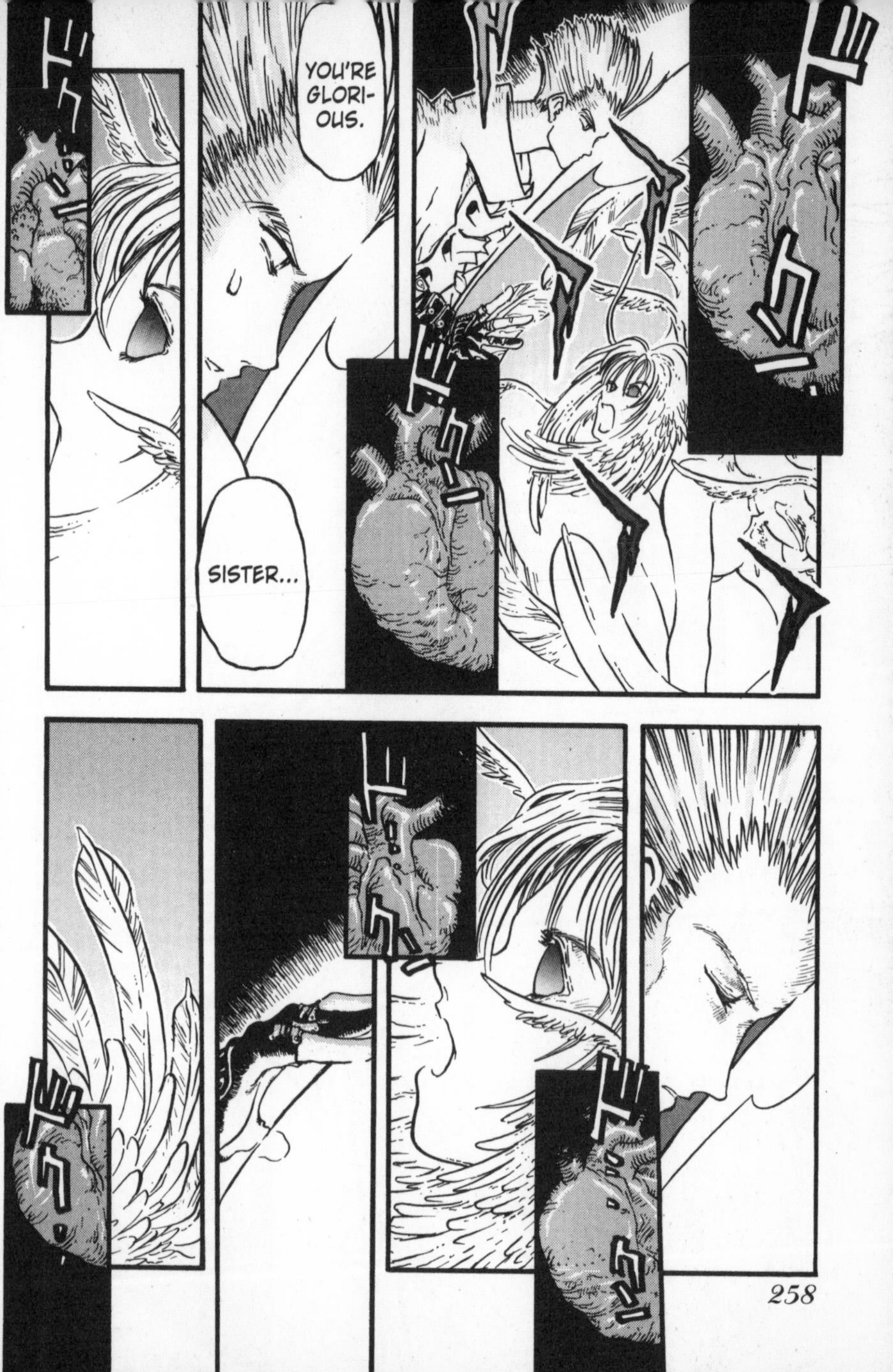
YOU'RE GLORIOUS.
SISTER...

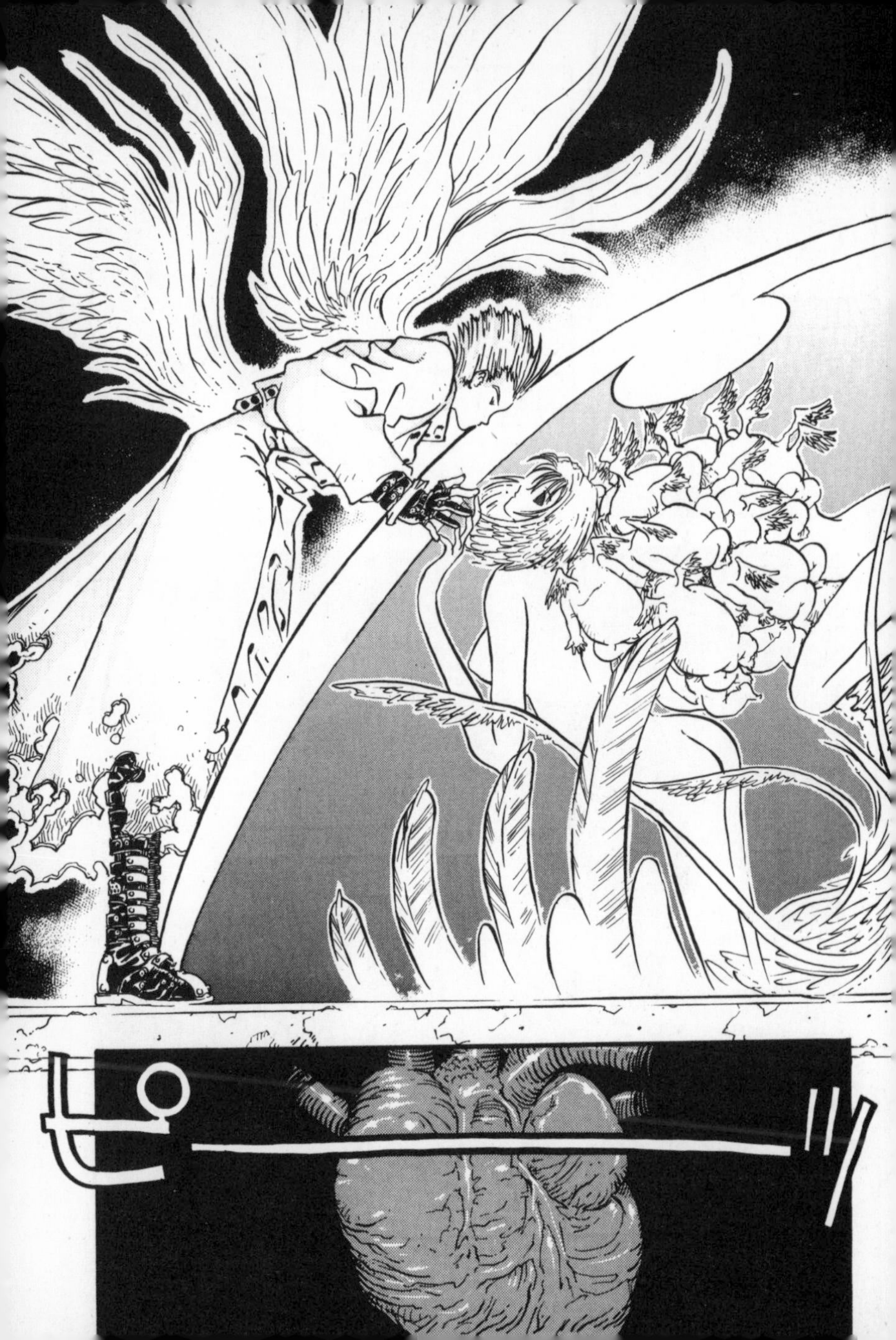
ピー

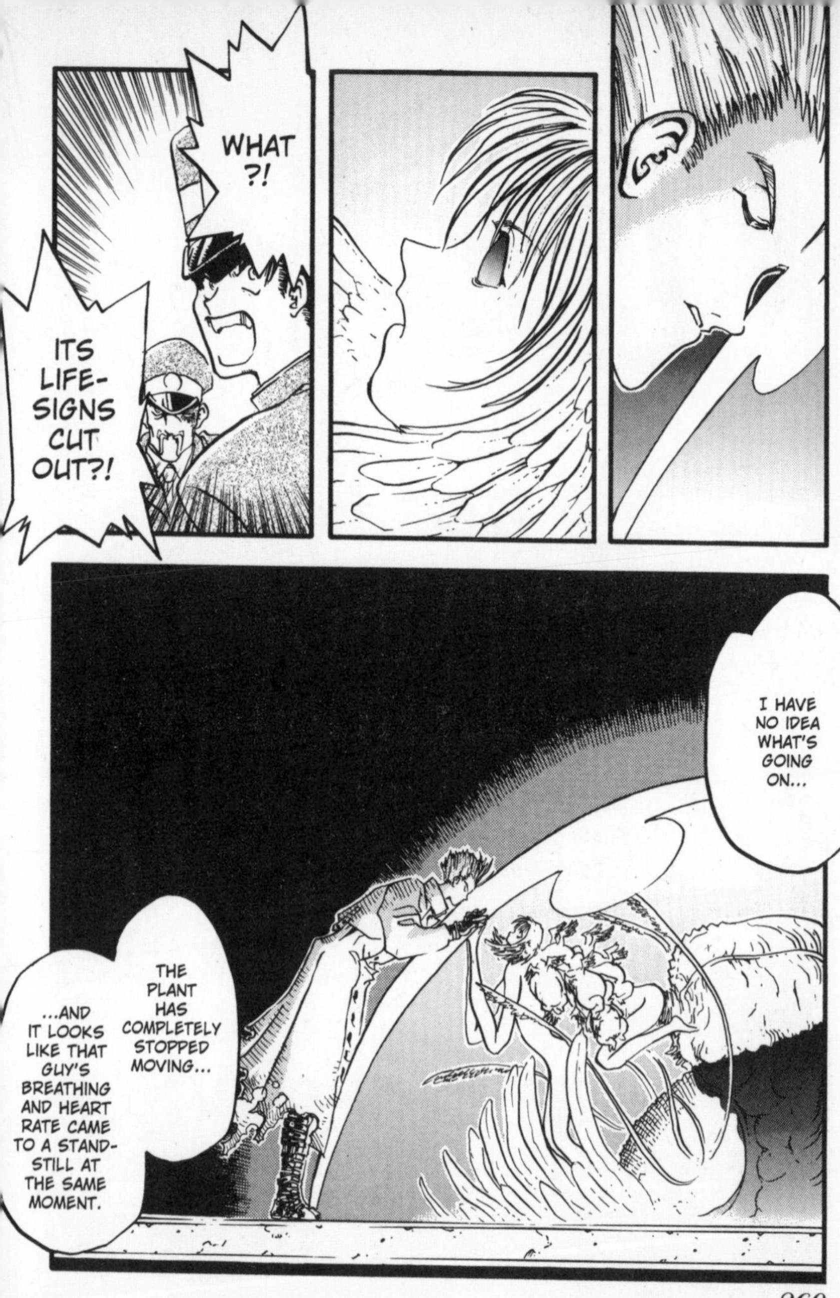
WHAT ?!
ITS LIFE-SIGNS CUT OUT?!
I HAVE NO IDEA WHAT'S GOING ON...
THE PLANT HAS COMPLETELY STOPPED MOVING...
...AND IT LOOKS LIKE THAT GUY'S BREATHING AND HEART RATE CAME TO A STAND-STILL AT THE SAME MOMENT.

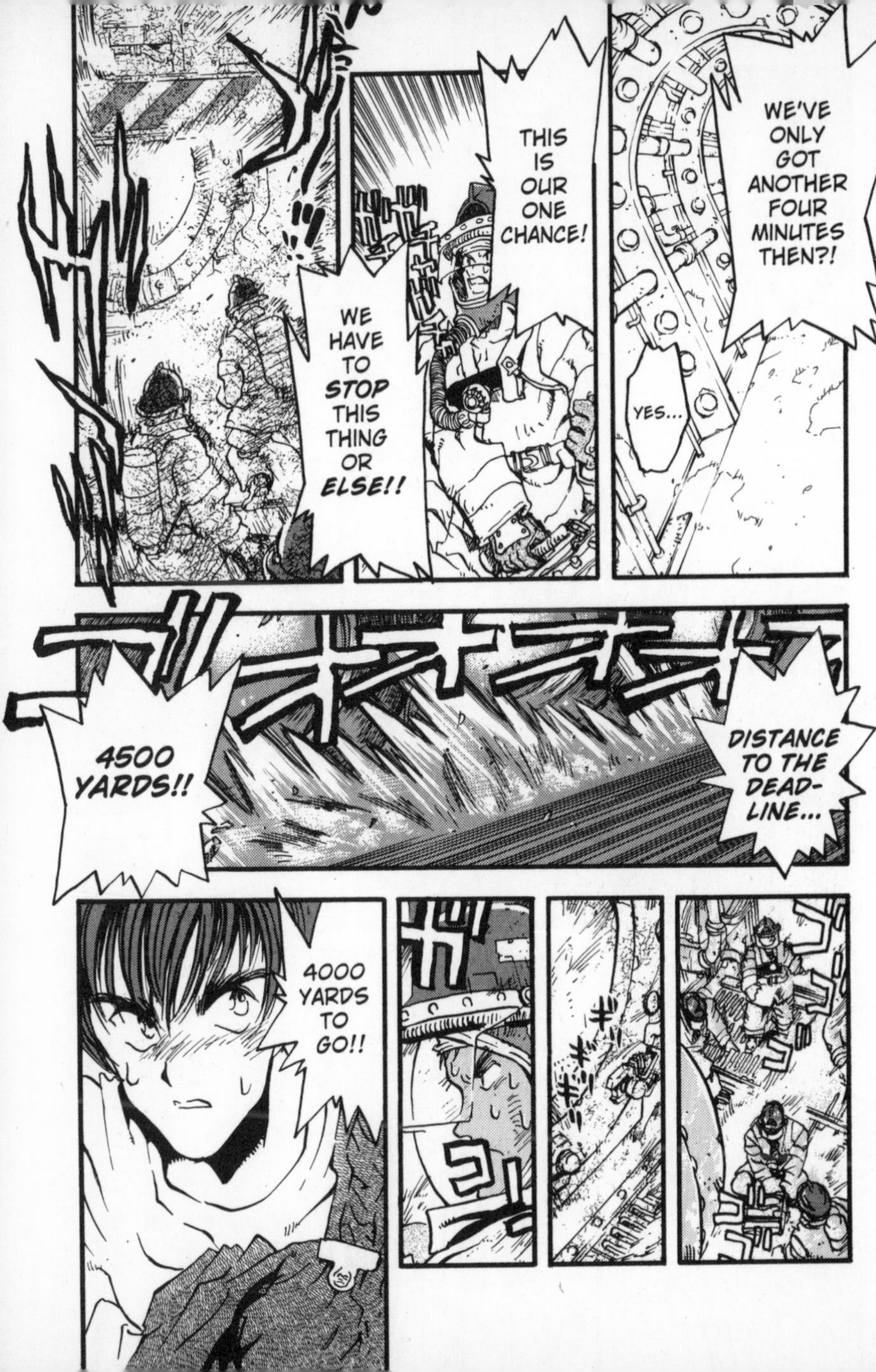
WE'VE ONLY GOT ANOTHER FOUR MINUTES THEN?!
YES...
THIS IS OUR ONE CHANCE!
WE HAVE TO STOP THIS THING OR ELSE!!
DISTANCE TO THE DEAD-LINE...
4500 YARDS!!
4000 YARDS TO GO!!

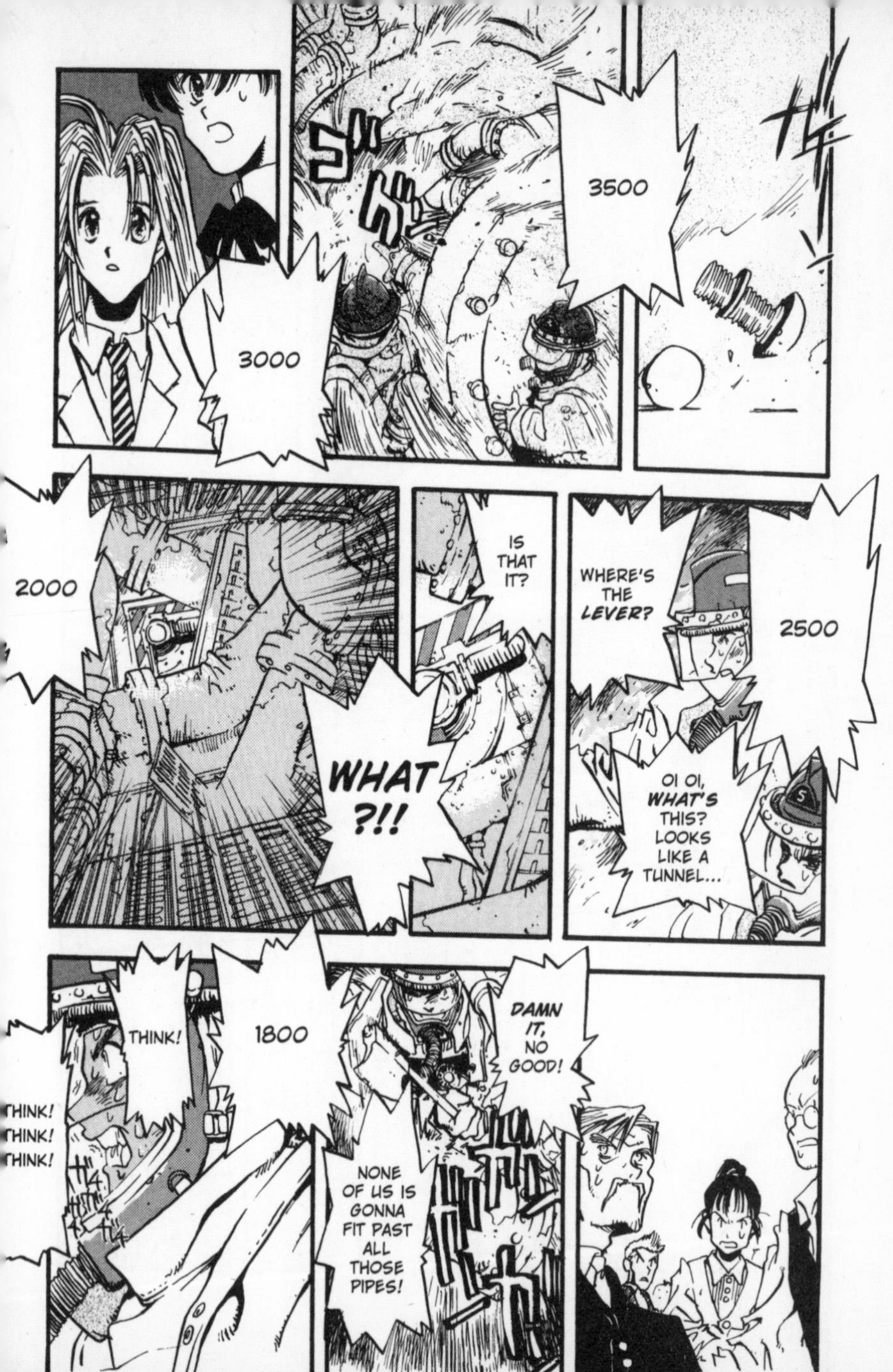
3500
3000
2500
WHERE'S THE *LEVER?*
OI OI, **WHAT'S** THIS? LOOKS LIKE A TUNNEL...
IS THAT IT?
**WHAT ?!!**
2000
***DAMN IT,*** NO GOOD!
1800
NONE OF US IS GONNA FIT PAST ALL THOSE PIPES!
THINK!
THINK! THINK! THINK!

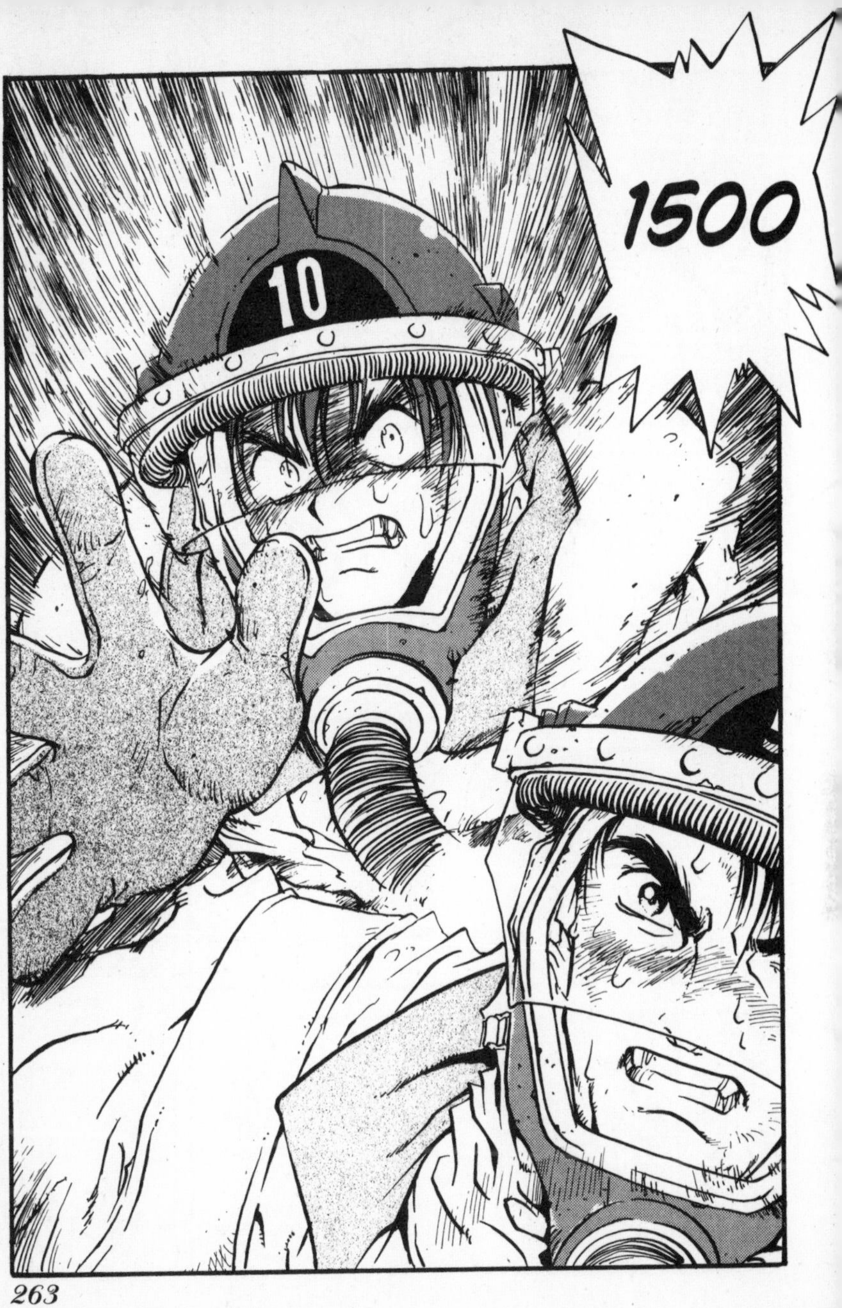
1500
10

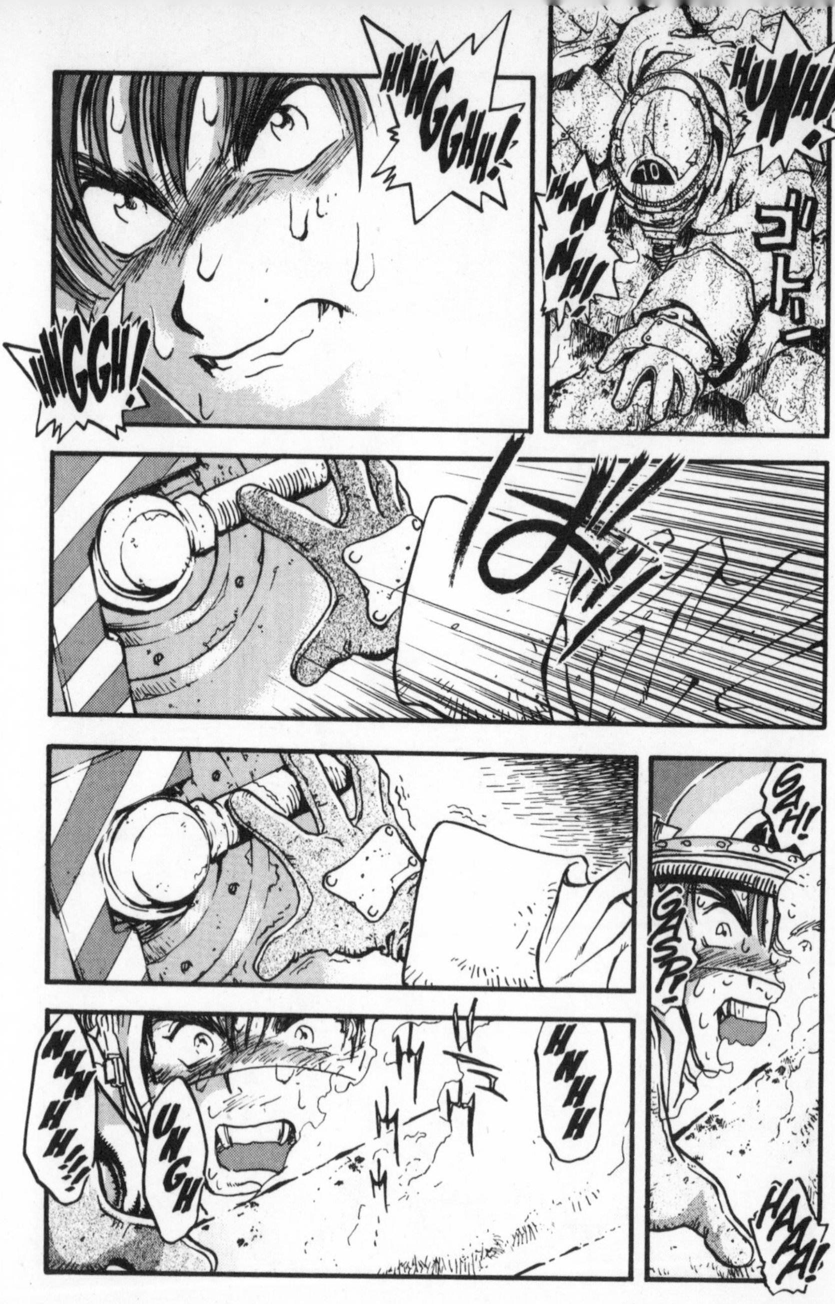
HUNH!
HNNNNH!
ゴトー
HHNGGHH!
HNGGH!
GAH!
GASP!
HAAA!
HNHH
UNGH
HNNNHH!!!!

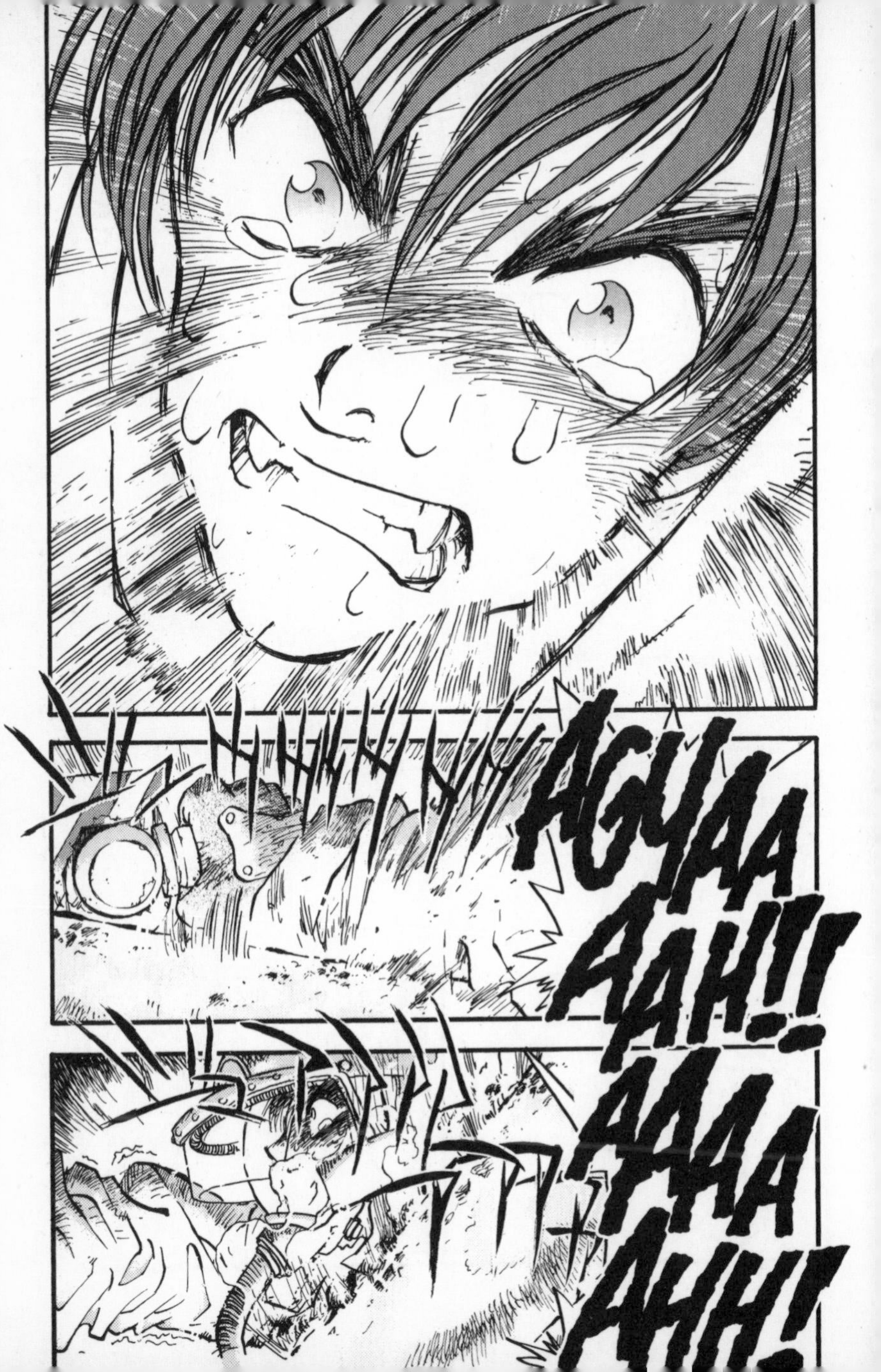
AGYAA AAH!! AAAA AHH!

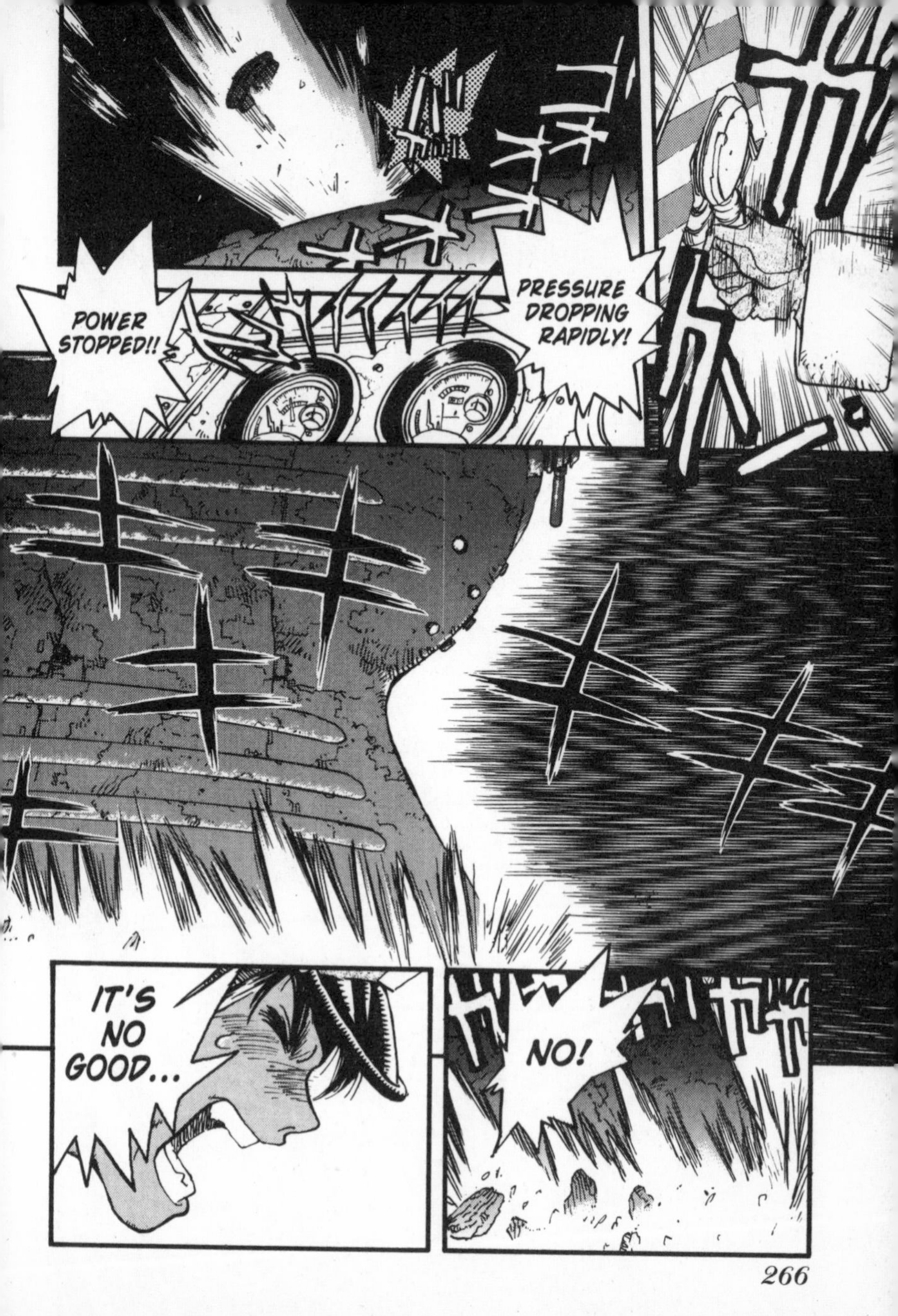
PRESSURE DROPPING RAPIDLY!
POWER STOPPED!!
NO!
IT'S NO GOOD...

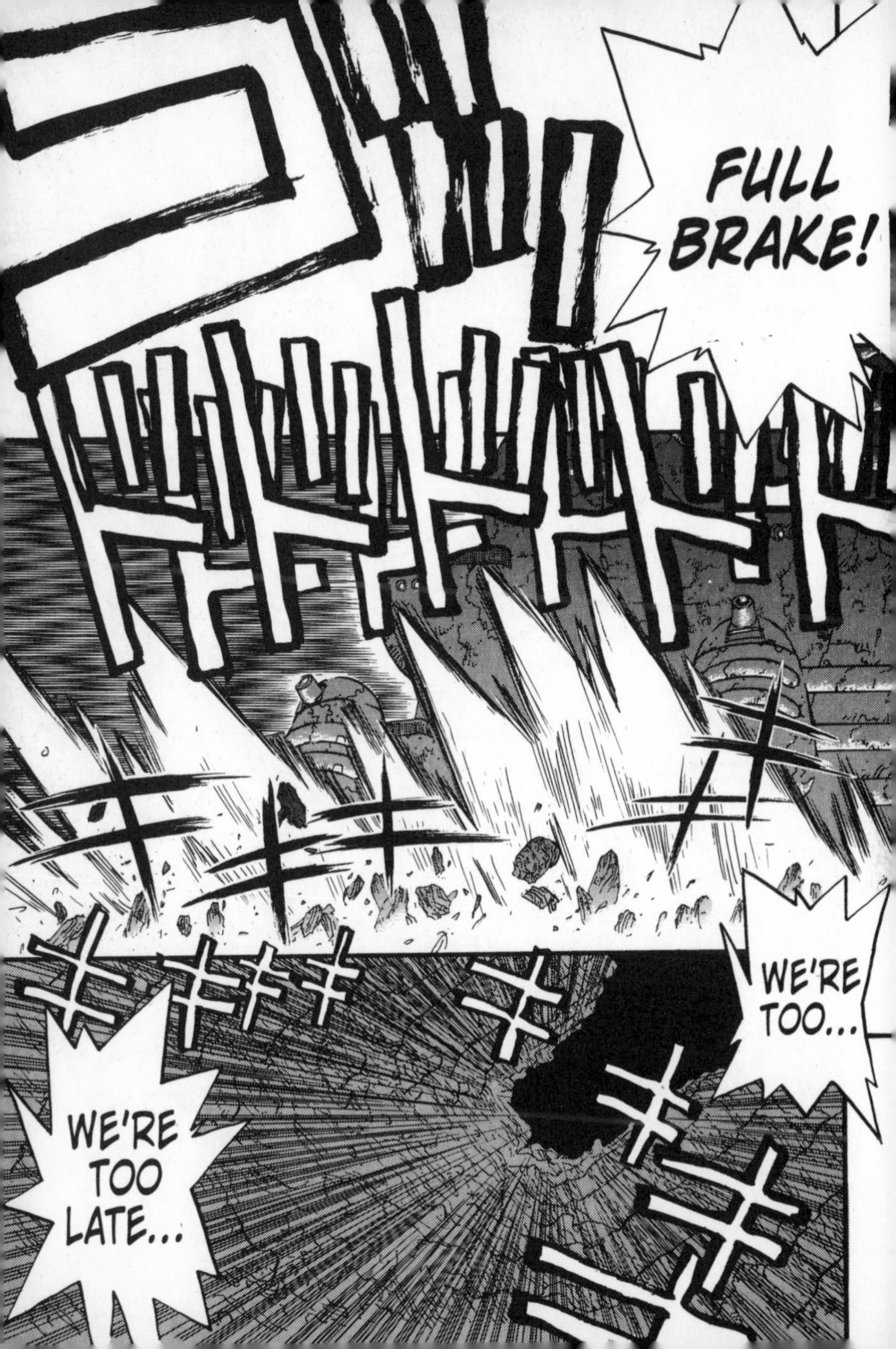
FULL BRAKE!
WE'RE TOO...
WE'RE TOO LATE...

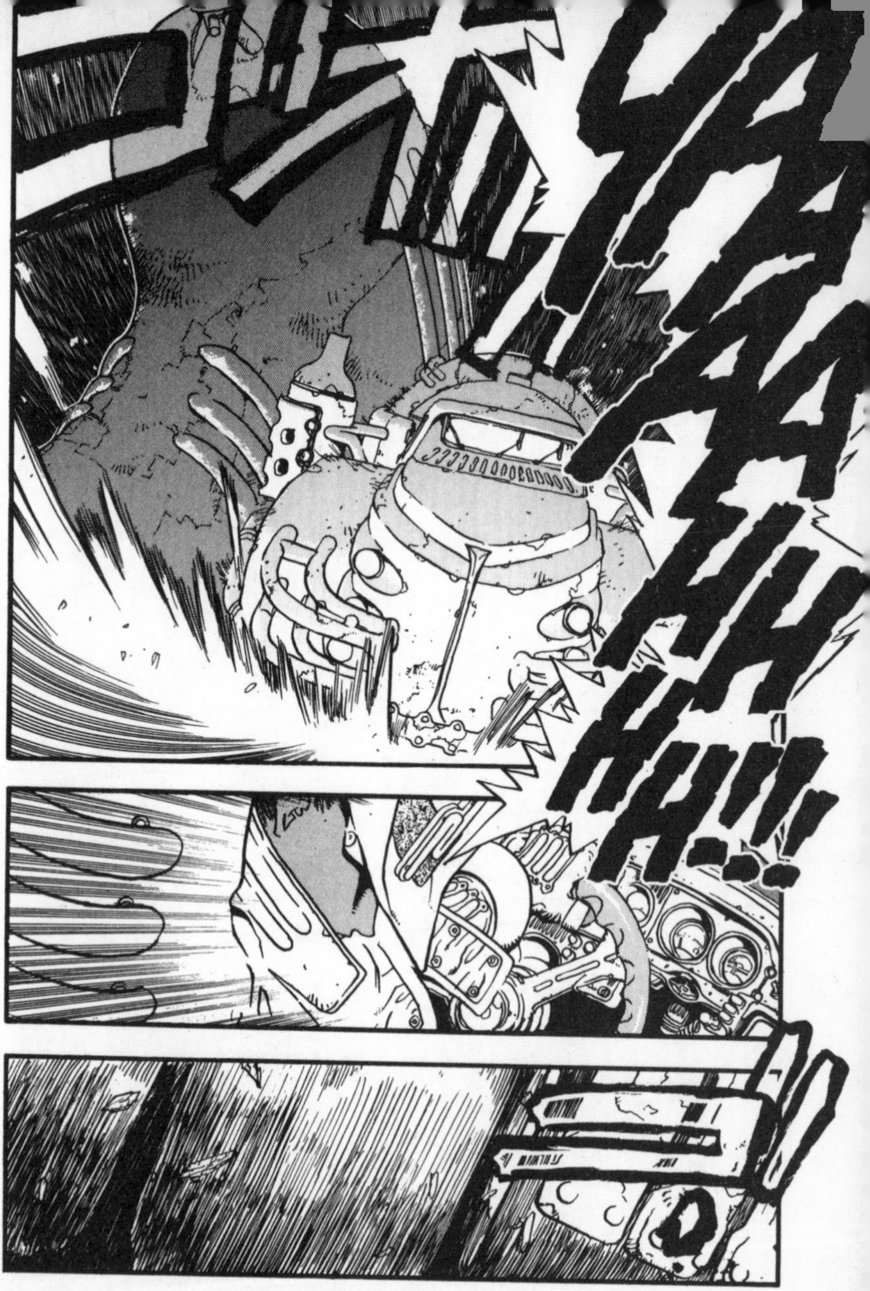
GYAAAAHHH...!!

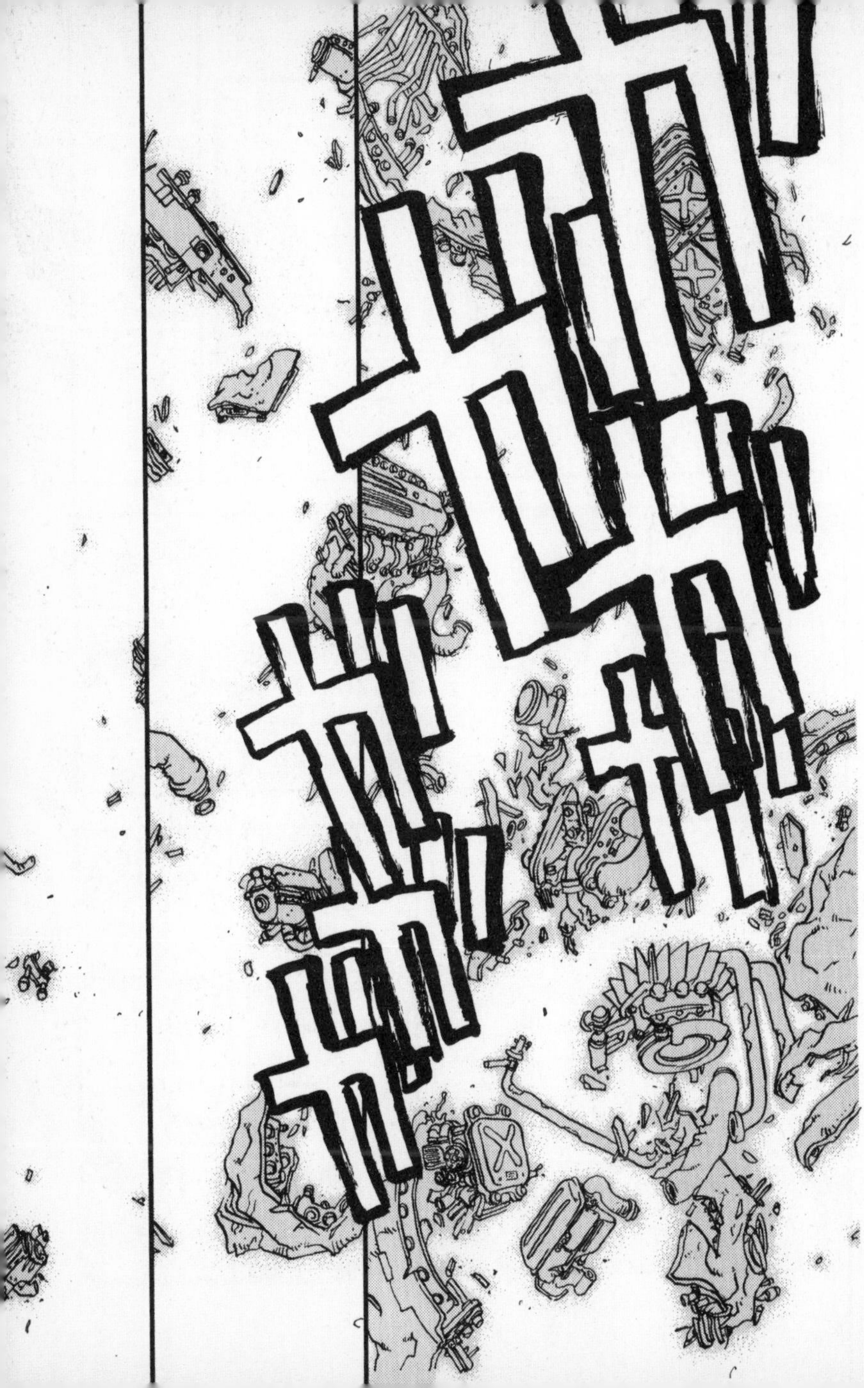

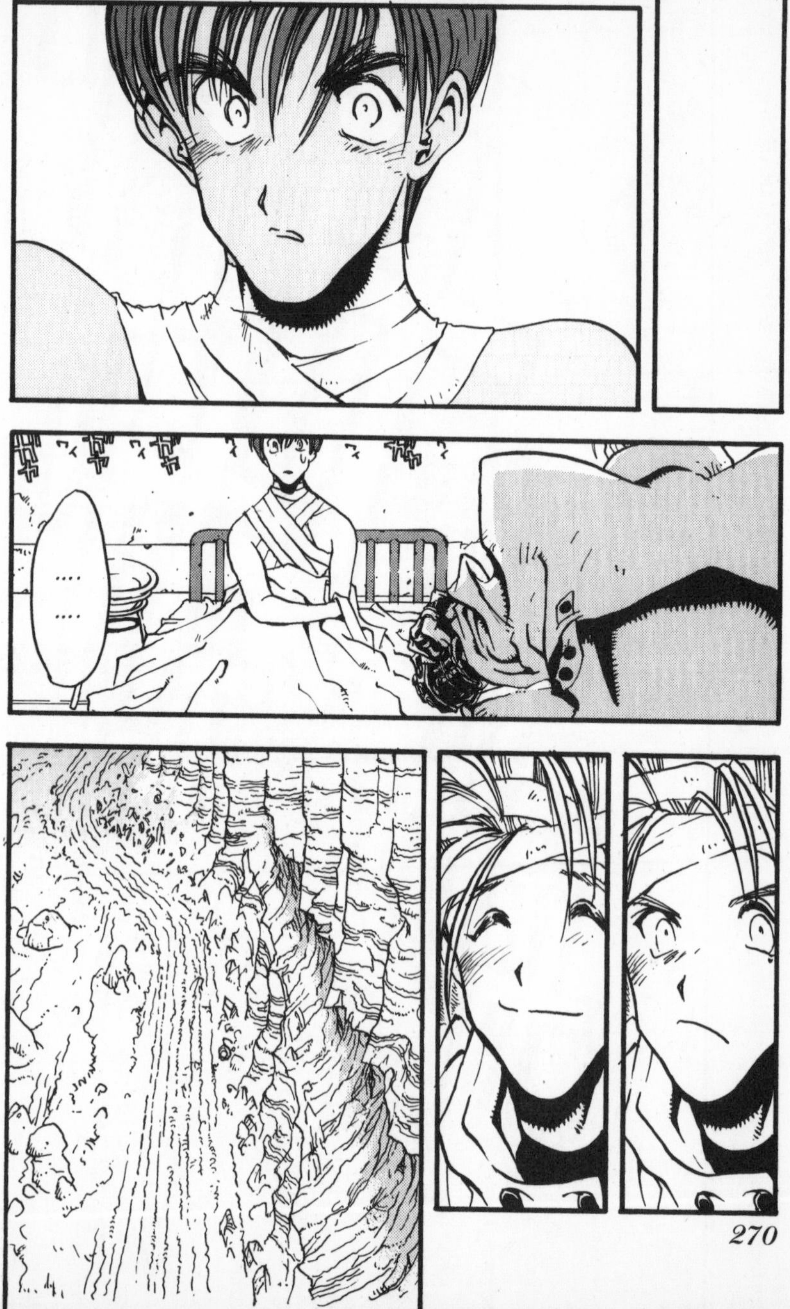
ワイ ガヤガヤ ワイ ワイ ガヤガヤ ワイ ガヤガヤ ワイ ガヤガヤ
....
....

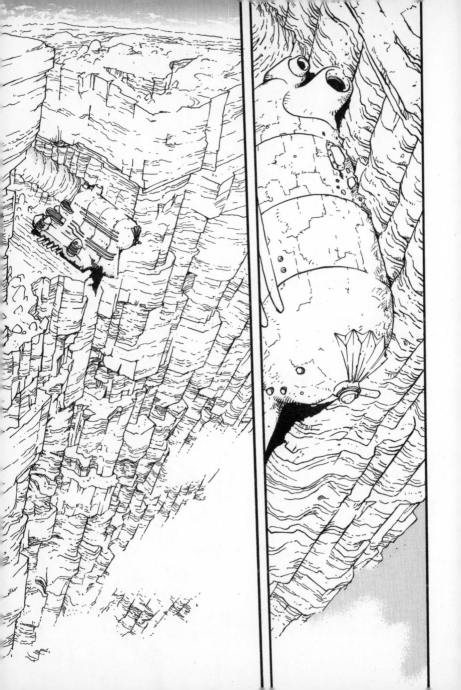

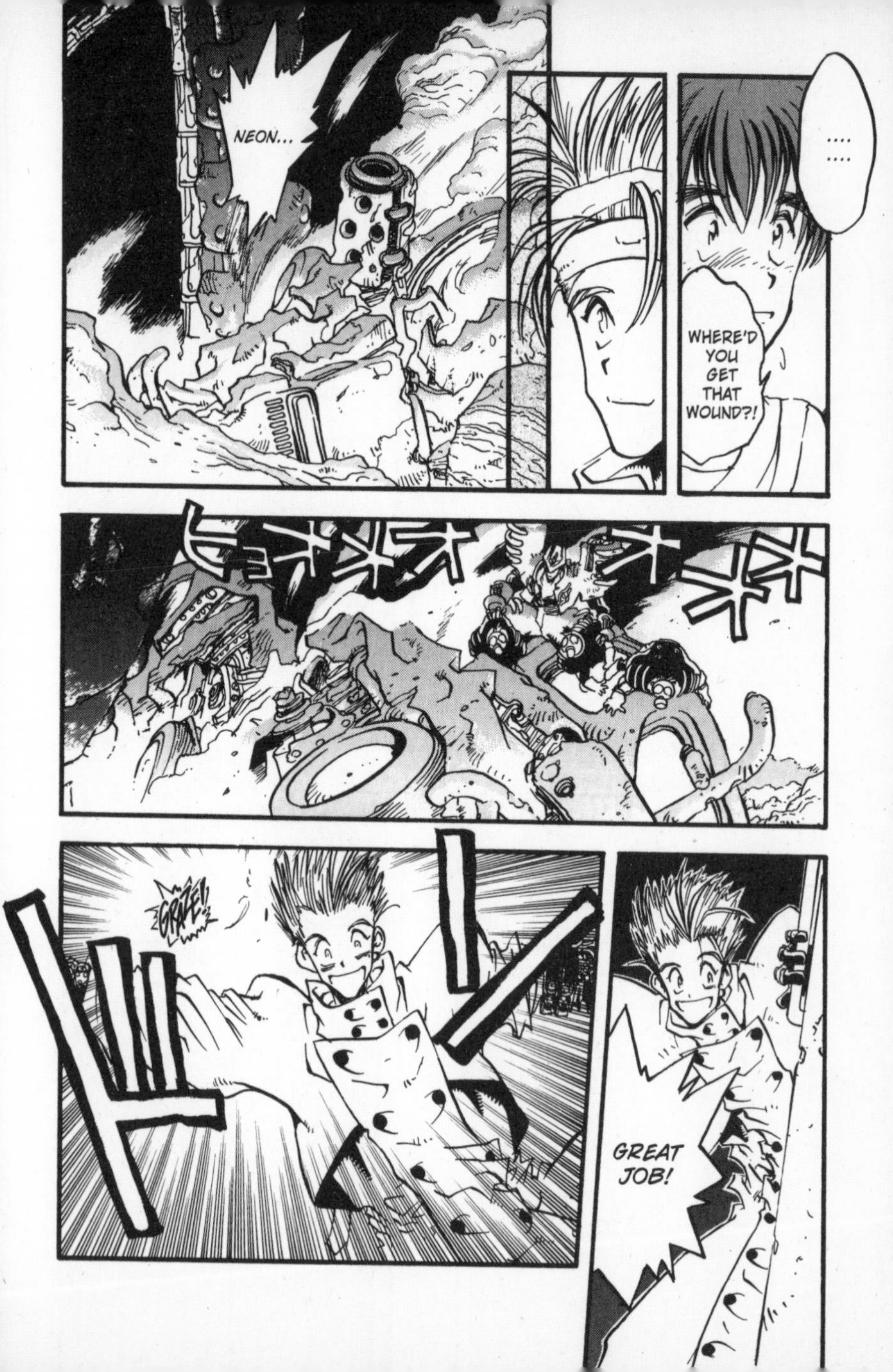

....
....
WHERE'D YOU GET THAT WOUND?!
NEON...
GREAT JOB!
GRAZE!

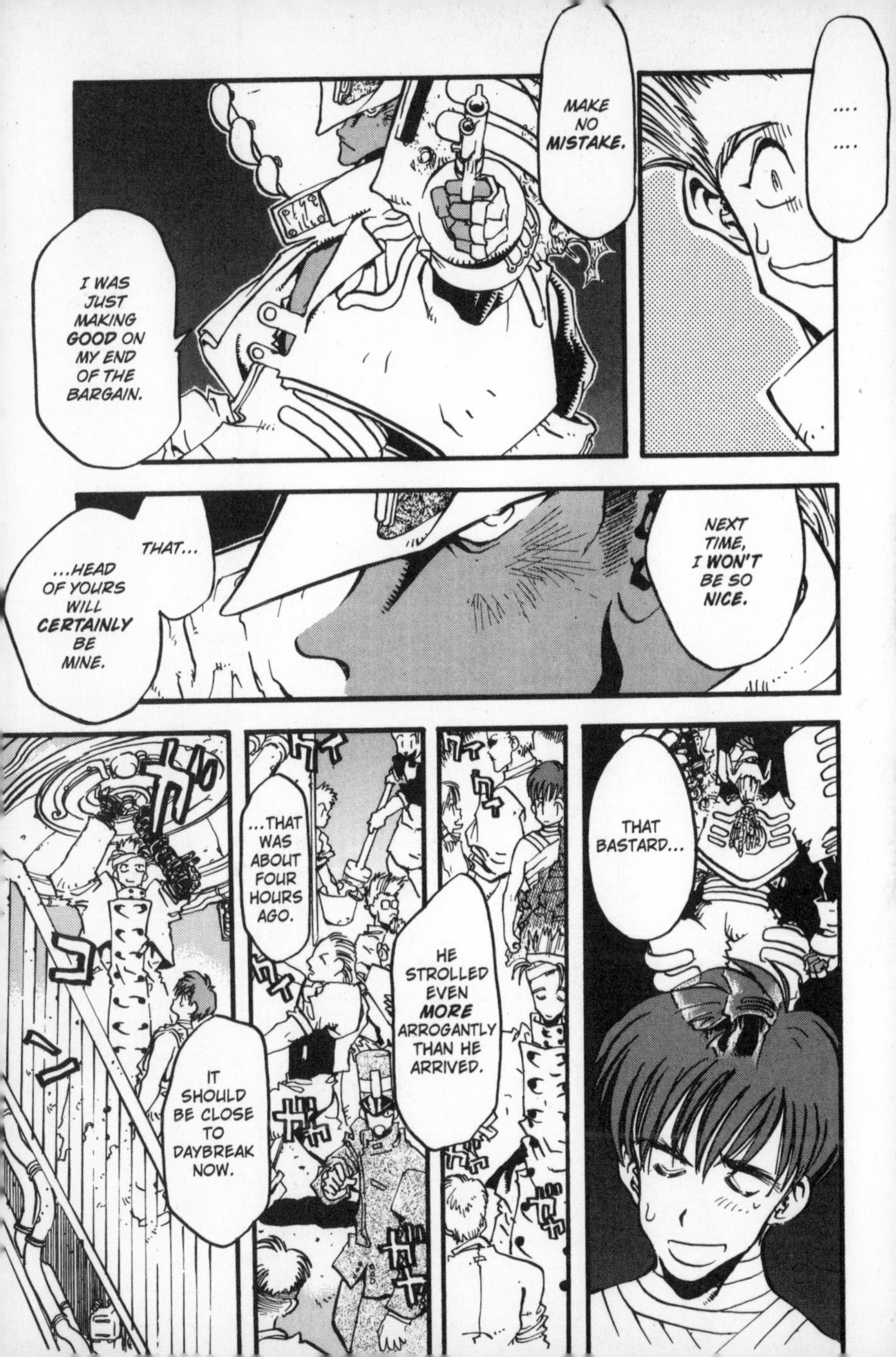
....
....
MAKE NO MISTAKE.
I WAS JUST MAKING GOOD ON MY END OF THE BARGAIN.
NEXT TIME, I WON'T BE SO NICE.
THAT...
...HEAD OF YOURS WILL CERTAINLY BE MINE.
THAT BASTARD...
...THAT WAS ABOUT FOUR HOURS AGO.
HE STROLLED EVEN MORE ARROGANTLY THAN HE ARRIVED.
IT SHOULD BE CLOSE TO DAYBREAK NOW.

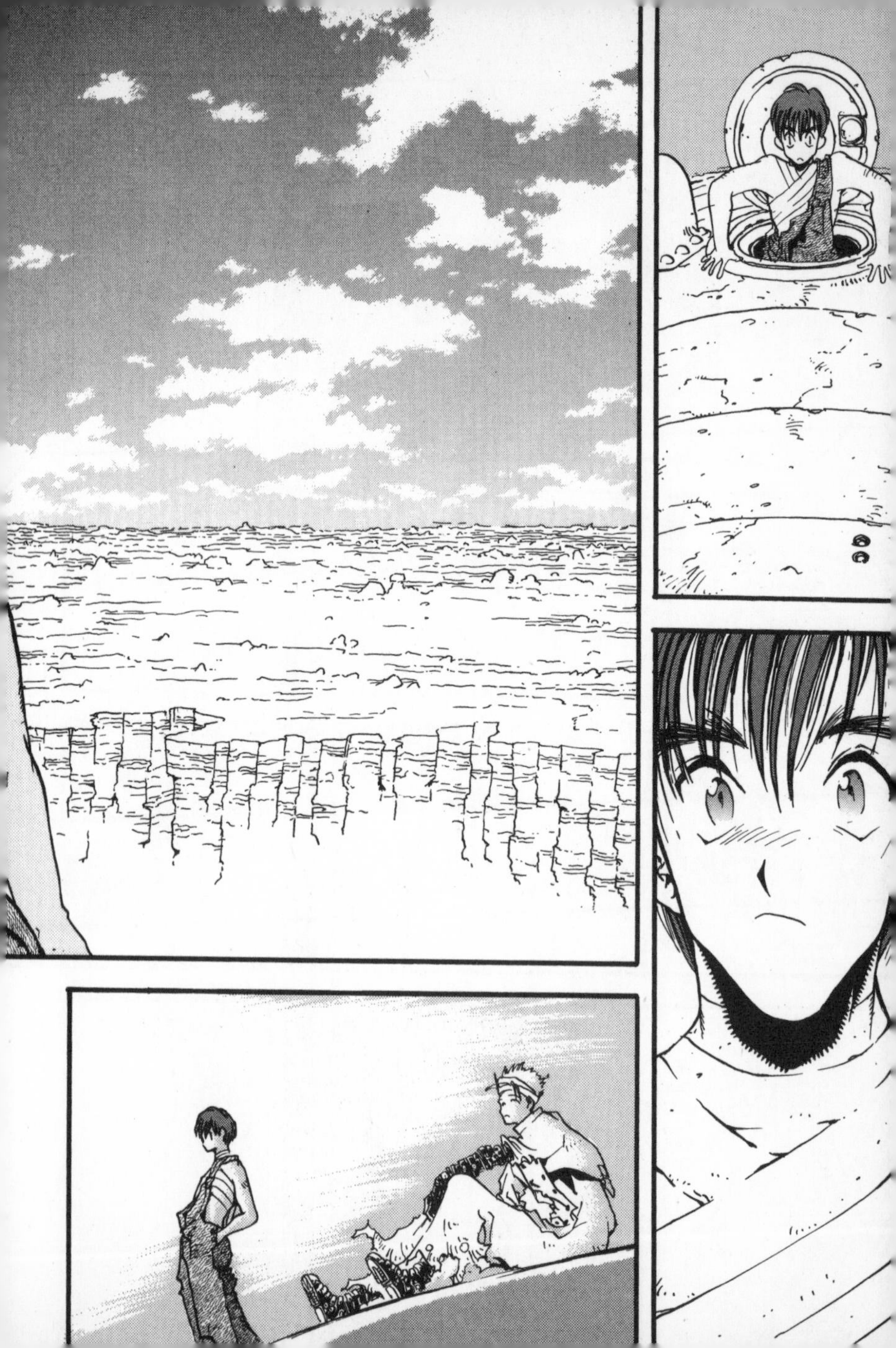

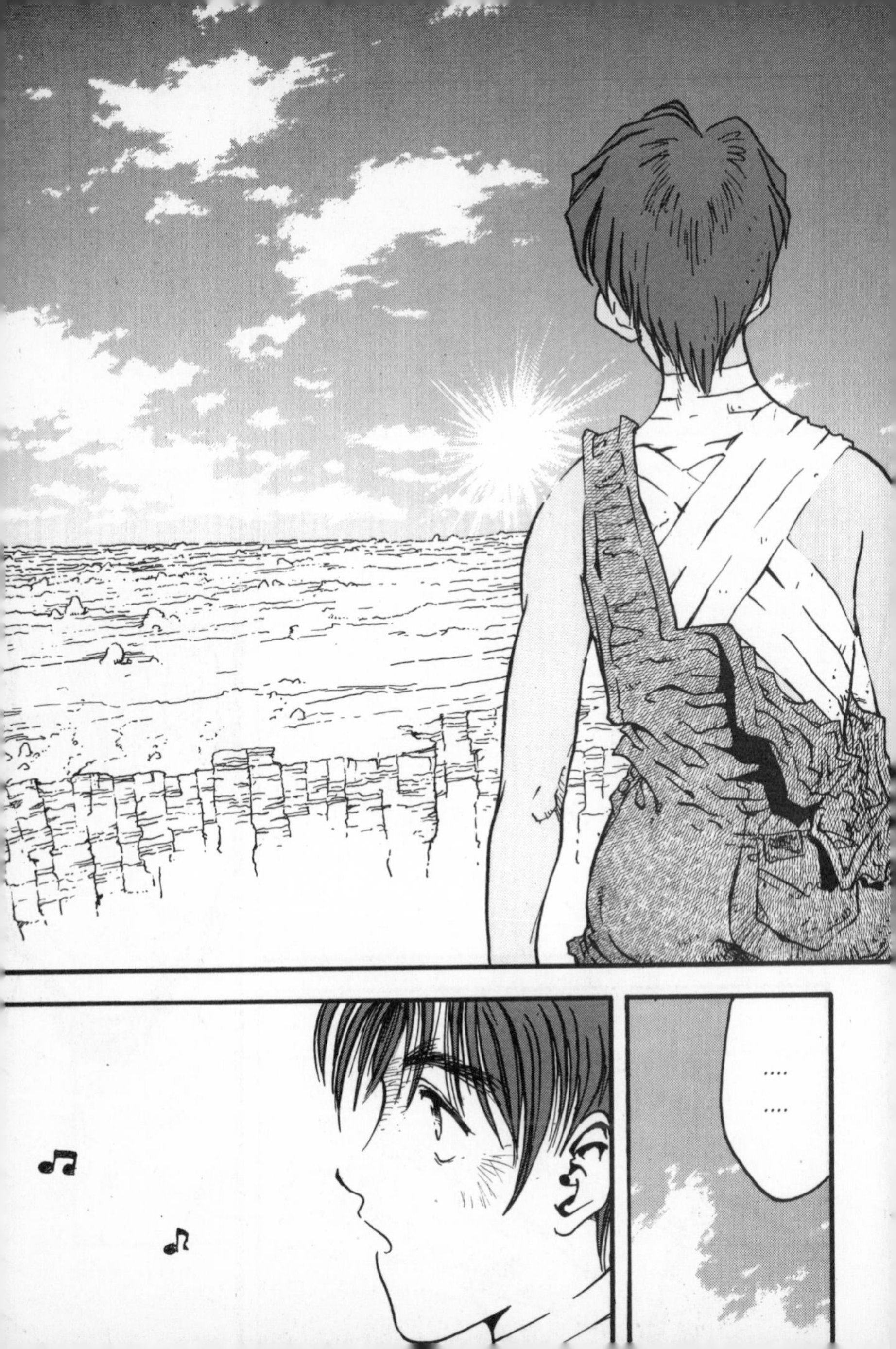
....
....

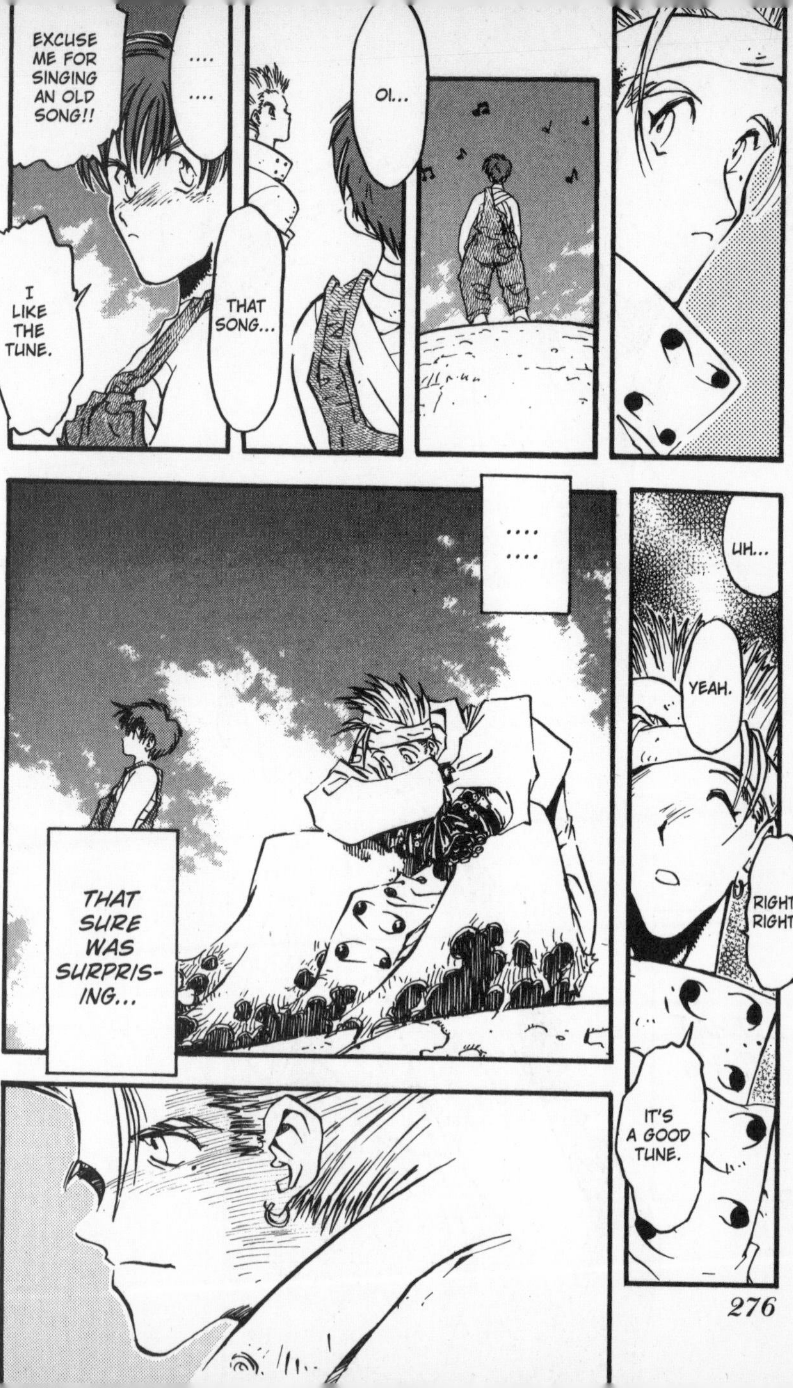
OI...
THAT SONG...
....
....
EXCUSE ME FOR SINGING AN OLD SONG!!
I LIKE THE TUNE.
UH...
YEAH.
RIGHT, RIGHT.
IT'S A GOOD TUNE.
....
....
THAT SURE WAS SURPRIS-ING...

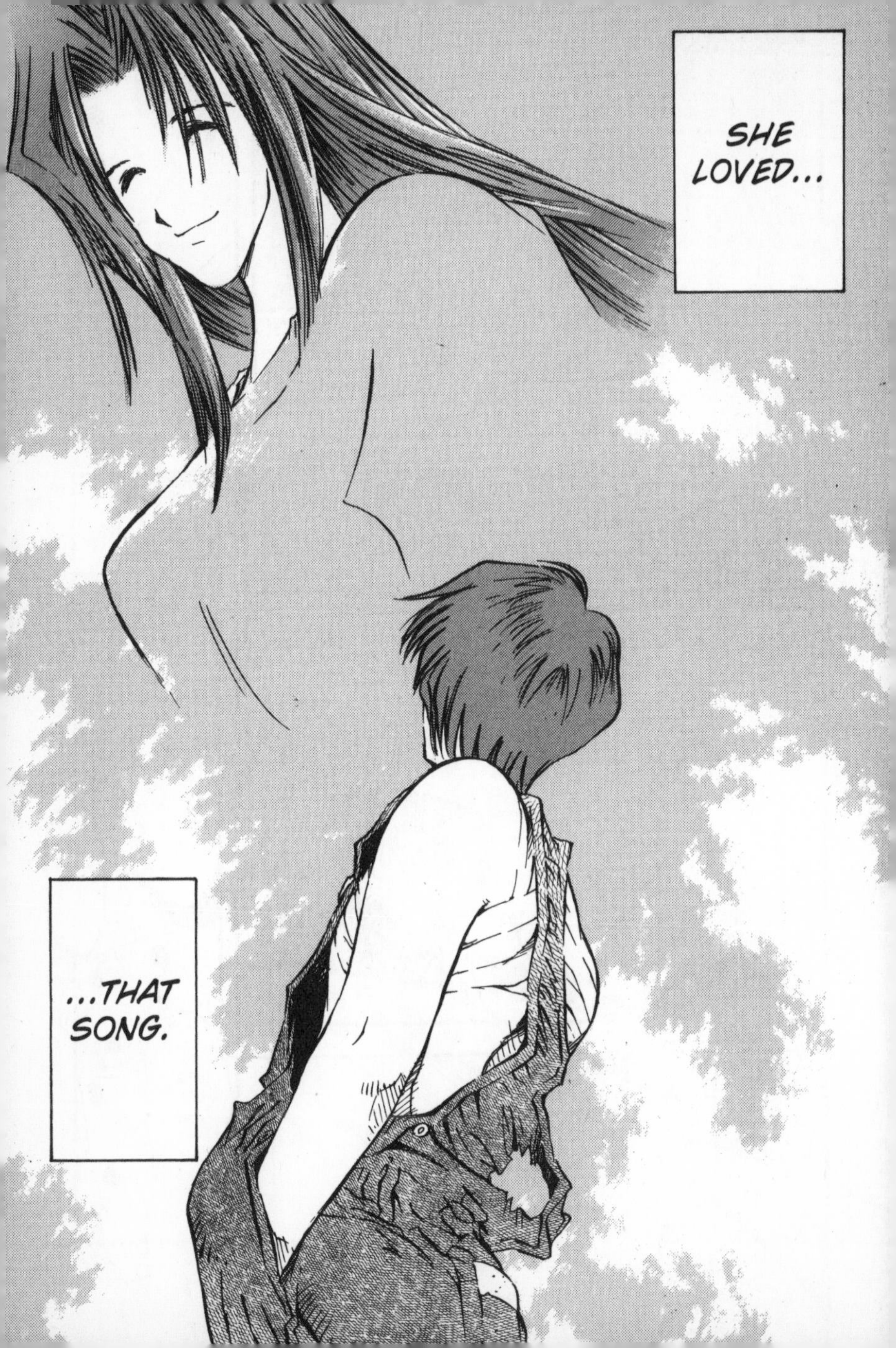
SHE LOVED...
...THAT SONG.

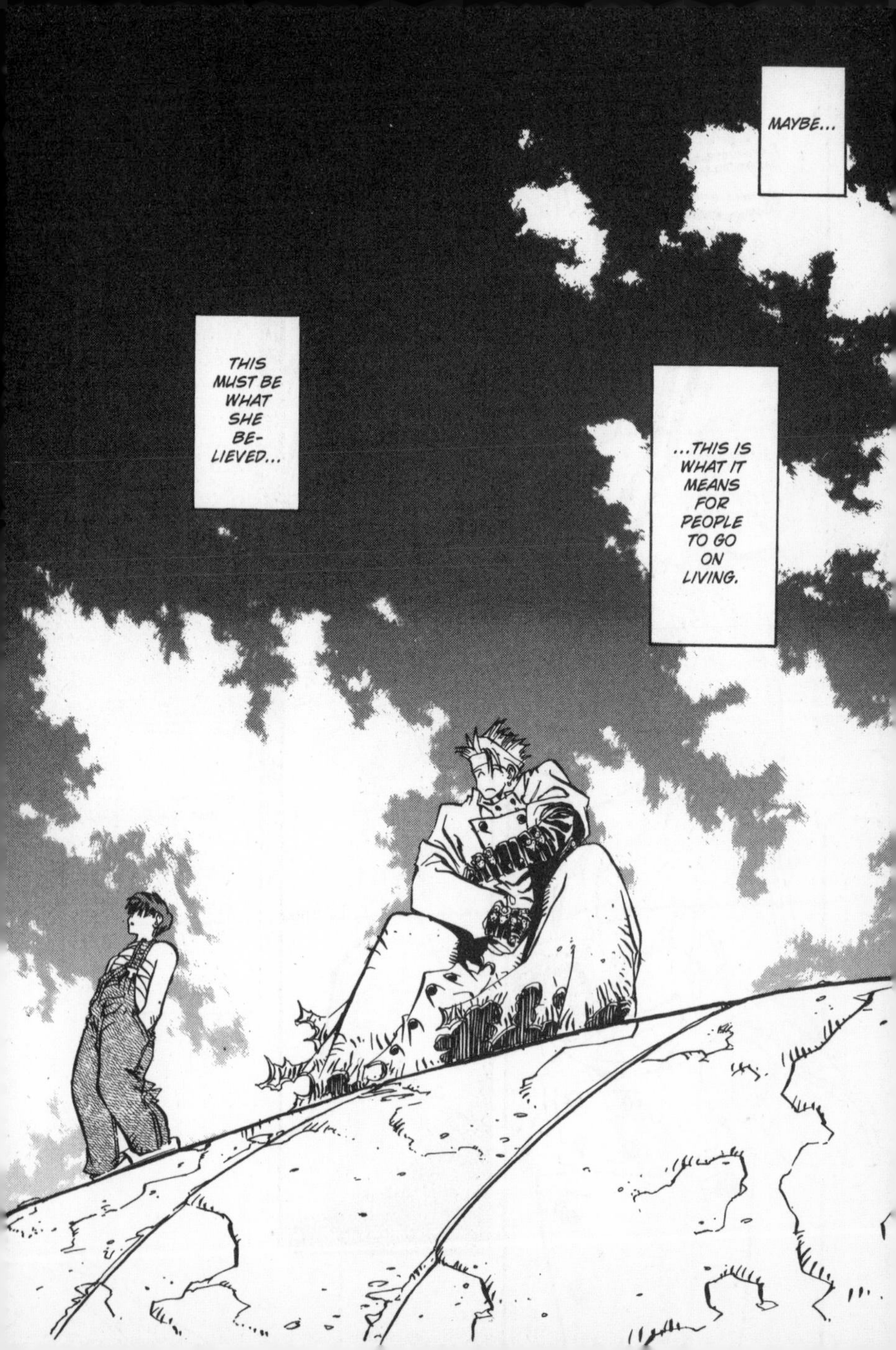
MAYBE...
...THIS IS WHAT IT MEANS FOR PEOPLE TO GO ON LIVING.
THIS MUST BE WHAT SHE BE-LIEVED...

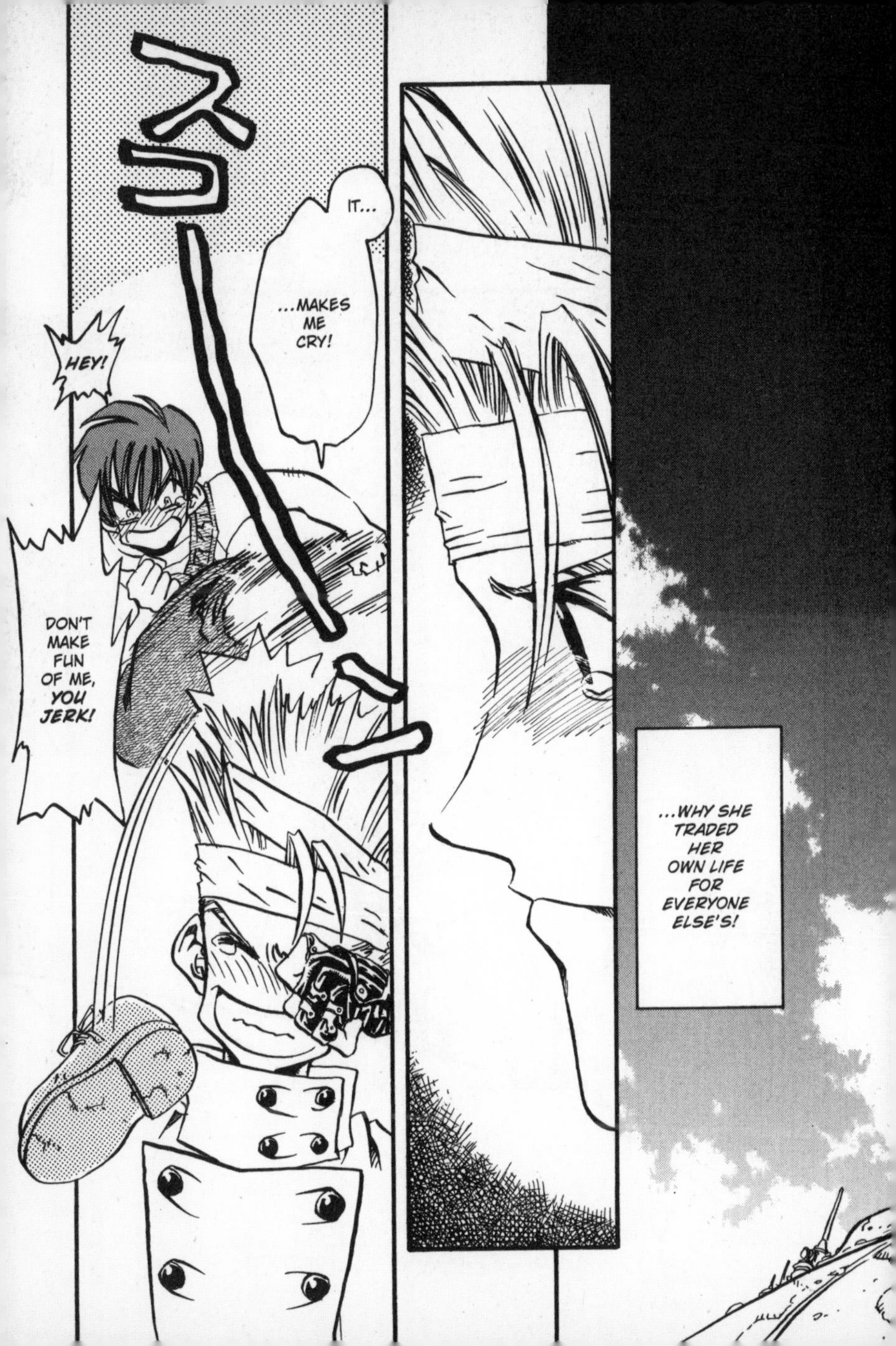
...WHY SHE TRADED HER OWN LIFE FOR EVERYONE ELSE'S!
IT...
...MAKES ME CRY!
HEY!
DON'T MAKE FUN OF ME, YOU JERK!

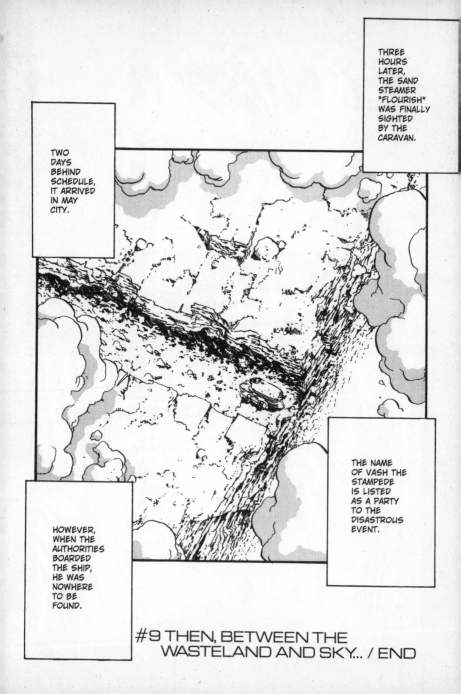

THREE HOURS LATER, THE SAND STEAMER "FLOURISH" WAS FINALLY SIGHTED BY THE CARAVAN.

TWO DAYS BEHIND SCHEDULE, IT ARRIVED IN MAY CITY.

THE NAME OF VASH THE STAMPEDE IS LISTED AS A PARTY TO THE DISASTROUS EVENT.

HOWEVER, WHEN THE AUTHORITIES BOARDED THE SHIP, HE WAS NOWHERE TO BE FOUND.

#9 THEN, BETWEEN THE WASTELAND AND SKY... / END

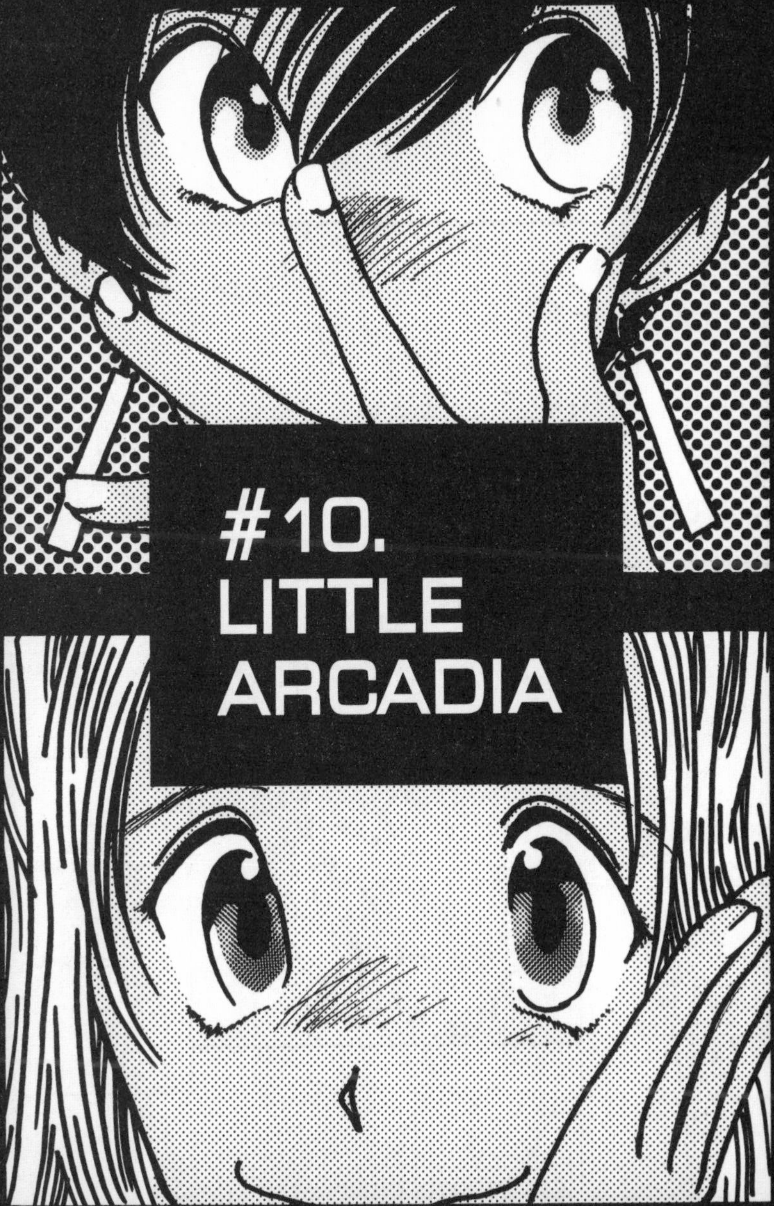

# #10. LITTLE ARCADIA

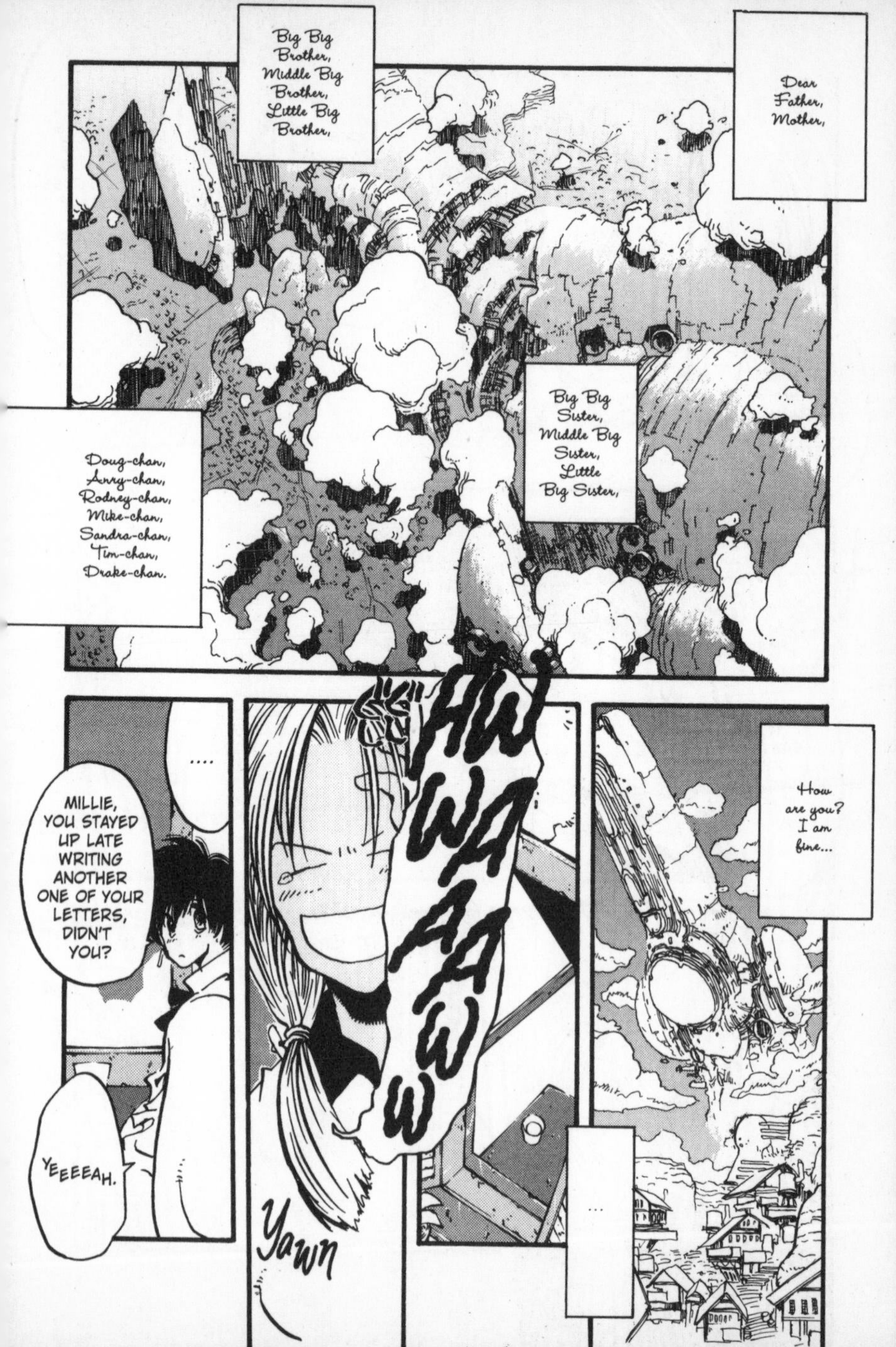

Dear Father, Mother,
Big Big Brother, Middle Big Brother, Little Big Brother,
Big Big Sister, Middle Big Sister, Little Big Sister,
Doug-chan, Anry-chan, Rodney-chan, Mike-chan, Sandra-chan, Tim-chan, Drake-chan.
How are you? I am fine...
...
AWWAAAAWW
Yawn
....
MILLIE, YOU STAYED UP LATE WRITING ANOTHER ONE OF YOUR LETTERS, DIDN'T YOU?
YEEEEAH.

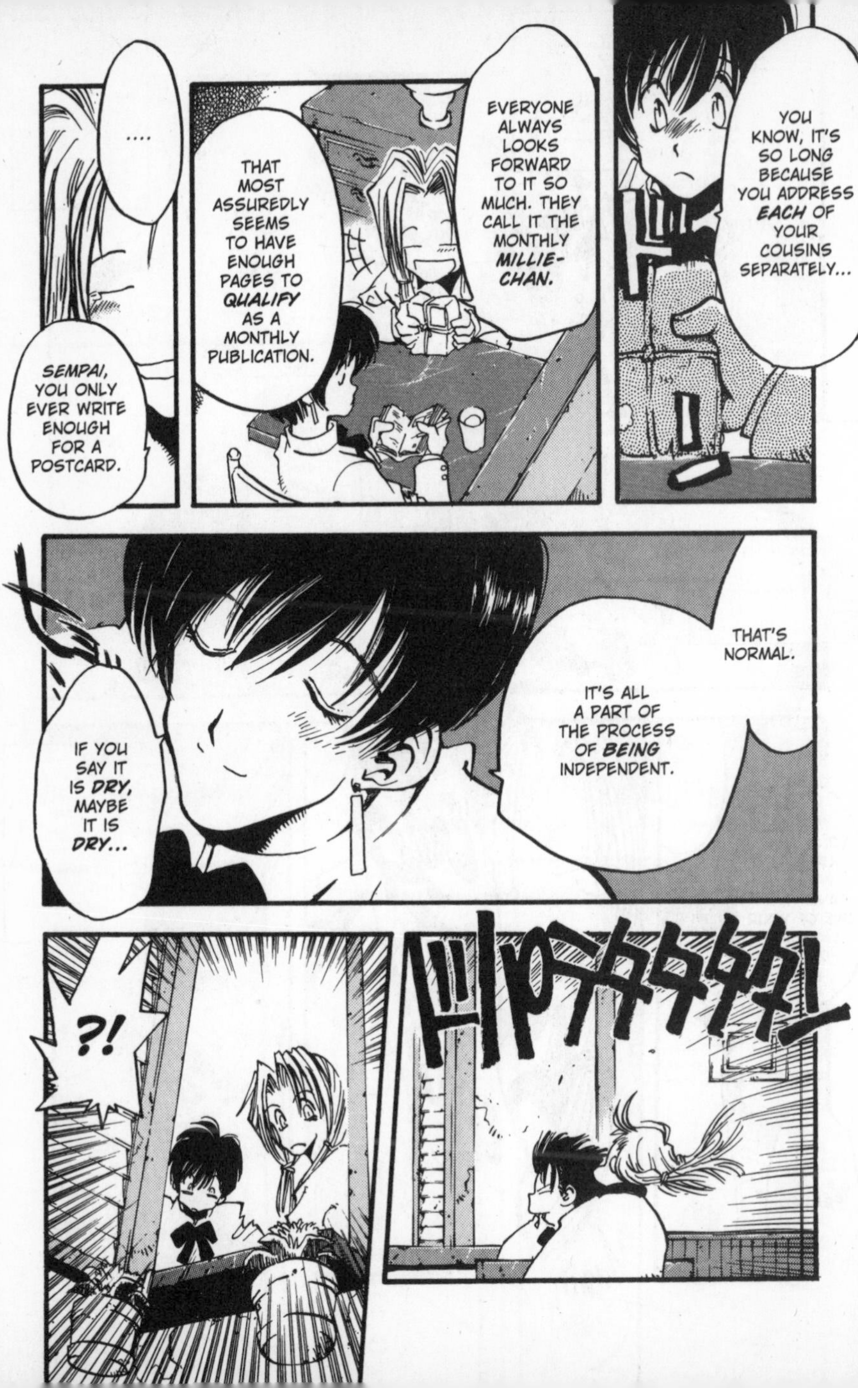
YOU KNOW, IT'S SO LONG BECAUSE YOU ADDRESS *EACH* OF YOUR COUSINS SEPARATELY...
EVERYONE ALWAYS LOOKS FORWARD TO IT SO MUCH. THEY CALL IT THE MONTHLY *MILLIE-CHAN.*
THAT MOST ASSUREDLY SEEMS TO HAVE ENOUGH PAGES TO *QUALIFY* AS A MONTHLY PUBLICATION.
....
*SEMPAI,* YOU ONLY EVER WRITE ENOUGH FOR A POSTCARD.
THAT'S NORMAL.
IT'S ALL A PART OF THE PROCESS OF *BEING* INDEPENDENT.
IF YOU SAY IT IS *DRY,* MAYBE IT IS *DRY...*
?!

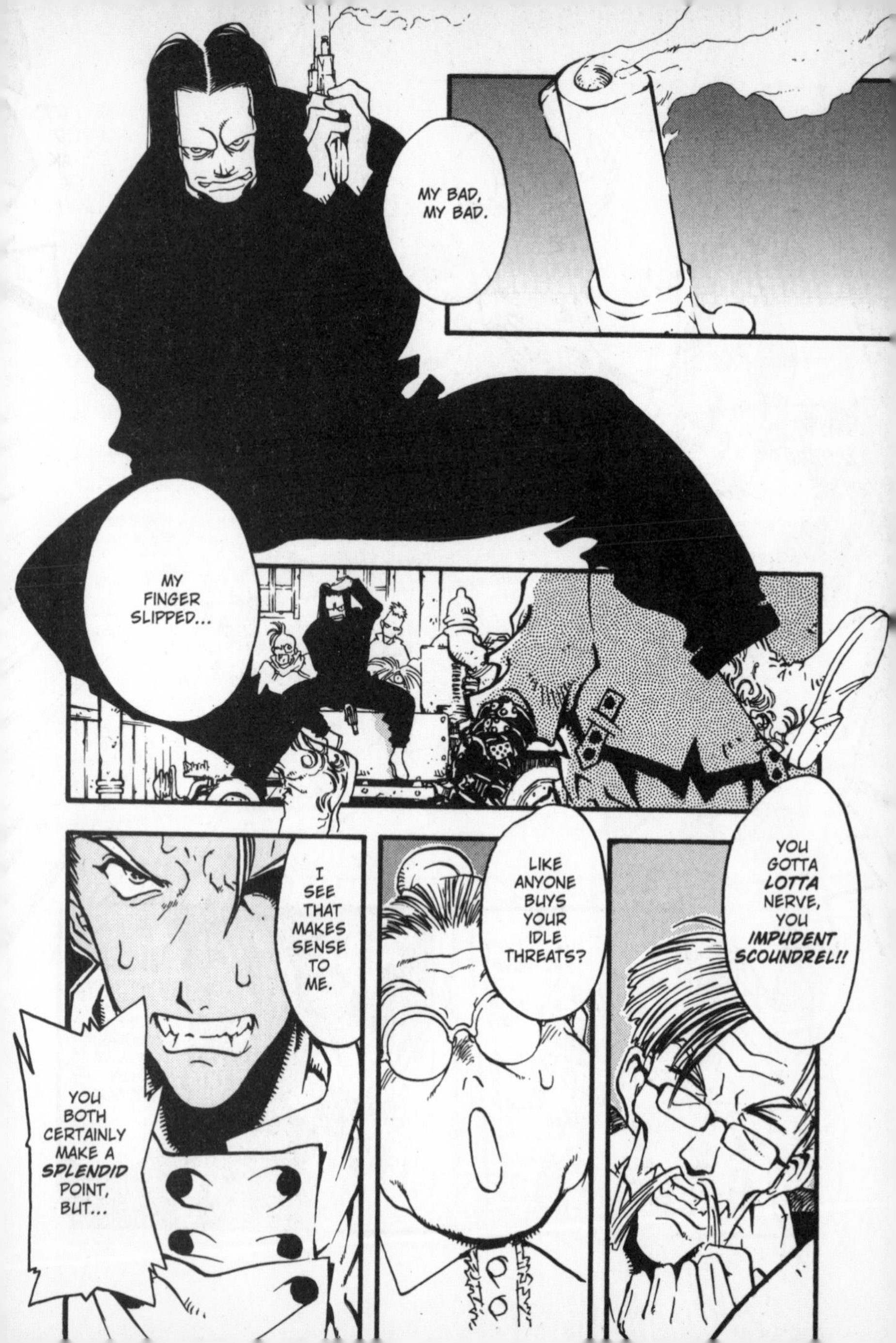
MY BAD, MY BAD.
MY FINGER SLIPPED...
YOU GOTTA *LOTTA* NERVE, YOU *IMPUDENT SCOUNDREL!!*
LIKE ANYONE BUYS YOUR IDLE THREATS?
I SEE THAT MAKES SENSE TO ME.
YOU BOTH CERTAINLY MAKE A *SPLENDID* POINT, BUT...

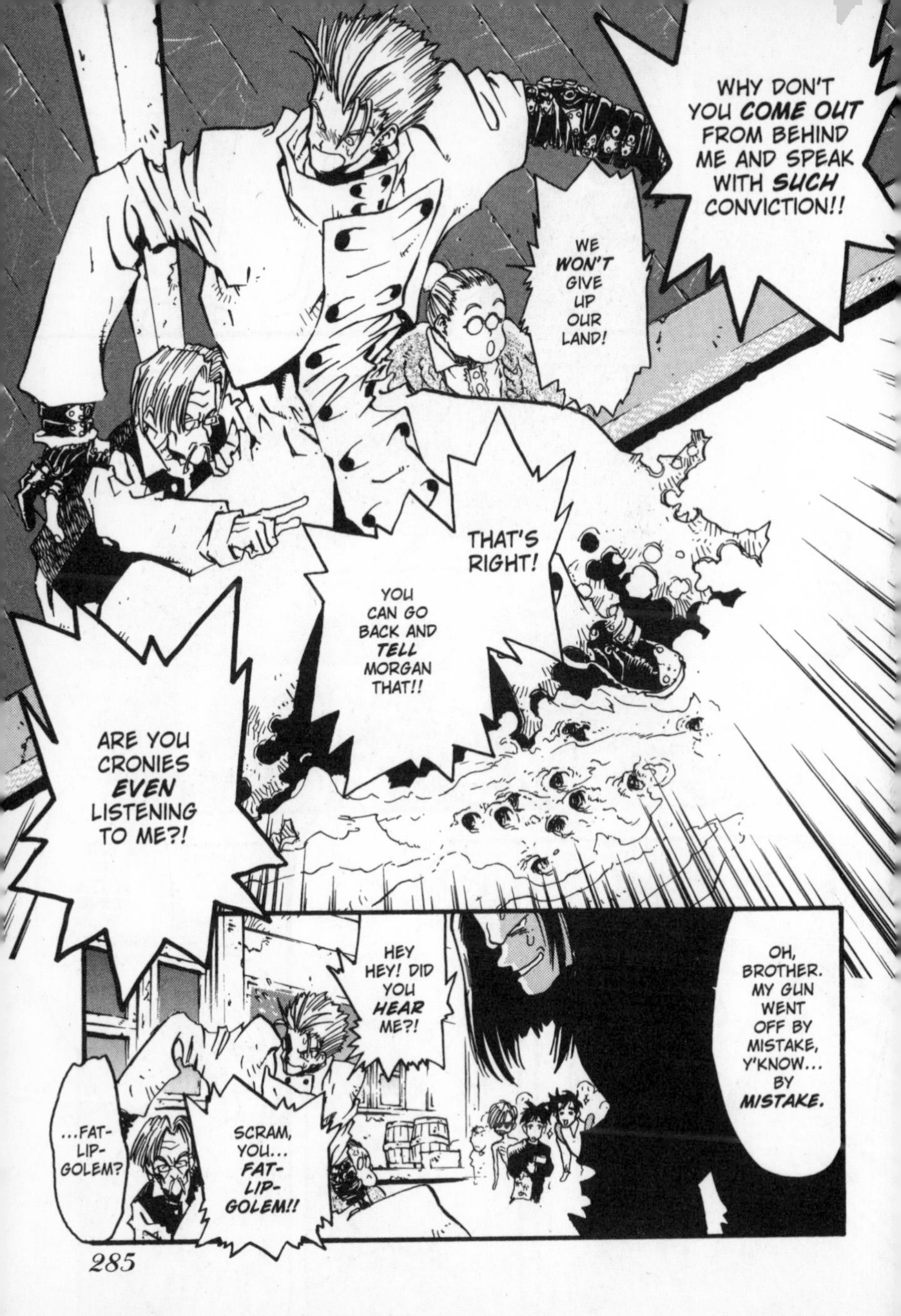
WHY DON'T YOU COME OUT FROM BEHIND ME AND SPEAK WITH SUCH CONVICTION!!
WE WON'T GIVE UP OUR LAND!
THAT'S RIGHT!
YOU CAN GO BACK AND TELL MORGAN THAT!!
ARE YOU CRONIES EVEN LISTENING TO ME?!
OH, BROTHER. MY GUN WENT OFF BY MISTAKE, Y'KNOW... BY MISTAKE.
HEY HEY! DID YOU HEAR ME?!
SCRAM, YOU... FAT-LIP-GOLEM!!
...FAT-LIP-GOLEM?

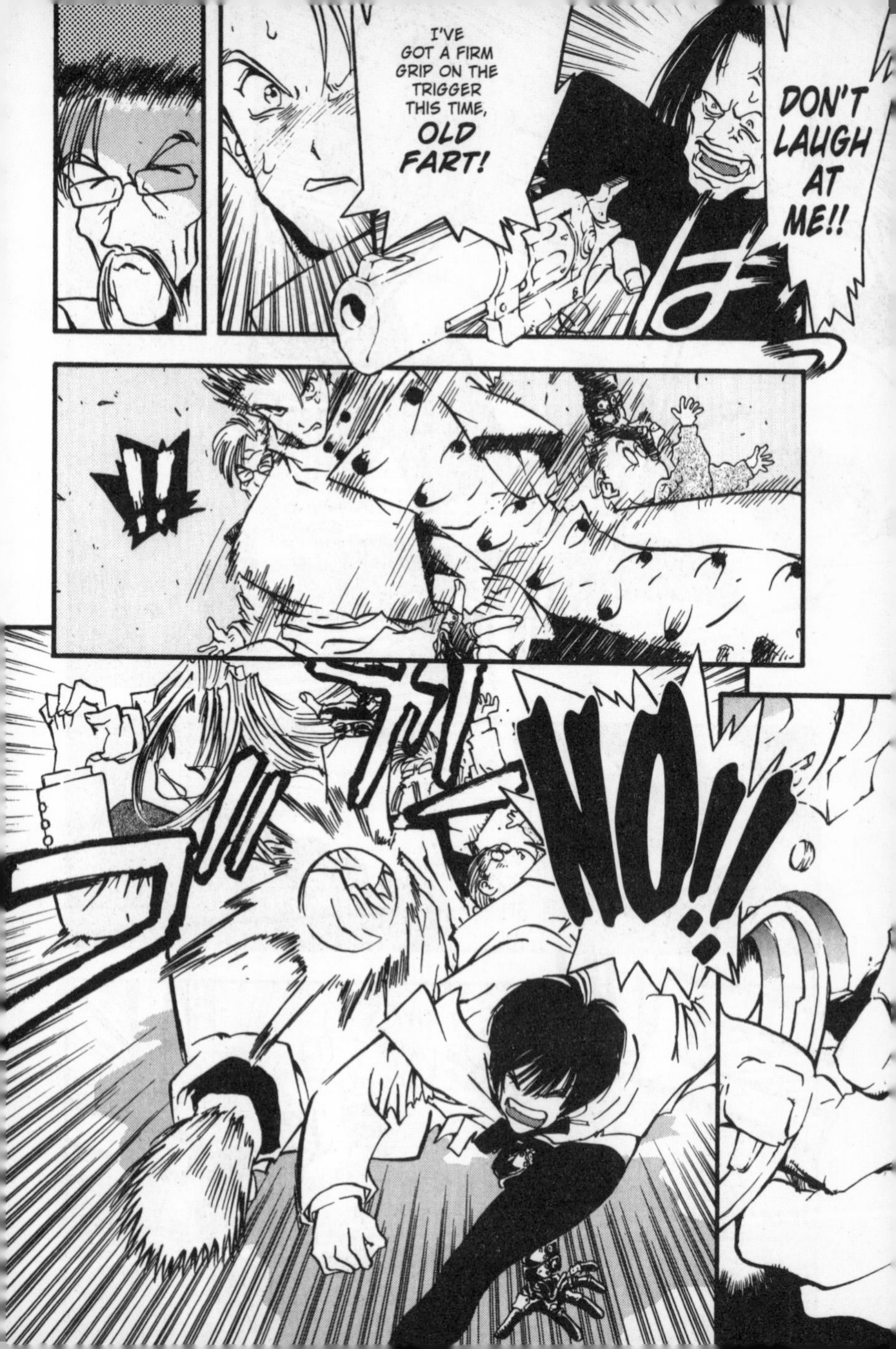
DON'T LAUGH AT ME!!
I'VE GOT A FIRM GRIP ON THE TRIGGER THIS TIME, OLD FART!
!!
NO!!

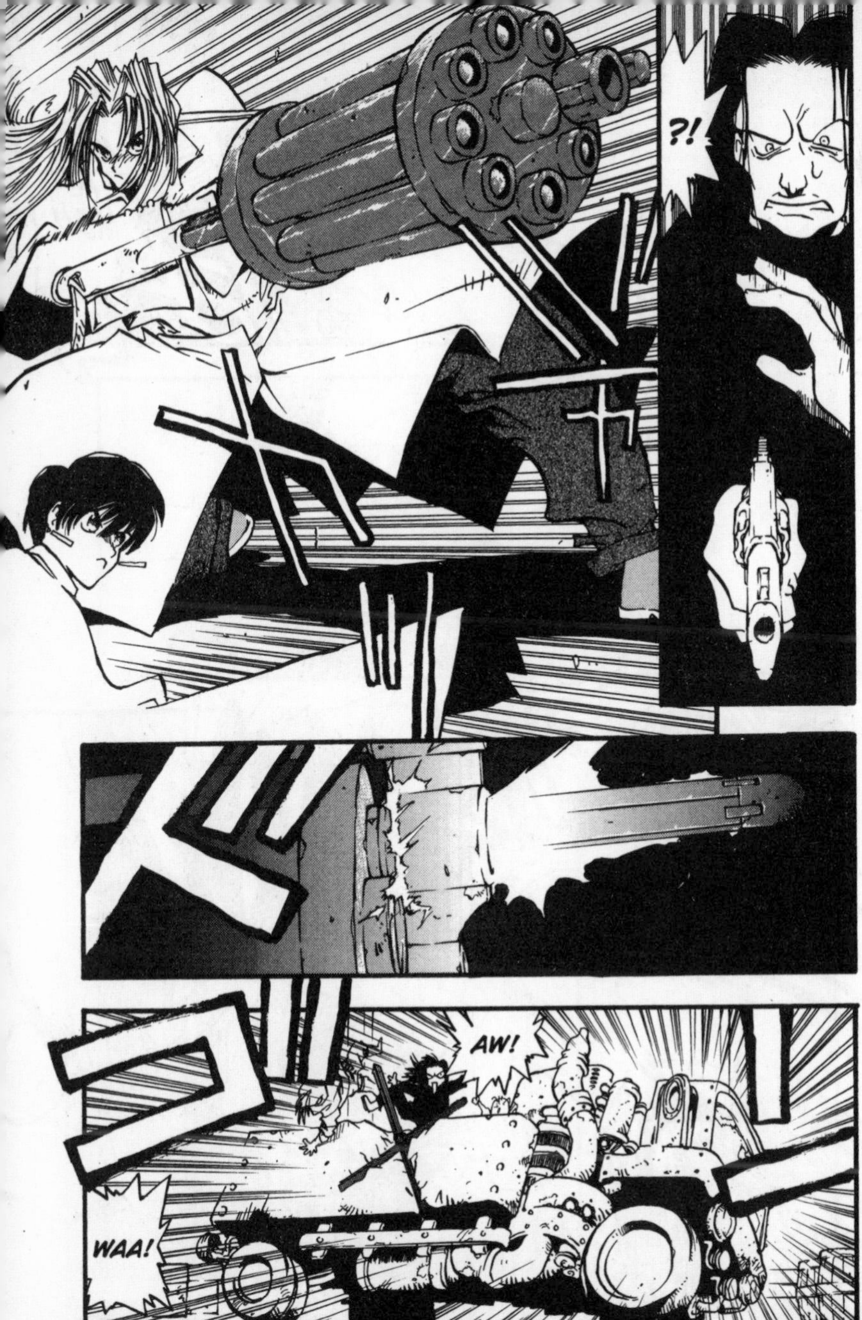
?!
AW!
WAA!

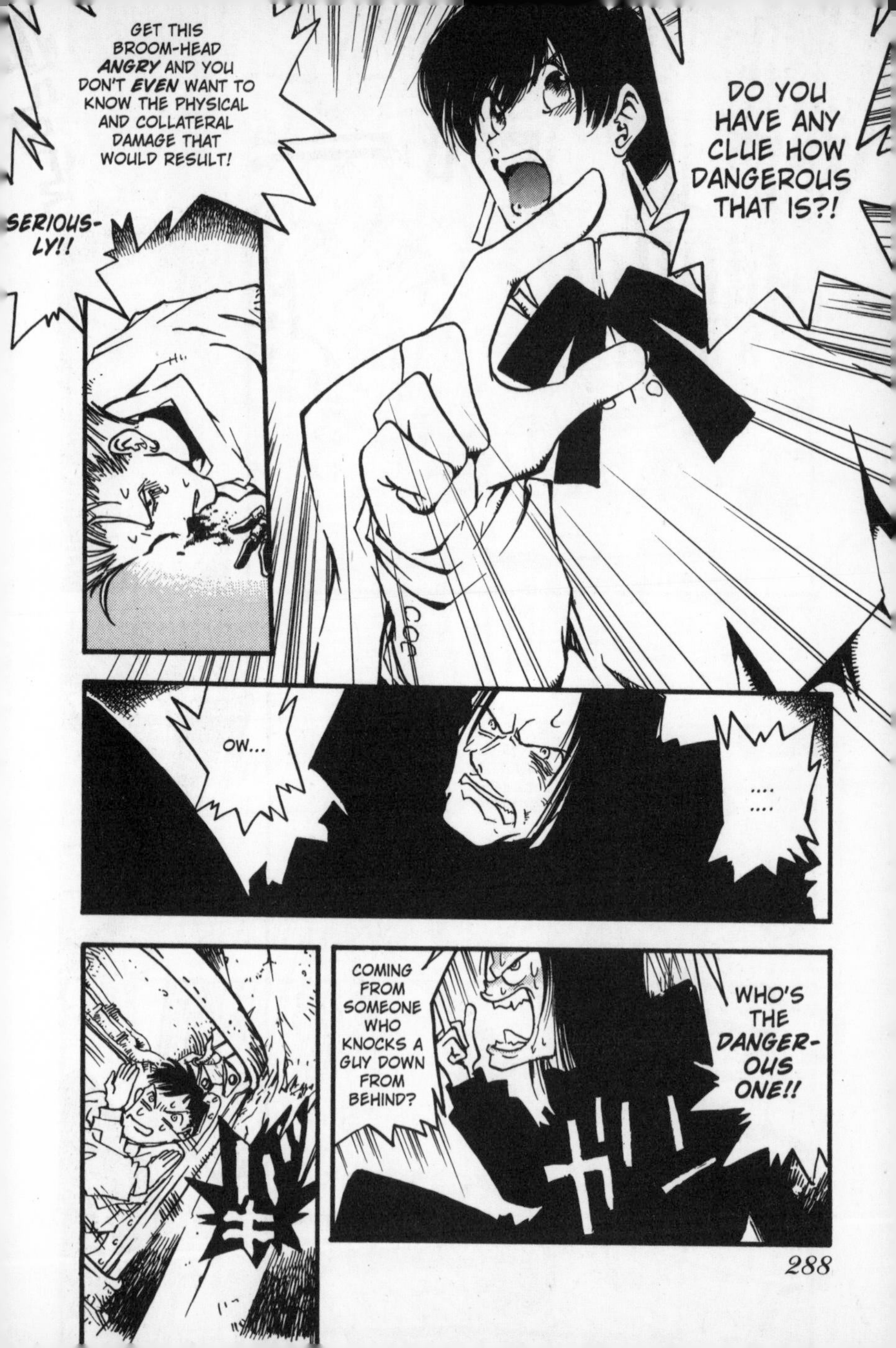
DO YOU HAVE ANY CLUE HOW DANGEROUS THAT IS?!
GET THIS BROOM-HEAD ANGRY AND YOU DON'T EVEN WANT TO KNOW THE PHYSICAL AND COLLATERAL DAMAGE THAT WOULD RESULT!
SERIOUS-LY!!
....
....
OW...
WHO'S THE DANGER-OUS ONE!!
COMING FROM SOMEONE WHO KNOCKS A GUY DOWN FROM BEHIND?

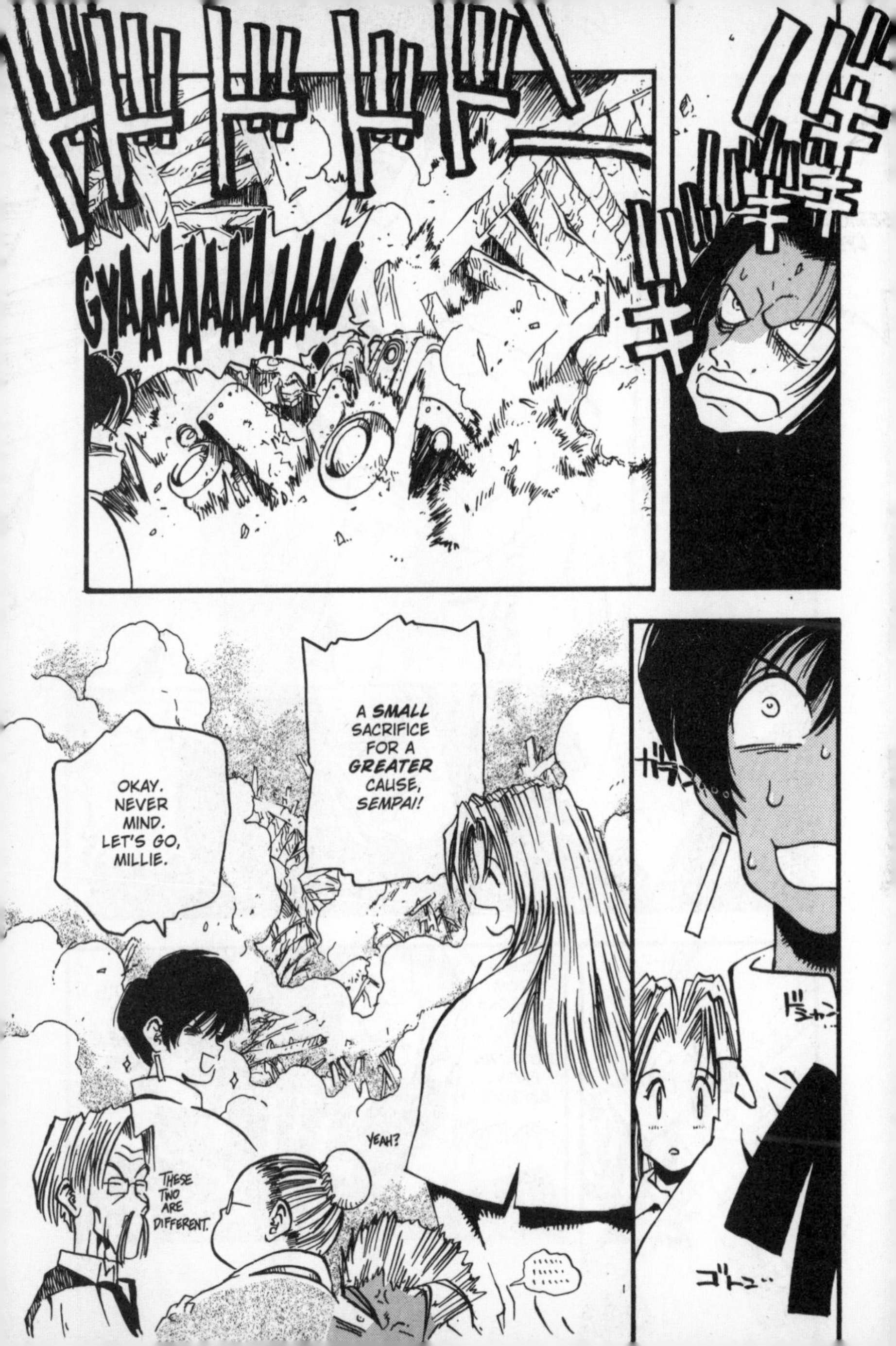
GYAAAAAAAAAA!
A SMALL SACRIFICE FOR A GREATER CAUSE, SEMPAI!
OKAY. NEVER MIND. LET'S GO, MILLIE.
YEAH?
THESE TWO ARE DIFFERENT.
......

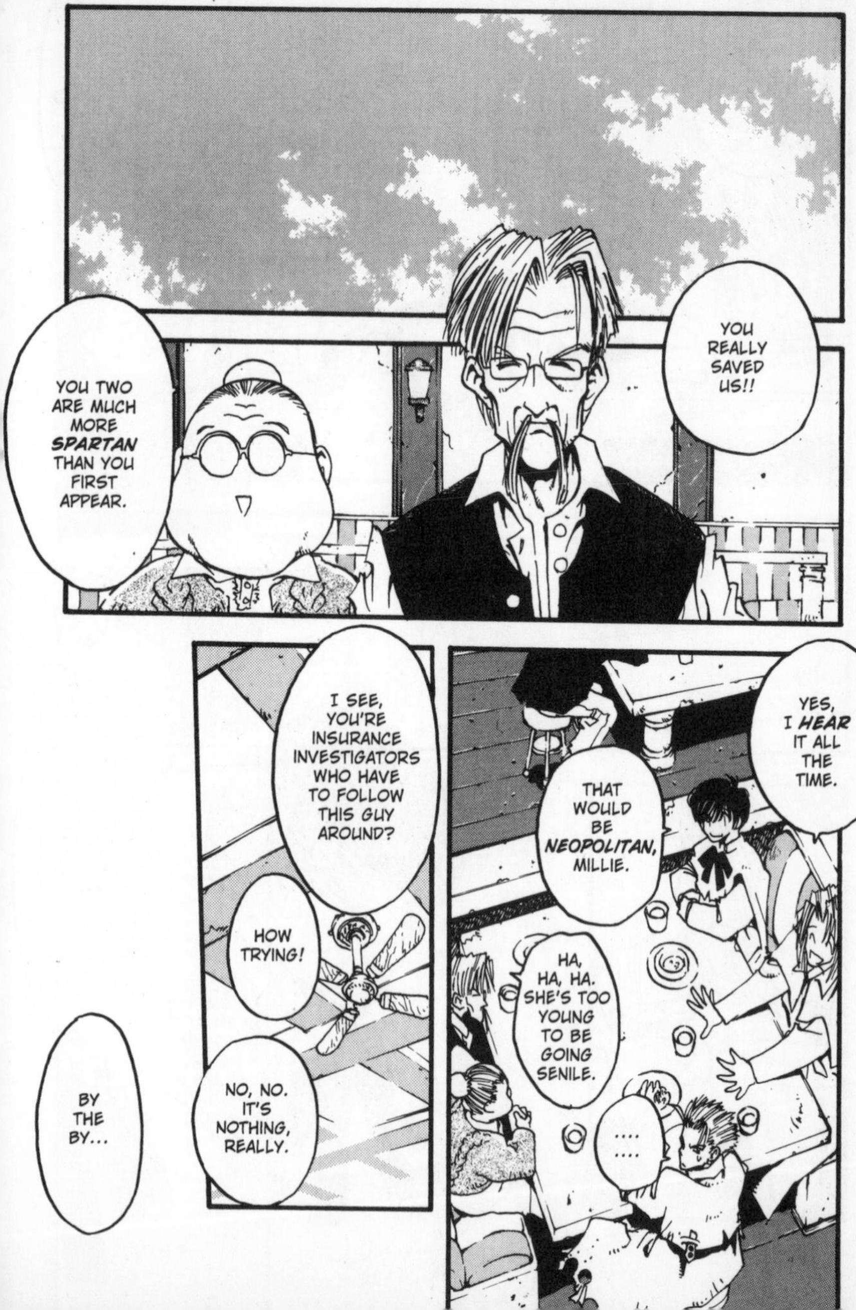
YOU REALLY SAVED US!!
YOU TWO ARE MUCH MORE SPARTAN THAN YOU FIRST APPEAR.
YES, I HEAR IT ALL THE TIME.
THAT WOULD BE NEOPOLITAN, MILLIE.
HA, HA, HA. SHE'S TOO YOUNG TO BE GOING SENILE.
....
....
I SEE, YOU'RE INSURANCE INVESTIGATORS WHO HAVE TO FOLLOW THIS GUY AROUND?
HOW TRYING!
NO, NO. IT'S NOTHING, REALLY.
BY THE BY...

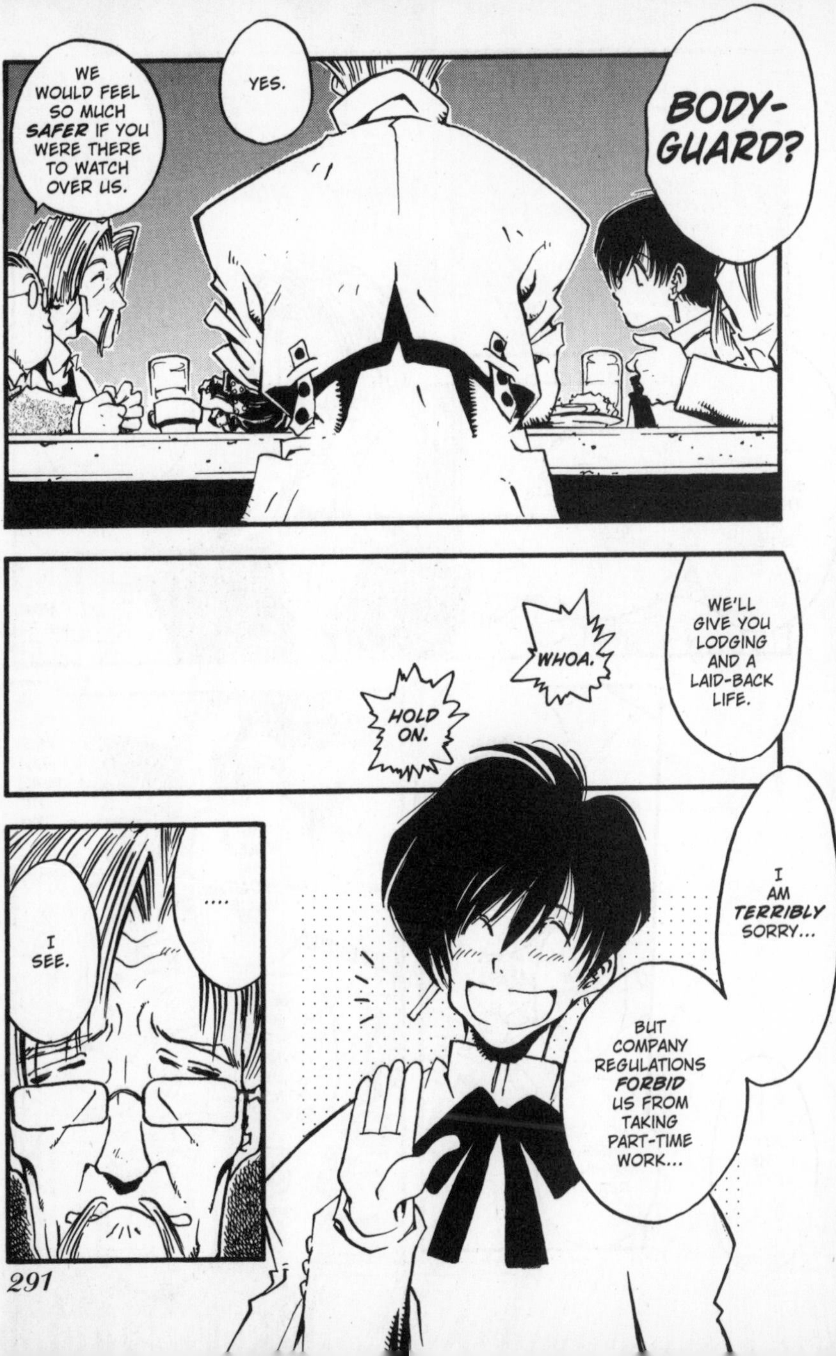
BODY-GUARD?
YES.
WE WOULD FEEL SO MUCH *SAFER* IF YOU WERE THERE TO WATCH OVER US.
WE'LL GIVE YOU LODGING AND A LAID-BACK LIFE.
WHOA.
HOLD ON.
I AM *TERRIBLY* SORRY...
BUT COMPANY REGULATIONS *FORBID* US FROM TAKING PART-TIME WORK...
....
I SEE.

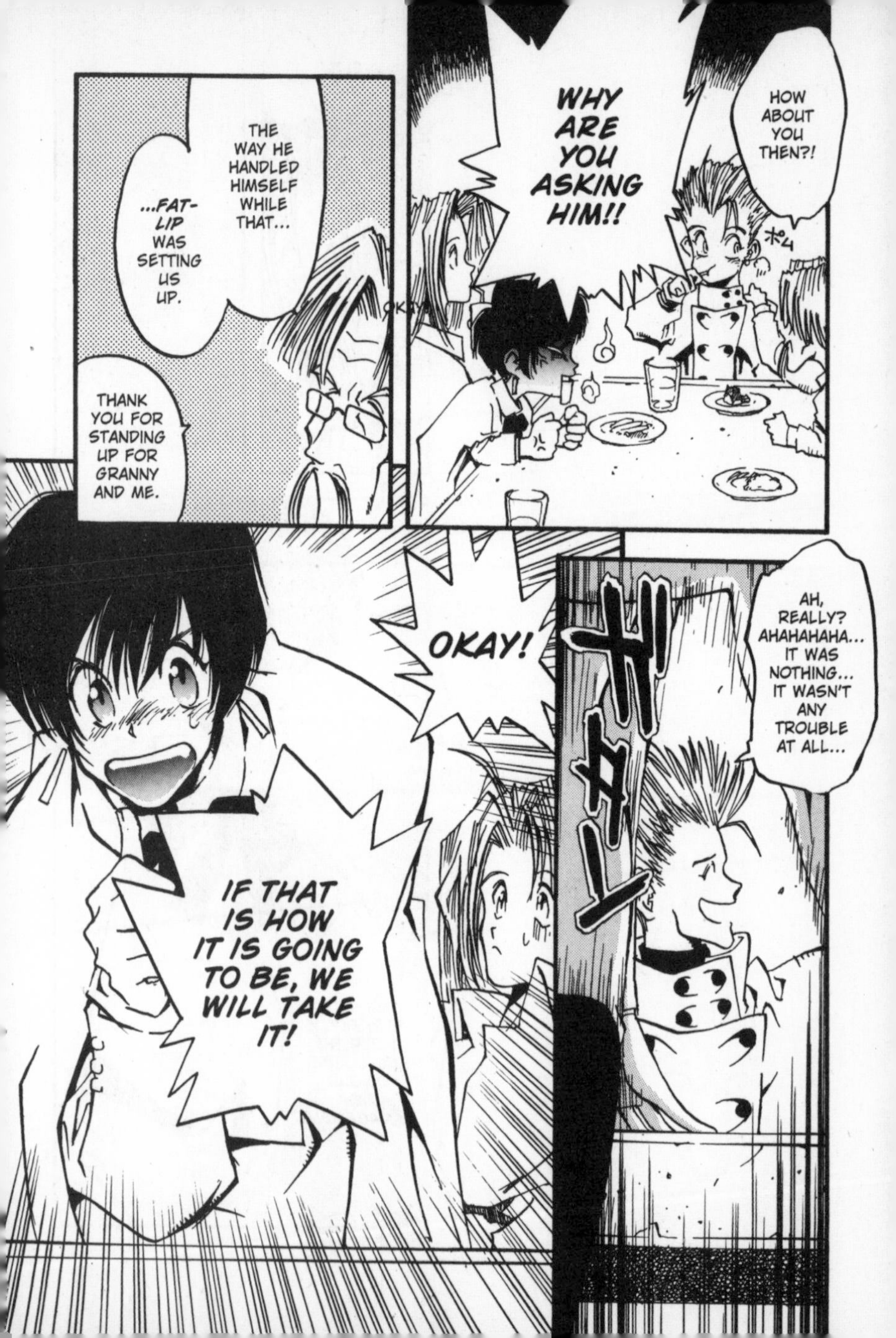
HOW ABOUT YOU THEN?!
WHY ARE YOU ASKING HIM!!
THE WAY HE HANDLED HIMSELF WHILE THAT...
...FAT-LIP WAS SETTING US UP.
THANK YOU FOR STANDING UP FOR GRANNY AND ME.
AH, REALLY? AHAHAHAHA... IT WAS NOTHING... IT WASN'T ANY TROUBLE AT ALL...
OKAY!
IF THAT IS HOW IT IS GOING TO BE, WE WILL TAKE IT!

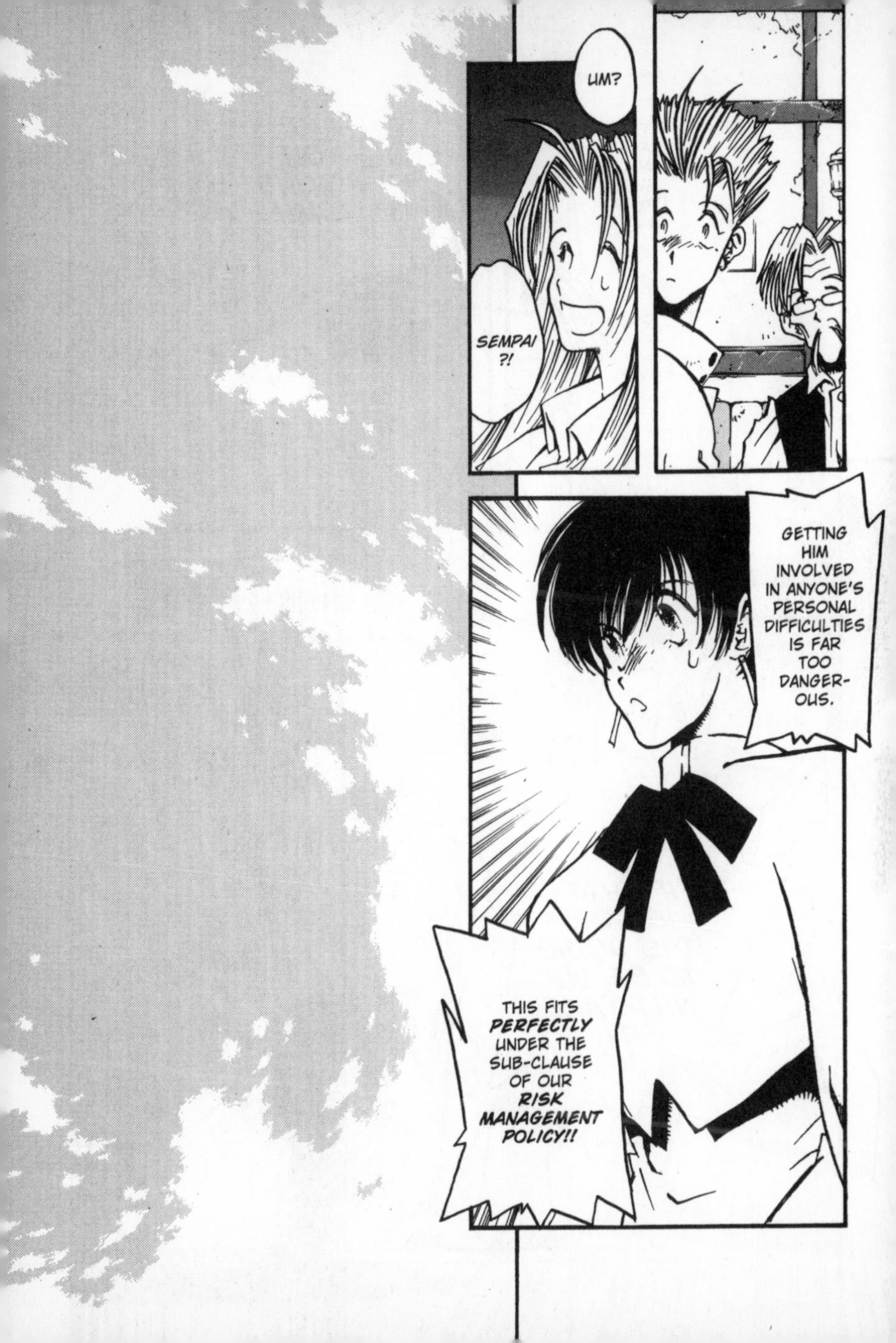
UM?
SEMPAI ?!
GETTING HIM INVOLVED IN ANYONE'S PERSONAL DIFFICULTIES IS FAR TOO DANGER-OUS.
THIS FITS *PERFECTLY* UNDER THE SUB-CLAUSE OF OUR ***RISK MANAGEMENT POLICY!!***

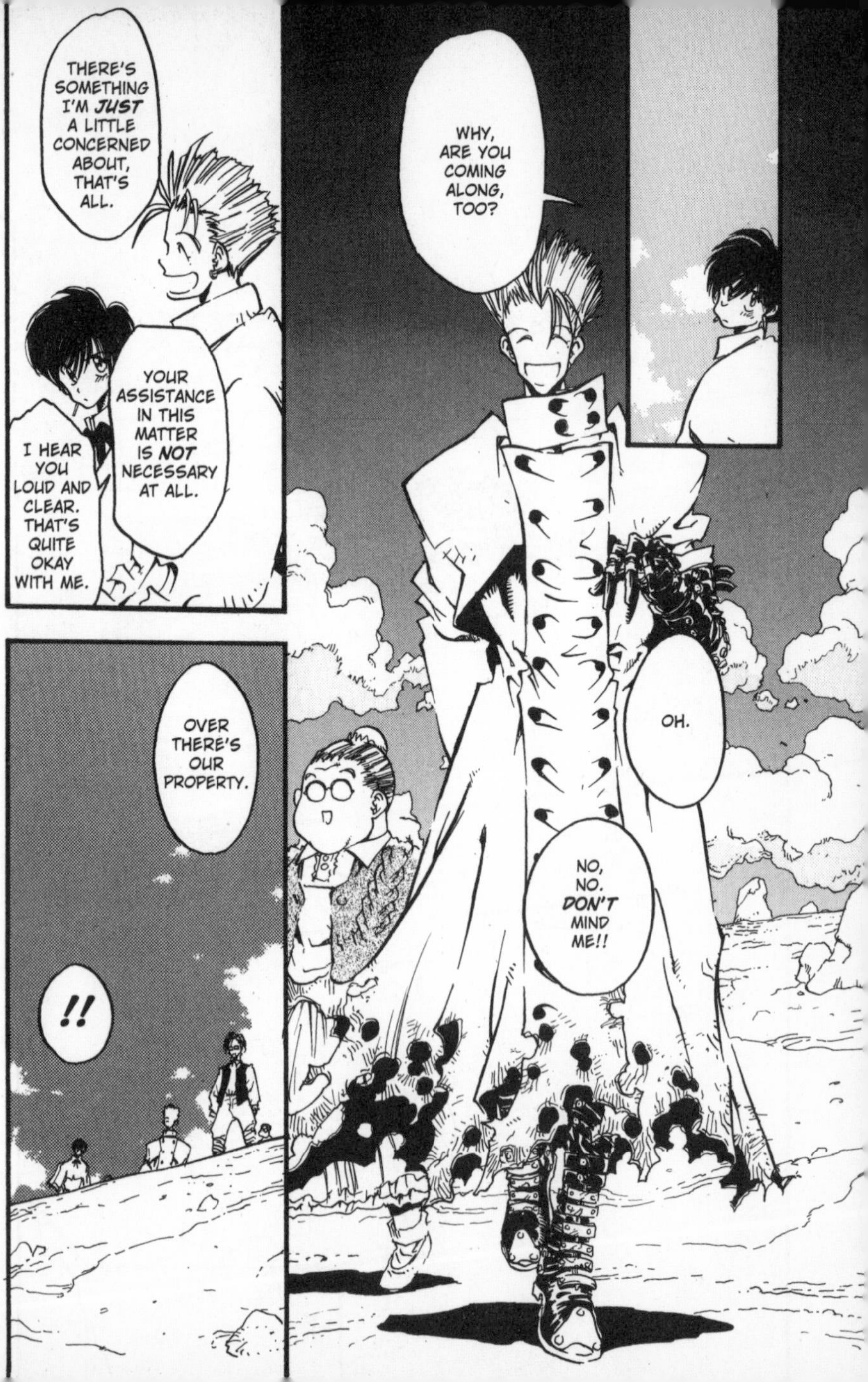
WHY, ARE YOU COMING ALONG, TOO?
OH.
NO, NO. **DON'T** MIND ME!!
THERE'S SOMETHING I'M **JUST** A LITTLE CONCERNED ABOUT, THAT'S ALL.
YOUR ASSISTANCE IN THIS MATTER IS **NOT** NECESSARY AT ALL.
I HEAR YOU LOUD AND CLEAR. THAT'S QUITE OKAY WITH ME.
OVER THERE'S OUR PROPERTY.
!!

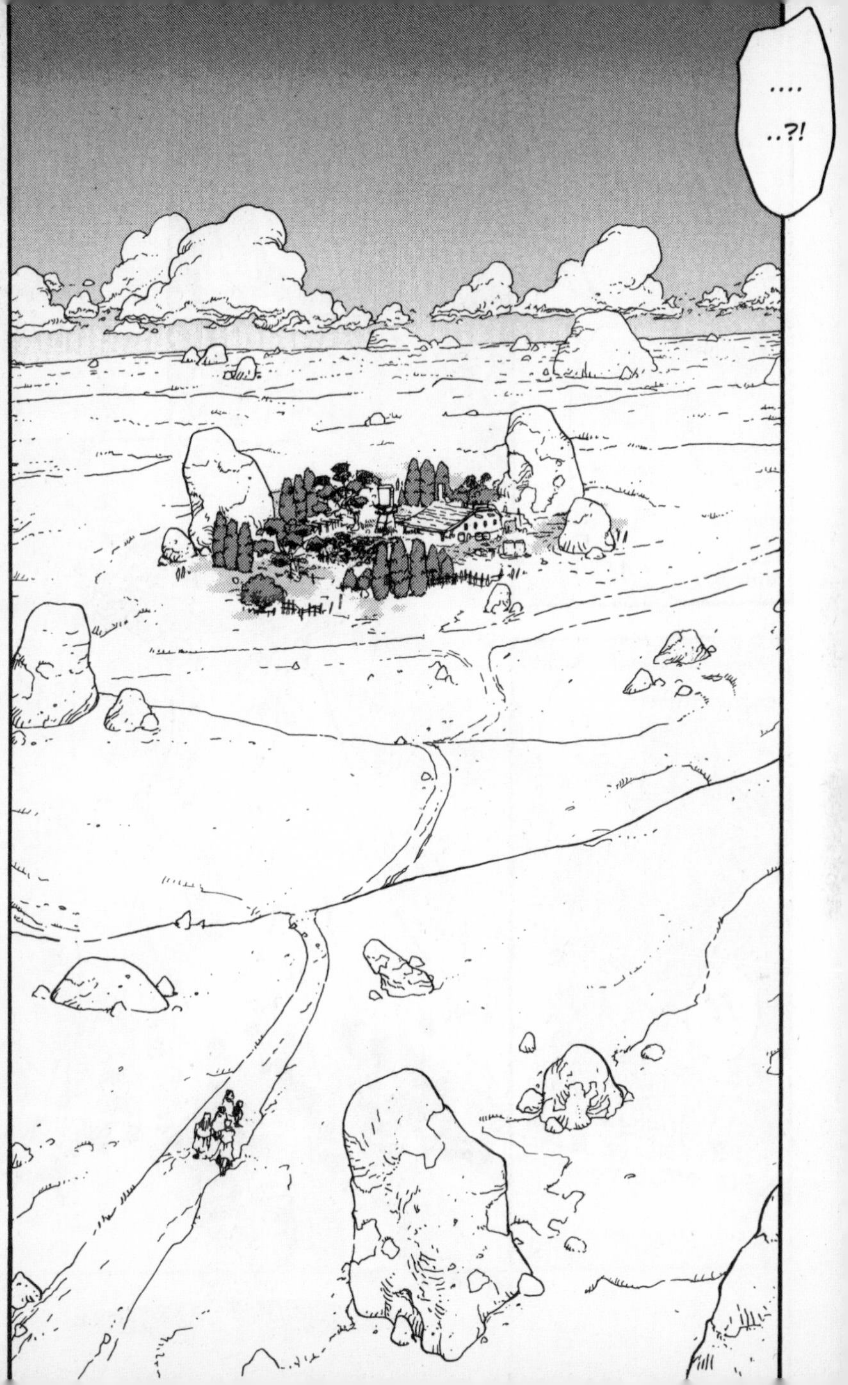
....
..?!

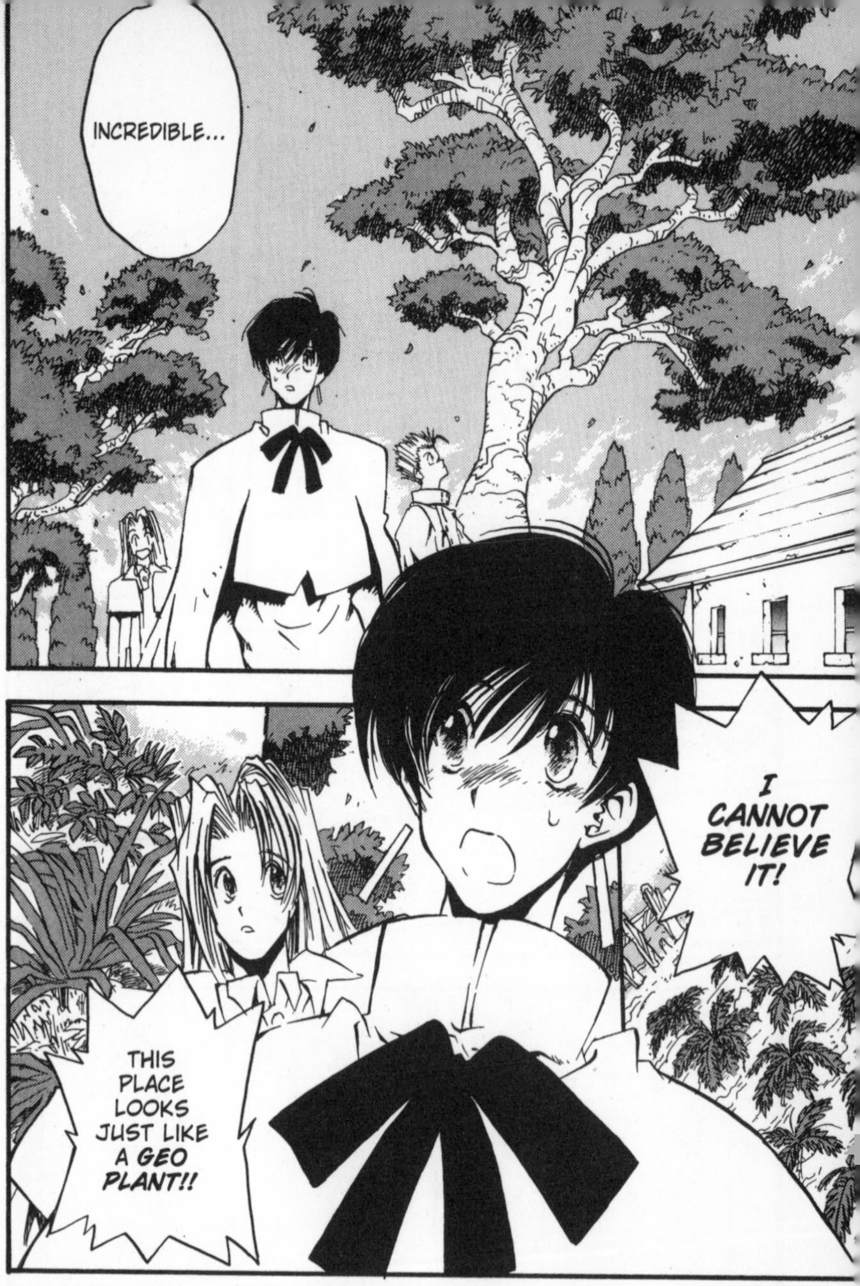
INCREDIBLE...
I CANNOT BELIEVE IT!
THIS PLACE LOOKS JUST LIKE A GEO PLANT!!

NO...

THIS
PLACE
*IS*
A GEO
PLANT.

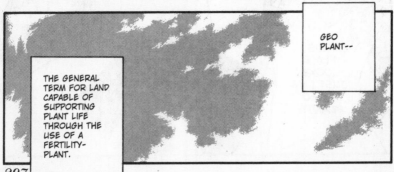

GEO
PLANT--

THE GENERAL
TERM FOR LAND
CAPABLE OF
SUPPORTING
PLANT LIFE
THROUGH THE
USE OF A
FERTILITY-
PLANT.

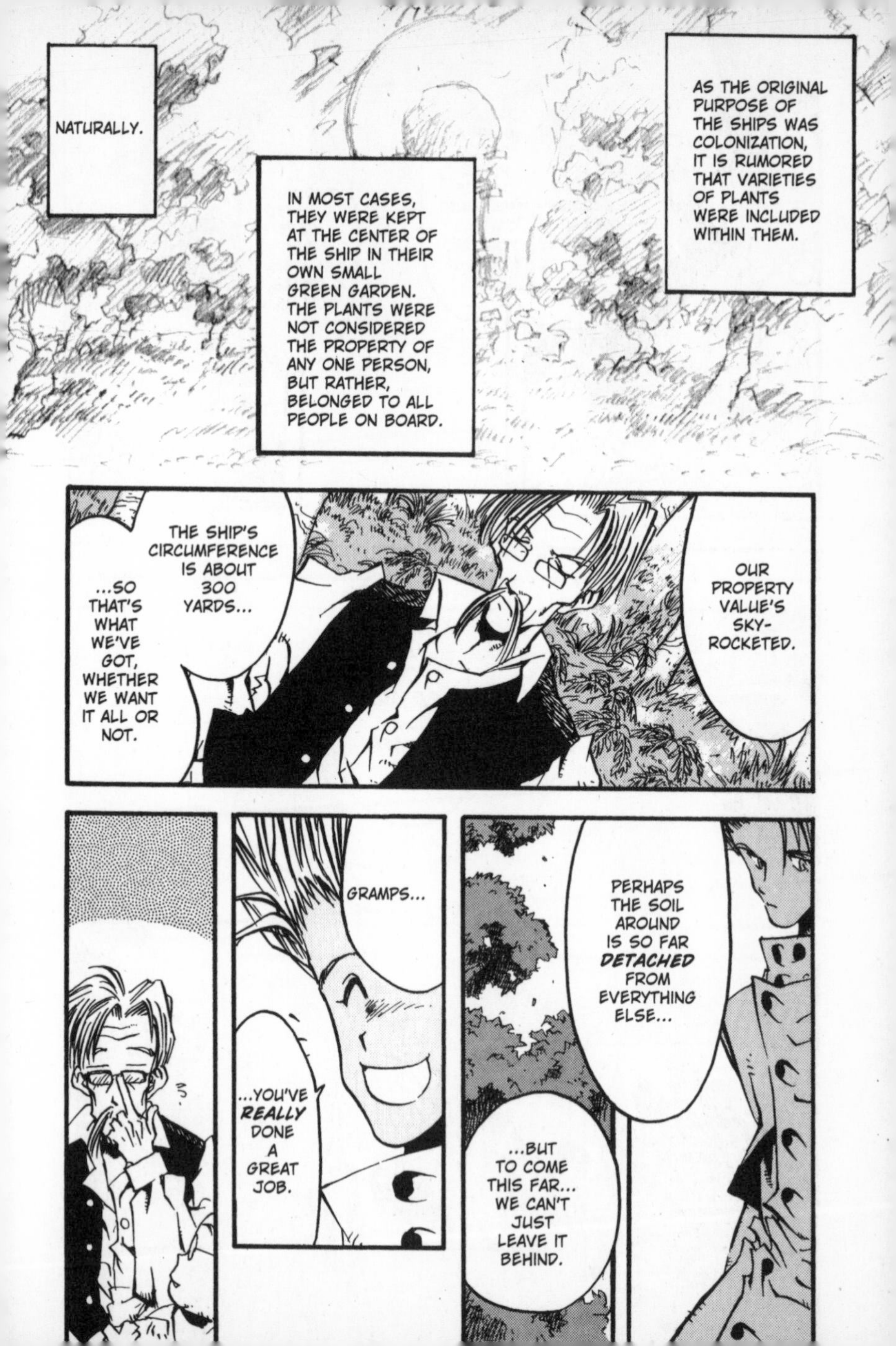
AS THE ORIGINAL PURPOSE OF THE SHIPS WAS COLONIZATION, IT IS RUMORED THAT VARIETIES OF PLANTS WERE INCLUDED WITHIN THEM.
IN MOST CASES, THEY WERE KEPT AT THE CENTER OF THE SHIP IN THEIR OWN SMALL GREEN GARDEN. THE PLANTS WERE NOT CONSIDERED THE PROPERTY OF ANY ONE PERSON, BUT RATHER, BELONGED TO ALL PEOPLE ON BOARD.
NATURALLY.
OUR PROPERTY VALUE'S SKY-ROCKETED.
THE SHIP'S CIRCUMFERENCE IS ABOUT 300 YARDS...
...SO THAT'S WHAT WE'VE GOT, WHETHER WE WANT IT ALL OR NOT.
PERHAPS THE SOIL AROUND IS SO FAR ***DETACHED*** FROM EVERYTHING ELSE...
...BUT TO COME THIS FAR... WE CAN'T JUST LEAVE IT BEHIND.
GRAMPS...
...YOU'VE ***REALLY*** DONE A GREAT JOB.

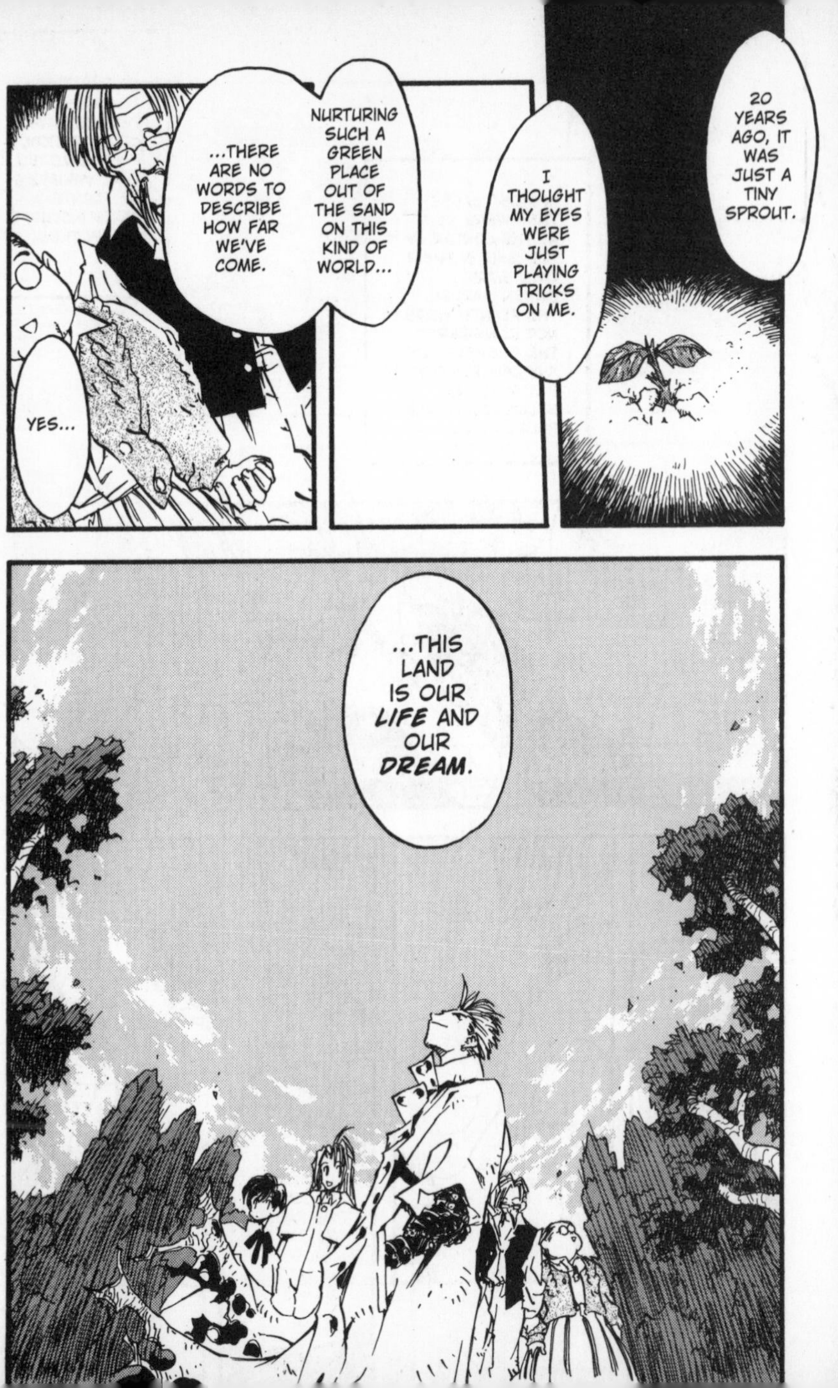
20 YEARS AGO, IT WAS JUST A TINY SPROUT.
I THOUGHT MY EYES WERE JUST PLAYING TRICKS ON ME.
NURTURING SUCH A GREEN PLACE OUT OF THE SAND ON THIS KIND OF WORLD...
...THERE ARE NO WORDS TO DESCRIBE HOW FAR WE'VE COME.
YES...
...THIS LAND IS OUR LIFE AND OUR DREAM.

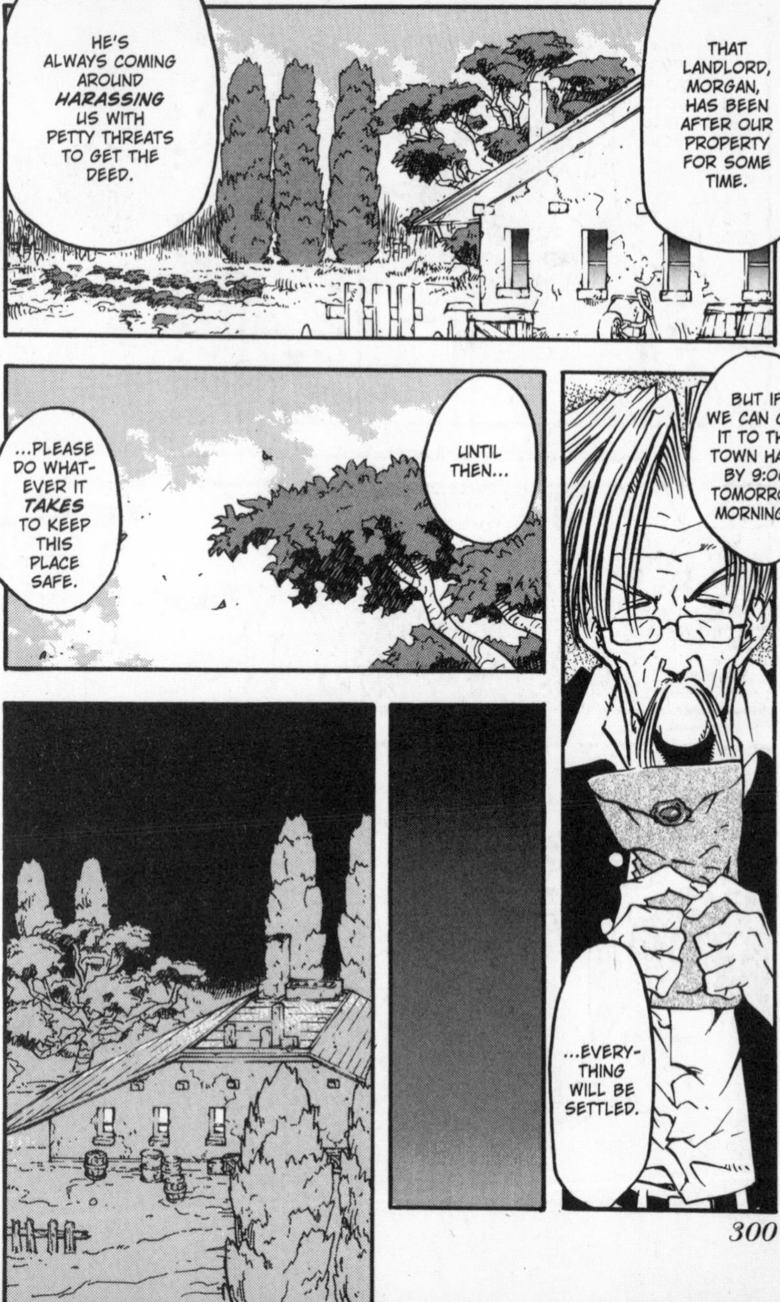
THAT LANDLORD, MORGAN, HAS BEEN AFTER OUR PROPERTY FOR SOME TIME.
HE'S ALWAYS COMING AROUND **HARASSING** US WITH PETTY THREATS TO GET THE DEED.
BUT IF WE CAN GET IT TO THE TOWN HALL BY 9:00 TOMORROW MORNING...
...EVERY-THING WILL BE SETTLED.
UNTIL THEN...
...PLEASE DO WHAT-EVER IT **TAKES** TO KEEP THIS PLACE SAFE.

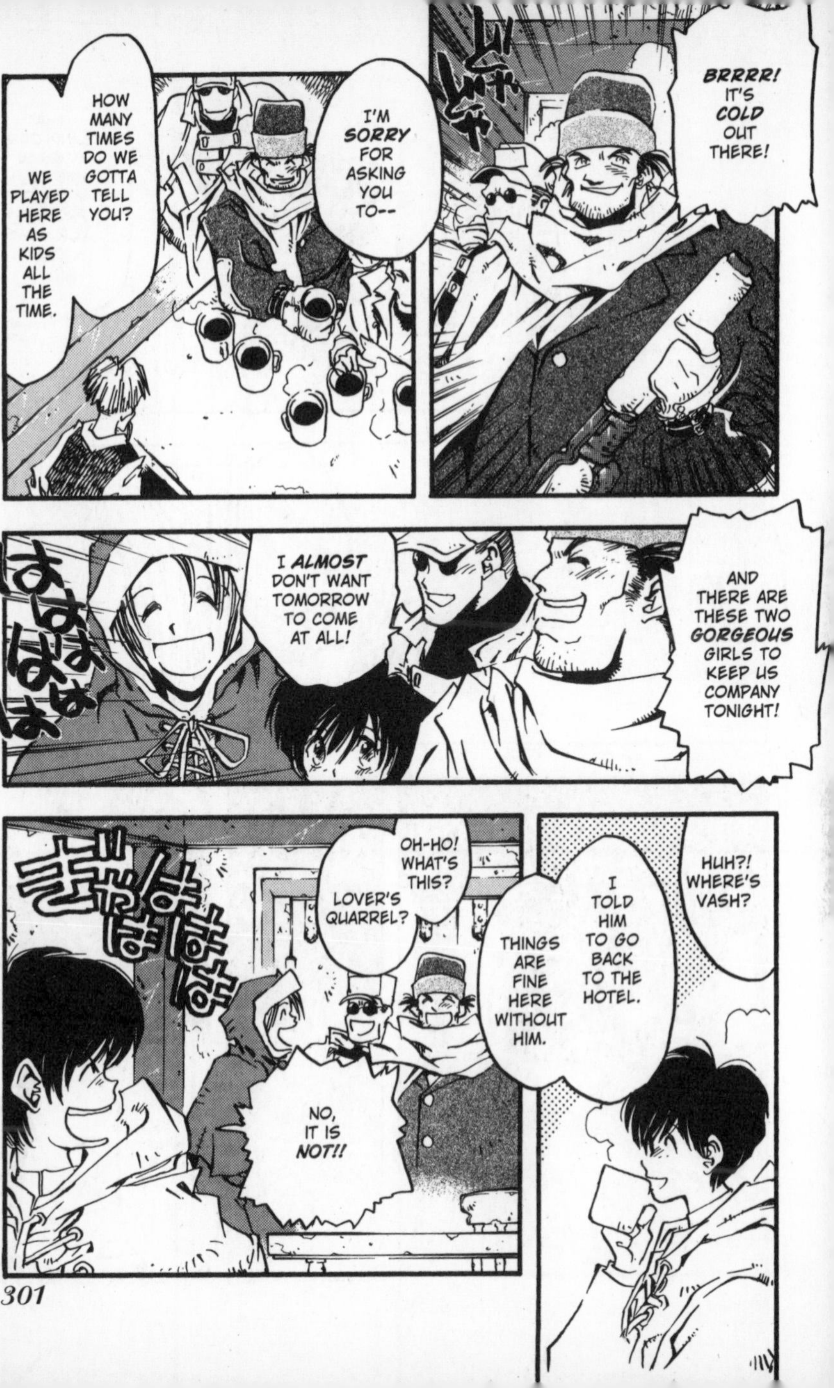
BRRRR! IT'S COLD OUT THERE!
I'M SORRY FOR ASKING YOU TO--
HOW MANY TIMES DO WE GOTTA TELL YOU?
WE PLAYED HERE AS KIDS ALL THE TIME.
AND THERE ARE THESE TWO GORGEOUS GIRLS TO KEEP US COMPANY TONIGHT!
I ALMOST DON'T WANT TOMORROW TO COME AT ALL!
HUH?! WHERE'S VASH?
I TOLD HIM TO GO BACK TO THE HOTEL.
THINGS ARE FINE HERE WITHOUT HIM.
OH-HO! WHAT'S THIS?
LOVER'S QUARREL?
NO, IT IS NOT!!

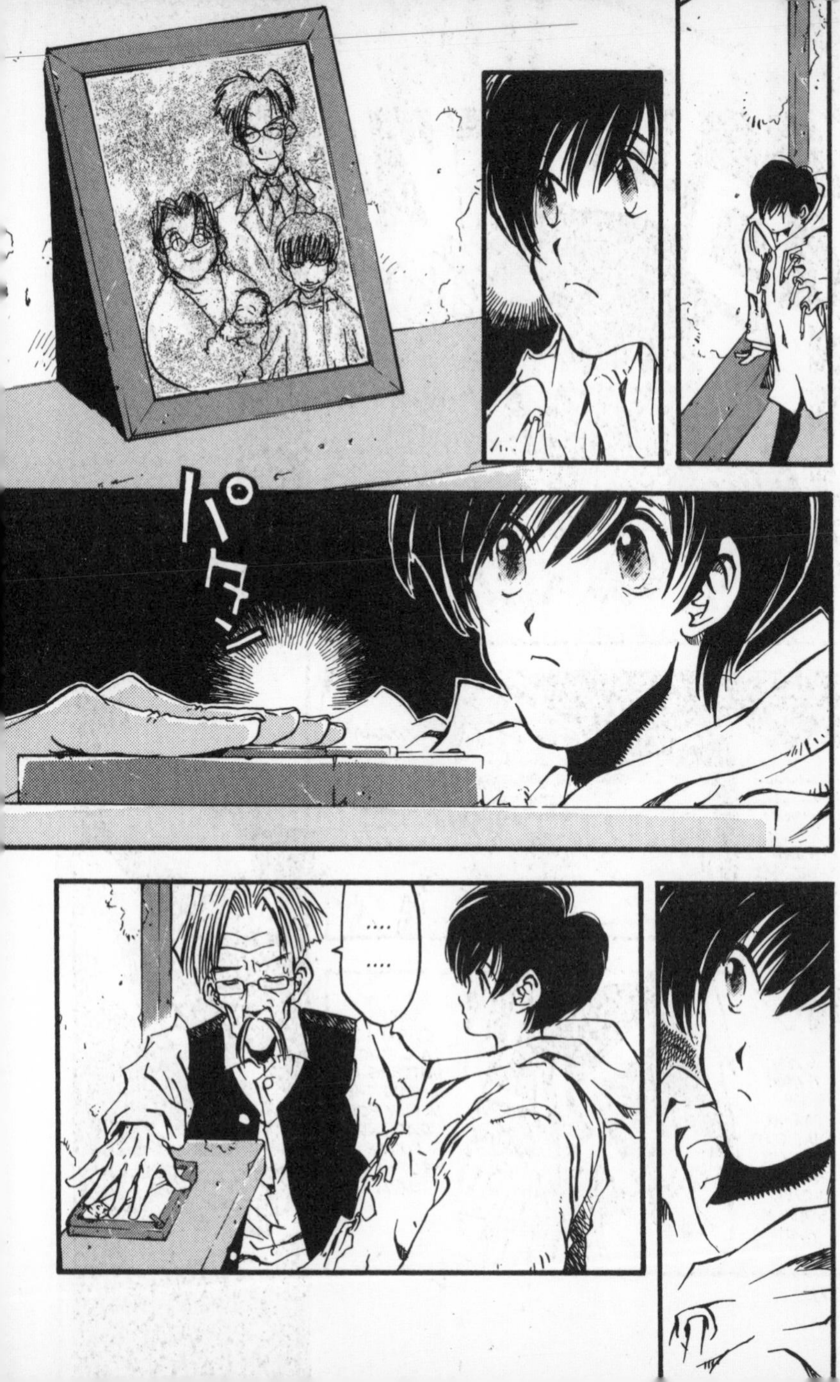
パタン
....
....

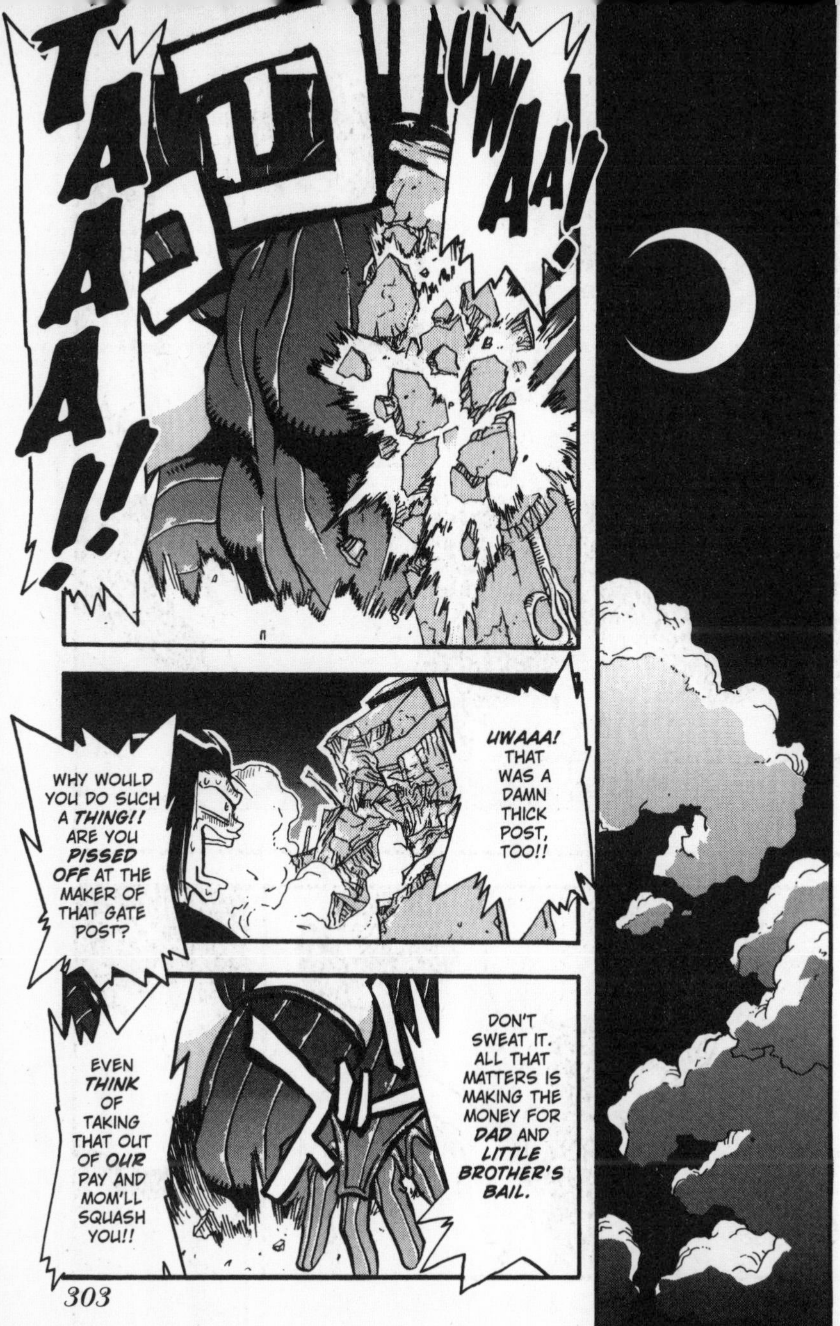
UWAAA! THAT WAS A DAMN THICK POST, TOO!!
WHY WOULD YOU DO SUCH A THING!! ARE YOU PISSED OFF AT THE MAKER OF THAT GATE POST?
DON'T SWEAT IT. ALL THAT MATTERS IS MAKING THE MONEY FOR DAD AND LITTLE BROTHER'S BAIL.
EVEN THINK OF TAKING THAT OUT OF OUR PAY AND MOM'LL SQUASH YOU!!

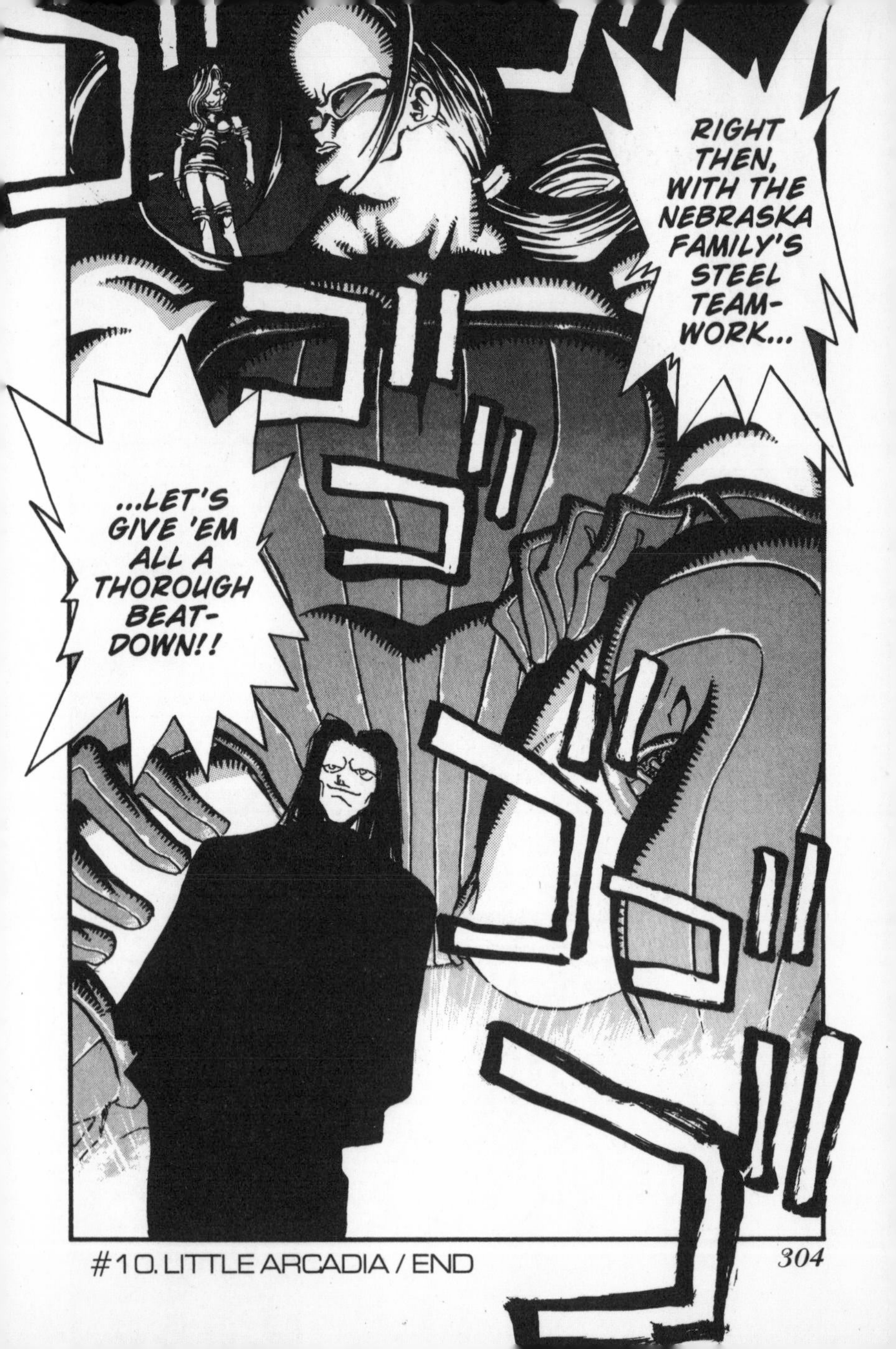
RIGHT THEN, WITH THE NEBRASKA FAMILY'S STEEL TEAM-WORK...
...LET'S GIVE 'EM ALL A THOROUGH BEAT-DOWN!!

#10. LITTLE ARCADIA / END

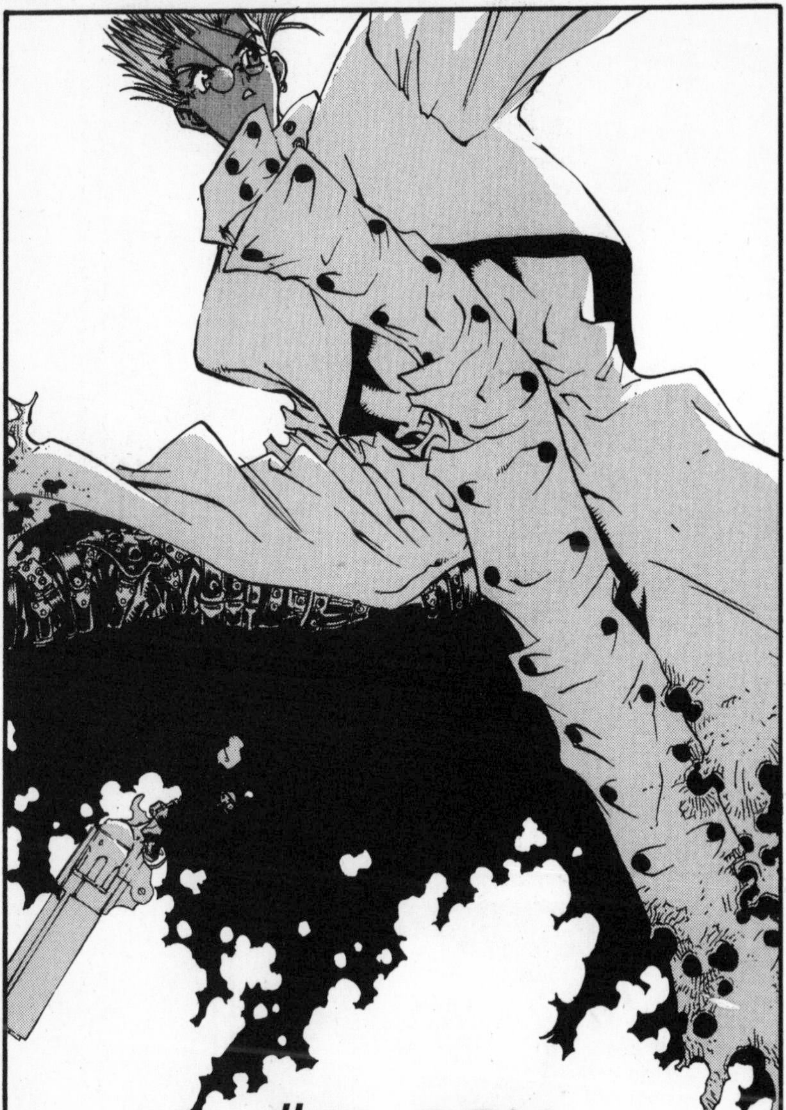

# #11. SON

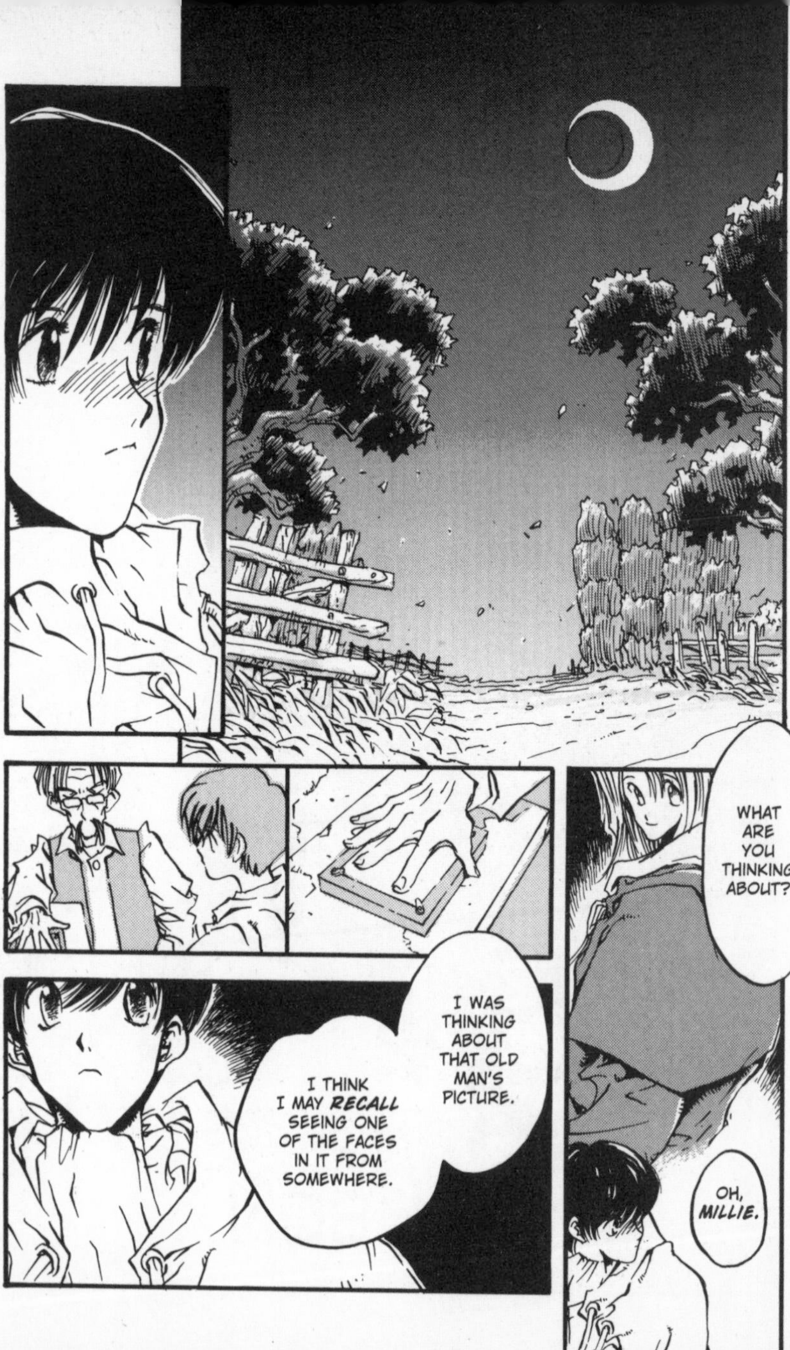
WHAT ARE YOU THINKING ABOUT?
OH, MILLIE.
I WAS THINKING ABOUT THAT OLD MAN'S PICTURE.
I THINK I MAY *RECALL* SEEING ONE OF THE FACES IN IT FROM SOMEWHERE.

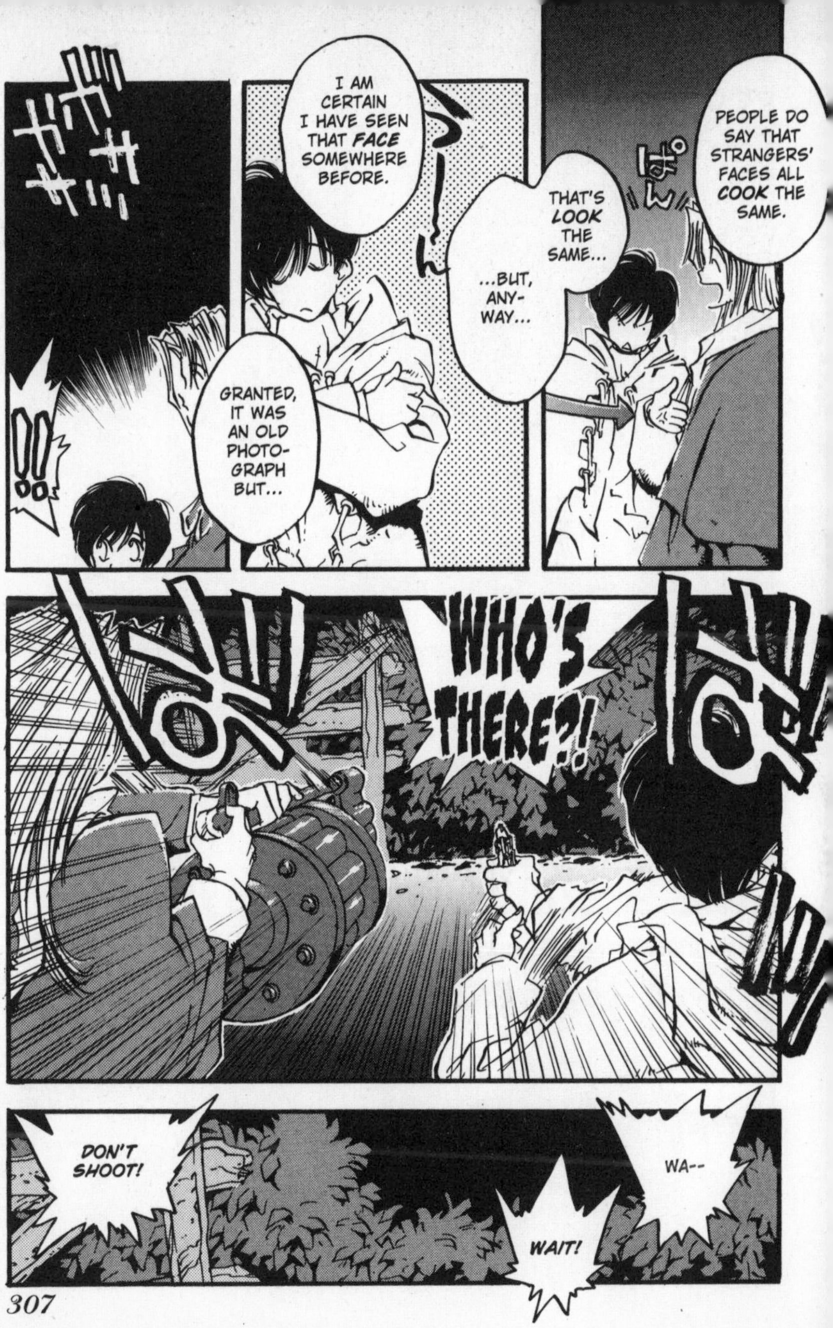
PEOPLE DO SAY THAT STRANGERS' FACES ALL COOK THE SAME.
THAT'S LOOK THE SAME...
...BUT, ANY-WAY...
I AM CERTAIN I HAVE SEEN THAT FACE SOMEWHERE BEFORE.
GRANTED, IT WAS AN OLD PHOTO-GRAPH BUT...
WHO'S THERE?!
WA--
WAIT!
DON'T SHOOT!

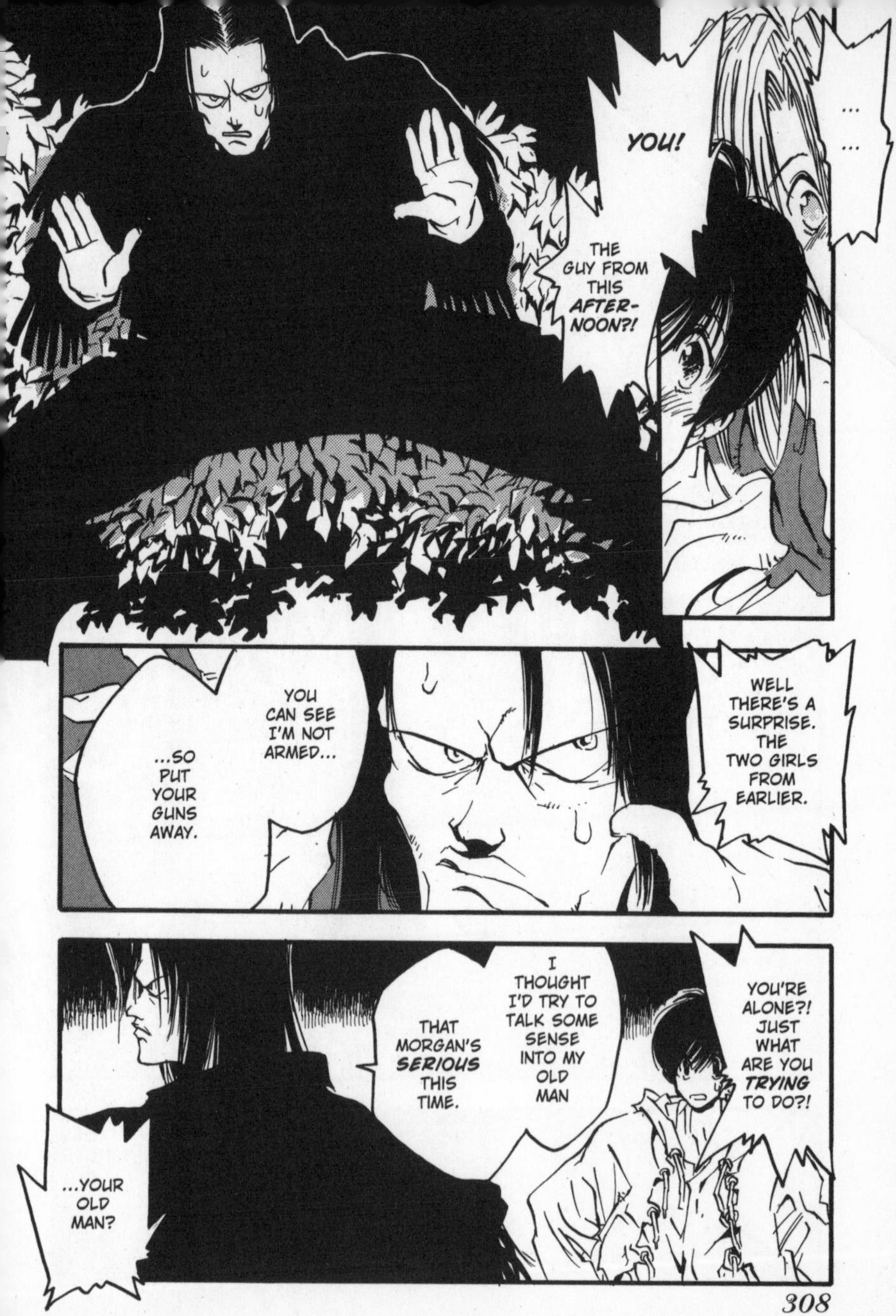
......
YOU!
THE GUY FROM THIS AFTER-NOON?!
WELL THERE'S A SURPRISE. THE TWO GIRLS FROM EARLIER.
YOU CAN SEE I'M NOT ARMED...
...SO PUT YOUR GUNS AWAY.
YOU'RE ALONE?! JUST WHAT ARE YOU TRYING TO DO?!
I THOUGHT I'D TRY TO TALK SOME SENSE INTO MY OLD MAN
THAT MORGAN'S SERIOUS THIS TIME.
...YOUR OLD MAN?

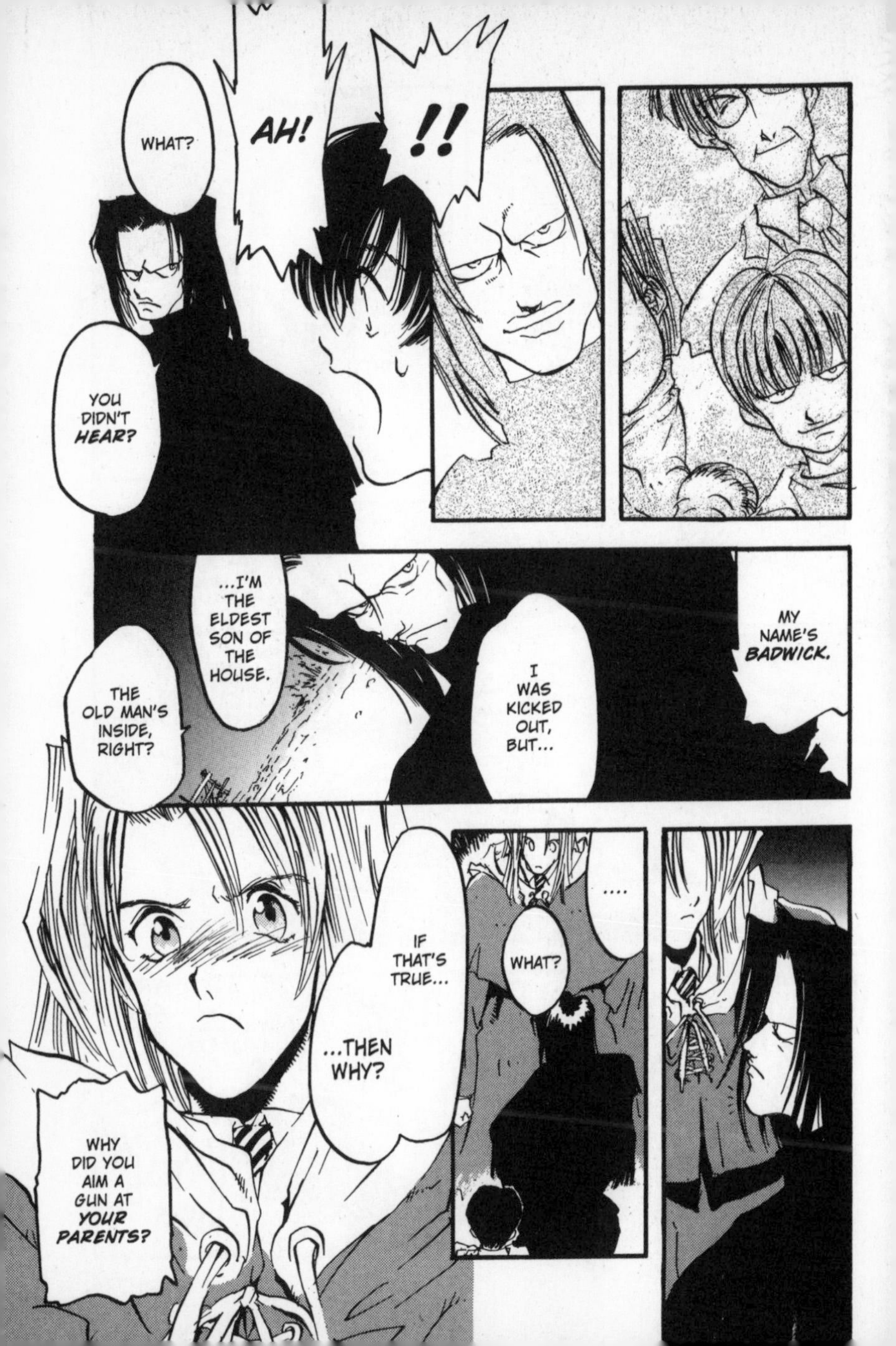
!!
AH!
WHAT?
YOU DIDN'T ***HEAR?***
MY NAME'S ***BADWICK.***
I WAS KICKED OUT, BUT...
...I'M THE ELDEST SON OF THE HOUSE.
THE OLD MAN'S INSIDE, RIGHT?
....
WHAT?
IF THAT'S TRUE...
...THEN WHY?
WHY DID YOU AIM A GUN AT ***YOUR PARENTS?***

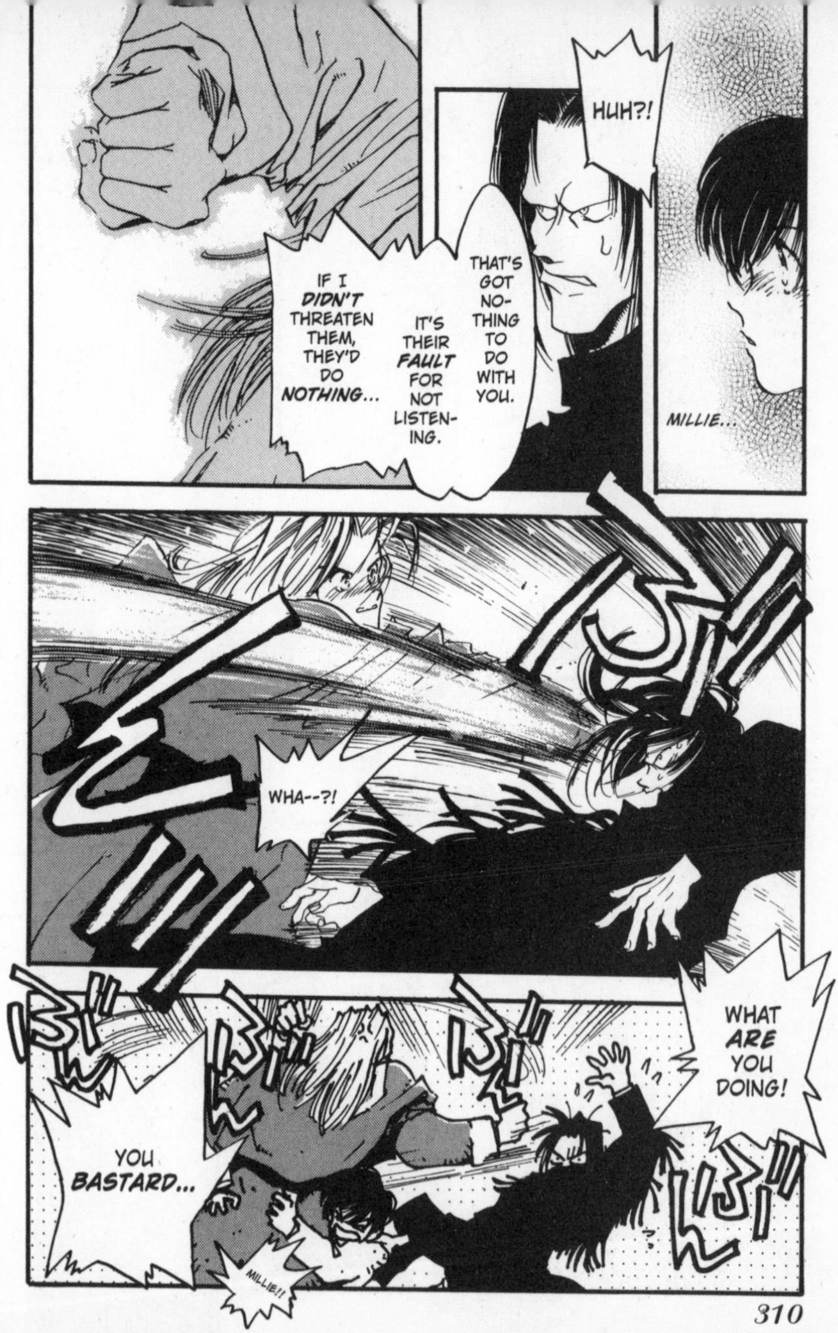

MILLIE...
HUH?!
THAT'S GOT NOTHING TO DO WITH YOU.
IT'S THEIR *FAULT* FOR NOT LISTENING.
IF I *DIDN'T* THREATEN THEM, THEY'D DO *NOTHING*...
WHA--?!
WHAT *ARE* YOU DOING!
YOU *BASTARD...*
MILLIE!!

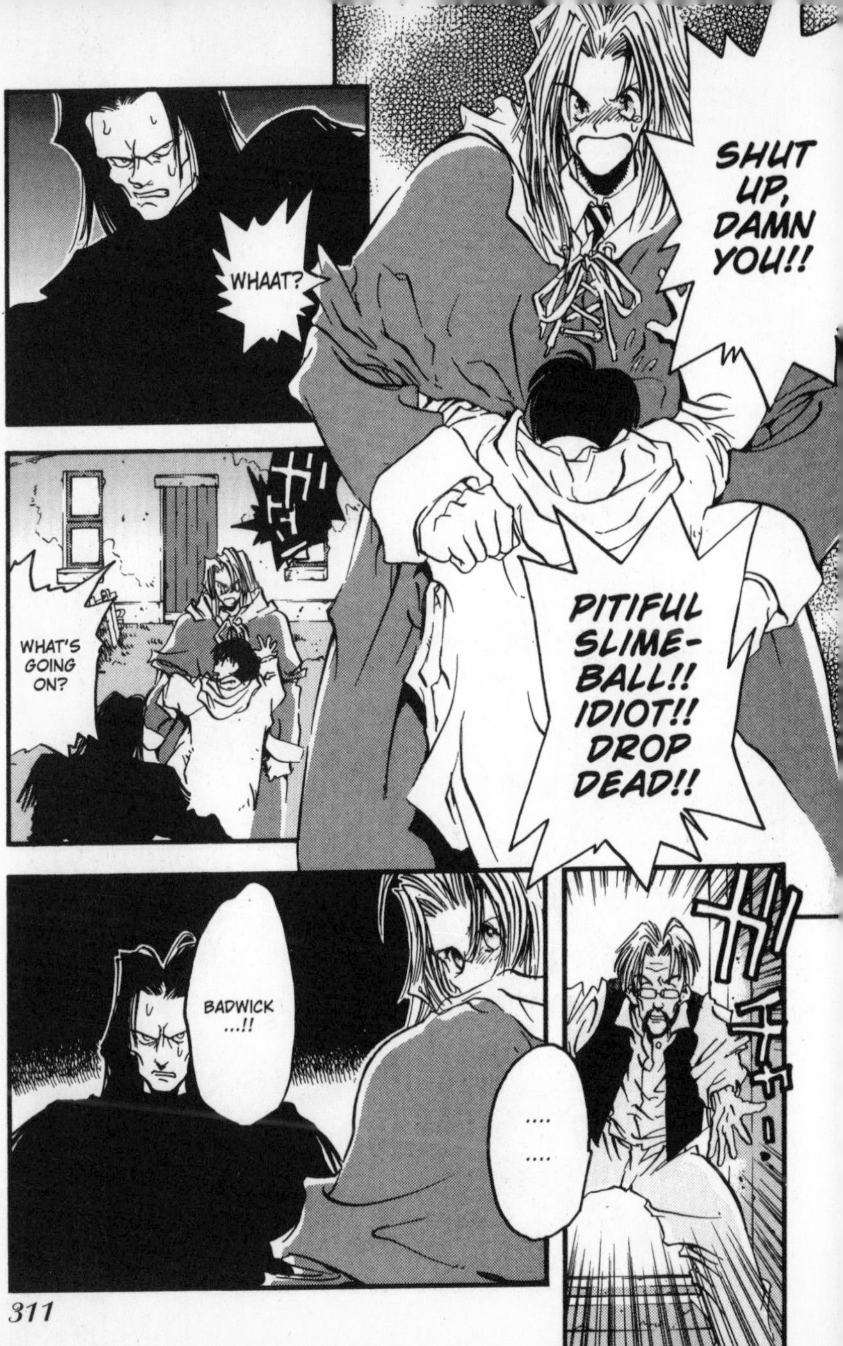
SHUT UP, DAMN YOU!!
PITIFUL SLIME-BALL!! IDIOT!! DROP DEAD!!
WHAAT?
WHAT'S GOING ON?
....
....
BADWICK ...!!

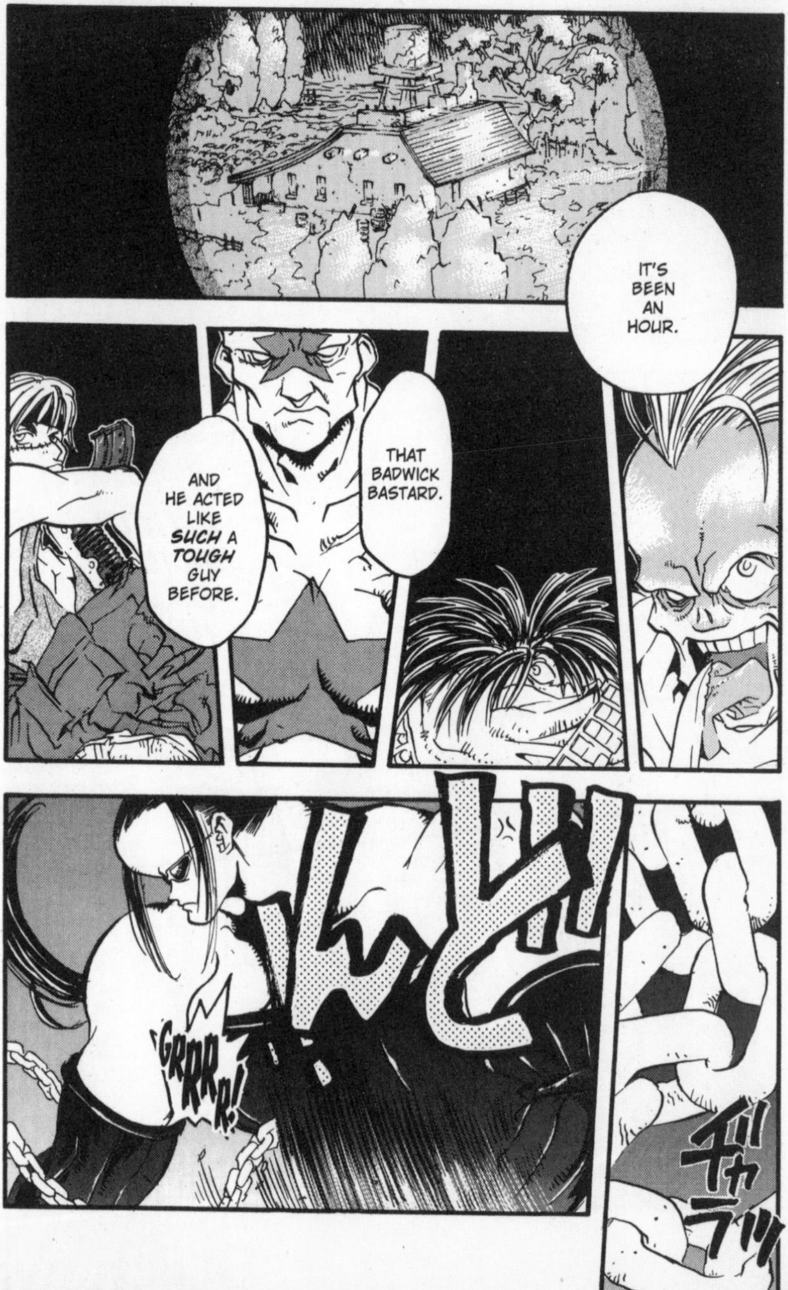
IT'S BEEN AN HOUR.
THAT BADWICK BASTARD.
AND HE ACTED LIKE *SUCH* A *TOUGH* GUY BEFORE.
GRRRRR!
ギャラッ

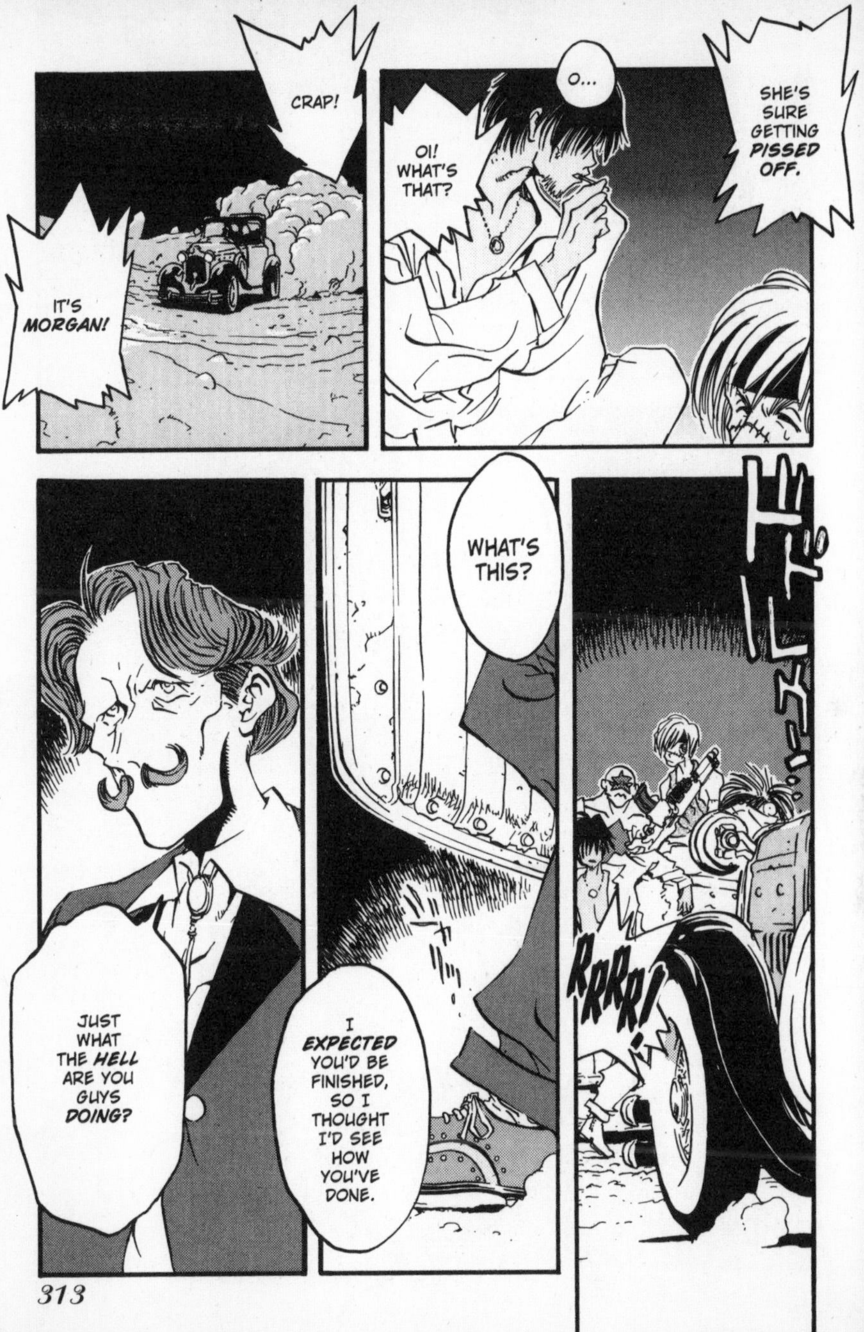
SHE'S SURE GETTING PISSED OFF.
O...
OI! WHAT'S THAT?
CRAP!
IT'S MORGAN!
RRRR!
WHAT'S THIS?
I EXPECTED YOU'D BE FINISHED, SO I THOUGHT I'D SEE HOW YOU'VE DONE.
JUST WHAT THE HELL ARE YOU GUYS DOING?

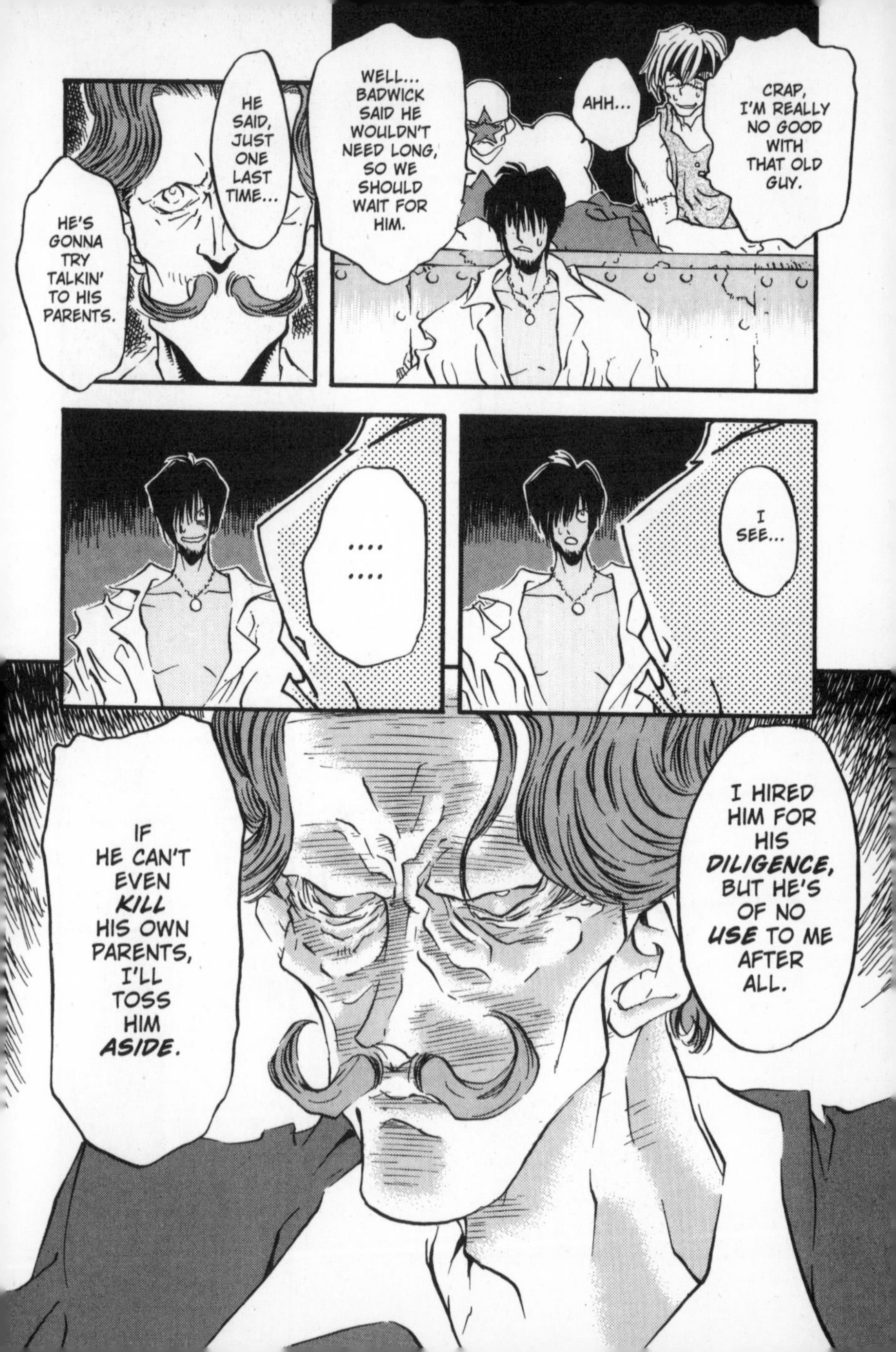
CRAP, I'M REALLY NO GOOD WITH THAT OLD GUY.
AHH...
WELL... BADWICK SAID HE WOULDN'T NEED LONG, SO WE SHOULD WAIT FOR HIM.
HE SAID, JUST ONE LAST TIME...
HE'S GONNA TRY TALKIN' TO HIS PARENTS.
I SEE...
.... ....
I HIRED HIM FOR HIS DILIGENCE, BUT HE'S OF NO USE TO ME AFTER ALL.
IF HE CAN'T EVEN KILL HIS OWN PARENTS, I'LL TOSS HIM ASIDE.

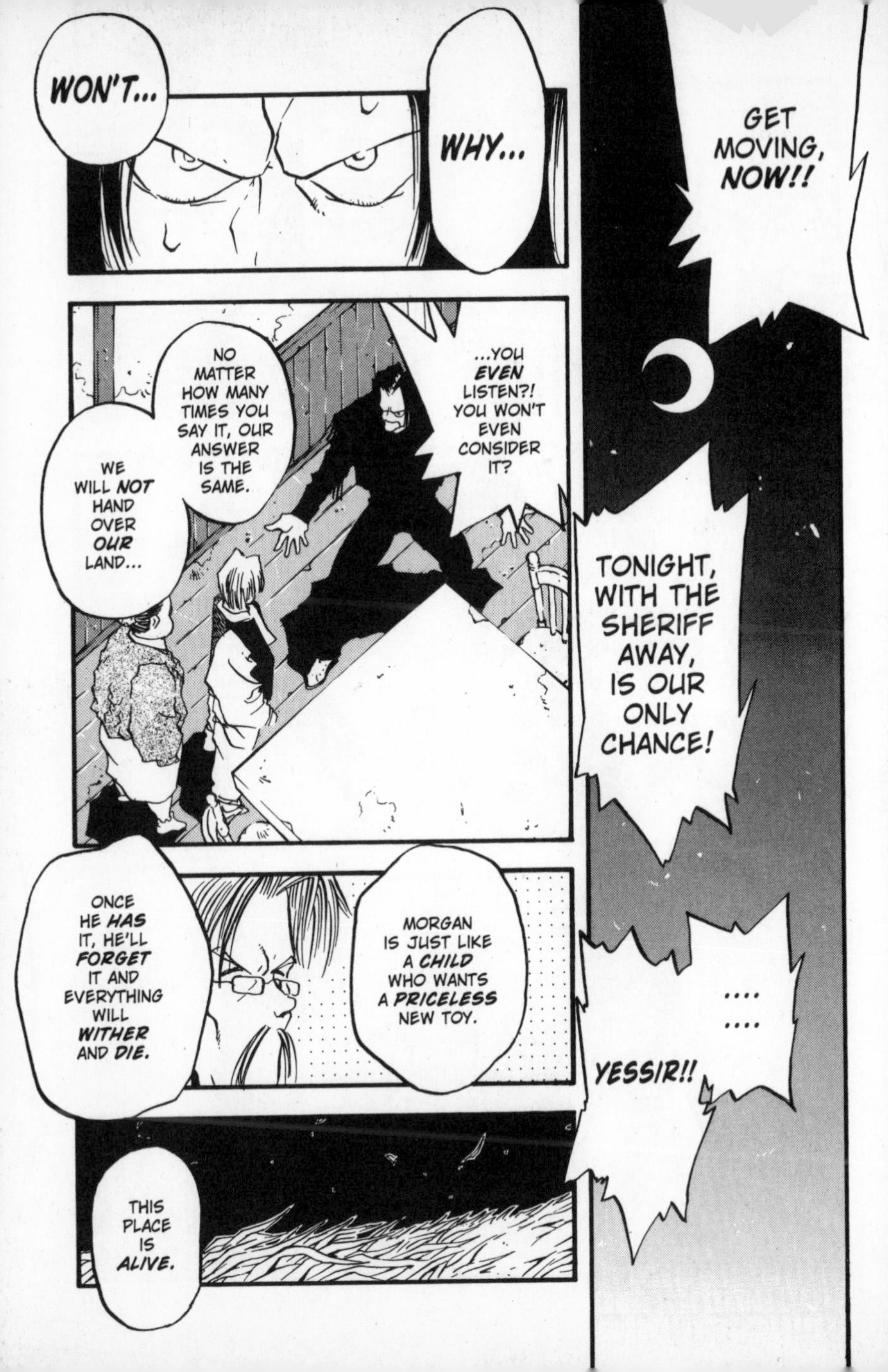
GET MOVING, NOW!!
TONIGHT, WITH THE SHERIFF AWAY, IS OUR ONLY CHANCE!
....
....
YESSIR!!
WHY...
WON'T...
...YOU EVEN LISTEN?! YOU WON'T EVEN CONSIDER IT?
NO MATTER HOW MANY TIMES YOU SAY IT, OUR ANSWER IS THE SAME.
WE WILL NOT HAND OVER OUR LAND...
MORGAN IS JUST LIKE A CHILD WHO WANTS A PRICELESS NEW TOY.
ONCE HE HAS IT, HE'LL FORGET IT AND EVERYTHING WILL WITHER AND DIE.
THIS PLACE IS ALIVE.

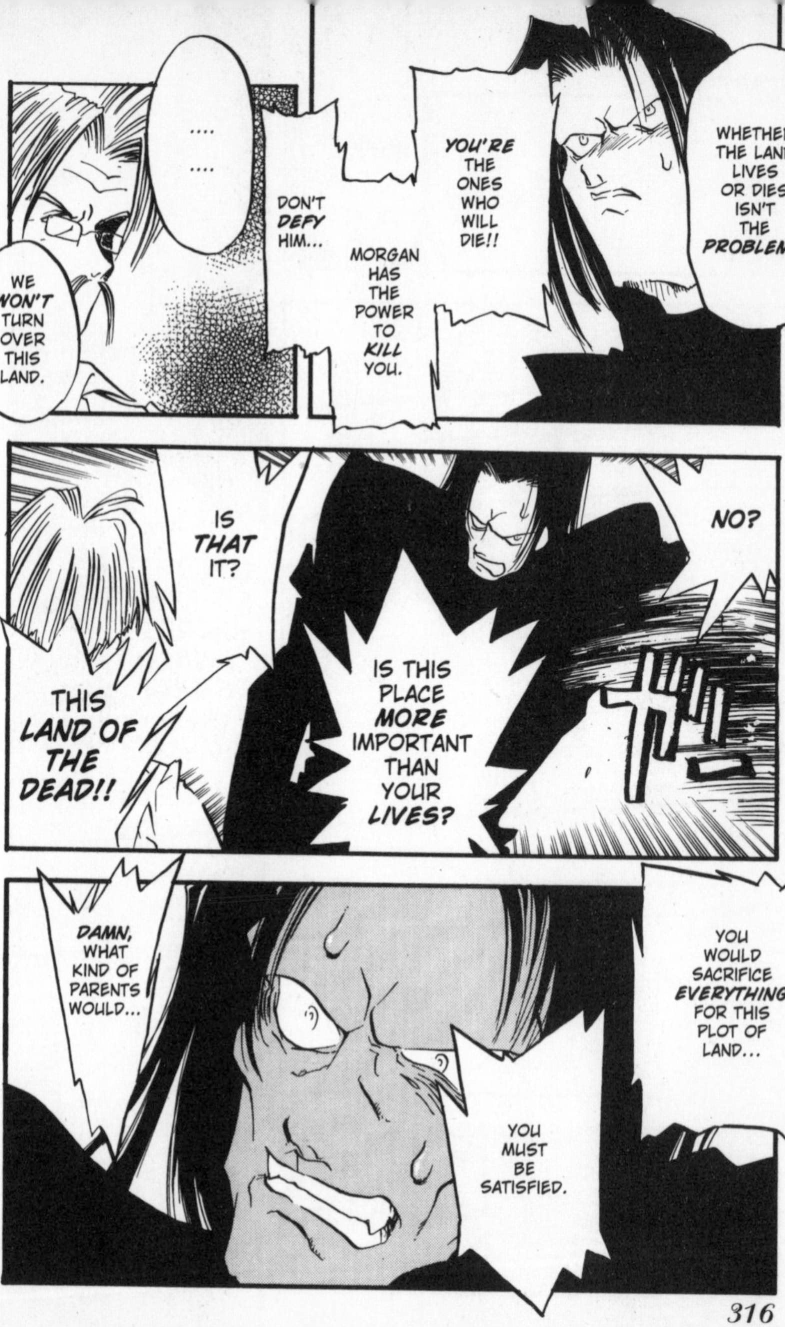
WHETHER THE LAND LIVES OR DIES ISN'T THE PROBLEM.
YOU'RE THE ONES WHO WILL DIE!!
MORGAN HAS THE POWER TO KILL YOU.
DON'T DEFY HIM...
....
....
WE WON'T TURN OVER THIS LAND.
NO?
IS THAT IT?
IS THIS PLACE MORE IMPORTANT THAN YOUR LIVES?
THIS LAND OF THE DEAD!!
YOU WOULD SACRIFICE EVERYTHING FOR THIS PLOT OF LAND...
YOU MUST BE SATISFIED.
DAMN, WHAT KIND OF PARENTS WOULD...

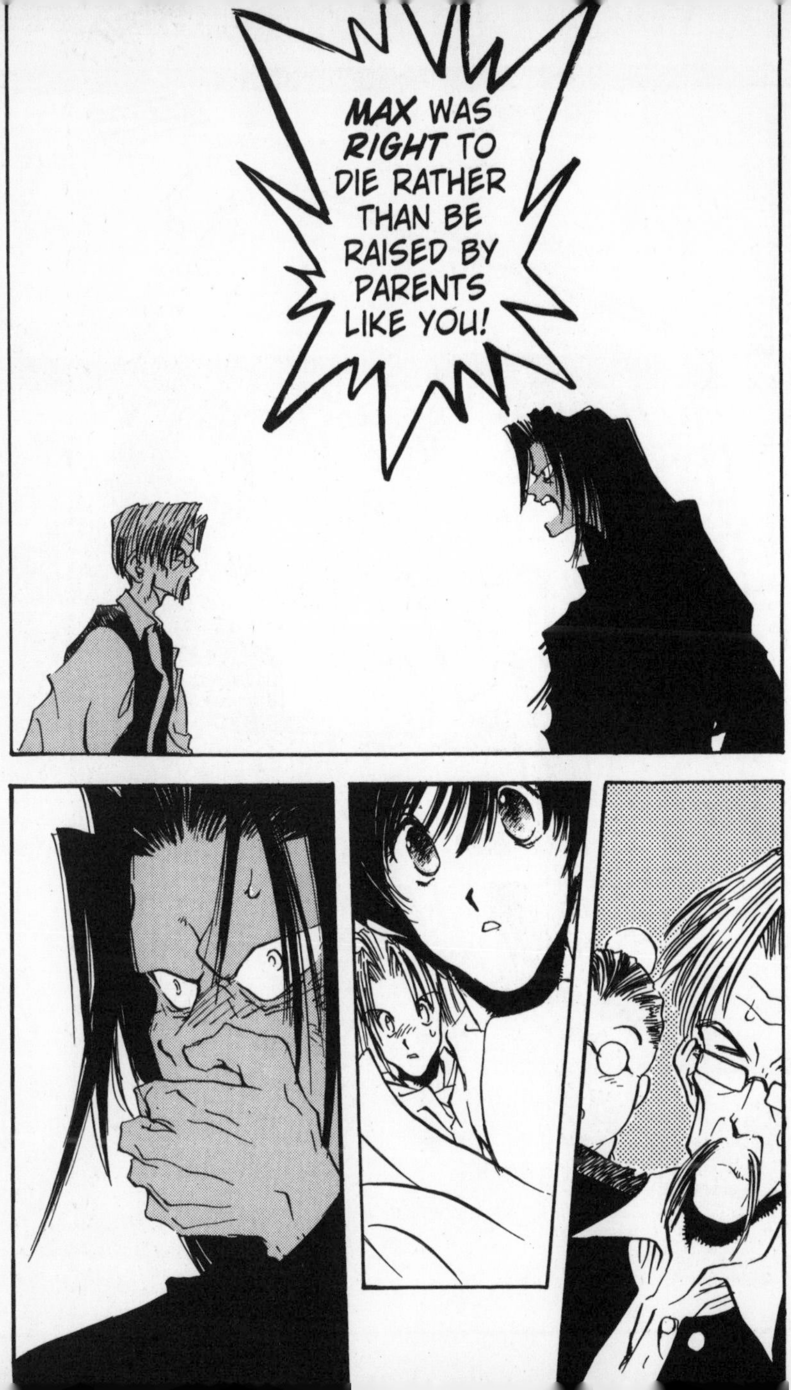
MAX WAS RIGHT TO DIE RATHER THAN BE RAISED BY PARENTS LIKE YOU!

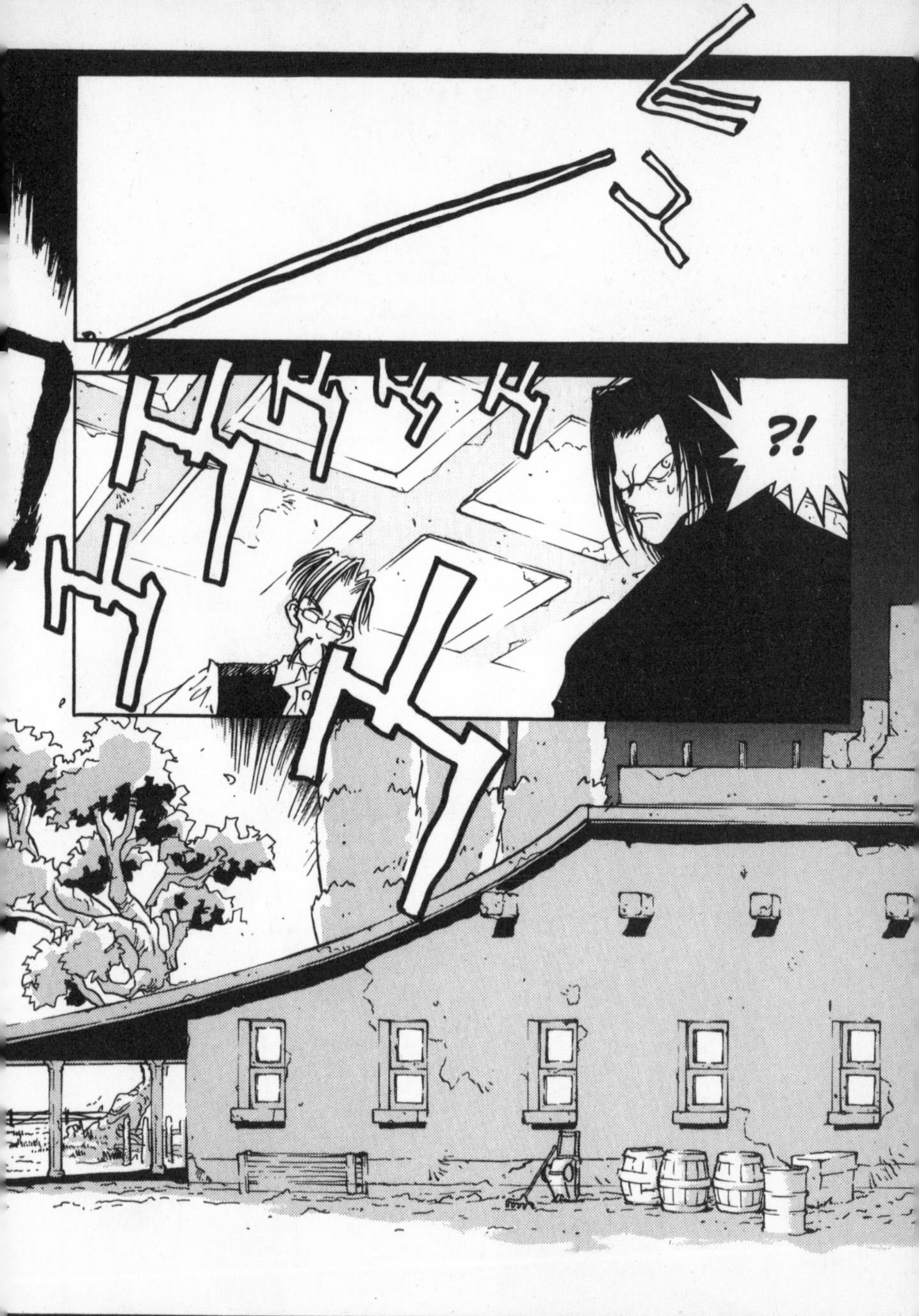
?!

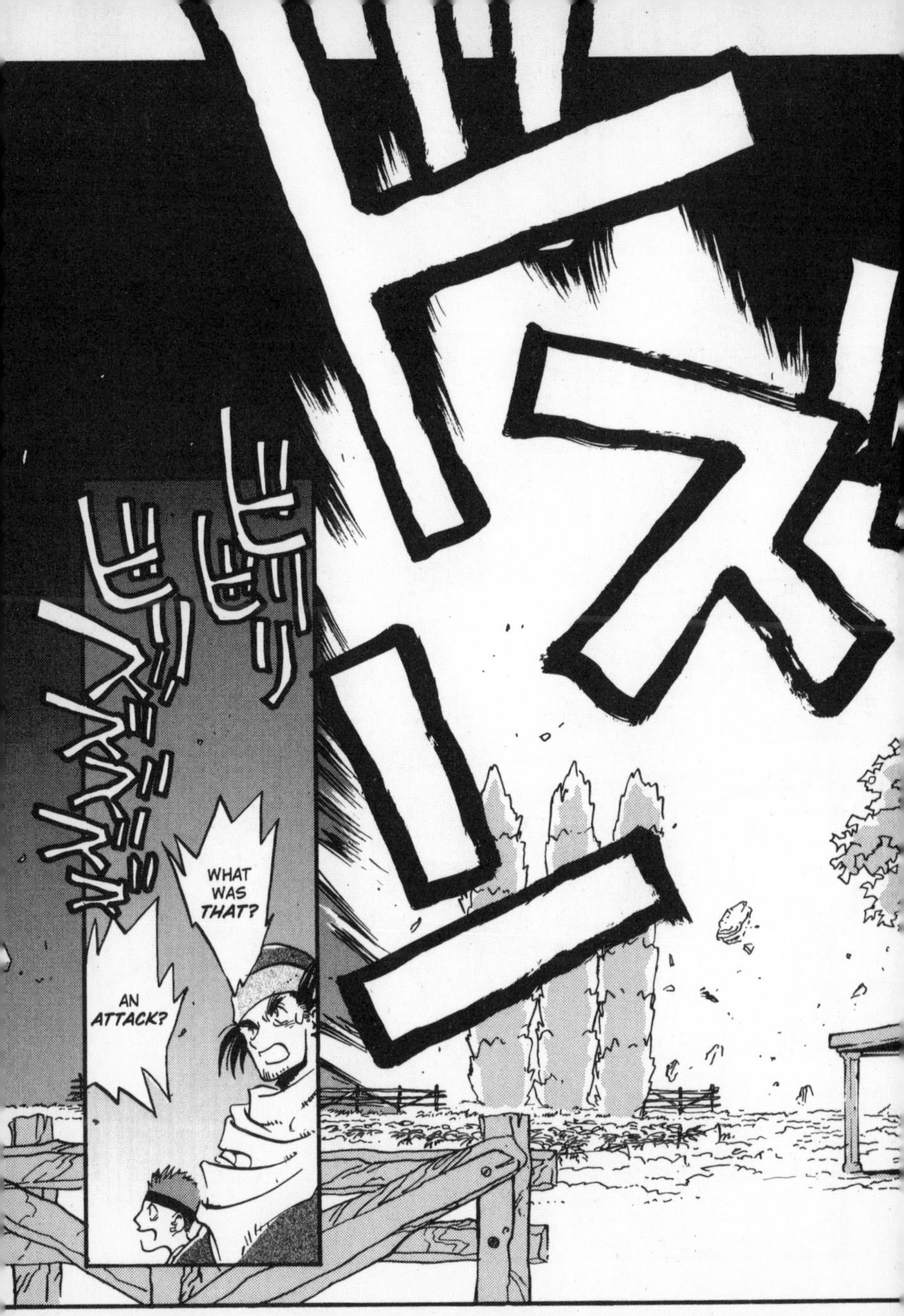
WHAT WAS THAT?
AN ATTACK?

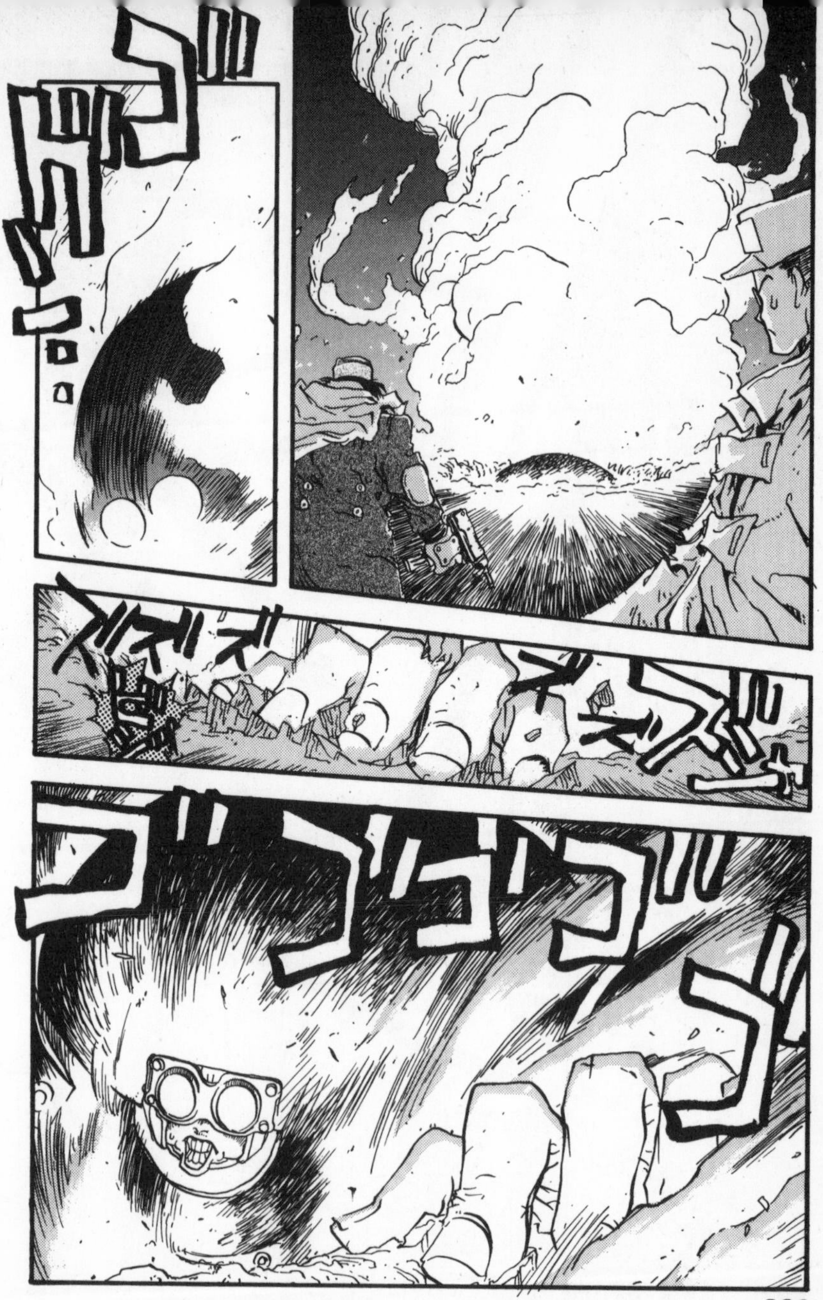

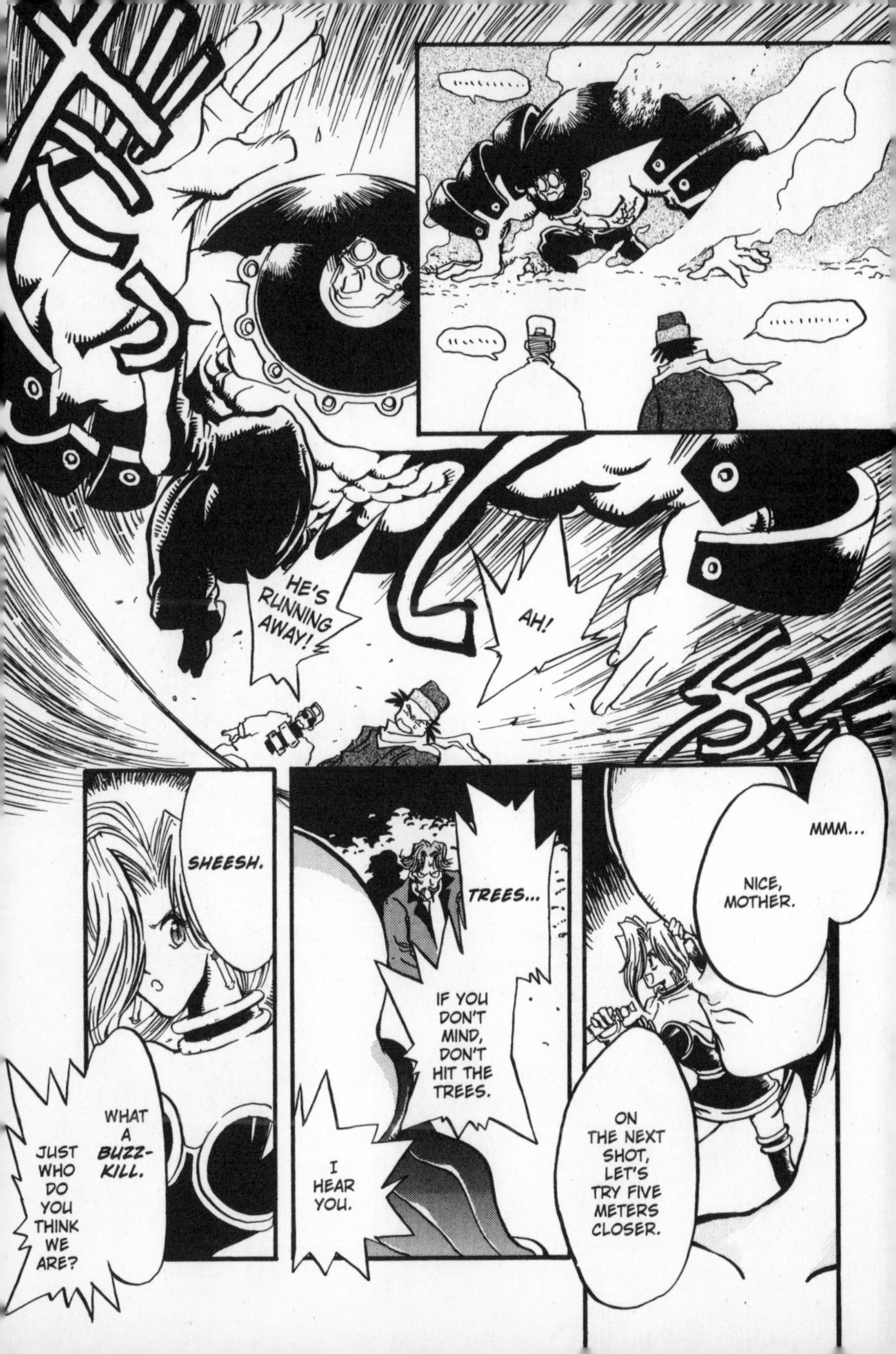
..........
........
......
AH!
HE'S RUNNING AWAY!
MMM...
NICE, MOTHER.
ON THE NEXT SHOT, LET'S TRY FIVE METERS CLOSER.
TREES...
IF YOU DON'T MIND, DON'T HIT THE TREES.
I HEAR YOU.
SHEESH.
WHAT A BUZZ-KILL.
JUST WHO DO YOU THINK WE ARE?

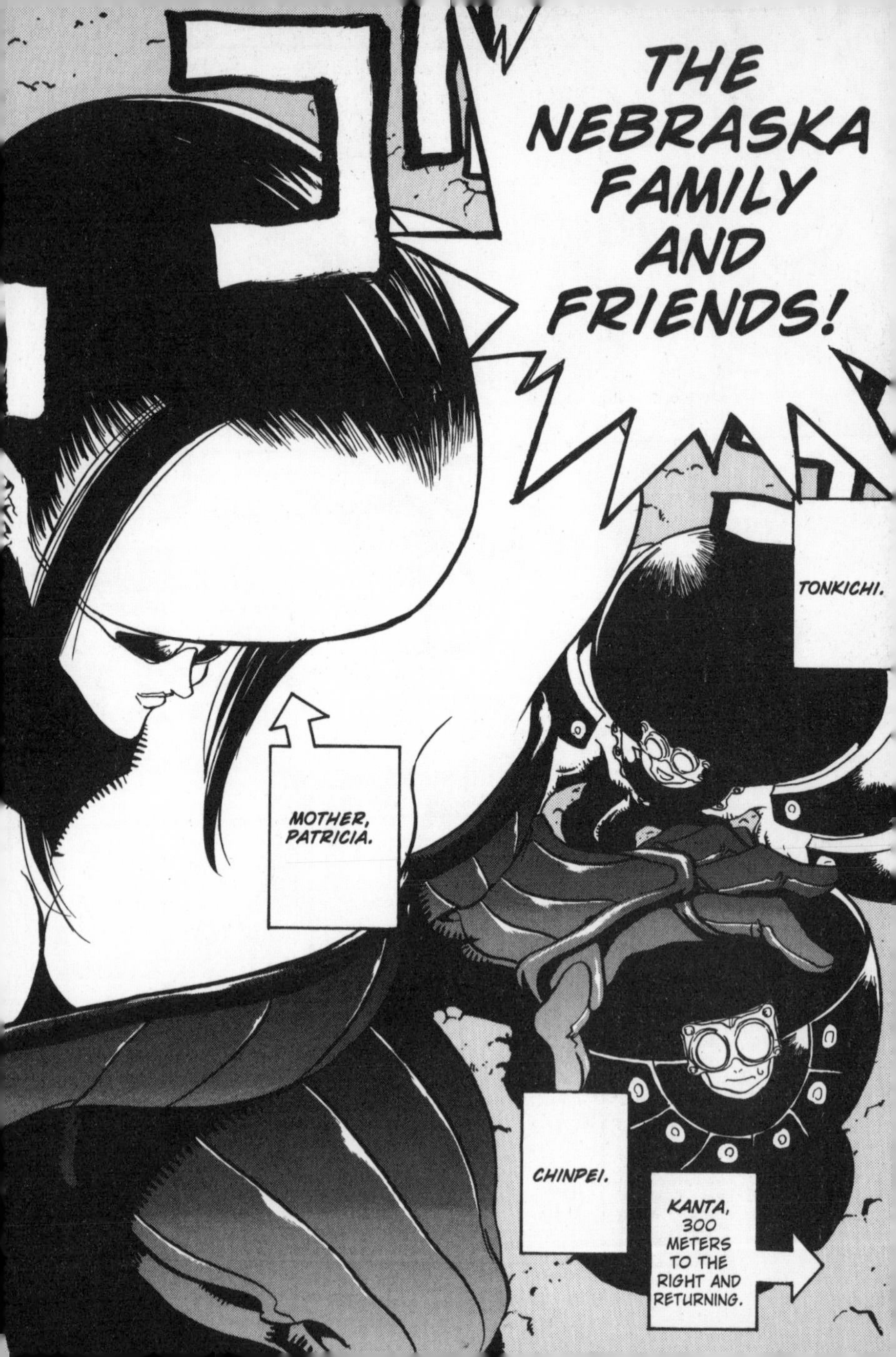
THE NEBRASKA FAMILY AND FRIENDS!
TONKICHI.
MOTHER, PATRICIA.
CHINPEI.
KANTA, 300 METERS TO THE RIGHT AND RETURNING.

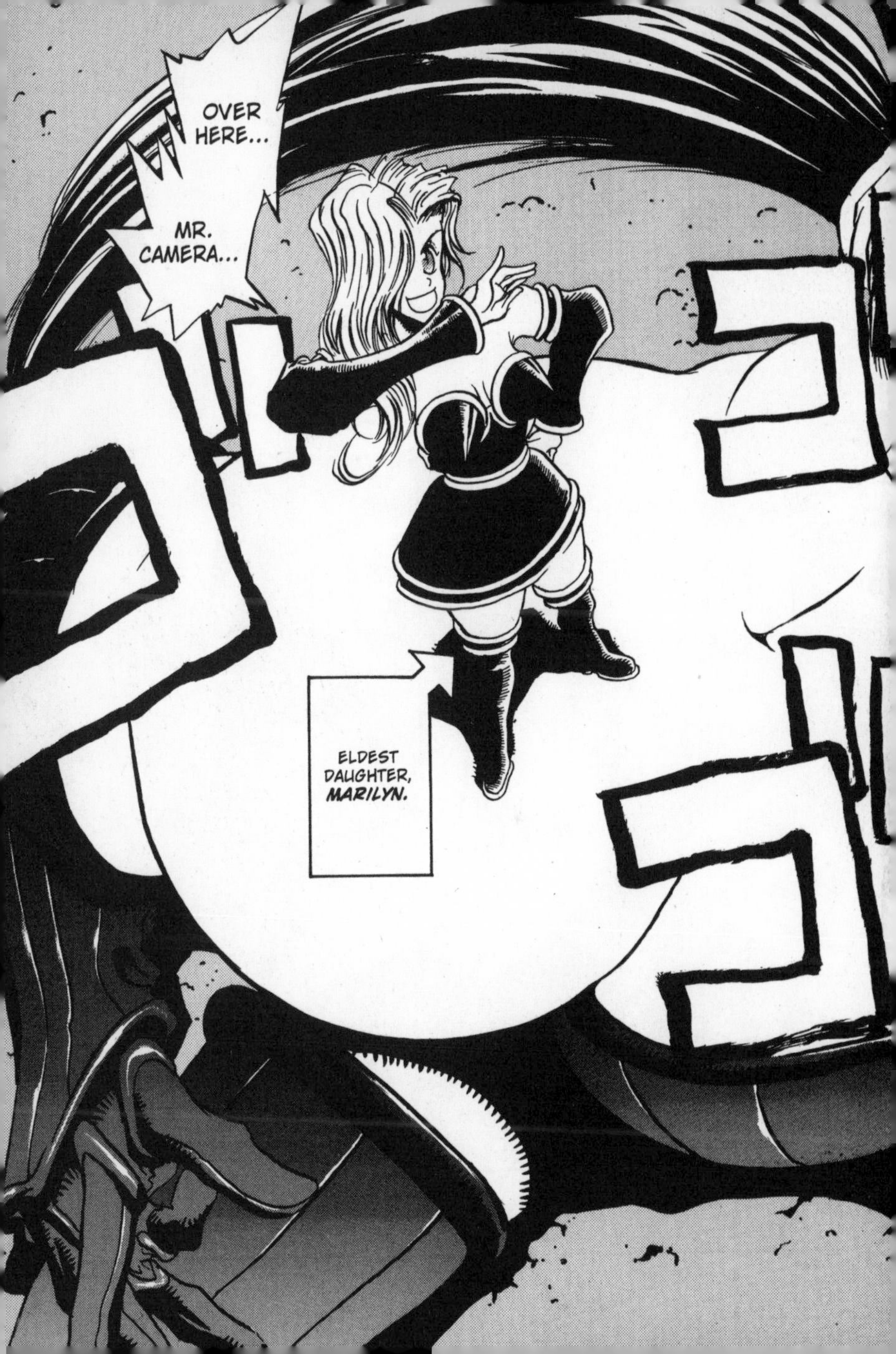
OVER HERE...
MR. CAMERA...
ELDEST DAUGHTER, MARILYN.

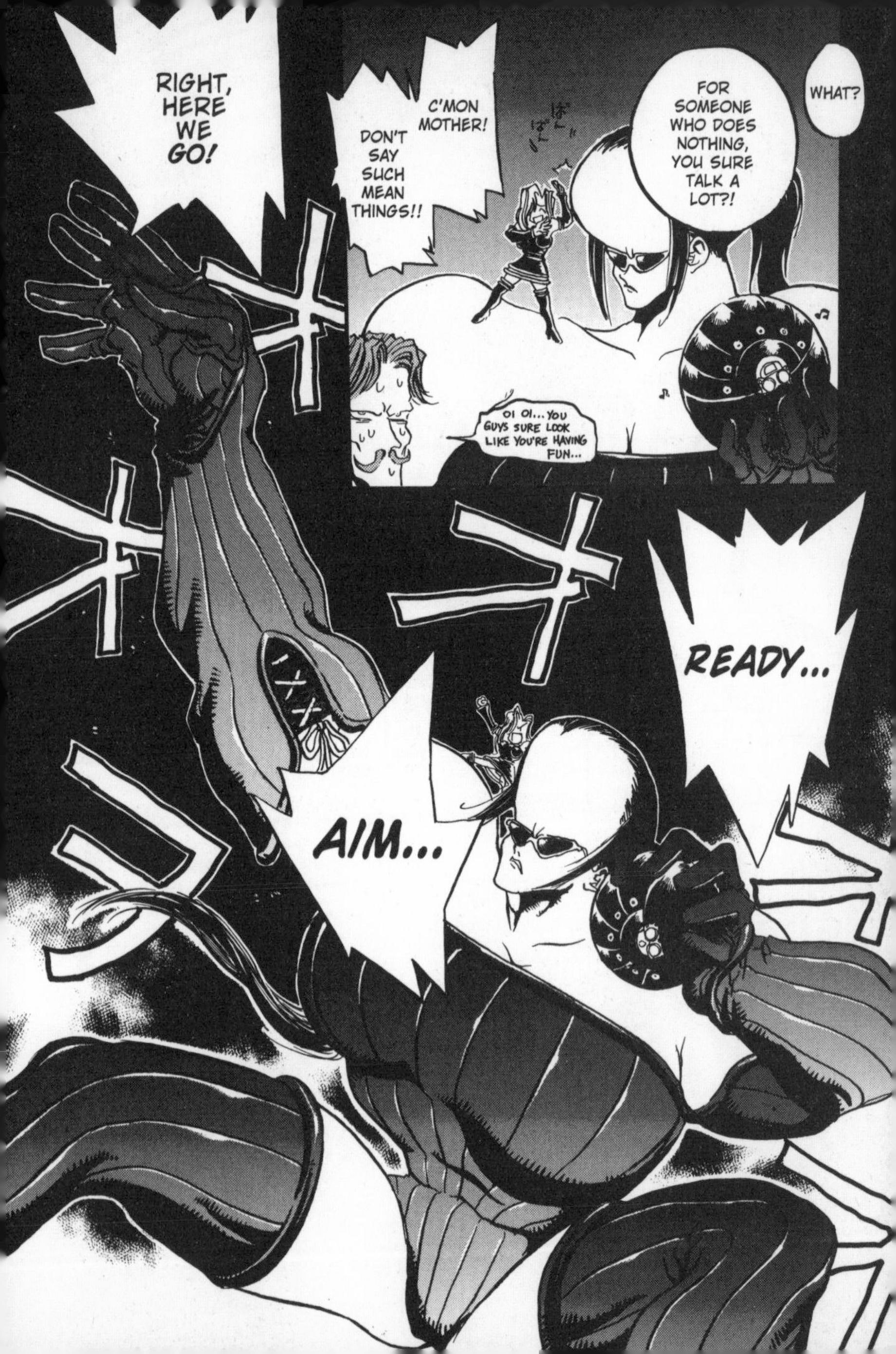
WHAT?
FOR SOMEONE WHO DOES NOTHING, YOU SURE TALK A LOT?!
C'MON MOTHER!
DON'T SAY SUCH MEAN THINGS!!
OI OI... YOU GUYS SURE LOOK LIKE YOU'RE HAVING FUN...
RIGHT, HERE WE GO!
READY...
AIM...

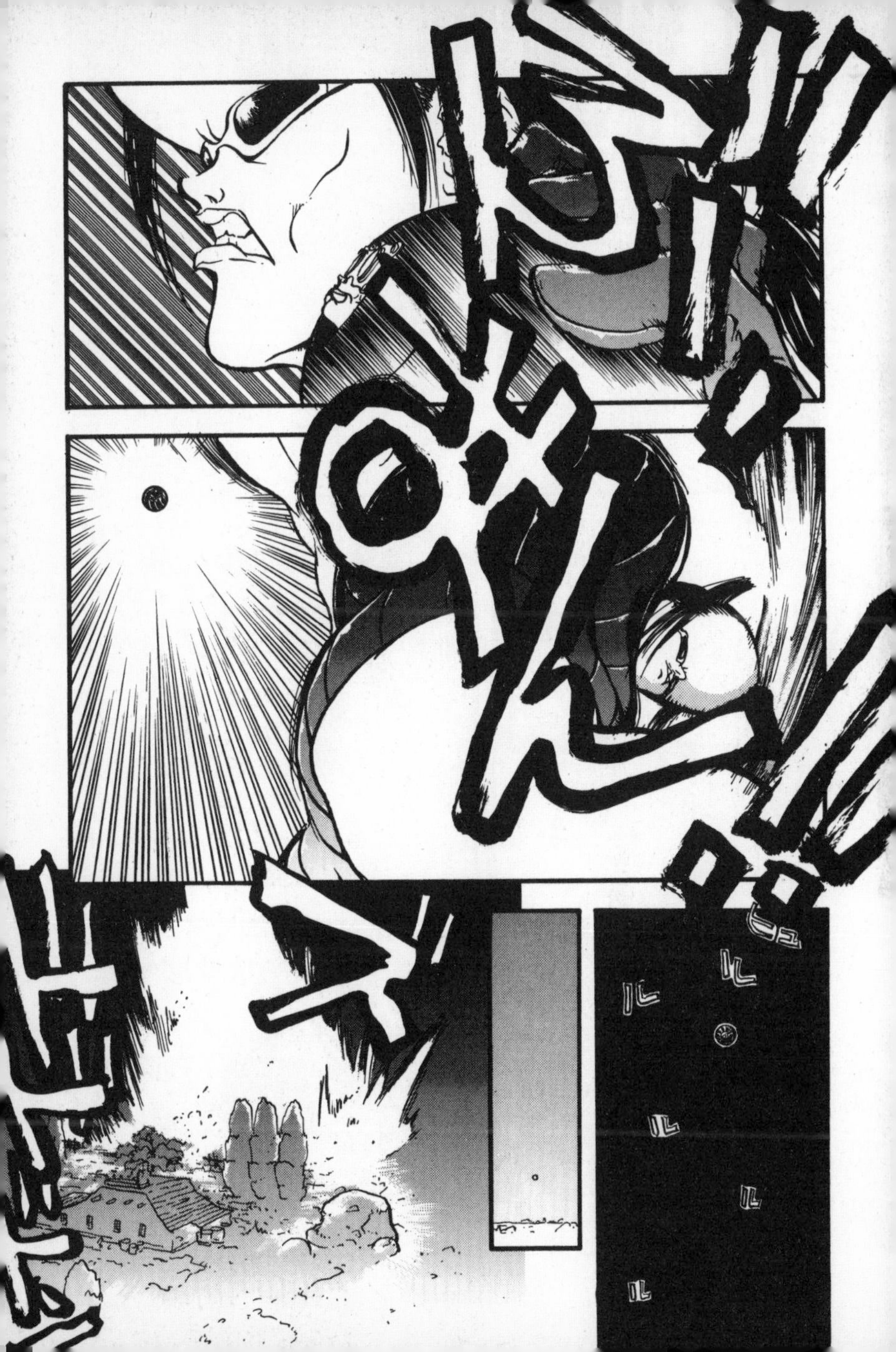

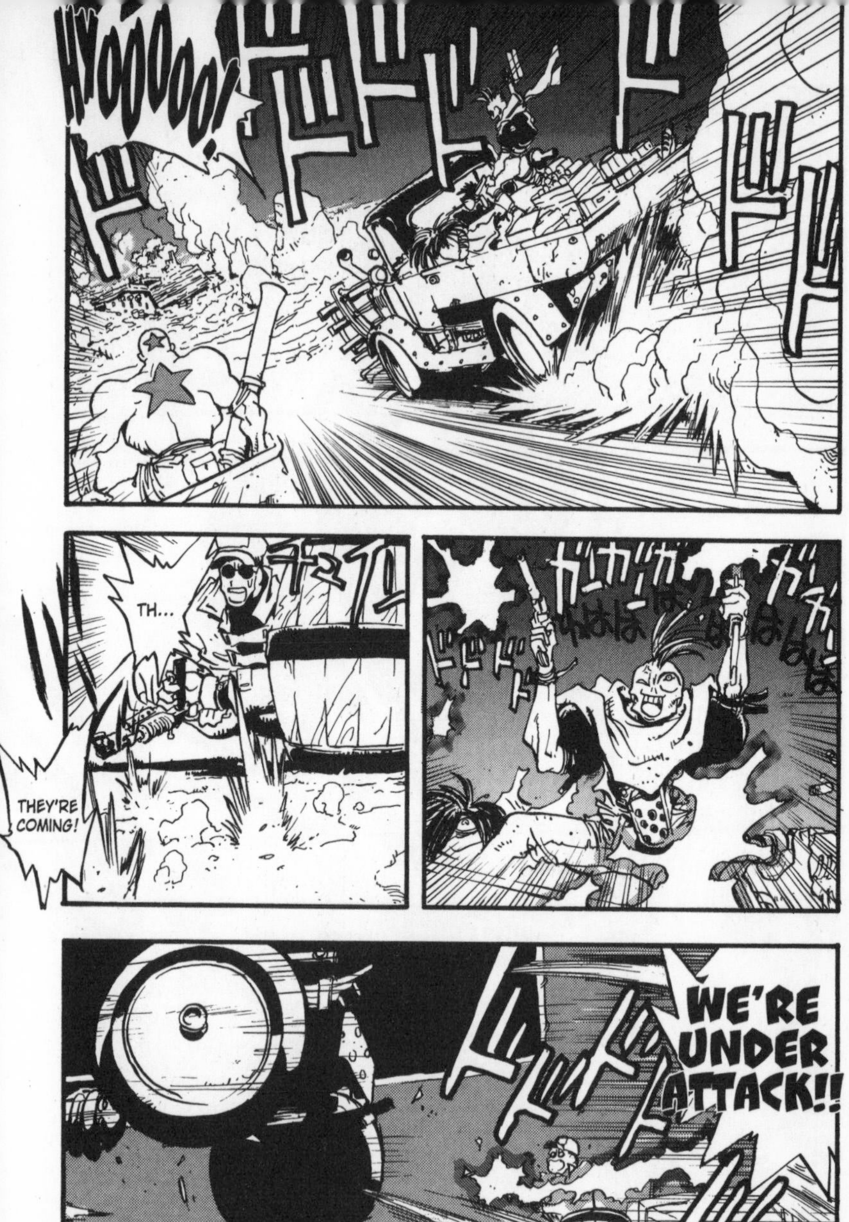
HYOOOOO!
TH...
THEY'RE COMING!
WE'RE UNDER ATTACK!!

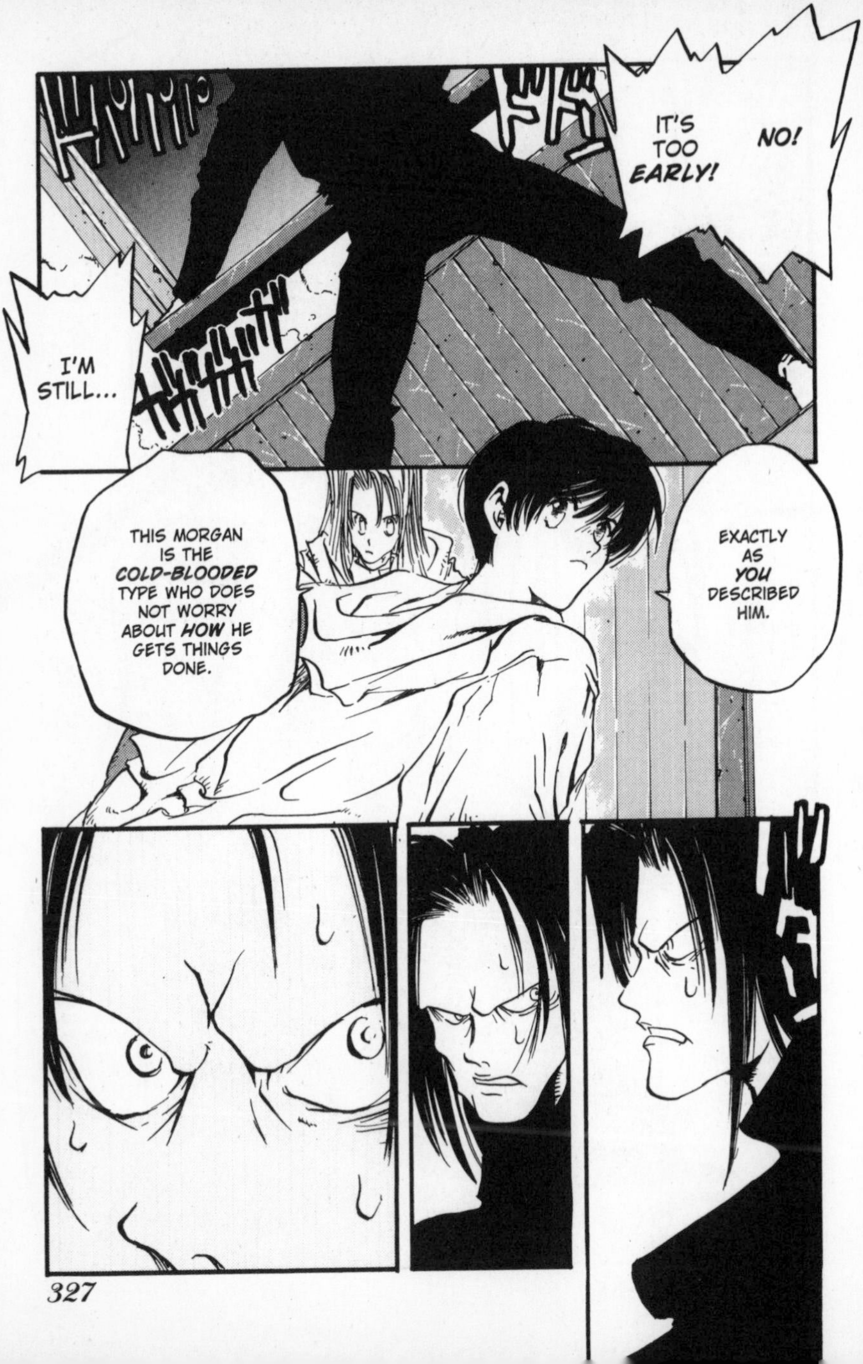
NO!
IT'S TOO *EARLY!*
I'M STILL...
EXACTLY AS *YOU* DESCRIBED HIM.
THIS MORGAN IS THE *COLD-BLOODED* TYPE WHO DOES NOT WORRY ABOUT *HOW* HE GETS THINGS DONE.

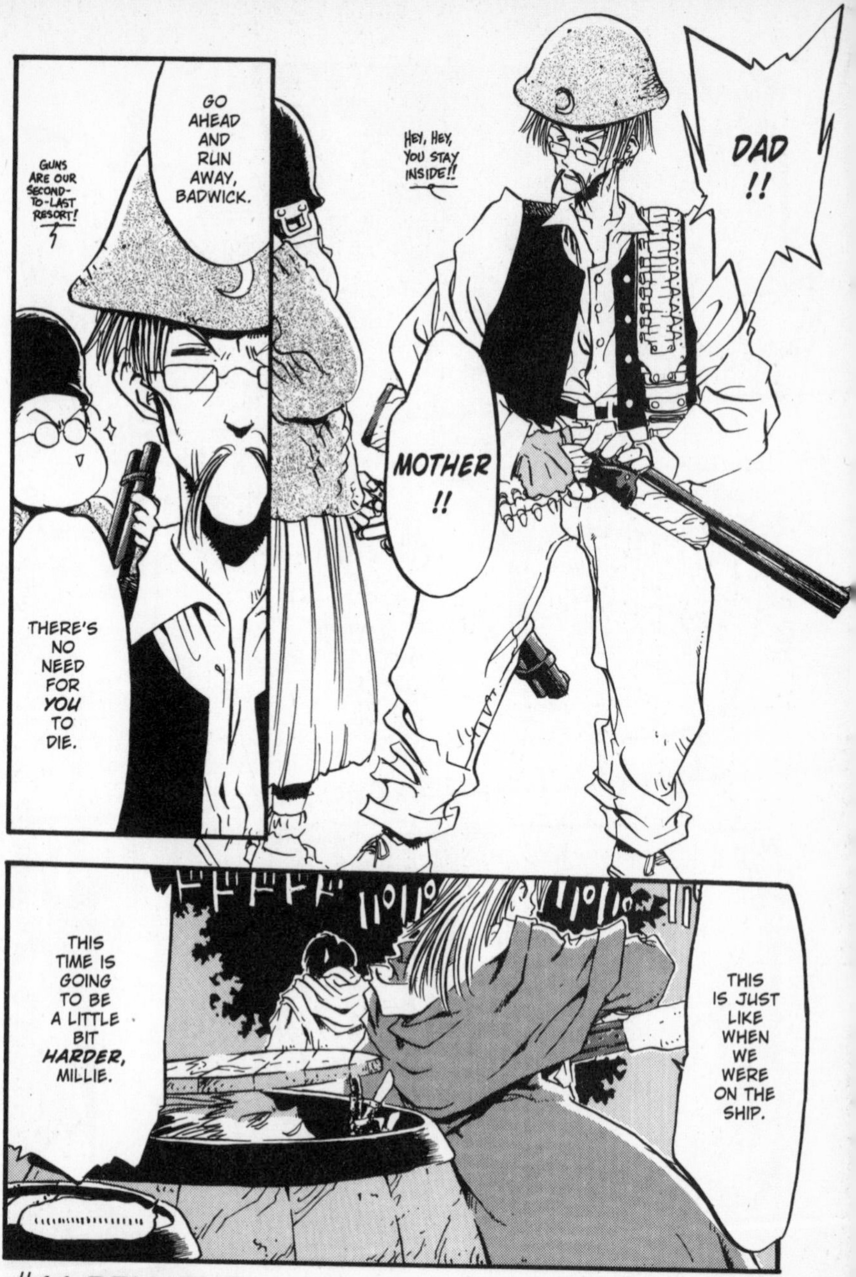
DAD !!
HEY, HEY, YOU STAY INSIDE!!
MOTHER !!
GO AHEAD AND RUN AWAY, BADWICK.
GUNS ARE OUR SECOND-TO-LAST RESORT!
THERE'S NO NEED FOR *YOU* TO DIE.
THIS IS JUST LIKE WHEN WE WERE ON THE SHIP.
THIS TIME IS GOING TO BE A LITTLE BIT *HARDER*, MILLIE.

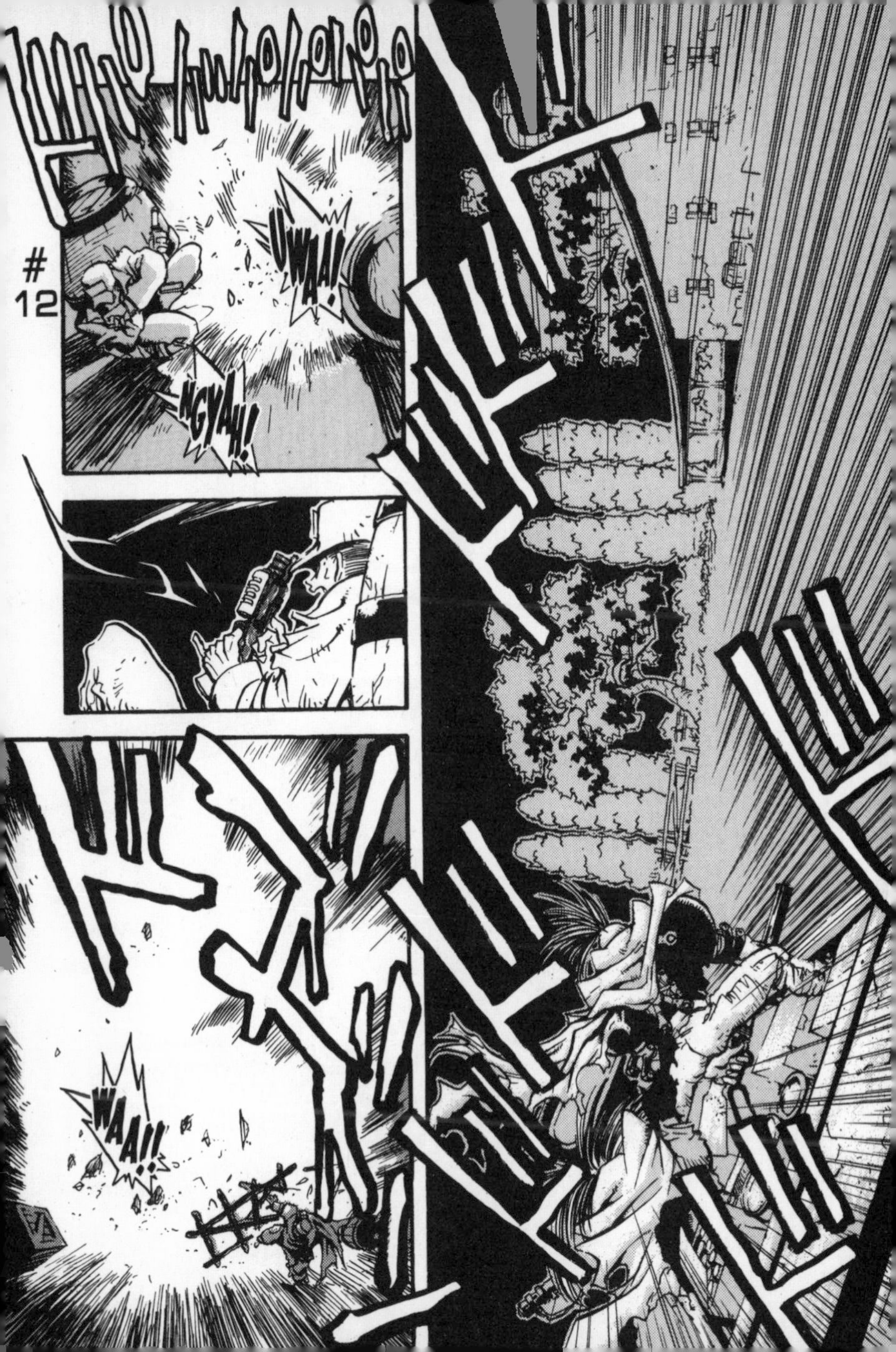

UWAAA!
NGYAAH!
WAA!!


# 12

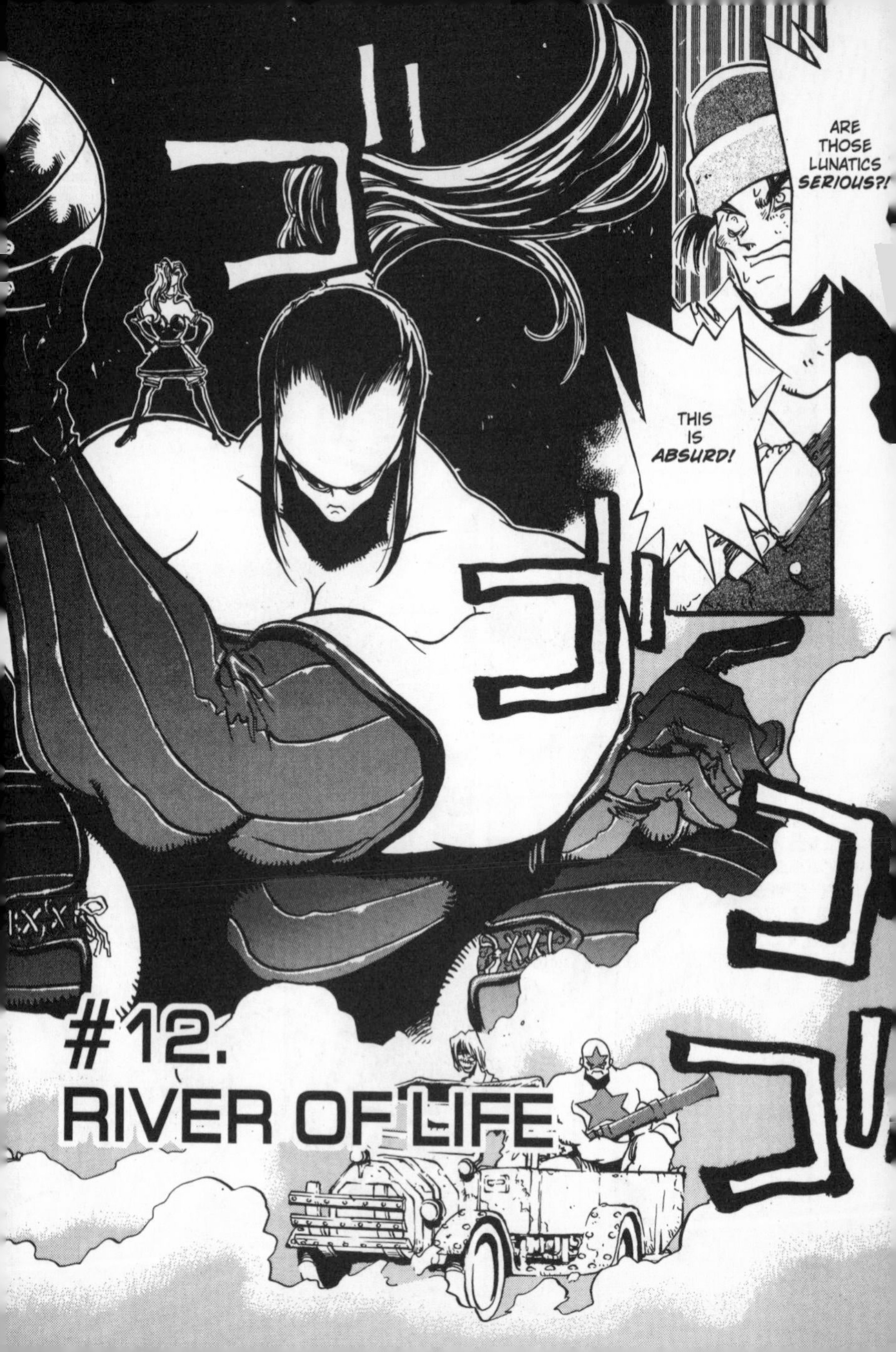
ARE THOSE LUNATICS SERIOUS?!
THIS IS ABSURD!
#12. RIVER OF LIFE

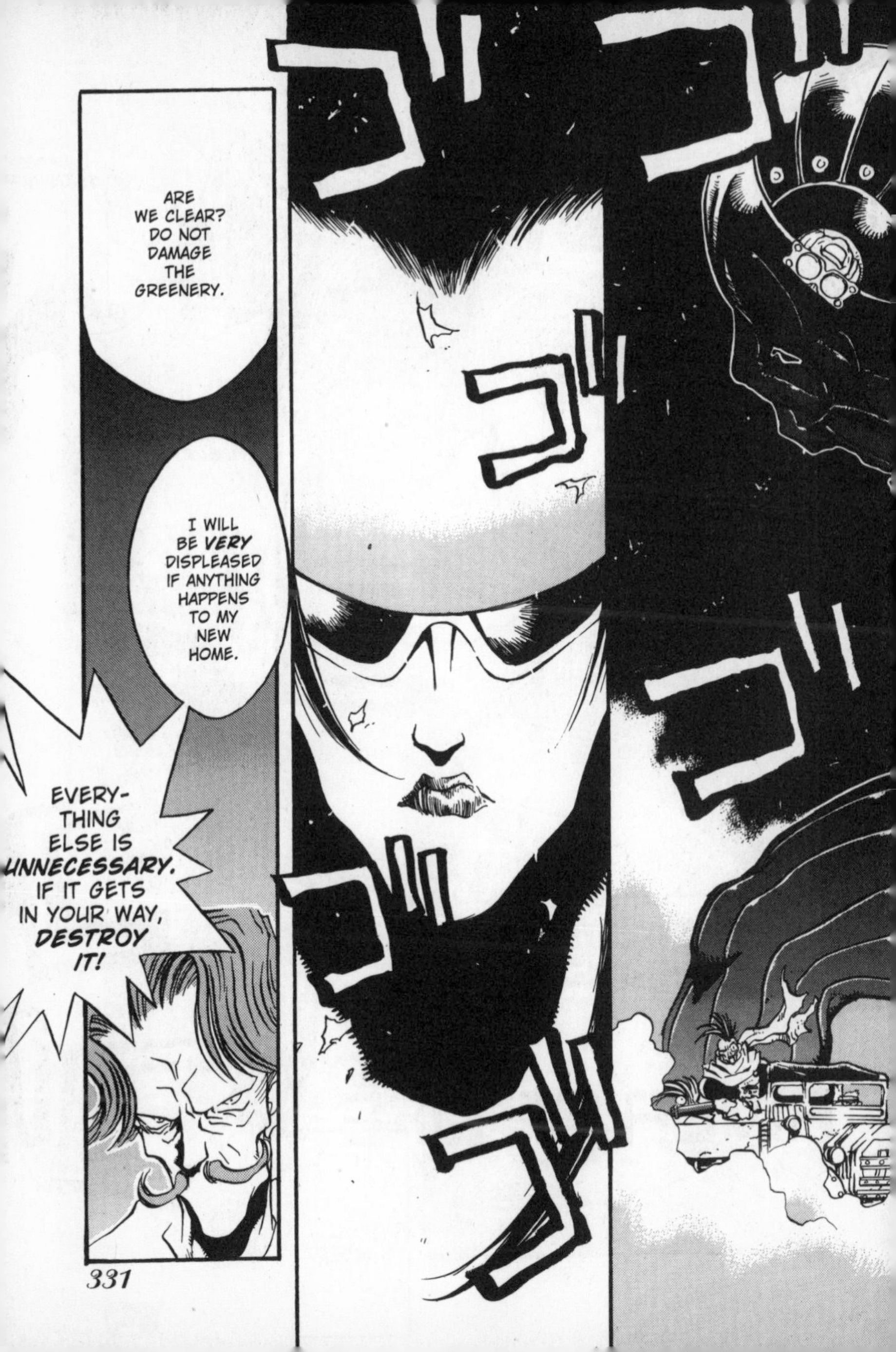
ARE WE CLEAR? DO NOT DAMAGE THE GREENERY.
I WILL BE ***VERY*** DISPLEASED IF ANYTHING HAPPENS TO MY NEW HOME.
EVERY-THING ELSE IS ***UNNECESSARY.*** IF IT GETS IN YOUR WAY, ***DESTROY IT!***

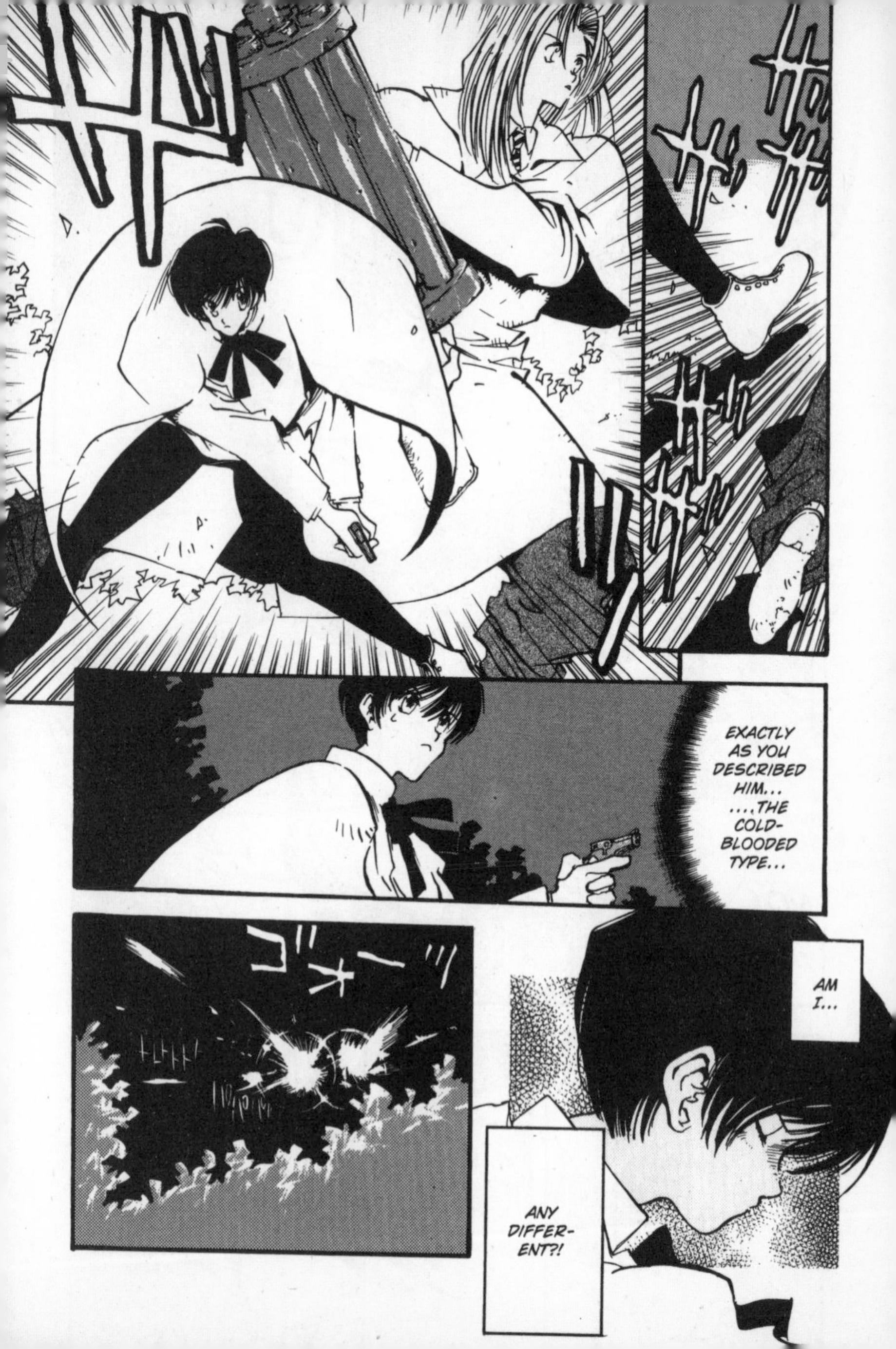
EXACTLY AS YOU DESCRIBED HIM...
....THE COLD-BLOODED TYPE...
AM I...
ANY DIFFER-ENT?!
ゴォーッ

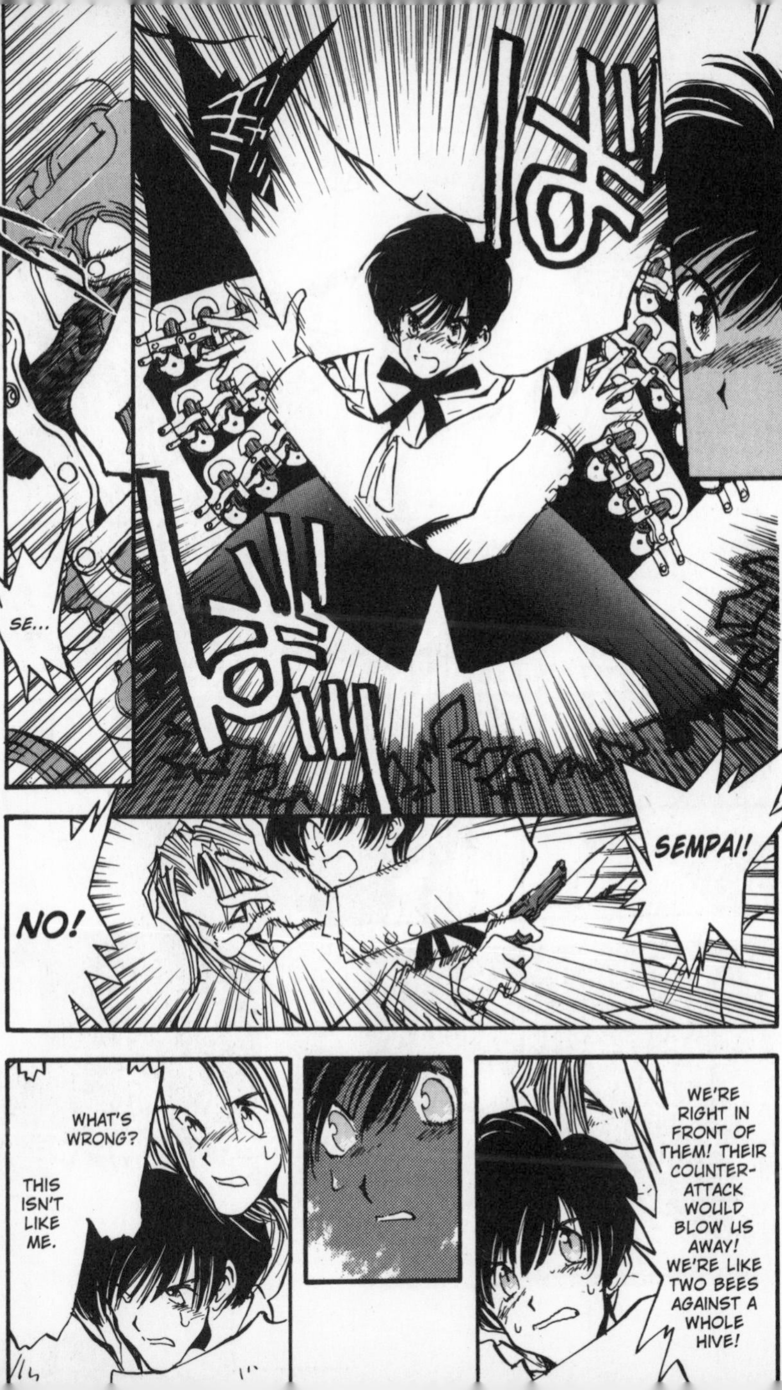
SE...
SEMPAI!
NO!
WE'RE RIGHT IN FRONT OF THEM! THEIR COUNTER-ATTACK WOULD BLOW US AWAY! WE'RE LIKE TWO BEES AGAINST A WHOLE HIVE!
WHAT'S WRONG?
THIS ISN'T LIKE ME.

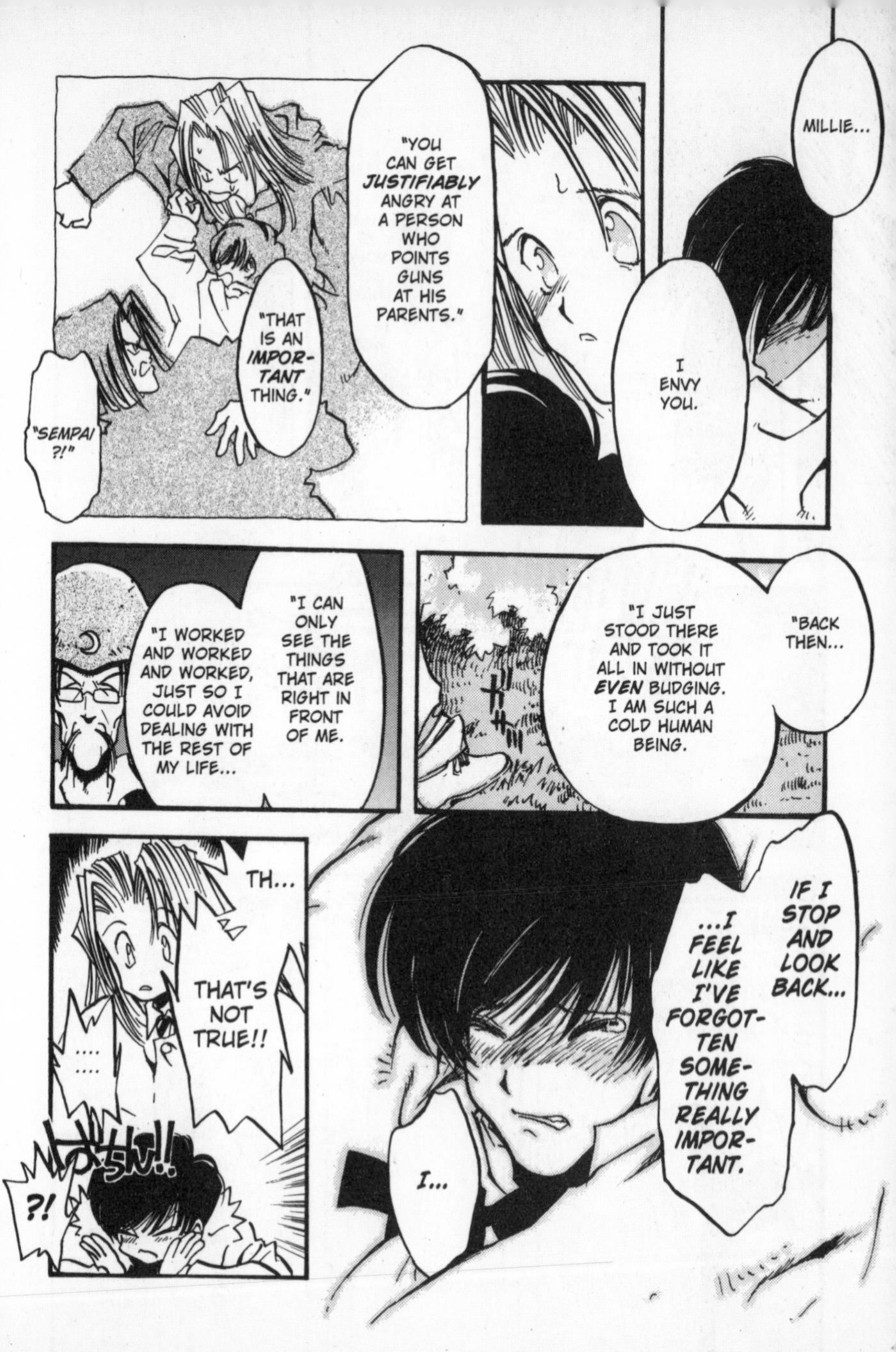
MILLIE...
I ENVY YOU.
"YOU CAN GET JUSTIFIABLY ANGRY AT A PERSON WHO POINTS GUNS AT HIS PARENTS."
"THAT IS AN IMPORTANT THING."
"SEMPAI ?!"
"BACK THEN...
"I JUST STOOD THERE AND TOOK IT ALL IN WITHOUT EVEN BUDGING. I AM SUCH A COLD HUMAN BEING.
"I CAN ONLY SEE THE THINGS THAT ARE RIGHT IN FRONT OF ME.
"I WORKED AND WORKED AND WORKED, JUST SO I COULD AVOID DEALING WITH THE REST OF MY LIFE...
IF I STOP AND LOOK BACK...
...I FEEL LIKE I'VE FORGOTTEN SOMETHING REALLY IMPORTANT.
I...
TH...
THAT'S NOT TRUE!!
........
?!

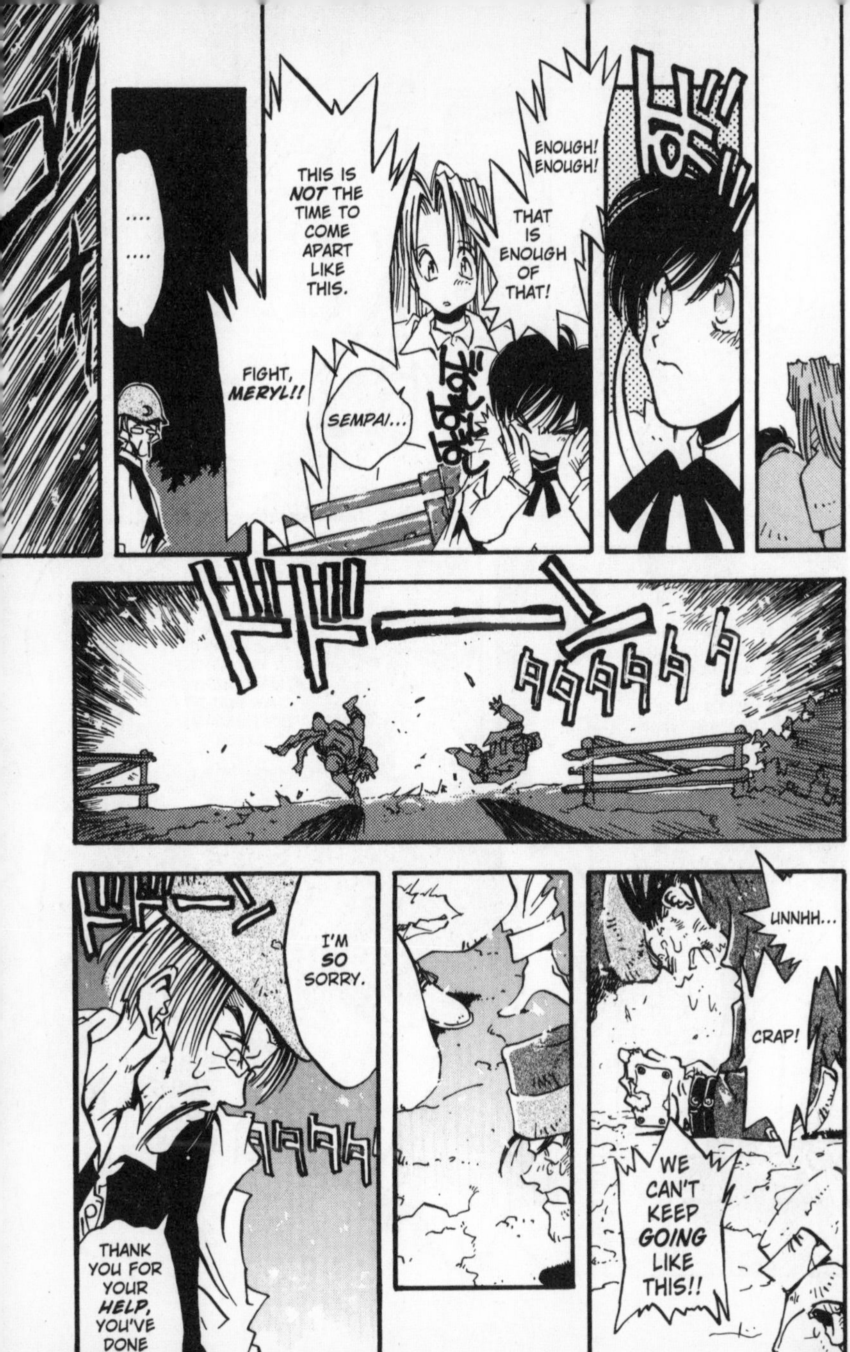
ENOUGH! ENOUGH!
THAT IS ENOUGH OF THAT!
THIS IS *NOT* THE TIME TO COME APART LIKE THIS.
SEMPAI...
FIGHT, *MERYL!!*
....
....
UNNHH...
CRAP!
WE CAN'T KEEP *GOING* LIKE THIS!!
I'M *SO* SORRY.
THANK YOU FOR YOUR *HELP,* YOU'VE DONE PLENTY.

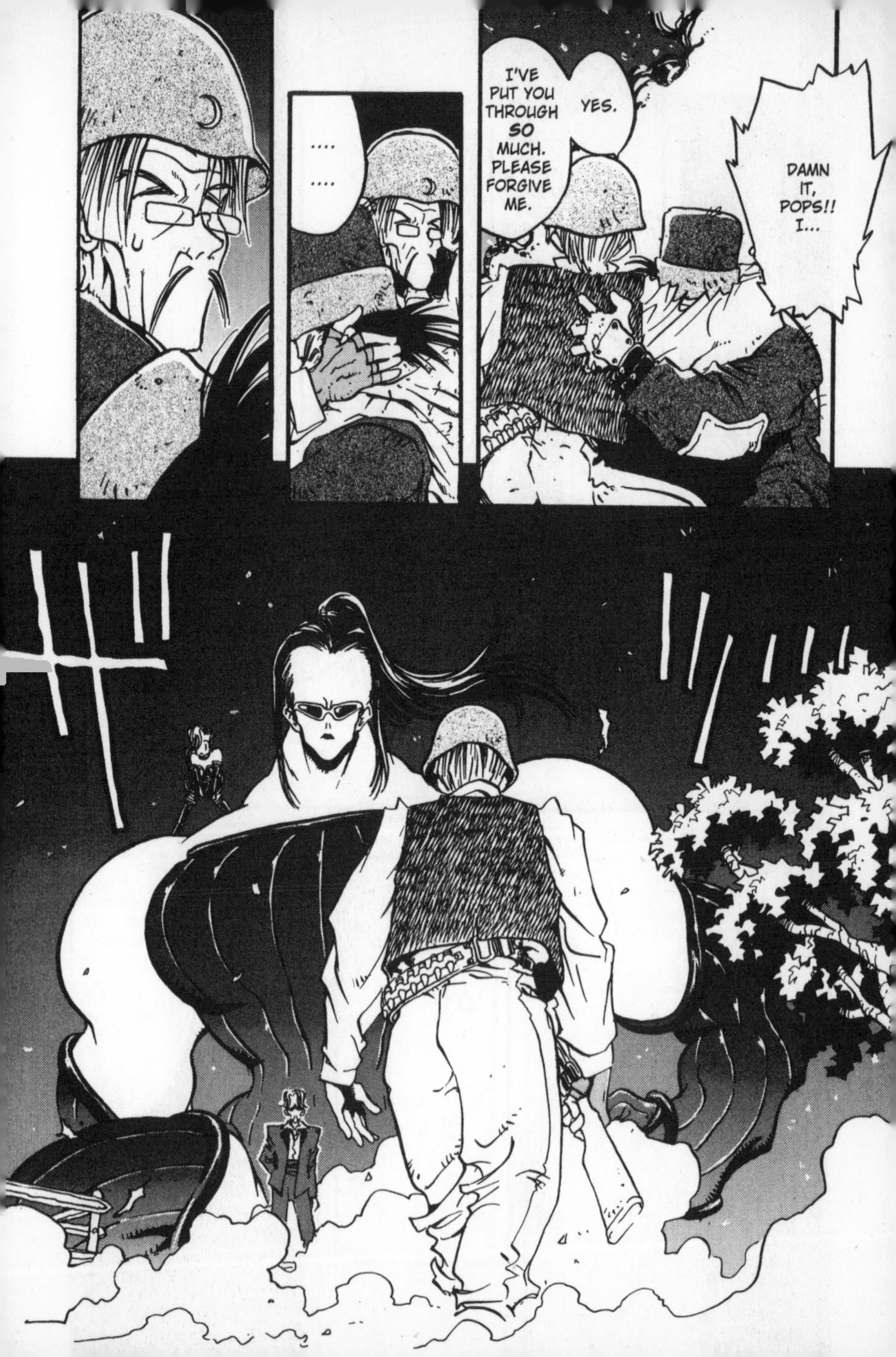

DAMN IT, POPS!! I...
I'VE PUT YOU THROUGH SO MUCH. PLEASE FORGIVE ME.
YES.
....
....

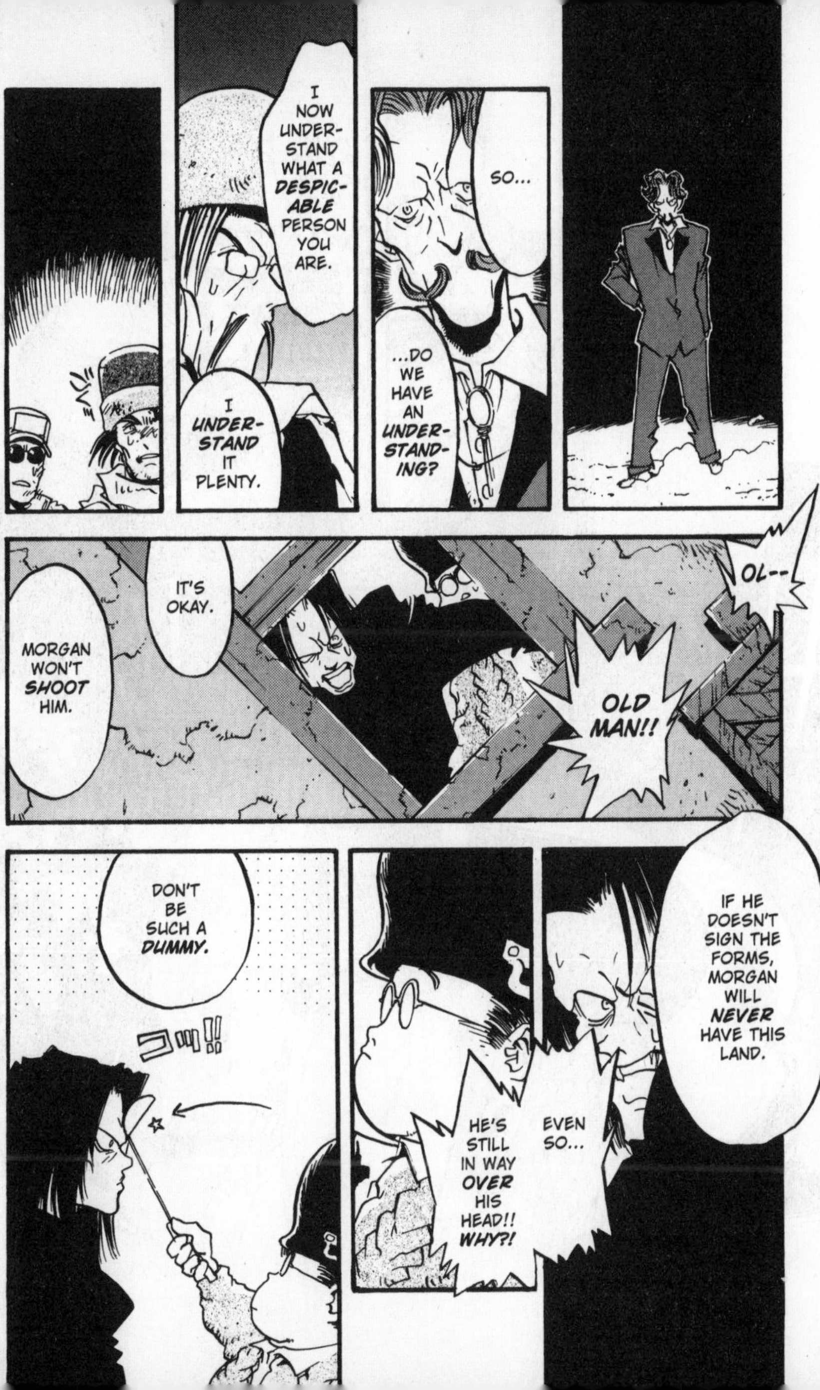
SO...
...DO WE HAVE AN UNDERSTANDING?
I NOW UNDERSTAND WHAT A DESPICABLE PERSON YOU ARE.
I UNDERSTAND IT PLENTY.
OL--
OLD MAN!!
IT'S OKAY.
MORGAN WON'T SHOOT HIM.
IF HE DOESN'T SIGN THE FORMS, MORGAN WILL NEVER HAVE THIS LAND.
EVEN SO...
HE'S STILL IN WAY OVER HIS HEAD!! WHY?!
DON'T BE SUCH A DUMMY.
コッ!!

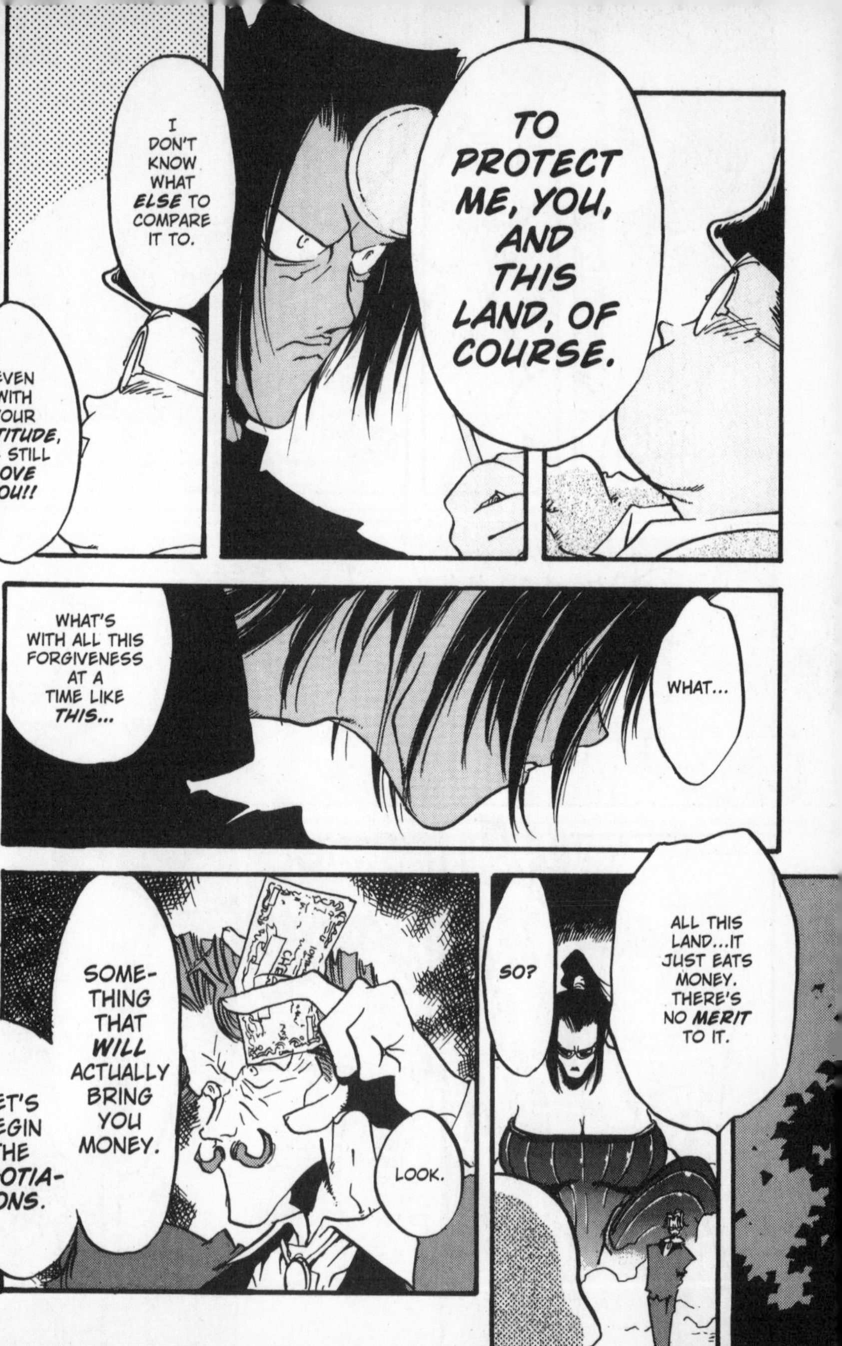
TO PROTECT ME, YOU, AND THIS LAND, OF COURSE.
I DON'T KNOW WHAT ELSE TO COMPARE IT TO.
EVEN WITH YOUR ATTITUDE, WE STILL LOVE YOU!!
WHAT...
WHAT'S WITH ALL THIS FORGIVENESS AT A TIME LIKE THIS...
ALL THIS LAND...IT JUST EATS MONEY. THERE'S NO MERIT TO IT.
SO?
LOOK.
SOME-THING THAT WILL ACTUALLY BRING YOU MONEY.
LET'S BEGIN THE NEGOTIA-TIONS.

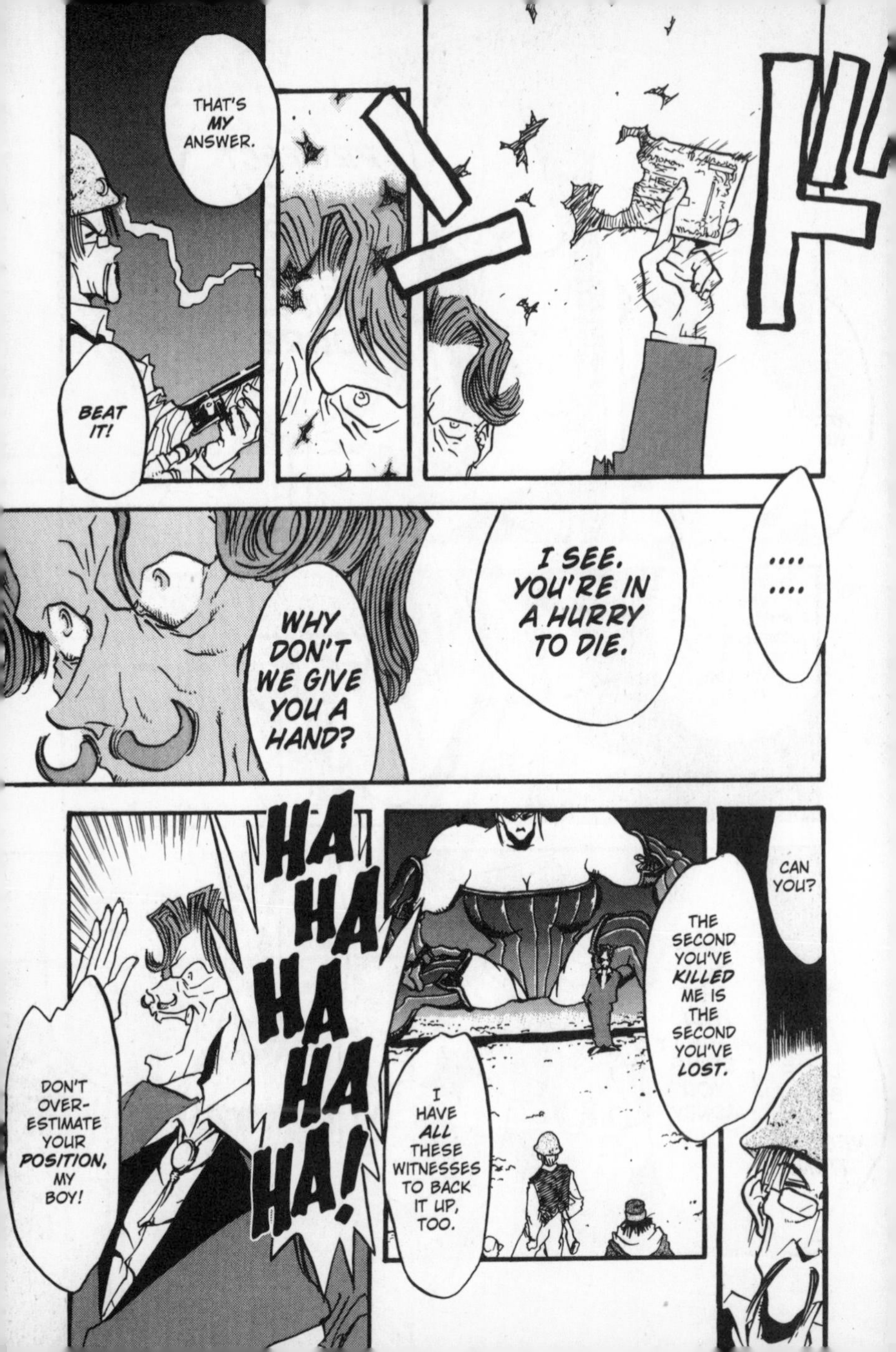
THAT'S *MY* ANSWER.
*BEAT IT!*
....
....
*I SEE. YOU'RE IN A HURRY TO DIE.*
*WHY DON'T WE GIVE YOU A HAND?*
CAN YOU?
THE SECOND YOU'VE *KILLED* ME IS THE SECOND YOU'VE *LOST.*
I HAVE *ALL* THESE WITNESSES TO BACK IT UP, TOO.
HA HA HA HA HA HA HA!
DON'T OVER-ESTIMATE YOUR *POSITION,* MY BOY!

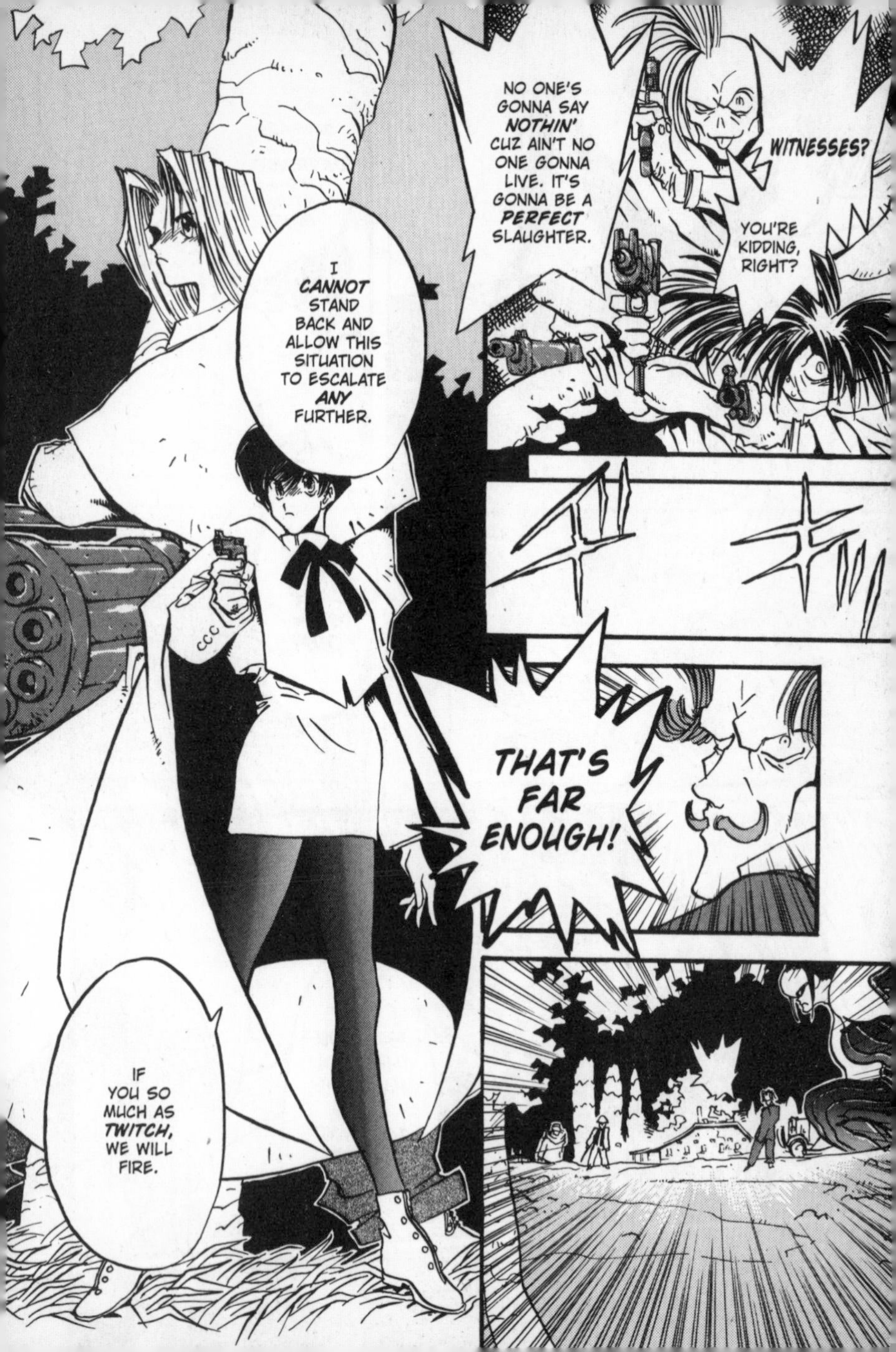
WITNESSES?
YOU'RE KIDDING, RIGHT?
NO ONE'S GONNA SAY NOTHIN' CUZ AIN'T NO ONE GONNA LIVE. IT'S GONNA BE A PERFECT SLAUGHTER.
THAT'S FAR ENOUGH!
I CANNOT STAND BACK AND ALLOW THIS SITUATION TO ESCALATE ANY FURTHER.
IF YOU SO MUCH AS TWITCH, WE WILL FIRE.

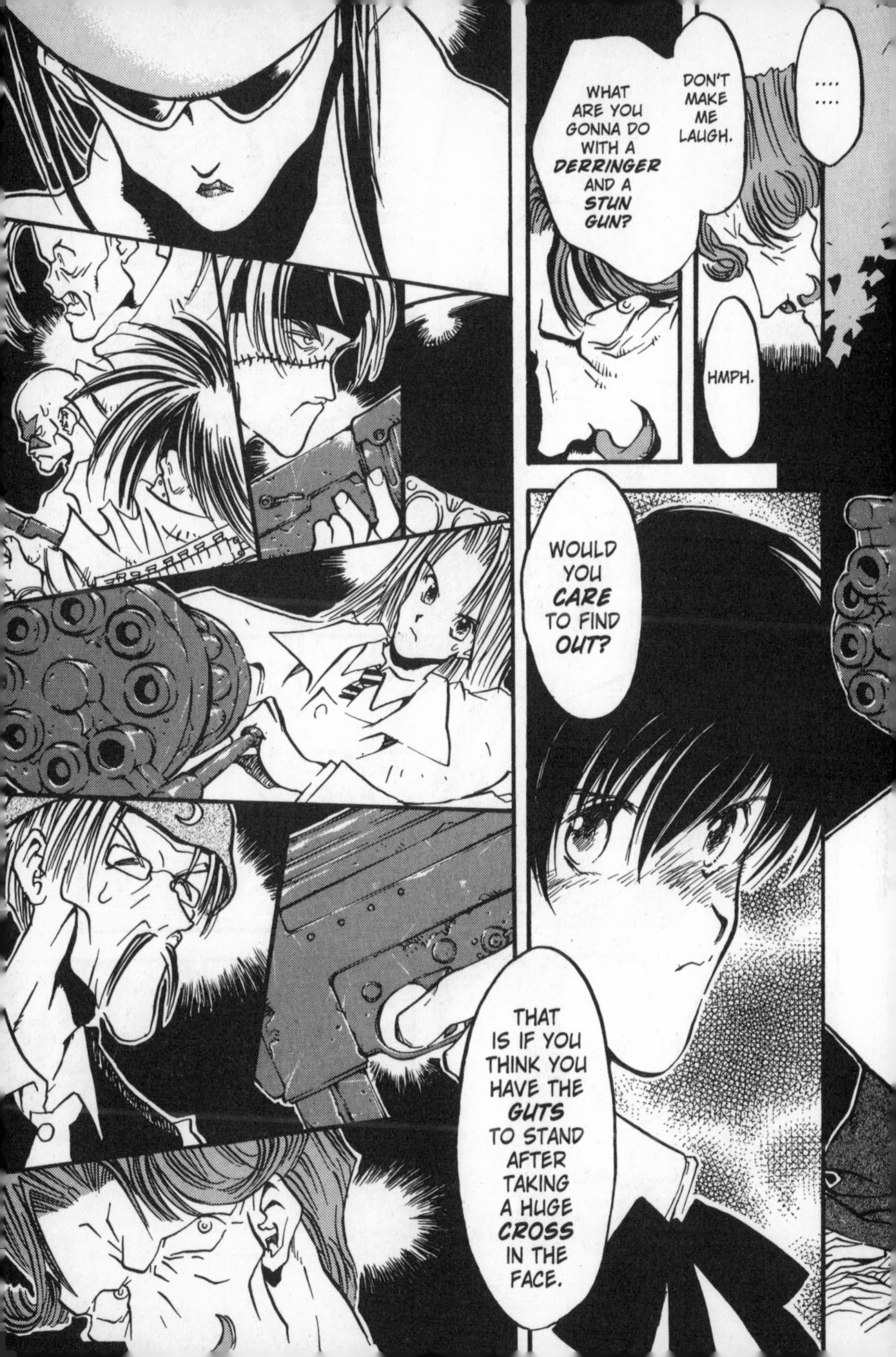
....
....
HMPH.
DON'T MAKE ME LAUGH.
WHAT ARE YOU GONNA DO WITH A DERRINGER AND A STUN GUN?
WOULD YOU CARE TO FIND OUT?
THAT IS IF YOU THINK YOU HAVE THE GUTS TO STAND AFTER TAKING A HUGE CROSS IN THE FACE.

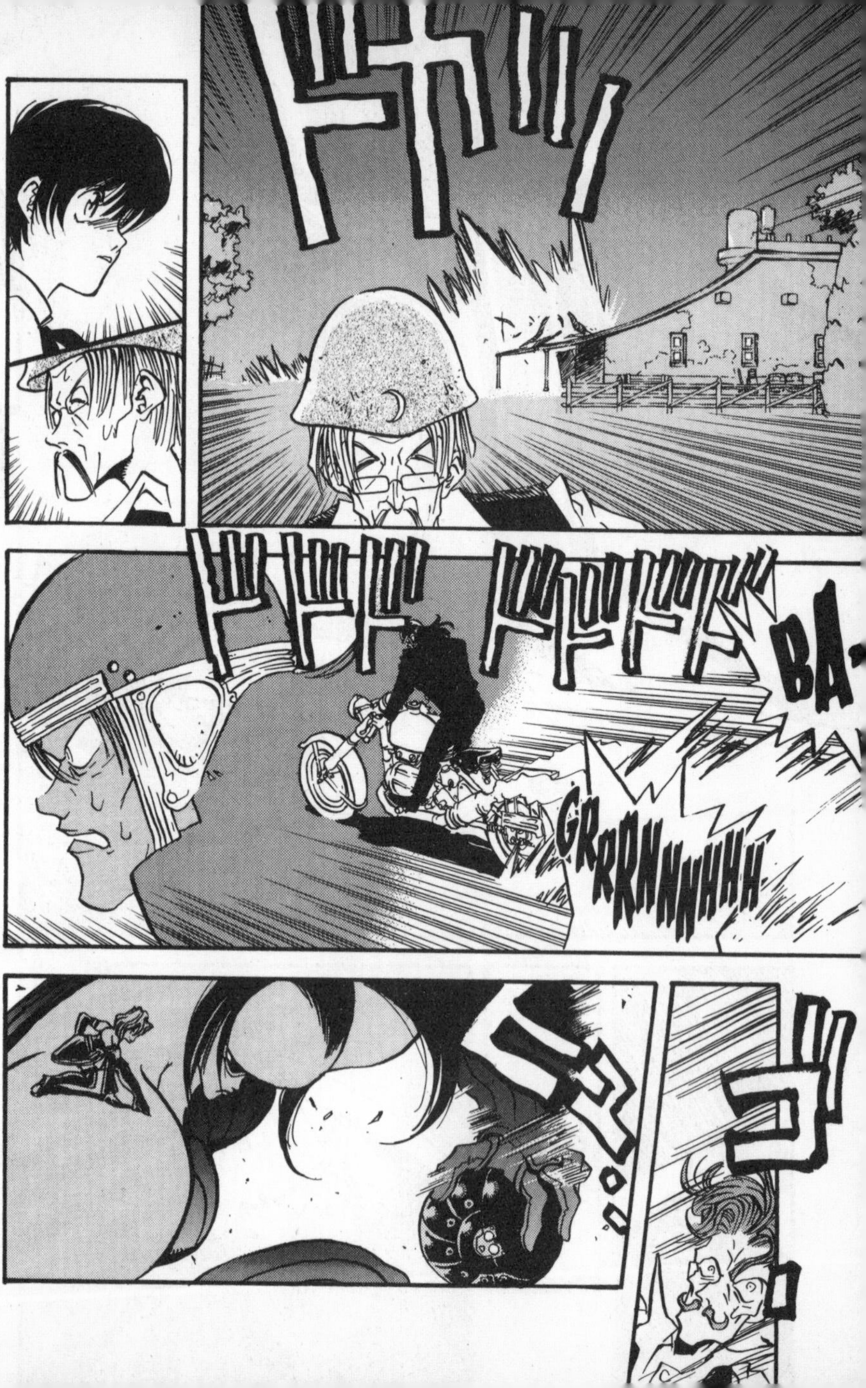
BA-
GRRNNHHHH

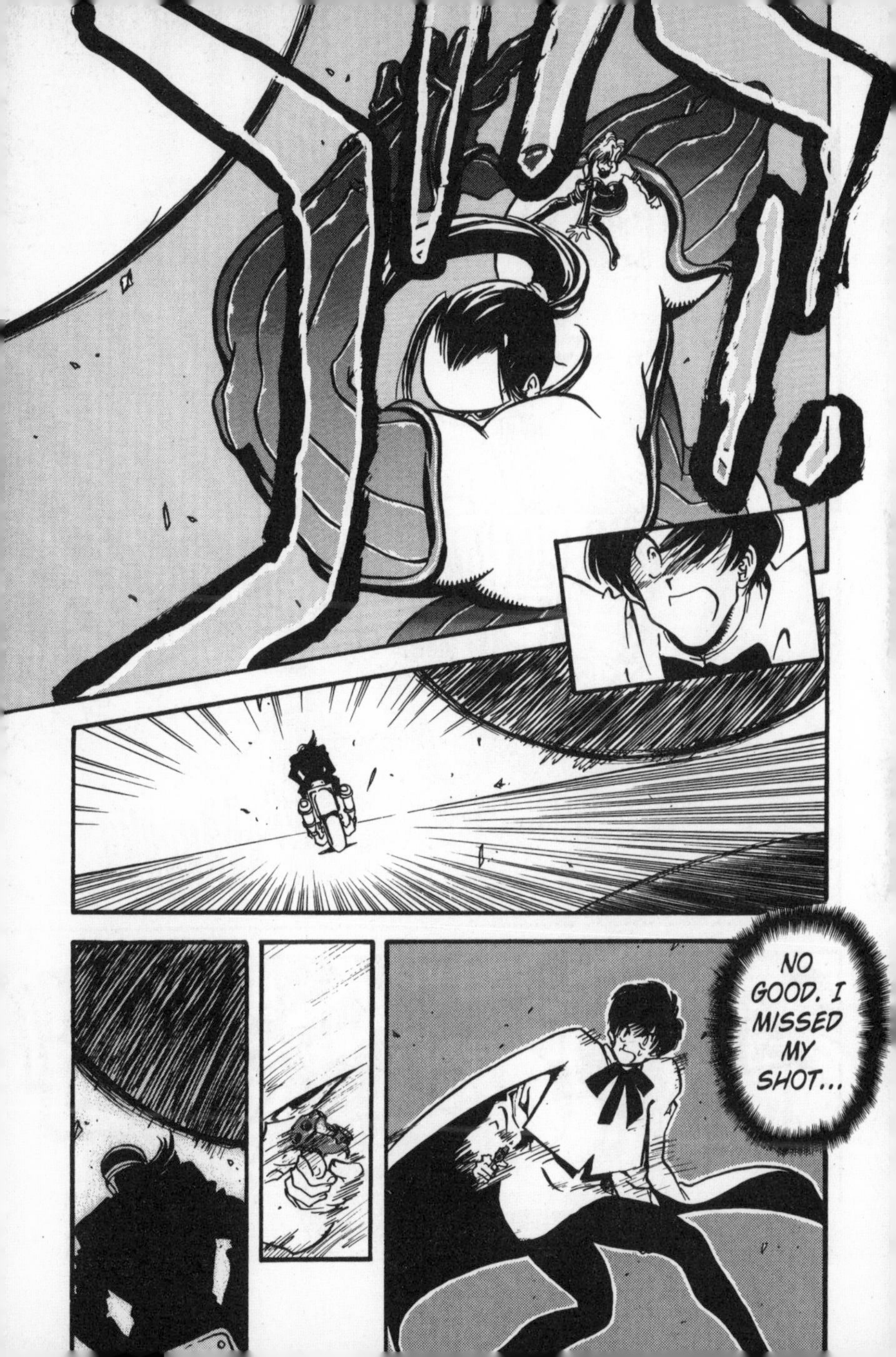
NO GOOD. I MISSED MY SHOT...

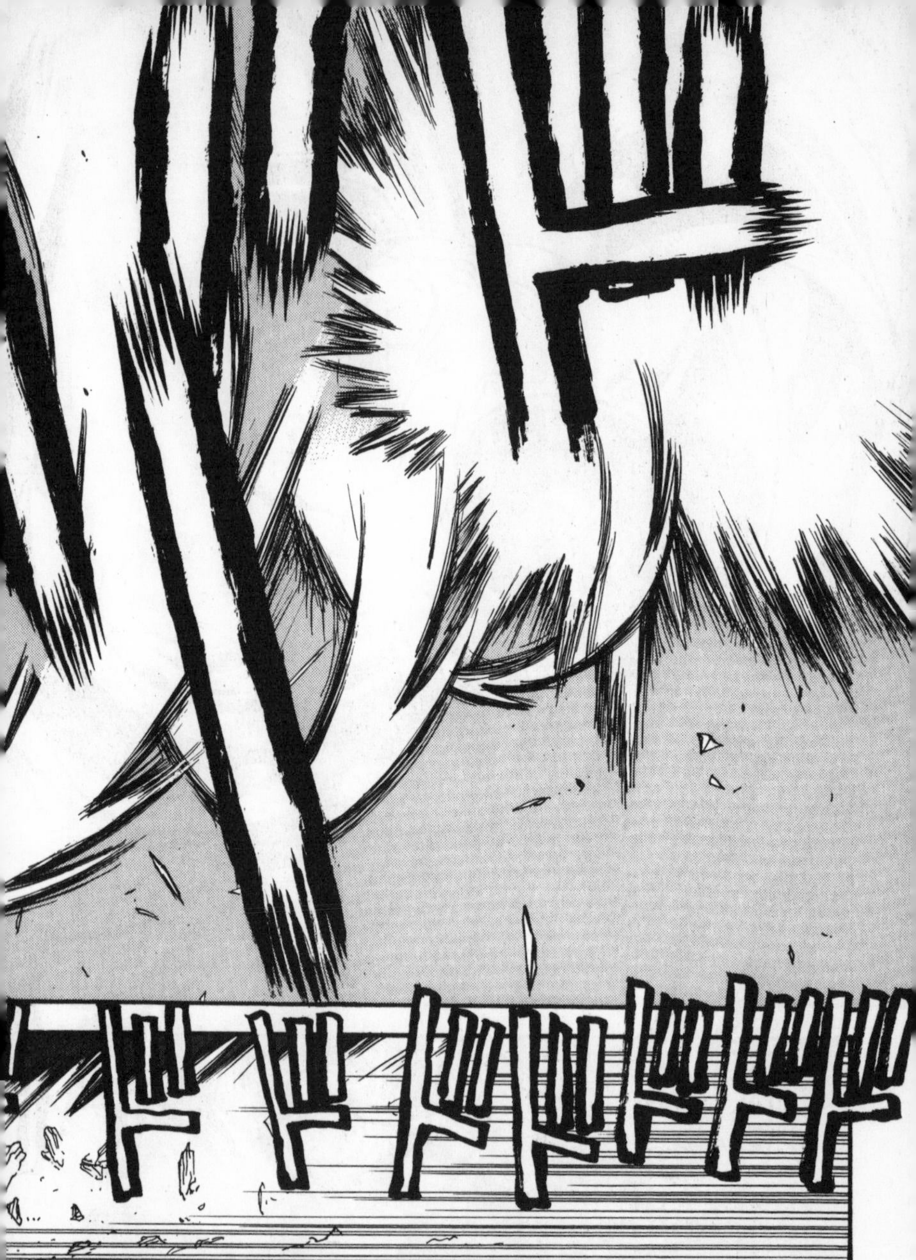
ドドドドドドド

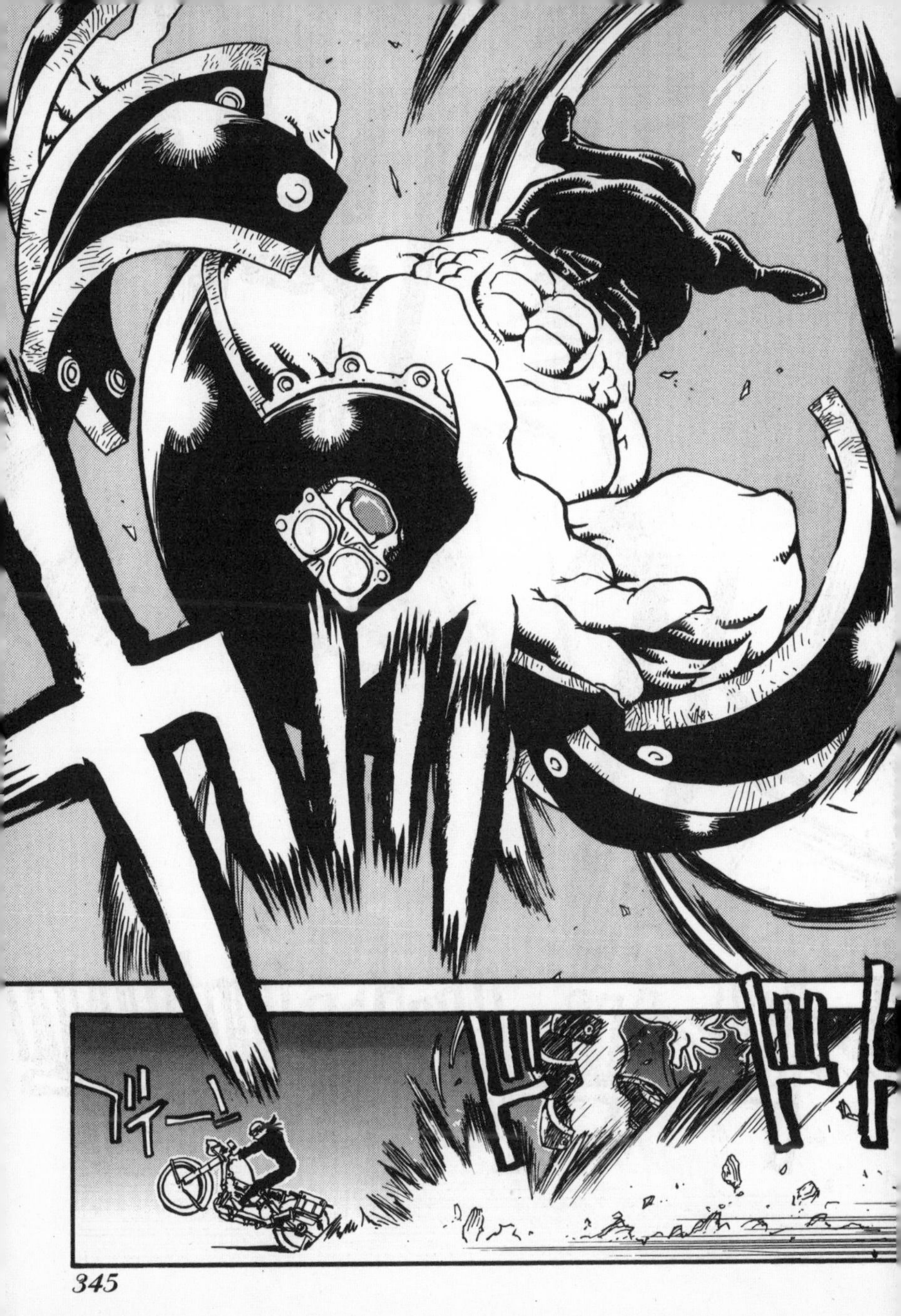
ブィーン

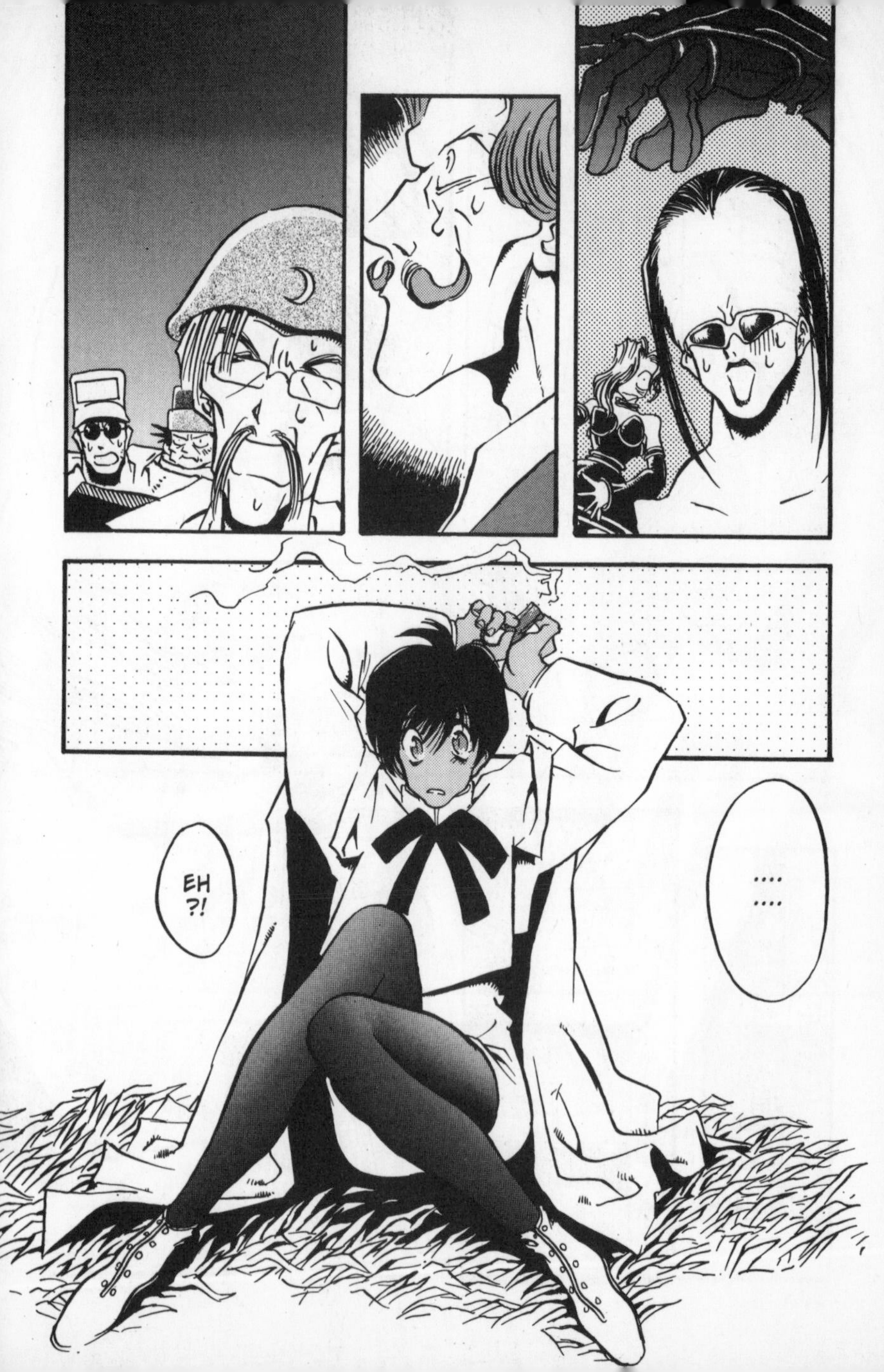
....
....
EH
?!

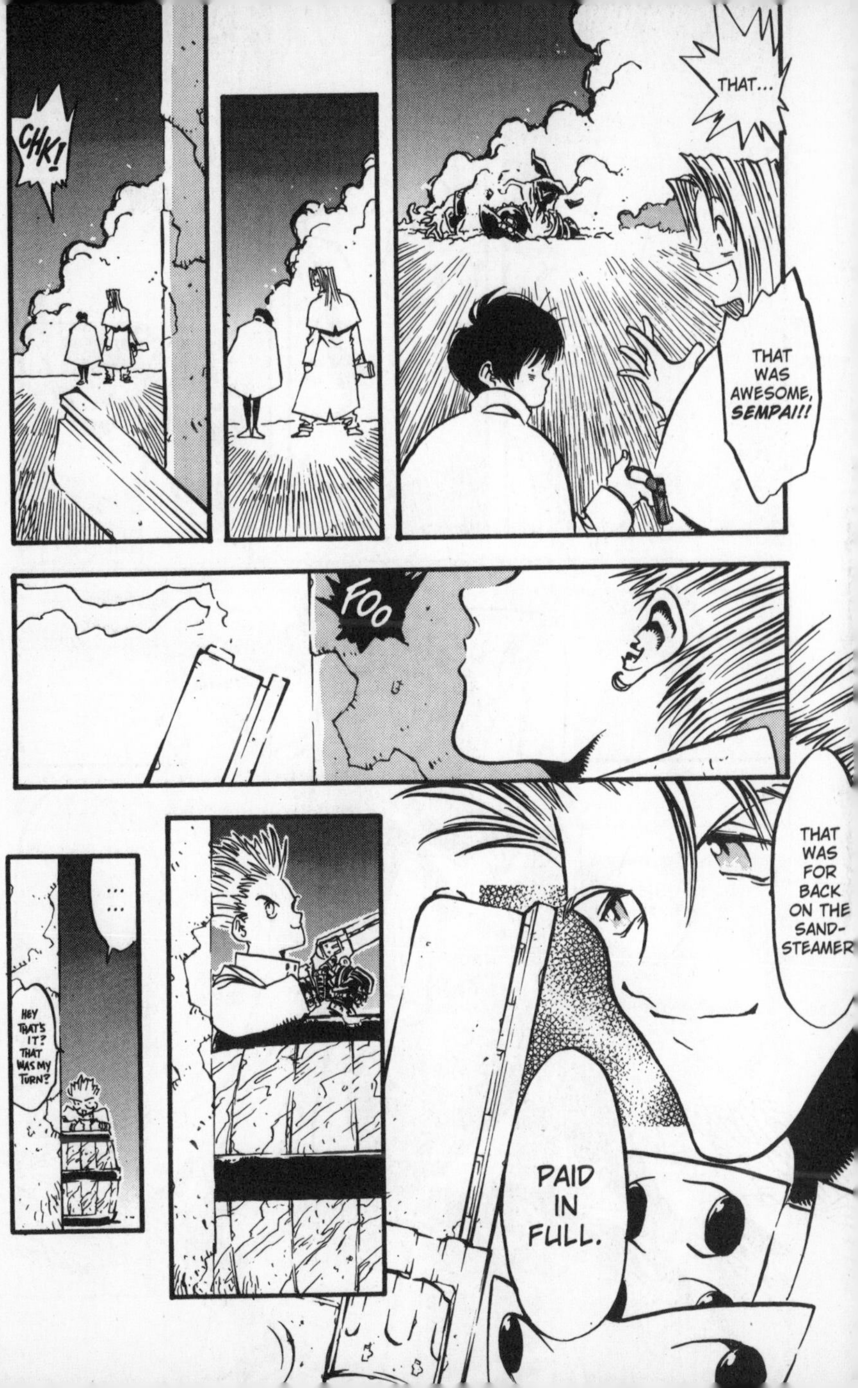
THAT...
THAT WAS AWESOME, SEMPAI!!
CHK!
FOO
THAT WAS FOR BACK ON THE SAND-STEAMER
PAID IN FULL.
... ...
HEY THAT'S IT? THAT WAS MY TURN?

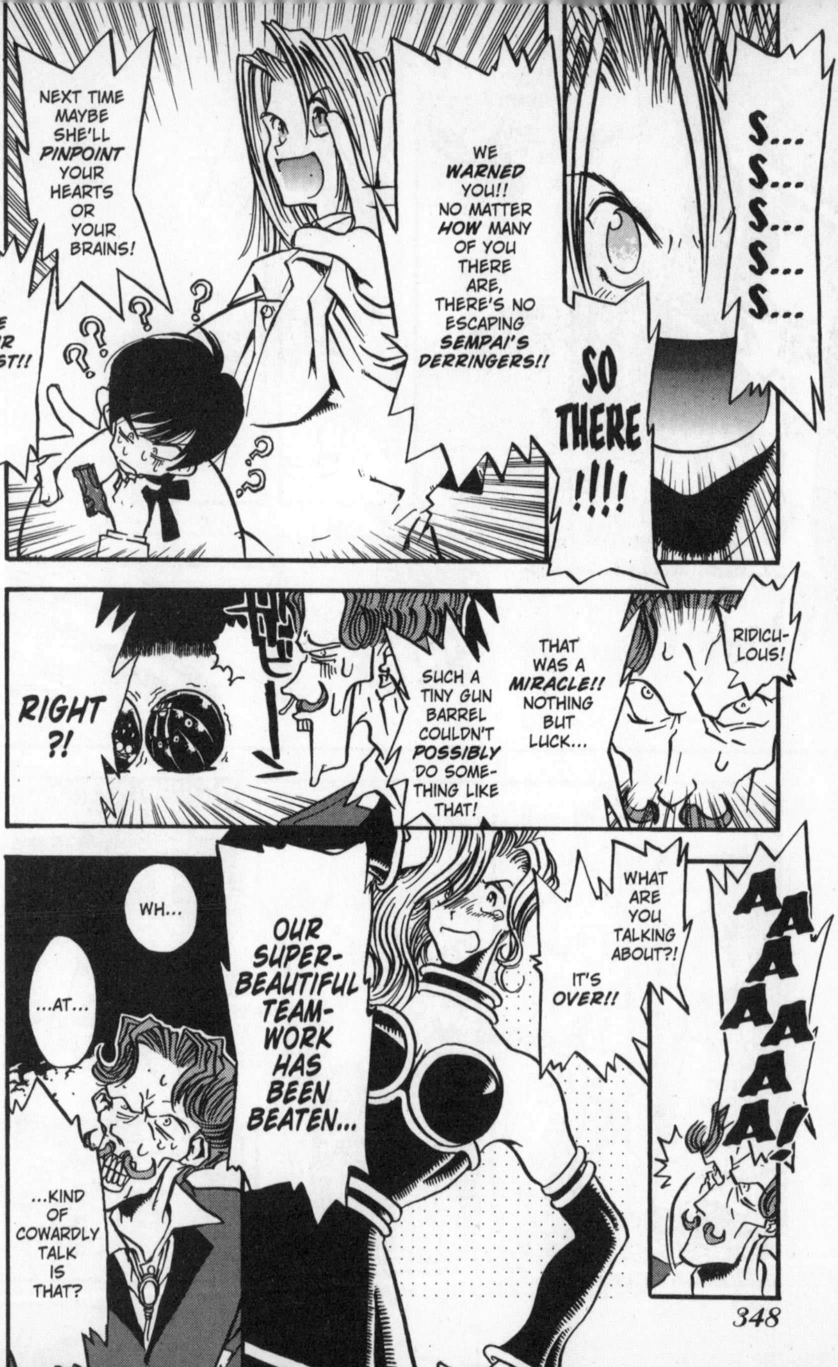

S... S... S... S... S...
SO THERE!!!!
WE WARNED YOU!! NO MATTER HOW MANY OF YOU THERE ARE, THERE'S NO ESCAPING SEMPAI'S DERRINGERS!!
NEXT TIME MAYBE SHE'LL PINPOINT YOUR HEARTS OR YOUR BRAINS!
BE OUR GUEST!!
RIDICULOUS!
THAT WAS A MIRACLE!! NOTHING BUT LUCK...
SUCH A TINY GUN BARREL COULDN'T POSSIBLY DO SOMETHING LIKE THAT!
RIGHT?!
AAAAAAA!
WHAT ARE YOU TALKING ABOUT?!
IT'S OVER!!
OUR SUPER-BEAUTIFUL TEAMWORK HAS BEEN BEATEN...
WH...
...AT...
...KIND OF COWARDLY TALK IS THAT?

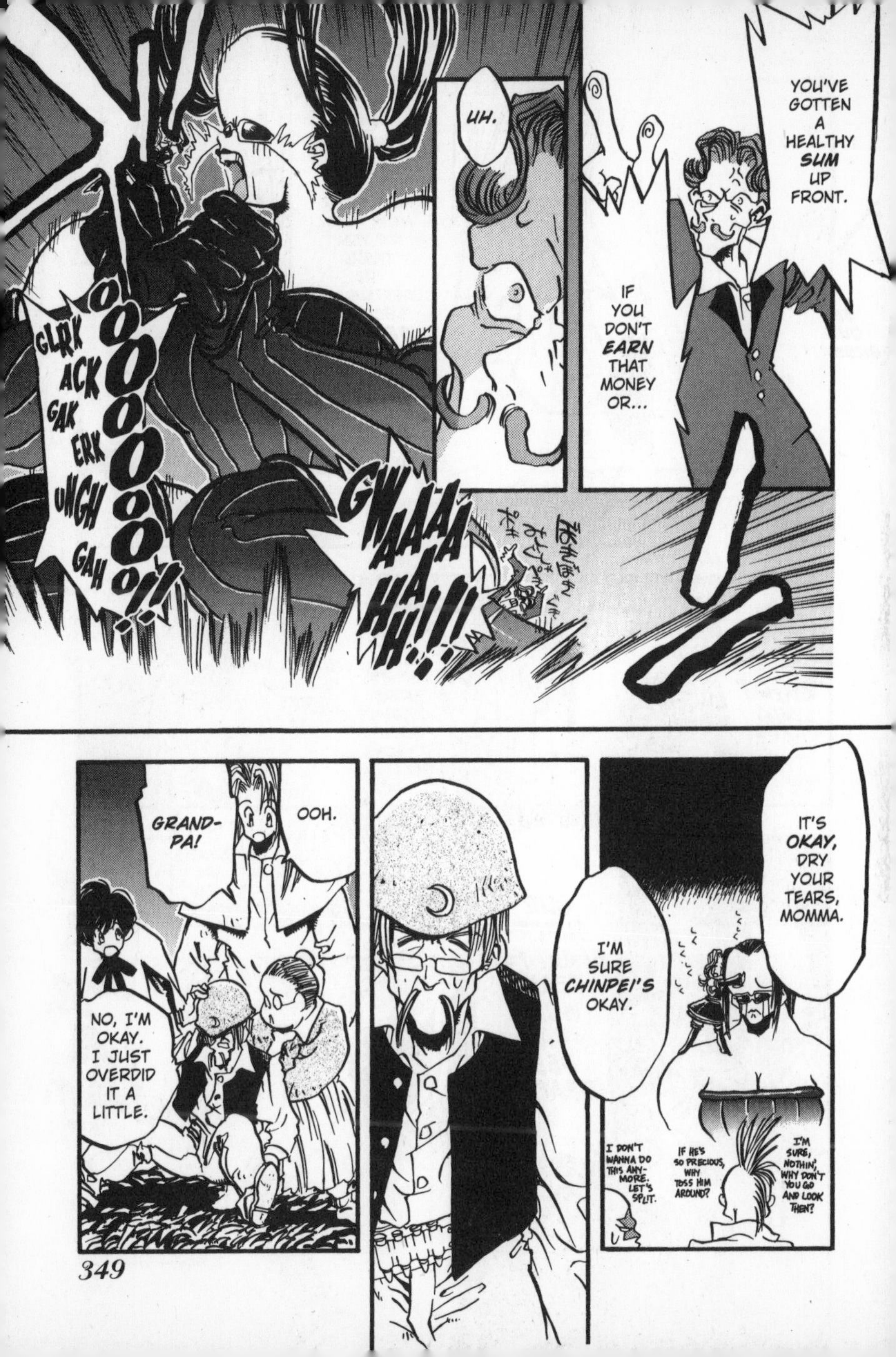
YOU'VE GOTTEN A HEALTHY SUM UP FRONT.
IF YOU DON'T EARN THAT MONEY OR...
UH.
GLRK ACK GAK ERK UNGH GAH
OOOOOOOOO!!..
GWAAAAAHH!!..
IT'S OKAY, DRY YOUR TEARS, MOMMA.
I'M SURE CHINPEI'S OKAY.
I'M SURE, NOTHIN', WHY DON'T YOU GO AND LOOK THEN?
IF HE'S SO PRECIOUS, WHY TOSS HIM AROUND?
I DON'T WANNA DO THIS ANYMORE. LET'S SPLIT.
OOH.
GRAND-PA!
NO, I'M OKAY. I JUST OVERDID IT A LITTLE.

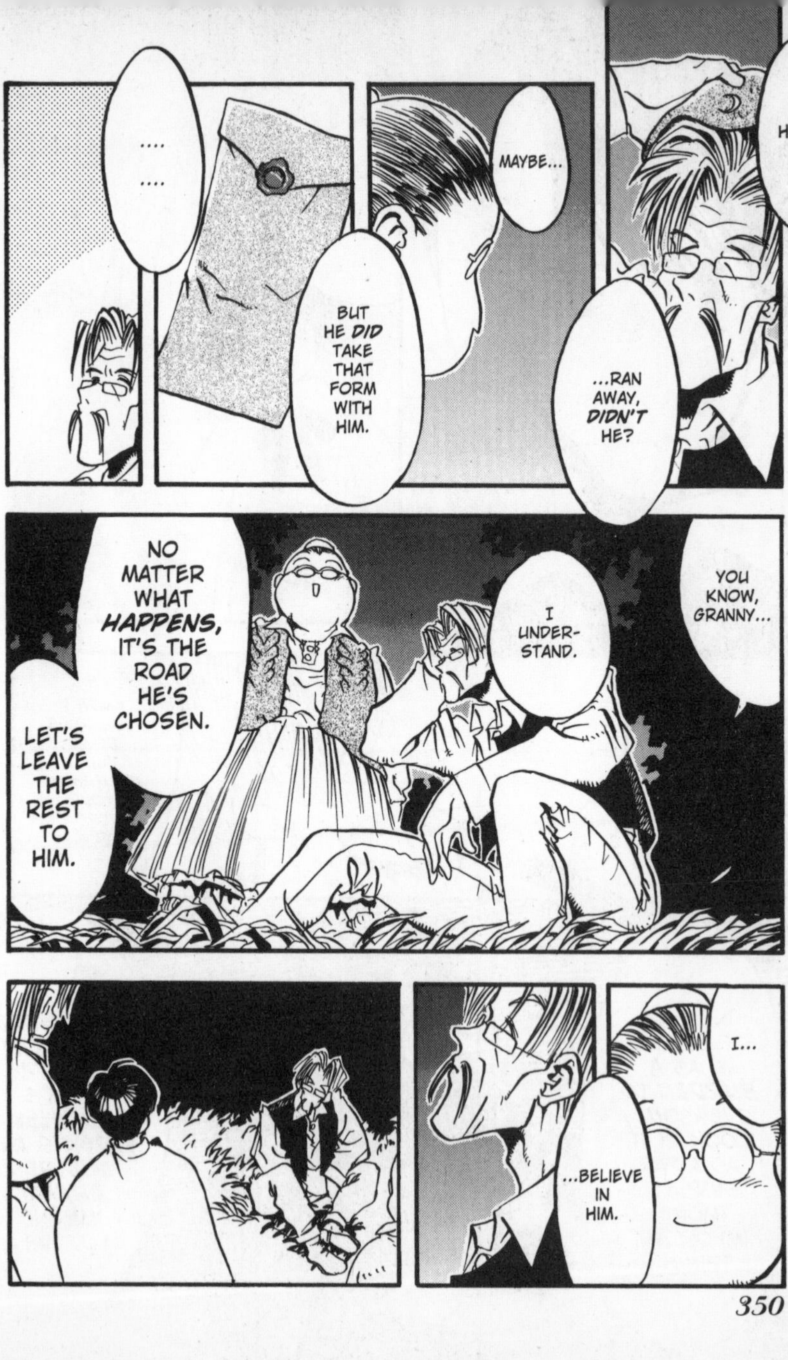
HE...
...RAN AWAY, *DIDN'T* HE?
MAYBE...
BUT HE *DID* TAKE THAT FORM WITH HIM.
.... ....
YOU KNOW, GRANNY...
I UNDERSTAND.
NO MATTER WHAT *HAPPENS,* IT'S THE ROAD HE'S CHOSEN.
LET'S LEAVE THE REST TO HIM.
I...
...BELIEVE IN HIM.

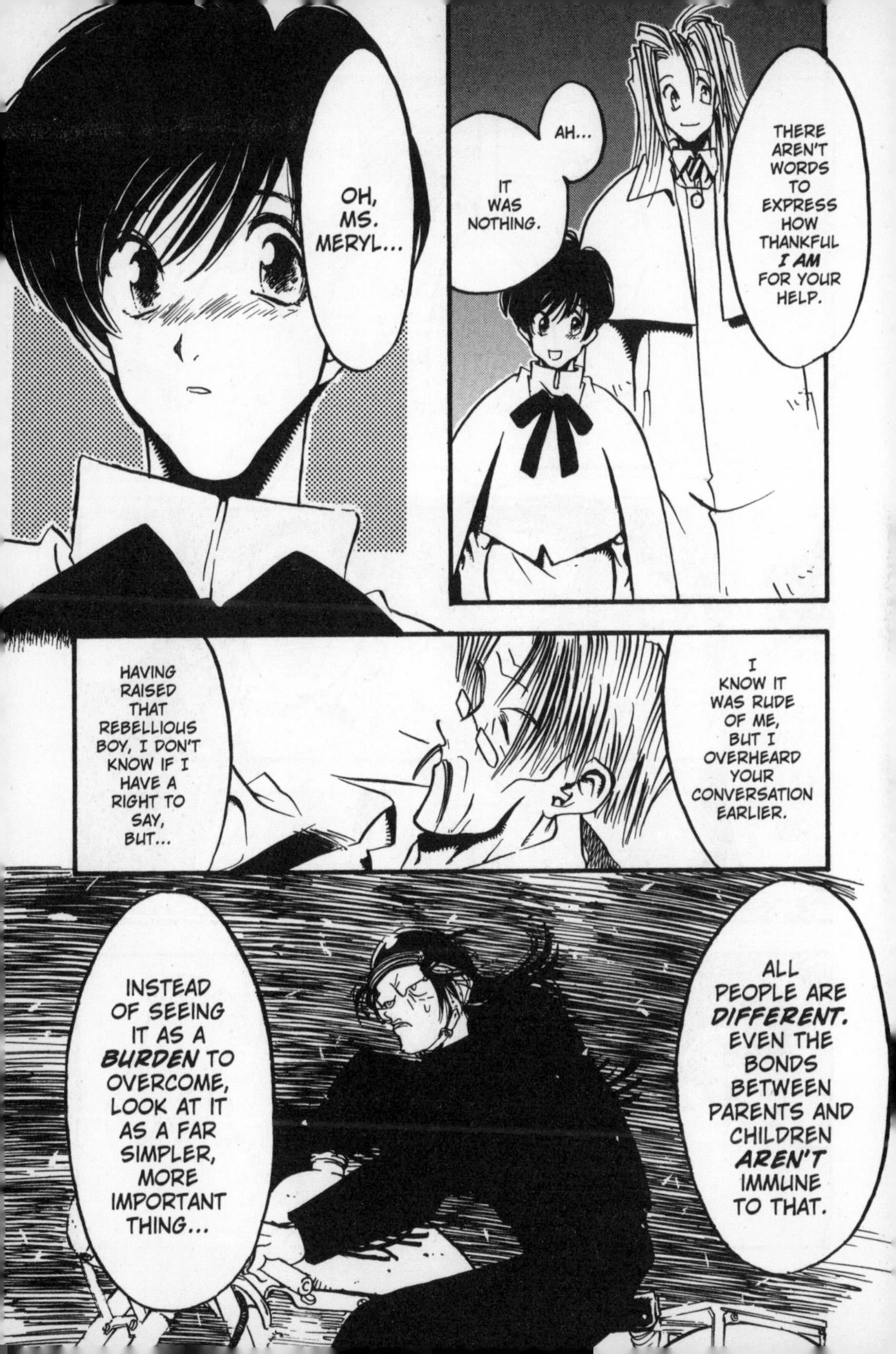
THERE AREN'T WORDS TO EXPRESS HOW THANKFUL I AM FOR YOUR HELP.
AH...
IT WAS NOTHING.
OH, MS. MERYL...
I KNOW IT WAS RUDE OF ME, BUT I OVERHEARD YOUR CONVERSATION EARLIER.
HAVING RAISED THAT REBELLIOUS BOY, I DON'T KNOW IF I HAVE A RIGHT TO SAY, BUT...
ALL PEOPLE ARE DIFFERENT. EVEN THE BONDS BETWEEN PARENTS AND CHILDREN AREN'T IMMUNE TO THAT.
INSTEAD OF SEEING IT AS A BURDEN TO OVERCOME, LOOK AT IT AS A FAR SIMPLER, MORE IMPORTANT THING...

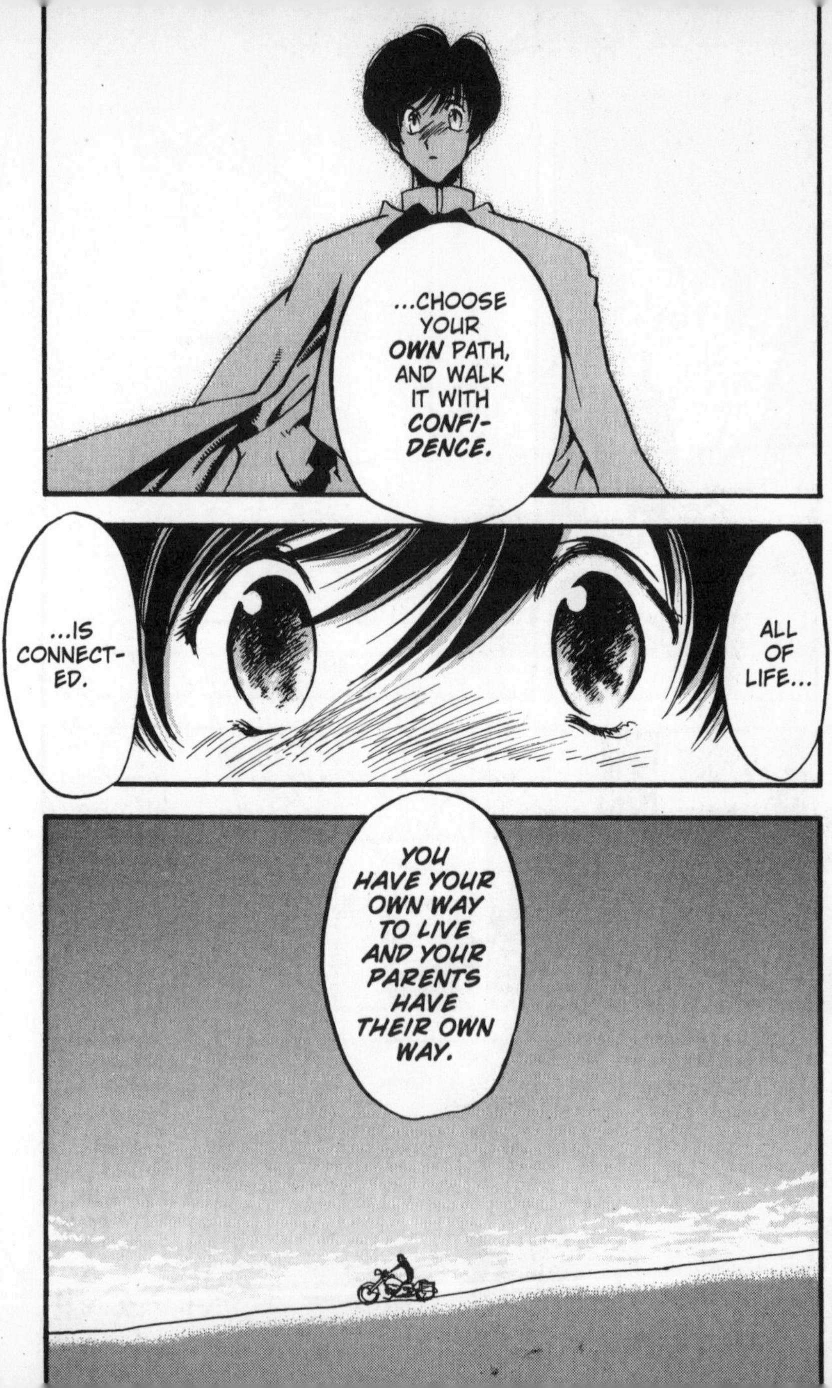
...CHOOSE YOUR OWN PATH, AND WALK IT WITH CONFI-DENCE.
ALL OF LIFE...
...IS CONNECT-ED.
YOU HAVE YOUR OWN WAY TO LIVE AND YOUR PARENTS HAVE THEIR OWN WAY.

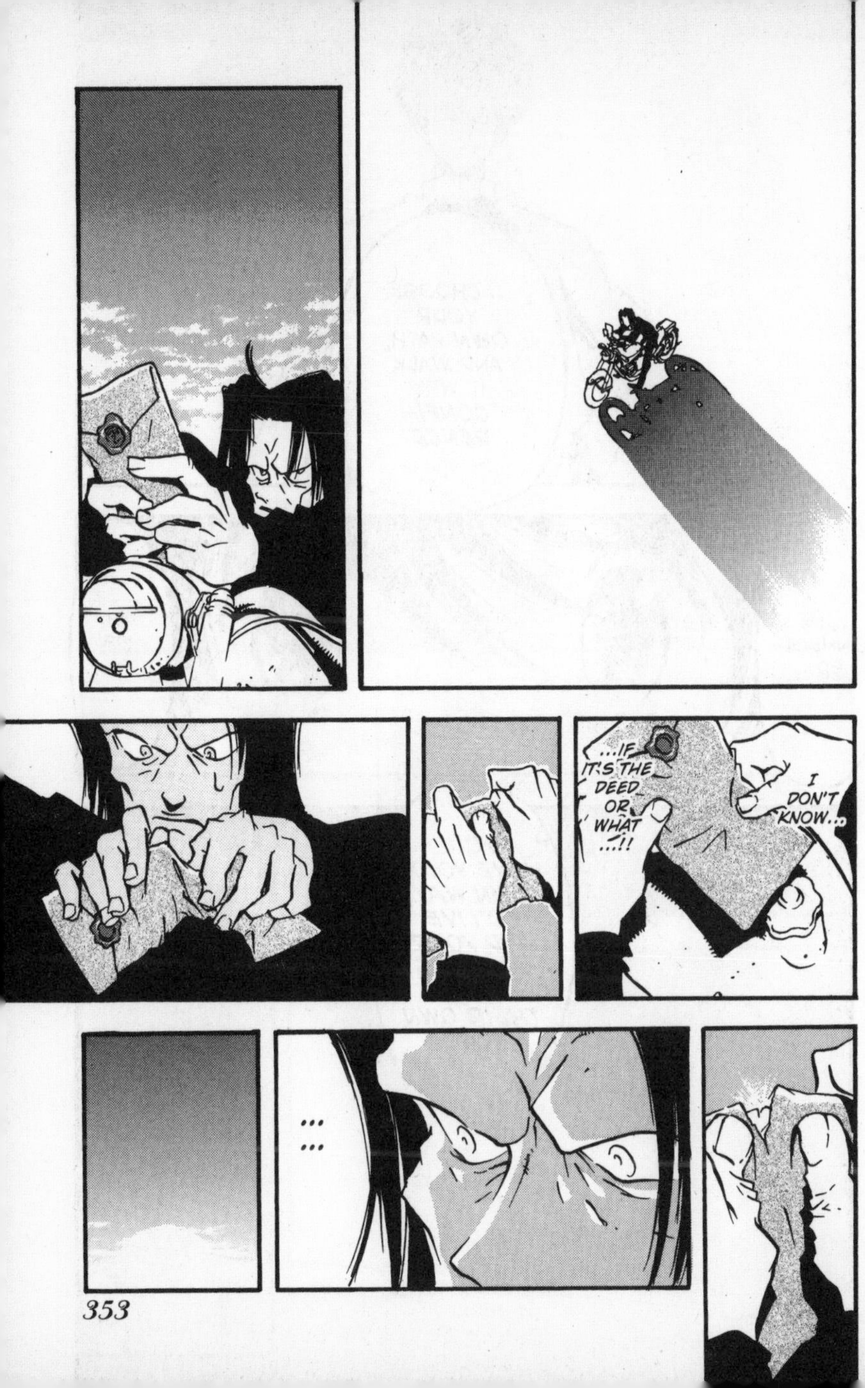
I DON'T KNOW...
...IF IT'S THE DEED OR WHAT ...!!
...
...

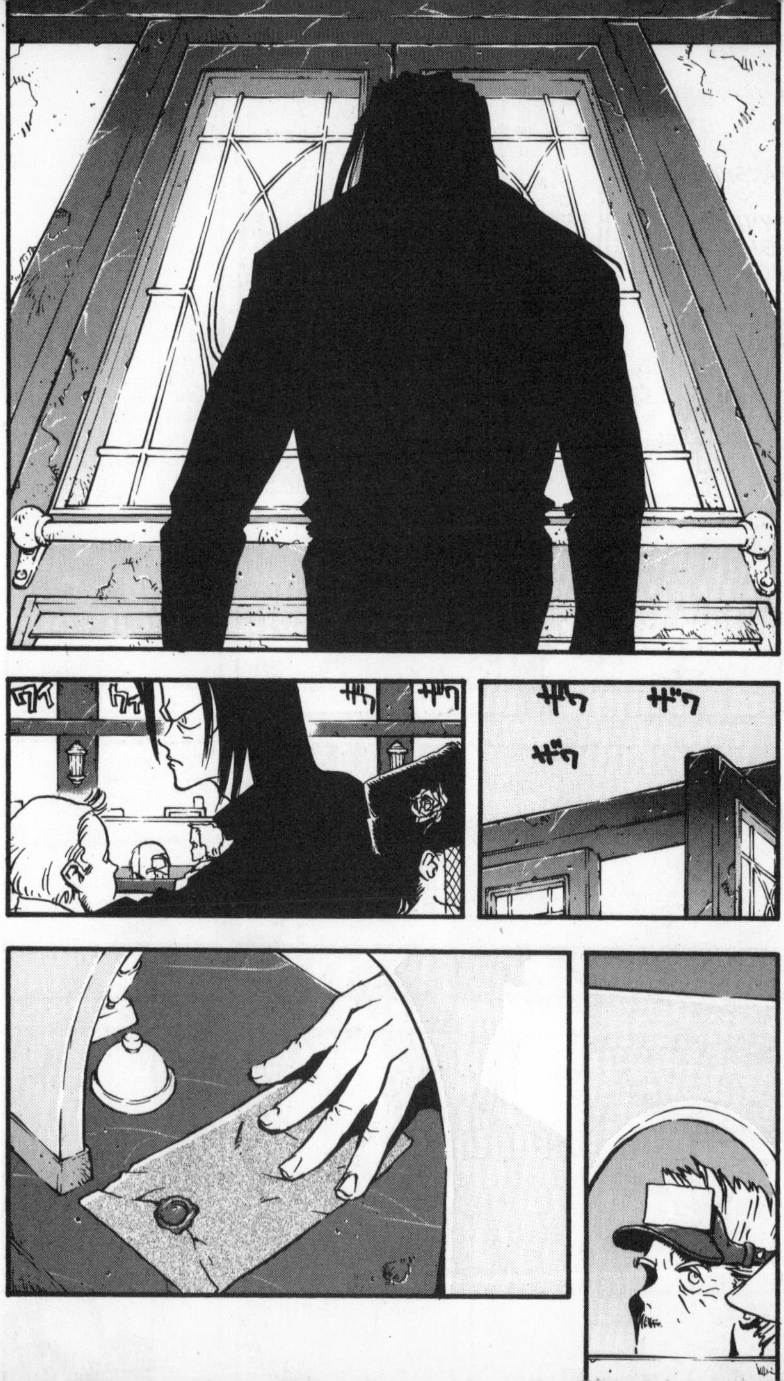
ザワ
ザワ
ザワ
ザワ
ザワ
ワイ
ワイ

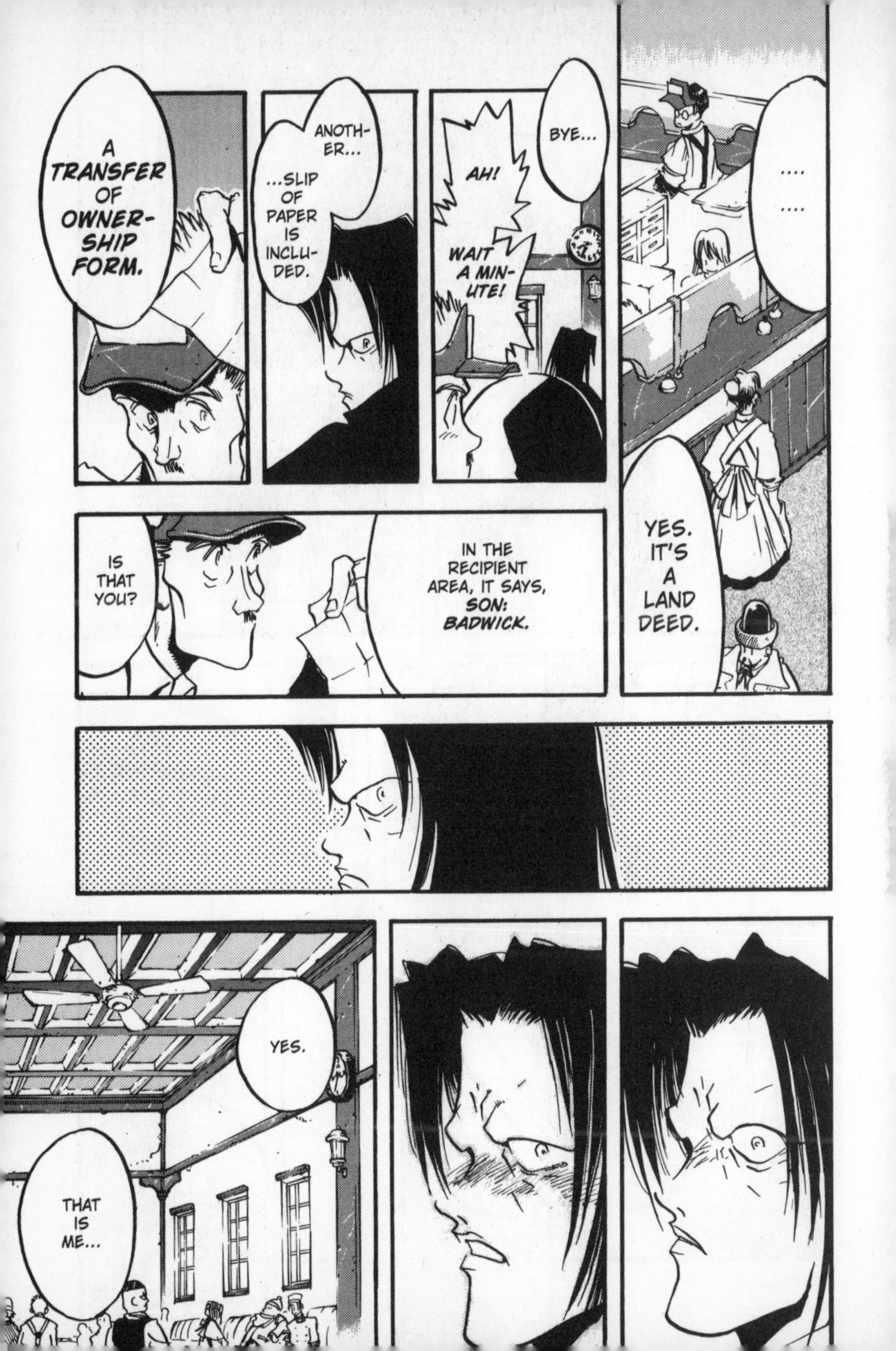
....
....
YES. IT'S A LAND DEED.
BYE...
AH!
WAIT A MINUTE!
ANOTHER...
...SLIP OF PAPER IS INCLUDED.
A TRANSFER OF OWNERSHIP FORM.
IN THE RECIPIENT AREA, IT SAYS, SON: BADWICK.
IS THAT YOU?
YES.
THAT IS ME...

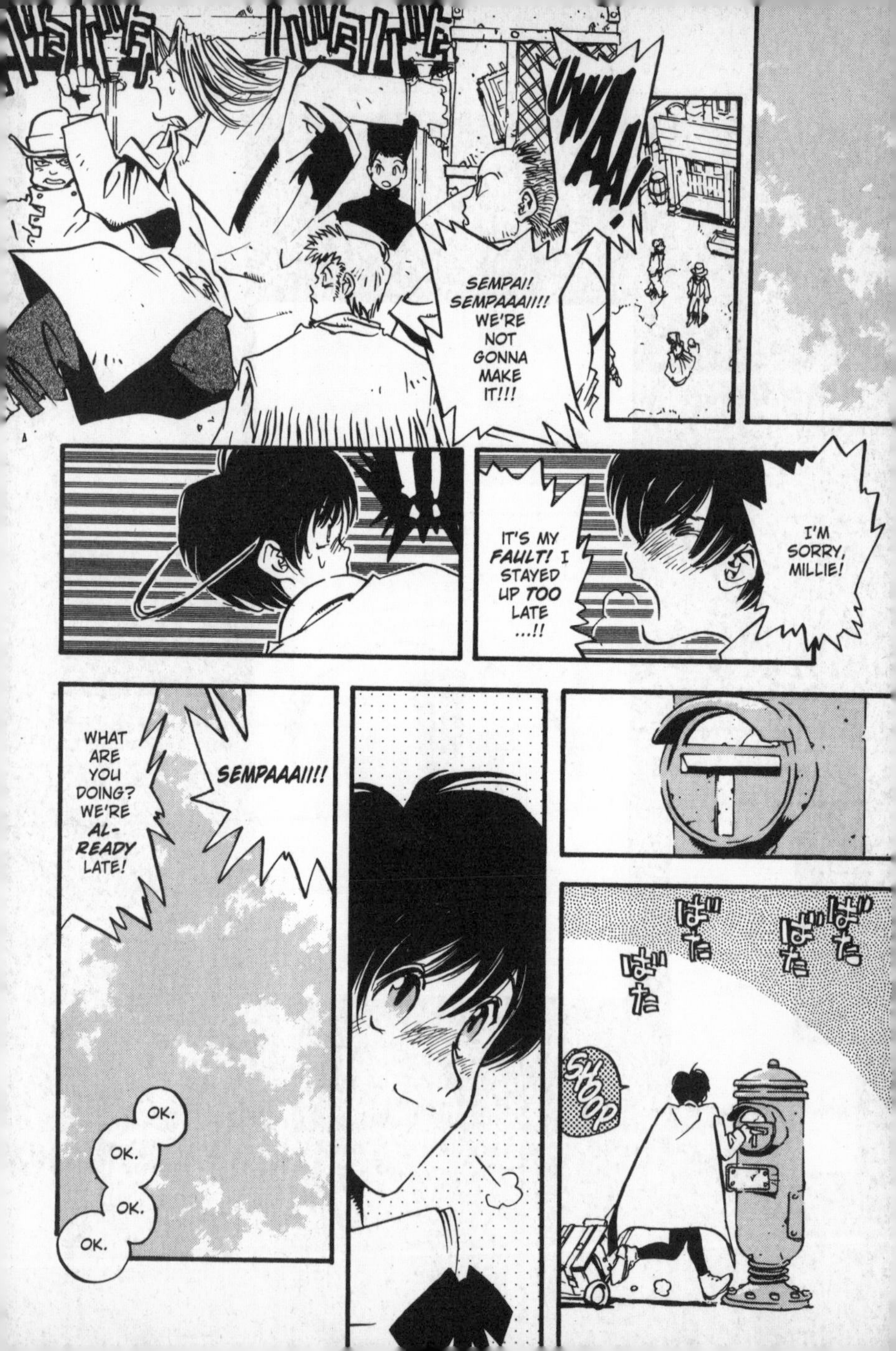
UWAAA!
SEMPAI! SEMPAAAI!!! WE'RE NOT GONNA MAKE IT!!!
I'M SORRY, MILLIE!
IT'S MY *FAULT!* I STAYED UP *TOO* LATE ...!!
ばた ばた
ばた ばた
ばた ばた
SHOOP
SEMPAAAI!!!
WHAT ARE YOU DOING? WE'RE *AL-READY* LATE!
OK.
OK.
OK.
OK.

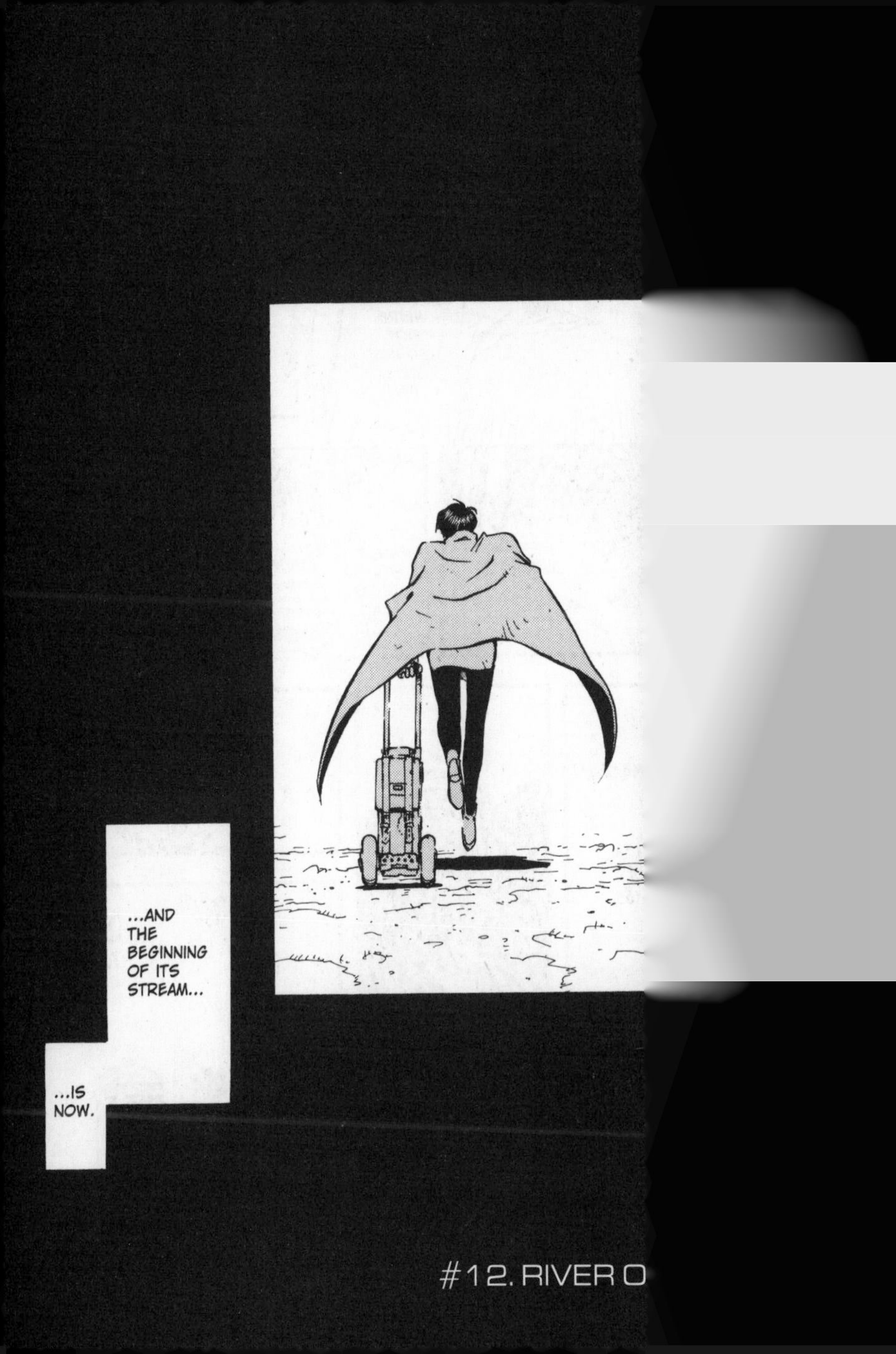
...AND THE BEGINNING OF ITS STREAM...
...IS NOW.
#12. RIVER O

TURN TO THE NEXT

TRIGUN YASUHIRO NIGHTOW

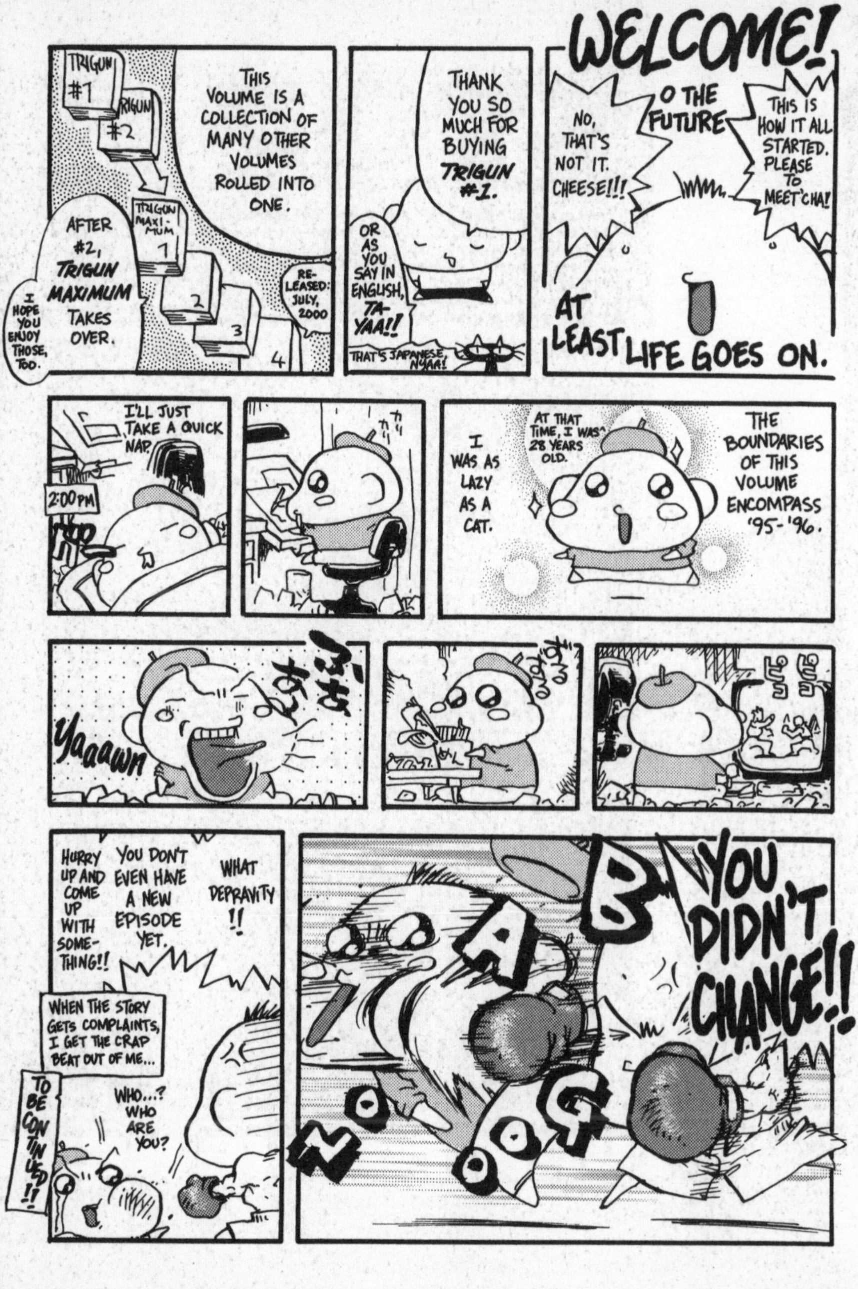
WELCOME!
THIS IS HOW IT ALL STARTED. PLEASE TO MEET'CHA!
O THE FUTURE
NO, THAT'S NOT IT. CHEESE!!!
AT LEAST LIFE GOES ON.
THANK YOU SO MUCH FOR BUYING TRIGUN #1.
OR AS YOU SAY IN ENGLISH, TA-YAA!!
THAT'S JAPANESE, NYAR!
THIS VOLUME IS A COLLECTION OF MANY OTHER VOLUMES ROLLED INTO ONE.
TRIGUN #1
TRIGUN #2
TRIGUN MAXI-MUM 1
2
3
4
RE-LEASED: JULY, 2000
AFTER #2, TRIGUN MAXIMUM TAKES OVER.
I HOPE YOU ENJOY THOSE, TOO.
THE BOUNDARIES OF THIS VOLUME ENCOMPASS '95-'96.
AT THAT TIME, I WAS 28 YEARS OLD.
I WAS AS LAZY AS A CAT.
I'LL JUST TAKE A QUICK NAP.
2:00 PM
ピコ ピコ
ふぁあ
Yaaawn
YOU DIDN'T CHANGE!!
WHAT DEPRAVITY!!
YOU DON'T EVEN HAVE A NEW EPISODE YET.
HURRY UP AND COME UP WITH SOME-THING!!
WHEN THE STORY GETS COMPLAINTS, I GET THE CRAP BEAT OUT OF ME...
WHO...? WHO ARE YOU?
TO BE CONTINUED!!

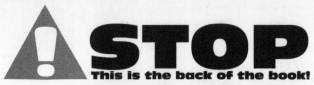

# STOP

## This is the back of the book!

**This manga collection is translated into English but oriented in right-to-left reading format at the creator's request, maintaining the artwork's visual orientation as originally published in Japan. If you've never read manga in this way before, take a look at the diagram below to give yourself an idea of how to go about it. Basically, you'll be starting in the upper right corner and will read each balloon and panel moving right to left. It may take some getting used to, but you should get the hang of it very quickly. Have fun!**

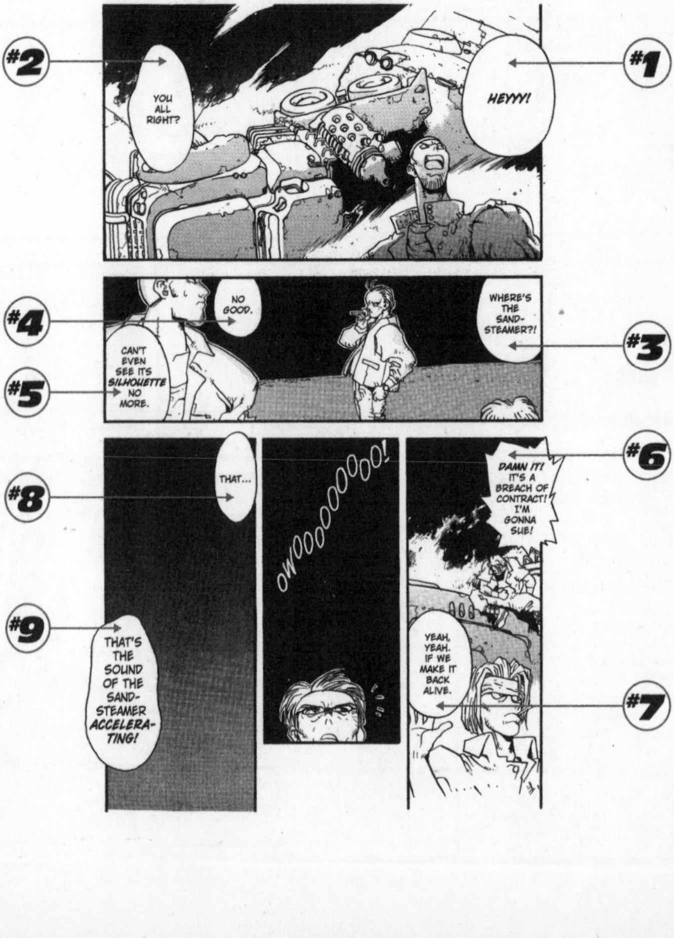

#1
HEYYY!
#2
YOU ALL RIGHT?
#3
WHERE'S THE SAND-STEAMER?!
#4
NO GOOD.
#5
CAN'T EVEN SEE ITS SILHOUETTE NO MORE.
#6
DAMN IT! IT'S A BREACH OF CONTRACT! I'M GONNA SUE!
#7
YEAH, YEAH. IF WE MAKE IT BACK ALIVE.
OWOOOOOOOOOOO!
#8
THAT...
#9
THAT'S THE SOUND OF THE SAND-STEAMER ACCELERATING!